The Mechanical Muse

The Mechanical Muse:
The Piano, Pianism and Piano Music, *c.*1760–1850

DEREK CAREW
Cardiff University, UK

© Derek Carew, 2007

All rights reserved. No part of this publication may be reproduced, stored in a retrieval system, or transmitted in any form or by any means, electronic, mechanical, photocopying, recording, or otherwise without the prior permission of the publisher.

The author has asserted his moral right under the Copyright, Designs and Patents Act, 1988, to be identified as the author of this work.

Published by
Ashgate Publishing Limited
Gower House
Croft Road
Aldershot
Hants GU11 3HR
United Kingdom

Ashgate Publishing Company
Suite 420
101 Cherry Street
Burlington, VT 05401–4405
USA

Ashgate website: http://www.ashgate.com

British Library Cataloguing-in-Publication Data
Carew, Derek
  The mechanical muse : the piano, pianism and piano music, c.1760–1850
  1. Piano music – 18th century – History and criticism 2. Piano music – 19th century – History and criticism 3. Piano – History
  I. Title
  786.2'09033

Library of Congress Cataloging-in-Publication Data
Carew, Derek
  The mechanical muse : the piano, pianism and piano music c.1760–1850 / Derek Carew.
     p.cm.
  Includes bibliographical references and index.
  ISBN: 978-0-85967-969-5 (alk. Paper)
  1. Piano music – 18th century – History and criticism. 2. Piano music – 19th century – History and criticism. 3. Piano – History. I. Title. II Title: Piano, pianism and piano music, c.1750–1850.

ML700.C37 2007-06-21
786.209'033—dc22

2006018630

ISBN 978-0-85967-969-5

Printed and bound in Great Britain by MPG Books Ltd, Bodmin, Cornwall

For Jan and Caitríona, who waited

Contents

Preface	ix
List of Figures	x
List of Tables	xi
List of Plates	xii
Editorial	xv
Introduction	xvii

I Instruments

1	History and Background	3
2	Action and Technique	28
3	Stringing	56
4	Sound Modification	86
5	Versatility	103
6	The Piano's Sound	116

II Influences

7	Character 1: Background	133
8	Character 2: Emotionalism	137
9	Character 3: Personification	144
10	Character 4: The Past	167
11	Character 5: Other Topics	184
12	Received Forms 1: The Minuet (and Scherzo)	217
13	Received Forms 2: The Rondo	241
14	Received Forms 3: The Solo Sonata	262

15	Received Forms 4: Variations	301
16	Received Forms 5a: The Concerto 1, Background and Presentation of Material	334
17	Received Forms 5b: The Concerto 2, The Solo	351
18	Received Forms 5c: The Concerto 3, Other Movements	362
19	Vernacular 1: General	375
20	Vernacular 2: Inclusion	393
21	Vernacular 3: Regional Styles	400
22	Improvisation 1: General	431
23	Improvisation 2: Types	442

III Integration

24	Accompaniment 1a: Chamber Music 1, Classical	459
25	Accompaniment 1b: Chamber Music 2, Romantic	474
26	Accompaniment 2a: Song 1	489
27	Accompaniment 2b: Song 2	517
28	Accompaniment 3: Piano Duet and Duo	523
29	Didacticism and Dissemination	531
30	The Dance	541
	Select Bibliography	557
	Index	565

Preface

This book was born of a fascination with, and love of, the piano, of the period chosen and of the 'period piano'. It has been far too long in preparation, a fact which, unfortunately, guarantees neither quality nor relevance; any such shortcomings are certainly not the fault of those who, in various ways, helped in its production. The early stages of my research were facilitated by a grant from the British Academy, for which I am grateful, as indeed I am to the School of Music at Cardiff University, for their contribution to the typesetting of the book's many musical examples and to the Librarian of the School's Music Library, Gill Jones, and her staff for their help and their collective amnesia around returns time, which was an enormous help. The encouragement and goodwill, over a long period, of Jim Samson has been a great resource and I thank my respective editors at Ashgate, Rachel Lynch and Heidi May for their patience and understanding over this long and complicated project and also their colleagues in various departments who were involved. My particular thanks goes to Ian Cheverton for his first-class typesetting and, especially, for the excellent quality of the musical examples; his skill and musicality was a great boon and nothing was too much trouble. Finally, my gratitude, now and over the years, goes to Jan and Caitríona for the kindnesses I may have forgotten and the love which I will not; their understanding, patience and support would have been far beyond the call of duty, if duty had been a consideration.

Derek Carew, Penarth, May 2007.

List of Figures

The figures are located on pp. 20–27.

1. Clavichord mechanism.
   Re-drawn from a version found in the *New Grove Dictionary of Music and Musicians*.

2. Action of the harpsichord: when the key is depressed the jack rises, plucks the string, returns, and damps it.
   Re-drawn from a version found in Jan H. Albarda, *Wood, Wire, and Quill: an introduction to the harpsichord*, The Coach House Press (Toronto, 1968).

3. Action of Cristofori's last surviving piano of 1726.
   Re-drawn from a version found in the *New Grove Dictionary of Music and Musicians*.

4. Prellmechanik action without escapement mechanism from an anonymous south German square piano, c.1770 (Royal College of Music, London); to allow space for the hammer, the rear of the key is narrower than the front; the dampers are beneath the strings and disengage when the hinged end rises with the key; the knee lever lowers the damper-support rod to disengage all the dampers simultaneously.
   Re-drawn from a version found in the *New Grove Dictionary of Music and Musicians*.

5. Prellmechanik, with escapement, in a Heilman piano of c.1785.
   Re-drawn from a version found in the *New Grove Dictionary of Music and Musicians*.

6. 'English single action' (from Cristofori by Zumpe) in a Kirchman piano of 1775.
   Re-drawn from a version found in the *New Grove Dictionary of Music and Musicians*.

7. Illustration of the 'compensated frame' from James Broadwood's patent of 1827.
   Re-drawn from a version found in the *New Grove Dictionary of Music and Musicians*.

8. Erard double-escapement action after the English patent drawing of 1822; the intermediate lever, pivoted to its flange, simultaneously lifts the hopper and pulls down the damper; the action is shown with the key depressed, the hammer having fallen back to its check.
   Re-drawn from a version found in the *New Grove Dictionary of Music and Musicians*.

List of Tables

1 Compass of eighteenth-century pianos (p.57)
Slightly adapted from p. 20, *Fortepianos and their Music* by Komlós, K. (Oxford, 1995). By permission of Oxford University Press.

2 Numbers of keyboard instruments advertised in Vienna 1760–1800 (pp. 112–3)
Slightly adapted from pp. 132–3, *Keyboard Instruments in Eighteenth-Century Vienna* by Maunder, R. (Oxford, 1998). By permission of Oxford University Press.

3 Overall plan of *The Glorious Victory of Salamanaca on the Ever Memorable 22nd of July 1812 ... dedicated to the Duke of Wellington and his Brave and Gallant Warriors* (p. 192)

4 Outline of the Baroque Venetian *ritornello* (p. 339)

5 Two versions of Clementi's variations on *The Black Joke* (p. 397)

6 A typical Hummel concert of 1824 (p. 432)
Taken from pp. 21–22, *Kapellmeister Hummel in England and France* by Sachs, J. (Detroit Monographs in Musicology Number Six; Information Coordinators Inc., Detroit, 1977). By permission.

7 Dance output of J.N. Hummel (p. 549)

List of Plates

Between pages 130 and 131

1 Grand piano by Bartolomeo Cristofori (1726)
  By permission of the Musikinstrumenten-Museum, Universität Leipzig

2 Metal bracing in grand piano by William Stodart (before 1837)
  Author's collection

3 Venetian Swell (open) in harpsichord by Shudi-Broadwood (1790)
  The Colt Clavier Collection. By kind permission of Stainer & Bell

4 Lodovico Giustini, Piano Sonatas Op. 1 (pub. Florence, 1732: extract)
  By permission of the British Library

5 Lyraflügel by Schleip (1825)
  The Colt Clavier Collection. By kind permission of Stainer & Bell

6 Clementi, Piano Sonata in A major Op. 33/1, title-page with 'additional keys'
  By permission of the British Library

7 *Due corde* block at right end of keyboard of grand piano by William Stodart (before 1837)
  Author's collection

8 Detail of *due corde* block on grand piano shown in Plate 7 (grand by Stodart, early 1830s)

9 Ludwig Berger, Piano Sonata Op. 7/*Introduzione*
  By permission of the British Library

10 John Field, *Nocturne* No. 6 in E flat major (Russian edition of c.1817)
   © The Musica Britannica Trust, reproduced by permission of Stainer & Bell Ltd., London, England

11 Bertini, *L'Ultima Fantasia*
   By permission of the British Library

12 Grand piano by Broadwood (1819)
   The Colt Clavier Collection. By gracious permission of the Curator, Mr W.G. Spiers

13 Detail of divided pedal on grand piano shown in Plate 12
   © The Open University, Milton Keynes

LIST OF PLATES

14 Piccolo piano by Wornum (*c.*1835)
Author's collection

15 Repair instructions inside piccolo piano shown in Plate 14

16 Giraffenflügel by ?Ehrlich (*c.*1840)
The Colt Clavier Collection. By kind permission of Stainer & Bell

17 Grand piano by Haschka, Vienna (*c.*1825)
The Colt Clavier Collection. By kind permission of Stainer & Bell

18 'Turkish Music' inside grand piano shown in Plate 17
The Colt Clavier Collection, by gracious permission of the Curator, Mr W.G. Spiers

19 Grand piano by Haschka (*c.*1810)
The Colt Clavier Collection. By kind permission of Stainer & Bell

20 Claviorganum by Merlin
The Colt Clavier Collection. By kind permission of Stainer & Bell

21 Portable piano by Verel (1783)
The Colt Clavier Collection. By kind permission of Stainer & Bell

22 Grand piano by Heilman (*c.*1775)
The Colt Clavier Collection. By kind permission of Stainer & Bell

23 Cottage piano by Broadwood (*c.*1825)
The Colt Clavier Collection. By kind permission of Stainer & Bell

24 Grand piano by Tomkison (1821)
The Colt Clavier Collection. By kind permission of Stainer & Bell

25 Square piano by Ganer (1779)
The Colt Clavier Collection. By kind permission of Stainer & Bell

26 Cabinet piano by Collard & Collard (1845)
The Colt Clavier Collection. By kind permission of Stainer & Bell

27 Harpsichord by Kirckman (1791)
The Colt Clavier Collection. By kind permission of Stainer & Bell

28 Upright grand piano by Clementi (1816)
The Colt Clavier Collection. By kind permission of Stainer & Bell

29 Table (square) piano by Pape (1834)
The Colt Clavier Collection. By kind permission of Stainer & Bell

30 Naval tactics (*Encyclopédie*)
By permission of the British Library

31 Upholstery (*Encyclopédie*)
By permission of the British Library

32 Mrs. Mary Delany *Halifax Rose* (paper mosaic) (1779)
© The Trustees of the British Museum

33 George Stubbs, *A Grey Hunter with a Groom and a Greyhound at Creswell Crags* (*c.*1762–4)
© Tate Gallery, London

34 James Ward, *Napoleon's Horse, Marengo, at Waterloo* (1824)
   © The Northumberland Estates

35 Eugène Delacroix, *Horse frightened by Lightning* (c.1813–14)
   © The National Gallery, London

36 Carmontelle, *Leopold Mozart and his children* (c.1763)
   © The Trustees of the British Museum

37 Johann Nepomuk della Croce, *The Mozart family* (c.1780)
   Mozart-Museum, Salzburg. © Internationale Stiftung Mozarteum (ISM)

38 Wright of Derby, *An Academy by Lamplight* (c.1768–9)
   By gracious permission of Hon. Hugh Crossley, Somerleyton House.

39 Thomas Gainsborough, *John Plampin* (c.1752)
   © The National Gallery, London

40 John Hoppner, *Mrs Williams* (c.1790)
   © Tate Gallery, London

41 Eugène Delacroix, *Baron Schwiter* (1828)
   © The National Gallery, London

42 Louis Daguerre, *The Ruins of Holyrood Chapel, Edinburgh, Effect of Moonlight* (c.1824)
   © National Museums Liverpool (The Walker Gallery)

43 John Gildon, *The Glorious Victory of Salamanca* (extract)
   By permission of the British Library

44 Lemière de Corvey, *La Révolution du 10 Aoust, 1792* (title-page)
   By permission of the British Library

45 Lemière de Corvey, *La Révolution du 10 Aoust, 1792* (extract)
   By permission of the British Library

46 Moore, *How dear to me the hour*
   By permission of the British Library

47 Muzio Clementi, *Variations on 'The Black Joke'* (freestanding set), last two
   By permission of the British Library

48 J.N. Hummel, *The Pretty Polly* (opening)
   Author's collection

49 J.N. Hummel, *The Pretty Polly* (Adagio)
   Author's collection

50 Figured bass in Hummel's Piano Concerto in A minor, Op. 85, first movement
   By permission of the British Library

51 Hummel, *New Vienna Waltz*, Trio 3
   By permission of the British Library

Editorial

All dates given are, where possible, those of the completion of the work, whether musical or otherwise. If this is not known, 'pub.' refers to its first publication and 'perf.' to its first known performance. Particular locations within pieces of music are identified by their Opus (Op.) number, or other appropriate designation, followed by the number or title of the piece(s) within that opus, followed by the movement number (in small Roman), and the bar or measure number (in Arabic) – all separated by forward slashes – with superscripts showing the beat(s) where desirable or necessary. Particular variations in a set are shown as 'var. 2', and so on, and bar numbers reckoned from the beginning of the particular variation. Thus, bar 10 of the second variation in the (slow) third movement of Beethoven's fifth string quartet (Op. 18 No. 5) would be Op. 18/5/iii/var. 2/10.

A note on nomenclature

Since many of the pianos made in the German-speaking areas of Europe used a mechanism perfected by an important group of makers in Vienna, I have kept the term 'Viennese', but used inverted commas where it can be determined that the instruments were not actually made in Vienna or referring to instruments that were made elsewhere on Viennese principles. The case with the so-called 'English' piano is different, not so much because of the fact that the piano was brought to the country by Germans who then developed it, since this situation also applied to a large extent to the 'Viennese' instrument, but because of non-English influences. I prefer to use the term 'British' in recognition of the vital Scottish (Broadwood, Stodart) and Irish (Southwell) contributions and because it harmonises with the usage both in Britain and abroad, since both of these countries – for better or worse – were part of the United Kingdom of Great Britain and Ireland for most of the period. I have adhered to the traditional 'London Piano School' (in inverted commas) of composer/performers because, even though the vast majority of the personnel involved are non-British, it was, at least, based largely in that city. The only remaining alternative, to use 'English' (in inverted commas) would, I think, be cumbersome and create more confusion.

General abbreviations

arr.	arranged	Op., Opp.	Opus, Opus (plural) or Opuses
aug	augmented		
b., bb.	bar, bars	perf.	first [known] performance
dim	diminished		
dim.	*diminuendo*	pf	piano[forte]
diss.	dissertation	posth.	posthumous
ed.	editor, edited (by)	pt, pts	part, parts
edn	edition	pub.	first published
Eng.	English	rep.	reprinted
facs.	facsimile	resp.	respectively
Fr.	French	rev.	revised
Ger.	German	r.h.	right hand
inc.	including	Sp.	Spanish
It.	Italian	trans.	translator, translated (by)
l.h.	left hand		
Mod	modulating	U.	University
MS, MSS	manuscript(s)	unpub.	unpublished
orc	orchestra	var.	variation
or.	original, originally	vol.	volume

Pitch

The system of pitches used in this book is a common modification of Helmholtz's, giving c^1 as middle C with the upper octaves as c^2, c^2, c^4 and so on, and the lower ones as c, C, C^1, C^2, and so on. So, the F♯ an octave and a half above middle C would be f♯^{2} and that of an octave a half below, F♯.

Bibliographic references

These are in the form of the author's name separated from the capitalised main (or first important) word in the relevant work's title or an obvious abbreviation: thus, 'Newman/SSB' refers to William S. Newman's *The Sonata Since Beethoven*. If the title is in a foreign language, the title-word is italicised, for example, Milchmeyer/*PIANOFORTE* refers to Milchmeyer's *Die wahre Art das Pianoforte zu spielen*. Where the personal name is that of an editor, the suffix '-ed' is added, as in Anderson-ed/BEETHOVEN for Emily Anderson's edition and transcription of Beethoven's letters, and when the source is wholly or largely music, the suffix '-m' is appended to the title-word as in the case of Koszewscy-eds/ KURPINSKI-m: Andrzej & Krystyna Koszewscy's edition of pieces by Karol Kurpinski. The addition of I, II, and so on, refers to the numbered (or un-numbered, if in a clearly numerical or chronological order) volumes in a source; for example, Landon/CHRONICLE II is the second volume of H.C. Robbins Landon's *Haydn: Chronicle and Works*; this particular volume is entitled *Haydn at Esterháza, 1776–1790*.

Introduction

All periods are periods of change, and our modern world and its preoccupations can, of course, be traced back to any and all of them but, it is fair to say, this particular ninety years (1760–1850) was a watershed, unleashing forces that still remain apparently unstoppable. The French Revolution changed our view of the state and its institutions and our ideas of democracy, law (and more); the Industrial Revolution changed our world in almost every other way. Most of the technological features that define our modern age would have been unthinkable without the innovations of the period discussed in this book; they include the steam train, the telegraph, gas lighting, photography and, just after our period, the use of electricity for lighting. We are used to a vastly accelerated rate of change today – to the point of bewilderment – but again it was during this period that the concept of change, especially when expressed in the guise of improvement, became a noticeable and necessary part of the political, social and industrial language of the merchants of 'progress' – and 'merchants' has a literal connotation here also.

Nevertheless, the enormous differences between the two worlds are more important than the similarities. At the beginning of our period, the journey by horse-drawn coach from London to Glasgow took 10–12 days on average; by the middle of the period it was half of this, and just after the end (1855), the journey from Cork or Southampton to New York could be made in nine to nine and a half days by the first iron steamer. Land transport was revolutionised by the steam train, which, in a matter of years after its invention, (the 1830s) could achieve speeds of up to 60 miles – or 90 kilometres – per hour; if powered flight and the TGV is excluded, the comparison with transport one and a half centuries later, is sobering.

To give some idea of the period's historical perspective, within a decade of its beginning we have Arkwright's first spinning mills, the discovery of the electrical nature of nervous impulses (Galvani), the opening of the first public restaurant (*Le Procope* in Paris), the completion of Goldsmith's *The Deserted Village*, of Laclos's *Les Liaisons dangereuses*, of Bürger's *Leonore*, Klopstock's *Odes*, Sterne's *Tristram Shandy* (and its author's death), Gainsborough's *Blue Boy*, and the births of Novalis, Humboldt, Hölderlin, Hegel, Tieck, A.W. von Schlegel, Wordsworth, Coleridge, Scott, Dalton, Malthus, Fourier and Canaletto as well as the openings of the British

Museum, the Sorbonne and the Kew Botanical Gardens; we also have the 'end of an era' with the deaths of Boucher and Tiepolo and the murder of Winckelmann. Musical matters of note were the appearance of Haydn's 'Sun' quartets (Op. 20), the first performance of the *Messiah* in the New World, the death of Telemann, the birth of Beethoven and the production of the first barrel organs in London.

At or near the end of the period, Britain annexed the Punjab, California became a US state, serfdom was abolished in Austria, the beginnings of Prohibition and the Gold Rush appeared in America, Haussmann began the reconstruction of Paris, France introduced insurance for the old and the British Factory Act of 1847 restricted the working day for women and children of 13 to 18 years of age to 10 hours. We have the first use of the concept and of the word 'evolution' (Spencer), the law of electromagnetic induction, Boole's *Mathematical Analysis of Logic*, the measurement of the speed of light (Fizeau), the appearance of Dickens' *David Copperfield* and *Bleak House*; Dumas *fils*'s *La Dame aux Camélias* (novel and play); Melville's *Moby-Dick*, Turgenev's *A Month in the Country*, Stowe's *Uncle Tom's Cabin*, the publication of *Jane Eyre, Wuthering Heights, Vanity Fair* and Millais' *Ophelia*; the births of R.L. Stevenson, Bell, Becquerel, van Gogh, Gauguin, Strindberg, Maupassant and Louis Daguerre; and the deaths of Tieck, Lenau, Poe, Wordsworth, Fenimore Cooper, Hokusai, and Turner. In music, there are the first performances of Verdi's *Macbeth, Rigoletto, Il Trovatore* and *La Traviata*, Flotow's *Martha*, Meyerbeer's *Le prophète*, Schumann's *Genoveva* and *Manfred*, the foundation of the Bach-Gesellschaft, Wagner's completion of his text for *The Ring* and the beginning of Steinway's piano production in New York with cast-iron frames. Chopin, Nicolai, Johann Strauss I, Lortzing, Donizetti and the Mendelssohns (brother and sister) died, and d'Indy, Stanford and Parry were born.

In terms of this book, the period (*c*.1760–1850) is that in which the piano first came into its own and encompasses, as neatly as is possible in such circumstances, its rise to prominence from the first appearances in public *c*.1764, to, as mentioned above, the founding of the Steinway company in New York and the beginnings of the modern concert grand *c*.1853. It also includes the first two generations of piano-composers and their close association with, respectively, the 'Viennese' and British ('English')[1] pianos and with French and later pianos, providing the new instrument with the first *tranche* of its great repertoire, which continues to furnish concerts and recitals with the vast bulk of their contents. The piano's ascendancy in so many ways – as instrument, cultural icon, social signifier, musico-social adjunct, piece of furniture – is without parallel in music history and it enjoys the widest repertory of any solo instrument, even when its appropriation of music from other media as arrangements is excluded.

In the realm of melodic instruments, the various keyboards are unique in that polyphonic music is produced by two hands, engaged in the same way and in equal measure, and separated from the sound-source by a more-or-less complex mechanism. Thus, in the matter of sound-production, only the player's hands are involved; the few exceptions to this are some types of organ (for air-supply) and the rare *Geigenwerk*

---

[1] See 'A note on nomenclature' above.

(in which the strings were excited by rotating belts or wooden wheels)[2]. For the purposes of this book, I view the diverse manifestations of keyboard music at the beginning of this period as being part of a single keyboard tradition, albeit a long one, since the earliest extant written examples of an already advanced practice survive from the early fourteenth century. I see this keyboard tradition, during the period, as being buffeted about by various influences, like winds – occasionally forceful – causing changes in substance and, occasionally, direction. These influences are social, cultural (including its narrower sense of fashionable) and technological, as well as purely musical and can be clearly discerned from the titles of my chapters. These are further grouped into three sections: Instruments, Influences and Integration. A further book (*The Companion to 'The Mechanical Muse: The Piano, Pianism and Piano Music, c.1760–1850'*) will appear shortly, containing a biographical index of the various musical personages mentioned, glossaries of works referred to and terms used.

Beginning in Section I ('Instruments') with a brief history and characterisation of the new instrument, the progress of the piano itself, in its various guises, can be traced from a sometimes ridiculed curiosity to the most desirable acquisition in any *salon* or drawing-room, the symbol of respectability, prosperity, artistic sensitivity, aesthetic acumen, fashionability and cultural arrival, and symbolic of a guarantee of all this in the marriageable daughters who played them. But the piano is also an 'influence' – the first and the most important of these – in that its construction and its methods of sound-production and sound-control demanded so strenuous a modification of existing keyboard techniques as to amount to an altogether new approach. Thus, the various features of the piano as an instrument give rise to modifications in the music (virtuosity, pedalling, and so on) and sometimes new genres, as in the case of the piano *Nocturne* and of the *Etude*.

Chapters in Section II chart influences in the more obvious senses of the word. The great interest in character, the heightened emotional content and the individuality in musical works, was occasioned by the sensitivity and expressivity of the piano as well as by the wider cultural changes in progress during the period. The vernacular grew into a virtual mania, especially in its guise of folk-songs, folk-tales, folk dances, vernacular buildings, dress and linguistic expression, and not only were these appropriated in settings – for example, variations and rondos – but many of their features inveigled their way into the musical style itself, eventually, in the later nineteenth century, becoming the cause of a rift between 'high' and 'low', or 'serious' and 'popular' styles – a fascinating development outside of my scope in this book. Another influence was the great popularity of improvisation, which, in our period, came to the forefront of performance as an item in itself, where the act of musical creation became a public spectacle – 'before the very eyes' of the audience. This, for good and bad reasons, has had very little attention in piano literature of the period, but needs to be addressed, as, in a similar fashion to vernacular music (in which *extempore* input is frequently encountered), many of its traits became part and parcel of musical style and expression as well as of performance practice. Again, this

---

[2] For this reason, and that of its extreme rarity, it will not be dealt with in this book.

was by no means confined to music, though it was to be seen at its most obvious and its most impressive there.[3]

Influences, of course, are usually reciprocal and the inherited forms that came as embedded in, or alongside of, the received keyboard tradition also had their effect on the piano's music in the period, and were themselves in turn affected by what was fast becoming a truly pianistic, as opposed to generally keyboard, tradition. Far from disappearing with so many other Baroque features and forms, the minuet continued in the Classical and early Romantic periods, long after it ceased to be danced in even the most aristocratic of *salons*, becoming enshrined in the sonata and then being transformed into the *scherzo*, while the rondo came into its own as a free-standing piece or as the best-loved finale for a sonata. Indeed, the sonata itself became the favourite small genre for the Classical period and, in addition, gave its name to that period's predominant and most distinctive musical form, while its relevance for the subsequent Romantic period, though buckling somewhat under the onslaught of the character-set, was still enough for composers – including those whose musical thinking was basically unsuited to its shape – to strive to do justice to it. It eventually became the most 'serious' form in the solo-piano performance, whether in private or in the public form of the piano-recital, which, in the last quarter of the period, began to establish itself as the solo counterpart to the symphony-concert and the more recently born chamber-concert. The variation-set blossomed – many would say went to seed – in this period and saturated the musical world of the *dilettante* and the drawing-room, and the concerto, long the favoured medium for solo display, became the most important vehicle for the piano in public, the genre in which the artist could be seen in his/her dual creative capacities as composer and performer: individuality personified.

The piano also has an important social role, some aspects of which are looked at in Section III: 'Integration'. The differences in the piano's use as an accompanying instrument is compared in the Classic and Romantic 'legs' of our period and its importance in helping to define the *Lied* and add to its capacity to encompass a miniature musico-dramatic world is paid tribute to. The more incestuous world of the piano duet and duo, as well as the reproductive function of the instrument in arrangements, is also mentioned, the piano's vital contribution to teaching across the musical spectrum is overviewed briefly, as is the importance of music printing and publishing, and the book ends with the piano's social use in accompanying dancing or appropriating the various dances as performed pieces.

In spite of my belief that musicology and musical historiography should combine various degrees of contextuality with as much musical depth as is possible or desirable, and of my attempts to deal with 'The Piano and its Music' in accordance with this belief, my book makes no claims to being comprehensive in any of these fields, either in scope or depth, and is intended only as a broad survey based upon – and, I am well aware, limited by – my own knowledge and perspective. The method used, however, might have some advantages: it allows the piano to be sited firmly in

---

[3] I intend to explore the subject of improvisation in art-music in a forthcoming book.

its socio-historic *milieu* and obviates the need to spend time on either 'explaining' the greatness of the Greats, or on apologising for not doing so. The 'greater' figures have been, and are being, dealt with in far better ways than this book aspires to and my wish is to consider as broad a spectrum of music as is practicable in a volume of this length – music which people daily played, sang, talked about, listened to and paid comparatively large sums to experience in concerts, and this encompasses composers of all ranks, of which the Greats are only a part and by no means always a large one, although they are accorded their place under various headings. The gift of hindsight is a two-edged sword – and an unwieldy one – and there is nothing inevitable about history: it is a construct, one of many possible, and has been frequently and successfully challenged. In this book I want to deal – as well as I can and weighing up the available evidence – with the music people in the period *actually* experienced, not what we now think they *should* have experienced.

PART ONE
Instruments

CHAPTER ONE

History and Background

(i) The beginnings

Unlike the violin, the piano was not a refinement of an extant, familiar instrument, in spite of its superficial similarity to several. Born in a climate in which the need for instrumental expressivity was increasing, its invention was a deliberate attempt to satisfy this need in terms of a keyboard instrument – a rather original attempt, though, on the face of it, somewhat unpromising at first.

It was original in the sense that it eschewed the familiar mechanisms of its sister instruments: the clavichord, in which the strings were sounded by being touched by tangents (see Fig. 1); the harpsichord, in which they were plucked by quills (see Fig. 2); and the rarer *Geigenwerk*, whose strings were 'bowed' by rotating belts or wheels.[1] It was unpromising in that striking strings would not seem at first sight to provide the solution to the problem of combining the controllable expressivity of the clavichord and *Geigenwerk*, with the harpsichord's loudness and brilliance. Striking strings seems to have found little favour with Western art-musicians; its prevalence in non-art traditions may have been part of the reason.

Nevertheless, the principle of striking has had a long pedigree in art-music. The medieval psaltery, a kind of small horizontal harp with a parallel soundboard played with the fingers, gave way to the hammered dulcimer, a zither-like instrument played with mallets. This appears to be the instrument depicted on a twelfth-century book cover.[2] The next reference to such an instrument occurs in the Arnaut Manuscript of 1440,[3] though the writer of the section relevant to this, the Netherlander Henri Arnaut de Zwolle, admits to basing his description on a manuscript from the end of the previous century. This is a mechanised form of dulcimer, the *dulce melos*, in which a keyboard causes hammers to strike the strings. No such instrument has survived, nor have any of the keyboard instruments in the possession of the Duke of Modena at the end of the sixteenth century, whose names include versions of '*pian e*[*t*] *forte*'.[4]

---

[1] As mentioned in the Introduction (fn. 2) we will not deal with this instrument.
[2] See 'Dulcimer' in New Grove/INSTRUMENTS.
[3] Bibliothèque Nationale, Paris (lat. 7295).
[4] For information on these and all other matters relating to the early piano, see Harding/PIANOFORTE, together with the other excellent monographs by Pollens/PIANOFORTE, Komlós/FORTEPIANOS, Cole/PIANOFORTE and Latcham/STRINGING.

They were also unknown to Bartolom[m]eo Cristofori, keyboard-instrument-maker to the Medici court in Florence, whose inventive ingenuity extended to all the common keyboard instruments. This appears to be the most authentic form of his name, since it remains so in the Medici court records; other forms of the surname include Christofori, Cristofali, and Cristofani. It may be misleading to credit him with the 'invention' of the pianoforte, since the principle had already been used in the past and since technicians in other countries seemed to be moving along similar lines, as in the various *clavecins à maillets* ('keyboard instruments with hammers') of Jean Marius (Paris, 1716) and possibly the hammered *'Clavier-Instrument'* of Christoph Gottlieb Schröter (Dresden, c.1721), although this claim is disputed.[5]

Cristofori's extra refinements over and above the basic striking action, resulting in an instrument fulfilling most of the expectations of a modern pianoforte, make him the main pioneer and the earliest, since he had constructed at least one such instrument by 1700 at the latest and probably by the early 1690s. In a manuscript inventory of the instruments at the court of Prince Ferdinando of Tuscany in Florence, dated 1700, an *'Arpicembalo di Bartolomeo Cristofori di nuova inventione, ... con ... martelli, che fanno il piano, et il forte'* ['A large keyboard instrument by Bartolomeo Cristofori, of new invention, ... with ...hammers, that produce soft and loud'] is described.[6] It is also of interest that his three surviving pianos date from late in his life, between the ages of 65 and 71, which would suggest the (very successful) end of a more-or-less lengthy period of experimentation and probably involving many instruments that have been lost, destroyed or converted (that is, their innards being replaced with other mechanisms, and so on).

The new instrument aroused much interest, particularly after the poet and playwright Scipione Maffei took the trouble to visit Florence in 1709–10, to see and, no doubt, hear, the new wonder and to interview its maker. His account, together with a drawing of piano action, was published in the prestigious *Giornale dei letterati d'Italia* (Venice, 1711).[7] That this honour was bestowed on a craftsman – the earliest known interview with a musical-instrument-maker[8] – was significant and presages the later interest which the piano would command. There are also other, more oblique, indications of Cristofori's importance and the esteem in which his work was held: his salary was quite a high one for such a position, and he confined himself to keyboard instruments, working at his home rather than within the Medici palace; he was 'brought in' from his previous home in Padua, even though there were a number of instrument-makers locally; also, it seems that he never felt the need to join the guild to which they all belonged, that of the *legnaioli*, or woodworkers, since there is no record of his membership. King João V of Portugal is reported to have paid a huge amount for his pianos.

Three of Cristofori's pianos survive: the first, dating from 1720, is now in the Metropolitan Museum of Art, New York, the second, made in 1722, is in the Museo

---

[5] See Harding/PIANOFORTE and, especially, Pollens/PIANOFORTE.
[6] Pollens/PIANOFORTE, p. 43.
[7] Information from ibid., Chapter 3.
[8] According to Pollens, ibid., p. 56.

Strumenti Musicali, Rome, and the Musikinstrumenten-Museum at the University of Leipzig (formerly the Karl-Marx-Universität) has the third (1726, see Pl. 1). Each shows refinements of various kinds: the action of the 1726 instrument is shown in Fig. 3. Some other keyboard instruments of his also survive and so do one each by two of his pupils, Giovanni Ferrini (a combination piano/harpsichord of 1746, the last remaining instrument from the school of Florence) and P. Domenico Del Mela (an upright piano – possibly the first of its type[9] – dated 1739).

In spite of this, the main advances in the construction of the instrument, even before Cristofori's death, were made elsewhere. Interest was already stimulated in the possibility of struck strings by the showmanship of a certain Pantaleon Hebenstreit, inventor of, and renowned virtuoso throughout Europe on, the hammered dulcimer, which was called, among other things, the *Pantalon,* a name which 'stuck' after the decree of a very impressed Louis XIV before whom Hebenstreit played in Paris in 1705. This was developed from the gut-stringed peasant dulcimer (*Hackbrett*) used to accompany dancing in a village inn frequented by Hebenstreit while he was a tutor to a local pastor's children. The keyboard-instrument-maker Gottfried Silbermann built a number of Pantalons, until a dispute with the inventor caused a cessation. The sound of the instrument can be gauged to some extent by the similarly-played cimbalom of present-day usage. Complication set in when a harpsichord keyboard was added to control the hammers, the gut strings became metal and stops were added to change the sound.[10] It is important to remember, however, that, in spite of these likenesses, any gradations in timbre or volume were not in question. Expectations of the sound 'seem to be locked into the aesthetic of the organ or harpsichord, where a change in dynamic level is achieved by adding or subtracting stops... Neither ... were ... crescendo or diminuendi ... or accents [expected.] ... In short, the Pantalon did not share the pianoforte aesthetic.'[11]

In spite of a German translation of Maffei's article on Cristofori (by the Dresden court poet Johann Ulrich König), published in 1711 and of its subsequent appearance, complete with the drawing of the action, in Johann Mattheson's *Critica Musica* (1722–5), it took the arrival of Cristofori's 1726 instrument in Germany to galvanise other instrument-makers. One of the first of these was G. Silbermann, who presented a piano to the Elector of Saxony, Frederick Augustus I. In fact, Silbermann was widely credited – even as late as 1806[12] – with the invention of the piano, in spite of the fact that his actions were almost identical with that of the 1726 Cristofori piano mentioned – including the hand-stops to shift the keyboard for single-string striking (the *una corda*) but with the addition of a stop to raise the dampers. Silbermann is, of course, principally remembered as the organ-builder associated with Johann Sebastian Bach, whose approbation he also, naturally enough, wished to elicit for his pianos. According to J. F. Agricola, when Bach tested one of his first two instruments he

---

[9] See Pollens/PIANOFORTE, pp. 107ff, for more information and a description of the instrument.

[10] I will return to this last aspect of the instrument in Chapter Six: 'The Piano's Sound'.

[11] Cole/PIANOFORTE, p. 30. Cole's treatment (ibid., pp. 23–39) of this fascinating and important byroad in piano-evolution is beyond my scope here, but is recommended reading.

[12] Schubart/*IDEEN,* p. 142.

praised the sound, even marvelled at it: however, he complained that the tone in the treble was too weak, and that it would be heavy to play. Hr. Silbermann, who could not endure criticism of his work, took this badly. He was annoyed with Hr. Bach for a long time.[13]

After years of effort, he improved his models and was rewarded handsomely during the 1740s, when Frederick the Great, a good flautist as well as a composer, bought all the fifteen pianos he had made to date.

Silbermann's reward was not only pecuniary, however, but also musical. When Bach, through the offices of his son Carl Philipp Emanuel Bach, who was Frederick's court accompanist, visited Potsdam in May 1747, he was rushed to Frederick's court straight from the coach. The evening concert was abandoned and Bach was asked to try out the Emperor's Silbermann pianos. As the party trooped from room to room, Bach extemporised, finishing up with an improvised fugue on a subject given by Frederick; this became the basis of the *Musical Offering* which, five months later, he had engraved and dedicated to the Emperor. The story was told to Bach's biographer, Johann Nikolaus Forkel, by another of Bach's sons, Wilhelm Friedemann, who accompanied him on this trip. Bach's endorsement was clearly not merely out of deference to his regal host, as he acted for Silbermann in the sale of a piano in 1749.[14]

Two of the King's Silbermann pianos survive today. Both belong to the collection of the Staatliche Schlösser und Gärten Preußischer Kulturbesitz, Potsdam. Although they both date from around the same time – one, 1746, the other very close to it – the difference in casework is striking: the dated one, in the palace of Sanssouci, has a plain black case and turned legs, and the other, in the Neues Palais, is in gold with highly ornate legs.

There were other, simpler, approaches to piano-building in Germany, however. In the early 1740s, the small square *Tafelklaviere* ('table-pianos', since they were placed on tables) begin to be found. These looked like clavichords and the resemblance didn't end there: the German *Prellmechanik* action, originally without escapement (see Fig. 4), later with it (see Fig. 5), was extremely close to that of a clavichord (Fig. 1), the main difference being the substitution of small hammers for clavichord tangents. The earliest surviving example is by the Bavarian maker Johann Socher dating from 1742.[15] The *Tafelklavier*, being cheap and space-saving, was by far the most popular type of domestic piano in Germany and remained so for most of the eighteenth century. It was furnished with various means for modifying the sound (see Chapter Four).

The importance of the Iberian peninsula as a haven for the early piano has only been appreciated comparatively recently. We have seen that the Italophile João V of Portugal was prepared to pay Cristofori well over the odds for one of his pianos,[16] and it was to his brother, the Infante Dom Antonio, that the first music expressly

---

[13] Johann Friedrich Agricola, in Adlung's *Musica Mechanica Organoedi* (1768) ii, pp. 116–7.

[14] Wolff/BACH, p. 403.

[15] The date is given on a label inside the instrument, but Pollens appears not to be entirely convinced (Pollens/PIANOFORTE, pp. 202–4).

[16] See above.

written for the new instrument was dedicated, a set of twelve *Sonate da Cimbalo* (1732) by Lodovico Giustini. João's daughter, Maria Barbara, brought her keyboard tutor, Domenico Scarlatti, to Madrid as court composer on her marriage to the prince of Spain in 1729, where the composer remained until the end of his life. An inventory after the queen's death shows five pianos, four of which were from Florence, and it is not surprising that their actions were closely modelled on that of Cristofori's – specifically the improved action of 1720. None of these pianos seem to have survived – in fact, despite a thriving Iberian industry towards the middle of the century, only five other instruments have survived, two from Spain (*c*.1745) and four from Portugal (1750s–60s); all their actions are copied from Cristofori's later action. Michael Cole's deduction is that the

> four instruments are relics of what may once have been a very flourishing tradition of Portuguese pianoforte-playing and instrument making, founded ultimately on instruments brought from Italy during the first half of the eighteenth century. Yet, for some reason, it is a tradition that did not move forward... and the pianos preserve the [piano-making] tradition of Cristofori so faithfully that, had we no surviving specimens from the Florentine maker, we could form a tolerably accurate impression of his work at second hand from these makers in far-away Lisbon.[17]

France's love of the colourful harpsichord and its military isolation from Britain for much of the eighteenth century offered no incentive to piano-builders, native or foreign. The French harpsichord-maker and inventor Jean Marius submitted models of four kinds of hammer-actions to the Académie des Sciences in 1716. It appears that because of mechanical imperfections, these *clavecins à maillets* remained on the drawing-board and it was not until considerably later in the century, with stimulation from Germany and England, that the French contribution became significant.

(ii) The later eighteenth century

If the French loved the brilliance and power of the harpsichord, the intimacy and expressiveness of the clavichord provided the point of departure for piano-making in the Austro-German and northern European lands. As noted above, the *Prellmechanik* (see Fig. 4), a modification of clavichord action with hammers taking the place of tangents, became the standard for square pianos and, with the addition of an escapement mechanism (to prevent the hammer from rebounding back to the string and re-striking it, see Fig. 5), probably by Johann Andreas Stein around the early 1770s, became the standard 'Viennese' piano so beloved of W.A. Mozart.[18] As with so much else in the history of the early piano, documentation is scarce and may be misleading. If the label dated 1773 on the Stein piano in the Musikinstrumenten-Museum at the University of Leipzig is correct, this may be the earliest surviving piano with *Prellmechanik* and escapement. Indeed, with slight modifications from

---

[17] Cole/PIANOFORTE, p. 19.
[18] His famous letter to this effect will be discussed later.

other makers, this action continued as the basis of the 'Viennese' piano for the first half of the nineteenth century.

Although later than the 'Viennese' piano, the other main type in the later eighteenth century was to be the British (so-called 'English'[19]) piano, and here we encounter the first of the several paradoxes which are associated with that instrument: the fact that it was German. According to Charles Burney, the first piano in England was by a 'Father Wood', an English resident in Rome. Burney used to play this during his first employment, from 1747, as Fulke Greville's music master, although it was brought to England a decade or so earlier. A copy was made, purporting to eradicate some problems mentioned by Burney – possibly to do with rate of note-repetition.[20] However, it is possible that there may have been another piano in London around this time. A friend of George Frideric Handel's mentions in a letter that the composer, 'played finely on the Piano-forte',[21] and the librettist of the *Messiah*, Charles Jennens, owned a piano in the mid-1750s – 'possibly the same one' according to Cole.[22]

The Seven Years War and its aftermath caused stringent economies, affecting industries of all kinds, and emigration to less hazardous environments was a temptation succumbed to by many. But an important instance, from our point of view, was the arrival in Britain of the rather obscure 17-year-old Princess Charlotte of Mecklenburg-Strelitz in 1761 to marry the recently-crowned George III, neither of whom had ever seen each other before this event. The princess, like all of the Germanic aristocracy, was well-versed in music and her arrival was a real boost for her countrymen, especially musicians, who had settled in Britain. Also, several musicians and music-technicians, either already famous, or soon to be, arrived around the same time or shortly after. They included: Johann [John] Christian Bach ('The "London" Bach'), who, within two years was advertising himself as the queen's music master; Americus Backers, inventor of the British grand piano action; Gabriel Buntebart, a keyboard-instrument-maker from Strelitz, who described himself in his will as 'grand Piano forte maker to Her Majesty'; and Johannes Zumpe who, after a short period with the Swiss harpsichord-maker Burkat (or Burkhardt) Shudi, set up in business for himself in 1761 and invented the British square piano. Shudi also appears under the names of Schudi, Tschudi and Tshudi: his firm and that of the Kirkman (Kirchmann, Kirckman) family were the foremost harpsichord-builders in Britain in the last half of the eighteenth century.

Zumpe, however, concentrated on the square piano, using a simplified Cristofori action which, because of its popularity, became known as the 'English single action' (see Fig. 6). A number of events worked in his favour, the principal of which was the fashion-conscious British public: everyone wanted the new instrument. It was comparatively easy and quick to make, portable, relatively cheap, and it took up little space; and, although playing it properly required specialised training, anyone who

---

[19] For my usage here, please see 'A note on nomenclature' in the Introduction.

[20] Cole's suggestion (*loc. cit.*, pp. 43–4).

[21] Rosemary Dunhill, 'Handel and the Harris Circle', *Hampshire Papers* (Winchester, 1995), 7; quoted in Cole/PIANOFORTE, p. 22.

[22] Cole, *loc. cit.*

could play any keyboard instrument could get a reasonable sound from it. When J.C. Bach took up residence in London in 1762, his expressed preference for the new instrument made him an important ally for Zumpe – and a good generator of business. The composer bought a square himself and publicly promoted it as a solo instrument in a benefit concert on 2 June 1768. Soon Zumpe was describing himself as 'Maker to Her Majesty and the Royal Family'.[23]

Bach's performance was by no means the piano's first public airing; its appearance in several European cities in the 1760s is an interesting phenomenon and marks the beginning of what would become an unstoppable rise. The instrument's first ever public outing seems to have been in Vienna, played by Johann Baptist Schmid in concerts on 6 March and 13 May 1763[24] and it was first played in public in England in 1767, when Charles Dibdin accompanied a singer at The Theatre Royal, Covent Garden, London. It seems that its first public appearances as a purely solo instrument were in Dublin on 19 May 1768 in performances by Henry Walsh, followed by Bach's in London on 2 June as mentioned above. It was first heard in public in Paris later in the same year (on 8 September) played by Mme. Lechantre at the *Concert Spirituel*. The fact that Bach's Op. 1 (1770) was a set of keyboard concertos dedicated to Queen Charlotte – the finale of No. 6 was a set of variations on *God Save The King* – and that he was officially her music master by 1764, guaranteed the piano respectability to go hand-in-hand with its novelty value.

Such was the demand that many builders were needed to satisfy it; according to Burney, 'After the arrival of John Chr. Bach in this country, and the stablishment of his Concert, in connection with Abel, all the harpsichord makers tried their mechanical powers at piano-fortes...'[25] Among these were Johannes Pohlmann, Schoene & Company (successors to Zumpe) and John Broadwood, who was responsible for the importance of the British School of piano-making. Broadwood moved from his native Scotland to Shudi's London workshop at the age of twenty-nine (1761), marrying his boss's daughter and becoming senior partner, and finally (1782) taking over the business. He made great improvements to Zumpe's action and began, as we shall see, to design grand pianos.

France appears less active during this period, the piano being somewhat suspect.[26] A combination of piano, carillon[27] and harpsichord was submitted to the Académie des Sciences in 1759, as was a piano combined with an organ, a type which found particular favour in France, known as the *pianoforte organisé*, in 1772.[28] In Strasbourg, Johann Heinrich Silbermann, nephew of Gottfried, made some of the earliest French pianos,[29] and Balbastre's wife owned a *clavecin à maillets* by

---

[23] In the *General Advertiser*, 1 February 1780.

[24] Maunder/KEYBOARD, pp. 97–8; I am grateful to Dexter Edge for first alerting me to these performances.

[25] Pollens/PIANOFORTE, p. 57.

[26] See the comments under (iv) 'The piano's early reception', below.

[27] For further information on the carillon, see Chapter Five (iv).

[28] See Peter Williams, 'The Earl of Wemyss' Claviorgan and its Context in Eighteenth-Century England', in Ripin/KEYBOARD, pp. 77–87, and New Grove/INSTRUMENTS, 'Claviorgan'.

[29] Announcement in *L'Avant Coureur*, 6 April 1761, pp. 219–20, quoted in Closson/PIANO, p. 86.

Blanchet; the bulk of the instruments, however, were of the Anglo-German type from London.[30] Pollens mentions that many Broadwood squares from this time bore instruction-labels in English and French – a fact that probably made them even more fashionable in England. The Flemish (French-naturalised) harpsichord-maker Pascal Taskin imported pianos from Buntebart and, later, Broadwood. Later in life, he made pianos based on Zumpe's models, as did some other local makers – Péronard, Goermans, Mercken, Zimmermann – but he also made the earliest grands in France in the late 1770s. The most important native figure is Sébastien Erard, who modified Zumpe's single action for his square pianos (producing his first in 1777) and the British grand action for his grands. His greatest contribution, however, belongs to the nineteenth century.

The sway of Zumpe's craftsmanship can be seen in other parts of Europe also, in Spain and, ironically, in the piano's home, Italy, as well as in Austria, where they were challenged by French imports – themselves close copies of Zumpe's originals – and in North America. The first mention of a (probably square) piano in America was in the *Massachusetts Gazette in* 1771, and it may have been this instrument which caused Thomas Jefferson to change his order for a clavichord.[31] Given the British presence in America, it is not surprising that the ubiquity of British squares was apparent here also, although both the cost and damage incurred in shipping instruments from Britain encouraged a burgeoning native industry together with, of course, the attraction of the country for immigrants; indeed, several piano-makers from London and Germany arrived in America in the 1780s. It would appear that the first indigenous instrument, a square, was built by an earlier German immigrant, Johann Bahrent (or 'John Brent') in 1775. The attraction of the square piano is clear from a report in a New York periodical of 1792:

> The Forte-piano is become so exceedingly fashionable in Europe that few polite families are without it. This much esteemed instrument forms an agreeable accompaniment to the female voice, takes up but little room, may be moved with ease, and kept in tune with little attention ... so that on that account it is superior to the harpsichord.[32]

By the middle of the nineteenth century, however, advances in technology would bring America to the cutting edge of the industry, an arrival which is beyond the scope of this book.

The grand piano's development was a different, though related, story. Being larger and more expensive, it tended to appear in only the very largest drawing-rooms and *salons*, as well as, of course, the public venues. Opinions differ on the nationality of the inventor of the 'English grand piano action', Americus Backers, although they lean towards Holland. He certainly had a wide experience of Continental pianos before settling in London *c.*1763. The oldest surviving British grand is one of his, with *Americus Backers No. 21 Londini fecit 1772* on the nameplate, complete with two

---

[30] Pollens/PIANOFORTE, pp. 221–2.
[31] See Cole/PIANOFORTE, pp. 86–7.
[32] *Loudens Register*, 19 September 1792, quoted in Cole/PIANOFORTE, p. 88.

pedals, sustaining and *una corda*.³³ Backers died in January 1778 and his work was continued by Robert Stodart, who arrived in London *c.*1765 and who, like his fellow-Scot John Broadwood, was apprenticed in the Shudi workshop, supervised by the latter. In 1775 he set up his own workshop in Wardour Street and, like Backers, also dedicated himself almost entirely to grands and had very little competition in this. It was only when Broadwood turned his attention to grands in 1785 that he began to collar the market, a story that will be taken up in Chapter Three.

(iii) The first half of the nineteenth century

By the first half-decade of the nineteenth century, three main centres of piano-construction, or 'schools', had polarised in the three largest musical centres, Vienna, Paris and London. Each type had its devotees and each tended to be associated with a particular kind of music.³⁴ The 'Viennese' type of grand held sway in the Habsburg Empire, representing work by a plethora of makers, the best-known of whom were Anton Walter, Johann Schantz, the Streicher/Stein and Brodmann/Bösendorfer dynasties, and Conrad Graf. It could be said to have been fully developed by the time W.A. Mozart was twenty and that later instruments were more in the nature of modifications than basic changes. Michael Latcham considers the work of Stein, the inventor of what he calls the German action, the '*Prellmechanik* with escapement' (*Prellzungenmechanik* – see Fig. 5), to be the acme of eighteenth-century piano-making, whereas he sees Walter, whose actions were derived from Stein's, as '[preparing] the way for the nineteenth-century developments. These were characterised by a search for a single ideal timbre and a demand for ever more volume.'³⁵ In this sense, Walter trod a similar path to that of Broadwood in 'standardising' the piano and its sound.

This century also saw the proliferation of small five-and-a-half octave Viennese squares, but problems caused by the desire to extend this compass switched the attention of makers to the upright, which caught on early in Vienna, especially the 'Pyramid style'. Because piano-making was not concentrated in the hands of a small number of makers, as, for example, in London, a much greater sense of individuality is evident in these instruments than elsewhere, as can be seen from the elaborate Pyramid piano, complete with Nubian slaves, in the Gemeentemuseum, The Hague, by the Viennese maker Conrad Graf *c.*1830. The music and style of performance associated with this 'school' was, as I have outlined before, clear and brilliant, and capable of articulating the finest nuances of dynamics and touch. As an indication of the size of the market, the Stein/Streicher firm's annual production rose from *c.*710 grands a year in 1805 to *c.*4,300 in 1850³⁶ and the workshops in 1816 were 'very extensive, ... [occupying] a large part of the house in which he only has a few rooms

---

[33] The instrument is at present on loan to the Russell Collection, Edinburgh.
[34] This will be dealt with below, see Chapter Two (ii).
[35] Latcham/STRINGING I, p. 10. Latcham prefers the phrase to the longer German term.
[36] Information taken from Graph 1 in Latcham/STRINGING II, p. 1.

as living quarters.'[37] An inventory on the day after Stein's daughter, Nanette Streicher, died in January 1833 includes beds for 17 apprentices.[38] Similarly, the industry grew from 'a handful of makers' in the 1780s to about 300 by 1825, including the ongoing firms of Hoffmann, Walter & Streicher.[39]

It is perhaps ironic that the nation – empire, rather – that earliest embraced industrialism and capitalism and therefore had the power and the market to benefit from it, was that in which grand piano-manufacture was concentrated almost exclusively in a handful of firms, and that handful itself dominated by a single workshop. (On the other hand, a glance at today's capitalism shows this principle writ large in the existence of the comparatively few global business conglomerates and the myth of the 'competition' principle.) Irony or not, the firm of John Broadwood and Sons led, by many lengths, a field that included W. Stodart and Son, Clementi & Company and, indeed, makers of all nationalities. The furious pace of improvements and patents levelled off during the first two decades of the new century. The more modest end of the domestic square market, however, provided a livelihood for a large number of makers and the competition was far keener, with exports ranging virtually throughout the known world. Clementi's European peregrinations to promote his pianistic hardware will be remembered here, ranging, *via* Beethoven in Vienna, to as far as St. Petersburg, where his erstwhile apprentice, the composer John Field, decided to remain.

If there was a feeling of *déjà-vu* about French pianos with respect to their British and German counterparts in the late eighteenth century, the piano-making industry burgeoned during the time of Napoleon, with the Erard brothers continuing their indigenous tradition to provide some of the most praised instruments in Europe, and the immigration of the Austrian composer-pianist Ignaz Pleyel during the first ten years of the nineteenth century. The latter also produced fine squares.

Much of the piano's nineteenth-century development stems from the quest for greater volume and durability and a need to keep mechanically abreast of the prodigious increases in technique. As we shall see in Chapter Sixteen (ii), the general increase in audience and concert-hall sizes in the early nineteenth century coupled with a rise in pitch gave the need for louder and stronger instruments generally. One of the criticisms[40] that emerges of French and British (as opposed to 'Viennese') grands was that their tone merged too much with that of the orchestra in concertos; the only remedy for these instruments was to modify or 'improve' them so that they would produce more volume. Among the modifications to the piano were the increase in string tension, the use of thicker strings and of stronger materials such as steel, and the various methods of bracing to counteract these, from stronger wooden cases and bracing, through metal bracing to the compensation frame. In this, patented by the Stodart firm in London in 1820, tubes of the same metal as the strings (brass or iron) would brace the instrument so that changes in temperature and humidity causing

---

[37] From an entry in the diary of Dr Karl Bursy, 24 June 1816, quoted in *op. cit.*, I, p. 8.
[38] *Loc. cit.*, fn. 14.
[39] *Loc. cit.*, p. 10.
[40] For example, see the quotation from Hummel/PIANOFORTE on pp. 21–2.

expansion or contraction of the strings would be compensated for by the same processes in the braces. Thus, the tension of the strings would remain substantially the same, preventing breakage and preserving tuning. Fig. 7, from Broadwood's patent of 1827 shows the principle of the system and Pl. 2 shows its application in my own William Stodart piano of before 1837. The next step along this particular road takes us to the end of our period with the full iron frame. In the case of domestic pianos, the space-saving trend led, among other things, to cross-stringing. The main advance with respect to technique was the patenting by Erard in London (1821, renewed in 1835) of the double-escapement (or repetition) action, allowing for greater rapidity in general and faster repetition of the same note in particular; this became the basis of all modern grand piano actions. Erard had the advantage of having a factory in London as well as in Paris, and a British patent for his invention represented a significant advantage; Fig. 8 is copied from this patent.[41]

(iv) The piano's early reception

The desire for a keyboard instrument with greater tonal flexibility and controllability had been made explicit on several occasions during the piano's infancy. In Maffei's description[42] (1711) of Cristofori's piano, he speaks of the delight of 'those who enjoy perfection in the art' of 'artful degrees [of] diminishing the voice little by little' and continues:

> Now, of this diversity and alteration of voice, in which are excellent, among others, bowed instruments, the harpsichord is entirely deprived, and the idea of constructing it so that it might have this gift would be deemed, by whomsoever it might be, a vain endeavour. Nevertheless, such a bold invention has been no less happily conceived than executed in Florence ... [43]

Even that most idiomatic of harpsichord-composers, François Couperin, could lament the instrument's inability 'to swell or diminish its sound' making the plea: 'I would be eternally grateful to anyone who, through infinite art supported by taste, would succeed in rendering this instrument capable of expression'.[44] It is not surprising, then, that attempts were made to do just this, to the extent that, as we shall see, some harpsichord makers, among them Marius, Weltman, Merlin and Geib, even added a separate piano-action to their instruments, in addition to the usual jacks and quills.

But these attempts provided for a choice of sounds and did not address the main problem, which was to create some kind of *crescendo/diminuendo* facility within the harpsichord itself. In fact, two methods of artificially implementing this were invented. The first was rather basic: a pedal attached to the harpsichord's lid so that the latter could be gradually raised and lowered – the 'nag's head swell'. The other was

---

[41] See Chapter Two (iii).
[42] See this chapter (i).
[43] Quoted and translated in Pollens/PIANOFORTE, p. 57.
[44] 'Je sçauray toûjours gré à ceux qui, par un art infini soutenu par le goût, pouront arriver à rendre cet instrument susceptible d'expression...' In the *Préface* to Bk. I of his *Pièces de clavecin* (Paris, 1713).

the 'Venetian swell', copied from the organ swell-box, in which hinged slats of wood, placed inside the lid over the strings, were gradually opened and shut creating artificial *crescendi* and *diminuendi*. This type became popular in the last quarter of the eighteenth century: Pl. 3 shows a Shudi-Broadwood harpsichord of surprisingly late date – 1790 – with the slats in open position.

There is no doubt that the piano's acceptability was hastened by the stylistic transition, broadly-speaking, from Baroque to Classical, which involved the development of newer styles having different melodic, harmonic and textural preoccupations from the basically monistic contrapuntality of the High Baroque. Two of J.S. Bach's sons were instrumental in this transition, each representing one of the two principal mid-eighteenth-century styles and each, to some extent, reacting against the music which their father exemplified.

With Johann Christian, the 'London' Bach (1735–82), this reaction took the form of a general lightening-up, a relaxation, of the rigours of Baroque polyphony in favour of a homophonic Southern European style, based on Italianate vocal models, exemplified in *opera buffa*. Like the vogue for polite conversation, this *style galant* rejoiced in pretty, well-turned melodies, couched in phrases that were well-balanced to the point of being occasionally foursquare, with unobtrusive but supportive harmonies of almost exclusively diatonic ilk: a musical analogue of the Augustan couplet of Pope *et al*. Ex. 1.1 gives the opening of his Piano Concerto Op. 7/6 in G major (1770).

Ex. 1.1: J.C. Bach, Piano Concerto in G major Op. 7/6/i, bb. 1–12.

Even the shape of the movements was an expansion of this principle, in which the busyness of the Baroque *ritornello* was replaced by the gentler extended binary form, allowing for a small measure of melodic contrast and tonal variety, in the shift to the dominant and the return to the tonic.

Carl Philipp Emanuel Bach's stylistic reaction took a different form, that of *Empfindsamkeit* ('feeling') or the *empfindsamer Stil* ['feeling style'] resulting in personal, emotionally charged music. This was more common in northern Europe, associated with the Germanic penchant for the intimately expressive clavichord, and characterised by dramatic and pathetic gestures, a high level of chromaticism and contrast, and an improvisatory freedom of expression. Ex. 1.2 is an instance from the second (slow) movement of the fifth of Emanuel's *Probestücke* Sonatas, illustrating the principles laid out in Part I of his *Versuch über die wahre Art das Clavier zu spielen* (1753) ['Essay on the true art of playing Keyboard Instruments'[45]].

Ex. 1.2: C.P.E. Bach, *Probestücke* No. 5/ii, bb. 1–9.

---

[45] See Chapter Two (iii).

The transformation of what could have easily been over-emotionalised self-indulgence into a public language was very much Emanuel's achievement and the style became an impetus, in the 1760s and 1770s, for the *Sturm und Drang* movement, a proto-Romantic upwelling which affected all the arts in the Germanic countries. Rhetorical rather than conversational, the kind of thematic material this style demanded, and its wider harmonic and chromatic range, was better suited to thematic and motivic development in the more rigorous sonata-form movements than the *galant* style, which was still represented, to an extent, in other movements. The fusion and transformation of these near-opposites in W.A. Mozart's hands would form a large part of his contribution to the mature Classical Style.

The north-European predilection for the clavichord mentioned earlier ensured a lively interest in the piano in those regions and explains the burgeoning of the industry, while it remained somewhat obscured in its country of origin, Italy. Ironically, the separating-out of melody and accompaniment in the homophonic *galant* style also favoured the piano, since this was possible without recourse to separate keyboards as on the harpsichord.

And yet, the piano's initial passage was slow, the older instruments still having influential adherents. C.F.D. Schubart could write a *paean* to the clavichord as late as 1785, the year in which Mozart completed and premiered his great D minor (K. 466) and C major (K. 467) concertos:

> Clavichord, this lonely, melancholy inexpressibly sweet instrument surpasses the harpsichord or piano when it is made by a master [craftsman]. Through the pressure of the fingers, through the oscillation and vibrato of the strings, through the strong or gentle touch of the hand, can be determined not only the immediate musical colorings but the middle tints, the swelling and dying away of the tone, the expiring trills melting away under the fingers, the portamento or glide – in a word, all the qualities out of which feeling is comprised. Whoever does not prefer to bluster, rage, and storm; whosoever heart overflows often and readily in sweet feelings – he passes by the harpsichord and piano, and chooses the clavichord ... [46]

In the end, however, even the reactionary anonymous writer in Cramer's *Magazin der Musik* of two years earlier (1783) had to give in, albeit with bad grace:

> ... adjacent melodic notes make a bad effect on this defective instrument, since no player has springs in his fingers. Composers must, therefore, change the character of their melodies so that the intervals are wider, in order to lessen the untimely sounding together of notes already heard.[47]

In France also, it was an uphill drive. As mentioned earlier, the harpsichord was the standard of measurement[48] and, according to the composer Claude-Bénigne Balbastre, would never be usurped by the piano.[49] The statement is odd in view of his owning a piano and, later, writing for it. The fact that it was directed to Pascal

---

[46] Schubart/*IDEEN*, pp. 288–9. Quoted in Newman/SCE, p. 83. C.F.D. Schubart was a poet also, immortalised in Schubert's settings of his *Die Forelle* [The Trout] and *An mein Klavier* [To my Piano].

[47] *Loc. cit.* (Cramer/*MAGAZIN I* (1783), p. 1238 tr. in Parrish/CRITICISMS, p. 439).

[48] It is interesting that even at the present time, French pianos tend to have a brighter sound than those of many other countries.

[49] Brancour/*INSTRUMENTS*, p. 92.

Taskin, the premier harpsichord-builder who had not yet embarked on his first piano, may explain this. For Voltaire, the piano was a 'boilermaker's instrument'[50] and Canon Trouflant was 'alarmed' at its internal complexity adding: 'Si les dessus en sont charmans, les basses dures, sourdes & fausses, semblent donner la consomption à nos oreilles françoises.'[51] ['If the treble is charming, the bass, hard, muffled and false, seems consumptive to our French ears'.] The Chevalier de Piis, a *vaudevilliste*, lampooned the piano thus:

> Fier de ses sons moelleux qu'il enfante sans peine
> Avec un flegme anglais le piano se traîne
> Et nargue, fils ingrat, le grêle clavecin.
>
> [Proud of its mellow sounds to which it gives easy birth
> With the reserve of the English the piano crawls along
> And, ungrateful child, derides the thin harpsichord.][52]

and the latent xenophobia is explained in the further jibe, reminding us of the almost constant hostilities between the two countries in the eighteenth and nineteenth centuries:

> Quoi, cher ami! tu me viens d'Angleterre?
> Pour quoi on lui déclare la guerre?
>
> ['What, my dear friend, you come to me from England?
> Why then [do we need to] declare war on her?'][53]

Despite the public bluster, it was clear that the new instrument was not only making inroads on the musical life, but attracting a following. Balbastre heard it in the Tuileries in 1774, but its first public outing in France was, as we have seen, in 1768 in the Concert Spirituel – 'not, however, with marked success', according to Ernest Closson.[54]

By 1791, when much in France had changed, Nicolas-Joseph Hüllmandel, in a French encyclopaedia article entitled 'Clavecin' must surely have been preaching largely to the converted when he wrote:

> The harpsichord lacks nuances. No way was found, after the addition of the second keyboard, of augmenting or diminishing the volume ... [except by complications that] denote the imperfections of [the instrument]. It requires too much skill from craftsmen and too much patience from performers ... moreover, should we seek to cling to false and puerile imitations? An instrument in which evenness and purity of sound and all the desired degrees of strength and gentleness speak to the heart without hurting the ear, fulfills the aim of music to a much greater degree ... To harpsichord music was assigned the role of harmony and execution, gracefulness and lightness, which are suitable to it ... [Now various authors,] by giving to their music graduated nuances, contrasts, and a melody suited to the tone and resources of the piano, have prepared or determined the downfall of the harpsichord.[55]

---

[50] A letter to the Marquise du Deffand of 8 December 1774, quoted in Parrish/CRITICISMS, p. 443.
[51] Quoted in Closson/PIANO, p. 59.
[52] Quoted in Parrish/CRITICISMS, p. 432.
[53] Quoted in Closson/PIANO, p. 86.
[54] Closson/PIANO, p. 90.
[55] Quoted in Hüllmandel/*CLAVECIN*, p. 34.

Burney links the popularity of the piano in England and France:

> Zumpé's [sic] [square] piano-fortes ... from their low price, and the convenience of their form, as well as the power of expression, suddenly grew into such favour, that there was scarcely a house in the kingdom where a keyed-instrument had ever had admission, but was supplied with one of Zumpé's piano-fortes, for which there was nearly as great a call in France as in England. In short, he could not make enough to gratify the craving of the public. Pohlmann, whose instruments were very inferior in tone, fabricated an almost infinite number for such as Zumpé was unable to supply.[56]

(v) The piano's early music

Burney was writing in retrospect, but even allowing for the fact that hindsight may have lent extra enthusiasm to these lines, it is clear that the piano was being seen less as a harpsichord with expressive possibilities and more as an instrument in its own right, for which an idiomatic literature was already being provided. Lodovico Giustini's twelve *Sonate da cimbalo di piano e forte detto volgaramente di martelletti* ['Sonatas for the soft and loud harpsichord called, commonly, with hammers'], Op. 1 (pub. Florence, 1732) the first known music to be written expressly for the piano, have already been mentioned.[57] As well as the expected *piano* and *forte*, available on a clavichord and two-manual harpsichord – and, possibly, with some considerable deftness and a change of timbre, on a single-manual one – one also finds *più forte* and *più piano* (see Pl. 4) indicating what would later come to be written as *crescendo* and *diminuendo*, or the familiar hairpin marks. The possibilities of simultaneous opposite dynamics were exploited by J.S. Bach in the 'Italian' Concerto, where the *piano* of the left hand accompaniment and the *forte* of the right hand melody appear on the same stave, but this is misleading, as two manuals are used for the effect, a fact that also accounts for the designation of the piece as a concerto.

The next works mentioning the piano included J.G. Eckard's Op. 1, *Six Sonates pour le Clavecin* (pub. 1763). One of the first title pages in English to mention the piano was that of John Burton's (1730–82) *Ten Sonatas for the Harpsichord, Organ or Piano-forte* (1766). Although many of the '*Pia*[no]' and '*For*[te]' alternations can be articulated on a harpsichord with more than one manual, or by agile application of pedals, stops or *genouillères*,[58] none of these could effectively carry out his dynamic instructions as given in bb. 93–7a. No doubt Burton, a well-known harpsichord and organ player, became acquainted with the piano during his concert tour of Germany in 1754.

Sir William[59] Herschel's *Sei Sonate per il cembalo cogli accompagnamenti di Violino e violoncello che si possone sonare anche sole* ['Six sonatas for keyboard accompanied by violin and cello, which can also be played solo' (that is, on the

---

[56] From an article written between 1801 and 1806 for Rees/CYCLOPAEDIA (pub. 1802–19).
[57] In (i), above.
[58] 'Knee-pedals': these will be discussed briefly in Chapter Four.
[59] German-born as Friedrich Wilhelm, he settled in England and became Astronomer Royal.

keyboard)] (pub. Bath, 1769), include *pianissimo, fortissimo, sforzando* and even a *piano – crescendo – forte* progression in the final work. Although the clavichord could fill the bill as the 'keyboard' here, it is highly unlikely.

The problem of assigning pieces to their proper instrument continues, and what muddies the waters is that the terms *cembalo* and *clavecin*, hitherto both meaning harpsichord, begin now to take on the more generic meaning of 'keyboard instrument', encompassing the piano and clavichord as well. Only in the case of certain composers can we be sure which is intended, and even then, the question as to exactly or approximately *when* their allegiance to the piano became paramount or exclusive remains only partly answered. Mozart's enthusiasm for the (forte)piano becomes apparent as soon as he settles in Vienna in 1781, although evidence using his title pages alone is misleading: the piano is specified only in the last two piano concertos, K. 537 (1788) and K. 595 (1791). Muzio Clementi, who used to be described as 'father of the pianoforte', did not become a devotee until later than was previously thought: the famous Op. 2 sonatas, which were traditionally cited as his claim to such a title, were not published until 1779 and, while other performers in London during the 1760s – notably J.C. Bach, as we have seen – were using the new instrument, Clementi continued to play on the harpsichord, at least until the middle of 1780.[60] Joseph Haydn's keyboard music from *c.*1770 on shows possible pianistic traits[61] and it can be safely said that Beethoven had the piano in mind from the start, certainly in the sonatas. Yet, his first sonatas up to and including the *Pathétique* Op. 13 were published for 'harpsichord or piano'. This is a reminder that, although the clavichord was out of favour by the 1780s, due partly to the fact that the piano was too close for comfort in terms of sound and possibilities, the harpsichord continued to be made and sold into the nineteenth century.

---

[60] See Plantinga/CLEMENTI, Chapter II.
[61] This is debatable and the evidence is briefly summarised in Chapter Two (i).

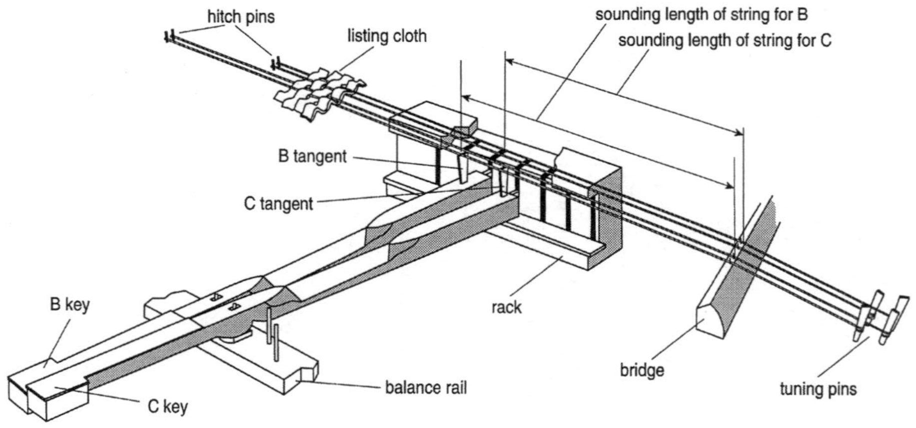

Fig. 1: Clavichord mechanism.

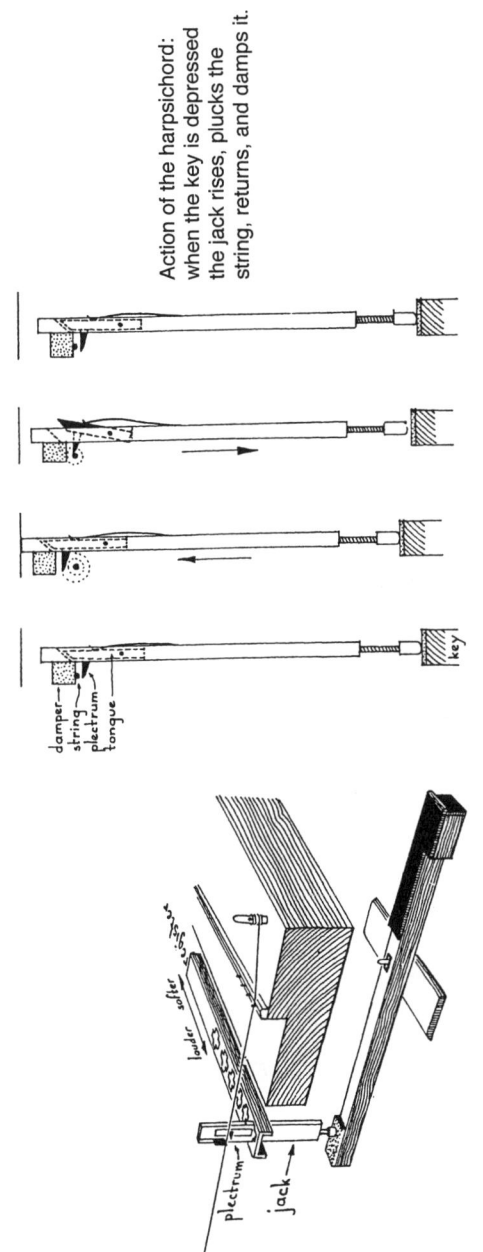

Fig. 2: Action of the harpsichord: when the key is depressed the jack rises, plucks the string, returns, and damps it.

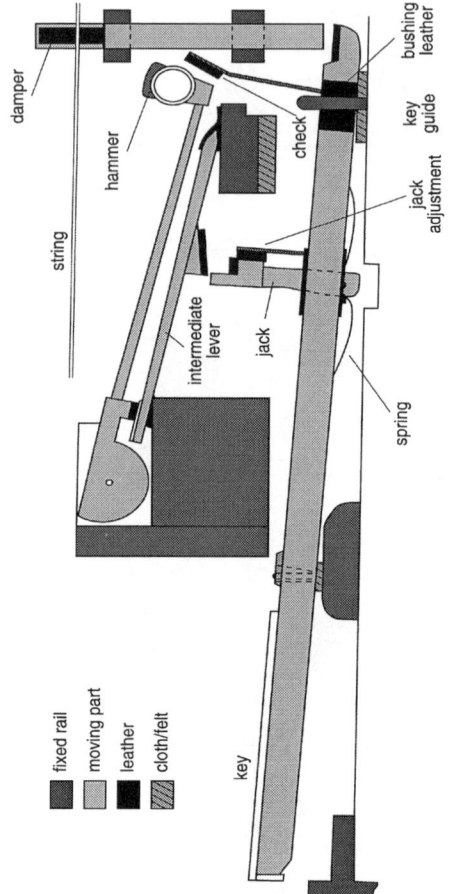

Fig. 3: Action of Cristofori's last surviving piano of 1726.

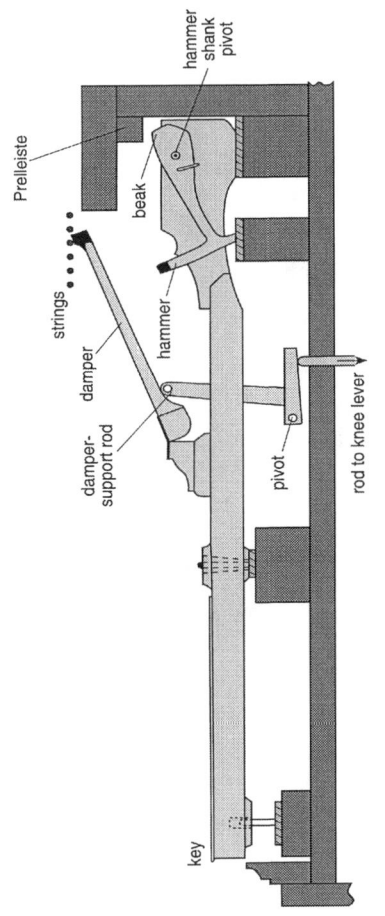

Fig. 4: Prellmechanik action without escapement mechanism from an anonymous south German square piano, c.1770 (Royal College of Music, London); to allow space for the hammer, the rear of the key is narrower than the front; the dampers are beneath the strings and disengage when the hinged end rises with the key; the knee lever lowers the damper-support rod to disengage all the dampers simultaneously.

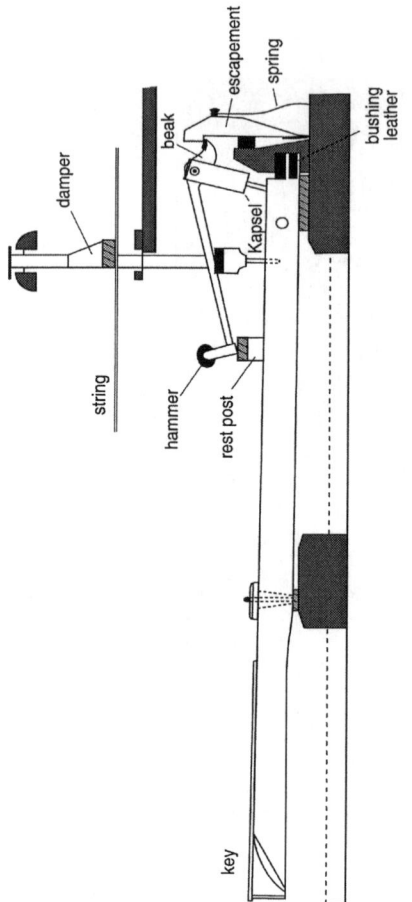

Fig. 5: Prellmechanik, with escapement, in a Heilman piano of c.1785.

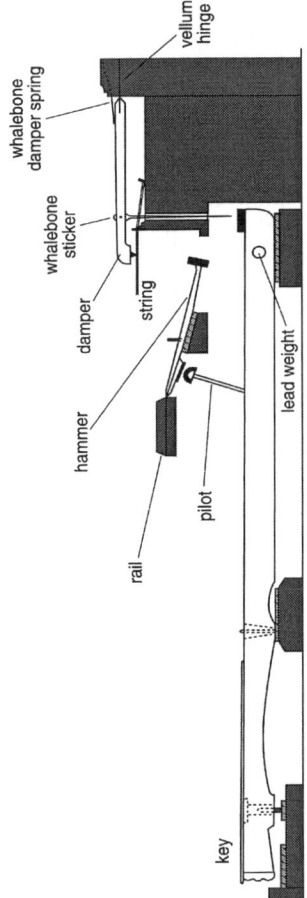

Fig. 6: 'English single action' (from Cristofori by Zumpe) in a Kirckman piano of 1775.

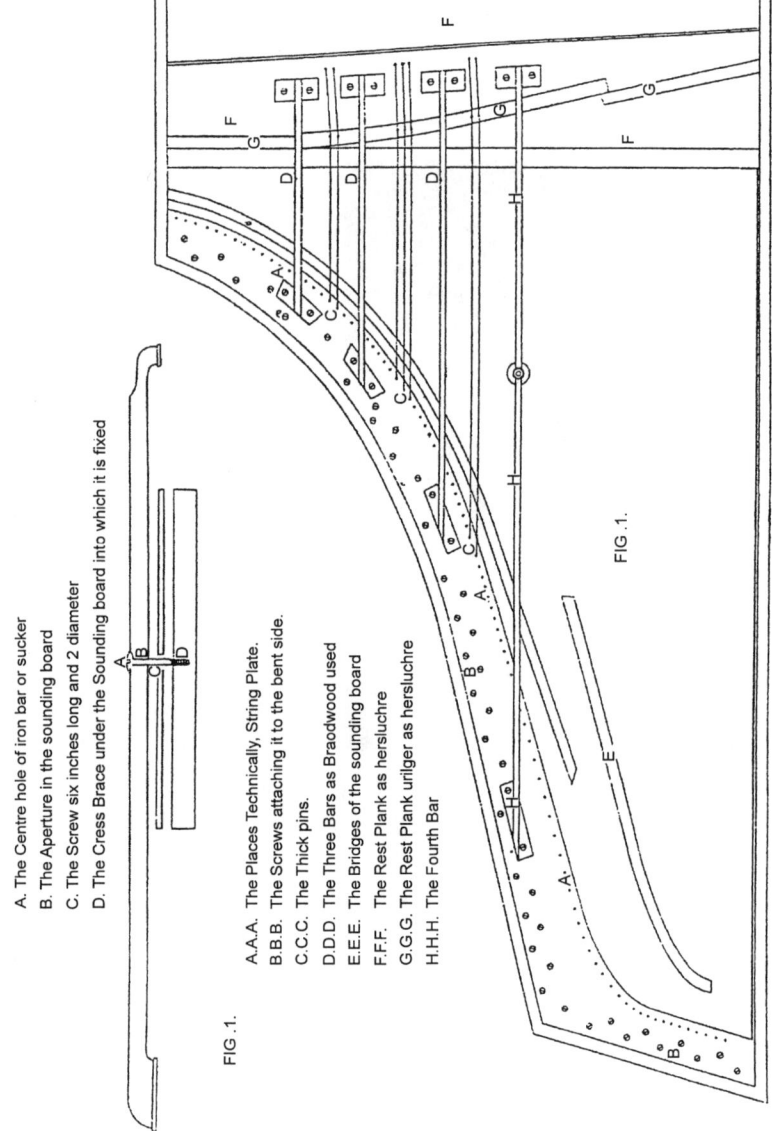

Fig. 7: Illustration of the 'compensated frame' from James Broadwood's patent of 1827.

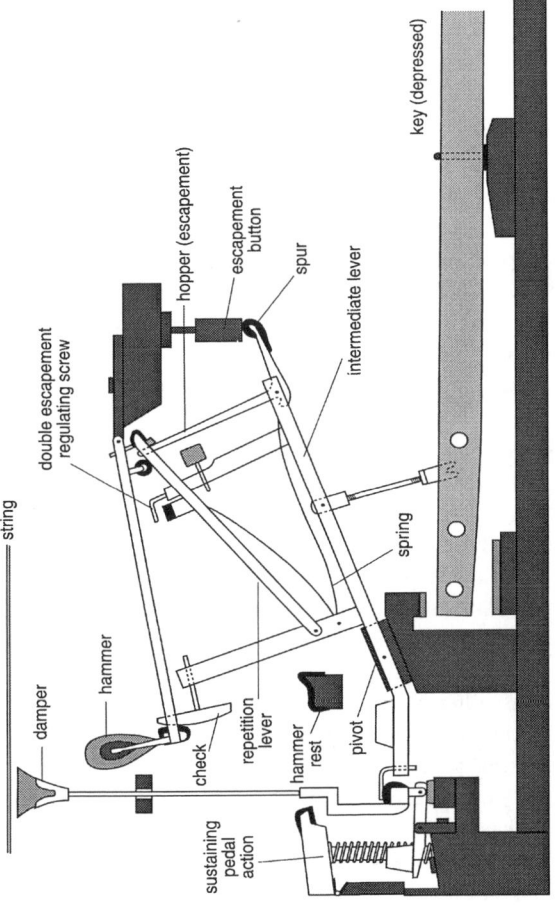

Fig. 8: Erard double-escapement action after the English patent drawing of 1822; the intermediate lever, pivoted to its flange, simultaneously lifts the hopper and pulls down the damper; the action is shown with the key depressed, the hammer having fallen back to its check.

CHAPTER TWO

Action and Technique

(i) Piano and harpsichord

We have seen that the ideal of the piano was to 'sensitise' the bright harpsichord or, to put it in terms which would be better recognised in the German-speaking lands, to combine the intimate expressive qualities of the clavichord with the power and brilliance of the harpsichord. The *raison d'être* of the piano and central to all its various designs was the gradability of tone and volume by touch. Few instruments, especially in comparatively recent times, had such a long gestation period, particularly in view of the high state of development of the earliest surviving instruments.

That the piano took almost a century to be fully and generally accepted in the sense that the harpsichord was, is another of the great paradoxes of its history. Various reasons have been put forward: the sheer ubiquity of the harpsichord and its versatility in tone, volume and colour (lacking only in gradability which, of course, could be achieved on the clavichord); the view of the piano as a version of the harpsichord; and its more complicated mechanism with greater chance of malfunction, which might not be understood by a local technician. To a much greater extent than quills, hammers and hammer-coverings were at the mercy of temperature and humidity, small changes in either of which could cause perceptible differences in the sound produced. The problem was compounded by the bewildering variety of materials involved in making a piano: different kinds of wood, of hide (pig, deer, sheep, cow), and of cloth, yarn, felt, sponge, cord, gutta-percha, parchment, cork, and various combinations of these, all giving different sounds and reacting differently to climatic changes; the fact that Alpine spruce was the clear favourite for soundboards does not negate this variety. A different approach to playing was also required, and a new style of performance needed to be learned. It may also be that the ubiquity and use of the domestic square *in situ* may have confined the piano's perception to the miniature and the family-oriented. There is also inertia, prejudice towards the new-fangled, and, of course, simple vested interest. All of these factors will have contributed in different places and in different degrees and combinations.

Nevertheless, as soon as the piano began to be considered as an instrument in its own right with idiomatic sound-possibilities, its progress was unstoppable.[1] Burney, admittedly an ardent fan, states that, after Merlin's improvements in mechanism and those of Broadwood and Stodart in tone, 'the harsh scratching of the quills of a harpsichord can now no longer be borne'. We cannot rule out the possibility of xenophobic overstatement here and, in an interesting reversion of contemporary French attitudes (see Chapter One (iv)), he lambastes the harpsichord in favour of the piano, singling out

> showy and brilliant lessons, which by mere rapidity of finger in playing single sounds,[2] without assistance of taste, expression, harmony, or modulation[3] enabled the performer to astonish ignorance, and acquire the reputation of a great player at a small expence. There is no instrument so favourable to such frothy and unmeaning Music as the harpsichord. Arpeggios, which lie under the fingers, and running up and down the scales of easy keys with velocity, are not difficult, on an instrument of which neither the tone nor tuning depends on the player; as neither his breath nor bow-hand is requisite to give existence or sweetness to its sounds ... At length, on the arrival of the late Mr. [J C] Bach, and construction of piano-fortes in this country, the performers on keyed-instruments were obliged wholly to change their ground; and instead of surprising by the seeming labour and dexterity of execution, had the real and more useful difficulties of taste, expression, and light and shade, to encounter.[4]

As Burney hints, its espousal by prominent eighteenth-century composers such as C.P.E. and J.C. Bach and, above all, Wolfgang Mozart, guaranteed the piano its eventual ascendancy and provided it with the beginnings of an idiomatic literature that is the most comprehensive in all instrumental music.

(ii) 'Viennese' and British pianos

As I have mentioned, the new instrument called for a completely new technique from its predecessors and this was not helped by the fact that the 'Viennese' and British schools of piano-making throughout the first half of our period remained distinct. The differences can be summarised briefly. The British instrument was altogether heavier and more solid with a thicker soundboard and three strings to a note (trichord) for most of the compass. The 'Viennese' piano tended to be bichord (two strings per note) and its soundboard was concave as opposed to the convex British. The latter's action was also a good deal heavier, with a deeper key-dip, and the size of the keys, in all three dimensions, larger. In addition, the hammer in the 'Viennese' instrument was, like the clavichord, mounted directly on the key, giving more – and more intimate – control.

---

[1] 'Harpsichord' in Rees/CYCLOPAEDIA.
[2] Burney is here referring to single-line music in one hand, without the complication of contrapuntal parts requiring more technical control.
[3] This is not used in our modern harmonic sense, but refers to modulation of tone and volume.
[4] Burney/HISTORY, vol. II, pp. 996–7.

But it was the different actions that attracted most attention and demanded different approaches from composer and, especially, player, and each action, at least until the very late eighteenth century, became associated with a fairly distinct literature. That of the composer-performers of the 'Viennese' school was characterised by rapidity, clarity and precision, the 'brilliant' style – the playing of Mozart's pupil Hummel, for example, was often referred to as *'perlenden'* ['pearly'] – in contrast to the 'legato' of the so-called 'English' or 'London' School. Burney had already commented on the lugubriousness of the first piano to arrive in England c.1752.

> The tone of this instrument was so superior to that produced by quills, with the additional power of producing all the shades of piano & forte by the finger, that though the touch and mechanism were so imperfect that nothing quick could be executed upon it, yet the dead march in Saul, and other solemn and pathetic strains, when executed with taste and feeling by a master a little accustomed to the touch, excited equal wonder and delight to the hearers.[5]

On the other hand, Mozart's *paean* to the instruments of his favourite maker, in a letter to his father, is well-known:

> This time I shall begin at once with Stein's pianofortes. Before I had seen any of his make, Späth's claviers had always been my favourites. But now I much prefer Stein's, for they damp ever so much better than [Späth's] Regensburg instruments. When I strike hard, I can keep my finger on the note or raise it, but the sound ceases the moment I have produced it. In whatever way I touch the keys, the tone is always even. It never jars, it is never stronger or weaker or entirely absent; in a word, it is always even. It is true that he does not sell a pianoforte of this kind for less than three hundred gulden, but the trouble and the labour which Stein puts into the making of it cannot be paid for. His instruments have this special advantage over others that they are made with escape action. Only one maker in a hundred bothers about this. But without an escapement it is impossible to avoid jangling and vibration after the note is struck. When you touch the keys, the hammers fall back again the moment after they have struck the strings, whether you hold down the keys or release them. He himself told me that whenever he has finished making one of these claviers, he sits down to it and tries all kinds of passages, runs and jumps, and he shaves and works away until it can do anything. For he labours solely in the interest of music and not for his own profit; otherwise he would soon finish his work. He often says: 'If I were not myself such a passionate lover of music, and had not myself some slight skill on the clavier, I should certainly long ago have lost patience with my work. But I do like an instrument which never lets the player down and which is durable.' And his claviers certainly do last. He guarantees that the sounding-board will neither break nor split. When he has finished making one for a clavier, he places it in the open air, exposing it to rain, snow, the heat of the sun and all the devils in order that it may crack. Then he inserts wedges and glues them in to make the instrument very strong and firm. He is delighted when it cracks, for he can then be sure that nothing more can happen to it. Indeed he often cuts into it himself and then glues it together again and strengthens it in this way.[6]

Even as late as 1827, Johann Nepomuk Hummel could still characterise the distinctness of the two piano-types:

---

[5] *Loc. cit.*

[6] Letter from Mozart to his father, Leopold, Augsburg, 17 October 1777. (Anderson-ed/MOZART, pp. 327–8).

The German [i.e. 'Viennese'] piano may be played upon with ease by the weakest hand. It allows the performer to impart to his execution every possible degree of light and shade, speaks clearly and promptly, has a round fluty tone, which in a large room contrasts well with the accompanying orchestra, and does not impede rapidity of execution by requiring too great an effort. These instruments are likewise durable, and cost about half the price of the English pianoforte.

To the English construction, however, we must not refuse the praises due on the score of its durability and fullness of tone. Nevertheless this instrument does not admit of the same facility of expression as the German; the touch is heavier, the key sinks much deeper, and, consequently, the return of the hammer upon the repetition of a note cannot take place so quickly ... this mechanism is not capable of such numerous modifications as to degree of tone as ours ...

In the first moment [i.e. on depressing the keys] we are sensible of something unpleasant, because, in forte passages in particular, on our German instruments we press the keys quite down, while here, they must only be touched superficially, as otherwise we could not succeed in executing such runs without excessive effort and double difficulty. As a counterpoise to this, however, through the fulness of tone of the English pianoforte, the melody receives a peculiar charm and harmonious sweetness.

In the meantime, I have observed that, powerfully as these instruments sound in a chamber, they change the nature of their tone in spacious localities; and that they are less distinguishable than ours, when associated with complicated orchestral accompaniments; this, in my opinion, is to be attributed to the thickness and fulness of their tone.[7]

Hummel, ironically enough, had the first British grand in Vienna, which he played in concert on 12 March 1794, not long after he returned from his visit to Britain; he was therefore in a particularly strong position to comment on the relative merits of the two types without having to rely on memory. The 'Viennese' type of piano, as he observed, is much shallower and more responsive than the British and the damping more efficient. 'The rhetorical, *sprechend* [speaking] manner of German keyboard music could only be communicated through perfect articulation; the more 'public' and flamboyant concert style of the London Pianoforte School, on the other hand, sought volume and a legato effect.'[8] This 'speaking' could approach the literal at times, as with, for example, Momigny's analogy of the first movement of Mozart's String Quartet K. 421 in D minor with Dido's monologue at Aeneas' departure, and with Gerstenberg's undertexting of C.P.E. Bach's C minor keyboard Fantasy with Hamlet's 'To be' monologue as well as with that of Socrates as he takes the hemlock.[9] In the case of the British piano's main quality, again we have a paradox: it was in fact the faulty and slightly sluggish damping which gave it the built-in *legato*, encasing each note in a slight 'halo', which was so effective in slow movements of the period by members of the 'London Piano School' – those brought up on, or spending most of their time with, this type of instrument, including Johann Baptist Cramer, Muzio Clementi and John Field. An example is given from the second movement of Clementi's Piano Sonata in G major Op. 40/1, (Ex. 2.1, pub. 1802). The dissonances are carefully chosen, especially in bb. 3 and 5.

---

[7] Hummel/PIANOFORTE, Part III, Section 11, Chapter iv, pp. 64–5.
[8] Komlós/FORTEPIANOS, p. 24.
[9] See Bent-ed/ANALYSIS, I, p. 27, fn. 20.

Ex. 2.1: Clementi, Piano Sonata in G major Op. 40/1/ii, bb. 1–11.

Ex. 2.2 shows the Adagio variation No. 7 from the second movement of J.B. Cramer's Piano Sonata in D major Op. 20 (*c*.1800); the arpeggios are particularly effective.

Ex. 2.2: J.B. Cramer, Piano Sonata in D major Op. 20/ii, var. 7, bb. 1–9.

INSTRUMENTS

(iii) Merging of features

It was clear that, in an odd mirroring of the piano's early history *vis-à-vis* the harpsichord and clavichord, the solution was to combine the advantages of both instruments[10] and, to an extent, this is what happened. A step in this direction had already been taken in the eighteenth century, when German and British modifications of Cristofori's action fused in what has been called the 'Anglo-German Action'. The combination of the strong resonant British tone, the 'Viennese' facility and precision, and the various mechanical means of strengthening the whole – the cast-iron frame being the final outcome – resulted in an instrument with sufficient power to be featured in large concerts, yet retaining 'Viennese' brilliance of execution.

This brilliance was greatly enhanced by the last great invention applied to the piano, that of the double-escapement mechanism, permitting notes to be repeated at high speed. The inventor, Sébastien Erard, had already patented an early version of this in 1808 and a piano of his with the mechanism fitted had been put through its paces by J.L. Dussek at a concert in the Odéon that year, to great acclaim. Work on the escapement was continued by Sébastien's nephew, Pierre, who patented his version in England in 1821 (Fig. 8 shows an English patent drawing of the action from 1822). The idea was to obviate the necessity for the hammer to fall back completely to its place of rest before re-striking, thus saving time and pressure and resulting in faster repetition. Ex. 2.3 illustrates its use in 'Reconnaissance' from Robert Schumann's *Carnaval* Op. 9 (1833–5)

Ex. 2.3: R. Schumann, *Carnaval* Op. 9/14, bb. 1–8.

and a more extreme example is to be found in Ex. 2.4, Henri Herz' *Fantaisie et Variations ... sur la Marche d'Otello de Rossini* Op. 67 for piano and orchestra, where the repeated notes imitate violin *tremolandi* when the piece is played as a piano solo.

---

[10] Harding in Harding/PIANOFORTE, pp. 38ff.

Ex. 2.4: Herz, *Fantaisie et Variations* ... Op. 67, Cadenza.

The Czech-born German pianist-composer Ignaz Moscheles interested himself in Pierre Erard's progress, not only in the case of the escapement action, but the general improvements the latter was making in other ways also. Although he still preferred his Clementi piano, by 1830 Moscheles was won over: his wife Charlotte described the sound of his Erard of that time as having 'an organ-like tone and full resonant sounds' and that the composer had 'every incentive to bring into relief these great excellences, and display them in his adagios'. Moscheles himself called the instrument a 'very violoncello'.[11]

Given the great improvements made in French pianos (which also included a process for treating and using felt for hammers by Pape), it is little wonder that pianistic interest centred on Paris, to where the later generation of virtuosi – Henri Herz, Franz Hünten, Johann Peter Pixis, Sigismond Thalberg, Friedrich Kalkbrenner and Franz Liszt – gravitated, especially in the winter, 'like swarms of locusts' according to Heinrich Heine.[12] It is also no accident that Frédéric Chopin was also attracted and his avowed preference for the pianos of Pleyel – while not dismissing those of Erard – is well known. The Polish critic Maurycy [Moritz] Karasowski

---

[11] Moscheles/LIFE, pp. 246–7.
[12] Quoted in Loesser/MEN, p. 376.

reports: '"When I feel out of sorts," Chopin would say, "I play on an Erard piano where I easily find a ready-made tone. But when I feel in good form and strong enough to find my own individual sound, then I need a Pleyel piano." '[13]

(iv) C.P.E. Bach and the piano: touch and fingering

From early on in its life, the piano's mechanical progress became a focus for composers and performers to an unprecedented extent – to Mozart's 'consultancy' with Stein and Streicher can be added that of J.S. Bach's to Silbermann, and Moscheles's to Erard (just mentioned) – and this progress can be charted in detail in the patents to which it gave rise and even in the comparatively small number of surviving instruments in which it can be seen. Similarly, the distinctive action, with the new and considerable demands that it made on players and composers – and these were almost universally one and the same at this time – gave rise to a plethora of 'schools' or 'methods': books for teaching technique with musical exercises to monitor progress. Since much of the earliest music written for or including the piano is based on harpsichord or clavichord technique, those composers and performers who were used to the latter instrument were clearly better prepared for the new one.

And it so happens that one of the greatest keyboard-players of the eighteenth century who also wrote the first comprehensive treatise on keyboard-playing, was a great champion of the clavichord. C.P.E. Bach's *Versuch über die wahre Art das Clavier zu spielen* ['Essay on the true art of playing keyboard instruments'], published in two parts in 1753 and 1762, was not only the first of its kind, but the best and most comprehensive; it was also widespread and very influential, and did much to familiarise players with techniques that were equally applicable to the piano. Bach also pays tribute to the new instrument:

> Of the many kinds [of keyboard instrument] ... there are two which have been most widely acclaimed, the harpsichord and the clavichord. The more recent pianoforte, when it is sturdy and well built, has many fine qualities, although its touch must be carefully worked out, a task which is not without difficulties. It sounds well by itself and in small ensembles. Yet, I hold that a good clavichord, except for its weaker tone, shares equally in the attractiveness of the pianoforte and in addition features the vibrato and portato which I produce by means of added pressure after each stroke. It is at the clavichord that a keyboardist may be most exactly evaluated.[14]

The 'vibrato' mentioned was the celebrated *Bebung* peculiar to the clavichord, in which the constant contact which the tangent – and indirectly the finger[15] – had with the string allowed the pitch to fluctuate when the key was shaken from side to side, or quickly pressed up and down, without re-sounding. Bach's 'portato', however, is ambiguous. Its antecedent usage on string instruments implied a *mezzo-staccato*, and Bach's description of 'notes that are both slurred and dotted' (here meaning staccato) and his notated examples confirm this (Ex. 2.5a and b). But he later declares that it

---

[13] Quoted in Eigeldinger/CHOPIN, p. 26.
[14] C.P.E. Bach/ESSAY, pp. 35–6.
[15] See diagram Chapter One.

only applies to the clavichord, and William J. Mitchell, in his footnote commentary, quotes later piano methods to show that the *portato* was a slightly slower variant of the *Bebung*,[16] also dependent on finger-pressure.

Ex. 2.5a/b: C.P.E. Bach, *Versuch ... Clavier zu spielen*, p. 156.

Whatever the truth, these are fine points of interpretation and if we consider non-controversial ones, such as those embodied in Ex. 2.6, where he says that (i) and (ii) may be played both on harpsichord and, more effectively,[17] on clavichord, but 'must not be corrupted to' (iii), it is clear how refined it was possible to be with clavichord performance-practice and how such nuances could, and would, be transferred to the piano.

Ex. 2.6: C.P.E. Bach, *Versuch ... Clavier zu spielen*, p. 157.

As well as his musical examples, Bach supplied *Achtzehn Probestücke in sechs Sonaten* ['Eighteen sample-pieces in six sonatas'] for Part One of the *Versuch* (1753) and *VI Sonatine Nuove* ['Six New Sonatinas'] for the revised edition (1787). The former are more-or-less graded with respect to difficulty.

Another aspect of touch which was not confined to the piano, but which achieved greater prominence because of it, was fingering, and this was one of the most important aspects of the *Versuch*. The prevailing system of keyboard fingering before the middle of the eighteenth century was governed by three basic features: finger-preference, stylistic change and instrumental development.

1. Finger-preference

Firstly, the use of fingers 2, 3 and 4 almost to the exclusion of the thumb, 1 and the little finger, 5, was preferred. Thus, in runs, the technique was to cross 3 over 4 as in Ex. 2.7a, and it also affected other aspects of playing in a manner that would seem unusual to us today (Ex. 2.7b and c).

Ex. 2.7a: Early 18th-century l.h. fingering and b/c: Couperin, *L'Art de Toucher le Clavecin*.

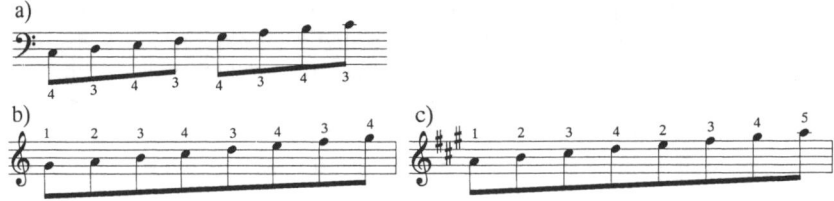

---

[16] C.P.E. Bach/ESSAY, p. 156, fn. 17. Page numbers in Exx. 2.5 and 2.6 refer to this edition.

[17] This phrase was added later by him in a footnote in the 1787 edition.

While he doesn't discard this method, Bach gives it as the least satisfactory of the possibilities – indeed, it would have been unwise to ignore it, given the quality of the players who continued to use it. There were, of course, partial exceptions to its usage, notably in England and France, and it is inconceivable that, judging from the demands of his *Essercisi*, Domenico Scarlatti was a practitioner of the method.

Wilhelm Friedemann Bach is reputed to have performed runs 'with smoothness and an astonishing rapidity',[18] according to Daniel Gottlob Türk, who goes on: 'I do not dare reject this fingering, although I would permit it in only a few cases'[19] – this, from a treatise published in 1789 and reiterated in the 1802 edition. However, the increasing demands of, on the one hand, virtuosity and, on the other, stronger and more expressive instruments, required a more inclusive approach, one that encouraged the use of the thumb and little finger on a more-or-less equal basis with the others. The greater flexibility achieved by using the thumb as a pivot in scalic and arpeggiaic passages was soon recognised. I should point out that F.W. Marpurg, in his treatise *Die Kunst das Clavier zu spielen* ['The art of playing the clavier'] of 1750 recommends fingerings for scales that are close to those in use today. However, he still preferred the earlier techniques in general.

2. Stylistic change

The second of the three features involving fingering is to do with musical style. There was a comparative avoidance of the keys with greater than three sharps and flats in music before the Classical period. This was also a matter of temperament and tuning[20] but the wider key-usage required greater flexibility, and more frequent and faster changes in hand-position, than two or three middle fingers could accommodate; not only would fingers 1 and 5 need to be used more, they would also need to be used on the 'black'[21] keys. More specifically, as well as the clear need for control in the *Empfindsamer Stil*, the homophonic bent of the *style galant*, with its Italianate melodies and *Alberti*-based accompaniments, also demanded digital control as well as differentiation between the hands.

Apart from its great value as an instrumental tutor along with the two other great mid-eighteenth-century musical treatises – Johann Joachim Quantz's *Versuch einer Anweisung die Flöte traversiere zu spielen* (Berlin 1752), which probably encouraged Bach in his own similar venture, and Leopold Mozart's celebrated *Versuch einer gründlichen Violinschule* of 1756 – Bach's *Versuch* also shares with them a comprehensive interest in musical stylistic matters in the broader sense.

A further indication of its 'modernity' and applicability to the new piano is to be seen from its influence on later, more piano-oriented treatises, such as those of Türk (1789, quoted from above) and J.P. Milchmeyer'[22] (1797). Nor were composers and performers slow to acknowledge their debt to him, either directly or indirectly. Even

---

[18] Türk/SCHOOL, p. 146.

[19] *Loc. cit.*

[20] This will be discussed in Chapter Three (ii).

[21] I refer to the sharp and flat keys here: the reason for the quotation marks is the prevalence of lightly coloured sharps and flats and dark naturals on earlier instruments.

[22] See next section (v) in this chapter.

Clementi, the acknowledged first pioneer in piano technique, said of the *Versuch*: 'Whatever I know about fingering and the new style, I have learned from this book.'

3. Instrumental development

The third feature governing fingering, the development of the instrument itself, implies not only the increasing power of the piano and its greater sensitivity, but also matters such as the greater depth of the keystroke, and changes in the width and length of the keys themselves, which required a well-developed all-round basic technique applicable to different kinds of instruments – within, as well as without, the piano family. These matters are so bound up with individual instruments at particular times in particular places, that it would be tedious to discuss them here. Nevertheless, even the early nineteenth-century professional lions of the keyboard, used to all sorts of pianos and conditions, must have spent many hours simply acclimatising themselves to the instruments variously assigned to them: even the greatest and most in demand of them could not always rely on their optimum type of piano being on the platform.

(v) Later piano treatises

The works mentioned above by C.P.E. Bach, L. Mozart and J.J. Quantz began a new breed of instruction books in which not merely the methods of playing the instruments – respectively, keyboard, violin and flute – were addressed, but musical matters generally (including interpretation of signs, decorations, and so on) and additionally, musicality of approach to the literature of the instrument. This may well reflect the larger and perhaps less homogeneous 'audience' than, say, Couperin's *L'Art de toucher le Clavecin* ['Art of Playing the Clavecin'] of 1716 or Saint Lambert's *Principes du Clavecin* ['Principles of [playing] the Clavecin'], both referring to the harpsichord and aimed at an aristocracy already schooled in 'taste'.

The next work of the more modern kind was the already mentioned *Klavierschule* of Daniel Gottlob Türk (Leipzig, 1789, revised and enlarged in 1802). Like Bach's *Versuch*, the focus is still the *Klavier*, that is, the clavichord, and, like Bach also, Türk was well aware of the newer piano and had respect for it. It was, however, a treatise that appeared in Dresden in 1797 – between the two editions of Türk's work – which placed the piano unequivocally centre-stage.

J.P. Milchmeyer's *Die wahre Art das Pianoforte zu spielen*[23] ['The true art of playing the piano'] echoes Bach's groundbreaking work in its title and lays its cards firmly on the table as early as page 2, taking fingering as its launch-pad:

> [Because of improper finger technique] I do not believe that the harpsichord as well as the clavichord (the clavier) are the right instruments on which one can learn to play correctly. Seeking to play expressively on the latter causes unending contortion of the fingers ... I rather believe that the student should begin immediately on the pianoforte and with the treble clef and set aside the old prejudice

---

[23] Milchmeyer/*PIANOFORTE*.

and obstinacy that there is nothing better than the clavichord and the discant clef.[24] In my way of thinking there is no one in the world who wants to learn an instrument and not ever be heard playing it.[25] ... But nowadays ... since all great composers ... write for the pianoforte, this instrument is all the more to be given preference .... The pianoforte can be played with all of its possible variations [in dynamic levels], it can be heard in the largest hall, and is finally a much more secure instrument in that one will not become accustomed to playing it with contortion and improper usage of the fingers.[26]

Milchmeyer's work is a link between eighteenth- and nineteenth-century piano 'schools'.

(vi) The *Etude*

The new instrument, and its swiftly expanding number of players and aspiring players of all standards, demanding a revision of existing playing techniques, produced, as we have seen, a number of 'schools' devoted to it. It called forth music to aid the study or practice of technique, as in C.P.E. Bach's *Probestücke* accompanying his treatise. As the nineteenth century arrived, however, this kind of music had become, on the one hand, much more technically focused, as in the exercise ([Fr.] *exercice*; [Ger.]*Übung*; [It.] *essercizio*) but also more musically oriented, as in the study ([Fr.] *étude*; [Ger.] *Etüde, Studie*; [It.] *Studio*).

The first of these, the exercise, is a mechanical type in which the main aim is to master a technical point or a problem of piano technique and consists simply of repetition of minimally musical figurations. Scales and arpeggios are, perhaps, the obvious examples here, but other pieces often partake of such a function also, as some of J.S. Bach's do. Instances are the first and second Preludes in a work that was partly didactic, Bk. I of the *Forty-Eight Preludes and Fugues* (Ex. 2.8a and b),

Ex. 2.8a: J.S. Bach, *Das Wohltemerirte Clavier* Bk. I/Prelude in C major, opening.

Ex. 2.8b: Prelude in C minor, opening.

---

[24] The older treatises used this, a C clef with middle C on the bottom line of the stave, whereas Milchmeyer favours the more modern treble (G) clef.

[25] Milchmeyer here refers to the low volume of the clavichord, and gives an example in underlining the impossibility of public concerto-performance.

[26] Milchmeyer, *op. cit.*, taken and slightly adapted from the translation in Türk/SCHOOL, p. xvii.

and, in our period, Ex. 2.9a–c from Clementi's *Gradus ad Parnassum* ['Steps to [Mount] Parnassus'], (issued 1817–26), which has remained a standard for this purpose until comparatively recently.

Ex. 2.9a: Clementi, *Gradus ad Parnassum,* No. 1.

Ex. 2.9b: *Gradus ad Parnassum,* No. 12.

Ex. 2.9c: *Gradus ad Parnassum,* No. 16.

In more basic vein is Hanon's famous *Le pianiste virtuose* (Ex. 2.10),

Ex. 2.10: Hanon, *Le pianiste virtuose,* No. 19.

Carl Czerny's *School of Velocity* Op. 299 and Potter's *Studies in All the Major and Minor Keys* (Op. 19, 1826), where in No. 3 (Ex. 2.11) the hands exchange their material later.

Ex. 2.11: Potter, *Studies in All the Major and Minor Keys* Op.19/3, bb. 1–3.

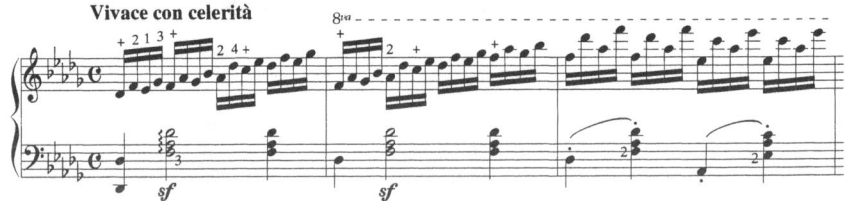

INSTRUMENTS 41

R. Schumann prefaced each of his *Studien nach Capricen von Paganini* Op. 3 (1832) with similar short exercises ('*Übungen*'), highlighting their accompanying pieces' technical problems, although they go beyond the specific needs of their respective studies, as in No. 3 in C major, where the preparatory exercise for the study – Ex. 2.12a gives the opening – involve pedagogical principles of a high order (particularly in Ex. 2.12e) and betray his acute sense of piano touch and tone (Ex. 2.12b–f).

Ex. 2.12a: R. Schumann, *Studien nach Capricen von Paganini* Op. 3/3 in C major, bb. 1–4 and b–f: *Übungen* for *Studien*/3, (a)–(e).

On a less exalted musico-technical level, this kind of preparation could, if published separately, be a good wheeze for increasing sales: Moscheles issued *50 Preludes in the Major and Minor Keys, intended as short INTRODUCTIONS to any movement, and as preparatory EXERCISES to the Author's Studies, for the Piano Forte, Composed, Fingered, and Dedicated to the Royal Academy of Music* Op. 73 in 1827. (The dedication certainly did his royalties no harm either.[27])

---

[27] See Chapter Nine (vi); this type of institutional dedication will be mentioned again in Chapter Twenty-Nine.

The more basic, mechanical types of study certainly have their use – although Liszt recommended his pupil Valérie Boissier to read a book while repeating them! – and there is something satisfyingly workmanlike about leaping through such pianistic hoops. But they were greatly outnumbered, if not superseded, by the more interesting studies, in which the aesthetic outweighed the anaesthetic and whose technical function was clothed in more musical garb. The later numbers in the Clementi's *Gradus* are of this kind and a pupil of his, Henri Bertini, published his *25 Elementary Studies* Op. 137, which, after the fashion of the Schumann *Studien*, are 'each preceded by a short exercise and prelude'.

However, the period's great penchant for character of all kinds – to be discussed in Section II – would unite with the technical impulse to produce pieces in which the aesthetic value was foremost, yet without losing sight of the workaday aspect. Chopin's 27 *Etudes* are foremost among these, but by no means the only ones and certainly not the first: he had a substantial literature to draw on.

Clementi's work again was one of the earliest, as the more advanced material from the *Gradus* shows, but J.B. Cramer, also in London, had produced the first examples of this type with his *Studio per il pianoforte* (two sets of 42 studies, issued 1804 and 1810). In a later (1815) set of six studies, which he entitled *Dulce et Utile* ['Pleasant and useful'[28]] we see Chopinesque figurations before their time (see No. 2, Ex. 2.13), so to speak, which were already beginning to become part and parcel of the virtuosos' *lingua franca*.

Ex. 2.13: J.B. Cramer, *Dulce et Utile*, No. 2, bb. 71–4.

Any good study, especially one for piano at this time, is as much a test of the instrument as it is of the practitioner: No. 1 (Ex. 2.14) taxes the player's subtlety in imparting structural linearity to the bass progression, aided by its registral integrity; the performer, however, cannot simply rely on the piano's distinct timbral layers, but must actually compensate for their differences if he or she is to articulate the interplay of the three individual voices while not overstressing any one of them.

---

[28] Subject to various translations, the title is probably a reference to the *Ars Poetica* of Horace: "Omne tulit punctum qui miscuit utile dulci / Lectorem delectando pariter monendo."[He who has combined usefulness with pleasure has won every point, by delighting the reader while instructing him.]

Ex. 2.14: J.B. Cramer, *Dulce et Utile,* No. 1, bb. 54–9.

The tricky changes in hand-position in No. 3 (Ex. 2.15) at Allegretto con brio also require more than digital mechanics to judge the octave transfer.

Ex. 2.15: J.B. Cramer, *Dulce et Utile,* No. 3, bb. 183–4.

This kind of subtlety requires intimate knowledge, not merely of the piano *per se* but of the individual instrument upon which one is performing – as, indeed, do the repeated-note figures in No. 4, the *Toccatina* (Presto), in the pre-double-escapement age (Ex. 2.16; see also bb. 48–54).

Ex. 2.16: J.B. Cramer, *Dulce et Utile,* No. 4, bb. 144–50.

For a performer with such a distinct style, remarked upon and admired by virtuosi of all schools, including Liszt, it is surprising that John Field left no 'school' or body of technical material. He was prepared to 'compose' and write out in his own hand some similar for his more talented pupils, such as Mme Caspari and Countess

Orlova.[29] There are, however, some published *Exercices* which, if they afford little musical insight, do show aspects of the instrument. The 'No. 1' in C major has a right-hand *perpetuum mobile* almost entirely in the upper register consisting of a repeated note alternating with a *quasi*-melody that Field clearly wishes not to be too obvious as such, since there is no separate bracing. Thus, the player is free to impose more subtle phrasing, difficult in this register, if one is to avoid the impression of a mandolin (Ex. 2.17a). The top 'melody' has an added third for reinforcement when the repeated note descends into the middle register (Ex. 2.17b).

Ex. 2.17a: Field, *Exercises* 'No. 1', bb. 2–4.

Ex. 2.17b: 'No. 1', bb. 8–9.

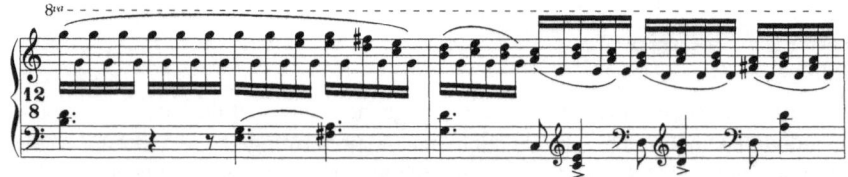

Field's '2^d *Exercice pour la main gauche*' again rests on instrumental articulation of a sort in which he excelled. After six initial promising bars, however, it settles for more standard fare. Those virtuosi of this period who taught regularly, as most of them did, were, like all good teachers, at their best in a 'hands-on' situation, but this did not prevent them from attempting to codify their methods in 'schools' in spite of the dilution and generalisation that this entailed. It is significant that neither Field nor Chopin left a 'school', although the latter intended to do so.

Commentators of the period, including the virtuosi themselves, revelled – in spite of their pious admonishments and *caveats* – in virtuosity, but they laid more stress on the *cantabile* quality of playing. Vocal metaphors are a constant presence, partly as a hangover from the previous century's ideal of the primacy of melody in general and vocal melody in particular; indeed, the very title of Thalberg's *L'art du chant appliqué au piano* ['The art of singing applied to the piano'] confirms this.

---

[29] I shall expand on this in Chapter Twenty-Nine: Didacticism and Dissemination.

Johann Nepomuk Hummel's set of *24 Grandes Etudes* Op. 125 were published a few months after Chopin's, but, as so often with his works, one cannot pinpoint when they were written. Certainly it might well have been some time before publication, as this was very much the norm for him, and a situation echoed by the other virtuosi who played a good deal in public. The overall emphasis in these studies is *legato* and highly controlled *legato* passages, frequently in several voices simultaneously, and as contrasting episodes in faster pieces; therefore I will return to them in the next chapter. Of the brilliant type, the first in C major partakes of the typical cut of many studies and other virtuoso works or movements in that key: fast scales and arpeggios, and some deft pivoting on the thumb is required. No. III is a 'Tempo di Polacca', if a rather restrained one: only the occasional syncopations suggest the genre. The accent is on thirds (and various articulations of them) for both hands, the hands being sometimes at odds with each other (Ex. 2.18). Thirds also feature in No. XV.

Ex. 2.18: Hummel, *24 Grandes Etudes* Op. 125/III, bb. 11–12.

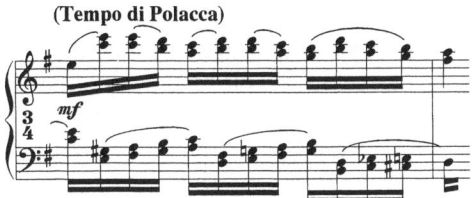

Clean and measured execution of decorations is featured in three of the studies, the skipping figure that pervades No. XIX in its several guises (Ex. 2.19),

Ex. 2.19: Hummel, *24 Grandes Etudes* Op. 125/XIX, bb. 10–18.

the *acciaccatura* in various voices and using various fingers in No. II (Ex. 2.20)

Ex. 2.20: Hummel, *24 Grandes Etudes* Op. 125/II, bb. 15–22.

and the mordent is treated similarly in No. XIII, with a key change to ensure that the decorated note appears on different degrees of the scale with the rather sneaky integration of mordent and melody-note (marked *x* in Ex. 2.21). No. XVII has compound leaps and the player's wrist- and finger-*staccato* is tested in No. XXIII.

Ex. 2.21: Hummel, *24 Grandes Etudes* Op. 125/XIII, bb. 15–25.

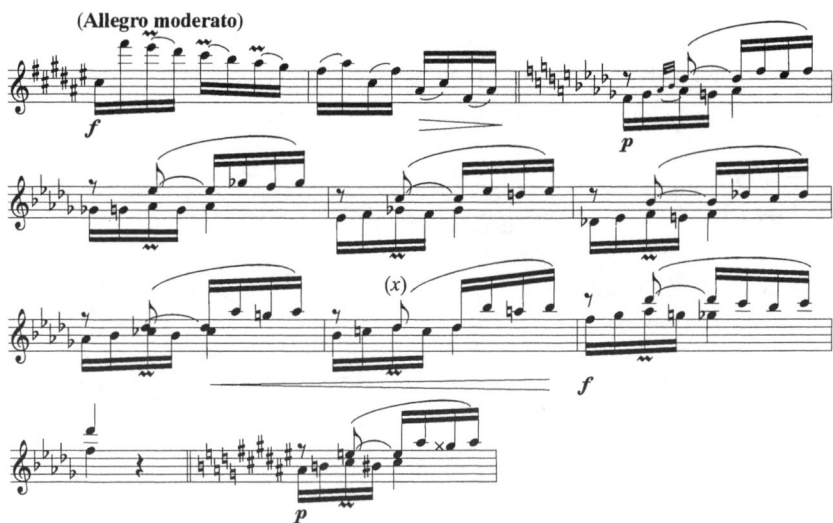

Hummel has endeavoured to make these works musically interesting and many of them are so; what is surprising is that, on the technical side, their difficulty is superseded by many instances in his other works. So it seems that these studies were intended as an introduction to the other works rather than as an end in themselves. As an example of this, his *Fantaisie* in E flat major Op. 18 requires pianism equal to, if not surpassing, anything in the *Etudes* – deft articulation in both hands (Ex. 2.22a)

and the tricky right-hand change in thirds (Ex. 2.22b, c and d) – all at Allegro con fuoco in *alla breve* time. There is nothing in the *Etudes*, either, to match the *alla breve* Presto of the octaves at the end of the piece (Ex. 2.22e).

Ex. 2.22a: Hummel, *Fantaisie* in E flat major Op. 18, bb. 23–32.

Ex. 2.22b: Op. 18, bb. 75–7.

Ex. 2.22c: Op. 18, bb. 127–33.

Ex. 2.22d: Op. 18, bb. 158–60.

Ex. 2.22e: Op. 18, bb. 587–93.

As we saw in the case of Clementi and Cramer, attention was often drawn to the character imposed by the addition to, or substitution of, the 'study' aspect of the title by something less severe, both of these composers' sets stressing the idea of musical achievement rather than digital drudgery. This was, of course, bound to appeal to the bourgeois sensibility of self-sufficiency, self-improvement and the fruit of honest labour rather than privilege – the Virgilian *labor omnia vincit*, or even perhaps *per ardua ad astra*.[30]

However, also in keeping with the times was a degree of something approaching characterisation in the titles, such as Charles Mayer's *Le Tremolo: Grande etude*, which turns out to be a measured trill at a Moderato cantabile speed (Ex. 2.23) and which later moves into the inner voice.

Ex. 2.23: Mayer, *Le Tremolo: Grande etude*, bb. 1–4.

Ignaz Moscheles calls his Studies *24 Characteristic Compositions*, meaning that each has a musical character, and explains in his preface:

> Not only a well grounded knowledge is here required, but that species of execution which is the effect of taste and sensibility; for it is not so much the author's intention to cultivate mechanical perfection, as to address himself to the imagination of the performer, and to enable him to excel in all the delicacies of light and shade, in contrast, sentiment, and passion – in short, to make him master of all that is implied by the comprehensive term *Style*.

---

[30] 'Work conquers all' from Virgil's *Georgics* I and 'Through hardship to the stars' (Anon), the motto of the British Royal Air Force.

It is worth quoting some of his remarks of a little later, on touch:

§1. The player must possess such controul [sic] over his fingers as enables him, by the weight and pressure of their extremities, to produce every shade and gradation of tone from the most delicate to the most powerful. Nor is this finely proportioned touch necessary only in passages having a succession of notes of equal strength but also in those where sudden changes in their degrees of force are required or where all the shades of distinction, betwixt delicacy and power, are nicely interwoven with each other.
In this Work, as well as in others of the latest production of distinct masters, these several gradations of strength of touch are carefully marked by the following signs of *f. mf. ff. p. sotto voce. mezza voce. pp.* and even *ppp*.

He goes on to talk of distinctions in voices in, for example, contrapuntal passages and that, 'in an uninterrupted sequence of fast notes' the first of every three or four notes must be accented. He cautions, however, that it is not so much force he has in mind, but 'slightly dwelling on the first note, but this must be done with great care and judgment, since its abuse will render the passage stiff and mechanical.' He marks this with a ∧ (as in Ex. 2.24a), and also makes a clear distinction between the two groupings in Ex. 2.24b. He draws attention to three kinds of staccato: the 'pointed dot' to which he assigns 1/4 of the value of the note (Ex. 2.24c), the normal 'round dot' at 1/2 value (Ex. 2.24d) and the 'slurred dot' (Ex. 2.24e–g), to which he assigns different durations depending upon whether an Adagio tempo is in question or not.

Ex. 2.24: Moscheles, *24 Characteristic Compositions*, Preface.

But again, something more characteristic, even fanciful, was required, especially for the ladies at home, at whom many of these didactic pieces were aimed. Examples of this kind of piece are Henri Bertini's 25 *études caracteristiques* Op. 66 (1832) and Moscheles's *Characteristic Studies* Op. 95, each of which has a suggestive title: Ex. 2.25 gives the opening of No. 4 'Juno'.

Ex. 2.25 Moscheles, *Characteristic Studies* Op. 95/4, bb. 1–6.

Ex. 2.25 continued

Virtuosity on one instrument stimulates the same in others and our period is unique in having an unprecedented example of this in the impact of the violin virtuosity of Niccolò Paganini, a talent which was, in some quarters, put down to demonic possession, or at least, agency. All of the pieces written with his brilliance in mind, whether in homage or in emulation, are technically oriented and many are sets of studies, stimulated by the violinist's famous and technically confounding *Caprices* Op. 1 They include Edward Eliason's *6 Characteristic Caprices dedicated to Paganini (with addition of a Farewell caprice ded to Eliason by Paganini)* of which the last is 'Adieu à mon ami Paganini', Moscheles's *Gems à la Paganini, a Brilliant Fantasia in the Style of this Performer* also dedicated to its subject 'in token of esteem and admiration' and Hummel's Fantasia *Recollections of Paganini (c.1831)*, not to mention R. Schumann's two sets of *6 études d'après des caprices de Paganini*, Op. 3 (1832) and Op. 10 (1835 – this set being entitled '*études de concert*') and, of course, Liszt's *Grandes Etudes de Paganini* (1851) as well as similar works by Brahms, outside the time-span of this book.

Liszt's interest in piano technique was paramount from the beginning. While still a child (1826), he decided to write an *Etude en 48 exercices dans tous les tons majeurs et mineurs* ['Study in 48 exercises in all the major and minor keys'], and managed to write 12 of them. In 1837, he planned a set of 24 *Grandes études* based on the youthful work; again, 12 were written and, when published two years later, were the most difficult piano works ever seen, remaining almost unplayable to this day. In Jim Samson's words, 'Liszt thought with his fingers at the keys, and he did so with a fluency as natural as breathing.'[31] His technical approach to the keyboard, in these and elsewhere, was unique, almost from first principles, and his solutions to technical problems grew from his basic absorption of the ideal of the first wave of Romantic virtuosi, Hummel, Field, and especially his own teacher, Carl Czerny: that of equality of the fingers, including the thumb. It is fair to say, however, that they

---

[31] Samson/VIRTUOSITY, pp 28–9.

would have hardly recognised the principle when carried to the lengths that Liszt did. One result of this, albeit a trivial one, was to enable him to indulge very occasionally in tricks *à la* Paganini, such as holding a lighted cigar between the first two fingers of his right hand while accompanying Joseph Joachim in the finale of the Mendelssohn E minor violin concerto.

Some examples of Liszt's unorthodox fingering will illustrate this. Ex. 2.26 is from the sixth of his *Paganini* studies, and the only one of the set not taken from the violinist-composer's *Capricci* Op. 1, being in fact the theme of the finale of Paganini's Violn Concerto No. 2 in B minor (1826). The example shows a harmonic minor scale (A minor) in thirds in contrary motion between the hands, where Liszt keeps the same fingers for the left-hand chords.

Ex. 2.26: Liszt, from *La campanella*, bb. 117–8.

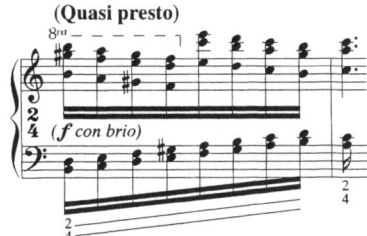

Liszt compounds this digital felony in his First *Hungarian Rhapsody* where a chromatic scale in thirds is divided between the hands, each od which maintains the same fingering for the successive chords (Ex. 2.27).

Ex. 2.27: Liszt, from the First *Hungarian Rhapsody*, bb. 287–90.

Another aspect of keyboard technique that he also extended – literally – was the use of leaps. These were hardly unusual, and were a speciality of Hummel, as the following example from the second movement of his posthumously-published Piano Concerto in F major Op. posth. 1 shows (Ex. 2.28).

Ex. 2.28: Hummel, Piano Concerto in F major Op. posth. 1/ii, bb. 53–4.

Liszt, however, goes much further, even as early as the fantasy *Clochette* of 1832, which contains a *variation à la Paganini* with plenty to occupy both hands and a texture reminiscent of violinistic technique (Ex. 2.29).

Ex. 2.29: Liszt, *Clochette,* opening.

It is also similar to the kind of (much more basic) texture which Schumann uses in his musical portrait of Paganini in his *Carnaval* Op. 9 (1833–5). Liszt's *La campanella* furnishes another famous example, where rapid leaps of up to two octaves are used to give the effect of a bell's overtones (Ex. 2.30); on the period piano this effect is much more telling because of the difference in registers and because of the predominance of upper partials.

Ex. 2.30: Liszt, *La campanella*, opening.

In this connection, it is interesting that Liszt, following the trend of characterisation, revised – in terms of technical simplification and thinning of texture – his *Grandes études* and published them as the *Douze études d'éxécution transcendente* ['Twelve Transcendental Studies'] of 1852 with new titles for ten of them, including his previously revised (1840) version of the fourth study now manipulated to fit a programme and published in 1847 as *Mazeppa*. The programme was based on a story, which Lord Byron and Victor Hugo also used and which Boulanger painted,[32] of a Hungarian count who, because of sexual misbehaviour, was lashed to a wild horse and set a-gallop through mid-eastern Europe.

A final reference to character might be seen in the publication of collections of studies by well-known virtuosi, such as Moscheles's and [François Joseph] Fétis's *Etudes de Perfectionnement,* part of their *Complete system of Instruction* for the

---

[32] *The Torture of Mazeppa* (1827).

piano (pub. 1840), which included works specially written for the publication by Moscheles himself and by Chopin (his *Trois nouevelles études* of 1839), Thalberg, Adolf von Henselt, Stephen Heller, Edouard Wolff, Jacob Rosenhain, Felix Mendelssohn, Julius Benedict, Theodor Döhler and Liszt. Some of these in turn sported character titles such as 'Playfulness' and 'L'Ambition'.

(vi) The Toccata

The toccata, a technical display-piece which was much in evidence in the Renaissance and, especially, the Baroque periods, had lain dormant during the Classical period, except for the famous 'duel' between Clementi and Mozart before the Emperor Joseph II in 1781, when the former played a toccata characterised by fast runs of thirds in the right hand, and published three years later with an accompanying sonata. The general conclusion of Leon Plantinga is that Clementi did not do himself justice either in his flashy playing or type of piece, but, whereas he was generous and appreciative in his judgement of Mozart, the latter unfortunately lapsed into some of his all-too-customary nastiness: 'Clementi plays well, as far as execution with the right hand goes. His greatest strength lies in his passages in thirds. Apart from this, he has not a *kreuzer*'s worth of taste or feeling – in short, he is simply a *mechanicus*.'[33] In fact, the episode seems to have 'bugged' Mozart for years and his letters show several later references to the event, each expressed in more venom than the previous one.[34] Is it perhaps in the nature of a sly dig at the great man that Clementi's 'Preludio alla Mozart' (from his *Musical Characteristics ... composed in the style of Haydn ...*[etc.], c.1787) is very toccata-like, while eschewing the fast thirds of the 'duel' ?

As can probably be gathered from Mozart's report alone, the toccata, resurrected from the Baroque period, preserved many of the features that characterised it at that time: manual dexterity, being of free episodic form, usually multi-sectional and often including a fugal section. Little vestige of the last-mentioned survived into the nineteenth-century toccata, and, in addition, it acquired a particular kind of choppy texture involving repeated and alternating notes, as shown in the following examples from J.B. Cramer (Ex. 2.31, the last piece, Toccatina, in his *Dulce et Utile*),

Ex. 2.31: J.B. Cramer, *Dulce et Utile,* No. 6, bb. 0–8.

---

[33] Quoted in Plantinga/CLEMENTI, p. 62.
[34] *Loc. cit.* ff.

Ex. 2.31 continued

Robert Schumann (Ex. 2.32), Cipriani Potter (Ex. 2.33), and Czerny (Ex. 2.34).
Ex. 2.32: R. Schumann, *Toccata* Op. 7, opening.

Ex. 2.33: Potter, from *Toccata* in G major (no opus number).

Ex. 2.34: Czerny, from *Toccata* in C major Op. 92.

There are also examples from Maria Theresia von Paradis and Kalkbrenner in the latter's *Traité d'harmonie du pianiste* ['Treatise on harmony for the pianist'], his Op. 185, a theoretical work; these are easier than the examples given, as they are intended for students, and the emphasis is on harmony rather than technique, as its name implies.

CHAPTER THREE

Stringing

Stringing involves the functions of range, pitch, tuning, and registers, all of which share, with the soundboard, the largest part in defining the characteristic sound of the piano.

(i) Range

The range of the piano at any given moment is a notoriously vexed question since, as the foregoing discussion implies, the generic term is of little value. There was not really a 'piano' for most of this period: there were pianos. Not only was there the general distinction between the 'Viennese' and the British types and the fact that these were joined by a French type that combined many of their characteristics, there were also the individual styles of makers and the fact that most instruments were built to commission, some of the terms of the commissions being quite specific. Perusal of any collection of period pianos, for example the Colt Clavier Collection, reveals several such commissions in terms of casework and presentation[1] but the composer-pianomaker relationships mentioned above (see Chapter Two (ii)) also show such demands.

There was also the question of the function of the piano (*continuo*, public, domestic) and, of course, the various forms of the instrument: grand, upright, square, cottage, and so on, as well as the more exotic forms (to be discussed a little later). Even the general truism that the range increased with time can be misleading when information about a certain maker, composer, performer or institution is sought. For example, of pianos made in, or very close to, 1825, a Broadwood Cottage has five-and-a-half octaves, a Henderson Cabinet six; and a Clementi Square, a Schleip *Lyraflügel* (see Pl. 5) – whose action, despite its name, was an 'English' one by Wornum – and a Haschka Grand ('Viennese', see Pl. 17), each with six-and-a-half, though disposed differently, ranging upward from F^1, D^1 and C^1 respectively.

Cristofori's surviving pianos have compasses of four and four-and-a-half octaves but as soon as later makers began to revive the instrument, five octaves (such as Mozart's grand) was the norm. Although Broadwood had built six-octave pianos to

---

[1] Several of these commissions are featured in the Plates.

commission in 1794 – for the composer-performer Jan Ladislaw Dussek (1760–1812) – and 1796, and Clementi a similar one in 1812, this compass was unusually wide at this stage, particularly in the latter instance since it was an upright in which a square had been turned on its side – by no means an unusual procedure, as will be seen. Six octaves would not become the norm until $c.1808$. Table 1 shows the extension of the compass in representative instruments in the eighteenth century:[2]

Table 1: Compass of eighteenth-century pianos

Instrument	Year	Compass
Cristofori grand	1726	$C - c^3$
J. Socher square	1742	$C - f^3$
G. Silbermann grand	1746	$F^1 - d^3$
J. Zumpe square	1767	$G^1 - f^3$
A. Backers grand	1772	$F^1 - f^3$
J.A. Stein	1784	$F^1 - f^3$
Broadwood grand	1787	$F^1 - f^3$
Broadwood grand	1790	$F^1 - c^4$
Broadwood grand	1794	$C^1 - c^4$

However, this is only a rough guide from surviving instruments, which represent a miniscule percentage of the total built. Michael Latcham cautions against trying to date pianos from their ranges, noting that $c.1800$, the customer's wish was paramount; a writer of the time states baldly that '... the compass of the piano was determined by the client.'[3] Indeed, one Viennese builder, Wachtl, offered extra keys over and above his standard $F^1 - c^4$ at 4 Gulden 30 kr[eutzer] each [4] In the domestic market, square pianos could be provided with extra keys (usually four or five) at the upper end of the keyboard. The first to do this was the pioneering Irish builder, William Southwell, in Dublin in 1794, with Broadwood following in 1796; soon it became usual to publish music with amendments capable of being played on instruments with or without these 'additional keys'. Pl. 6 illustrates the opening page of the first movement of Clementi's Sonata in A major Op. 33/1, dedicated to 'His Pupil Miss Theresa Jansen' in a London edition by Longman and Broderip, the title page of which states that, 'The First Sonata is composed for Instruments with or without additional Keys.' It is clear from Pl. 6 and the other instances in the sonata that the expected range ended at f^3 and in the example shown here, there is clearly a loss of some climactic punch on instruments without the additional keys. The PRIMO part in Moscheles's *Rondeau brillant (La belle Union)* Op. 76 for piano duet has the note 'N.B. Wherever a single Note is found beyond the compass of

---

[2] This is slightly modified from Komlós/FORTEPIANOS, p. 20.

[3] Wilhelm Lütge, in an article 'Andreas und Nannette Streicher', 1927; as quoted in Latcham/STRINGING I, p. 17 and fn. 57.

[4] *Op. cit.*, p. 18 and fn. 59.

Instruments up to C, (as in the first and seventh bars,) it may be left out, without any detriment to the effect of the passage.' Broadwood widened the compass further from 1810, this time downwards, from F^1 to C^1, and Wornum's six-octave upright ($F^1 - f^4$) of 1830 sounded the death-knell of the squares; by 1850, the full seven-octave span common today was achieved, with the aid of iron bracing or the cast-iron frame.

(ii) Pitch and tuning

The relative standardisation of pitch in the modern musical world is a comparatively recent development: International Standard Pitch was settled on by agreement in 1939 as a^1 = 440 Hertz (Hz). During the period of this study, however, pitch depended upon an enormous variety of factors: the country or region, the city, the venue — whether church, court, or public hall — the instruments (wind, brass, strings or combinations), and the preferences of individual performers or music-directors. Thus, for example, Baroque organs by German makers could be as much as a tone and a half higher than the contemporary norm, while orchestral strings could be tuned slightly sharp to accommodate the progressive sharpening of the winds due to heating of air, and woodwind players in the early nineteenth century were supplied with several slightly different versions of the same joints, which could be substituted in the (common) event of differences or changes in pitch. Indeed, during the late eighteenth and early nineteenth centuries, there were two widely used pitches in German-speaking countries, *Chorton* (choir pitch) and *Kammerton* (chamber pitch), which were fixed at a tone apart, the former being the higher. Singers frequently demanded a sharpening of pitch to add brilliance to their performances, although the opposite could also be required, as in 1824 when the Paris *Opéra*'s pitch was lowered for an ageing *prima donna*. Once the nineteenth century got under way, however, there was a general rise in pitch. This was prompted by the desire for more brilliance — itself a result of the burgeoning of public concerts, and especially the growing audience-numbers requiring larger halls and larger orchestras. This is particularly true of the balls and dances and even more so of, for example, Philippe Musard's hugely popular promenade concerts in London in the early 1830s. There is also the greater contribution of the orchestral brass due to the gradual adoption of valves and, indeed, it has been suggested that the rise in pitch began with the presentation of sets of new sharper instruments to several Austrian military bands during the first two decades of the nineteenth century. Since orchestras, especially those in the theatre, were heavily dependent on these bands to supplement their basic quotas of brass players, the result was a rise in pitch. This was especially noticeable in Vienna, where it is estimated that between Mozart's lifetime and the 1820s, pitch rose by almost three-quarters of a tone.[5] The trend, however, was a general one and could cause havoc on the occasions when a piano was involved, because of the time and difficulty involved in tuning and retuning. Hummel who, as an international travelling virtuoso, was in a better position than most to

---

[5] More details can be found in Harding/PIANOFORTE, p. 214.

comment on such matters, bewails the situation in his Pianoforte School (written 1821–5 and published in 1827):

> It is much to be wished that a uniform mode of tuning were universally introduced. To what disagreeables are we not exposed, particularly with regard to wind instruments. Sometimes they are not in tune with the piano forte, at other times in the orchestra not with one another. One is constructed according to the mode of tuning in use at Dresden, another to that of Vienna, a third to that of Berlin. One gives the pitch more usual in the chamber, another that in the theatre, and another again that in the Church. How is it possible, among all this diversity, to obtain a pure and equal mode of tuning? At all times Singers have been the greatest impediment to this arrangement.[6] Would that in all countries they would agree upon some uniform system of tuning and upon a pitch neither too high nor too low to employ it alike in the theatre, as alla camera, and, where possible, also in the Church. By this means they would everywhere meet with their accustomed pitch, and would sing with less exertion, without being compelled to have recourse to transposition.[7]

The unnamed writer of an article on pitch in the Berlin musical periodical, the *Allgemeine Musik-Zeitung,* in 1827, paints a similar picture, and mentions yet a third pitch, *Cornetton,* cornet pitch, as well as the *Chorton* and *Kammerton*. He suggests that the first two are obsolete (or at least obsolescent) and that the problem now (1827) is the constant manipulation of the *Kammerton*:

> [V]ery arbitrary and, in different cities and countries, very unequal changes have been made such that by now Babylonian confusion is rife and there is scarcely anyone who can still say what is meant by chamber pitch [*Kammerton*]. There are now as many tunings (claimed as chamber pitches) as cities of any importance in Europe and, what is more, even in one and the same city there is a plurality of recognised tunings.[8]

Things had not changed by 1835, when the critic and writer G.W. Fink echoes the *AMZ* article in his encyclopedia entry on '*Chorton*', saying that in Vienna alone there were three different pitches in use in the theatres and adding that 'from all reports it is clear that the chamber pitch was driven ever higher'.[9] It has been suggested that Germanic piano-makers designed their instruments so that they could withstand tuning up to semitone higher,[10] but there are also several extant examples of transposing pianos obviating the need for retuning – as well as to facilitate transposition in, for example, vocal accompaniment.[11] It was not until 1859 that the French government fixed a standard pitch (of $a^1 = 435$), with England following in 1899 ($a^1 = 439$).

Similarly, the universal use of equal temperament, by which the octave is tuned not according to natural principles, but mathematically, by dividing it into 12 equal

---

[6] It is worth noting that Hummel was happily married (since 1813) to the famous soprano, Elisabeth Röckel; no doubt his remark was carefully considered.

[7] Hummel/PIANOFORTE, Part III, Section II, Chapter VI, fn. p. 69.

[8] Quoted in Latcham/STRINGING I, pp. 95–6.

[9] Quoted in ibid., p. 96.

[10] Ibid., p. 97. The semitone is because there is evidence that, by this time, the two main pitches were that interval apart rather than a tone.

[11] See Chapter Five (v).

semitones, was to have particular relevance for keyboard instruments. In this tuning system, unlike all others, all the semitones are rendered theoretically equal; thus it imposes enharmonic identity, whereas in other systems there is a perceived distinction, however minute, between, for example, F♯ and G♭. When it is borne in mind that the ambit of keys – both in the sense of the basic keys of pieces and movements (including a greater preponderance of minor keys) and in the sense of modulations within keys – was much increased in the early nineteenth century, and not forgetting that the increasingly widespread practice of public improvisation would have suffered significantly from restrictions in modulation,[12] the advantages of equal temperament would seem to guarantee its universal adoption.

This, however, was not the case, and various kinds and adaptations of temperaments were used, the scope of which is beyond a general book such as this. In fact equal temperament itself was, in practice, an approximation, a compromise between the skill of the piano-tuner and the prescription of the performer. Even in the case of the most famous work to imply the term in its title – J.S. Bach's set of 48 Preludes and Fugues – two for each of the major and minor keys, *Das wohltemperirte Clavier* ['The Well-tempered Clavier'] – its use is by no means guaranteed, as there were several other tuning systems at the time of its composition that would have allowed all the pieces to be played in tune.

All of these factors, the rise in pitch, the widening of the instrument's range, the increase in the number of strings per note and their thickness, the increase in string tension to provide better sound-quality,[13] the more widespread use of steel and the general need for greater volume of sound – 'probably the most important factor [from 1795 on]'[14] – meant that the tension, which had ultimately to be borne by the case, increased enormously. One estimate puts the increase in tension on a piano made in 1820 as double or triple that of one made in 1785.[15] While it is true to say that this was lessened in practice by using shorter strings (shorter scaling), the increase was still considerable and in many cases led to further strengthening of the casing, including the compensated frame[16] and of course, ultimately, the cast-iron frame in the early 1850s. A further advantage of shorter scaling was that, as the bass range increased, it did not need to be matched by a corresponding lengthening of the casing which, in many instances, would have resulted in a piano of over 13 feet (4 metres) in length!

However, one can say, in summary, that the general sound of the piano of the period was much warmer and much more characteral than the comparatively standardised tone of modern-day instruments.

---

[12] See Chapter Twenty-Two.

[13] 'The closer a sounding string is to breaking point, the better the harmonics are in tune with the fundamental.' Latcham/STRINGING I, p. 92.

[14] According to Latcham/STRINGING I, p. 85.

[15] *Op. cit.*, p. 83.

[16] See Chapter Two (iii) and Pl. 2 (Stodart).

(iii) Registers

One of the most noticeable differences between the modern piano and its counterparts during our period was the latter's respect for individuality of register, in that the preservation of a degree of timbral distinction between bass, middle and treble registers was a deliberate and desirable feature. This, again, is in contrast to the modern ethos of standardisation and contributes enormously to the characterful-ness of the instrument. The exact location of the register-changes cannot, of course, be universally determined and, in any case, they would have varied from maker to maker. However, as a very rough guide, it would seem that the bass/middle divide occurred somewhere between f and c^1 and the middle/upper in the region of c^2 'or a little higher'.[17]

A large number of factors contribute to this property of the period piano, mainly the materials, tension, thickness (gauge), length and striking-point of the strings, as well as the number of strings to each note. The strings are thickest and longest in the bass register, with the core usually of brass and overspun (wound) with copper and sometimes coated with another metal, such as silver. This also helped to prevent rusting and, together with overspinning, allowed for greater mass without greater weight and without affecting the tone. The resultant sound, at a normal finger-pressure, is a mellow 'twang', rich in overtones. The rest of the instrument was strung in iron, until about the late 1820s, when British steel strings were used for the top (third) register. It is necessary to generalise here: many other factors are involved, which cannot be gone into in detail here and the reader is directed to more specialist material.[18] These other factors include: the different types of brass (principally 'red' with 85-90 per cent zinc, and 'yellow' with 70-75 per cent); the various trace metals, present either by accident or design; and the fact that British and American pianos used steel more commonly and earlier than most of their European counterparts. There are also the various methods of tempering the strings (for which many patents exist), their different shape – conical, thicker in the middle, and so on – the casing, overstringing, and whether the hammers were up- or down-striking.

The point at which the string was struck affected the sound also, allowing for it to be brightened or darkened, although few makers agreed on the best place. One of the first to approach this methodically was John Broadwood, who experimented ceaselessly to determine the optimum position for the more desirable harmonics. Although Alfred Hipkins insists[19] that this is one-ninth of the distance along the length of the majority of the strings (except the most extreme ones), Michael Cole disputes the exactitude of the ratio and the impression given that it was fixed at an early date. His only concession is that 'a tendency can be observed that is fairly suggestive of a convergence towards the numerical aim that Hipkins states'.[20] In smaller domestic forms of piano where volume was less of a consideration a striking-

---

[17] According to Sandra Rosenblum in Rosenblum/PERFORMANCE, p. 38.
[18] For example, Harding/PIANOFORTE.
[19] In *Encyclopaedia Britannica*, 9th edition. (London, 1885), 'Pianoforte'.
[20] Cole/PIANOFORTE, p. 138.

point closer to the centre of the string was preferred, giving a mellower tone. Broadwood enlisted the help of Tiberius Cavallo and others to help him in his acoustic experiments. Cavallo (1749–1809), made a Fellow of the Royal Society in 1779, was a Neapolitan scientist who wrote on electricity and magnetism among other things. One of the most important results of his collaboration with Broadwood was the divided bridge, by which the iron strings making up the tenor and treble registers could be at a higher tension compared to the brass bass strings, giving a more even tone throughout. This shift towards uniformity, however, was not entirely a blessing and, interestingly, those 'Viennese' makers who were influenced by British (and French) pianos – as evinced, for example, in the instruments they gave J. Haydn and Beethoven – did not choose to adopt these innovations. '[Their] reluctance ... indicates a stronger reliance on an approach based in the craftsman's tradition.'[21]

Also contributory in terms of sound quality was the number of strings used for each note. Single overspun strings in the deep bass gave way to double (bichord) stringing in the upper bass and middle, while the treble notes had three (trichord) or, at the extreme, four strings per note (tetrachord) to counteract the harshness and metallic quality of the steel strings. When the distinction between them was relevant – until the 1830s, say – the 'Viennese' piano tended to have less strings per note than the British. As mentioned above, the bewildering variety of materials used for the hammers also affected the sound. Generally speaking, although it was more common in France, the use of felt, as in modern instruments, did not become widespread until the very end of our period, leathers of various kinds being preferred.

(iv) The soundboard

But probably the most important factor of all was the very heart of the piano, the soundboard, which amplifies the vibrations of the strings, rendering them audible; here again, because of the many varieties and methods, a few general observations must suffice.

The wood itself and the manner in which it was cut and seasoned and, if necessary, the way the pieces were fixed together, were important and often reflected local availability and the prevalent tree types: on the Continent, for instance, pine and fir were preferred. Soundboards' thicknesses varied with the density of the wood used and also within the instrument, the bass end being thinnest, since it required less help than the weaker higher registers. Because the bridge was fixed to the soundboard, the latter had to be sufficiently strong to be able to withstand the proportion of the tension imparted. This usually required braces, which had to be carefully placed, and it was also necessary to take into account the grain of the wood.

Seasoning was an art in itself. Mozart's description (given above on page 30) of his favourite builder, Stein's procedure of alternate exposure to rain and sun and filling in the cracks one by one, was clearly not appropriate once demand for the instrument grew, and other faster methods involving steaming and drying were used.

---

[21] Latcham/STRINGING I, p. 79.

(v) The music

The aggregate of all these factors was, as I have said elsewhere in this book, instruments possessed of unique sonic qualities, which make them the best vehicles for the performance of the music of the period. One of the most important of these was the registral difference, as outlined above, and it was clearly a matter of concern for composers in the period who viewed it, like other aspects of the sound, as a positive feature, at least until the cold hand of standardisation and global mass-production began to tighten its grip on modern commerce. We see this throughout our period in the great number of composers either strongly oriented toward the piano – Joseph Haydn after *c.*1770, Ludwig (or Louis) Spohr, Friedrich Kuhlau – or specifically piano-composers, of whom the first were W.A. Mozart, Clementi and J.L. Dussek.

Muzio Clementi

Clementi, if he did not quite earn the title of 'Father of the Pianoforte' – which was bestowed upon him by many and various musical eminences and is inscribed on his gravestone in Westminster Abbey – he probably deserved it. Even if the 'audacious novelties' of the Op. 2 piano sonatas (pub. spring 1779), until recently taken as very early and easily arguable examples of piano music, were first heard by the London public played by him on the harpsichord,[22] the musical substance of the works had great impact and influenced later composers, including Ludwig van Beethoven. Clementi's keyboard technique – founded on the harpsichord – was, by the late 1770s, of the kind that the next generation of (travelling) virtuosi would champion. In fact, he was himself an early example of their breed.

Ludwig van Beethoven

From the beginning, the piano was part of Beethoven's musical make-up, not only because he was, in his early years, a brilliant performer, but also because he used it throughout his career as a stylistic testing-ground, and wrote some of his greatest works for it, as well as providing pianists, in his 32 piano sonatas, with an encyclopedic collection of the order of J.S. Bach's '48'. Indeed, the two collections are often referred to respectively as the pianist's 'Old and New Testaments'.

Beethoven's career as a virtuoso was, however, 'nipped in the bud' by his deteriorating hearing with the result that, although he continued to write for the piano, his technique, in comparison with his contemporaries, did not develop in the same way. This is not, of course, to say that he did not write virtuoso works or that the music is un-pianistic, but there are awkwardnesses at times, which are overlooked – as indeed they should be – in the face of the music's quality. What is interesting is that if his outer ear could not be trusted, his inner ear was impeccable. Apart from the times when no piano of any kind was any good for him, or when the enthusiasm of a new acquisition was at its height, it was the Viennese piano that he favoured and whose sound was engraved on his musical memory in later, deafer, years. The sense

---

[22] Plantinga/CLEMENTI, p. 289.

of the instrument and its capabilities is always in the music he writes for it; in terms of the subject of this chapter, registers and range are in question. It is clear that Beethoven always wanted more from his pianos in power and responsiveness as well as range, and he shows this in his immediate exploitation of the qualities of each new instrument.

In the first movement of his very first published piano sonata, Op. 2/1 in F minor (1793–5), the highest note is trumpeted as the culmination of a progression on several levels. Bb. 20–41 of Ex. 3.1 come from the end of the second subject in the exposition. In terms of phraseology, the exposition had been characterised by a conflict between two and four-bar phrases, often the result of overlapping. With the advent of the second subject, a more leisurely two plus two-bar shape seems to be happening. The second of these, however, is answered (bb. 26ff) by a panting two-bar figure, which again is an overlap, beginning a series of what threaten to be two-bar phrases but which further fragment in bb. 28–30, to be followed by two bars that finally arrive at b. 33 as the natural end of the process and the beginning of another group of longer, four-bar phrases; this is the point at which the highest note f^3 occurs. Melodically it also a culmination, as part of a progression leading through the harmony-notes A♭, B♭, C, D, E♭ (marked with asterisks in bb. 26–7 of Ex. 3.1). By octave-transfer this continues with an as yet unresolved harmony note F♭ (part of the diminished chord in bb. 29 and 30), which is finally resolved with the f^3 in b. 33, coinciding with its also being the resolution of the further stepwise progression of the *appoggiaturas* B♭, C, D♭, E♭, F, and repeated for added emphasis in b. 37. The harmony in both of these cases is a return to the new local tonic-chord of A flat major and the dynamic is the *forte* end-point of the only sustained *crescendo* so far in the movement. There is another melodic-harmonic climax here also, in that the f^3 as the major sixth degree of the scale is a vindication of the 'unsullied' major modality of A flat, in (again triumphantly) contradicting the F♭ minor sixth, which was a feature of the second subject proper (bb. 20, 22 and 24).

Ex. 3.1: Beethoven, Piano Sonata in F minor Op. 2/1/i, bb. 0–108

Ex. 3.1 continued

Ex. 3.1 continued

Ex. 3.1 concluded

He similarly teases the uppermost note in the first movement of the *Waldstein* Sonata (Op. 53, 1803–4), where the a^3 is also presented as the vindicating major sixth after having had two bars of the minor version, changing the $V^{\flat 9}$ to a V^9 (Ex. 3.2a, b. 234).

Ex. 3.2a: Beethoven, Piano Sonata in C major Op. 53/i bb. 231–9.

Ex. 3.2a continued

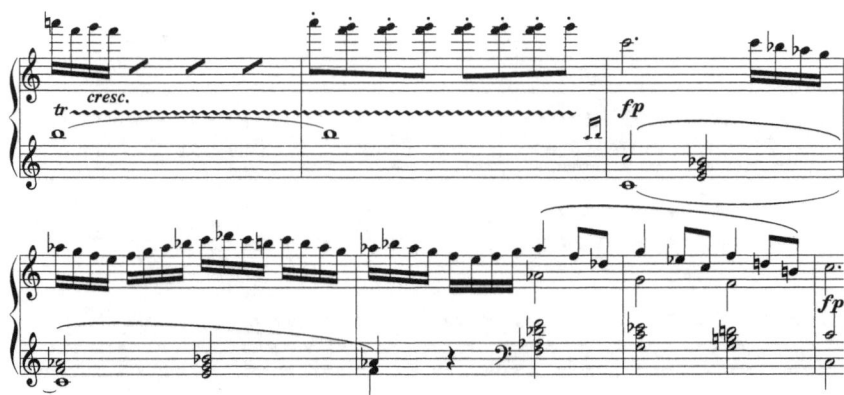

If this passage – the return of the second subject in the tonic key in the reprise – is compared with its corresponding one in the exposition, the extra degree curtailment of the later passage can be seen (Ex. 3.2b, bb. 72–3) lacking the high D to match the previous F♯.

Ex. 3.2b: Beethoven, Op. 53/i, bb. 71–4.

In the early virtuoso Op. 2/3/i in C major, the top F is touched on as the highest point of the cadenza and of the coda's octaves. Curtailment of the music by the piano's range can also be seen in, for example, Op. 10/1/i/128, with the omission of the top G♭, and Op. 10/3/i/22, the enharmonic F♯ suffering the same fate. Beethoven takes less advantage of the increased range in the late piano sonatas. It occurs covertly in a soft passage in the first movement of the *Hammerklavier* (Ex. 3.3 b. 313); however, there is much more exploitation of the instrument in other ways in these works, as we shall see in Chapter Six.

Ex. 3.3: Beethoven, Piano Sonata in B flat major, Op. 106/i, bb. 313–4.

Use of the lowest note in the piano's compass is less common, but usually of importance in other musical ways also. Its presence can be felt in the missing low E in Op. 10/3/i/15 and it appears as the quiet centre of the middle episode (in F) of the sonata-rondo finale of Op. 2/3 and also *ff* and *sf*, as part of a local dominant seventh, in Op. 2/2/ii. This particular movement is an early example of the range of Beethoven's interest in pianistic effects, and I will return to it in the next chapter.

It is fascinating that, although Beethoven is reported to have been delighted with the full bass sound – which he apparently 'felt' through his hands and chest, rather than properly heard – of the Broadwood gift of a six-octave (C^1– c^4) grand in 1816, he still stays within the compass of his earlier pianos, not going below F^1, although in the Adagio sostenuto of the *Hammerklavier* (Op. 106/iii, 1817–18), it is a teasing E♯ (b. 5 for example).

The truism of the inadequacy of musical notation in almost all periods becomes even more blatantly apparent in this one when one looks at the question of registers. Their use is certainly colouristic – what composer with half an ear (inner or outer) could ignore the possibilities? – but in much of the music there is a structural usage also. Beethoven, in the *Pathétique* Sonata (Op. 13 in C minor, *c.*1797–8), builds it into both his subjects in the sonata-form first movement. The *tremolando* accompaniment to the first is sited firmly in the bass register, while the right hand careers from the bottom of the middle into the top, only to descend again (Ex. 3.4).

Ex. 3.4: Beethoven, Piano Sonata in C minor Op. 13/i, bb. 11–19.

The delineation of register is even clearer in the second subject (Ex. 3.5) where, after a few bars' settling in the lower part of the middle register, the accompaniment, a mixture of held and repeated notes, remains in the middle while the theme indulges in a dialogue with itself between the interrogative bass and the answering upper strata. The character of the music remains appropriate for their distinction also, the decorations being reserved for the more supple treble of the piano. A little later, both are combined, with the highest and very nearly the lowest notes appearing close together (Ex. 3.6) and the whole is summarised, so to speak, in the last bars of the codetta, with the functions of the hands, as they appeared in the first subject, reversed:

this time, near-static right hand and a downward-moving *tremolando* in the left (bb. 125–32).[23]

Ex. 3.5: Beethoven, Piano Sonata in C minor Op. 13/i, bb. 48–67.

Ex. 3.6: Beethoven, Piano Sonata in C minor Op. 13/i, bb. 101–31.

---

[23] I shall return to this movement in discussing its introduction in Chapter Six (ii).

Ex. 3.6 continued

The theme of the first sonata's finale (Ex. 3.7, bb. 1–9) would hardly exist if it were not for its sound-quality – the *p* – *f* contrast and that of the registers, in both hands, and the further difference in texture, again in both hands, in bb. 5–6.

Ex. 3.7: Beethoven, Piano Sonata in F minor Op. 2/1/iv, bb. 1–9.

Ex. 3.7 continued

Articulation and register also conspire with each other to add interest to the opening theme of the A major Sonata Op. 2/2 (Ex. 3.8)

Ex. 3.8: Beethoven, Piano Sonata in A major Op. 2/2/i, bb. 0–17.

and informs the transition of Op. 2/3/i, and the serene beauty of parts of its slow movement would be much the poorer without the sensitive exchanges of bass and treble (Ex. 3.9).

Ex. 3.9: Beethoven, Piano Sonata in C major Op. 2/3/ii, bb. 19–21.

Much of the clod-hopping humour of the mock-fugue that ends the F major Sonata Op. 10/2 (1796–7) has to do with the registers chosen, especially in the relentless movement upwards or downwards, particularly and comically evident in the hammering out of the left-hand's circle-of-fifths sequence (Ex. 3.10).

Ex. 3.10: Beethoven, Piano Sonata in F major Op. 10/2/iii, bb. 51–63.

The *Waldstein* is one of the most registrally conscious of all the sonatas, from the dramatic contrast of the opening theme – also subjected to orchestral interpretation in the critical literature – through the slow movement, an extended modulation between the flanking movements where the music is often reduced to harmony and registral colour (Ex. 3.11) – to the finale, where the bass, a reminder of the physical body, gently anchors the floating soul – the falconer, to paraphrase Yeats, which the falcon cannot see.

Ex. 3.11: Beethoven, Piano Sonata in C major Op. 53/ii, bb. 20–5.

This feeling becomes more apparent later in the finale with the addition of the inner trill and the scales traversing bass and middle registers (Ex. 3.12).

Ex. 3.12: Beethoven, Piano Sonata in C major Op. 53/iii, bb. 168–72.

Although the striking leap-and-trill at the beginning of the *Hammerklavier*'s fugue-subject need not span two registers – since the leap is only an octave-and-a-half – Beethoven almost always causes it to do so, due to his placing of it near the top or the bottom of a particular register (Ex. 3.13a).

Ex. 3.13a: Beethoven, Piano Sonata in B flat major Op. 106/iv, bb. 16–26.

Ex. 3.13a continued

This is particularly audible when the head of the subject is separated out for motivic interplay (Ex. 3.13b) and further eviscerated later (Ex. 3.13c). The remainder of the subject, a convoluted falling scale (see Ex. 3.13a), does, however, cover more than one register.

Ex. 3.13b: Beethoven, Op. 106/iv, bb. 47–52.

Ex. 3.13c: Beethoven, Op. 106/iv, bb. 113–30.

Ex. 3.13c continued

There is a fascinating insight into Beethoven's awareness of the physical and sonic aspects of the piano in the revisions which he made to his Fourth Piano Concerto in G after its publication. Barry Cooper has examined and annotated these[24] and the vast bulk of them concern articulation and register. These 'result in a more complex and imaginative articulation than before, with some interesting new antiphonal effects between different registers.'[25] Ex. 3.14a shows the beginning of the development section in the first movement's published edition, and Ex. 3.14b the changes that Beethoven made.

Ex. 3.14: from Beethoven, Piano Concerto No. 4 in G major Op. 58/i.

Similarly, an ethereal quality is given to the piano's continuation out of the cadenza later in the movement, by the addition of a sustained trill instead of the original plain octaves (Ex. 3.15a and 3.15b).

---

[24] In Cooper/REVISIONS.
[25] Ibid., p. 88.

Ex. 3.15: from Beethoven, Piano Concerto No. 4 in G major Op. 58/i.

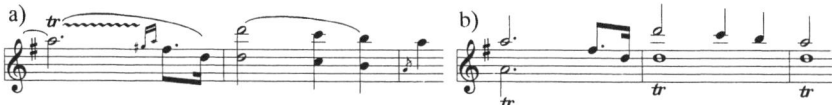

Robert Schumann

Register is also used in this period to characterise its musical material, very often when that material is less characteristic in the usual melodic/harmonic ways. As an example, Schumann encloses the set of character pieces that make up his *Carnaval* Op. 9 (1833–5) between a 'Préambule' and an extended 'Marche' (though in 3/4). There are various reminiscences of the former in the latter, and Ex. 3.16a and 3.16b give two of them as they appear in the 'Préambule'; Ex. 3.17a and 3.17b show how they reappear, respectively, in the 'Marche', each at a higher pitch.

Ex. 3.16a: Schumann, *Carnaval* Op. 9/'Préambule', bb. 62–7.

Ex. 3.16b: Schumann, Op. 9/'Préambule', bb. 79–83.

Ex. 3.17a: Schumann, *Carnaval* Op. 9/'Marche', bb. 252–7.

Ex. 3.17b: Schumann, Op. 9/'Marche', bb. 187–91.

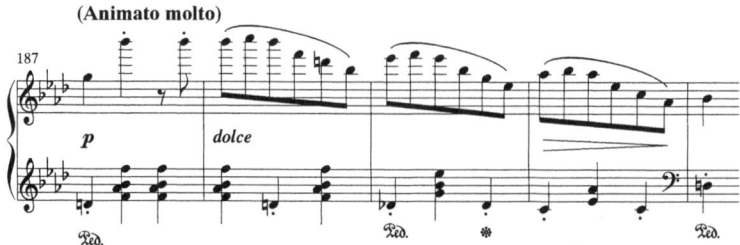

In both these parallel cases, it is the use of right-hand register and the gap between it and the left hand that, in spite of the intervening pieces, cause the link between the two. It is worth mentioning that the first appearance of the turn figure itself comes as a strong registral and textural contrast to what preceded it (Ex. 3.18).

Ex. 3.18: Schumann, *Carnaval* Op. 9/'Préambule', bb. 22–9.

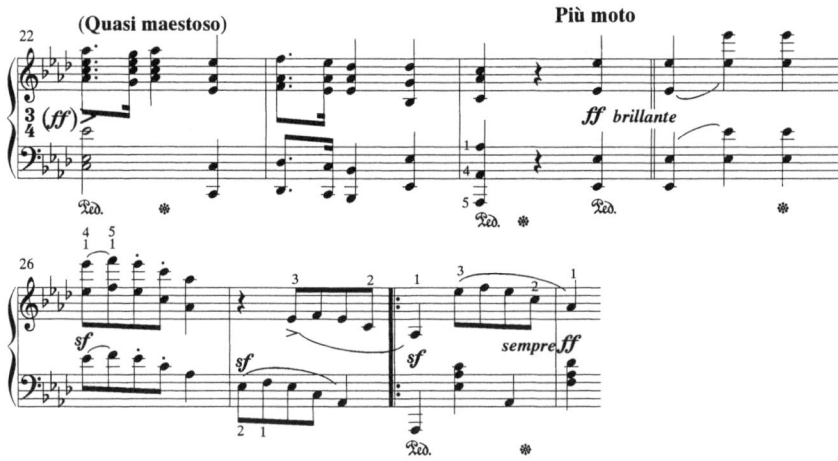

Register-highlighting also has other effects here; the different ficklenesses of 'Arlequin', 'Coquette' and 'Florestan' are shown by unexpected leaps into the more-or-less extreme top register (Ex. 3.19a–c).

Ex. 3.19a: Schumann, *Carnaval* Op. 9/'Arlequin', bb. 1–8.

Ex. 3.19a continued

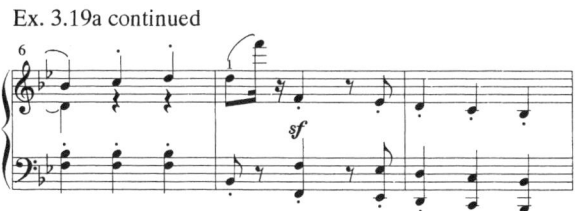

Ex. 3.19b: Schumann, Op. 9/'Coquette', bb. 1–11.

Ex. 3.19c: Schumann, Op. 9/'Florestan', bb. 1–8.

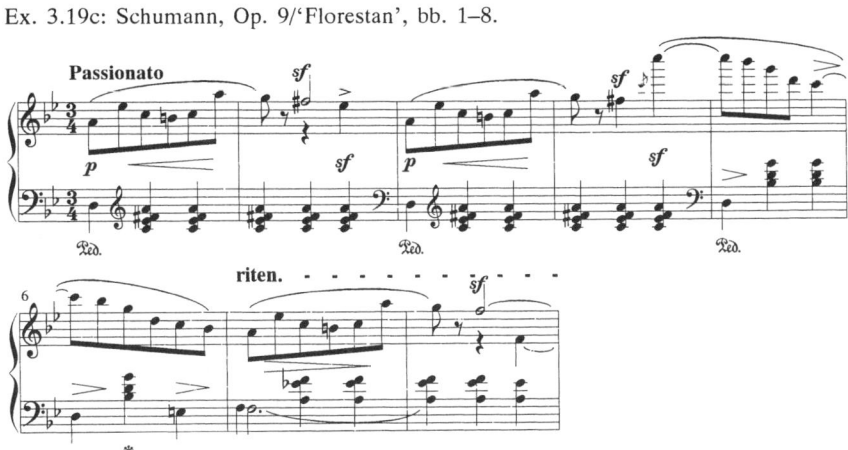

The clear three-register structure of 'Chiarina' (Schumann's name for his then-estranged bride-to-be, Clara Wieck) carries the main melodic burden, the syncopated scales, which, in turn, generate the harmonic movement (Ex. 3.20).

Ex. 3.20: Schumann, *Carnaval* Op. 9/'Chiarina', bb. 0–16.

Frédéric Chopin

Such awareness of the period piano's possibilities imbues all of Chopin's work. His delicate and frequently understated colour-counterpoint can be seen to great advantage in the first of his *Préludes*, Op. 28/1 in C major with tenor and treble shadowing each other in a timbral paperchase. His first *Etude* is coruscating colour-change in its entirety, and the unexpected middle section of Op. 10/3 in E major (Ex. 3.21) is a frightening (not least for the player) contrast to the gentle and beautiful melody that opens it.

Ex. 3.21: Chopin, *Etude* in E major Op. 10/3, bb. 37–52.

Part of the immense power of the so-called 'Revolutionary' (Op. 10/12 in C minor) is the sharp, frequently dissonant treble and its contrast with the angrily ominous bass line (Ex. 3.22). It is difficult not to see the flash and to hear the thud of the cannon here, especially on a period Erard. The piece ends, appropriately, on the lowest note of the piano, C^2. The beautiful extended dialogue/argument between upper and lower parts that is Op. 25/7 in C sharp minor is, of course, much more than a matter of registral sparring, but register is nevertheless inseparable from the totality of the effect: Ex. 3.23a illustrates part of the dialogue and Ex. 3.23b, part of the argument.

Ex. 3.22: Chopin, *Etude* in C minor Op. 10/12, bb. 28–33.

Ex. 3.23a: Chopin, *Etude* in C sharp minor Op. 25/7, bb. 2–9.

Ex. 3.23b: Chopin, Op. 25/7, bb. 22–8.

Sigismond Thalberg and Franz Liszt

The famous 'three-handed' effect that was a prominent feature in the music and performances of Thalberg is a clear expression of the registral zones of the period instrument. Ex. 3.24 shows its use in his *Grande fantaisie de concert on Verdi's 'Il trovatore'*, where the middle melody (mostly played by the thumbs), and its wide-ranging accompaniment, are both shared between the hands.

Ex. 3.24: from Thalberg, *Grande fantaisie de concert on Verdi's 'Il trovatore'*.

The first of his two *Airs Russes variés* Op. 17 (pub. 1834) shows an organ-like texture, more specifically a *quasi*-chorale-prelude (Ex. 3.25).

Ex. 3.25: from Thalberg, *Airs Russes variés* Op. 17/1.

Equally clear is the use, especially by Liszt, of three staves for a solo piano piece, as shown in Ex. 3.26, from the first of his *Drei Konzert-Etüden* S 144 (c.1848, pub. 1849) with its apotheosising repetition of the right-hand scalic figure.

Ex. 3.26: from Liszt, *Drei Konzert-Etüden* S 144/1.

Ex. 3.26 continued

Liszt, however, never needed the convenience of three staves to liberate his use of the keyboard; the entire range was his province and he was a frequent visitor to the extreme outposts. The differences between the first and final (1851) – at times *quasi-*orchestral – versions of the *12 Grandes Etudes* are a case in point and, from just within our period, Ex. 3.27 (from *Funérailles* 1849) needs no further comment.

Ex.3.27: Liszt, *Funérailles*, bb. 14–18.

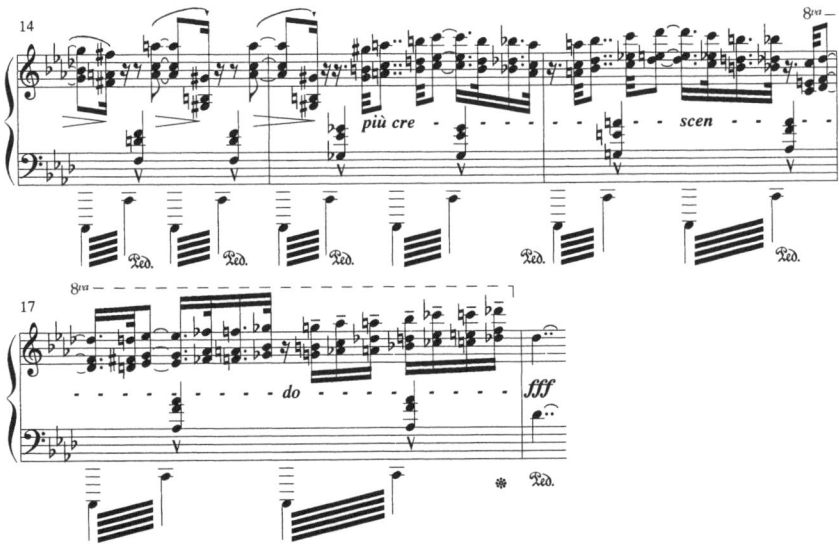

CHAPTER FOUR

Sound Modification

As well as control over the pianos by touch alone and the 'built-in' colour of the registers, other methods of altering the sound also became a concern for performers, composers, and ultimately, piano-makers. The versatility of the harpsichord was enviable here and, although it was mechanically extremely cumbersome to couple several octaves simultaneously with the given register on the piano, there were, nevertheless, several instruments built with, and patents taken out for, such mechanisms. These involved either the coupling of another set or two of strings to the given octave, as in the harpsichord, or giving the player the opportunity of shifting the action of the piano to include one or more strings tuned an octave above and/or below, striking them all with one hammer.[1]

However, less prosaic means were devised to provide the new instrument with possibilities for added colour.

(i) Stops and *genouillères*[2]

During the eighteenth century, however, these various mechanisms were operated not by pedals, but by stops, which were usually mounted either above the keyboard, or to one or both sides. The Merlin 'Claviorganum' in Pl. 20 shows two, one under the centre of the keyboard and the other in the recess below: their functions will become clear later. These stops were familiar to all organ-players and to most harpsichord-players of the period, and they functioned in the same way, requiring a matter of a few seconds or less to change registration. However, when any kind of gradation was called for, such as the gradual shift from three strings to one, giving a kind of *diminuendo*, or the more accurate kind of damper-control required for early nineteenth-century piano music, it soon became clear that hand-operated mechanisms were cumbersome and required the hand to be removed from the keyboard.

One solution was to have *genouillères*, or knee-levers, placed under the keyboard and worked by knee-pressure, and these are still to be found on some harmoniums.

---

[1] See Harding/PIANOFORTE, pp. 106–8.

[2] For more detailed information on pedals, etc., the reader is referred to Harding/PIANOFORTE and the excellent monograph Rowlands/PEDALLING.

INSTRUMENTS

The Schleip 'Lyraflügel' in Pl. 5 shows three of them under the keyboard; the devices can sometimes be folded away, as on the Louis Dulcken grand of 1794 in the Gemeentemuseum in The Hague. *Genouillères* in turn gave way to pedals, at first attached to the side legs of the piano, and then, as the nineteenth century approached, being moved into the centre as in present-day usage. Foot-pedals were not in themselves new. They had already been in use on the harpsichord in the 'nag's head swell' and the 'Venetian swell', devices fitted to the harpsichord to give the illusion of graded dynamics.[3] As with all other matters, the development was a gradual and unevenly distributed one: there were instruments in which stops, *genouillères* and pedals coexisted in various combinations and some even duplicated to allow for left- or right-hand (or -foot) usage. In 1783, John Broadwood took out a British patent for a pedal to raise and lower the dampers as in today's 'loud pedal' and this became standard on British grands. From *c.*1840, the two pedals found on the modern grand piano began to become more and more standard.

(ii) 'Instrumental' imitation and the soft pedal

Taken directly from the harpsichord were the imitations of the sound of the lute, or harp (often called *Sordino*), by arranging for a piece of felt or other cloth to be placed between the hammers and the strings, and of the bassoon, with a piece of parchment laid on the strings to give a 'buzzing' sound. Although the scarcity of references to them in music of the period would suggest that their use was left to the performer's discretion, they were called for on a number of occasions. It is surprising, for example, to find Hummel, who was fairly sparing in his use of even the usual pedals – see the quotation from his *Piano School* in (iii) below – calling for the use of the 'Pedal di Fagotto' in the first ('à la Suisse') of his *Trois Amusements en forme des Caprices* Op. 105 (Ex. 4.1).

Ex. 4.1: Hummel, *Trois Amusements en forme des Caprices* Op. 105/1, bb. 144–8.

The proliferation of stops, etc., was used as a reason for scorning the piano: thus, according to Johann Friedrich Reichardt, '[a]ll newly-invented *Claviere* with 6 and 12 different stops are patchwork and childsplay against a Silbermann clavichord.'[4]

To the lute and bassoon pedals, another was added, with which we are now familiar as the 'soft' pedal. This existed in three forms during the period (as indeed it still

---

[3] See Chapter One (iv) 'The piano's early reception'.
[4] Quoted in Rowland/PEDALLING, p. 65.

does) depending on whether a grand or upright piano was in question. Two of these forms were found on uprights: one is the type by which the action is moved closer to the strings, thus shortening the blow, and this has remained virtually unchanged into our own today. The other type on uprights, variously known as 'moderator', *piano*, *pianissimo, Jeu Céleste, Jeu de buffe* or *Pianozug*, called for strips of soft leather, rather than cloth, to be applied between hammers and strings, as in the lute imitations. These could occasionally give rise to subtle differences, depending on how much of the string was damped with the leather, but the principle is the same in all cases. It is this pedal that Schubert wants the player to hold down constantly when he writes *'durchaus mit dem Pianissimo'* at the beginning of his *Morgenlied* (to Werner's text) (D. 685, 1820).

The grand-piano version of the soft pedal was the now-familiar lateral shift of the keyboard allowing the hammer to strike only one of the two or three strings, the *una corda*. This is the only stop incorporated in the last two (1722 and 1726 (Pl. 1)) of Cristofori's three surviving pianos, the earliest (from 1720) having none. Many instruments had two of these types together with the *forte* pedal, although it is interesting that British grands had the *una corda* as early as the 1770s, whereas they were introduced on a large scale in Vienna only *c*.1810.

The *una corda* pedal was itself subjected to modifications, such as the existence of a *'due corde'* possibility, in which not one, but two of the (in most cases) three strings could be struck, giving a median between minimum and maximum. This, although sounding as though it might be an elaborate mechanism, was simply a tiny block of wood or piece of metal embedded in the wood at the right (usually) of the keyboard, which, when depressed, would stop the action at the two-string point. Pl. 7 and Pl. 8 show this mechanism on my William Stodart grand of between 1822 and 1830. It was also possible to create a kind of sonic *diminuendo* and *crescendo* by gradual depression and raising, respectively, of the shift pedal. There will be more detailed discussion of these possibilities in the next two chapters.

(iii) The sustaining pedal

Cristofori's three extant pianos (see Pl. 1) were, like the harpsichord, fitted with a damper for each note, which was raised when that note's key was pressed, allowing the struck string to vibrate freely. When the key was released, the damper returned to deaden the string. Thus, this feature was a permanent fixture in pianos from the very first. The clavichord, because of the quick decay-time of its sound, needed no such damping, and there were also a number of pianos (mostly earlier German ones) made without dampers. Soon, a method of raising the dampers *en masse*, as distinct from – but in addition to – the individual key operation, also became an expected and eventually a necessary feature of the piano. This was called, variously the *'forte'*, *'Fortezug'*, 'damper pedal' or 'forte pedal' during the period and was later known as the 'loud' pedal; I shall refer to it as the sustaining pedal from here on. Once composer-performers and composers began to become more used to the piano as an instrument in its own right rather than as a substitute for the clavichord and harpsichord, they began to use the pedal as a musical feature rather than as an effect.

An example of this is the basic case of allowing the strings to vibrate freely. In the performance of music of this period on a modern piano, after a very short time the result is a kind of aural silt. On the period instrument however, it produces a pleasant 'halo' of sound that was much admired at the time. It is used in the finale, 'Rondo Pastorale', of Potter's Sonata in C major Op. 1 (1818, or before) (Ex. 4.2a), where the sustaining pedal is held down for each of the parts of the theme, supported by the tonic pedal, five and a half and four bars respectively.

Ex. 4.2a: Potter, Piano Sonata in C major Op. 1/iii, bb. 0–13.

It also appears a number of other times in the movement, such as the passage in bb. 55–7 (Ex. 4.2b), where the use of the top of the keyboard and the unusual but interesting dissonances combined with the held sustaining pedal is particularly effective.

Ex. 4.2b: Op. 1/iii, bb. 55–8.

The effect is not overused: the final appearance of the theme has *sostenuto* without any pedal-direction (which I take to be subject to the usual interpretation, although it is a moot point). One other passage – the longest of the examples – has the same pedal-effect: the dominant preparation, over a dominant pedal-note, for the return of the theme (Ex. 4.2c). This is an extended V^7 chord with, at the beginning of the example, a few dissonances and this usage is also very effective.

Ex. 4.2c: Op. 1/iii, bb. 239–50.

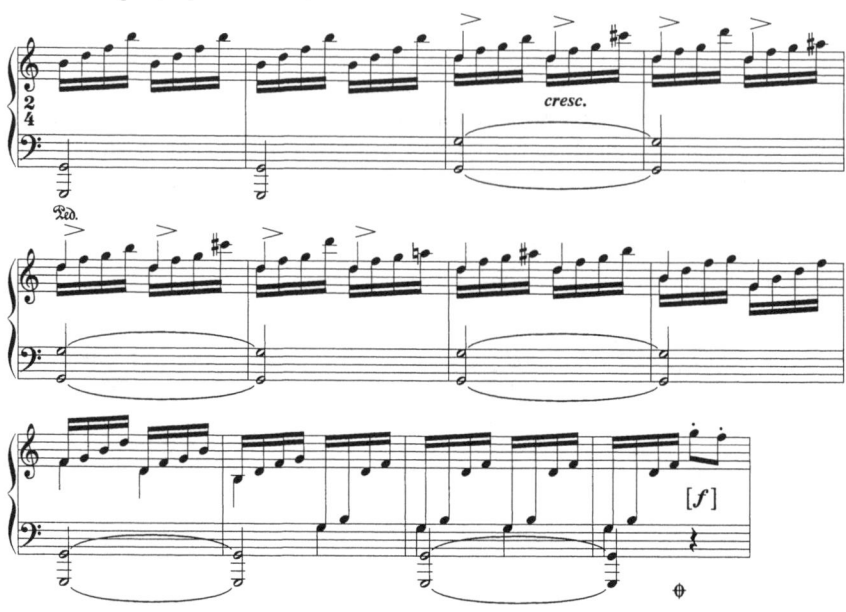

The finale of Augustus Kollmann's two-movement Piano Sonata in A flat major, Op. 1/3 (pub. 1808, at the age of 19) also uses the raised dampers, creating, in the decorated right hand, the sound of a distant bell (Ex. 4.3).

Ex. 4.3: Kollman, Piano Sonata in A flat major Op. 1/3/ii, bb. 101–8.

This halo effect was particularly associated with pastoral pieces, such as Potter's (discussed above) and, in fact, Louis Adam, in his *Méthode* (pub. 1802) recommended it for

> pastorals and musettes, tender and melancholy airs, romances, religious pieces, and generally in all expressive passages where the melodies are very slow and only rarely change dynamic.

[... les pastorales et musettes, les airs tendres et mélancoliques, les romances, les morceaux religieux, et en général dans tous les passages expressifs dont les chants sont très lents et ne changent que très rarement de modulation.]⁵

Indeed, the example Adam gives (No. 84 in the *Méthode*) is itself a *Pastorale* (Ex. 4.4). Another example involves a Swiss melody sung by mountain herdsmen popular around Europe at this time, *Air Suisse nommé le ranz des vaches imitant les echos* [Swiss air called *ranz des vaches* with imitations of echoes]. It is *tremolando* almost throughout and various pedal-combinations are used for the different kinds of echoes. Adam remarks that the use of both pedals together gives a smooth sound, without the individual notes being distinguishable.⁶

Ex. 4.4: L. Adam, *Méthode*/Air Suisse, bb. 0–8.

It is clear that Adam was aware of, and revelled in the use of, pedals in various combinations before many other 'Schools', and one would expect French composers and those attracted to France, to show familiarity with pedalling techniques, which seems to have been the case. The second (and final) movement of Boieldieu's First Piano Concerto is a 'Pastorale con variationi' in which the first variation is *poco f* 'Sans Pedalle' and the coda repeats the theme *pp* 'Avec la grande Pedalle'. The pianist-composer Daniel Steibelt was something of an experimenter in this field: in a French edition (1799) of his Third Concerto in E major (perf. 1798, called *'L'orage'* because of the storm episode in its pastoral finale) he gives pedalling directions on the title-page:

Ce signe indique de mettre le pied de dessus la Pédale qui étouffe le son [that is, press the damper pedal]
Ce sign indique de toucher la Pédale qui fait le Piano [press the soft pedal]
Ce signe indique de lever le pied de dessus les Pédales qu'on vient de toucher [release pedal(s)]

The London edition of this work, published by Clementi, omits these instructions, though it uses the second symbol for the soft pedal and the third for its cancellation

---

⁵ Adam/*METHODE*, pp. 219–20.
⁶ *Op. cit.*, p. 220.

in the little cadenza near the end of the first movement. Steibelt later published the '*Orage*' alone, justifying this by saying that it will serve as a study for the pedals and their effects, adding that the piece depends essentially on fingering, and that the given fingering best fulfils his musical intentions: 'Cette Pièce servira à l'étude des pédales, et à connaître leurs effets. L'effet de cette Pièce dépendant essentiellement du doigté; j'ai cru devoir donner celui qui rempli mieux mon intention.'

Ludwig Berger's *Grande Sonate pathétique* Op. 7 (1813–4), with exactly the same descriptive title and key as Beethoven's Op. 13 (C minor), dogs its model further by also having a slow – in this case Adagio – introduction, which, again like Beethoven, recurs in a modified form later in the movement. The sustaining pedal is directed to be held for at least ten bars in each case, although the release-point is different and one, possibly, a misprint: Pl. 9 is a facsimile of this introduction. The combination of *tremolo*, semi-hemi-demi-semi-quaver [*sic*] notation with dissonances, three-note chords in the lower-middle register and (in its second appearance) close-position four-note diminished chords anchored on the lowest note of the piano, coupled with a *fortissimo* dynamic – all these and not least the very appearance of the music promises extreme turgidity. Again, however, the period sound saves the day and the build-up is quite effectively handled. John Field's statement of the theme in his variations on the Russian tune *Kamarinskaya* (*c.*1808) is over a tonic octave pedal and asks for 'Due Pedali' after the left-hand has sounded the B♭ octave and joins the right hand for the harmony (Ex. 4.5).

Ex. 4.5: Field, Variations on *Kamarinskaya*, bb. 1–11.

Field is generally recognised as being the pioneer of the pedal, in the sense of integrating it into the fabric and make-up of his music, rather than using it as an accessory. One of the great advantages of the increasing effectiveness of the sustaining pedal, especially after the turn of the century, was that it freed the left hand from the close-set *Alberti* figuration necessary to prolong the harmonies when the piano had less sustaining power. But it also allowed for a greater range of accompanimental figurations, including, through the use of the bass's extended compass, the compound, wide-ranging arpeggios characteristic of much nineteenth-century music, and found typically in the nocturne style (which *genre* Field first brought to the public ear) and shown in typical configuration in his twelfth Nocturne (pub. 1834, Ex. 4.6). Like Handel before him, Field was also a great believer in recycling: this piece was also published as the second movement of his Seventh Piano Concerto, and is but one of many rewritings, reissuings and renamings.

Ex. 4.6: Field, Nocturne No. 12 in G major, bb. 1–4.

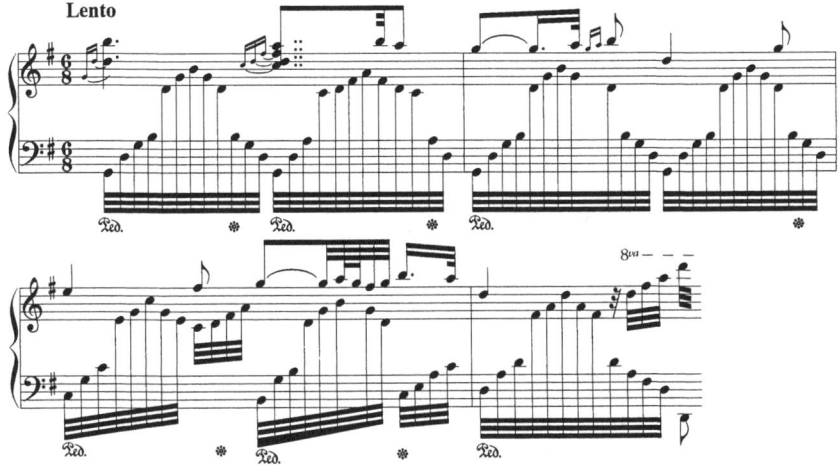

Pl. 10 shows a copy of a *c*.1817 Russian edition of Field's Sixth Nocturne in which the pedal-markings are very meticulous, a particular note being highlighted, in most cases, for the raising of the sustaining pedal (by the asterisks, *). This gives a subtle prominence to the last semiquaver of many of the beats, and these are occasionally dissonant. When the music moves very high up on the piano (for example at b. 7), the pedal is held for longer stretches in spite of the running demisemiquavers. The *Pastorale* in A major (pub. 1831), is the third of the solo piano versions of a movement originally appearing as part of a piano quintet. All three are slightly different, including their lengths, and the number of issues indicates what a popular piece this was. The piece also shows the use of the pedal for other than simply sustaining (Ex. 4.7a). The first bar would be very unsatisfactory in terms of sonority and, indeed, harmony if the pedal did not prolong the bass tonic through the fleeting touch of dominant and the, on the face of it, rather awkward accompaniment-line A – E – D – C♯.

Ex. 4.7a: Field, *Pastorale* in A major, bb. 0–10.

The coinciding of the left hand's rest with the damping results in the isolation of the right's last quaver C♯ and highlights its anacrustic function, which comes into its own as the basis of the little punctuating commentary at the end of b. 3, extending this function ⌣ - ⌣ -. This figure appears in various guises throughout the piece and has the last word (Ex. 4.7b).

Ex. 4.7b: *Pastorale* in A major, ending.

Piggott draws attention to the pedal-markings of Field's manuscript for one of the versions of the Fifth Nocturne ('Serenade') where the ♯ii^7 (b. 1) and V$^{♭9}$ (b. 3) are lovely chromatic ripples on this cool diatonic pool, simply fading in and out of the surrounding chords without needing any of the emphasis that all but the most subtle of pedalling on the modern piano entails (Ex. 4.8).

Ex. 4.8: Field, Nocturne No. 5 in B flat major, bb. 1–4.

The extension of accompanimental figures in the music of Chopin also demands *sostenuto* pedalling, which he usually provides. The pedal-changes in the D flat major Nocturne Op. 27/2 (Ex. 4.9) certainly coincide with the chord-changes, the long dreamy D♭ with a haze of added passing-notes and *appoggiature* settling on the full-bar harmonic *appoggiatura* of b. 5. But then pedalling is used to draw attention to the anchoring linear bass-progression[7] of bb. 6–8: D♭ – C – B♭ – B♭ – A♭ (the last as the dominant) while the treble indulges in decorative figuration traversing the upper and upper-middle registers.

Ex. 4.9: Chopin, Nocturne in D flat major Op. 27/2, bb. 1–12.

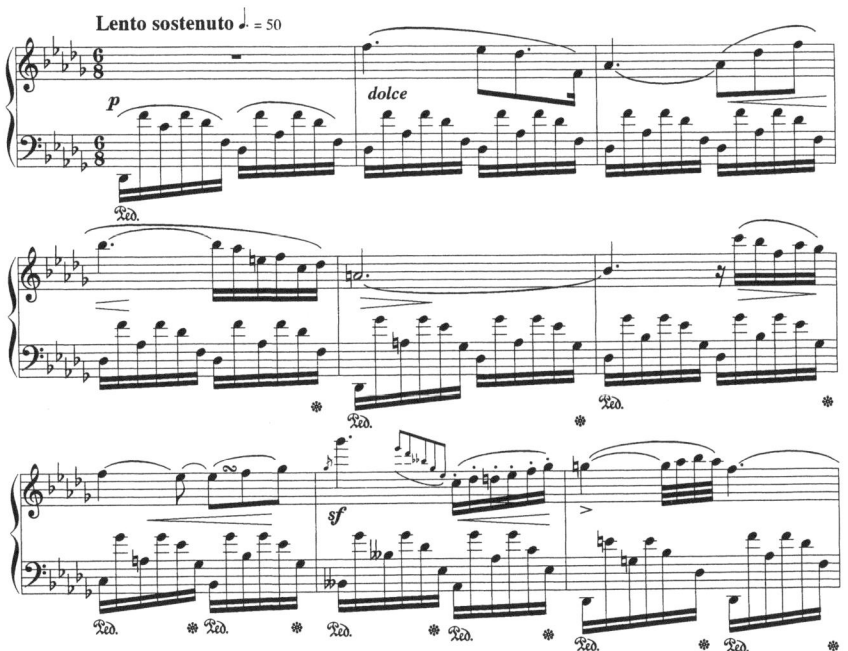

---

[7] This will be further discussed in Chapter Eleven (vi) Nocturne.

Ex. 4.9 continued

Ex. 4.10, from its companion-piece Op. 27/1, reminds us that a two-bar held sustaining pedal at *fff* on, say, one of Chopin's favourite Erards, does not entirely preclude the left-hand articulation of the *staccati*.

Ex. 4.10: Chopin, Nocturne in C sharp minor Op. 27/1, bb. 49–50.

At the beginning of the Second Nocturne in E flat major Op. 9/2 (1830–32) the pedal is again held only for the duration of each beat, each one having a different harmony. One result of this is an accentuation of the dissonance between the bass line and the melody at the end of the first bar, pointing towards the move to the supertonic in the next, although given the overall mood, I suspect that Chopin has half-pedalling in mind here. Also, the exposed octaves involving an upward octave leap in both hands to the Cs – and including a change of register in the right hand – makes these notes too prominent. On the other hand, the passage in b. 6 (Ex. 4.11) and the cadenza in the antepenultimate bar, have dampers raised, as does a similar free passage in the next Nocturne, Op. 9/3 in B major, giving the typically early nineteenth-century chromatic halo effect (Ex. 4.12).

Ex. 4.11: Chopin, Nocturne in E flat major Op. 9/2, bb. 6–7.

Ex. 4.12: Chopin, Nocturne in B major Op. 9/3, ending.

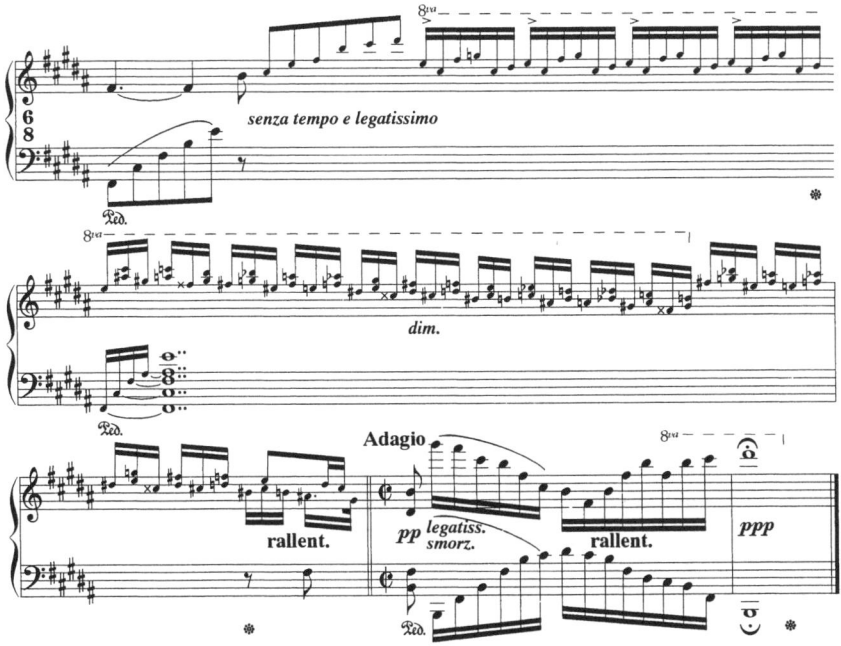

A similar kind of quality was often noted in Chopin's own performance: his pupil Elizavieta Cheriemietieff, a young Russian aristocrat, wrote in her unpublished journal: 'His playing is out of this world, something airborne, misty: one imagines angels when listening to this music.'[8] Léon Escudier, co-founder of the weekly *La France musicale*, waxes even more numinous: '... one might well believe one is hearing small fairy voices sighing under silver bells, or a rain of pearls falling on crystal tables.'[9] Similar qualities are praised in a performance of the master's works by another of his pupils, Tellefsen, by the critic in *Revue et gazette musicale de Paris*: 'Few will be able to interpret better the hazy, slightly mystical poetry whose gentle breath the Polish composer has imparted to all his works.'[10]

This is very much the same effect which Schumann evokes in b. 10 of his portrait of Chopin in *Carnaval* (1833–5, Ex. 4.13). For the first nine bars, he directs that the pedal be depressed at the beginning of each change of harmony, on the bar and half-bar, including several dissonant decorative notes. He does not, however, specify the points at which it should be raised, implying either that the player would interpret this as we would today on the modern piano, – that is, raised just before the change of harmony – or that it was only to be partly raised. A third possibility is that once the direction for depressing the pedal is followed, the raising is at the player's

---

[8] From her unpublished *Journal*, 17 November 1842. Quoted in Eigeldinger/CHOPIN, p. 162.
[9] *La France musicale*, V/9, 27 February 1842. Quoted in ibid., pp. 294–5.
[10] *Revue et gazette musicale de Paris*, 1851/18, 3 May, p. 141. Quoted in ibid., p.185.

discretion. This is an interesting experiment, but raises too many possibilities, however intriguing, for me to discuss here. In view of the meticulousness of Schumann's pedal-marking in general, I would opt for part-pedalling, which is very effective in this context. The result, on the single occasion on which he does use the raise-pedal asterisk (Ex. 4.13)

Ex. 4.13: R. Schumann, *Carnaval* Op. 9/'Chopin', b. 10.

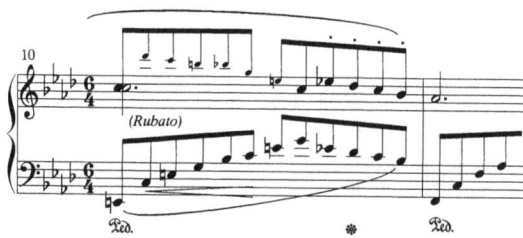

is that the last two quavers (with the suggested *rubato* and the *mezzo-staccato*, and isolated by the raised pedal) are yet another manifestation of the omnipresent two-crotchet anacrusis in this piece. The overall dynamic, *forte*, announced in the first bar, is the only explicit one given – there are hairpins and a '*cresc.*' – and Schumann directs the repeat of the piece to be played *pianissimo*: the contrast is illuminating when Ex. 4.13 is re-heard at this dynamic level with the pedalling observed.

It is clear that Schumann experimented much with the sustaining pedal, and some of the results remain in the published music. Even in his Op. 1 of 1829–30, the 'Abegg' variations, he shows a remarkable ear for sonorities that are impossible on our modern instrument. Just before the end of the last coda-variation, he writes as in Ex. 4.14,

Ex. 4.14: R. Schumann, 'Abegg' Variations Op. 1/Finale, bb. 73–4.

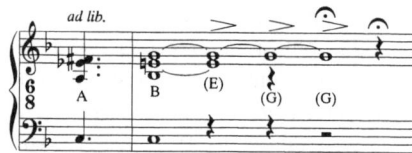

and the end of *Papillons* Op. 2 (1829–31) does something similar. Here the chord of the dominant seventh is sounded and the notes slowly released one by one, giving the effect of a slow retrograde re-playing of the initial arpeggio-spread. This in itself is only the end of an even more striking passage, a miniature sound-scene with a town-clock ringing six as the sound of a Shrovetide carnival recedes. This entire passage is worth reproducing for its long depression of the sustaining pedal and the strange effect produced (Ex. 4.15).

Ex. 4.15: R. Schumann, *Papillons* Op. 2, ending.

Ex. 4.15 continued

Since I cannot include, at this stage in her career, his wife-to-be Clara – a vignette of whom appears as No. 11, 'Chiarina' – as such, the only other prominent musical personality portrayed in *Carnaval* also shows experimentation and a novel effect. The last three bars of 'Paganini' are given as Ex. 4.16:

Ex. 4.16: R. Schumann, *Carnaval* Op. 9/'Paganini', bb. 35–7.

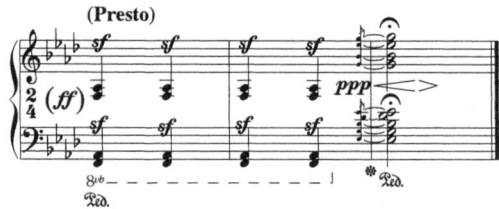

four *sf fortissimo* chords of F – on the piano's lowest note – and A♭, doubled two octaves above, with the dampers up. Before these are dropped on the strings, a grace-note chord of V⁷ on E♭ is to be played *ppp* and tied to the same chord – the dominant of the key of the next piece, A flat – as a minim with a pause. Schumann instructs: 'Nur bei genauer Beobachtung der Vorschrift für den Pedalgebrauch wird der beabsichtigte Effekt erreicht' ['Only by precise attention to the indications for the use of the pedal will this effect be obtained'].

It seems that Schumann does not actually wish this dominant chord to be heard in the normal way at all, but the notes to be depressed soundlessly and held: the instrument does the rest, by allowing the strings of the chord, already vibrating in sympathy with the previous *sf* chords, to be heard only as overtones. The point to remember – already made in several previous chapters – is the greater capacity for overtones in the early piano due, in particular, to the materials used in the making of the strings and their much lesser tension than in the present time. The effect, to be sure, is a subtle one, but it is also a magical one and gives the impression, already described, of the still-vibrating strings of a violin and the magnetic residue of Paganini's personality, having left the stage. One of the most *outré* examples of experimentation in respect of the sustaining pedal is that of Bertini in *L'Ultima*

Fantasia published in 1844: the composer's own description (Pl. 11) will obviate any commentary on my part.

In spite of the detail in Adam's *Méthode* (see above), it is interesting that several piano schools, in keeping with the views of their authors, warn against over-use of pedals. Czerny, in his *Pianoforte School* (written very much in the spirit and on the model of Hummel's) calls such pedals 'childish toys of which a solid player will disdain to avail himself'.[11] Hummel, for example, having gone so far as to say that if many of his performing contemporaries were forbidden to use pedals they would be unrecognisable, writes:

> 2. Though a truly great Artist has no occasion for Pedals to work upon his audience by expression and power, yet the use of the damper-[sustaining] pedal, combined occasionally with the piano-pedal (as it is termed) [moderator] has an agreeable effect in many passages, its employment however is rather to be recommended in slow than in quick movements, and only where the harmony changes at distant intervals: all other pedals are useless, and of no value either to the performer or the instrument.
> 3. Let the Pupil never employ the Pedals before he can play a piece correctly and intelligibly. Indeed, generally speaking, every player should indulge in the use of them with the utmost moderation; for it is an erroneous supposition that a passage, correctly and beautifully executed without pedals, and of which every note is clearly understood, will please the hearers less, than a mere confusion of sounds, arising from a series of notes clashing one against another.[12]

Nevertheless, he does give a few examples, including the use of both sustaining and soft pedals. My own feeling is that he is being rather 'cagey', since his own style of piano-writing is admirably suited to a variety of pedalling techniques. It is clear that here, as on so many other occasions to do with the period piano, a healthy sense of comparativeness must be maintained. Paramount, of course, is the quite different sound and sustaining powers of this instrument, which I will summarise in the next chapter.

(iv) Divided pedals

Additionally, pedals could be divided: this is to say that the upper and lower halves of the instrument (breaking about middle C) could be controlled independently, either by separate pedals, or by, literally, dividing the pedal, as in the Broadwood of 1819 in Pl. 12 whose *forte* pedal is so constructed, as the detail in Pl. 13 shows. This was not just an early version of the 'third pedal' on some modern grands, which allows a single bass note only to be sustained, but in recognition of the greater difference in the early instrument between the volume and quality of sound between the three registers, or, in this case, the different halves of the keyboard. Use of this kind of pedal seems to have been left to the performers' discretion as I have not found any directions for it in music of the period. In Field's Introduction and Rondo on *Come*

---

[11] Czerny/PIANOFORTE, p. 152.
[12] Hummel/PIANOFORTE, Vol. II, Pt. 2, p. 35.

Again, Come Again there appears the direction '*Ped: à Gauche.*' on a *pp* passage at the end of the Introduction. There is a tantalising possibility that this might refer to the left half of a divided sustaining pedal but, given the fact that most of the passage is in the bass register and appears after a *dim[inuendo]*, it would seem that one of the versions of the soft pedal is in question.[13]

---

[13] See Temperley-ed/LONDON-m, Vol. 13, p. 95.

CHAPTER FIVE

Versatility

(i) Early forms of the piano

The piano showed its versatility in many ways, as we shall see, and not least in its purely physical manifestation. By the end of the eighteenth century, it existed in three main forms, the two older of these reflecting its origins in, first, the harpsichord (giving the concert grand, or 'wing' piano – *Flügel, Flügelklavier* or *Hammerflügel* in German – with the strings stretching from the broad (keyboard) end to the narrow), and, secondly, in the clavichord, giving the domestic 'square' (though really oblong) model in which the strings are more or less parallel with the keyboard. Outside of those countries in which the clavichord was common, the spinet, or 'square' harpsichord can be seen as the progenitor of the square piano. The third form, the upright, was intended as a space-saving compromise by placing the strings and soundboard perpendicular to the keyboard; even grands were adapted in this way – see Pl. 28 – accounting for the unusual height of these instruments compared with our modern upright. Early attempts at upright pianos include one attributable to Christian Ernst Friederici, a pupil of Silbermann, made in or before 1745. Rosamond Harding shows a photograph of an elaborate German model from about 1740, now in the *Schloss Museum* in Berlin.[1]

By 1795, William Stodart had built his upright grand – which was praised by Joseph Haydn during a visit to his London shop in that year – and William Southwell of Dublin made an upright square, which he patented in 1798, although it seems that few were made or sold. The modern form of the upright came in 1800 when Matthias Müller in Vienna and John Isaac Hawkins of Philadelphia (USA) independently dispensed with the stands of these pianos, having the strings stretching down to the floor. Such instruments were given various distinguishing names – Müller called his the 'Dittanaklasis', and Hawkins' name was the 'Portable Grand Pianoforte'. 'Portable' may have been a little misleading, as these instruments still remained large and cumbersome, with the extra disadvantage that, in a domestic situation, the player would be facing in the direction of the wall against which the piano was placed. This presented difficulties from the point of view of accompaniment, which was the most useful function of the instrument and several

---

[1] Harding/PIANOFORTE, Plate III(a), facing p. 32.

possible solutions were investigated, including the production of smaller versions, not needing to be placed against a wall. There was also Southwell's construction of what he called the 'Piano sloping backwards' in 1811, which reduced the height[2] and a Broadwood upright of *c*.1835 with a dip in the back for the same reason,[3] as well as fitting a mirror in front of the player (see the Collard in Pl. 26).

However, it was Robert Wornum who secured the popularity of these domestic instruments and patented several versions. They were known by various names – *pianino*, cottage piano, cabinet piano, *piano vertical* in France – but the most enduring was Wornum's 'piccolo piano' (see Pl. 14), whose action has changed less *vis-à-vis* its modern counterpart than in any other type of piano in our period. Wornum clearly viewed his instruments in this category as being 'enduring' in a more literal sense also, as a set of printed instructions for repairs aimed at the early nineteenth-century do-it-yourself homemaker pasted on the inside of this instrument ends, 'These directions are given as matters of information; but from the great stability of this Action they are not likely to be necessary.'(see Pl. 15) Brave words indeed! Nevertheless, this 'stability' and their compact size and visual appeal guaranteed their popularity. It is a little unexpected, but none the less interesting that, according to one of his star pupils, Camille Dubois-O'Meara, 'Chopin had always a cottage piano [*pianino*] by the side of the grand piano on which he gave lessons' and that, in accompanying his concertos on it, he 'performed the rôle of the orchestra most wonderfully [*d'une façon prodigieuse*]'.[4]

The German/'Viennese' version of the upright began as the 'Giraffe' piano ('Giraffenflügel'): Pl. 16 shows a later version (from *c*.1840, probably by Ehrlich of Bamberg). These were scaled down for domestic use and soon such instruments, especially the small French pianos from 1827 onwards – the '*piano droit*' for example – saw the end of the square piano. They were also responsible for one of the most important nineteenth-century advances in useful design, cross- or over-stringing. Intended to save further space, this had the advantages of more evenly distributing the string-tension within the case or frame and helping to keep the instrument in tune for longer.

An idea of the different kinds and models of piano available in the early nineteenth century can be gleaned from advertisements of the time. D'Almaine & Co billed themselves as 'Manufacturers of Improved Square, Piccolo, Boudoir, Cottage & Cabinet, Piano Fortes' at their 'Royal Piano Forte & Music Saloon, 20, Soho Square'[5] and Willis & Co had their 'Royal Musical Library in London and Dublin ... where may be found every variety of PIANO-FORTES BY THE MOST EMINENT MAKERS at the lowest manufacturer's prices'. In addition, the firm was 'appointed sole Agents in London for the sale of PAPE'S PATENT TABLE PIANO-FORTES ... ' and they also had 'a splendid variety of ... Harps, Seraphins, &c. &c, ...'

---

[2] There is a line drawing in Harding/PIANOFORTE, p. 228.
[3] Ibid., Plate XV, facing p. 268.
[4] Eigeldinger/CHOPIN, p. 63.
[5] British Library, Hirsch Collection 1272.

The piano also showed versatility in its many capabilities in terms of sound production and modification, and the varying rôles in which these allowed it to shine. It had the ability to stand alone in solo performance, to be the ideal accompanying partner (as we shall see in Section III) and even – anachronistically invoking the terms of later Romanticism – to 'oppose' a larger group or the orchestra. This was not the whole story, however. Even greater versatility was sought in adding to and modifying its sound-possibilities, although some commentators considered – and many still do consider – that at least some of these overstepped the bounds of musicality.

These possibilities varied from instrument to instrument, although they were generally more common than many histories of the piano would suggest and, even though some of the modifications and/or additions were controlled by pedals, stops, or *genouillères*, I have treated them separately from the last chapter, as they are less intrinsic to the music than the usual pedals with which we are familiar. Section (v) below deals with the instrument's versatility in other than strictly musical ways.

(ii) Turkish music

The Viennese Haschka grand of *c.*1825 in the Colt Collection (see Pl. 17) has five pedals: a keyboard shift (*una corda*), sustaining, bassoon, moderator and Turkish music. The craze for things Turkish – fashions, symbols, and so on – had begun in the eighteenth century because of the Turkish wars, and the military music of the Sultan's private bodyguard, the Janissaries, was well-known to the servicemen who had been involved in the hostilities; such 'Janissary music' had a strong impact on military music in the West. After the treaty with the Ottoman Empire, many European army regiments incorporated Turkish instruments into their own bands. Western potentates also vied with each other in forming private Turkish bands, including Catherine the Great, the King of Prussia and the Austrian Emperor, some of them taking the trouble to seek advice from Turkish musicians and even employing them. By the late eighteenth century 'a standardised Turkish percussion section had become a part of European regimental music.'[6] The sound of the music was characterised by contrasts between the shrill, penetrating tones of the several Turkish hautboys, flute, cymbals and triangle, and the dull sound of kettle- and bass drums, and the fact that they played in unison or octaves.

The westernised parody of the style is immortalised in the rondo finale, *Alla Turca*, of Mozart's Piano Sonata in A major, K. 331, which work is itself something of a rarity among the sonatas, having a set of variations in A major for its first movement, a Menuetto in the same key and this *Alla Turca* finale in the parallel minor with a recurring episode in the major, in which mode it ends. The finale has the traits traditionally associated with 'Turkish music' – a simple melody, more rhythmic than melodic and heavily reliant on repeated figures, a four-square, regular accompaniment of the 'um-cha' type and a very restricted harmonic ambit, basically

---

[6] See the fascinating Head/ORIENTALISM, p. 58.

diatonic and confined to the three primary chords, a slow rate of harmonic rhythm and the use of the dominant minor (Ex. 5.1a).

Ex. 5.1a: W.A. Mozart, Piaano Sonata in A major K. 331/iii, bb. 0–8.

The implied effects (Ex. 5.1b and c) suggest the cymbals, triangle (or bells) and bass drum that later pianos equipped with Turkish music could provide, although a drum alone could also be found, occasionally operable by a different pedal.

Ex. 5.1b: K. 331/iii, bb. 88–92.

Ex. 5.1c: K. 331/iii, bb. 116–21.

Pl. 18 shows the devices inside the Haschka grand pictured in Pl. 17 – in fact they can also be discerned in that plate. The cymbal sound is made by the wire under the protruding bar which is lowered onto the bass strings, and the triangle sound by the bell. In most cases (as here), these were operated by the same pedal which could also couple a bassoon mechanism (parchment placed against (usually lower) strings: see Chapter Four (ii)). The 'drum' is the actual soundboard hit by a felted beater on a foot-pedal as in a modern drum-kit, although some instruments were instead fitted with one or more small drums and could have a number of bells. This is the case with the Van der Hoef piano in the Gemeentemuseum in The Hague, which has six pedals including Drum and 'Triangle', in this case small bells.

On pianos with several pedals, some were duplicated to allow for more combinations, depending upon which foot was free at any given time. The Giraffe piano (c.1825) by the Amsterdam maker Joannes van Raay, which is also in the Gemeentemuseum, has six pedals (left to right): 1. sustaining, 2. bassoon, 3. and 4. moderator, 5. *una corda*, and 6. triangle-with-drum. Such multi-pedal instruments (whether these included Turkish music or not) were by no means rarities: a drawing of Rossini shows him standing with a square piano with six or more pedals and Carl Maria von Weber had a piano with four, while Napoleon owned an Erard piano of 1802 with five pedals. Beethoven's friend and lawyer, Jan [Johann] Nepomuk Kanka possessed a beautiful 'Viennese' Empire style piano (c.1800) with six pedals which the composer frequently played during his visits to Kanka's house in Prague, and a very similar instrument of c.1810, (another Haschka in the Colt Collection) is shown in Pl. 19 with the pedals (left to right): 1. drum, 2. bells and cymbal, 3. moderator, 4. *una corda*, 5. sustaining, 6. bassoon, 7. second moderator.

Nor were these confined to grands: many surviving squares have a range of pedals, and also include combinations of pedals with *genouillères* and even stops. A Beyer (London) square of c.1783 in the Gemeentemuseum, The Hague (on loan from the Rijksmuseum), was extremely well-endowed in this respect, having originally had three hand-stops (divided sustaining 'pedal' and lute), a *genouillère* (also working the lute attachment) and two pedals (sustaining and lid-swell), giving a number of possible combinations. It is probably fair to say that a piano of the first half of the nineteenth century with only two or three pedals, as in modern instruments, was the exception rather than the rule.

(iii) Orchestral effects

These effects reinforce the view of the piano as a kind of universal instrument. Its possibilities of gradation of tone and volume comparable to the more expressive instruments (and above all, the voice) and its enormous range, made it suitable for reproducing orchestral works, especially with the extra pedals and effects. Not for nothing was it called the 'orchestra in the drawing-room' and we will see its suitability for the very popular 'battle' pieces later.[7]

Other experiments, stranger and more short-lived, included the various inventions for sustaining the sound on the piano so that it could more closely match strings, winds or voice. One of these was a mechanism to keep the hammers hitting the strings rapidly, as long as the key was depressed, by means of a toothed cog-wheel. These 'Sostenente' pianos, as they were called, allowed the player a kind of *Bebung*

---

[7] See Chapter Twelve (ii).

effect similar to that obtainable on the clavichord.[8] Another device was a band of gut or flexible metal between pulleys operated by a treadle which was used to 'bow' the piano-strings, giving the impression of a string orchestra. As early as 1802, the American piano-maker John Isaac Hawkins of Philadelphia, produced an upright of this kind which he called the 'Claviol'; it was seen in London eleven years later. The names used by other makers or patentees were similarly evocative: 'Violicembalo', 'Piano-Viole', 'Plectroeuphon'. I have already mentioned an ancestor of this kind of instrument – the *Geigenwerk* in which the strings were mechanically bowed – in the Introduction and in Chapter One (i). In other experiments, currents of air were applied to the struck strings to keep them vibrating and once again the names are suggestive: 'Eolodicon' and 'Animo-Corde' are examples. The equally evocative 'Euphonicon' by Dr John Steward of Wolverhampton, *c.*1840 (see front cover), constitutes one of the strangest experimental instruments of this type, in which the upper parts of the vertically strung strings are open to view. In addition, instead of the usual soundboard, the instrument had three sound-boxes of different sizes, shaped like the (neckless) bodies of a violin, viola and cello respectively, and complete with *f*-holes. Some early pianos even sported a soundboard amplified by a copper timpani-case.

In whatever light our modern sensibilities cause us to view these additions to our beloved piano, they had the blessing and encouragement of key figures in the period. It is perhaps not surprising that the pioneer of orchestration, Berlioz, should enthuse over them, as this quotation from his *Traité d'instrumentation* shows:

> The sustaining device is the most important recent invention in the manufacture of keyboard instruments. This invention ... allows the player to sustain a note, a chord, or an arpeggio indefinitely in any part of the keyboard with a simple knee movement after the hands have been lifted from the keys. While several notes are being held in this way the player can use the freedom of his hands to strike new notes which are not part of the sustained chord and also those which are being sustained. It will be clear what a wide range of different attractive combinations this invention can make available on the ... piano. These are truly orchestral effects, like string instruments playing four or five independent parts against a sustained chord in the wind ... or better still like the wind playing in several parts against sustained harmony on divided violins, or when the harmony and the melody move above or below a pedal.[9]

He also recommends three or four staves for notating music using such effects.[10]

(iv) Imitations of other instruments

From its earliest times the piano had been subjected to modifications and mechanisms by which it could be made to sound otherwise. Indeed, as mentioned above,[11] piano actions had, fairly often, been included in harpsichords as an extra resource. The use of uncovered wooden hammers in combination with the lute stop could simulate a

---

[8] As described above Chapter Two (iv).
[9] Berlioz/TREATISE, pp. 314–15.
[10] Ibid., p. 315.
[11] See Chapter One.

clavichord's sound and, used without the lute stop, strongly suggested the sound of the harpsichord. So it is not surprising to find yet another stop, the *Cembalo* stop, being applied. This was based on the same principles as the lute and bassoon stops, but, instead of cloth or parchment, a hard substance was interposed between hammers and strings; ivory, brass and whalebone were used, among others. Again, as we have seen, these harpsichord/piano combinations were not uncommon.[12]

The carillon – a French word imported into English, the German for which was *Glockenspiel* – has already been mentioned in Chapter One (ii). It was a set of tuned bells either in a church or civic spire, and rung by hand or by large keyboard, sometimes with a pedalboard as well. In the nineteenth century there were attempts made to provide it with a piano-type keyboard but finger-pressure regulation was a problem. Partly for this reason and partly because the closely-guarded secret of making accurately-tuned bells died out with the last of the the bell-makers' families, the instrument was already part of the nostalgic past, with connotations of the passing of time and the peal of the Angelus. The piano, however, was well-suited to producing a kind of muted carillon sound in passages in the upper register when the dampers were raised, as in the finale of J.B. Cramer's Piano Sonata in E flat major Op. 25/3, which is a 'Rondo en Carillon' showing several slightly different 'carillon' textures: Ex. 5.2a and 5.2b give two of these, the latter continuing for a further 8 bars before closing the piece *perdendosi*.

Ex. 5.2a: J.B. Cramer, Piano Sonata in E flat major Op. 25/3/iii, bb. 0–5.

Ex. 5.2b: Op. 25/3/iii, ending.

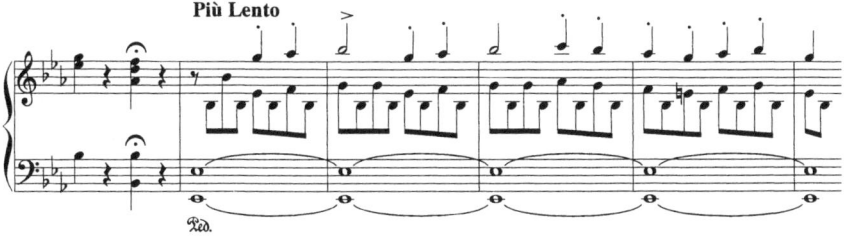

No. 2 of Moscheles's *4 grandes Etudes de concert* ('Le Carillon', Allegro giocoso) has a similar texture (Ex. 5.3).

---

[12] Some, by Marius, for example, are described in Chapter One.

Ex. 5.3: Moscheles, *4 Grandes Etudes de concert* Op. 111/2, bb. 0–1.

(v) Combination instruments

As well as mechanisms to alter or sustain the sound of the piano, there were also more complicated attempts in this direction. This impulse to combine or couple instruments sprang from the same necessity to impart variety which gave rise to the various additions and modifications described above. Octave coupling has already been mentioned as a means for increasing the hands' coverage and swelling the sound so that an orchestral range might be approximated. Another consequence of this was the pedal-piano, in which a foot-operated keyboard was added in the manner of an organ's pedalboard. This could either, with its own mechanism and hammers, operate the same strings as the manual, or be an independent 'instrument' with its own strings, hammers and so on. Examples of both types exist throughout our period, although surviving instruments of the latter type are all nineteenth century. As with the pedal-harpsichord and pedal-clavichord – known at least as early as the fifteenth century, on the evidence of Paulirinus of Prague (*c.*1460) and of a drawing of one from the same period – there was the added benefit of allowing for organ music to be played. Some of these also incorporated an octave-coupler, so that each of the pedal notes also sounded the octave below. Pedal-pianos were by no means mere curiosities: such an instrument called forth Schumann's sets of *Studien* [Studies] Op. 56 and *Skizzen* [Sketches] Op. 58, Alkan's *11 grands préludes et une transcription* Op. 66 and (perhaps appropriately) *Impromptu sur le choral de Luther* Op. 69, as well as Gounod's concerted *Fantaisie sur l'hymne national russe* and his *Suite concertante* – also with orchestra.

As well as underlining the versatility of the piano, its social aspect as a domestic instrument capable of being played by more than one performer is also shown.[13] The class of instrument called 'Duoclave' ('double-keyed'), for example, either had two keyboards, or had provision for a second one to be added at a later date. Duoclaves could be uprights or grands.

Even more versatile, perhaps, were the instruments that combined a piano with another keyboard instrument and mention has been made[14] of a combination of piano, carillon and harpsichord in Paris as early as 1759, and a piano and organ in 1772. The Colt Clavier Collection possesses a similar instrument, a highly interesting 'Claviorganum' by the Flemish maker John Joseph Merlin (see Pl. 20), who spent

---

[13] This will be dealt with in more detail in Chapter Twenty-Eight.
[14] See Chapter One (ii).

most of his life in London, and was also the inventor of the Bath chair and the roller-skate! Of the two handstops on this instrument, one disengages the hammer mechanism and engages the small organ, a single 8 foot stop– that is, the same pitch as the piano – with wooden pipes. The other is an *una corda*. The pedal fulfils the same function as that on a small organ or harmonium, to pump air into the wind reservoir. C.F. Colt observes that it is difficult to sustain a constant supply of air with such a small reservoir (*c*.18 inches square) and a single pedal, but that the organ tone is very sweet. Another possibility is the incorporation of an armonica (a glass harmonica) into a piano: this will be discussed briefly in Chapter Twenty-One (iii).

Another hybrid by Johann Stein (1777), in Castelvecchio, Verona has a piano at one end (as in a normal grand) but, at the other, a two-manual harpsichord with the third (lowest) manual also coupled to the piano mechanism. The piano's two handstops (for raising the treble and bass dampers respectively) are also duplicated at the harpsichord end, and the coupling can be seen inside the case, travelling along the two side-edges of the instrument, allowing for the piano to be played at either end.

Raymond Russell[15] describes a similar combination harpsichord/piano of 1780 by the ever-inventive Merlin in the Deutsches Museum in Munich. The harpsichord has three sets of strings, 16 foot – sounding an octave below pitch, the only English harpsichord Russell knew of that had this – as well as 8 foot (normal pitch) and 4 foot (an octave above), with harp and 'Celestial Harp' stops. The latter is a device for raising the dampers on the 8ft register, allowing them to vibrate in sympathy with the other strings. The piano department has its own strings, but the (down-striking) hammers hit these as well as those of the harpsichord's 8 ft set. Such combinations were by no means late developments: a privately owned instrument in Antwerp is a two-manual harpsichord with a completely separate spinet inset at the side, made by Jan Coenen in 1734. It is interesting in that the naturals are white and the accidentals black, as on later and modern instruments. Michael Cole suggests that '[j]udging by the number of schemes announced in patent applications and newspaper advertisements, [such combination instruments] may have been a lot more common than their meagre survival might lead us to imagine.'[16]

The intriguing conversion of pianos into harpsichords in Spain is in teasing defiance of the progressive view of history and, as Stewart Pollens observes,

> surprising, as the pianos [both Florentine] were extremely rare and expensive instruments. The conversions suggest either that the escapement mechanisms were too complex for local makers to regulate or repair or that there was greater need or preference for the conventional harpsichord. The removal of hammer actions and installation of registers and jacks would have been a fairly straightforward procedure for local harpsichord makers.[17]

Another result of piano-makers' eagerness to experiment and improve was the transposing piano. The earliest types, at the middle of the eighteenth century, used an extension of the same mechanical principle as that used for the *una corda* shift by

---

[15] Russell/HARPSICHORD, Plate 79.
[16] Cole/PIANOFORTE, p. 239.
[17] Pollens/PIANOFORTE, p. 120.

which the mechanism could be moved laterally to strike one or all three strings. Two of Silbermann's surviving pianos – of 1749 in the Germanisches National-museum, Nuremberg and of 1746 in Frederick the Great's collection in the palace of Sanssouci in Potsdam – have the facility of semitone transposition.[18] Although this was useful in overcoming some of the problems of pitching,[19] in practice it was still subject to the limitations on harmonic range since, before equal temperament, only the more-or-less closely related keys could be used anyway. The transposing piano was, however, a great facility for the piano-playing public, sparing the less well-trained amateur the embarrassment of not being able to transpose when accompanying singers.

(vi) The functionality of the piano

It is yet another irony of its history that the piano, first seen as a cheaper and more-easily maintained alternative to the harpsichord (in that it did not need to be re-quilled periodically) should replace it so completely. Once the new instrument had emerged from its initial period of evolutionary torpor, the rapidity of its rise from being a curiosity to becoming the first mass-produced and mass-consumed household instrument was certainly phenomenal by the timescale of its period, even if the harpsichord remained by its side in a number of households[20], in some cases into the nineteenth century. This is also illustrated in Richard Maunder's table showing the numbers of keyboard instruments advertised for sale in Vienna in the *Wienerisches Diarium/Wiener Zeitung* during the eighteenth century. This is given in modified form as Table 2 below.

Table 2: Numbers of keyboard instruments advertised in Vienna 1760–1800.

Year	Harpsichord	Spinet	Clavichord	Fortepiano	Clavier	Total
1760	1					1
1761	1				1	2
1763	4					4
1764	6					6
1765	2	1				3
1767	1					1
1768	4	1				5
1769	2				1	3
1770	3				2	5
1771	2	1	1			4
1772	11	3	1			15
1773	2	1			2	5
1774	7	1			2	10

---

[18] Pollens/PIANOFORTE, p. 183.
[19] See Chapter Three (ii).
[20] Cole/PIANOFORTE, p. 239. He mentions the examples of Thomas Twining, Mme. Brillon and the experiences of a Hertfordshire piano-tuner between 1770 and 1790.

Year	Harpsichord	Spinet	Clavichord	Fortepiano	Clavier	Total
1775	4				1	5
1776	6				5	11
1777	8	2		2	5	16*
1778	8				4	12
1779	6	1		1	4	11*
1780	12			1	10	23
1781	13	3	3	1	12	32
1782	13	3	1	4	5	26
1783	15	2	1	3	9	30
1784	14	2	2	12	8	37*
1785	17	3	1	12	5	37*
1786	12		3	21	12	48
1787	9	1		21	5	36
1788	16	2	1	29	9	57
1789	7		1	22	10	40
1790	2	1		32	5	40
1791	8	1	4	37	2	52
1792	8	2	2	50	10	72
1793	12		2	55	10	79
1794	6	1	2	39	5	53
1795	11	1	2	42	13	69
1796	9	1		42	10	62
1797	12	2	4	55	7	80
1798	10	1		59	8	78
1799	6	3	2	75	9	95
1800	8			54	3	64*
TOTALS:	298	40	33	760	194	1325*

Notes:
(1) In cases markes with an asterisk (*) the 'total' figure differs from the sum of the others, because combination instruments (Piano/Harpsichord etc.) are entered under two headings.
(2) Pantalons and organs are not counted, although combination-organs appear under the alternative heading (eg. Piano/Organ under 'Fortepiano').
(3) 'Clavier' refers to keyboard instruments not otherwise identifiable.

Apart from the grand, square and upright versions of the instrument, the sheer variety of other forms, types, shapes and sizes has already been remarked upon. Again, our view of the modern, heavy, iron-framed instrument does not equip us for the prevailing tendency of the early instrument to be so small and light as to be quite portable.

Most pianos, especially, but by no means exclusively, the 'Viennese', rested on trestles or tables and thus legs were not integral. Many were indeed constructed with portability in mind, such as the Verel portable (1783) with dimensions of 38 inches long by 13 inches wide and 5.75 inches high (see Pl. 21), and the ones invented by Röllig in 1795 (the 'Orphika'), which could be strapped to the player when in use.

Mozart was thought to have had a portable piano, suitable for travelling by coach, made by Späth and Schmahl of Ratisbon. In Britain, the portable instrument was often called a 'Conductor's piano'; Sir George Smart, a founder-member and the conductor of the Philharmonic Society, had such an instrument and was reputed to have carried one with him when travelling.[21] When one recalls that Smart belonged to the age when conductors predominantly presided at the keyboard rather than at the rostrum, the convenience of his mechanical travelling-companion can be appreciated.

One consequence of the addition of foot-pedals, however, was the fact that, in contrast to the eighteenth-century model without legs, allowing for the instrument to be stored when not in use, the piano became a permanent household fixture and therefore an item of furniture (and in an age still largely dominated by craftsmanship, it would have to take its place among other items of drawing-room furniture). Consequently, an aesthetic dimension was superimposed on that of utility, and the variety and sheer beauty of a large proportion of these instruments is astounding. The early 'Viennese' and German instruments have a classic simplicity: Pl. 22 shows a Heilman grand of c.1775 in walnut with tapered legs. Rosewood was also popular, as in the Broadwood cottage piano of c.1825 (see Pl. 23) with brass inlay – 'surely ... more likely to grace a lady's boudoir than an artisan's cottage' as C.F. Colt observes.[22]

Using the same combination of brass and rosewood, the Tomkison grand of 1821 (Pl. 24) is, however, of quite a different order, with beautifully carved and decorated lyre legs, having been made for King George IV to be housed in Brighton Pavilion, and the meticulous beauty of a piano made by the Erard brothers, (now in the Gemeentemuseum, The Hague) bespeaks its commissioner, Louis Bonaparte, who ordered it for his wife, Hortense. Equally upmarket in appearance and also with French connections, is the Haschka grand of about 1810 in stained cherry with exotic features (here, partly-gilt caryatid legs) associated with the 'Empire style' (Pl. 19).

Pl. 25, a British square of 1779 by Christopher Ganer (one of the eighteenth century German *émigrés* to London mentioned in Chapter One), shows a very popular wood, mahogany, with satinwood crossbanding and elegant square tapered legs, and the Merlin 'Claviorganum' mentioned in the previous chapter has the same features (see Pl. 20). Mahogany became very widespread after the first quarter of the nineteenth century because of its strength and rich colour: it was also common to stain other woods to look like it[23] or to use it as a veneer on softer timbers, which resulted in a cheaper, yet good-looking, instrument. In the nineteenth century, piano legs began to be lathe-turned which helped to reduce prices and increased the demand for cheaper models. The resultant degree of uniformity could be offset to an extent by other factors: the turned legs could be tapered, as in the Broadwood Cottage piano in Pl. 23 (above), with reeding (see Pl. 28), and in other combinations.

---

[21] There is a photograph (Plate XIV, opposite p. 266) in Harding/PIANOFORTE.
[22] Colt/COLLECTION, p. 80.
[23] The case of the c.1810 Haschka grand mentioned recently (see Pl. 19) is actually made of cherry wood, stained for this reason.

Lathes and a few other matters notwithstanding, the Industrial Revolution made comparatively little impact on the piano as a whole during most of the period of this book, partly because much of the work involved in its construction – choosing, cutting, seasoning and fixing of soundboards, or stringing, for example – required hand-crafting, or at least close monitoring. Most workshops were in the maker's own home or close by.[24] In any case, in keeping with the general individuality of the makers, the various forms produced, and the fact that they were to take their place as (increasingly important) items of furniture, meant that a craft-ethos prevailed. What is, therefore, difficult to explain, is the practice, occasionally found, of instrument-makers 'buying-in' pianos from others to sell under their own names. Perhaps an order for which they were unprepared, or too busy to fulfil, was too good to turn down – or, perhaps, a gesture of friendship for another maker. One is reminded of the use of insertion arias in operas of the period, and, indeed of composers helping out others, as in the case of Mozart's Symphony No. 37 (K. 444 (425a)) in G major, which is actually by Michael Haydn, the introduction having been written by Mozart because of his friend's indisposition. This craft-ethos was, of course, somewhat compromised as the market burgeoned, but remarkably little so when set beside comparable industries, such as furniture-making generally. Only during the later part of the nineteenth century and later – especially with the universal adoption of the iron frame – would this change.

Once pianos became, as I have said earlier, items of more-or-less fixed furniture, they were often called upon to justify their space to fulfil other functions also. Some incorporated drawers for music, candles, and so on, or mirrors which, although they might, perhaps, be distracting, were nevertheless useful when accompanying – especially dancing – or for throwing the light back into gloomy Victorian rooms, as in the case of the Collard cabinet piano of 1845 in the Colt Collection (Pl. 26). Drawers were familiar even on some earlier instruments, as the Kirckman harpsichord (1781) in Pl. 27 shows – and others had useful hidden shelves (Pl. 28) for books or music, and many, especially the squares, did duty as tables, such as the several Papes in the Colt Collection. Pl. 29 is an example of these, a type which Field used in his Paris concerts of 1833 and whose description as 'square' or, sometimes, 'table' should not blind us to the fact that these 'down-striking' instruments (that is, the strings were struck by the hammers falling from above) were robust and sonorous in tone, and quite a match for an orchestra in concertos, as Field's first performance of his Seventh Concerto in the great *Salle du Conservatoire* showed.[25] Another useful device was one that Southwell fitted to the music desk of his aforementioned 'Piano sloping backwards': a 'Volto Subito', which allowed the player to turn the music-page by operating a pedal.[26]

---

[24] See Chapter One (iii).
[25] See Piggott/FIELD, pp. 105–6.
[26] See drawing in Harding/PIANOFORTE, p. 228.

CHAPTER SIX

The Piano's Sound

(i) General

This may be a good time to remind ourselves of the rich variety of piano-sounds in the early period, up to, say 1800. Not only those of the British and 'Viennese', but also the differences between grand and square (and, slightly later, upright), between particular makers and, last but not least in this pre-industrial system, between individual instruments, not forgetting the fact that, in addition, all of these could be further affected by the use of various stops, pedals, and so on, whose effect was by no means uniform. And when one takes into account the 'natural' but significant modification of a piano's sound at different stages of its lifetime due to, for example, atmospheric conditions and the hammer-coverings having altered with wear and tear, it becomes clear that the kind of standardisation so manically sought after in later periods, in all aspects of life, had no part in this sound-world.

However, the seeds of a uniformity already beginning to stifle variety in other areas, were being sown in the musical field also, and an instrument as desirable and fashionable as the piano would not be allowed to revel in its profligate motley for too long before donning the overalls of utility and profit, especially in the industrially-revolutionised climate of Britain. Michael Cole, is, as so often, perspicaciously aware of both sides of this development: referring to the British grand c.1800, 'wooden-framed, trichord, with the Backers-Stodart action and Broadwood's tonal improvements', he writes that it

> had become a standardised product in which one could discern hardly any variation whether one bought from Clementi, Broadwood, Joseph Kirkman, Stodart ..., or one of the smaller manufacturers, such as Rolfe or Tomkison. Except in trivial matters of decoration or the niceties of voicing, there is little to distinguish one from another. Culturally one might see this as a loss, as the diversity seen in eighteenth-century experiment and innovation disappeared. The pianoforte had entered upon an age of mass manufacture, with many firms already employing specialist craftsmen as action makers, case makers, finishers, or whatever; men whose standards of workmanship were beyond previous imagining, but whose knowledge rarely strayed outside their specialism within a small part of the manufacturing process. The

precision and durability of their work can only be marvelled at, but such standards were achieved only at the expense of individuality.[1]

Cole contrasts this market-driven attitude with, for example, the 'restless experimentation' of Stein,[2] working in an as yet comparatively unindustrialised Austria.

It is, on the one hand, the bewildering variety of piano sounds available during the first part of our period and, on the other, the fast-gathering trend towards standardisation in the second part that prompts me to concentrate on the more general differences in sound between the early piano as a whole during the period, and the modern instrument of the later twentieth- and twenty-first centuries, with whose sound we are most familiar. This standardisation has been compounded with the advent of electronic pianos and of the various electronic keyboards, with their array of instrumental effects. The usefulness of these to the composer and teacher, as well as to the performer, cannot be denied; it is, again, an uneasy question of the effects on musical perception – and the perception of music – as a whole, and the ever-increasing distance between music, people who make music, and people.

Another kind of perception gives rise to a whole 'new' question, of course, and one which adds to the confusion: that of our present-day perception of the early pianos' sound(s), influenced as we are by soundscapes undreamed-of by even our comparatively recent forbears. This is a real mare's nest of a problem, and I am relieved to be able to legitimately invoke the 'beyond the scope of this book' clause to sidestep it. A prevalent view of these early instruments, perhaps conditioned by those discovered in attics or in the possession of old relatives, was that the sound was 'tinny' and 'out-of-tune'; such a view is by no means laid to rest. The final paradox of the pre-c.1850 piano is that this is exactly the sound that was required and admired, and which the instrument was designed to produce. First of all, the 'tinniness', to summarise the previous chapters, resulted from the composition of the strings, with more brass than modern ones, and the fact that they were held at a much lower tension. As an instance, the combined tension on the frame of a modern grand is about 16,400 kilograms (nearly 18 tons), whereas that of an 1844 grand is c.10,421 kg (a little more than half) and of a square piano of that same year, 4,348 – just over a quarter. As a further comparison, the tension of a French piano of 1803 is given as 918 kg for one string per note, 1,836 kg if bichord and 2,754 kg if trichord.[3] The result was a sound rich in overtones, especially the higher ones. The other perceived quality of early pianos, 'out-of-tuneness', again, could simply be the result of tuning-pin slippage, and/or of the greater responsiveness of the early instruments to atmospheric conditions. It is more likely (depending on date), to be the result of a system of tuning other than equal temperament.[4]

With respect to the various devices for modifying the sound visited upon the piano in the period – unusual, even bizarre, though these incorporations seem to us today –

---

[1] Cole/PIANOFORTE, p. 140.
[2] *Op. cit.*, p. 192–3.
[3] Figures taken from Harding/PIANOFORTE.
[4] See Chapter Three (ii).

it is important not to dismiss them on a Darwinian 'survival-of-the-fittest' principle when compared with later pianos. Indeed, Milchmeyer recommends the square over the grand because the latter has 'fewer tonal changes [*Veränderungen*]' than the former.[5] These devices illustrate a number of wider concerns in their period: the *frisson* generated by the still-novel instrument on which so much attention was being focused from all quarters, the equally exciting 'buzz' in the air of a musical style-shift, the evolution of late Classicism into what would become high Romanticism, exemplified in many of Mozart's works but most clearly seen in the 'transitional' composers – most of them, significantly, piano-virtuosos, such as Clementi, Field, Moscheles, J.L. Dussek and Hummel – as well as Beethoven. These agents of sound-modification also evince the spirit of an enterprise born of the Industrial Revolution with its technical innovations, in the general culture of 'improvement' and in the sense of individual, thrusting entrepreneurship, together with its already advanced cognisance of marketability. It is not surprising that the new social ascendancy, the middle classes, with which these traits can be associated and who were, indeed, responsible in no small degree for the change of climate itself, should have taken the piano to their collective bosom and into the inner sanctum of their homes, the drawing-room. To the early nineteenth-century *bourgeoisie*, the piano had become what the harpsichord had been to the eighteenth-century aristocracy. In technological and cultural terms, its development and somewhat belated ascendancy is as iconic of the age as is the steam train or the telegraph.

(ii) Classical

In matters of piano technique, increasing in importance as the period wore on, Mozart's writing for the instrument is deceptively simple – until one actually plays it properly[6] – and, together with that of Clementi, his piano music represents the first body of high-quality music for the piano that clearly, and in almost every bar, shows the tactile awareness of the piano composer-performer, that easy intimacy with the instrument which produced idiomatic piano writing for the first time. A clear indication of this is the manner in which expression-marks from other instrumental groups are applied to music for the piano. The slur, for example, was certainly to be found in harpsichord music and its significance went well beyond a simple ligature or tie – for example, its use by the French *clavecinistes* – finding a place in the many ornaments and signs that served to distinguish individual notes in the absence of touch-responsiveness. But in the Classical period, its implication is vocal, or strings-generated, either in the sense of 'in one breath' or 'on one bow' when encompassing several notes, or of implied stress when applied to two; there is a quantitative as well as a qualitative implication, and it is usually associated with the expressive *appoggiatura*, and the accented passing-note. Similarly the wedge (') becomes more

---

[5] Milchmeyer/*PIANOFORTE*, p. 57.

[6] I can't resist quoting Cortot's wonderful dictum when asked why he played so much 'simple' Mozart: 'Ah Mozart! easy for children, difficult for artists'.

of a *martellato* than a *staccatissimo*, again with a quantitative usage. Thus a passage such as the second subject of the finale of Mozart's very first sonata, K. 279 (189d) in C major (Ex. 6.1), while certainly making sense to a harpsichordist, would suggest much more to a pianist, whose instinct would be to *crescendo* through the repeated notes to the strong beat and then articulate the graceful left-hand figure.

Ex. 6.1: W.A. Mozart, Piano Sonata in C major K. 279 (189d)/iii, bb. 22–6.

Because of his investiture of the piano sonata with high-quality music of occasionally *quasi*-symphonic cut and, especially in his first works, his casting of it in the four movement-shape of the Classical period's greatest musical achievements, the string quartet and symphony rather than the two- or three-movement shape of that period's piano sonatas, Beethoven's attitude to it has often been characterised as 'symphonic'. It is also generally recognised that he used the piano sonata as a testing-ground for many processes and effects that would later be used in these larger, and hitherto more 'important' forms.

But in another way too, this symphonic approach can be discerned, and has been commented upon, in the 'orchestral' quality of much of the music. This is apparent in, for example, the second movement of Op. 2/2 in A major from the outset, with the sonorous chords underpinned by a slightly ominous staccato bass line[7] (Ex. 6.2). This line is marked with great care; demisemiquavers separated by rests, with *staccato* dots and the reminder *staccato sempre*, which is repeated wholly or partly on each reappearance, as is the top line's *tenuto* or *tenuto sempre*. This '*pizzicato*' is itself tempered by '*arco*' on occasion (b. 4) and the music dons full orchestral dress later in the movement.

Ex. 6.2: Beethoven, Piano Sonata in A major Op. 2/2/ii, bb. 1–11.

---

[7] Denis Matthews suggests horns with *pizzicato* bass in Matthews/BEETHOVEN.

Ex. 6.2 continued

As will be seen in Chapter Twenty-Three (i), the antecedent of the *Prélude* was the improvisatory 'warming up' with which the performer flexed his or her pianistic muscles and at the same time checked out the characteristics of the instrument. These functions were also partly responsible for the musical introduction, although this, of course, became a musically integrated section also.

Since, as we have seen, the early piano of whatever provenance was such a variable instrument, each individual machine having its own mechanical profile, so to speak, which made for really quite different responses in touch, speaking, damping, variety and effect of pedals, stringing, and the various combinations of these as well as their sum in the instrument's overall sound-quality and possibilities, it would be unthinkable for the performer to attempt a piece in public without a thorough acquaintance of the particular instrument in question. I do not wish to exaggerate this aspect. Performers are, and always have been, performers and the show must go on: they quickly become used to the instrument at their disposal. My point here is that, even though the qualities of a modern Bechstein or Steinway are shared by others from the same house, as, indeed one can also say of an 1830s Erard or Broadwood, for example, the possibility for diversity was much greater in the earlier period. Luckily, many concerts in that period, and virtually all recitals, took place in the recital room (as we would call it now) of the local piano-maker's workshop or factory, and who, in fact, was usually the arranger of the concert or recital and frequently offered the visiting artist the hospitality of his or her own home for the duration of the visit. The performer usually had time and privacy to become acquainted with the particular instrument and it was in everyone's interest that he or she did so. Nevertheless, a glance at any introduction to a piano piece of the period, especially, but by no means exclusively, in the nineteenth century, will show that by the introduction's end, many aspects of the instrument will have been, so to speak, 'sussed out'.

The *Grave* introduction to Beethoven's *Sonate pathétique* (Op. 13 in C minor of c.1797–8) is one such and revels in the colours of the period piano, albeit the darker colours (Ex. 6.3). This is the first of his piano sonatas to drop the 'for harpsichord or piano' provision in its title, there remaining only the unequivocal '*für das Pianoforte*'. It is worth mentioning that Beethoven, of course, wrote for the piano more-or-less from the beginning, whatever the title said.

Ex. 6.3: Beethoven, Piano Sonata in C minor Op. 13/i, bb. 1–10.

attacca subito il Allegro

The range of the introduction covers that of the whole piano of the time, except for the lowest note, F^1 and the very first musical direction on the first chord presents a problem: two low full four-note chords of C minor, a crotchet tied to a dotted semiquaver, are marked *fp*. Mozart had used this in his first piano sonata (Ex. 6.4)

Ex. 6.4: W.A. Mozart, Piano Sonata in C major K. 279 (189d)/ii, bb. 39–41.

but this is no more than a stress on the first of the triplets (the left hand is silent here). There are several solutions in Beethoven's work. One of these is common in modern performances, to simply play the chord *forte(/issimo)* and the second chord *piano*; if he had wanted this, it would have been simple to place the *p* under the second chord. This highlights a perennial problem in modern performances of this composer: the temptation, given all the resources of the modern instrument, to exaggerate dynamics. Too many *fortes* become *fortissimi*, and in the case under scrutiny, a little less than a full *forte* in Beethoven's terms would go some way towards allowing sufficient time for the sound to subside to the required *p* without too long a wait. Bearing in mind the characteristics of the period piano, one could play the chord *forte* (not *fortissimo*) and simply wait until a *piano* is achieved, a rather shorter time than on the modern instrument. This is, in essence, Sandra Rosenblum's suggestion, noting that the '...incisive attack and rapid decay of sound on the fortepiano also produce an *fp*. [The] opening chord ... collapses suddenly to a *piano*, creating a dramatic change.'[8] The suddenness of the collapse would, of course depend on the piano used, to mention no other factor, but I cannot say that I have found this collapse as striking as the suggestion here. As so often with period instruments, it depends on the individual piano.

To produce what Beethoven asks for – and he was from the start precise in his requirements as well as in his manner of demanding them – another possibility suggests itself, one that takes into account fully the qualities of the contemporary instrument. This is to play the chord as directed, *forte*, release it, immediately catching the sound with the sustaining pedal and, when the requisite level of *piano* is achieved – which will be quite quickly – silently re-depressing the keys before moving on to the second chord. In this way, the drop to *piano* and the prolongation of the sound is achieved and the 'gap' between the chords that is inevitable is preserved by the re-depression and release.[9]

The first three bars are a progression upward through the bass and middle registers with the octave leap (end of bb. 1 and 2) serving to highlight the contrast, and the *fp* marking discussed is abandoned after the third iteration in favour of *sf*, showing the composer's awareness of the very different sound qualities of these two on the period

---

[8] Rosenblum/PERFORMANCE, p. 86.
[9] This is similar to Rosenblum's suggestion for realisation on the modern piano, but without her 'vibrato' pedalling. (*Loc. cit.*)

instrument. In b. 4, we are given the sequence '*sf p cresc. sf*' within five notes, the *crescendo* being articulated not only by the player but also resulting from the fact that the notes themselves – in this instance, chords – take a short time to reach maximum fullness. In the second half of b. 4, the performer has the first opportunity to test the response of the piano in runs.

Then comes the dynamic interplay, *piano* in upper-bass and middle registers (and right-hand octaves) against *ff* in lower-middle and bass (left-hand octaves), after which (bb. 7–8) the registers appear simultaneously between the hands as they draw apart, with right hand on the piano's topmost note; here, because of the register, the *sfp* marking is perfectly viable, and the *fp* (b. 10) much easier. Apart from one note – the F minor chord in b. 4 – all of the foregoing music has been *legato* or unspecified; now a *mezzo-staccato* is called for and the movement's introduction closes with a chromatic run from almost the top to the lower-middle register. The change of colour, hardly perceptible on a modern instrument, is quite clear – often dramatic – on any piano from any part of our period. The registral contrast built into both the sonata-form subjects in the succeeding Allegro has already been discussed.[10]

(iii) Piano sonority in late Beethoven

At a much later date in Beethoven's career, the time of the late sonatas (1816–22), the composer was just about clinically deaf. Spohr, who heard him in April 1814 rehearsing for one of his last public appearances (the first performance of the *Archduke* Trio) wrote that

> ... the piano was badly out of tune, which Beethoven minded little, since he could not hear it; ... there was scarcely anything left of the virtuosity of the artist which had formerly been so greatly admired. In *forte* passages, the poor deaf man pounded on the keys till the strings jangled, and in *piano* he played so softly that whole groups of tones were omitted, so that the music was unintelligible unless one could look into the pianoforte part.[11]

Although Spohr was not particularly well-disposed towards Beethoven, there is independent corroboration for this kind of occurrence.

Nevertheless, despite his deafness, there is even more awareness of the colouristic possibilities of the instrument of the period in the late piano works, particularly the sonatas. The approach to the exposition of the fugue in the *Hammerklavier* Sonata is, on one level, a kind of pianistic throat-clearing (Ex. 6.5). By the time the initial trills begin (Allego risoluto), the held chord in the left hand (un-pedalled) is merely a ghost and the long stretch of chords in which the hands move gradually apart to the extremes of the keyboard has finished. Coupled with this are increases, and reversals, in dynamics (*p* through *cresc.* to *ff*, and *dimin.* to *pp*), speed (Largo through *accelerando* to Prestissimo and *ritardando* to Allegro risoluto).

---

[10] See Chapter Three.
[11] Thayer/BEETHOVEN, Vol.II, p. 269.

Ex. 6.5: Beethoven, Piano Sonata in B flat major Op. 106/iv, bb. 9–17.

This last section of five bars (Allegro risoluto) is a kind of *précis* of the foregoing unmeasured, much longer, bar in its six-octave distance between the hands and its *pp* – *cresc.*– *f* – *ff* – *p* dynamic curve. Overlapping the first bar of the subject's entry, the right hand traverses from high-upper to mid-bass registers with a presage of the convoluted countersubject (bb. 14–16). Earlier, in the previous (third) movement of the same sonata (Adagio sostenuto: *Appassionato e con molto sentimento*), Beethoven combines the registral and dynamic colour possibilities of the trichord six-octave (C^1–c^4) piano which John Broadwood sent him as a gift from London in 1816, although he does not go below F^1, remaining within the compass of his earlier pianos. Despite this, the movement, if not the sonata as a whole, can in fact be seen as a sound-portrait of the instrument.

Ex. 6.6a (bb. 45–99) begins with one of the registral duets of the kind described above in the *Pathétique* Sonata but much more biased towards the bass. Here, three of the four voices – both those of the accompaniment and the lowest – are in the bass and are answered by the high-upper and treble; the implied dynamic is *p* and the effect is of lapping water, as 'romantic' a sound as almost any of the contemporary pictorial pieces for piano. There is more turbulence in bb. 53ff which *crescendo*es and subsides to *una corda* in b. 57. This, of course, refers to the shift pedal, which moves the action so that the hammer strikes only one of the three strings, thus not only decreasing the volume, but also giving a 'duller' tone; a bar later Beethoven calls for *tutte le corde*, the normal tone. B. 59 is only one of several extraordinary examples of the music being specifically designed to illustrate the instrument, the hands converging on the middle register with a *diminuendo* to *pp*. In the next bar, this *pp* is deftly contrasted with *una corda*, and the difference is much more striking on a period Broadwood than on a modern instrument. He now explores this particular sonority, (bb. 60 (end) to 67) with different registers and combinations of them, single notes against chords and between bb. 67 and 69, we get an opportunity to remind ourselves of the distinctions between the *una corda* and normal sound.

Ex. 6.6a: Beethoven, Piano Sonata in B flat major Op. 106/iii, bb. 45–99.

Ex. 6.6a continued

Ex. 6.6a continued

Ex. 6.6a concluded

After the change of key-signature (b. 76), more radical experimentation begins from the still-prevailing *una corda*, with the combination of the directions '*cresc.*' with *poco a poco due ed allora tutte le corde* ['little by little two and then all [three] strings']. This is an example of what I have termed a 'sonic *crescendo*'[12] and the effect is quite unique, and specific to period instruments: the sound swelling in volume, required by the *cresc.*, and its gradual enrichment due to the build-up of overtones as more and more strings throughout the instrument vibrate, is like the sun coming out. And, in playing this on such an instrument, I heard the *smorzando* in b. 86, for the first time in my experience, as precisely that: a real *smothering* of the sound.

Another surprise occurs in the section bb. 88–93, when the internal melody, requiring no help from the player, takes on a life of its own in its middle register,

---

[12] See Chapter Four (ii).

resulting in an intriguing timbral conversation with its *alter ego* in the top register. Beethoven, having already directed '*sempre legato*', gives us here, not a redundant slur, but a phrase-mark for this inner melody, which is a restatement of the equally sonority-conscious presentation in b. 69. This is an extraordinary moment, a glimpse of the inner Beethoven, a movingly intimate record of the 'dialogue between Self and Soul' so characteristic of the last period.

Ex. 6.6b (bb. 113–25) is also a restatement, but with more extreme registral usage, of previous material, again couched in the timbral counterpoint of the four voices, the two pedal-notes (left-hand D and right-hand F♯) in widely separated registers against the high, improvisationally generated, self-absorbed melody and the rapt accompaniment, a presage of the ethereal ending of his last sonata. To hear this music performed, however wonderfully, on the modern piano only, is to miss some of its innermost feeling.

Ex. 6.6b: Beethoven, Op. 106/iii, bb. 113–25.

Ex. 6.6b continued

(iv) Conclusion

I have spent some time on Beethoven partly because, without wishing to go as far as Marshall McLuhan in averring that 'the medium *is* the message', I feel that the greatness of the music can blind us to the fact that the connection between medium and message is a symbiotic one. I have also chosen to illustrate it in a period of Beethoven's life when the actual living sound was hardly a factor and in which, furthermore, he has been characterised as, and criticised for, over-stretching the particular medium – especially in the case of the piano and the string quartet – in which he wrote. Even if the effect is occasionally somewhat strained, there is little music which gets as close to the heart, soul and mind of the early piano than Beethoven's in his late period. And, referring to Schindler's account of Beethoven's (private) playing and improvising in his last years, where he would use left-hand discordant clusters of notes to drown out (to the hearers, if any were nearby) 'the music to which his right [hand] was feelingly giving utterance',[13] Maynard Solomon writes, 'He did not wish his musical thoughts to be overheard. Thus, even at the end, the piano remained Beethoven's most intimate means of self-communication.'[14]

Of the late piano works we can say, in paraphrase of the inscription on Elgar's Violin Concerto, '*Aqui esta encerrada el alma de ... Beethoven*'.[15]

---

[13] Schindler/BEETHOVEN, pp. 179–80.
[14] Solomon/BEETHOVEN, p. 423.
[15] 'Herein is enshrined the soul of ... Beethoven'. The Elgar work's inscription lacks a name, making it even more enigmatic.

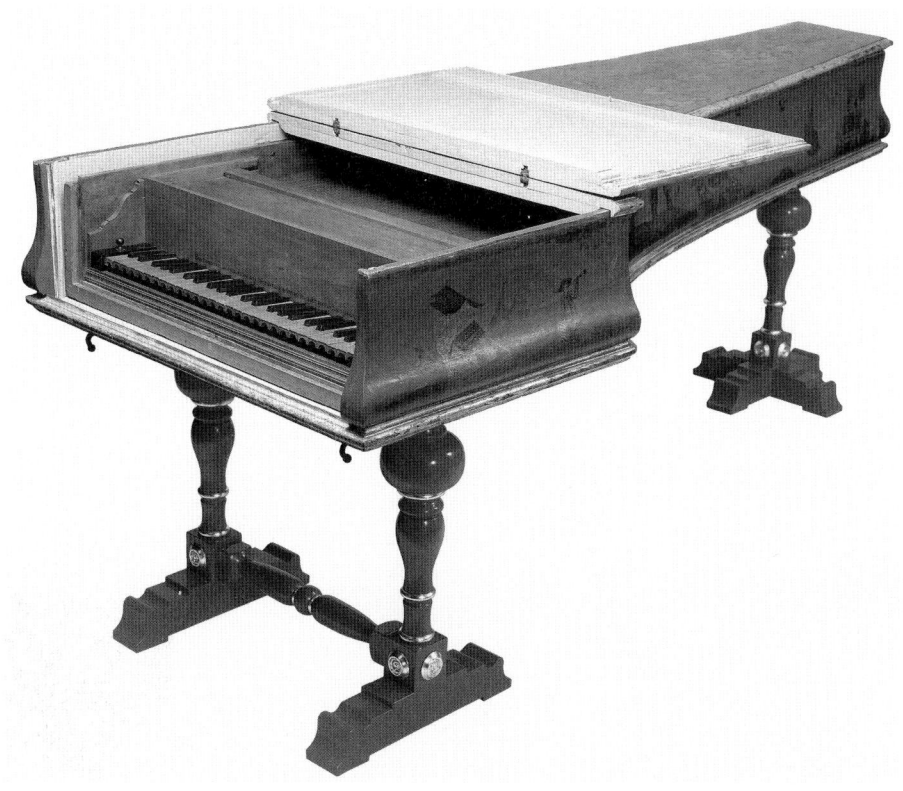

1 Grand piano by Bartolomeo Cristofori (1726)

2 Metal bracing in grand piano by William Stodart (before 1837)

3 Venetian Swell (open) in harpsichord by Shudi-Broadwood (1790)

4 Lodovico Giustini, Piano Sonata Op.1 (pub. Florence, 1732: extract)

5 Lyraflügel by Schleip (1825)

6 Clementi, Piano Sonata in A major Op. 33/1/I, title-page with 'additional keys'

7 *Due corde* block at right end of keyboard of grand piano by Stodart (early 1830s)

8 Detail of *due corde* block on grand piano shown in Plate 7 (grand by Stodart, early 1830s)

9 Ludwig Berger, Piano Sonata Op.7/*Introduzione*

Nocturne 6
(1817)

JOHN FIELD (H.40)
Edited by Robin Langley

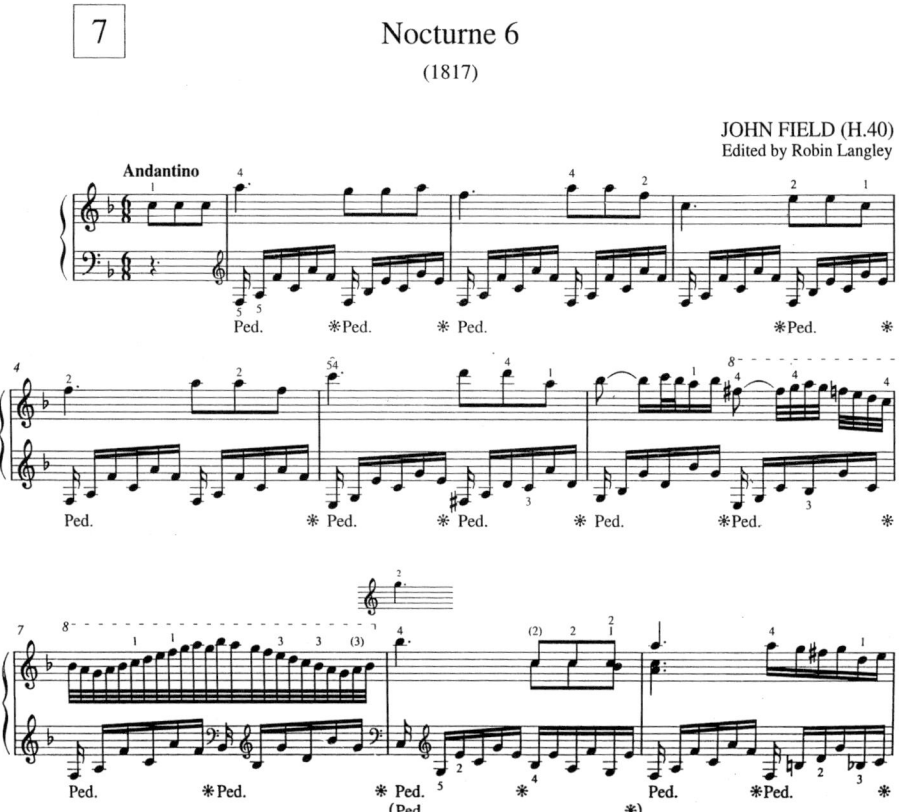

10 John Field, Nocturne No. 6 in E flat major (Russian edition of *c*.1817)

4.

The author thinks that he cannot express better than he has done in this and the following page, his idea for producing an effect quite different from that of playing, in the usual way, either without or with the pedal which raises the dampers. The figures 1,2,3,4,5,6, marked at equal distances one from the other, represent the six quavers contained in each bar, and are marked here in order to facilitate the student in keeping perfect time. The demi-semi-quaver rests *thus*, on one line under the figures 1,2, 3,4,5,6, show that the foot must be entirely off the pedal during the rest; and the pedal acted upon immediately after, and kept down till the next rest. The mark P (for brevity's sake) is here made use of, instead of the word "pedal." The quavers and the dotted crotchets are, of course, the only notes that are to be played *stenuto* by keeping the thumb down, while the other notes, on the contrary, are to be played *staccato* as written. The proper movement of the six quavers contained in each bar, may be easily ascertained without the aid of a *metronome*, by refering to the fifth bar of this page and playing the four successive chords as quickly as possible.

NB. This and the following page must be played *forte* till the word *dolce* is marked.

12   Grand piano by Broadwood (1819)

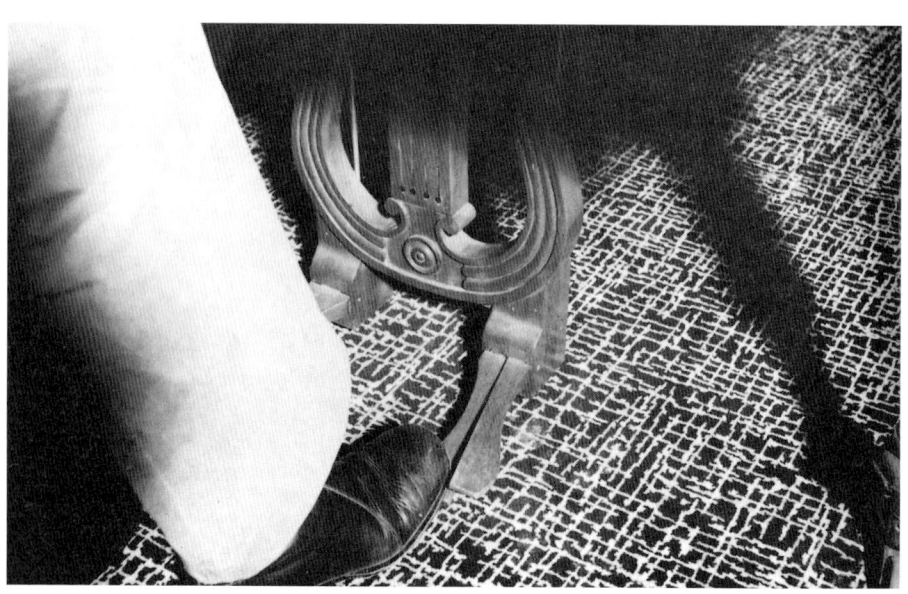

13   Detail of divided pedal on grand piano by Broadwood (1819) in Plate 12a

14   Piccolo piano by Wornum (*c*.1835)

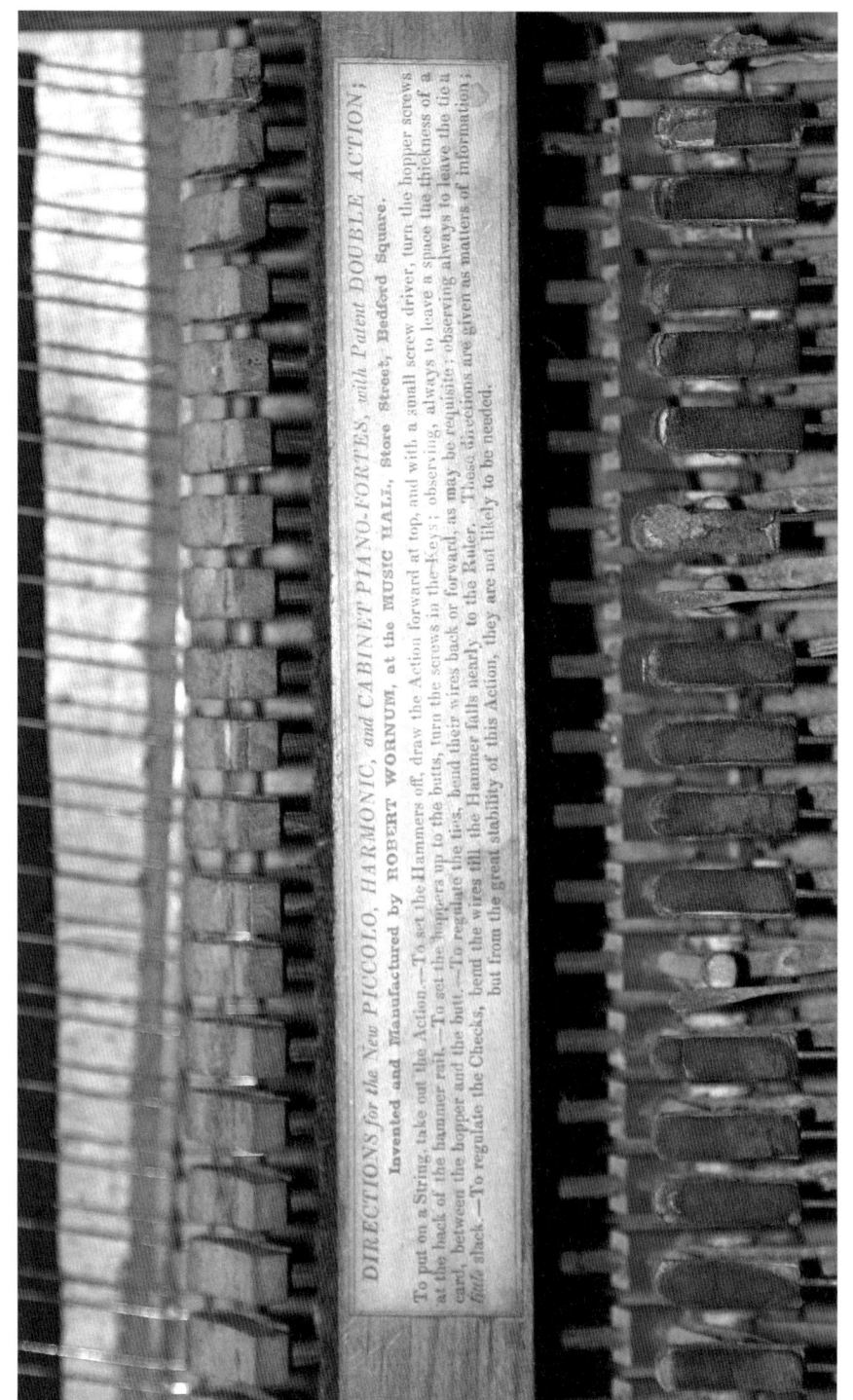

15 Repair instructions inside piccolo piano by Wornum (c.1825) in Plate 13

16   Giraffenflügel by ?Ehrlich (*c*.1840)

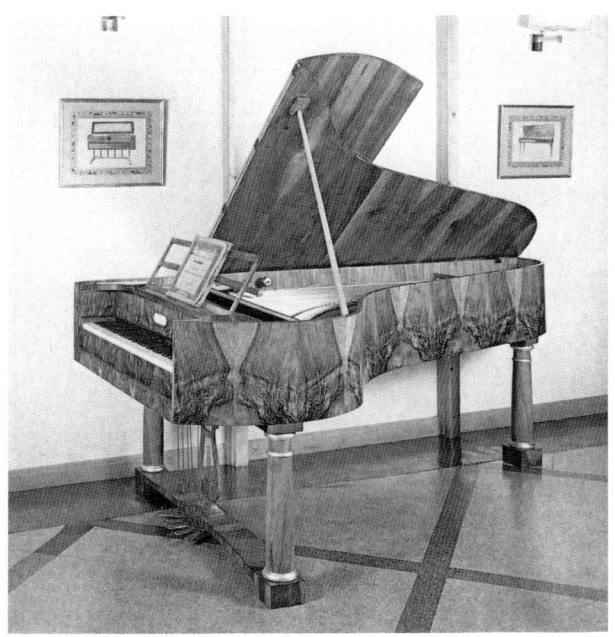

17   Grand piano by Haschka, Vienna (*c*.1825)

18 'Turkish Music' inside Haschka (*c*.1825) in Plate 17

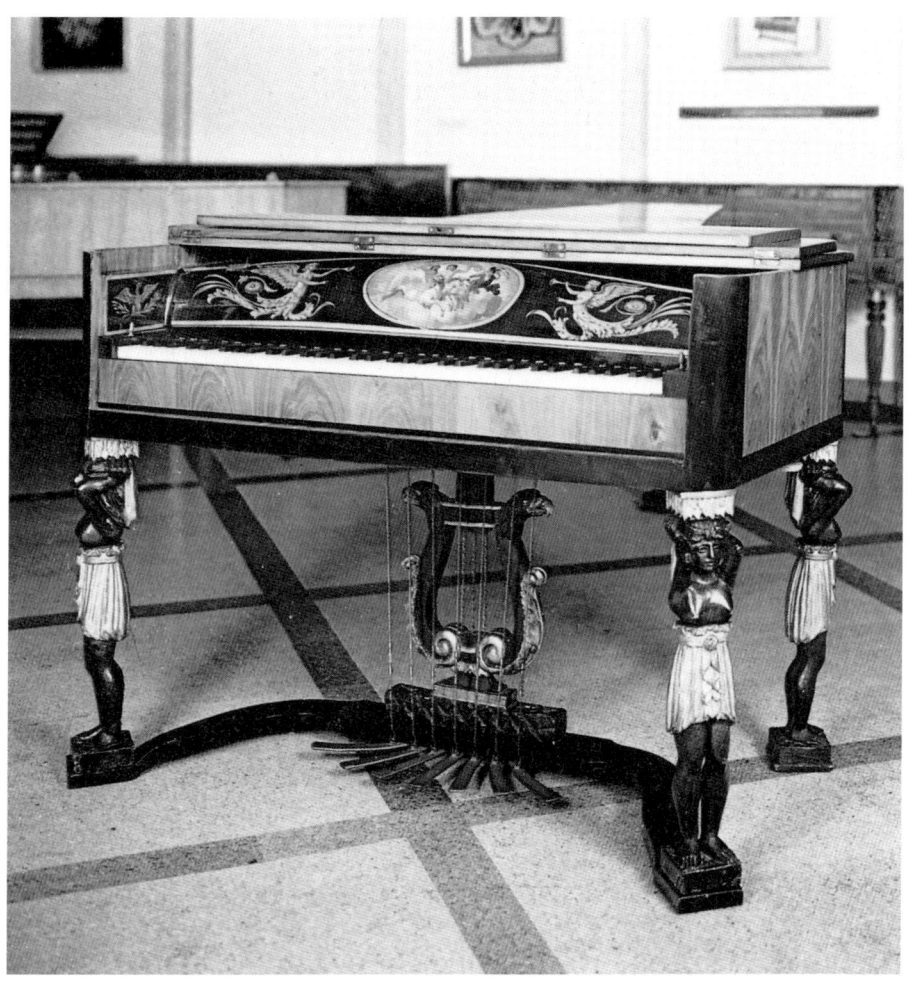

19 Grand by Haschka (*c*.1810)

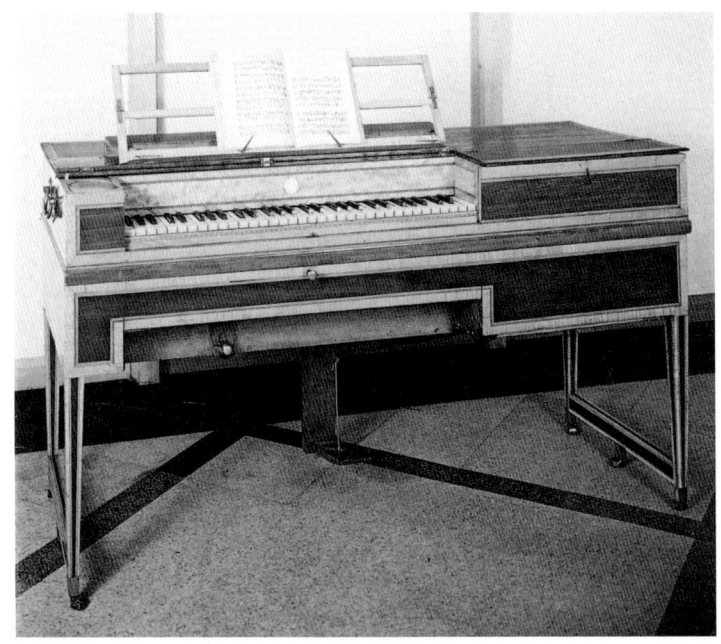

20 Claviorganum by Merlin

21 Portable piano by Verel (1783)

22 Grand piano by Heilman (c.1775)

23 Cottage piano by Broadwood (*c*.1825)

24 Grand piano by Tomkison (1821)

25 Square piano by Ganer (1779)

26 Cabinet piano by Collard & Collard (1845)

27 Harpsichord by Kirckman (1791)

28 Upright grand piano by Clementi (1816)

29 Table (square) piano by Pape (1834)

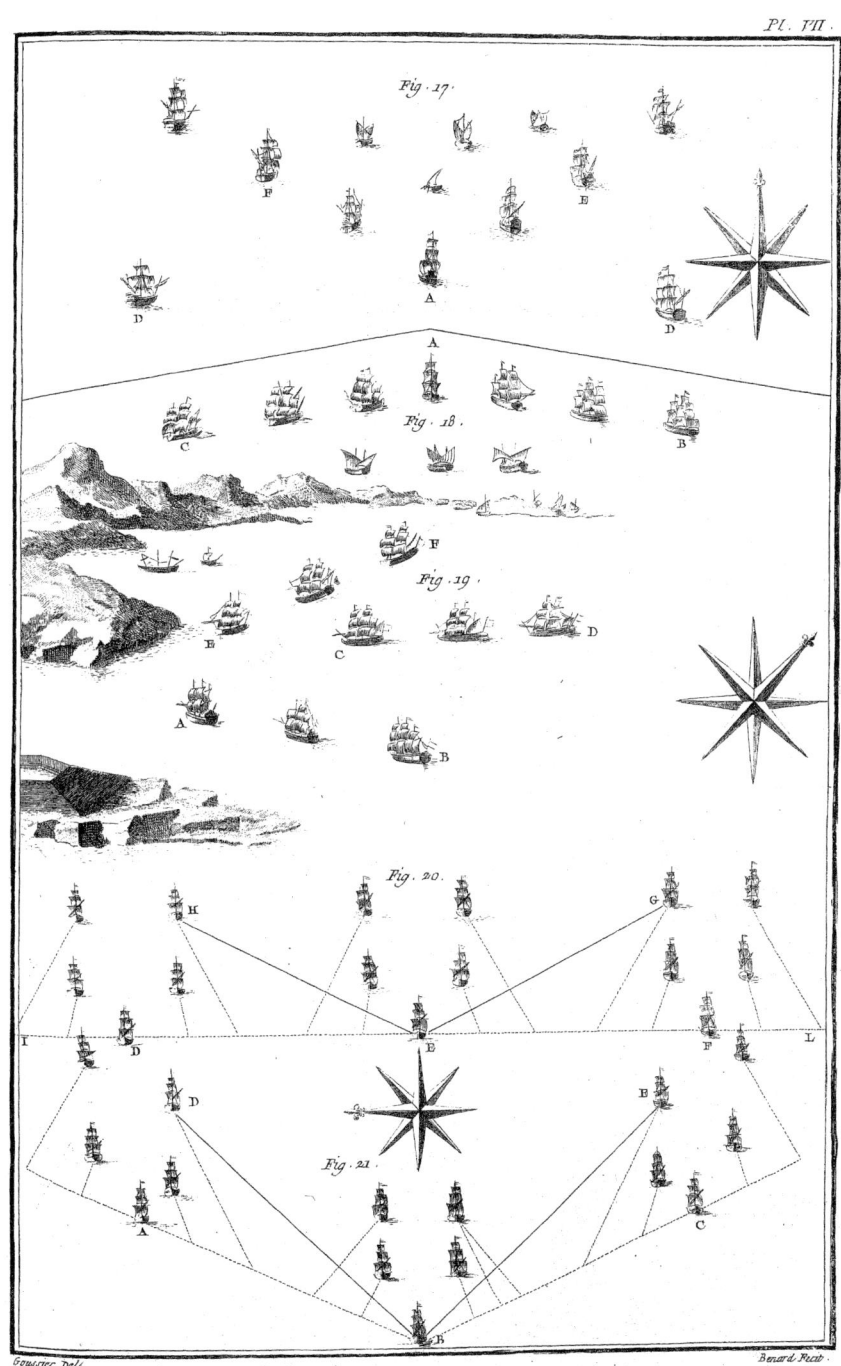

Marine, Évolutions Navales.

30 Naval tactics (*Encyclopédie*)

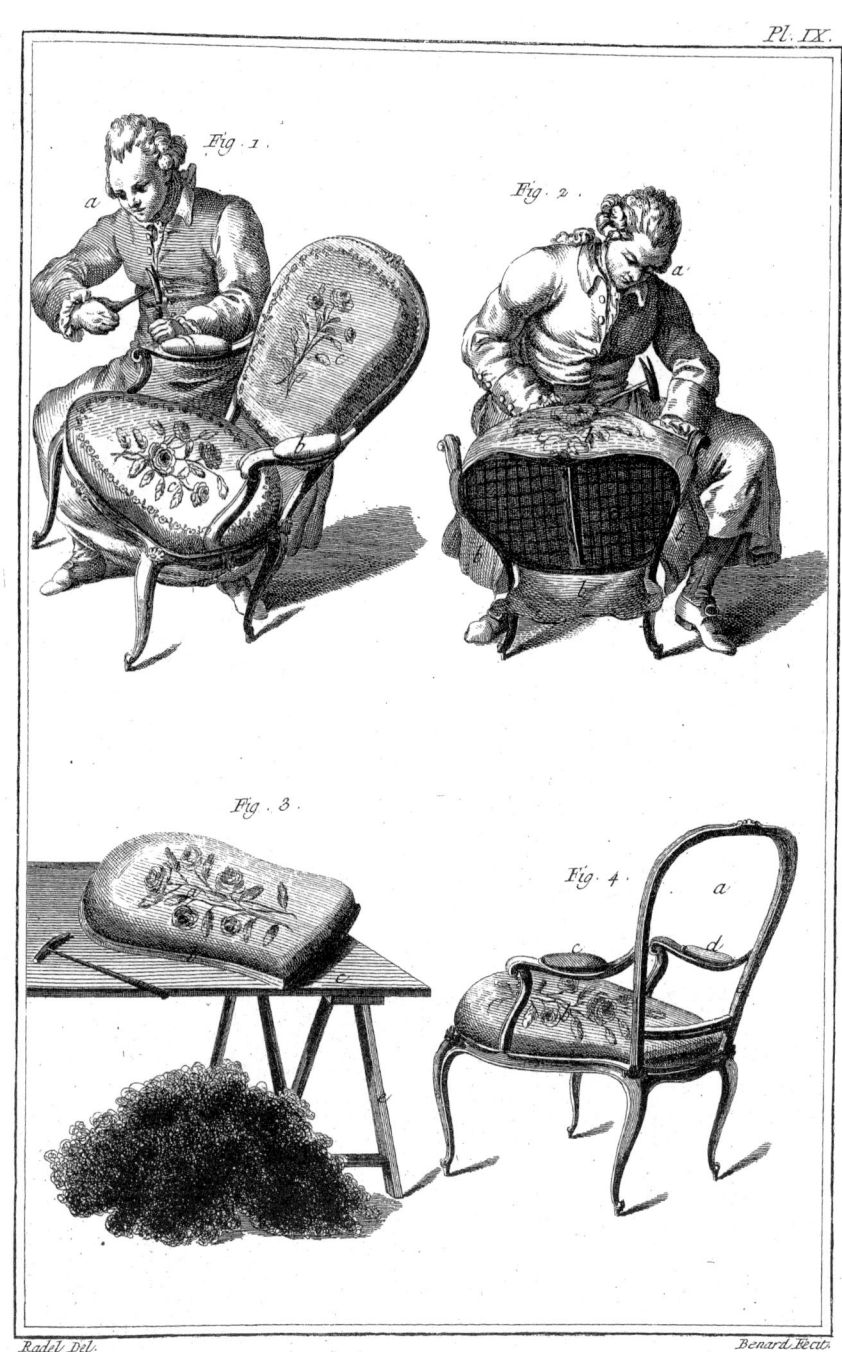

31 Upholstery (*Encyclopédie*)

32 Mrs Mary Delany, *Halifax Rose* (paper mosaic) (1779)

33 George Stubbs, *A Grey Hunter with a Groom and a Greyhound at Creswell Crags* (c.1762–4)

34 James Ward, *Napoleon's Horse, Marengo, at Waterloo* (1824)

35 Eugène Delacroix, *Horse frightened by Lightning* (1835)

36 Carmontelle, *Leopold Mozart and his children* (*c*.1763)

37 Johann Nepomuk della Croce, *The Mozart family* (c.1780)

38 Wright of Derby, *An Academy by Lamplight* (c.1768–9)

39 Thomas Gainsborough, *John Plampin* (c.1752)

40 John Hoppner, *Mrs Williams* (*c*.1790)

41 Eugène Delacroix, *Baron Scwhiter* (1828)

42 Louis Daguerre, *The Ruins of Holyrood Chapel, Edinburgh, Effect of Moonlight* (c.1824)

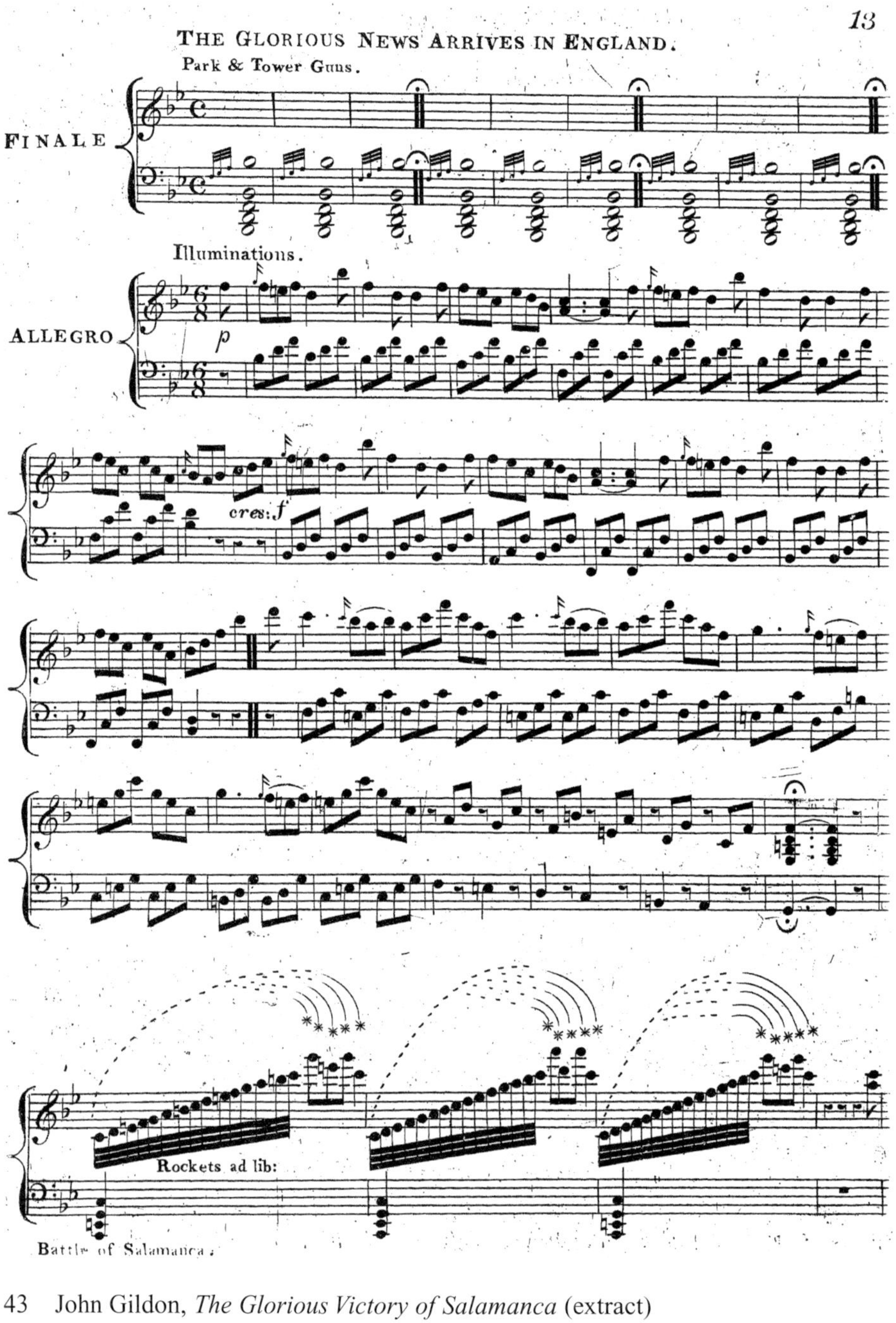

43 John Gildon, *The Glorious Victory of Salamanca* (extract)

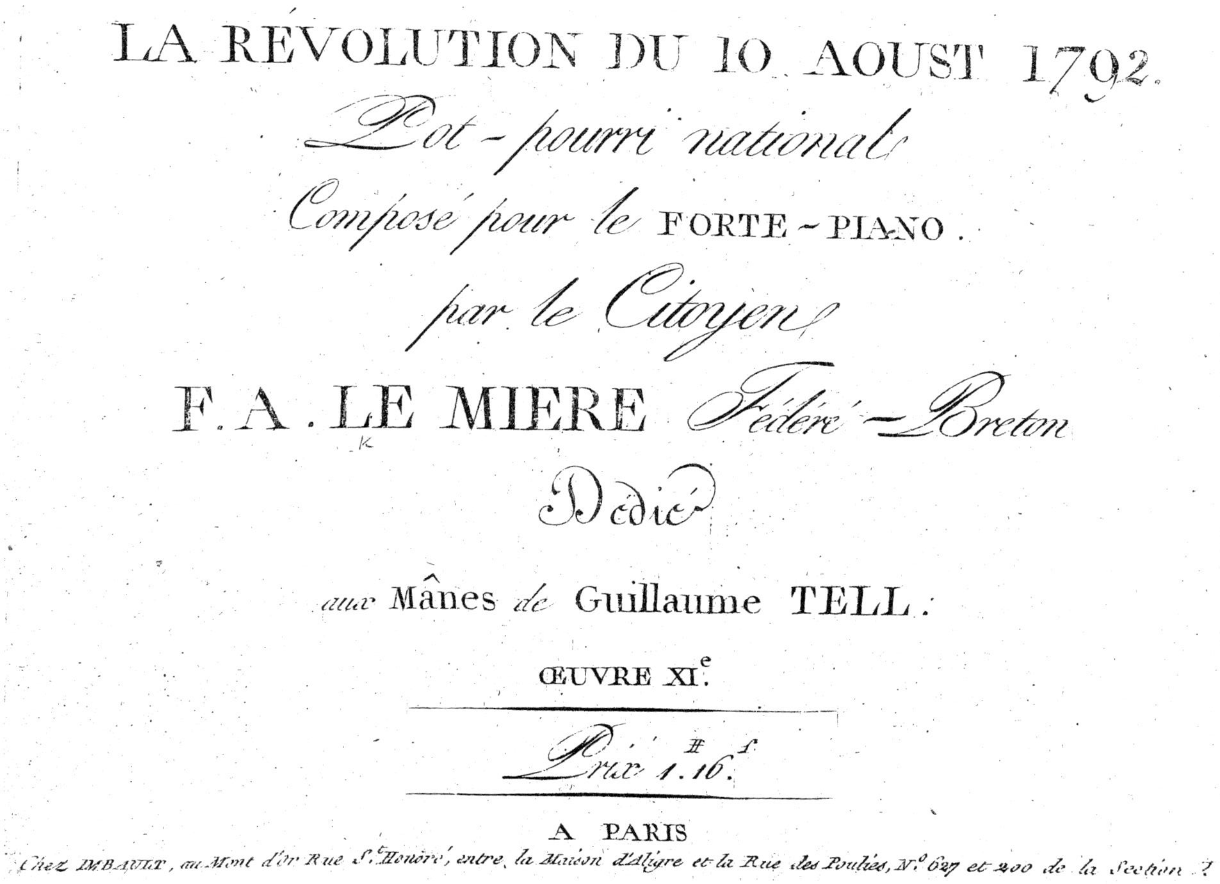
LA RÉVOLUTION DU 10 AOUST 1792.
Pot-pourri national
Composé pour le FORTE-PIANO.
par le Citoyen
F. A. LE MIERE Fédéré-Breton
Dédié
aux Mânes de Guillaume TELL.
ŒUVRE XIe.
Prix 1.16.
A PARIS
Chez IMBAULT, au Mont d'or Rue St. Honoré, entre la Maison d'Aligre et la Rue des Poulies, No. 627 et 200 de la Section

44 Lemière de Corvey, *La Révolution du 10 Aoust, 1792* (title-page)

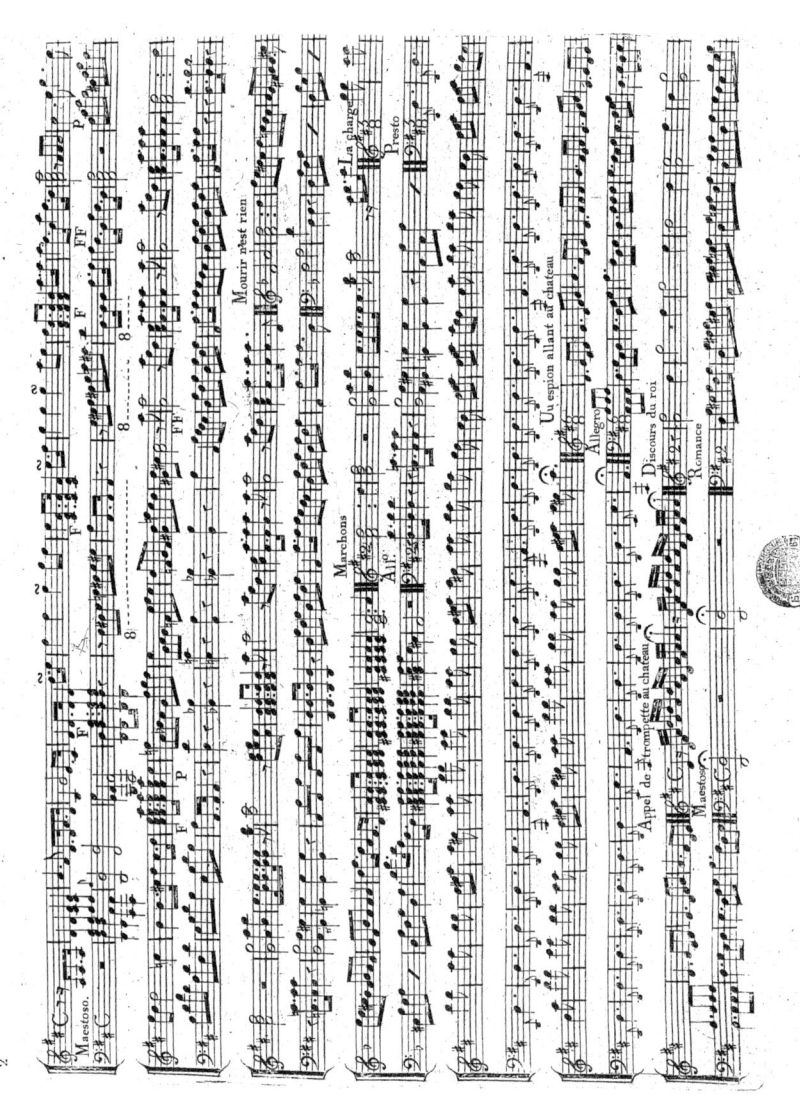

45 Lemière de Corvey, *La Révolution du 10 Aoust, 1792* (extract)

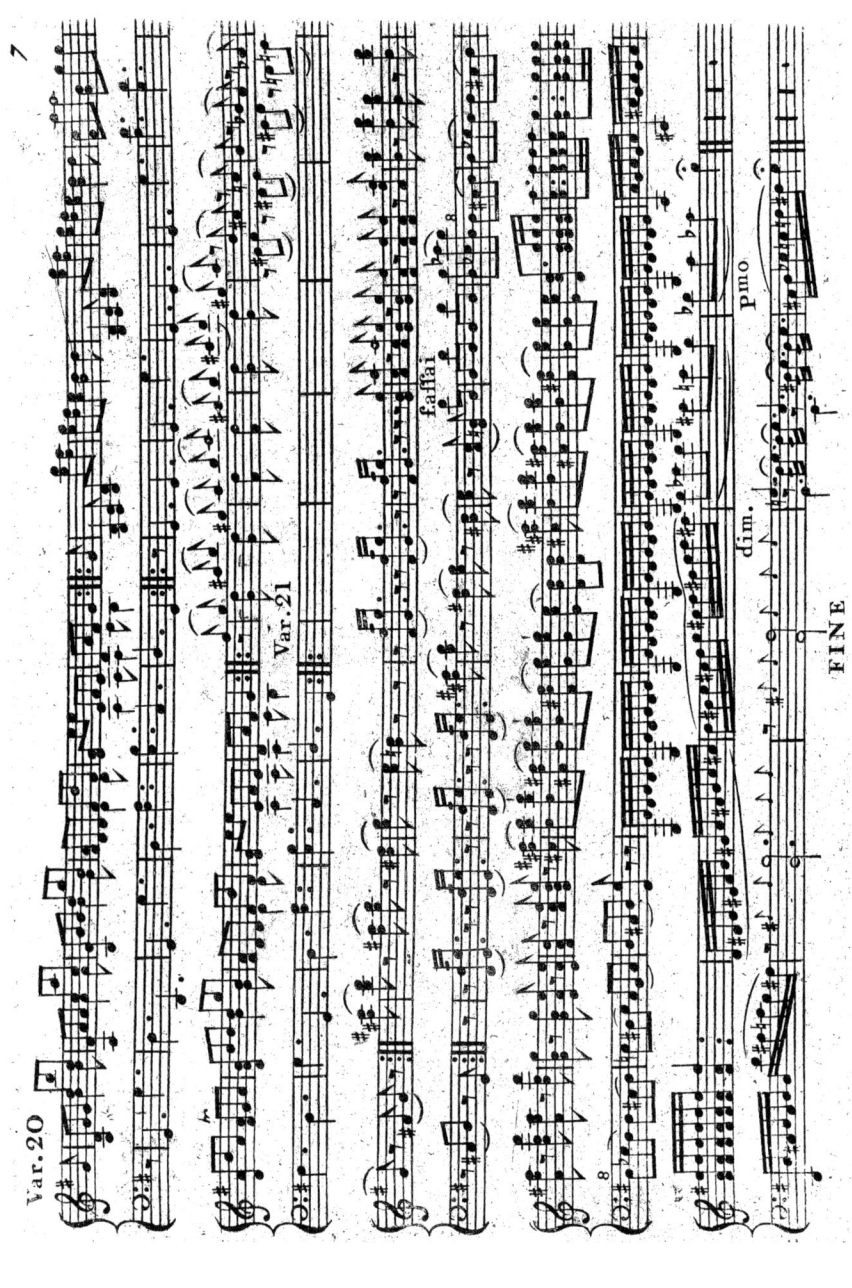

47 Muzio Clementi, *Variations on 'The Black Joke'* (freestanding set), last two

48 J. N. Hummel, *The Pretty Polly* (opening)

49　J. N. Hummel, *The Pretty Polly* (Adagio)

50 Figured bass in Hummel's Piano Concerto in A minor, Op.85, first movement

51 Hummel, *New Vienna Waltz*, Trio 3

PART TWO

Influences

CHAPTER SEVEN

Character 1: Background

(i) General

One of the greatest achievements of the eighteenth-century Enlightenment was its classificatory impulse, evident principally in its attempt to collect together and codify knowledge. This knowledge was for the most part what would later be recognized as scientific, and indeed those of our present-day sciences that were not actually born in this century were transformed. The painstaking gathering, classifying and processing of information that we accept as scientific method became characteristic of the century, and the trial-and-error of experimentation as opposed to reliance on received authority gave new meaning to the Euclidean 'Q.E.D.'.

Apart from this new 'scientific' attitude abroad, what further distinguished the eighteenth century from earlier ones was the promulgation and presentation of this knowledge to an increasingly more literate public through publications and compilations that, however exclusive they may appear to us in retrospect, were aimed more and more at the equivalent of a mass market. The tone is set, at the opening of the century, with John Harris's *Lexicon technicum*, the first encyclopaedia of the known sciences, followed by the work of the Swedish scientist Carolus Linnaeus (Carl von Linné) (1707–78) whose taxonomic work on plants still remains basic to botany. His *Systema naturae fundamenta botanica* of 1735, *Genera plantarum* of two years later, and the *Species plantarum* (1753) – the fruits of his widespread geographical explorations – outline the binomial system of identification, most of which is still in use. Samuel Johnson's ambitious *Dictionary of the English Language* appeared in 1755, and the British Museum (and its incorporated British Library), doing for international artefacts what Johnson had done for English words, opened in 1759, with the Botanical Gardens in London's Kew opening the following year.

Perhaps the most far-seeing project of this kind was the *Encyclopédie* edited by Denis Diderot and Jean D'Alembert, whose 35 volumes appeared between 1751 and 1780. The full title, *Encyclopédie, ou Dictionnaire raisonné des sciences, des arts et des métiers, par une société de gens de lettres* [Encyclopaedia, or analytical dictionary of the sciences, the arts and the professions, by a society of writers] indicates its full scope as a compilation of all contemporary knowledge, an investigative summation with wonderfully detailed illustrations. Pl. 30 shows naval signals and battle-manœuvres and Pl. 31, in complete contrast, some of the illustrations accompanying the instructions for upholstering a chair.

But the system was to be hoist on its own petard; the very questioning that set the Enlightenment in opposition to the Baroque was to be turned back on itself by a later generation. Countering what more and more people came to see as the oppressing generality and hierarchisation of the eighteenth century came the need for an assertion of individualism of various kinds and in various degrees – from particular traits and qualities, to the wholesale overlaying of a complete personality. It was less a case of out-and-out revolt as of the extrapolation and enhancement of features already embedded in the Enlightenment *ethos*, albeit hidden or even dormant. What mattered to Linnaeus, Johnson, and those who used their work, was not the individual flower or word, for example, but to what extent these conformed to type or definition and so represented and justified their grouping. A corresponding typification was applied to people as well, most obviously seen in the uniforms and liveries of those in military and domestic service, under which latter heading would have been classed musicians from, occasionally, the greatest of composers to the lowliest of fiddlers. The right or opportunity to express individualism within society in the ways which the West takes for granted today was then confined to the aristocracy. After the French Revolution, however, servants in France no longer wore livery, widely seen as the badge of slavery, while the individually distinguishing coats-of-arms were removed from the aristocrats' town houses.

An example of the shift in attitude to classification and its uses is instanced in the beautiful and immensely skilful paper-mosaics of flowers by [Mrs] Mary Delany. Pl. 32, *Rosa alpina (Halifax)* (1779) is probably modelled on one of the real flowers that she acquired or that one of her many interested friends sent her from their gardens. One of almost a thousand completed in the last seventeen years of her life (1700–88), it is a collage of small pieces of coloured paper occasionally touched up with watercolour; 'I have invented a new way of imitating flowers' she wrote to her niece. These 'paper mosaicks' combine botanical accuracy with respect for the individuality of the specimens, whose names – botanical, common and, in many cases, local – and dates she carefully recorded on her mosaics, a fine instance of the merging of Enlightenment generalism with Romantic particularism.

(ii) **Background**

It is in this changing context that the proliferation of one of the most quintessentially Romantic of musical genres, the character (or 'characteristic') piece must be seen, and it is no accident that it should have been associated almost exclusively with the piano. Typically, it is relatively short and self-contained, expressing one (or two associated) ideas or moods, which immediately calls to mind the Baroque Doctrine of the Affections (*Affektenlehre*), in which a piece or movement is governed by a single emotion, or 'affect'.

Indeed, this kind of piece had a long and respectable lineage, in part perhaps because such pieces were often didactic or otherwise functional in intent. Instances include J.S. Bach's fugues and D. Scarlatti's Sonatas and *Essercisi*, as well as Johann Kuhnau's Biblical Sonatas, the six *Musicalische Vorstellung einiger biblischer Historien*, illustrating incidents from the Old Testament, such as *David and Goliath* and *Saul cured by David through Music*. There was also a growing literature of what one might call – until the nineteenth century at any rate – the diversionary piece, and it is this category that exhibited the greatest fecundity in post-Baroque music, splintering into many sub-genres that can all be described loosely as character pieces.

'Self-contained' need not, of course, imply free-standing, and several types of piece began life as parts of larger works, such as the rondo, the scherzo and the variation-set, before seeking their fortune in the wider world. Having done so, the tendency to flock together seems to reassert itself, and the pieces appear in groups – either of short pieces in compilations such as Schumann's *Carnaval* (of which more later) or longer pieces in short groups, such as the issuing of Chopin's Nocturnes in sets of two (or three in the case of the first set, Op. 9).

An interesting halfway-house exists in the sonatas of Domenico Scarlatti (originally issued as '*Essercizi*') some of which, while being individually so-titled, often appear to be grouped in pairs either by key-association or on other musical grounds. Scarlatti's patron, Queen Maria Barbara of Spain, for whom most of them were written, had pianos in all of her residences, and it is tantalising, but inconclusive, to speculate on whether Scarlatti had this instrument in mind for some of the works. Though primarily for harpsichord (to which their unique combinations of sonorities seem ideally suited) some include organ stops, and, remembering the closeness of the fortepiano sound of the early eighteenth-century to that of the harpsichord, it is unlikely that a keyboard pioneer like Scarlatti could not have been intrigued by the digitally controllable possibilities of the new instrument. The sonatas certainly lose little in performance on the modern piano.

The term 'character' in this context is capable of a plethora of implications. On occasion, it has been used without any specific character being apparent, as in Ignaz Moscheles' two books of Studies: '*24 Characteristic Compositions*', the Preface to which gives some justification:

> ... it is not so much the author's intention to cultivate mechanical perfection, as to address himself to the imagination of the performer and to enable him to excel in all the delicacies of light and shade, in contrast, sentiment, and passion – in short, to make him master of all that is implied by the comprehensive term *Style*.

Similarly, of Kalkbrenner's *Essais sur différents caractères* (pub. early 1818) only two have a character in more than the most general sense of tempo-markings, No. 2 in C sharp minor, an Adagio melancolico and No. 5 in F major, Andante grazioso.

'Characteristic' in various languages is also used superfluously, such as in Czerny's 25 *Character Etudes*, Op. 755 and *Grand Characteristic Studies*, Op. 785; the title seems to have been used to generate interest in what might otherwise be seen as just another set of (Czerny) studies. At its loosest, it can describe the cut and pace of the music – slow, fast – and the general association of slow with dark, and fast with happy, emotions (other things being equal) usually ensues.

The use of descriptive titles involving human emotions or emotional states, occupations, nationalities, dances, places, and so on, is another category, as is the further step into the realm of 'programme music', where, according to Liszt (who invented the term) purely 'musical considerations, although they should not be neglected, have to be subordinated to the action of the given subject.'[1]

As is so often the case in the process of categorisation, the distinction between these many sub-genres lies somewhere along a continuum bounded at one end by pieces in pre-existent forms such as rondos and at the other by pieces having varying degrees of 'free-ness', in which the form is determined, to differing extents, by the content, whether this be purely musical or suggested by external, possibly non-musical, factors.[2] The very existence of the character-piece is ultimately a consequence of what might be called the emancipation – from didacticism and from an accompanimental function – of instrumental music, and its appropriation and development by early nineteenth-century composers goes hand-in-hand with the existence of an instrument that was equally self-contained and capable of doing justice to its versatility. Given the increasingly greater emphasis on expressiveness and individualism, and the willingness to expose these, it is not surprising that one of the earliest manifestations should be seen in the escalation and intensification of tempo directions and of expression and dynamic markings.

---

[1] Liszt/*SCHRIFTEN*, iv, p. 69.

[2] These 'extremes' are dealt with in separate chapters: Chapter Thirteen (Rondo), Chapters Twenty-Two and Chapter Twenty-Three (Improvisation).

CHAPTER EIGHT

Character 2: Emotionalism

The elevation of emotion to the level of a religion in the Romantic era is something of a truism; a very un-aristocratic displaying of the emotions was more and more considered a measure of sensitivity and sensibility and characterised the arts in the period. It was even extended to animals, and many painters of the early nineteenth century moved from more-or-less distanced, symbolic imputation of such attributes as nobility and pride – intended, of course, to reflect on the animal's owners or subjugators – to more directly emotional, even 'human' ones such as sorrow and fear. The hare in Wordsworth's 'Resolution and Independence' (1802)[1] is a case in point; this first reference is one of three – each with the same sentiments – in the poem:

> ... on the moors
> The Hare is running races in her mirth;
> And with her feet she from the plashy earth
> Raises a mist which, glittering in the sun,
> Runs with her all the way, wherever she doth run.[2]

This shift towards emotionalism is particularly clear when one examines the enormously popular depiction of horses (or horses and their grooms or owners), such as many of those of the master horse-painter, George Stubbs. His *A Grey Hunter [Hack] with a Groom and a Greyhound at Creswell Crags* (c.1762–4, see Pl. 33), in which the horse and its pose are modelled on Greek friezes, is a *paean* to possession: the groom, the dogs, as well as the rocky setting which frames the prize commodity, the horse, all belong to the local landowner. Even Stubbs' several pictures of horses frightened by lions never quite lose their objectivity, excellent though they are. The contrast with, on the one hand, *Napoleon's Horse, Marengo, at Waterloo* (1824, Pl. 34) by James Ward, in which the Emperor's favourite charger is shown alone on the deserted battlefield in the evening after the defeat of his master's forces, watched by a raven, symbol of death, in a bloody sunset; and, on the other hand, Géricault's *Horse frightened by lightning* (1835, Pl. 35), in which the magnificent piebald is transfixed in terror, with muscles knotted, in a baleful and almost featureless landscape, shows the trend clearly. As it happens, Ward's paintings were greatly admired by Géricault and generally in France, as were those of Landseer, whose later more reflective work,

---

[1] Also known as 'The Leech-gatherer' (from *Poems in Two Volumes*).
[2] Ibid., ll. 10–14.

exemplified in the famous *The Monarch of the Glen* (1851), betrayed a salutary change of heart from his earlier glorying in the blood and thunder of the hunt.

In the case of music, the similar and, perhaps, more subtle and more gradual transition to Romantic sensibility and emotionalism is to be found in tempo indications and qualifiers, and in directions relating to dynamics.

(i) Tempo indications

Many Classical and most pre-Classical pieces and movements had no indication of tempo, since this could normally be deduced from other information. Paramount here was, when specified, the piece's genre or title; dance-movements were usually clear in this respect, and, if they were to be otherwise, an explanatory direction would be added, such as the Presto in the Gigue of Handel's Sixth Keyboard suite in F sharp minor and the Adagio-Presto change in the *Ouverture* of the Seventh in G minor, where the section after the double barline is not, at first sight, anything more than a continuation of the prevailing *notes inégales* movement (Ex. 8.1).

Ex. 8.1: Handel, Suite VII in G minor/*Ouverture*, bb. 18–23.

Similarly, in the C minor Praeludium in Bk. I of J.S. Bach's *Wohltemperirte Clavier*, although the piece has no initial tempo direction, the section beginning bar 28 is marked Presto since, again at first sight, the texture, apart from bar 28's pedal-point, hardly differs from the previous *perpetuum mobile*. The following two bars, marked Adagio, could scarcely be anything else, but the last four bars do need some indication, resuming, as they do, the *perpetuum mobile*; they are marked Allegro (see Ex. 8.2). On the other hand, the opening *Sinfonia* of Bach's Second Keyboard Partita is marked 'Grave. Adagio', and is followed after eight bars by an Andante section, so-headed. But when, after a further 22 bars the time-signature changes from ₵ to 3/4 and the texture becomes two-part and contrapuntal, he clearly sees no necessity to indicate that this is to be played at an obviously faster tempo.

Ex. 8.2: J.S. Bach, *Wohltemperirte Clavier* I/Praeludium II, bb. 33–8.

Additionally, the location of a movement in a multi-movement piece other than a dance-suite often suggests its tempo and type, opening and closing movements being traditionally fast or medium-fast – and this tends to prevail even in a two-movement work – and inner movements being on the slower side. In the absence of such aids as title and placement, the general cut of the music was often an unequivocal indicator, and notation could also suggest pace, as, for example, the more leisurely cut of music using 'white notes' – minims, semibreves and even breves. It would be difficult to mistake the first movement of J.S. Bach's *Italian Concerto* for anything other than a medium- to fast-paced curtain-raiser for a significant work aimed at an audience, however select, despite its lack of initial tempo or dynamic indications.

The question of tempo indications, or lack of them, has to be seen against a background of a more-or-less instinctive *Tempo giusto* or *ordinario*, a kind of 'neutral' speed that fitted with what was deducible from the music. Beethoven, who was aware of these terms, may have had this in mind when he headed the finale of the E major Piano Sonata Op. 14/1 with Allegro commodo; Cramer also uses it in No. XL of his *Studio* (1804). The principal tempo indications were broad and few, ranging from the fastest, Presto, through Allegro and Moderato, with the occasional Andante, to Adagio. Presto was generally reserved for finales and, in the case of Joseph Haydn's sonatas, is characteristically allied to the racy movements of this kind with the 'smaller' time signatures (3/8, 2/4, and, less commonly, 3/4), as shown in Ex. 8.3. First movements were characterised by Allegro and slow ones by Adagio – C.P.E. Bach refers to the former's 'briskness' and the latter's 'tenderness'[3] – and they were frequently and increasingly qualified by such words and phrases as *non troppo*

---

[3] C.P.E. Bach/ESSAY, p. 149.

('not too much'), *molto* ('much' or 'very') and later, the rather cavalierly applied *assai* (used for both 'very' and 'rather') and [*un*] *poco* ('a little'). Thus quantitative and qualitative indications were mixed.

Ex. 8.3: J. Haydn, Piano Sonata in A major H:XVI:26/iii, opening.

However, the need for directions or qualifiers to convey more specifically the mood and emotional character of a piece to the performer soon becomes more noticeable. This is an indicator of several important historical processes, all of which would come to fruition in our period. Firstly, it signified an almost instinctive awareness of the increasing distance between the composer and his or her composition resulting in a weakening in the lines of control due to the separating-out of the functions of composer and performer, a process that would be well on the way to completion by the end of the period of this book. Secondly, this distance was exacerbated by a further detour in the composer/consumer line, through the printing, publishing and distribution of music – all of which were ultimately of great service to the composer, but representing a further depersonalisation.[4] Thirdly, as a result of printing and publishing, allied to the increasing importance in wealth and prestige of the *bourgeoisie*, the exposure of the composer's music to a wide, but musically amateur, public required more, and more detailed, guidance as to the composer's intentions and the most effective way to perform the piece.

Lastly, with the growing importance of music-criticism which, by the end of the period could make or break reputations[5] as well as affect income, it behoved a composer to ensure that his or her intentions were clear. It was not unheard-of for the critic to get the wrong end of the stick, so to speak, and for a composer to be – justly or unjustly – accused of shortcomings which, perhaps because of editorial censorship, of his or her absence, or of ignorance of the charges, would be damaging, and remain either not answered, or too belatedly so to prevent the damage. Not even the greatest were immune: Joseph Haydn, writing to his Viennese publishers, Artaria, felt obliged to 'cover himself' with a prefatory remark when he used the same theme for two different movements in a set of piano-sonatas dedicated to the Auenbruggen daughters, XIV: 35–39 and 20.[6] In general, the greater attention that composers paid to such matters as directions and dynamics shows their awareness of their own individuality and of their music, whether in performance or as hard copy, as their artistic property.

---

[4] This will be dealt with in Chapter Twenty-Nine (ii).

[5] One need only think of the influence of Robert Schumann's criticisms in *the Neue Zeitschrift für Musik* (Leipzig) in the cases of Chopin and Brahms.

[6] See Landon/CHRONICLE II, pp. 430–32.

Indeed, Joseph Haydn, whose keyboard sonatas appear throughout most of his creative life (1765–1794/95[7]), is a typical case. The early works follow the expected pattern of general tempo and dynamic indications, but as soon as we reach the 1770s, there is more care and detail. To be sure, the *Sturm und Drang* called forth an almost unheard-of expressiveness in Germanic art, which would account for the more daring features of his works of this period, and it may be that, because of the heightened expressiveness, Haydn's thoughts turned towards the new expressive instrument.

It is, unfortunately, not possible to state categorically when Haydn first had access to a piano in Esterháza but Robbins Landon suggests, on the evidence of a portrait of the composer, that it might have been by c.1770, and, on musical evidence, by 1771.[8] There is, however, some controversy over the matter. Ex. 8.4a and 8.4b show markings suggestive of pianoforte usage appearing in the autograph of the Piano Sonata in C minor H:XIV:20/i of 1771[9] which, on the other hand, would be quite possible on a two-manual harpsichord, in spite of their relative rarity. Indeed, Richard Maunder suggests this as a possibility and speculates as to whether Haydn's employer Prince Esterházy had acquired one.[10] Certainly, the idea of the left hand taking the *forte* notes on a louder lower manual is no more far-fetched than this dynamic effect itself is bizarre.

Ex. 8.4a/b: J. Haydn, Piano Sonata in C minor H:XIV:20/i, bb. 18 and 13–15.

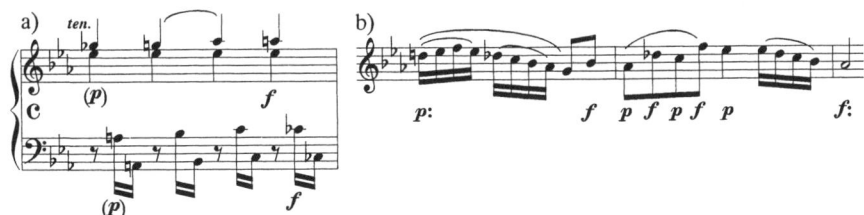

Maunder argues convincingly for such a two-manual instrument in the case of several passages in sonatas from the same period. Ex. 8.5, from the E flat major Sonata XIV:38/i (?c.1770–75) implies a number of subtleties in both articulation and syncopation

Ex. 8.5: J. Haydn, Piano Sonata in E flat major H:XIV:38/i, b. 6.

and Ex. 8.6 (Sonata in F major, XIV:29/i of 1774) is also an example of articulation, although the *p* added to the *f* coupled with the slur may signify an agogic accent

---

[7] There are doubtful works dating from c.1750.

[8] See the argument in *op. cit.*, pp. 343ff.

[9] Robbins Landon, describing a similar passage in the same movement, mentions in a footnote the possibility that these markings may have been added to the autograph when it was revised for printing in 1780, but does not discuss the matter (*op. cit.*, p. 343, fn. 1).

[10] Maunder/KEYBOARD, pp. 100–102.

rather than a dynamic alteration; this movement also sports a *'cresc.'*, and Haydn was soon to include directions such as *innocentamente* and *sostenuto*.

Ex. 8.6: J. Haydn, Piano Sonata in F major H:XIV:29/i, b. 10.

(ii) Tempo qualifiers

Many earlier (Baroque and early Classical) qualifiers were less a matter of mood than of fixing the tempo with more precision, such as Adagio ma non troppo lento and Allegro ma non tanto, the increasing use of *con moto* and *quasi*, and the use of multiple directions – Allegro moderato, Allegretto moderato, Allegretto più tosto Allegro and Allegro non presto. Occasionally, less common forms of the main directions were used: Prestissimo, Vivacissimo, and so on, become more prevalent, and Allegramente (Beethoven, *Bagatelles*, Op. 119/10), Allegrissimo (in Vol. I of Clementi's *Gradus ad Parnassum*, pub. 1817–26) and Allegretto moderatissimo (in the solo piano part of J.L. Dussek's Piano Concerto in E flat major Op. 70/iii). Directions for ways of playing were also used, the most common being *cantabile*, less so *energico*, and later *spiritoso*, together with *delicato*, *con delicatezza*, and by 1801, Beethoven's atmospheric Op. 27/2/i in C sharp minor (giving the sonata its nickname of the 'Moonlight') carried the inscription 'Si deve suonare tutto questo pezzo delicatissimamente e senza sordini' ['The whole of this piece must be played with the utmost delicacy and without dampers.'].[11]

But mood and emotion would also soon make inroads. The addition of the more general *espressivo* was followed by *con* [*molto* or *molt'*] *espressione* and *con grand' espressione* (Clementi, *Gradus ad Parnassum* I/39 (pub. 1817) and Hummel's *Gesellschaftsrondo* Op. 117/Introduzione) and by the slightly more specific *con sentimento* and *sentimentale* – compare Cramer's Op. 89, *All'amica lontana*: Adagio sentimentale of 1825 – as well as *soave, maestoso, appassionato, innocente, semplice, grazioso* and *agitato*. The works of J.B. Cramer are a treasure-store of such markings, and in particular his *Studio* (studies) Book I of 1804, with Vivacessimo [*sic*], Il più prestissimo possibile, Spiritoso assai, Maestoso Energico, Allegro Moderato ma energico. Book II of 1809 has 'Ex. XXVII' headed Allegro Strepitoso, and his *New Studio* of 1835 included Allegrissimo, *tranquillo*, Quasi Allegretto, *e Sentimentale*, *Con affetto, e Soave*, Larghetto affettuoso, and others.

The evocation of more specific emotions ensued. Mozart had used Andante qualified by cantabile and later grazioso in the Piano Sonata in B flat major K. 333 (315c, 1783)/i and /ii respectively, and even before this, Andante amoroso in his Third Sonata K. 281 (189f) in B flat major of early 1775; similarly, Philip Cogan used amoroso with Adagio in his Piano Sonata in B flat major Op. 40/1/ii of 1787.

---

[11] For the implication of the latter injunction, see Chapter Four.

He also used mesto qualifying Adagio in Op. 8/1/ii (1799). With the direction *patetico*, the very un-Classical practice of heart-on-sleeve is illustrated. Clementi's Piano Sonata in F sharp minor Op. 25/5 has a slow movement, Lento e Patetico in B minor, and Book I of the *Gradus ad Parnassum* (1817) has a *Scena patetica* (No. 39). Weber's 'Last Thought' (as it was billed by the *Harmonicon* in 1826) was his Adagio patetico in C sharp minor (1826) and in Moscheles's *Studies* Book I – also called *24 Characteristic Compositions* (pub. 1825–6, of which more later) – No. 11 is headed Allegro Moderato e patetico.

(iii) Dynamics

The change in musical style from Baroque to Classical, in which the predominantly contrapuntal style was to a great extent replaced by a homophonic, melody-with-accompaniment one, also demanded that differentiation between the two elements was possible on a single keyboard instrument as it was in other musical media. Both the gentle, languid *style galant* and the hyper-emotional *empfindsamer Stil* pointed, in their different ways, to the new instrument, even though the latter did so *via* the clavichord.

By the time we approach the High Classical period, however, the piano was championed for the first time by composers, including those of the first rank, who saw its potential and wished to use it to the full. This led to increased interest in dynamics and dynamic markings, and increased attention to their notation, one aspect of which might be described as an emotionalisation, even personalisation, of dynamics. Sandra Rosenblum suggests that, even in cases where only absolute dynamics (that is, *pp*, *p*, *mp* and so on) are given, 'gradual dynamic change seems desirable'.[12] A *diminuendo* or *decrescendo* would be replaced, in the 1780s and 1790s, by the more graphic hairpin[13] ══════ or, later, a more general, subjective word that sought to convey not only the dynamic, but the entire mood associated with it; this usually involved variations in tempo as well. Cogan's Piano Sonata in B flat major, Op. 7/1/i (1794–8) has *calando nel tempo*, (a cooling-down to the [original] speed) and other directions of this sort include *smorzando* ('smothering'), used, among many others, by Beethoven in his Op. 10/3/ii, and by the ever-resourceful Cogan as early as 1780, in the Rondo in his *A Favourite Lesson and Rondo* WO1 in C major. The term is particularly apposite to the pianos of this period, in that the sustaining pedal, in attenuating the strings' higher frequencies, muffled the tone as well as lessening its volume.[14] Czerny also uses *smorzando* (as well as *morendo* (dying)) in *La Reine, Nocturne*, Op. 647 (?1840) and *perdendosi* also appears. Méhul heads the second of his *3 Sonates* Op. 1 (in C major, 1783) Fièrement (proudly).

---

[12] Rosenblum/PERFORMANCE, p. 69.
[13] Loc. cit. Rosenblum finds much earlier sporadic appearances of the hairpin (ibid.).
[14] See Chapter Six (iv).

CHAPTER NINE

Character 3: Personification

(i) Introduction

Just as the generalised descriptions of the pace and type of movement earlier in the period (as embodied in headings, titles and dynamic indications) gave way to more emotionalised directions, and so on, so these in turn began to show a greater degree of more specific humanisation and even personification. One of the clearest illustrations of this trend in the period is, not surprisingly, portrait-painting and the manner in which the more faithful rendering of the features and traits of the sitter gradually takes precedence over the conventional 'staging' or a more-or-less idealised image – the sitter as they would wish to be seen. The famous watercolour portrait by Louis Carrogis de Carmontelle of the Mozart family (*Leopold Mozart and his children,* *c.*1763, see Pl. 36) shows a relative stiffness in spite of the fact that the subjects are absorbed in music: little Wolfgang, sitting bolt upright at the clavier in almost aristocratic garb (complete with sword), and sister Nannerl, equally formal. In fact it is only Leopold who shows any hint of ease, with his relaxed pose and crossed legs. The nonchalance is, however, diminished in the setting, with the calf of Leopold's right leg being echoed in the gently curved legs of the stool and of the harpsichord, which latter's curvature is subtly neutralised by the opposing curve of the stool; the strong verticals and horizontals also dwarf any hint of ease, and the diagonal of the violin is transmuted into downward motion by being transferred through to Wolfgang's upright back, as well as being opposed by the music-stand's diagonal. Similarly, Nannerl is denied any real feminisation, as her dress is hidden by the harpsichord and the trees above her are insufficient to do anything very much to soften the pillar's verticality, of which she partakes: she is somewhat marginalised, and it is clear that it is the little *Wunderkind* who gets the limelight. Indeed, there is very much the feeling of a stage-set about the painting. The stiffness is the more telling since it is children, for the most part, who are being portrayed here, and this same quality is also evident in another portrait of Nannerl (*c.*1763, probably by Pietro Antonio Lorenzo) in the Mozart Museum in Salzburg and (albeit to a lesser extent) in a later portrait of the family *c.*1780 by Johann Nepomuk della Croce (see Pl. 37).

Indeed, the very method of art training in the eighteenth century favoured the conventional, at least in terms of the outward forms. Students learnt by copying the

Classical and Renaissance masters – the latter themselves very often more-or-less faithful channels of the former. Joseph Wright (of Derby's) *An Academy by Lamplight* well illustrates this, where the students in the life class of a painting school (which may well refer to the Royal Academy, founded in 1768) are sketching a Classical sculpture (see Pl. 38). The irony of Wright's unconventional and pioneering techniques of lighting, frequently using a single and usually artificial source – a candle or lamp – in the service of a conventional scene was probably not unintentional. In Britain, portraiture was paramount, a market that, unlike Continental countries, eventually outstripped other kinds such as history-painting – at least where living artists were concerned, since the old masters were avidly collected. Joshua Reynolds (later Sir), who, as the son of a schoolmaster, clergyman and a former Fellow of Balliol College Oxford, was well aware that he was socially a cut above the usual run of painters of his time, capitalised on this market for portraits – although his own inclination was towards the 'grand manner' in which he did not excel – and, instead, set about raising the status of what was called, derogatively, 'face-painting'. His success – as well as his views on art – made him the ideal choice for the first presidency of the Royal Academy of Art on its foundation in 1768 and for the inevitable knighthood that followed a year later. Reynolds' fifteen *Discourses*, which he delivered at the Academy's annual prize-giving, are, together with the work of Edmund Burke, the prime examples in English of the Enlightenment philosophy applied to art. Hence the emphasis here is on the timeless (Classical) rather than the ephemeral (modern), the general rather than the particular; one should aspire to *ideals* of beauty and truth and not let mere observed reality stand too much in the way. As soon as he became the spokesman of the Academy, however, he put portraiture in its place as a 'lower form' and his Tenth Discourse expounds his artistic *credo* clearly:

> ... it happens in a few instances, that the lower [style] may be improved by borrowing from the grand. Thus if a portrait-painter is desirous to raise and improve his subject, he has no other means than by approaching it to a general idea. He leaves out all the minute breaks and peculiarities in the face, and changes the dress from a temporary fashion to one more permanent, which has annexed to it no ideas of meanness from its being familiar to us... It is very difficult to ennoble the character of a countenance but at the expense of the likeness, which is what is most generally required by such as sit to the painter. [1]

His ideas were the counterpart of his friend Dr Samuel Johnson's theory of poetry, that is, that 'the whole beauty and grandeur of art consists in being able to get above all singular forms, local customs, particularities, and details of every kind.'[2]

Happily, there is a divergence between Reynolds' practice and his preaching. It is true that he chooses antique garb and attitude for his upper-class sitters, such as the *Apollo Belvedere's* pose for both *Captain Keppel* (1753) and *Omai* (1776) a Tahitian 'Noble Savage' (whose nobility was obviously insufficient to shine through modern dress) and this is especially true in the case of women of all ranks, such as *Three Ladies Adorning a Temple of Hymen* (also known as '*The Irish Graces*') (1773). In similar manner, the pose of the eponymous actress in his *Mrs. Siddons as the Tragic*

---
[1] Reynolds/DISCOURSES 10, p. 56.
[2] Johnson/LETTERS, p. 88.

Muse (1789) is that of one of the Prophets on the Sistine Chapel ceiling, Reynolds being a great admirer of Michelangelo. But he chose less exalted attitudes for his lower-status subjects, such as his friend Johnson, whom he painted five times. Reynolds is best remembered in works in which his sitters' personality is more important than external personal or social trappings, such as in his portraits of children, in *Nelly O'Brien* (1760–62) and in the magnificent *Garrick between Tragedy and Comedy* (1762) in which the great actor – another close friend – chooses the 'wrong' figure and faces Tragedy with a rueful smile.

Johnson's ideas (above), which Reynolds, Burke and others espoused, are directly antithetical to Romantic ideals, in which the individual is paramount and the particular eclipses, or should strive to eclipse, the general. Later portraiture revels in the particular and the personal, although it is fair to say that this may contain an ulterior motive, as in the portrait by Gainsborough of John Plampin (*c.*1752, see Pl. 39), whose easy relaxation shows a fashionable man-about-town with expectations – fulfilled some five years later, in 1757 – of the country estate in the background, large and well-worked (and therefore profitable) with not a peasant in sight: an advertisement for an eligible bachelor if ever there was one. His dog, however, may, in his obedient but cowed pose, tell us more about the sitter than he would wish us to know. John Hoppner's portrait of Mrs. Williams, (*c.*1790, see Pl. 40) is something similar, although much more charming, in its portrayal of a young, pretty woman in a simple bonnet and dress with gentle suggestivity – the *décolleté* dress and the escaped curl, emphasizing her cleavage and neckline respectively (and respectably). Although there is a hint of personality in the picture, it still remains closer to the Enlightenment's notions of beauty, soft, feminine, vulnerable and desirable as opposed to the rugged sublime, associated with the male. In Ferdinand-Victor-Eugène Delacroix's portrait of the ennobled landscape painter, who is the subject of his *Louis-Auguste Schwiter* (1828, see Pl. 41), something of this last quality lingers in the wild and mysterious background, but here the predominant feeling is one of sensitivity rather than power or awe. It is interesting that the vase has possibly been removed from the pedestal to the floor to show the view in the background: the flowers it contains also blend into the foliage of the wall of trees behind, forming a link between foreground and background and echoing the Baron's hand and watch-fob. He himself stands between his house and his lands, without any of the smugness of Plampin, but something more akin to shyness, as if posing for a photograph with little warning, and undecided as to what to do with his hands.

Photography was, of course, the great artistic discovery in this period, opening up new horizons in terms of fidelity and ease; even though exposures were, by our standards, very long, they were as nothing compared with hours of daily posing over weeks or months. Unicity and individuality went hand in hand here and Louis Daguerre succeeded in fixing images from a *camera obscura* as early as 1816. (Pl. 42, *The Ruins of Holyrood Chapel...* (*c.*1824) gives an example of Daguerre's painting, the precision of which suggests a photograph.) As a footnote, I find it remarkable that in what seems to be a bid for artistic acceptability, a number of the early portrait-photographs still relied on Classical and Renaissance modelling in terms of poses and body-types.

(ii) Musical directions

It would be surprising if the art of music were not to be influenced by these changes and tendencies and, as we shall see, it, too, partook of the personalising drift of the age, again, in directions and, of course, titles. Given the increasing emotional range and intensity of music in general, and of piano music in particular, during the period under discussion, it was inevitable that tempo qualifiers and directions should move away from the abstract generality of fast, slow, and so on, to convey the more particular and human emotions – happy, sad (and so on). In a sense, of course, this was already the case: Allegro, for example, meaning cheerful, implied a brisk tempo, but for non-Italian-speaking musicians, the tempo signification would have been (and still remains) paramount, if not exclusive. Also, as has been mentioned, the need for the composer to project through the performer (when they were not the same person) to the listener is apparent here. Also apparent is the need for more specific direction in the case of the new market for such pieces, the domestic drawing-room players, almost exclusively women, upon whom human qualities or attributes applied to the manner of performing would have much more immediate impact than a generic direction; 'passionately' or '*appassionato*' was much more involving and would have elicited a more appropriate performance than a mere Allegro. I have already touched on this in the last chapter with the use of *patetico*, and others soon followed in a similar vein.

There was, perhaps, another general reason also, in that the emotional and personal would posit an antidote to the emphasis on the rational and, given the contemporaneity of the Industrial Revolution, the mechanistic and quantitative. Richard Leppert, dealing with the mathematical ideas of the musical theorist John Keeble, notes that he 'locates music in mathematics, in phenomena that in turn can be 'objectively' measured and systematised'. The system 'is legitimated on the claim that it is structured on 'natural' [mathematical and acoustical] principle, and on that basis it becomes law'.[3] Leppert refers to Keeble as one who, 'like others of his time, virtually fetishises numbers as the embodying principle for both truth and progress ...'[4] The poet William Blake suggests a similar 'fetishisation' involving the Industrial Revolution, at whose inception he was present and of the abuses of which he was a persistent critic. In *Jerusalem* [5] he contrasts older, simpler mechanisms based immediately on natural principles and with the – in his view – unnecessary over-complication of the machinery associated with industrialisation. This he sees as resulting in dehumanising workers whose labour is too immediately directed at the minute task in hand, rather than being part of – or even being able to see – the totality to which they are contributing so much for so little return:

> And all the Arts of Life. they changed ito the Arts of Death in Albion.
> The hour-glass contemnd because its simple workmanship.

---

[3] Leppert & McClary/MUSIC, p. 73.
[4] Ibid.
[5] This refers not to the well-known extract from his *Milton* (beginning 'And did those feet') also called 'Jerusalem' but to a later poem.

> Was like the workmanship of the plowman, & the water wheel,
> That raises water into cisterns: broken and burnd with fire:
> Because its workmanship. was like the workmanship of the shepherd.
> And in their stead, intricate wheels invented, wheel without wheel:
> To perplex youth in their outgoings, & to bind to labours in Albion
> Of day & night the myriads of eternity that they may grind
> And polish brass & iron hour after hour laborious task!
> Kept ignorant of its use, that they might spend the days of wisdon
> In sorrowful drudgery, to obtain a scanty pittance of bread:
> In ignorance to view a small portion & think that All.[6]

At another point in the same poem, he talks of 'Reasonings like vast Serpents / Infold around my limbs, bruising my minute articulations . ..'[7]

Among the German-speaking *bourgeoisie*, a parallel, but opposite, shift during the first part of our period is noted by Mary Sue Morrow in her book dealing with musical criticism in German-language magazines and journals: 'the development of an aesthetic vocabulary for instrumental music ... during the last four decades of the eighteenth century',[8] a shift from the rational to the emotional, going hand in hand with a critical vocabulary that was gradually being augmented with terms that were becoming more emotional and personal: 'pieces were found to be "touching" (*rührend*) or "full of feeling" (*gefühlvoll*), or "heartfelt expression".[9] *Charakter* also appears from time to time in reviews. 'Character associated adjectives included naive, sentimental, melancholy, mournful (*schwermütig*) and similar words pertaining to human moods and personality.'[10] She also gives some striking examples from reviews in the 1770s and 1780s. In a review of keyboard sonatas by some amateur composers in 1787, the following appears:

> The first sonata has an ingratiating Gratioso ... and a flowing rondo that is full of feeling. The second sonata has ... a short Andante that sneaks by, a tender minuet, and a lively rondo ... The third begins with a short, dark, mournful Andante maestoso, which soon breaks into passionate Allegro assai that seems to die out at the end ... [and] concludes with a lively Allegretto.[11]

Similarly, C.F. Cramer, writing in 1783, waxes lyrical in reviewing a rondo by C.P.E. Bach (W. 58/1):

> It is always difficult to say something definite about an instrumental piece without simply breaking out in general exclamations or going into detail with barren lists of harmonic beauties, modulations, etc. Nonetheless, in order to justify my sentiments in some measure, I generally try to think of a character that could correspond to an excellent piece. Thus I perceive, for example, that this Rondo theme and its realisation resemble a charming girl who has set her cap for something that she wishes to achieve through humor and amiable insistence.[12]

---

[6] Blake/POETRY, *Jerusalem: The Emanation of the Giant Albion*, Plate 65, ll. 17–27. The poet's orthography has been preserved.

[7] *Loc. cit.*

[8] Morrow/CRITICISM, 2.

[9] Ibid., 77.

[10] *Loc. cit.*

[11] *Neue Leipziger gelehrte Zeitungen* III/2 39 (March 1787), 618–19 (quoted in *Op. cit.*, 77/8).

[12] Cramer/*MAGAZIN*, I/2 (17 December 1783), pp. 1238–55 (quoted in *Op. cit.*, 127).

Although the exception rather than the rule, this shows a shift away from technical criticism towards the kind of emotive and personifying description that is more characteristic of the nineteenth century.

Faced with what was, for the new sensibility, a limited vocabulary of markings and directions, composers endeavoured not only to widen it, as we have seen, but also began to appropriate terms previously unused, or rarely used, in a musical context. Thus, Potter, in his *Studies* of 1825 uses *Con precisione ed accento*; *Maestoso con precisione; con gusto*; *pulito* (clean); *Solemno, lento e sostenuto*, and in *The Enigma Vars & Fantasia on an Irish Air* of the same year, var. 5 is headed L'originale: *Con grandissima precisione*.

At times it seems almost as if composers were vying with each other in the complexity, the proliferation and even the grammatical forms of directions that to some extent had implications for dynamics: J.L. Dussek's Piano Sonata in E flat major Op. 44 ('The Farewell', pub. 1800) has *con passione, il più forte poſsibile, dolcissimo* (with the utmost sweetness), *delicatamente* (delicately), *plangendo,* (weeping), *mancando* (dying away), *smorzando, sempre calando, con espressione, sotto voce* (beneath the [main] voice or part – effectively, softly), *semplicamente* (simply), *perdendosi* (dying), *con molta espressione, amoroso, con passione, con amore, languendo* (languidly). Not to be outdone, Moscheles, in his *Characteristic Tribute to Malibran* (the famous soprano), gives us *tenero* (tender), *animando* (animatedly), *calando, teneramente* (tenderly), *con delicatezza* (with delicacy), *tranquillo* (peacefully), *con moderazione* (with moderation), *con dignità* (with dignity), *affettuoso, appassionato, calmato* (calming), *flebile* (plaintively), *agitato, con tormento* (tormentedly), *con disperazione* (with desperation), *sempre agitando, energico assai, veemente* (vehemently), *con smania* (with restlessness), *mancando* (dying away), *vacillando* (swaying, hesitant), *morendo*, and '*smorz.*'. Just outside of our period (*c.*1853), Theodor Kullak, in his Ballade 'Lénore', Op. 81, would add *parlando, tempo misurato quasi marcia, con somma passione, quasi arpa, sempre dolce arpeggiato: ma la melodia espressivamente marcata, con somma grazia, ff con grandezza, grazioso l'accompagnamento,* and *precipitato*.

(iii) Musical portraiture

Considering its popularity and lucrativeness in art, as mentioned above, it is to be expected that portraiture should have begun to invade music also, difficult though it would be in an abstract art form. No doubt the fact that a well-loved soprano was the subject of the Moscheles *Tribute,* as described above, accounts for the humanisation of the terms, and it provides another indication of the influence of opera and its dramatic and lyrical range and conventions on piano music. It is also an excellent example of that most personalised of character-pieces, the musical portrait, of which there are many in the period, usually of the 'Reminiscences of ...' or 'Gems *à la* ...' type. Contributing to the former are Moscheles's *Hommage à Weber ... Grand Duo sur des Motifs d'Euryanthe et Oberon* Op. 102 (*c.*1842) and his *Hommage à Haendel*

Op. 92 (for two pianos, 1822–3), showing a great sensitivity towards music of the Baroque period.

The *Characteristic Tribute to Malibran* appears to be a portrait of the performer rather than the person, and shows her wide range of 'characters'; this necessarily results in a series of stylised vignettes, but Moscheles's skill allows him to glide through the costume-changes quite well. There is a passage *con dolore*, with a hint of orchestral accompaniment under a *rubato* melody (Ex. 9.1a) – a striking prefiguring of the scene in the church in Act IV of Gounod's *Faust*, though it is also reminiscent of an aria, 'The parent bird in search of food', from Handel's Oratorio *Susannah* – a *con dignità* passage, the free repetition of a melody, originally *affettuoso*, now *con disperazione* (Ex. 9.1b) and some vocal agility to boot (Ex. 9.1c).

Ex. 9.1a: Moscheles, *Characteristic Tribute to Malibran*/ii, bb. 9–11.

Ex. 9.1b: *Malibran*/ii, bb. 68–9.

Ex. 9.1c: *Malibran*/ii, bb. 99–100.

I have also already mentioned other pieces in Robert Schumann's *Carnaval* Op. 9 (1833–5), such as 'Arlequin' and 'Florestan' and, like the latter, but in opposite vein, 'Eusebius' is also a self-portrait, a depiction of the dreamy aspect of Schumann's own multi-charactered nature. This is beautifully conveyed by the meandering septuplets against the two crotchets of the 2/4 bar, with the left-hand changes of harmony gently nudging them along, and especially when juxtaposed with the normalised four-quaver fall (Ex. 9.2a).

Ex. 9.2a: R. Schumann, *Carnaval* Op. 9/'Eusebius', bb. 1–4.

The effect in the middle section of the piece is of the reverie moving a step nearer to reality with the more 'rational' quintuplet-plus-triplet, which keeps to the basic two beats (Ex. 9.2b). The dreaminess is also supported by the inconclusive chords, first and second inversions mostly, with the tonic reaching root-position only once in the entire piece's 32 bars.

Ex. 9.2b: Op. 9/'Eusebius', bb. 17–18.

The movements 'Chopin' and 'Paganini' in the same set are of a similar type in that they seek, I think, to show not primarily the person or his music, but to provide an impression of the performance-styles of each – the flashy Paganini and his prodigious technique, which Schumann tries to re-adapt for the piano, and, as already stated,[13] the electricity remaining after he has bounded from the stage, strings still sounding. With 'Chopin', the opposite is portrayed: the self-absorbed quietude[14] with which he is constantly associated, even when improvising.[15]

Perhaps 'Chiarina', ('Little Clara', referring to his love and wife-to-be) is also a self-portrait, or, at least, personal emotion shared between them, with its straining lines moving in opposite directions and all the beats coinciding with dissonances that accumulate unresolved until the last half of the second of the 3/4 beats in the final bar of each section. He uses a 'motto' in the 'alto' voice of this piece, a falling line A♭–G–F–E♭–D, (see Chapter Three, Ex. 3.20) which she herself had used several times in her own compositions and which became a bond in common in subsequent works, notably in Robert's great *Phantaisie* in C major Op. 17 (1836–8).

In contrast, the movement 'Estrella', supposed to depict his recent love Ernestine von Fricken, although it also has a touch of tension rather similarly articulated (Ex. 9.3a), the overall feeling, in returning to the opening, is more self-reliant (Ex. 9.3b).

---

[13] See Chapter Four (iii) and Ex. 4.16.
[14] See Eigeldinger/CHOPIN *passim*.
[15] Examples from these movements are to be found in Chapter Four (Exx. 4.13 and 4.16).

Ex. 9.3a: R. Schumann, *Carnaval* Op. 9/'Estrella', bb. 13–17.

Ex. 9.3b: Op. 9/'Estrella', bb. 29–32.

In a letter to his mother, Schumann described Ernestine as one of two

> gorgeous women [who] have entered our circle ... daughter of a rich Bohemian, Baron von Fricken – her mother was a Gräfin Zettwitz – a wonderfully pure, childlike character, delicate and thoughtful. She is really devoted to me, and cares for everything artistic. She is remarkably musical – everything, in a word, that I might wish my wife to be.[16]

His decision to drop her like the proverbial hot cake shortly after may have been due to his discovery of her illegitimacy, or it may have been his new love for Clara; such matters aren't always entirely clear with Schumann.

The final number in *Carnaval* (No. 21) is the March (though in 3/4 time) of the League of David (*Davidsbündler*) – the 'Good Guys' in terms of musical taste and modernism – against the Philistines, represented by a '*Thème du XVIIème siècle*', the *Grossvatertanz* (Grandfather's Dance) with which they are lampooned appearing first in the bass (Ex. 9.4a),

Ex. 9.4a: R. Schumann, *Carnaval* Op. 9/'Marche des "Davidsbündler" contre les Philistins' bb. 50–4.

and then varied in the treble (Ex. 9.4b)

Ex. 9.4b: Op. 9/'Marche des "Davidsbündler" contre les Philistins', bb. 67–70.

---

[16] Schumann/*JUGENDBRIEFE*, p. 243.

to become transmogrified into a quotation from the finale of Beethoven's 'Emperor' Piano Concerto, in a form in which it appears in the development section of that movement.

Schumann also paints musical portraits of fictional characters and, given his abiding interest in literature, it comes as no surprise to find him dealing thus with characters from his favourite writers. The *Kreisleriana* Op. 16 (subtitled '*Fantasien*'), written in four days in April 1838, are based on a character from E.T.A. Hoffmann, Kapellmeister Kreisler, a representation of the eccentric pianist and composer Ludwig Böhner of Gotha. Although Schumann thought of the piece as also portraying Clara and their love in separation, the work is dedicated to 'His friend, F. Chopin'.

Kreisleriana is, of course, an example of a figure being not only portrayed but made a character in a mini-drama. There are others similar, often in the melancholic or heroic vein, such as Graf von Gallenberg's *Phantesie der Trauer am Grabe des beweinten Jünglings* ... (Fantasy of the mourning at the grave of the lamented youth) Op. 35, including the unexpected entry of '*eine Stimme*', a voice singing a few lugubrious phrases of *quasi*-recitative as a song of farewell (Ex. 9.5).

Ex. 9.5: Gallenberg, *Phantesie der Trauer* ... Op. 35, bb. 79–89.

Works such as Liszt's seven *Hungarian Historical Portraits* (1870–85) and his explicit *La marquise de Blocqueville, portrait en musique* (S190, 1868) lie well beyond the time-span of this book, as do the sentimental *salon*-oriented *The Dying Poet* (1863–4) and *The Maiden's Blush* (1859) of Gottschalk.

(iv) Human types and attributes

There is also the kind of process whereby a type of person is depicted, or a generalised view is given in the name of a particular individual. The most extensive body of examples of this kind of procedure is that of the harpsichord music of the French classical school of composers of the seventeenth and eighteenth centuries, particularly the *Ordres*, or Suites, of François Couperin, many of which have descriptive titles embodying human types and attributes. Writing of his procedures, he says:

> In composing these pieces, I have always had an object in view, furnished by various occasions. Thus the titles reflect ideas which I have had; ... it would be as well to point out that the pieces which bear [these titles] are in a sense portraits which appeared under my fingers, ... and that the majority of these flattering titles

are given to the amiable originals which I wished to represent rather than to the copies which I took from them.

[J'ay toûjours eu un objet en composant toutes ces piéces: des occasions différentes me l'ont fourni. Ainsi les Titres répondent aux idées que j'ay eues; on me dispensera d'en rendre compte; cependant, comme, parmi ces Titres, il y en a qui semblent me flater, il est bon d'avertir que les piéces qui les portent sont des espéces de portraits qu'on a trouvé quelques fois assés ressemblans sous mes doigts, et que la plûpart de ces Titres avantageux sont plûtôt donnés aux aimables originaux que j'ay voulou representer, qu'aux copies que j'en ay tirés.][17]

Many of the titles are human attributes and mostly in the feminine gender – 'La ténébreuse' ('The Brooding' or 'Obscure One', *Ordre* 3), with its low tessitura and clinging to the lowest notes of the harpsichord, 'La laborieuse' ('The Industrious One'), an Allemande having regular four-semiquaver groupings and comparative lack of the groupings which characterise so many of his Allemandes, and 'La diligente' ['The Diligent One'] (*Ordre* 2), with its 6/8 and running semiquavers giving a lighter sense of busy-ness. There is also the marvellous set of 'Les folies françoises' (from *Ordre* 13) a *tour de force* of satirical portrayal ('La virginité', 'La poudeur', 'L'ardeur', 'La coquetérie' and so on), as well as nature references, each sonically but subtly suggestive of their subjects – 'Les abeilles' ['The Bees'], (Ex. 9.6a)

Ex. 9.6a: F. Couperin, *Premier Ordre*/ 'Les abeilles', bb. 10–17.

or '*Les Papillons*' ['The Butterflies'], (Ex. 9.6b)

Ex. 9.6b: F. Couperin, *Second Ordre*/'Les papillons', bb. 41–7.

– and titles based on place-names, such as 'La florentine', ['The Florentine Girl'] (Ex. 9.6c) whose 12/16 and characteristic leaps and auxiliaries remind one of a *saltarello*.

---

[17] Preface to the first edition, Paris, 1713.

However, this title, like several of Couperin's, is ambiguous: the use of feminine gender may be in agreement with the understood 'Piece' (*la pièce*). It could also mean simply 'Florent's piece', referring to his pupil Florent Dancourt.

Ex. 9.6c: F. Couperin, *Second Ordre*/'La florentine', bb. 7–11.

This kind of titling fell into decline in the second half of the eighteenth century, except for such composers as Claude-Bénigne Balbastre, who, although primarily an organist, published a set of keyboard pieces in 1759, with titles in the tradition of Couperin and Jean-Philippe Rameau (often involving place-names) such as '*La de Belombre*', '*La Courteille*' and '*La d'Héricourt*'. There were also isolated pieces such as Mozart's comic *Marche funebre del Sig^r Maestro Contrapunto* [Funeral March of Maestro Counterpoint].

The nineteenth century would rediscover, or perhaps reinvent, this kind of title: Ferdinand Ries' 'The Melancholy' (the eighth of his *Twelve Trifles* (pub. 1815) in E flat minor), Sterndale Bennett's *L'amabile* and *L'appassionata* of Op.26 (?1844), Moscheles' *La tenerezza* and 'Il Sensibile' and 'L'originale' in Potter's *The Enigma Vars & Fantasia on an Irish Air* (1825), for example. But they were more often used as a sign of the fashionable times: '*La cappriciosa*' ['The Capricious One'] by Ries, or, better still, '*La Bella Capricciosa*' ['The Beautiful Capricious One'] (Hummel) sounded so much more intriguing than plain '*capriccio*' or even '*caprice*'. And speaking of fashion, French – or a title that clearly suggested a French origin – was, significantly enough, often used, as in Moscheles's *La petite babillarde* ['The little chatterbox'], Kalkbrenner's *La femme du marin*, ['The sailor's wife'], Czerny's *Le page inconstant* (also known under its English title of 'The Page Inconstant') and in Heller's *La petite mendiante* ['The little beggar-girl'] (pub. 1844), in which one hopes the meaning associated with *affetto* in the direction (Allegretto con sentimento ma senza affetto) is 'without affectedness', rather than 'without feeling'.

The Moscheles piece mentioned (*La petite babillarde*) is subtitled *A Brillant Rondo* and well illustrates the type. After a short, showy introduction, the chattering begins (Ex. 9.7a) and Mother tries to insist on moderation, but is pushed too far and finally puts a foot down (end of Ex. 9.7b): with the subsidence of the chattering (Ex. 9.7c), the comparative normality of the opening section returns.

Ex. 9.7a: Moscheles, *La petite babillarde*, bb. 5–9.

Ex. 9.7b: *La petite babillarde*, bb. 25–9.

Ex. 9.7c: *La petite babillarde*, bb. 32–7.

In the first episode[18] in the dominant, Mother seems to be getting heard (Ex. 9.7d)

Ex. 9.7d: *La petite babillarde*, bb. 71–4.

and some conversation even gets under way, with happy triplets outlining the main chords (Ex. 9.7e).

Ex. 9.7e: *La petite babillarde*, bb. 86–90.

The babbling threatens to become a problem once more, but is carefully controlled by an insistent left hand (Ex. 9.7f)

---

[18] Rondo form is discussed in more detail in Chapter Thirteen.

Ex. 9.7f: *La petite babillade*, bb. 94–6.

and again the opening returns and the dominant episode reappears in the tonic, G. As before, however, matters begin get out of hand with the subsequent 'slow burn' and explosion (Ex. 9.7b) as before, but this time the return to the opening brings chatter that, though still a little breathless, is more thoughtful and more phrased, while the chord-progression is structured in a more cadential way (Ex. 9.7g).

Ex. 9.7g: *La petite babillarde*, return of opening.

I have dwelt a little on this piece because it is a particularly successful example of this kind of early nineteenth-century character-piece, as well as being a useful technical study and at the same time embodying a 'programme' that would very much appeal to familiar and familial sentiments.

(v) Moods and emotions

On its least 'personal' level, the attribution or evocation of human moods and emotions in the case of musical pieces or passages was, of course, by no means a Romantic innovation. The general lessening of interest in keyboard music in France after Couperin was balanced by the increase in importance and wider dissemination of Teutonic music, aided by the cosmopolitanism of Handel. His preference, like J.S. Bach and, to a more limited extent, D. Scarlatti, was for pieces – *capriccios*, variations, fugues, single-movement sonatas – and, more commonly, sets of pieces – suites, preludes and fugues, multi-movement sonatas – in which the content and style were more-or-less readily deducible from their titles.

However, the preference of the Teutonic countries and Britain for the clavichord and piano, contrasting with the French loyalty to the harpsichord, also helped to focus on the more emotional and expressive side of keyboard music, and, coupled to the other, more general changes during the passing of the eighteenth century into the nineteenth, began to be reflected in titles. This was partly because, apart from the piece-types mentioned above (*capriccio*, etc.) individual items, such as rondos and even free-standing variation sets, required some distinguishing mark apart from the title of the material on which they were based. In the case of rondos, it could be argued that the very fact of their detachment from the apron-strings of their host-sonatas was as a result of their possessing a character that was stronger, or at least different enough, to make them more popular than their more domesticated sibling-movements.

The detaching of the *Grosse Fuge*, from Beethoven's String Quartet Op. 130 in B flat major, at the request of his publisher Matthias Artaria,[19] is such a case. Artaria considered it too much of a strain on listeners and players, and therefore bound to adversely affect sales. This is an example in opposition to the norm, in which such a separated piece was detached for its individual popularity (although the *Grosse Fuge* does, in fact, enjoy life after excision). Such pieces would then become '*favori*'/'favorite' [*sic*] or '*célèbre*'/'celebrated' and these were also applied to pieces destined for cyclic works that were replaced, but too good to waste, such as Beethoven's Andante in F major ('*Andante favori*' WoO 57) originally the slow movement of the *Waldstein* Sonata Op. 53. Such appellations could also be used second-hand, so to speak, in sets of variations or rondos based on well-known or well-loved airs by earlier composers, such as Ries's *Trois Airs Favoris*, the third of which is based on an *Air célèbre de Mazzinghi*.

It soon becomes evident, however, that a more specifically emotional appeal was being made in titles and headings and, again, Beethoven had dallied with such ideas in, for example, his early piano piece *Lustig und traurig* ['Happy and Sad'] WoO 54 and in his late period the Piano Sonata in A flat major Op. 110/ii, he indulges in a *Klagender Gesang* [Mournful Song] marked *Arioso dolente* ['Sad aria'] and later has *ermattet, klagend* ['exhausted, mournful'] *Perdendo le forze* ['losing force'], *dolente* ['sadly'] and *Nach und nach wieder auflebend* ['reviving little by little'].

However, like some of our earlier examples, there occasionally seems little reason for some titles except to be in fashion or to avoid the simple bald genre-titles. Walter Cecil Macfarren's *L'Amitié. Caprice for the Piano Forte* (pub. 1848, Ex. 9.8) seems hard put to justify its 'Friendship' in purely musical terms unless one takes into account the easy-going opening melody, with the cut of an early twentieth-century popular song.[20]

Ex. 9.8: W.C. Macfarren, *L'Amitié*, bb. 1–5.

---

[19] Not to be confused with the more famous publishing house, Artaria & Co.

[20] In particular the signature tune of the *Workers' Playtime* programme on the BBC during the 1940s and 1950s.

The 'friendship', however, may be implied in the piece's dedication to a 'Mr Henry G. Fanner'. It was quite common in the period to add some indication if a friend was the dedicatee[21] – 'to his friend (so-and-so)' was widely used; perhaps English reserve prevents the use of the formula here. This salon piece is also not particularly capricious.

Following Beethoven's *Sonate pathétique* Op. 13 came a host of other similar works. The feeling is exemplified in, especially, the introductions and in second subjects,[22] but this became more sentimentalised later. Berger's second movement in his Piano Sonata sharing Beethoven's title and his key, C minor, shows this in its heading of Adagio patetico (though it is in E flat major), with a slightly cloying effect (Ex. 9.9).

Ex. 9.9: Berger, Piano Sonata in C minor Op. 7/ii, bb. 0–2.

More convincing is Weber's Adagio patetico in C sharp minor, known as the composer's 'last Thought' (Ex. 9.10),

Ex. 9.10: C.M. von Weber, Adagio Patetico, bb. 0–4.

as is Clementi's *Scena patetica* in B flat (No. 39) from the first book of the *Gradus ad Parnassum* (1817) and his sonata Op. 25/5/ii (*Lento e patetico*).

The same composer's Sonata in G minor Op. 50/3 is an extended example of several of this chapter's and of some previous chapters' preoccupations. It involved the Queen of Carthage, Dido, and her abandonment, at the command of the Gods, by Æneas, to whom she had given refuge and with whom she had fallen in love. Entitled *Didone Abbandonata* [Dido abandoned], it begins with an *Introduzione,* called, in turn *Scena tragica* and headed Largo Patetico e Sostenuto, and the directions throughout perpetuate or intensify such emotions: Allegro ma con espressione with *'Deliberando, e Meditando'*, an Adagio Dolente for the slow movement including the direction *languente* and a *'Lamentando'* section, and this also appears in the finale, Allegro Agitato, e con Disperazione, which at some points progresses through *con anima* to become *con furia*.

---

[21] See section (vi) in this chapter.
[22] See Chapter Three, Exx. 3.4 and 3.5.

The first bars of the introduction (Ex. 9.11a) give the basis for the entire sonata: an opposition of wounded stateliness and barely restrained desperation; the dotted sobbing motif, and the repetition of notes; the lugubriousness of the minor, especially of that most pathetic of keys, G minor; the dissonance of the short notes at the opening, compounded when it appears doubled in the bass register – itself a recurrent textural treatment – at the end of the example; there is even an embryonic form of the ♭3–♯7 fall, marked x, which is the basis of the sonata's entire thematic material.

Ex. 9.11a: Clementi, Piano Sonata in G minor Op. 50/3/i, bb. 1–8.

Ex. 9.11b gives the main theme of the Allegro on its second statement, and the motif is marked x1, x2, x3 and x4.

Ex. 9.11b: Op. 50/3/i, bb. 41–61.

Ex. 9.11b continued

Similarly, it makes its presence felt, together with augmented seconds and diminished harmonies, in the slow movement (Ex. 9.11c) and in the finale (Ex. 9.11d).

There are various operatic, if not melodramatic, touches throughout, such as the little *recitativo*-like lead-in to the first subject's restatement (Ex. 9.11b, bb. 43–6) and the *coloratura* commentary on the subject in the bass (Ex. 9.11b, bb. 54ff), also apparent in Ex. 9.11c and elsewhere.

Ex. 9.11c: Op. 50/3/ii, bb. 1–11.

Ex. 9.11d: Op. 50/3/iii, bb. 0–8.

This fine work ends resolutely in the minor, with a final reference to the basic cell (Ex. 9.11e).

Ex. 9.11e: Op. 50/3/iii, ending.

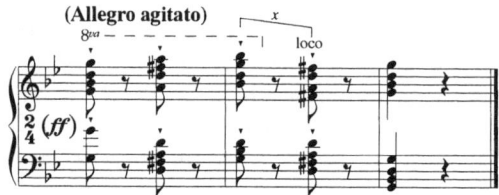

Moscheles' *Concerto pathétique* (No. 7) in C minor Op. 93 (1835–6) has a good example of a pathetic melody as its first subject, and his third, Op. 60 in G minor (1820), an even better one, making it equally worthy of the C minor's descriptive title, if not more so (Ex. 9.12).

Ex. 9.12: Moscheles, Piano Concerto No. 3 in G minor Op. 60/i, opening.

Henselt heads the opening of his F minor Concerto Op. 16 *Allegro pathetico*, and his *Sonate mélancolique* in F sharp minor Op. 49 (1814) exhibits yet another popular appellation. Ries entitles the eighth of his *Twelve Trifles* – called 'Bagatelles' in the German edition – Op. 58 (pub. 1815) The Melancholy, in the unusual key of E flat minor with a suitably lugubrious opening (Ex. 9.13).

Ex. 9.13:Ries, *Twelve Trifles*/'The Melancholy', bb. 1–5.

Mozart's son, W.A. Mozart (*Fils*) wrote a set of *Quatre Polonaises mélancoliques* Op. 22, three of which are in minor keys, and Gottschalk's *La scintilla* (*L'etincelle*) (1848/9) is, in spite of its suggestive name ('The Spark'), a *mazurka sentimentale*. The two books of three *Essais sur différents caractères* Op. 34 which Kalkbrenner published in 1818 has an Adagio *melancolico* as No. 2 and an *Andante grazioso* for No. 5. The former is the only one in a minor key in which the opening melancholy melody (the top line in Ex. 9.14a) is intensified chromatically – though not too much so – by the accompaniment in a subsequent appearance (the whole of Ex. 9.14a), and the transition from the middle section's tonic major (in A flat) to the minor is like a restrained wordless recitative (Ex. 9.14b).

Ex. 9.14a: Kalkbrenner, Op. 34/2, bb. 0–4 (top); bb. 27–30 (with accompaniment).

Ex. 9.14b: Op. 34/2, bb. 70–5.

Ex. 9.14b continued

It seems that the more downbeat aspects of human nature were preferred; Hummel's No. 3 from the *Bagatellen für Klavier* Op. 107 (pub. c.1825) is entitled '*La Contemplation. Petite Fantaisie*' and well depicts a mood of gentle contemplation (Ex. 9.15a), even in the *con anima* section (Ex. 9.15b).

Ex. 9.15a: Hummel, *Bagatellen* Op. 107/3, bb. 1–4.

Ex. 9.15b: Op. 107/3, bb. 9–13.

Similar states of mind, with a touch of J.J. Rousseau, are implied in works such as Heller's *Promenades d'un Solitaire: 6 Characteristic pieces* Op. 78 (pub. 1851), which range from a thigh-slapping first through a more leisurely No. 2 with a real sense of movement and distant horizons (see Ex. 9.16), No. 3 *Allegro vivo, con melanconia* [sic] in B flat minor, and No. 4 *Piu* [sic] *lento*, and back to the happier mood of the opening.

Ex. 9.16: Heller, *Promenades d'un Solitaire* Op. 78/2, bb. 1–5.

Henry Hugo Pierson's *Musical Meditations* No. 1 (pub. 1844, Ex. 9.17) is entitled 'Lost Happiness. *Entflohenes Glück*' and headed by a suitably dolorous quotation from Dante.

Ex. 9.17: Pierson, *Musical Meditations*/'Lost Happiness', bb. 1–6.

Moscheles often uses titles such as *L'Ambition*, *Tendresse et Exaltation* [Tenderness and Elation], *La Fougue* [Enthusiasm], and Cramer, directions such as Moderato innocente, and Adagio sentimentale, while Heller requires his *Les Maturins* Op. 49/2 to be delivered *Vif et avec une expression de naïveté*.

(vi) A note on dedication[23]

The common practice of dedicating pieces to people, or even institutions often overlaps with some of my sections above. A piece may embody a trait or attribute of its dedicatee, especially if he or she is royal or noble, or, for example, have a military connection.[24] The case of Beethoven's change – and re-change[25] – of heart with his *Eroica* Symphony and its dedicatee Napoleon is the most famous example, but his dedication of some of his greatest works to a small number of (mostly noble) patrons bespeaks gratitude as well as flattery, though he would have been the last to admit it. Dealing only with pieces involving the piano, to the Lichnowsky family were dedicated the Piano Sonatas Opp. 13 (*Pathétique*), 26 and 90, the Variations WoO 69, WoO 45, and those with the Fugue Op. 35 (the *Eroica* Variations) and the Rondo in G major Op. 51/2; to the von Browne family the three Piano Sonatas of Op. 10 and that of Op. 22 as well as the *Gellert Lieder* Op. 48 and the Variations WoO 71; the dedication of the great *Waldstein* Sonata speaks for itself.

---

[23] There will be mention of this again in Chapter Twenty-Nine, Didactic music.
[24] I will give some examples of these in Chapter Eleven, Character 5 (i).
[25] See Solomon/BEETHOVEN Chapter 13 for a discussion of the events surrounding the dedication.

Into this category also falls J.L. Dussek's Piano Sonata in F sharp minor, and his *'Elégie harmonique sur la mort du Prince Louis Ferdinand de Prusse'* of 1806–7. Dussek, ever a royalist, was the *Kapellmeister* to the prince – a first-class composer and performer himself, and the dedicatee also of Beethoven's Third Piano Concerto in C minor. In fact, according to Ferdinand Ries, Beethoven told the prince that his playing was 'not that of a king or a prince but more like that of a thoroughly good pianoforte player'.[26] In addition to their professional relationship, the prince and Dussek were also friends, if not entirely good influences upon each other in terms of strong drink and roistering. Equally wordy dedications are those of Pixis's Grand Concerto *'Très humblement Dédié à Sa Majesté Impératrice d'Autriche, Reine de Hongroie, de Bohême, $\&^a$, $\&^a$, $\&^a$'*, and of Czerny's *Souvenir à Schönbrun, Seconde Grande Marche de Coronation pour S.M. Anna Maria Carolina.* Following J.B. Cramer's dedication of his *Twelve New Studies* Op. 92 to Prince Albert, his publisher produced a sumptuous gothic title page complete with knights in armour and *'Dieu et mon droit'* to the left, with *'Gott und mein Schwert'* to the right.

Occasionally members of a composer's family would be favoured: Moscheles was very much a family man and his *Rondeau Exprefsif ... sur un air favori de la Collection de Romances* [by Cramer] was *'dédié à son Épouse'*, his *Rondeau brillant (La belle Union)* Op. 76 for two pianos was *'Composé et Dédié à son Ami / J.B. Cramer, / et sa Nièce / Mifs Antonetta Cramer'* and his *Romance & Tarantella brillante* Op. 101 was *composeé par sa fille Emilie.*

But there are also, on the one hand, looser titlings, such as Sir George Alexander Macfarren's Sonata No. 2 (*Ma Cousine*) pub. 1845, and, on the other, the building up of a personally oriented portrait or tribute into what is in effect a whole scene. Some examples are Gallenberg's already-mentioned[27] *Phantesie der Trauer am Grabe des beweinten Jünglings ...* Op. 35, and Liszt's well-known essays in this genre, such as *St. Francis of Assisi preaching to the birds* and the more extended 'Dante' Sonata: the latter is entitled *Après une lecture du Dante: Fantasia quasi sonata*. Begun in late 1839, the extant version dates from Liszt's completion and revision (by 1853) and it was from then that the sonata gained its title, borrowed (erroneously) from Hugo's poems called *'Après une lecture de Dante'*. It is in essence a picture in music of Dante's *Inferno*, with portraits of hell (the descent in tritones of the opening), the *lamentoso* wailing of the damned souls, and a vision of paradise at the end.

---

[26] Thayer/BEETHOVEN, Vol. I, pp. 196–7.
[27] See above, this Chapter, section (iii), and the accompanying Ex. 9.5.

CHAPTER TEN

Character 4: The Past

(i) General

Nostalgia is, of course, a permanent feature of the human psyche and manifests itself in all ages in ways that are characteristic of those ages, but one of the most striking characteristics of the period of this book is the reverence for, approaching at times obsession with, the past in general and certain ages in particular – ages that had not been the subject of such a degree of interest previously, such as the Medieval.

The result of a complex intertwining of reasons, this revivalist impulse was a powerful one, and produced new directions and movements, not only in literature and the arts, but in politics and political institutions also. Many of these factors are, naturally, outside the scope of this book, but some general comments are called for.

One reason for the retrospection is shared with other similar ages, ages that are, for various reasons, characterised by great changes, and/or a rapid rate of change, resulting in a need for security, typified by memory of a happier, or at least more tranquil or less stressful, past. The memories can be personal (for example childhood), national (past history) or racial, (evocations of the vernacular, or 'folk') and they rarely come as single spies.

Where change or the speed of change is concerned, no previous eras even approached the one under discussion.[1] The Agricultural, French and Industrial Revolutions changed mankind for ever, politically, culturally (in the broadest sense) and in all aspects of everyday life, many of the repercussions being more-or-less immediate, and occasionally devastating, for many people. Without doubt, the almost constant wars involving many nations and people, many deaths and mutilations, many causes, and, not least, profound and frequent alterations of national or territorial boundaries, brought with them a yearning for less complicated, more peaceful and, ultimately, happier days.

There is also, perhaps, a hint of rehabilitation of the past here also, since the eighteenth-century Enlightenment, with its appeal to reason rather than precedent, and its entrepreneurial, experimentative, pragmatic approach, resulted in a rejection of many aspects of its own past. It could be that the over-reaction so common – even understandable – in such situations called for a readjustment that was itself an

---

[1] This has been alluded to in the Introduction.

overswing of the pendulum. It was not only the sciences, or what passed for them, that were to wilt in the bright glare of this rational sun – a common symbol, Masonic and otherwise, for the pursuance of Reason: religion also suffered a series of body-blows that left it changed utterly.

Yet, in its turn, religion (in its broadest undenominational sense), gained from the subsequent anti-rationalist reaction, which ended by placing the numinous above the nominalist, the transcendental above the pragmatic, the intuitive above the rational, the Fichtean *Ich* above the Newtonian cogwheel. Part of that reaction was, on the one hand, a preference for the more ritualised religions with communal forms of public worship (which, to a large number of people in this period, meant Catholicism) in contrast to the comparatively more austere manifestations, exemplified by the Protestant ethic. Protestantism itself would also suffer attack from within, with the various evangelical non-conformist movements: democratist Presbyterianism, proselytising Methodism and others.

One result was a kind of European 'north/south' divide, the Protestant, rational north and the Catholic, intuitive south that, in spite of its patent geographical over-simplification, was accepted in principle by many thinkers and artists, Madame de Staël being a prominent one. Her *De la littérature* of 1800, (English trans., 1812), was enormously influential and took sides in favour of a northern superiority.[2]

A further intensification of this reaction against the rational and impersonal was soon to give rise to a fascination for the less psychologically healthy aspects of the human psyche, such as dreams, the morbid or sordid, and the supernatural, and their manifestation in such diverse manners as the Gothic and 'horrid' novels of Horace Walpole, M.G. Lewis, W. Beckford – the first cousin of Peter Beckford, Clementi's patron – Mrs Radcliffe, and their German-speaking counterparts, Ludwig Tieck, Achim von Arnim and E.T.A. Hoffmann. Walpole's *The Castle of Otranto: a Gothic Story* (1764) was an instant hit and began a wave of such novels of ghosts, graveyards – hence the 'Graveyard Poets' (Gray of the famous *Elegy*, Parnell, Young) – monastic cells, gloomy castles and eerie forests, while Lewis was nicknamed 'Monk' Lewis after his equally famous Gothic novel, *The Monk*. The trend continued with the American master of the macabre, Poe. The Gothic style was well-represented in architecture also, with Walpole's house *Strawberry Hill*, outside London and, at the highest level, the new Houses of Parliament in London designed by Charles Barry and decorated by Auguste-Charles Pugin. Similar developments can be seen in the art of the period and later, in as diverse manifestations as, for example, Giovanni Piranesi, John Fuseli, Blake and Daguerre – Pl. 42 shows his *The Ruins of Holyrood Chapel, Edinburgh, Effect of Moonlight* (*c*.1824), the quality of his reproduction here reminding us that he was a pioneer in photography[3] – in fairy painting in Britain, in the work of Géricault and Francisco Goya in Europe and, for moral and political ends, in Honoré Daumier and George Cruikshank.

The evolutionary tendencies of the period also focused the collective vision on the past as progenitor of the present (and the future) together with the ideas of

---

[2] Staël/*LITTERATURE*.
[3] See Chapter Nine (i).

improvement and perfectibility. Connected with this was the construction of The Canon, a series of Great Men stretching back (and, by implication, forward) through whom the development and perfection of all sorts of movements and human endeavours – including, of course, the arts – could be traced; or, as Daniel Chua[4] puts it so well, 'a genealogy in which composers begat one another in a line of culture from Bach to Brahms, spawning numerous children to squabble for legitimacy in the pantheon of "Great Masters"'. Contact with past civilisations, whether through travel, as in the Grand Tour, or discoveries, due, as was frequently the case in our period, to the expansion of wars into far-flung areas, also rekindled interest in the cultural Other and the past, often resulting in reappraisals and breakthroughs in understanding, many of which continue to be of influence in our own time. One of these – selected almost at random – was the recovery of the ancient Egyptian language through the final decipherment of the hieroglyphs by Jean-François Champollion in the mid-1820s, opening up a 'dead' civilisation for the first time.

(ii) Classical Antiquity: the pastoral

Study of Classical Antiquity – the Greek and Latin languages, literature, mythology, history, above all art – was held in the highest regard in the eighteenth century, and it was the cornerstone of aristocratic education. Its importance as the basis of aesthetic theory had been established through scholars such as Johann Joachim Winckelmann and the classics were kept alive in the works of the poets and dramatists, in Germany especially by Goethe and Schiller, and even by their Romantic successors, the *Frühromantiker*, particularly Kleist and Hölderlin: indeed, the journal in which they launched their theories was called the *Athenäum*, whose name was echoed in an English musical periodical of a slightly later date, the *Athenaeum*. In France, La Harpe's *Lycée, ou Cours de littérature ancienne et moderne*, published in 1799, puts the achievements of the Neoclassical movement in France on a par with those of Classical Antiquity and thus it lived on. Napoleon's predilections in this area are well-known, not least his choice of title, First Consul, and his encouragement of the painter Jacques Louis David and other neoclassicists.

In Britain, the first half of the literary eighteenth century was called the Augustan Age and included Pope, Addison, Steele and Swift. The name itself refers to the age of the Roman emperor Augustus, and his patronage of Horace, Ovid and Virgil. But even in the early nineteenth century, 'strong belief in the value of a classical education ... was ... far from rare';[5] indeed the very idea of 'Georgian' calls forth Neoclassic buildings, decoration and images and the architectural and decorative work of Robert Adam, nicknamed 'Bob the Roman'. The displaying of the carved marble friezes and sculptures removed by Lord Elgin from the Parthenon in Athens (the 'Elgin Marbles') in a shed in Park Lane, London in 1807 was a major event for British artists and had great influence on portraiture and sculpture especially. At the

---

[4] Chua/ABSOLUTE, pp. 240–41.
[5] Lloyd-Jones/BLOOD, p. 112.

Royal Academy, student painters – including the revolutionary Turner – first attended the 'Antique Class', where they copied casts of Greek sculptures before moving on to the 'Life Class', which was based on the same principles. Both classes seem to be combined in Joseph Wright of Derby's *An Academy by Lamplight*, which shows, as I have remarked earlier[6] students sketching a Classical sculpture, and which also combines, ironically, antique subject-matter and revolutionary use of light (see Pl. 38). The favourite author of Gladstone – who himself held degrees from Oxford in classics and mathematics – was Homer, while such titles as *Epipsychidicon, Prometheus Unbound, Adonais, Endymion, Biographia Literaria, Anima Poetae,* 'Porphyria's Lover', 'Pictor Ignotis', *Ulysses* (Tennyson), the many Odes – *on the Intimations of Immortality, to a Grecian Urn, to Psyche* etc. – and others, testify to the poets' abiding interest. Classical myths and incidents still provided the basis of many of the opera libretti, though in practice there was a great deal of recycling of certain favourites. Even though fealty to the Classics was waning in the nineteenth century, it never quite disappeared and its influence in various ways can be discerned in the most unlikely places.

A particular aspect of antiquity, the pastoral, had a long artistic and musical lineage dating from the Renaissance. The style was associated with the idealised self-sufficient country life 'emptied of dung and toil'[7] enjoyed by shepherds and shepherdesses in Arcadia and their predilection for lyrical poetry, music and amorous pursuits. Arcadia was the romanticised setting of Virgil's *Eclogues* (see below), even though the historic area itself was mountainous and woody. Presiding over them is the god Pan, himself a symbol of the closeness of men and animals in his hybrid appearance. 'The pastoral is the world as a garden, a secular Eden conjured by the desires of the urban imagination, where work is play ...'[8] No composer born at any time during the eighteenth century could escape the pastoral as a topic and there is a large body of work alluding to it, most of it associated with instrumental interludes in oratorios, with the pastoral mass of Advent or pertaining to Christmastide and the worship of the Christ-child by shepherds. In addition, more specific references can be found, the six programme symphonies of Dittersdorf based on Ovid's *Metamorphoses* being an excellent example.

Although there was to be an attenuation, this reverence for Classical Antiquity remained in the nineteenth century, especially its first half. Beethoven's *Pastoral* Symphony, of course, springs immediately to mind, itself a high point of hundreds of years of pastorally influenced works. Two of Hummel's ballet-suites, subsequently arranged for solo piano, are entitled *Helene und Paris* and *Sappho von Mitilene* – subtitled *Ein großes heroisch-mythologisches Ballet*, in the unlikely event of the point being missed. The seventh number of this work is a *Pastorale* and his first attempt at an orchestral piece, and the Variations for piano and small orchestra Op. 6, was based on an aria from Vogler's opera *Castor et Pollux*, who, according to one tradition, were the twin sons of Zeus and Leda and among Jason's Argonauts involved

---

[6] See Chapter Nine (i).
[7] Chua/ABSOLUTE, p. 29.
[8] Ibid. p. 79.

in the Trojan Wars. Tomásek, in the spirit of Theocritus, and of course the *Eclogues* of Virgil (which the poet called *Bucolica*[9]), composed seven sets of six *Eclogues*; the first, Op. 35, published in 1807. He also wrote 15 rhapsodies and 3 dithyrambs.

These pieces very well suggest a series of generally pastoral scenes, the musical portrayal of which conforms to a small number of conventions – harmonically, a firm preference for the diatonic with a slow rate of harmonic change, with stretches of the same chord and a tendency to give more prominence to the subdominant than is usual, including a very early move to it whether as a key or a degree. Melodically, the repetition of particular figures that are not in themselves striking, and the repetition of particular rhythms are characteristic; time-signatures tend to be compound, frequently 6/8, and the texture is usually homophonic with the use of pedal-points or drone basses and the 'shadowing' of the melody at the third and, particularly, the sixth. There also appears to be a predilection for the flat keys, especially F and B flat, but D and A also occur with some frequency. The opening of the fourth of Tomasek's *Eclogues* in C major is typical (Ex. 10.1),

Ex. 10.1: Tomásek, *Eclogue* No. 4, bb. 0–4.

and so is No. 2 in F major: Ex. 10.2a gives its scene-setting opening, Ex. 10.2b the passage leading to the middle section, complete with droning fifths.

Ex. 10.2a: Tomásek, *Eclogue* No. 2, bb. 1–5.

Ex. 10.2b: *Eclogue* No. 2, bb. 52–66.

---

[9] The Greek word, *ekloge* means 'extract' or 'piece' after grammarians' habit of simply calling the individual items Piece 1, Piece 2, and so on. *Ecloga* was in later times furnished with the spurious root *Aig-loga* ['goat-talk'], supplying the pastoral connection.

Ex. 10.2b continued

Fine

The bucolic as well as the gentle side of the pastoral is shown in the Andante movement of Haigh's Sonata in E major Op. 41/1 (pub. 1809) (Ex. 10.3a and 10.3b),

Ex. 10.3a: Haigh, Piano Sonata in E major Op. 41/1/ii, bb. 19–20.

Ex. 10.3b: Op.41/1/ii, opening

and in Dussek's *Fantaisie* in F major C. 248, Op. 76 (pub. 1811) the same two sides are apparent in the *Menuet du Carême* (Ex. 10.4a and 10.4b).

Ex. 10.4a: J.L. Dussek, Fantaisie in F major C. 248/Menuet, bb. 0–8.

Ex. 10.4b: C. 248/Menuet, Majore

Heller's *La Petite Mendiante* mentioned already, was published together with an *Eclogue* in 1844, although they were actually part of a set of three *Miscelannés*, of which the other (first) one was a 'Rêverie'. *La Petite Mendiante* is in E flat major and 6/8 and sounds decidedly pastoral (Ex. 10.5) whereas the *Eclogue* is in A major, 2/4 and marked Allegretto con moto. Similarly, although his *'Silvana' Une Pastorale* is in A major, it is also in 6/8 and the B section of its ABA outline is in F major.

Ex. 10.5: Heller, *La Petite Mendiante,* bb. 0–4.

The heading of the second movement of Cramer's Third Piano Concerto in D major is *Pastorale e sostenuto* (in G major, Ex. 10.6, over a tonic pedal)

Ex. 10.6: J.B. Cramer, Piano Concerto No. 3 in D major/ii, bb. 1–8.

and he manages to include a range of styles in his *Harvest Home: A Pastoral Divertimento* for piano with *ad lib.* flute. The second movement is an *Allegretto spirituoso en Militaire* and the third, a rondo headed Allegro rustico which includes a *Carillon*[10] section and an *innocente* passage, a direction that he could as easily have applied to the opening (Ex. 10.7).

Ex. 10.7: J.B. Cramer, *Harvest Home*/iii, bb. 0–4,

---

[10] The carillon has already been discussed in Chapter Five (iv).

The Larghetto affettuoso of his Sixth Concerto in E flat major Op. 51/ii (in A flat major) has a 3/8 time-signature and opens over a pastoral-ish drone. Dussek's Piano Sonata in B flat major C. 96 of 1793 – which also appeared as Op. 23, Op. 24 and Op. 27 as well as being arranged for piano and violin – has a *Pastorale* headed Allegretto moderato *con espressione* as its second (and final) movement whose phrasing of 4 + 2 + 4 bars and chromatic touches of ♯ii^7 and ♯vi^7 nicely compensate for its overall regularity (Ex. 10.8). Ex. 4.2a (see Chapter Four) gives an example of a pastorale by Potter, this one being in simple duple time. The general tone of these pieces is tranquil and undisturbed, with the tempo-qualifiers frequently hammering the point home, as in Heller's *'Silvana' Une Pastorale* in A major, which has Allegretto tranquillo.

Ex. 10.8: J.L.Dussek, Piano Sonata in B flat major C. 96/ii, bb. 0–11.

Another indication of the persistence of the style in the first half of the century is the ease with which it became transmuted in works other than those entitled 'pastoral(e)' such as *Carillons* (mentioned already), and the occasional more general evocation of a pastoral tranquility. There is a suggestion of this at the opening of the finale of Haigh's Piano Sonata in E flat major Op. 31/2 (pub. *c*.1805, Ex. 10.9).

Ex. 10.9: Haigh, Piano Sonata in E flat major Op. 31/2/ii, bb. 0–5.

Latrobe, in his set of three sonatas Op. 3 (pub. ?1793 and dedicated to Haydn), has an *'Andante Paſtorale'* as the first movement of No. 3 (after an Adagio introduction), but the slow movement (Lento in D major) of the second of the set also has a pastoral air to it both at its opening and whenever it recurs, even when varied or transposed (Ex. 10.10a and 10.10b).

Ex. 10.10a: Latrobe, Piano Sonata in D minor Op. 3/2/ii, bb. 9–12.

Ex. 10.10b: Op. 3/2/ii, bb. 55–8.

Field wrote several *Pastorales,* and some of these were issued as Nocturnes, such as No. 9, a *Pastorale* in A major originally written for piano quintet, which exists in three subsequent solo-piano versions, all with important differences. Although it does share some of the pastoral traits outlined above, it is mostly in its tranquil mood that it suggests pastorality. This is the very style that Field transmuted to his Nocturnes, many of which inhabit the same dreamy groves, and which will be discussed later.

Even the most dewy-eyed of Arcadian adherents, however, could not deny that the sun didn't always shine, and the less clement face of pastorality, the storm, also became a minor sub-genre closely associated with it. Czerny's *Storm Rondo; Impromptu,* Op. 715 is very descriptive, with its thunder and lightning and calmer B major section, as is Field's Fifth Concerto in C major entitled *L'incendie par l'orage* with added orchestral colouring (Ex. 10.11).

Ex. 10.11: Field, Piano Concerto No. 5 in C major/*L'Orage.*

In fact, a Parisian edition of this concerto gives a part for a second piano during the Storm episode, stating that 'Le seconde Pianoforte est indispensable, lorsque le Concerto est executé avec tout l'orchestre; parsque un seul Pianoforte seroit trop faible pour exprimer l'orage.' ['The second piano is essential when the concerto is played with full orchestra, since a single piano would be too weak to depict the storm.']. Steibelt highlights the storm element in his *L'orage: Rondo Pastoral* in E major (from his third concerto, perf. 1798) and, like Beethoven's in the Sixth Symphony, the storm, when it finally breaks out, is sited in the key of the flattened sixth (C major).

(iii) Past styles

The Cramer *Divertimento (Harvest Home)* mentioned earlier is one of a number of pieces which, in addition to their specific mention, or use, of the pastoral vein, also appeal to a more generalised past, by virtue of choosing old or archaic styles or techniques. He is much more explicit in his contrasting of earlier pastiche with contemporary music in *The Two Styles, Ancient and Modern* of 1842, by which time nostalgia was a major factor in all areas of cultural life. In this piece, subtitled *A Musical Effusion*, the *Stile Antico* (Grave in D minor) with which it opens (Ex. 10.12a), is a mixture of chromaticism and modalism, cadencing in V/V and dominant minor. The opening flourish suggests at first a movement in French Overture style by Handel, but the dots or double-dots are not to be found, except in a few isolated moments, such as b. 3), and the four-part chorale-ish writing also suggests an earlier style, together with the 'white' appearance of the predominating minims and the rather drawn-out (*Più lento*) old-fashioned cadence with which it closes (Ex. 10.12b).

Ex. 10.12a: J.B. Cramer, *The Two Styles*/i, Stile Antico, bb. 0–8.

Ex. 10.12b: *The Two Styles*/i, Stile Antico, ending.

Other aspects of this style – or perhaps one should say 'these styles' as there is little coherence – are treated in the last movement, Tempo giusto. Again there is an *anacrusis*, this time a less striking triplet leading to a *perpetuum mobile*, beginning with a perambulating bass in quavers, reminiscent of a rather stilted organ-pedal line (Ex. 10.13a), if not a *pedal-exercitium*. The emphasis in the right-hand is full chords and a carefully-notated rhythm (b. 3), which might possibly have called to mind in a contemporary listener the openings of Arne's *Rule, Britannia* and/or Handel's *Zadok the Priest*. The sharing of the movement with other voices and the frequent use of simple imitative repetition (Ex. 10.13b) also suggests 'antique-ness'.

Ex. 10.13a: J.B. Cramer, *The Two Styles*/iii, Stile Antico, bb. 0–5.

Ex. 10.13b: *The Two Styles*/iii, Stile Antico, bb. 43–6.

Cramer, however, can do much better than this, and when we look at the central '*Stile Moderno*' movement, with its Andantino grazioso ed espressivo heading and flighty rhythms[11] contrasting with the stiff regularity of those flanking it, we realise that parody is the order of the day. The skittish 'Classicism' of Ex. 10.14 with its decorated *galant* cadences, sniggering echoes in bb. 3 and 4, and the sly dig at a Mozartian 'fill-in' (marked x, but also found in bb. 8, 12, 20 etc.), complete with the affected middle section in the parallel minor, is 'over the top' enough for us to see the intent, but not, at this distance in time, the target(s) if it/they are in any way specific.

Ex. 10.14: J.B. Cramer, *The Two Styles*/ii, Stile Moderno, bb. 0–5.

---

[11] Cramer only calls for the use of the (sustaining) pedal in this central movement, in spite of its appropriateness in the outer two.

I suspect it is a protest against what Cramer sees, on the one hand, as shallow virtuosity and skin-deep sentiment, and on the other, the self-satisfied pomposity attendant on the *Concerts of Antient Music*. These were founded in 1776 by noblemen, and granted royal patronage in 1785 when George III became a subscriber. The king was devoted to Handel's music, but he was matched in this by the directors, with the result that this composer was almost the sole representative of older music. The society was frequently criticised for lack of variety and folded in 1848.

Hummel's Op. 106 Piano Sonata in D major (1824) has a *Scherzo all' antico* (or '*in stilo antico*'), whose close imitations and inversions, couched at times in hemiola rhythms, have a flavour of past styles in their deliberateness and weight, even though the sonority is curiously 'Brahmsian' (Ex. 10.15a). The lighter *Alternativo*, however, gives the game away in that the emphasis here is clearly on *Scherzo* rather than *antico* (Ex. 10.15b).

Ex. 10.15a: Hummel, Piano Sonata in D major Op. 106/ii, bb. 0–20.

Ex. 10.15b: Op. 106/ii, bb. 39–43.

When, two years later, Cipriani Potter published his first book of piano Studies, he directed the fourth, a 6/8 Moderato in the rare key of B flat minor, to be played *Con precisione ed accento. Piùtosto nello stile antico*, and although the seriousness of this piece appears to rule out joking (Ex. 10.16a, later harmonised, Ex. 10.16b), there seems little justification for the rubric – in fact the final cadence sounds typically Victorian (Ex. 10.16c).

Ex. 10.16a: Potter, *Studies*, Book I/4, bb. 1–2.

Ex. 10.16b: Book I/4, bb. 11–12.

Ex. 10.16c: Book I/4, ending.

Similarly, in the slow movement of the – in view of his age of just 17 years – astonishing C minor Sonata of 1802–3, Pinto creates a subtle aura of nostalgia, partly through the slow-minuet evocation but also using the same kind of hemiolas (Ex. 10.17) mentioned above in connection with Hummel's Op. 106.

Ex. 10.17: Pinto, Piano Sonata in C minor/ii, bb. 68–78.

Moscheles evokes the 'Ancient Style' twice in Book I of his *24 Characteristic Compositions,* the Piano Studies Op. 70. The preface to No. 7 in B flat major, gives us some hint as to what was expected in this style in the period:

> This lesson being written in the Ancient Style, requires a bold and energetic manner of execution. Except as to the usual change from *forte* to *piano*, and the reverse, its style of performance is not so much to be characterized by expression and feeling, as by giving to the individual parts of every bar a particularly bold and distinct accentuation.[12]

The French version is more informative as to this last sentence, ' ..*d'en rendre les différents traits avec une énergie égale dans chaque mesure.*' ['in giving equal force to the individual features of every bar']. The point seems to be to imitate the precision and crispness of the harpsichord (Ex. 10.18); there are only four instances of graded dynamics in the 70 bars of the piece and no pedalling. There are, however, plenty of *sf*'s distributed throughout what is mostly a three-part texture.

Ex. 10.18: Moscheles, *24 Characteristic Compositions* Op. 70/7, bb. 0–4.

The more specific reference to the ancient style is in the preface to No. 10, and the French adds nothing on this occasion:

> This Study written in the ancient Style (somewhat in that of Scarlatti,) is to afford a practice of Shakes, which must uniformly be executed with a rapid and elastic change

---

[12] Augener edition, 1870.

of fingers; without however, disturbing in the least the quiet and stately character of the whole.

Here also, although the terraced dynamics are not exclusive, they are in the vast majority, and the edition by E. Pauer (Augener, pub. 1886) gives very few examples of 'elastic' finger-changes. There is nothing here specifically reminiscent of the Italian master mentioned, although perhaps there is an 'old-fashioned' feel to the harmonic scheme of the opening four bars in Ex. 10.19a (I–V–V–I), which set the pattern for much of the piece.

Ex. 10.19a: Moscheles, *24 Characteristic Compositions* Op. 70/10, bb. 0–4.

Perhaps there is also a touch of the quirky virtuosity of some of Scarlatti's sonatas suggested near the end in the tricky passage in Ex. 10.19b, which also exploits the piano's range and registral sonorities.

Ex. 10.19b: Op. 70/10, bb. 55–66.

What is interesting in cases such as these, whether humour is intended (as with Cramer) or not, is the lack of stylistic fidelity, which is why, I think, that a kind of generalised past is intended, the musical equivalent of Arcadianism. Certainly these composers were well aware of the true models, Handel, various Bachs – not least J.S.

– and Scarlatti. Moscheles had, in the first of a series of 'Historical Soirées' (London, Feb 1837) attempted to illustrate the differences between 'modern' and 'ancient' music, playing as well as piano music by Weber, Beethoven and himself, some of Bach's '48' and pieces by Scarlatti and Handel on the harpsichord. All the piano schools of the period prescribe a good dose of these composers.

The 'ancient styles' are best found unannounced – and comparatively unalloyed – in unexpected locations in music of the period. I choose as examples some passages from Hummel's *24 Grandes Etudes* Op. 125: the exercise in dotted-note precision evoking Baroque stateliness and restraint (No. IV, Ex. 10.20);

Ex. 10.20: Hummel, *24 Grandes Etudes* Op. 125/IV, bb. 0–8.

the Fughetta of No. VI where the epigrammatic stiffness of the short subject is softened in each of its progressive entries; the delicacy and gentle minor-mode melancholy of the French school of *clavecinistes* can be discerned in No. XX, a delightful butterfly of a piece in E flat minor (Ex. 10.21)

Ex. 10.21: Hummel, *24 Grandes Etudes* Op. 125/XX, bb. 1–2.

and perhaps also in No. X in E minor (Ex. 10.22), with its constant filigree decoration whose similarity to Chopin's in the same key (Ex. 10.23) seems too close to be coincidental.

Ex. 10.22: Hummel, *24 Grandes Etudes* Op. 125/X, bb. 1–3.

Ex. 10.23: Chopin, Etude Op. 25/5, bb. 0–3.

Chopin's was written 1832–4 and published in 1837, Hummel's published in 1833. There is no record of any kind of contact between the two at this period; Chopin remained in Paris and Hummel, based in Weimar, toured only in England in the early 1830s. Speculation is tempting, however.

Hummel's set concludes with another piece having an 'archaic' feel, a fugal exposition in four voices with a redundant entry attached, followed by a coda. Each of the entries (with real answers) is a harmonic and textural variation and requires the utmost digital control and command of keyboard colour: the opening is shown as Ex. 10.24a while Ex. 10.24b gives the fifth ('redundant') entry.

Ex. 10.24a: Hummel, *24 Grandes Etudes* Op. 125/XXIV, bb. 1–4.

Ex. 10.24b: Op. 125/XXIV, bb. 13–16.

The whole set, though not in Chopin's league, requires full, rounded, mature musicianship and knowledge of styles – 'ancient' as well as 'modern' – to do it justice in performance; it well repays the effort.

CHAPTER ELEVEN

Character 5: Other Topics

(i) The military style

The military character is one of the most prevalent during the period, not surprisingly perhaps, considering that for a good deal of this time Europe was at war. The features of the military character are as one would expect: martial dotted rhythms, arpeggiaic fanfares – and the use of brass and high flutes in orchestrated works – and swaggering chords. Mozart rarely referred overtly to events on the world stage, but he does so in two of his orchestral *Contredanses*, both in C major. K. 535, which exists in a piano reduction, is called '*La Bataille*' (The Battle, 1788) referring to the siege of Belgrade (1788–9), and K. 587 of 1789 is called '*Der Sieg vom Helden Coburg*' [The Victory of the Hero, (Coburg-Saalfeld), 1789], commemorating Austrian victories over the Turks. There are also references to the style in other works, notably the variation-finale of his C minor Piano Concerto, K. 491 (1786), both in the opening of the theme and its orchestration, punctuated by timpani and trumpets, and in several of the variations.[1] His satirical *Marche funèbre del Sgr. Maestro Contrapunto* [Funeral March for Maestro Counterpoint] (Ex. 11.1) is a less exalted, but comical instance.

Ex. 11.1: W.A. Mozart, *Marche funèbre del Sgr. Maestro Contrapunto* K. 453a, bb. 1–8.

---
[1] See Chapter Fifteen (ix), Ex. 15.36.

INFLUENCES

Haydn's use of the military style is well known in his *Missa in tempore belli* [Mass in Time of War, called 'Paukenmesse' [Kettledrum-Mass] in Austria and Germany, 1796–7] and, especially the *Missa in angustiis* [Mass in Time of Trouble] known as the 'Nelson' Mass, after the brief visit to Esterháza of the hero of the naval victory over the French at Aboukir. Beethoven's *Three Marches* Op. 45 (pub. 1804) for piano duet were also associated with a public figure, being dedicated to the Princess Maria Esterházy. The *Marcia Funebre sulla morte d'un Eroe* [Funeral March on the Death of a Hero] from the Piano Sonata in A flat major Op. 26 and the second movement of the late Sonata in A major Op. 101, headed *Lebhaft. Marschmässig.* and Vivace alla Marcia [Lively, in the style of a march] testify, among other pieces, to his continued interest in the topic.

Very often such works included, or were based upon, familiar military tunes, as in Carlo Minasi's descriptive *Fantasia on British Infantry Marches*, having the 'British Grenadier's March' as an introduction and also including the March of the 42nd Highlanders and 'The Girl I Left Behind Me'. Another favourite was *Partant pour la Syrie* which was a mixture of folk, operatic and military elements (Ex. 11.2).

Ex. 11.2: *Partant pour la Syrie.*

A tune that became well-known in Britain was *The Rataplan*, a *chansonette* composed by the singer Madame Malibran (Ex. 11.3).

Ex. 11.3: Mme Malibran, *The Rataplan.*

Czerny treats this with a degree of respect in his *Rondo Militaire on the Rataplan*, Op. 415, prefacing it with a long introduction (in F major) and supplying highly contrasting episodes in D and D flat majors, the latter, *dolce legato cantabile*, marked *con duolo* at one point. Czerny also published *Six Military Rondos* Op. 646 as well as Arne's celebrated *Rule, Britannia* and *God Save the Queen*, both arranged as rondos, and he hammers home the military message in his *Grandes Variations Brillantes et Finale Militaire sur une Marche française* for piano with orchestra or with string quartet, Op. 236.

The title-page of a concerted piece of his gives information as to its first performance on site, so to speak: *Le Retour de Kalisch! / Intro / Vars de Concert / sur / Une Marche Favorite executée à Kalisch / Pendant / 'La Revue Des Empereurs' / pour le Piano Forte, / dédiées à Monsieur G.F. Kiallmark, à Londres* with five contrasting variations, the last of which is headed Andante sostenuto alla Marcia, and a coda.

Cramer seems to harness the best of both worlds in celebrating a then recent defeat of the Napoleonic army and using an aria by Handel to do it: his *Kutusoff's Victory, an impromptu* was 'Founded on Handel's celebrated Air of Disdainful of Danger' [2] and combines the military and the Baroque in its canonic opening (Ex. 11.4). (It must be remembered that Handel had been adopted by the British as their national composer.)

Ex. 11.4: J.B. Cramer, *Kutusoff's Victory*, bb. 0–6.

Cramer's *Harvest Home: A Pastoral Divertimento* (already alluded to in Chapter Ten (ii)) for piano and flute *ad lib* has the unusual format of two pastoral movements, a gentle Aria (*dolce* in G major) and a Rondo, Allegro *rustico*, flanking an Allegretto spiritoso en Militaire in E flat major (Ex. 11.5).

Ex. 11.5: J.B. Cramer, *Harvest Home*/ii, bb. 0–4.

One finds strange bedfellows also in Ries: his *Grand Military Divertimento* (which was dedicated to the Duke of York) has a march followed by a rondo *a la Tedesca*. Indeed, this could be the apologia for the title of a Cramer piece dedicated to the 'Duchefs' of Newcastle, *Variety, / a / Fourth Divertimento / for the / Piano Forte / with an Appropriate Prelude / to which is added a / THIRD Grand March. / ...*; the other movements are a waltz and an aria.

---

[2] The battle, difficult to identify, was probably that of Berezina (27–9 November 1812), the inconclusive outcome of which was presented by Russian propaganda as a victory. Casualties on the French side were some 25,000 military and 30,000 non-combatants as opposed to Russian losses of some 20,000. It did, therefore, weaken Napoleon's *Grande Armée* further in its retreat into Poland. The aria, from the oratorio *Deborah*, is now known as 'All dangers Disdaining'.

The opening movement of Field's Sixth Piano Concerto in C major is a Tempo di Marcia, and Dussek's Op. 40 is a *Grand Military Concerto* in B flat major in which, after a surprisingly gentle expression of the military character in the opening movement (Ex. 11.6a and b), the milk of human kindness is entirely banished: the piece lacks a slow movement with the first passing straight to the finale's Allegro Militaire. Evidently this concerto appealed to a wide audience: according to one edition it was 'Perform'd at Opera-House Concerts and Oratorios at Covent Garden'.

Ex. 11.6a: J.L. Dussek, Piano Concerto in B flat major Op. 40/i, first subject (opening).

Ex. 11.6b: Op. 40/i, second subject (opening).

Another popular work was Moscheles's *Alexander Variations* Op. 32 for piano and orchestra, based on '*Marche d'Alexandre; The Fall of Paris*', which preserves the theme's military ebullience at each re-appearance (Ex. 11.7). As an example of nationalism in the period, the full title is worth quoting:

Abschieds-Marsch / das / löbl Infanterie Regiments / KAISER ALEXANDER / bey Gelegenheit seines Ausmarsches von Wien am 12ten April 1815, / zum grafsen Kampfe für Deutschlands Freyheit, und Selbstständigkeit. / Comp und für pf eingerichtet Moscheles.

Ex. 11.7: *Marche d'Alexandre (The Fall of Paris).*

S.S. Wesley's march in *March & Rondo* of 1842 stresses the ominousness of the genre with good understanding of the piano's orchestral possibilities (Ex. 11.8).

Ex. 11.8: S.S. Wesley, *March & Rondo*/March, bb. 24–41.

The *Septett Militaire* in C major, Op. 114 of Hummel (1829) owes its military cut mainly to the inclusion of the trumpet, unusual in a chamber work of this period – 'probably the first trumpet part to appear in chamber music since the time of Bach'.[3] – and to its bold octave opening (Ex. 11.9)

Ex. 11.9: Hummel, *Septett Militaire*/i, opening.

and perhaps also to its rather savage Menuetto in C minor, a demonic scherzo in all but name (Ex. 11.10a). The other instruments – flute, violin, clarinet, cello, double bass and piano – were also a challenging ensemble in a chamber-setting. The trumpet

---

[3] Hellyer-ed./SEPTET-m, Preface.

part is uninteresting for the player, being rather too typically orchestral in its confinement to the lower harmonics; one looks in vain for the writing of Hummel's Trumpet Concerto, although it is perhaps unfair to expect this, since, like Haydn's, it was written for the virtuoso Anton Weidinger and his keyed trumpet, which partook of some of the agility of its valve-endowed descendants. Hummel uses his natural trumpet tellingly, however, in the Menuetto mentioned (Ex. 11.10a)

Ex. 11.10a: Hummel, *Septett Militaire*/iii, bb. 0–8.

and its distant rallying-call sets the tone of the trio in C major (Ex. 11.10b).

Ex. 11.10b: *Septett Militaire*/iii/Trio.

Domenico Corri's Sonata in B flat major of 1808 entitled *L'Augurio Felice* [The Happy Portent] has the finale finishing with a Martiale section, perhaps unexpectedly, as is the case with Cramer's variations on (Mozart's) *'Deh! prendi un dolce amplesso'* headed Alla Marcia, while his namesake, Henri Cramer heads the second of his Four Characteristic Pieces of 1849, (Ex. 11.11), a *Marche Orientale* in G minor, Maestoso lentamente.

Ex. 11.11: H. Cramer, Four Characteristic Pieces/2, bb. 1–4.

The military or martial character was also very popular in other forms, such as variation-sets, in which its absence, in fact, was a rarity. Ries underlines this in his *Fantasia à la mode* by including a Tempo di Marcia as var. 5. Similarly, many of the various sets of dances for public dancing in the early nineteenth century had *militaire* or *alla marcia* numbers. There are also a number of concerted pieces – Dussek's *Military Concerto* has already been mentioned – but there is also Czerny's *Grandes Variations et Finale Militaire sur une Marche Française* Op. 236 (1830) and the *Fantaisie Militaire* of Pixis, both for piano and orchestra.

Many pieces contained sections in military style: Ries has a *Tempo di Marcia* section in the unexpected context of his piano-piece called *The Dream* (to be discussed below) and Dussek's *Fantaisie* in F major Op. 76 (C 248[4]) sports a *Marche Solenelle* Larghetto maestoso ma con moto (Ex. 11.12).

Ex. 11.12: J.L. Dussek, *Fantaisie* in F major C 248/V, bb. 0–4.

The small output of Pinto's short life contains a number of military references, whether so labelled or not. Berlioz, of course, does the same sort of thing in the 'Marche au supplice' [March to the Scaffold] of his *Symphonie fantastique* Op. 14, but the dream by then has become a nightmare and goes on to include a Witches' Sabbath.

Related matters and topics, such as soldiers, castles, etc., appear too: Heller's *Soldatenlied*, the second of a set of three character-pieces Op. 73 (1849) – interesting for having its *Tempo di marcia* theme presented in E flat major while the rest of the

---

[4] The 'C' numbering refers to the Thematic Catalogue of Dussek's works by Howard Allen Craw.

piece is in C major – was also published separately with the more romanticised title of *L'Adieu du Soldat* and contains much dotted-rhythm writing and cymbal-crashings. It would appear that even the highest were not immune to the musical military: Goulding and d'Almaine published (?1810) a piano arrangement of *Bonaparte's March / Quick Step, / and / Josephine's Waltz. / Composed by the / Emperor.*

(ii) Battle Pieces

A particular manifestation of the military style produced a sub-genre of considerable popularity during our period, the Battle Piece. This commemorated a, usually recent, military victory on land or sea and included one or several popular patriotic tunes. Most of them follow the same or a similar sequence of events: after some kind of introduction, the first of the protagonists arrives or becomes noticeable on the scene, heralded usually by its National Anthem or some other obvious nationally-oriented musical signifier. The second appears, similarly announced. There is often a reference of some kind to the day, either in terms of climate – the literary device of 'pathetic fallacy' being invoked at times – or in some other way, such as a reference to a saint in the case of a saint's day – perhaps the musical equivalent of Shakespeare's 'St. Crispin' speech of Henry V at Agincourt. Preparations for the battle (bugle-calls, and so on) are followed by engagement, with representations of general militariness and, more specifically, of cannons and shot. After the battle (which may be in several stages), there is always a ghoulish 'cries of the wounded' section which is swiftly overtaken by a triumphal march and victorious apotheosis with copious lashings of national fervour; again, a National Anthem or similar tunes are prominent.

The battle-piece type is fairly common in orchestral music; Beethoven's 'Battle' Symphony, *Wellington's Victory* and Tchaikovsky's *1812 Overture* – which, though later, refers to this period – are well-known examples. However, given the versatility of the piano, and especially the many stops (including 'Turkish music'[5]) and other ways of changing the tone, it is to be expected that solo pieces would be written with the same subject-matter; indeed, Beethoven himself arranged his 'Battle' Symphony for solo piano. One of the earliest of this type was *The Battle of Prague*, by the Bohemian composer Franz Kotzwara (properly Frantisek Koczwara), which was published in Dublin about 1788, for piano or harpsichord with accompaniments for violin and cello, and drum *ad lib*. It became a *succès fou* throughout Europe and North America in its solo and two-piano arrangements, and could be a useful endorsement to aid sales of other similar pieces, as with J. Blewitt's *The Battle of Salamanca: A grand descriptive Sonata in the style of the Battle of Prague* which he dedicated to the 'Marquis of Wellington'. In John Gildon's piece commemorating the same battle, *The Glorious Victory of Salamanca on the Ever Memorable 22nd of July 1812 ... dedicated to the Duke of Wellington and his Brave and Gallant Warriors* not only are the violin and cello accompaniments *ad lib*, but illuminations and rockets are also; Pl. 43 shows this on the score.

---

[5] See Chapter Five (ii).

The overall plan of this piece is echoed in the bulk of such pieces as shown in Table 3 below:

Table 3: Overall plan of *The Glorious Victory of Salamanca on the Ever Memorable 22nd of July 1812 ... dedicated to the Duke of Wellington and his Brave and Gallant Warriors*

Section	Type	Event	Key
I	March		B flat major
II	Bugle Call		
III	Andante	July 15th Marmont's Army moving & concentrating between Toro & San Romain	D minor
IV	Quick march	Ld Wellington moves the Allies to Concentrate on the Guarana (Drums & Fifes)	
V	Band	[da capo drums & fifes]	G major
VI	Slow march	4th and Light Divisions of Infantry & Major General Auson's brigade of Cavalry marching to Castrejos	F major
[VII]		Close attack with Broad-Swords	
[VIII]	con furia	Grand and Ever Memorable Attack	
[IX]	Adagio	Groans of the Wounded in the Streets & Hospitals	B flat minor
[X]	Bugle Call	God Save the King. Illuminations, Rockets ad lib.	B flat major

Although in Britain little, if any, was seen of the 'other side's' situation, that other side also, of course, commemorated its victories. A battle-piece by a career military-man and composer, Citoyen J.F.A Lemière de Corvey commemorates *La Révolution du 10 Aoust 1792* (see Pl. 44). This '*Révolution*' refers to an incident on the date mentioned in which the Duke of Brunswick, with a Prusso-Austrian army, invaded France and approached Paris, where they were faced with a semi-armed group who, in the nick of time, were saved by the appearance of an army of their countrymen, under Generals Doumouriez and Kellermann. Although the outcome of the battle was inconclusive militarily, it was an enormous political and moral boost for France. A list of the section-headings is sufficient to give the feel of the action:

> La générale battant dans Paris (Moderato) – Le tocsin – Appel de Trompette (Maestoso) – Une Patriote courant dans les fauxbourgs (Allegro moderato) – Chanson de guerre (Gayment) – Etonnement et tumulte dans les fauxbourgs (Allegro) – [the Marseillaise (untitled)] (Maestoso) – Mourir n'est rien – Marchons [from the Marseillaise] (Allegro) – La charge (Presto) – Un espion allant au Chateau (Allegro) – Appel de trompette au chateau (Maestoso) – Discours du roi (Romance) – S'il faut ici presser ma vie (Allegro) – Les Aristocrates (Plus vite) – Vive le roi (Plus lente) – Presto, Arrivée des Patriotes – Combat (Maestoso) – La Générale (Moderato) – Le tocsin – Presto. Les secours arrivent – Le combat continue – Trompette – Trompette – La Gendarmerie donne – La Victoire (Gay) – La Carmagnole (Plus gay)– Ah ca [sic] ira – La Carmagnole (Tres gay).

INFLUENCES 193

This was a popular piece appearing in several editions, with slight differences. Pl. 45 gives page two of the earliest one, from the (untitled) *Marseillaise* to the King's *Romance*.

This piece, dedicated to 'the Shade of William Tell' ['*aux* Mânes *de* Guillaume Tell', see Pl. 44] eschews gloating and the salaciousness of the groaning wounded, and even shows some sympathy for the king, who is allowed a measure of dignity. One does not expect the highest musical quality in such pieces, but they have some interest; however, at their worst – Thomas Smith's *Napoleon's Fall, or the Rise of Paris,* for example – they degenerate into tawdry tub-thumping.

(iii) The hunting style

Another very common type was the hunting style, identified by the subtitle *La chasse,* – sometimes spelt '*chace*' as in Corri's Sonatina in G major/iii, *Allegretto: Rondo a la Chace* – and very occasionally *Die Jagd,* as in Heller's Op. 29, which gives both the French and the German, in a gesture probably more economically than educatively oriented. This style stood halfway between the pastoral and the military and shared some of their features[6]. From the pastoral came the compound (usually 6/8) rhythm and the crotchet-quaver repetition over stretches of the same or similar harmony with occasional pedal-points and drones. From its more bellicose cousin came the fanfare, scaled-down to horn-calls – but with no less menace for the fox or stag, however – and a version of the martial rhythm, this time transmuted to the compound-time ⁶⁄₈ ♩. ♪♪ ♩ ♪ .The opening of Czerny's *Rondeau de chasse* in D major Op. 660 is typical, and the piece goes on to refer to various tunes – *Tom Moody, Whoop Whoop Tally ho! Tally ho!, The Road* and *The Fox Chase.* In the finale of an early piano sonata (appearing as Op. 25 and probably arranged from an accompanied sonata) in F major, J.L. Dussek becomes more specific, entitling it *The Fife Hunt* and although the tune itself possesses none of the 'hunt' characteristics listed above, it does have a folksy lilt about it (Ex. 11.13).

Ex. 11.13: J.L. Dussek, Piano Sonata in F major Op. 25/iii, opening.

Much more amenable, however, is his *La Chasse,* also in F major (1796), which has a slow introduction curiously reminiscent of Beethoven's *Andante favori* and in the same key and register (Ex. 11.14a). This leads to an Allegro fanfare and the theme proper (Ex. 11.14b), both forming the first subject in a sonata-form movement. The second suggests the scurrying of the fox (Ex. 11.14c).

---

[6] See Chapter Eleven above.

Ex. 11.14a: J.L. Dussek, *La Chasse*, Introduction.

Ex. 11.14b: *La Chasse*, bb. 16–20.

Ex. 11.14c: *La Chasse*, second subject.

The English composer John Burton, similarly, and much earlier, alternates these two types – quavers and twisting semiquavers in 6/8 – in the first movement of his First Sonata 'for Harpsichord, organ, or piano Forte' of 1766–7.[7] There is further 'folkiness' here in the snap rhythm (Ex. 11.15a), pedal-points and applied decorations (Ex. 11.15b).

Ex. 11.15a: Burton, Sonata No. 1 in D major/i, bb. 0–4.

---

[7] This work has already been referred to in Chapter One (v).

Ex. 11.15b: Sonata No. 1, bb. 49–54.

Herz's rather disjointed *Fantaisie chivalresque* Op. 202, with an *Introduction* in Spanish rhythm, and a *marcia* followed by a *variation* with many changes of tempo, ends with a finale *Allegro giojoso* speeding up to a *Doppio movimento* (a double speed *Alla breve*) at the end. The last of his *Trois airs variés* Op. 39/3 (on the Scottish tune 'We're a' nodden') has a finale (var. 6) *La chasse*, Allegro molto. This was a popular finale-type in sonatas or as free-standing rondos, and was still going strong at the end of our period, as testified by J.B. Cramer's *The Chase* Op. 114 of 1851, one of his very last pieces, written when he was eighty. After a moderately paced *Introduzione,* the main movement comes, headed *Stile di caccia* and it revels in the characteristic fanfares (Ex. 11.16, bb. 0–8), the horses' jogging (bb. 9–16) and the zigzagging fox (bb. 17 to the end).

Ex. 11.16: J.B. Cramer, *The Chase* Op. 114, bb. 0–32.

Ex. 11.16 continued

(iv) Nature pieces

The piano literature of the period shows several other topics that became miniature genre-types, the handy titles of which encouraged sales and provided moulds, however plastic, into which the composer could pour his or her musical plaster.

A number of these can be seen as sub-genres of larger ones,[8] such as nature-pieces, being more specifically descriptive of animals, insects, birds, plants, and so on. There was, of course, no shortage of this topic in the other arts in the early nineteenth century. From a concern for nature as an organism – already implicit in Hegel's *Weltgeist* – with its symbiosis of plants, animals and man, to emotional and spiritual identification with them, concern for, and participation in, nature (or personified Nature) is one of the primary traits of Romanticism. The polymathic Goethe was a botanist as well as an artist and his concern for nature always shines through, not only, for instance, in his poem *Die Metamorphose der Pflantzen*, ['The Metamorphosis of Plants'] being named after his botanical treatise of the same title, but in the detail of many poems, such as *Frühling übers Jahr* ['Perennial spring']:

> Primeln stolzieren
> So naseweis,
> Schalkhafte Veilchen,
> Versteckt mit Fleiß;
> Was auch noch alles

---

[8] Some of these are looked at under various headings in this book.

> Da regt und webt,
> Genug, der Frühling,
> Er wirkt und lebt.

['Primroses swagger so cheekily, and mischievous violets are carefully hidden – and much else too, moving, and weaving in and out: in a nutshell, spring is [here,] active and alive.'][9]

Schiller's concern is enshrined in his dictum *'Raum für alle hat die Erde'* ['The Earth has room for all'] from the poem *Der Alpenjäger* (1805)[10] spoken by the spirit of the mountain in restraining the hunter from killing a gazelle. We have already seen the same sentiments in art from the early nineteenth century and examples abound in English poetry also: one will suffice, from John Clare, who set new standards of nature-bonding, being very much a man *of* the country as well as *in* it. In 'The Robin's Nest' (1830) Clare, like Byron's Childe Harold, sees himself as part of the natural order, though in a less all-embracing, more intimate and loving way:

> The birds unbid come round about to give
> Their music to my pleasures; wild flowers live
> About as if for me; they smile and bloom
> Like uninvited guests that love to come,
> Their wildwood fragrant offerings all to bring,
> Paying me kindness like a thronèd king.
> Lost in such ecstasies, in this old spot
> I feel that rapture which the world hath not,
> That joy like health that flushes in my face
> Amid the brambles of this ancient place,
> Shut out from all but that superior power
> That guards and glads and cheers me every hour,
> That wraps me like a mantel from the storm
> Of care, and bids the coldest hope be warm,
> That speaks in spots where all things silent be,
> In words not heard but felt ...[11]

Music also partakes of the nature-cult on all levels and to it belong such categories as the ever-popular butterfly pieces, for example, William Sterndale Bennett's 'Der Schmetterling', No. 5 of his *Preludes and Lessons* Op. 33 (1853), two rondos entitled *Les Papillons* by, respectively, Bochsa (Op. 35, pub. 1810) and Hérold (Op. 18 pub. c.1820), Steibelt's Rondo *Les Papillons* (with typical note-painting, Ex. 11.17a and b),

Ex. 11.17a: Steibelt, *Les Papillons*, Introduction, b. 3.

---

[9] Goethe/SELECTED; my translation.
[10] Schiller/*GEDICHTE*.
[11] Clare/POEMS.

Ex. 11.17b: *Les Papillons*, bb. 31–3.

and Schumann's *Papillons* Op. 2 (1829–31). Also representative of this category are flower-pieces, like the same composer's *Blumenstück* Op. 19, and H. Cramer's *La Rose. Pensée sympathétique* (Ex. 11.18), a slightly cloying *pièce de salon* (though not so called) and *La Violette. Etude brillante*, whose 'brilliance', however, holds little threat for anyone beyond the first couple of grades.

Ex. 11.18: H. Cramer, *La Rose. Pensée sympathétique*, bb. 1–4.

In a laudatory article in the *Neue Zeitschrift für Musik* in 1855, Liszt wrote of the close link between Schumann's titles (mentioning *Papillons* among others) and the music itself: 'They exhibit the most subtle differences between the gentle gleam of the flower and the butterfly's fluttering around rose cups ...'[12]

Perhaps the most extreme, if not the most entirely serious, case of the invasion of music by nature is the music of 'Flora' an amateur composer/teacher in London, in which the notes, and so on, of the scores are depicted as delicately coloured flowers (see back cover); I expand a little on this in Chapter Twenty-Nine: Didactic music.

(v) Dream pieces

Liszt's flowery prose in describing Schumann's music brings to mind another topic that is exemplified in his own *Liebesträume* ['Love-dreams'], pianistic depictions of dreams or reveries. Much of the time, such pieces have the aura of general 'dreaminess' rather than recalling a specific dream. They often have the feel of the early nocturne, with their pastel chromatics, unobtrusive rhythm and slow rate of harmonic change, even when allied to other types, as in Voss's *Rêverie à La Valse* (pub. *c.*1850) (Ex. 11.19) whose tranquil mood remains undisturbed even in the central dominant episode.

---

[12] Quoted in Todd-ed./SCHUMANN, p. 355.

Ex. 11.19: Voss, *Rêverie à La Valse*, bb. 0–9.

The very title and directions – *Rêverie et Allegresse,* Con sentimento melanconico – of the first of Moscheles's *Quatre Grandes Etudes de Concert* Op. 111 suggests a similar tone.

Very different is the same composer's 'Der Traum' [translated as 'A Dream'], No. 11 from the twelve *Charakteristische Studien* Op. 95 (pub. 1836). Addressing what one might still call the Freudian elements of the dream often results in pieces of some ingenuity, and Moscheles creates an effect of something slightly more unsettling than the expected dreaminess almost from the first bar, with the wide gap between the hands and the murmuring inner voice becoming more ominous as it descends into the bass register (Ex. 11.20a).

Ex. 11.20a: Moscheles, *Charakteristische Studien* Op. 95/11, bb. 1–18.

Ex. 11.20a continued

The simple device of keeping the general shape of this figure (marked (*x*) in b. 2), especially providing it with an octave 'shadow', mostly in a lower register and thereby rendering the piece effectively a *perpetuum mobile*, suggests the feeling, so common in dreams, that things are both what they appear to be and yet contain other meanings at the same time. This amalgamation of different personalities in one person and multiple places in one location is also to be seen in the 'reinventions' of a motif from the theme (marked (*y*), bb. 7–8 in Ex. 11.20a) and Ex. 11.20b and c – each an *alter ego* of the other – during the central *Grandioso* section in the mediant major (D) where the four semiquaver figure becomes triplets.

Ex. 11.20b: Op. 95/11, bb. 81–3.

Ex. 11.20c: Op. 95/11, bb. 59–61.

There is also a hint of this in the subtlety with which these triplets themselves are reconverted into the undulating figure for the return of the opening (Ex. 11.20d).

Ex. 11.20d: Op. 95/11, bb. 91–6.

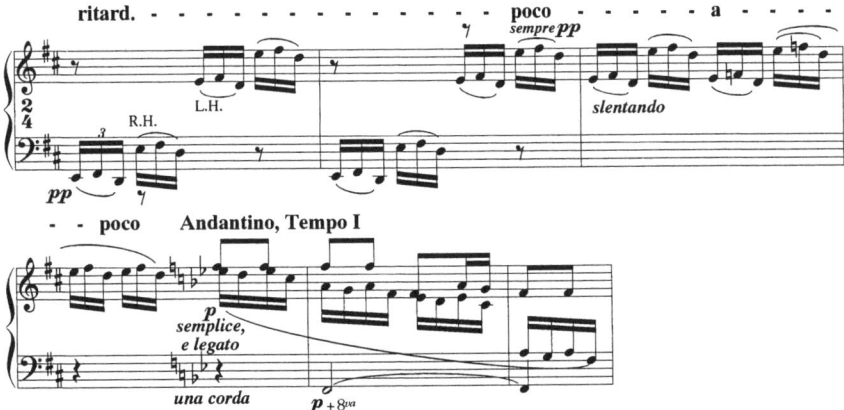

Another kind of 'shadowing' is discernible in the relationship between the bass and treble lines which are very often the same rhythmically, even in the syncopated bars (bb. 13–17 in Ex. 11.20a above). The piano's registers are used effectively, especially the bass, as in the ending (Ex. 11.20e),

Ex. 11.20e: Op. 95/11, ending.

and there are even rapid eye movements, though Moscheles prefers a more poetic tag, as Ex. 11.20f shows.

Ex. 11.20f: Op.95/11, bb. 55–6.

Moscheles joins a number of 'minor' composers in this period who remain seriously underestimated by our present-day acquiescence to judgements, which are neither always purely musical nor based on a fair sampling of their works.

Some of these dream features are apparent in a fine and much earlier dream piece from another neglected composer, Ferdinand Ries. *The Dream*, which Beethoven called '*Il Sogno*', was singled out by him as 'particularly delightful' after he heard the Archduke Rudolph play it.[13] Nicholas Temperley says of this piece: '[it] is full of Beethoven references ... but it also contains superbly original passages, and is remarkable for the degree of unpredictability that it adds to a sonata-based structure. It seems to follow an external program, whose details, however, have not been preserved.'[14]

The opening Larghetto *con moto* (Ex. 11.21a) abounds in harmonic instability, interrupted cadences and chromatic movement, and commences with a low scale where, at the last minute, the hands get 'out of sync'. There is also a flutter of terror and register-contrast, before settling into a more *cantabile* section (Moderato *e molto espressivo*) with a similar kind of top/bottom parallelism to the Moscheles piece dealt with above.

Ex. 11.21a: Ries, *The Dream*, bb. 1–29.

---

[13] Anderson-ed./BEETHOVEN, Vol.II, p. 571.
[14] Temperley-ed./LONDON-m/15, p. xv.

Ex. 11.21a continued

Also similar is the way in which this theme reappears in different guises, although Ries is more radical here. First, it is transferred to the middle register against a lovely countermelody (Ex. 11.21b),

Ex. 11.21b: *The Dream*, bb. 31–5.

and later, in an episode in F sharp major, it is given in 3/8 (Ex. 11.21c).

Ex. 11.21c: *The Dream*, F sharp major episode.

In another section, it dons full military uniform for the *Tempo di Marcia* (Ex. 11.21d) and in the final section of the piece, a varied reprise of the main theme, it appears in 6/8 (Ex. 11.21e), together with its transference to the middle voice with counter-melody analogous to its similar treatment before.

Ex. 11.21d: *The Dream*, March episode.

Ex. 11.21e: *The Dream*, Final section.

Schumann's rapt 'Träumerei' ['Dreaming'], although of the 'dreamy' type mentioned, gets this quality not from the impulse towards drawing-room sentiment, but from the fact that it belongs to the set *Kinderszenen* [*Scenes from Childhood*] Op. 15: this dreaming is that of childhood innocence. It, too, has different facets of the same theme, but these are less radically articulated. What changes here is the upward leap at the end of the phrase (marked *), giving rise to new harmonies and harmonic functions each of the four times it appears (discounting repeats). Ex. 11.22a–d demonstrate these.

Ex. 11.22a–d: R. Schumann, *Kinderszenen* Op. 15/7 bb. 0–3, 6–7, 10–11 and 22–3.

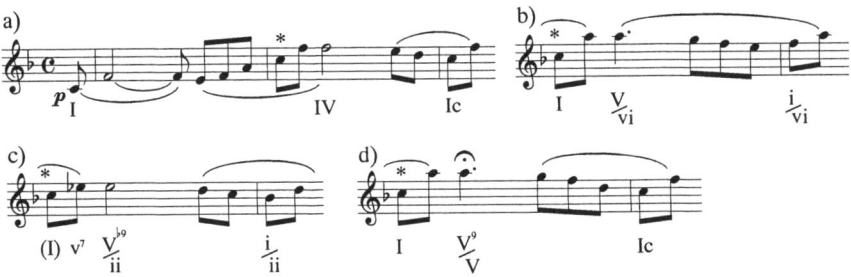

(vi) The Nocturne

I mentioned above the similarity of mood between a certain type of dream piece and the early nocturne. This genre is, of course, in large part the very embodiment of such a style, and the choice of name given to Field's pioneering pieces of this kind bears testimony to this fact, in spite of the variety of mood present. In fact, Liszt, in the preface to his edition of some of Field's nocturnes, writes of the Irish composer-performer 'dreaming' rather than 'playing' these works in concerts. This most quintessentially Romantic genre has been so thoroughly and excellently documented that it is unnecessary for me to spend much space on it here, except to make a few observations centred on the instrument.

The nocturne was bound up with the development of the piano, especially the British and French instruments and was the piano's first dedicated genre-type. Field is credited with its invention, although the familiar *bel canto* melody with more restricted arpeggiaic accompaniment is also to be found in French piano music straddling the change of the century.[15] The texture implies the possibilities of the period piano – as, indeed, does the *Song Without Words* – in its essential layout of more-or-less sustained melody and subordinate accompaniment, although in fact it is more accurate to speak of distinct melody- and bass-lines, and accompanimental layer. This implies opportunities for a relationship between the outer parts, which may be harmonic, linear – *quasi*-contrapuntal – colouristic, or any combination of these.

Thus, in Field's first Nocturne,[16] (before 1812), the left hand has a double *Alberti*, based on the quavers ('x' in Ex. 11.23) as well as the dotted crotchets. It revels in an interesting mixture of dissonance and consonance on different levels, an example being the *échappé* note F in b. 1, which is dissonant with the prevailing E flat major harmony of the bar, but consonant (or at least neutral) with the B♭ of the larger-scale *Alberti* (the x-s); the case of the right-hand C in the next bar is similar. The pattern of the larger *Alberti* in b. 3 is altered in a later revision (1831) to avoid consecutive

---

[15] See Rowland/NOCTURNE, pp. 36ff.

[16] The numbering of Field's Nocturnes is beset with problems, due to different editions, frequent revisions, and the inclusion of pieces that also exist in different genres, such as Pastorale and so on. I am using the numbering and dating in Langley-ed./FIELD-m.

octaves with the melody. On the other hand, Field is not shy of using this technique to highlight the linear motion through the first chromatic passing-note in a piece which has very few (bb. 9–10). This flattened note was also a later revision.

Ex. 11.23: Field, Nocturne No. 1 in E flat major, bb. 0–11.

In the next Nocturne, he draws attention to the compound *Alberti* by directing the larger to be sustained for the whole beat (Ex. 11.24).

Ex. 11.24: Field, Nocturne No. 2 in C minor, bb. 0–4.

On occasion, the inner accompanimental layer can also contribute more by 'pointing out' the melody in some way, as in Nocturne No. 17A (*c*.1809, also published as *Pastorale*) (Ex. 11.25a) where it provides momentary harmony to the B in b. 1, and Field extends this into the textural basis for the continuation of the tune later (Ex.

11.25b). Interesting also here is his use of a characteristic piano flourish to return to the prevalent keyboard register in which the melody is sited when his little 'fill-in' cadential figure led elsewhere (see b. 4 in Ex. 11.25a).

Ex. 11.25a: Field, Nocturne No. 17A in A major, bb. 0–4.

Ex. 11.25b: No. 17A, bb. 8–12.

Parallelism in highlighting moments in the melody by the inner part is also to be found in No. 4 (1817) and Field indulges in a similar technique to that used by Robert Schumann in *Träumerei*, mentioned under the last heading (v), that of sending the melody in a different harmonic direction at each subsequent reappearance (marked 1, 2, 3 and 4 in Ex. 11.26).

Ex. 11.26: Field, Nocturne No. 4 in A major, bb. 1–16.

Ex. 11.26 continued

Occasionally, this inner action attains independence and, in No. 7 in C major (comp. 1821 and sometimes called the *Rêverie-Nocturne*) becomes the melody of the piece, forming an interesting relationship with the right-hand's single, but subsequently decorated, note and underpinned by the tonic pedal (Ex. 11.27).

Ex. 11.27: Field, Nocturne No. 7 in C major, bb. 0–13.

This extremely inventive use of the contemporary piano also reminds us that Field's accompanimental figures – like Chopin's, but to a lesser extent – are quite considerably more varied than the 'textbook' nocturne suggests, however. This is attested to by the chord-arpeggios of No. 6, the unrolling of the accompaniment from a single note in No. 11 (1832, Ex. 11.28),

Ex. 11.28: Field, Nocturne No. 11 in E flat major, bb. 1–10.

and the complex texture of six interactive but independent voices of No. 3 (1812, Ex. 11.29). Apart from their intrinsic value, these Nocturnes were a worthy launch pad for Chopin's stratospheric flight.

Ex. 11.29: Field, Nocturne No. 3 in A flat major, bb. 1–6.

(vii) Religious character

Although the *Consolation* – French pronunciation being implied in almost every case – is rarely overtly religious, it is possible to place it within this category, if near the boundary; it also partakes of something of the peaceful aspect of the dream. J.L. Dussek's *La consolation* in B flat major (C 212, appearing both as Op. 61 and Op. 62, pub. 1807) derives its overall feeling of reassurance from the theme itself, with clear outline melodically, rhythmically and harmonically, lack of real opposition between melody and accompaniment, repetition of short cells and 'feminine' cadences (Ex. 11.30a).

Ex. 11.30a: J.L. Dussek, *La consolation* in B flat major Op. 61(62), bb. 0–8.

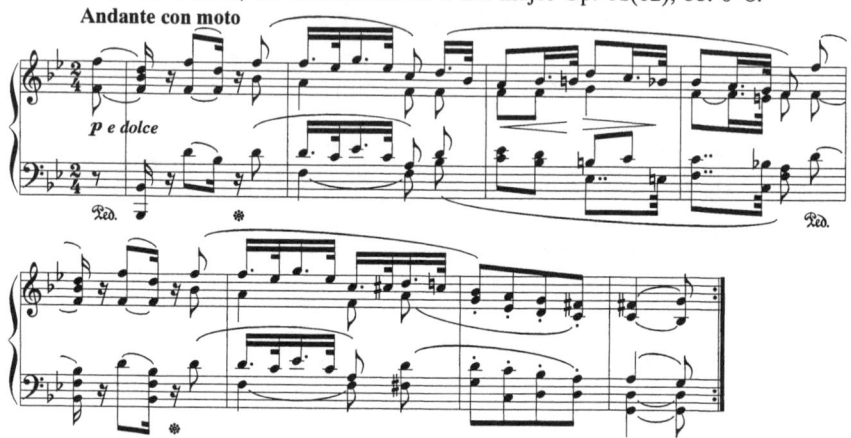

In both of the episodes of its rondo outline, some kind of opposition – one might almost say adversity – is encountered. In the first, in the tonic minor, the running semiquaver bass, firmly under the control of the slightly self-righteous top-line (Ex. 11.30b), begins to dictate the character of the music, but is subdued before the theme appears.

Ex. 11.30b: Op. 61(62), bb. 24–32.

This is followed by an arpeggiaic version of itself in triplets (Ex. 11.30c).

Ex. 11.30c: Op. 61(62), bb. 66–8.

Something similar happens in the second episode with demisemiquavers, which are also vanquished and, this time, the returning theme is followed by another variation of itself in demisemiquavers (Ex. 11.30d).

Ex. 11.30d: Op. 61(62), bb. 133–4.

Liszt's set of six *Consolations* (1849–50) are of a sentimental-religious type, and include a nocturne (No. III) and a chorale-ish one (No. IV), though neither are so-called. The former, in D flat major, makes much of third-related keys, the second phrase of the long strung-out melody cadencing into F minor and moving from there to A flat major: this is the key into which the piece sidesteps without warning for a short cadenza with sustaining pedal held, before ending with a first inversion third (F and A♭).

The religious side of Liszt – and it is an ever-present one – shows itself more obviously much later than this period, with works such as *Urbi et orbi, bénédiction papale, Sancta Dorothea, In festo transfiguronis*, and the two *Légendes*, dealing with St Francis of Assisi and St Francis de Paul respectively. It is, however, represented in an early collection of pieces which would be revised 1845–52, the *Harmonies poétiques et religieuses* (S 154, 1834, published the following year). The title is that of the set of poems by Lamartine (1830) that inspired it, and to whom the work was dedicated, and it marks the emergence of Liszt as a mature composer. The general tenor is of the poetic *rêverie* kind and it ends with an Andante religioso; the same spirit pervades another religiously entitled work of the same year, the three *Apparitions* (S 155).

The later revised version (S 173, 1845–52) of the *Harmonies* are much more specific in their religious intents, as a mere listing of the ten titles will show: 1 Invocations, 2 Ave Maria, 3 Bénédiction de Dieu dans la solitude, 4 Pensée des morts, 5 Pater noster, 6 Hymne de l'enfant à son réveil, 7 Funérailles, 8 Miserere d'après Palestrina, 9 Andante lagrimoso, 10 Cantique d'amour. Liszt adds to the religiosity by incorporating liturgical elements, such as his block-chordal intonation of the plainsong *De profundis* in 'Pensé des morts' as a *recitativo*, in which he approximates the Fourth Psalm-tone (Ex. 11.31).

Ex. 11.31: Lizst, *Harmonies Poétiques et Religieuses*/4, bb. 58–61.

Uniting the holy realms and the landscape of the solitary wanderer are the three books of the *Album d'un voyageur* [*Diary of a Traveller*] S 156, (1835–6, pub. 1842). Some of them are overtly religious, such as 'Les cloches de G...'[Genève] (The Bells of Geneva) and 'La chapelle de Guillaume Tell' (The Chapel of William Tell); the rest are of a pastoral kind, and/or folk-based.[17] These pieces which were also revised during the Weimar period and reissued in 1855 as the first of the *Années de pèlerinage: Suisse* (*Years of Pilgrimage: Switzerland*). Czerny's Op. 580 is subtitled *Chant réligieux des Orphelins de Vienne* [*Religious chant of the Orphans of Vienna*]: the title, however, is *Impromptu Sentimental*, one of several pieces so-called, and the chord-scheme of the introductory bars is that of Gounod's *Ave Maria* (Ex. 11.32).

Ex. 11.32: Czerny, *Improptu Sentimental* Op. 580, bb. 1–10.

The last of Henri Cramer's *Four Characteristic Pieces* (pub. 1849) is a *Chanson religieuse*, a lugubrious Adagio, (Ex. 11.33) and Pinto abbreviates what appears to be

---

[17] Some are mentioned in Chapter Nineteen.

the same word – '*Reliege*' – to which is appended in handwriting '*e u x*' in variation 8 of the second of his *Three Favorite Airs* Op. 2.

Ex. 11.33: H. Cramer, *Four Characteristic Pieces*/4, bb. 1–16.

Very occasionally one comes across the direction *Religioso* to denote the same kind of approach as in the pieces mentioned. One of Bertini's *25 Etudes Faciles et Progressives* Op. 100 includes a *Religioso*, and the opening movement of Henselt's Piano Concerto in F minor (headed Allegro pathetico) has in its development section a '*quatuor con sordini*' (a muted string quartet playing a *religioso* chorale in C major (♩ = 112) (Ex. 11.34).

Ex. 11.34: Henselt, Piano Concerto in F minor/i, development section.

The other side of the religious coin is, of course, evil, often personified in the devil, and the closely related macabre, and, in the music of our period, the dark has a higher profile than the light. Again, many of the works showing the 'diabolic' side of Liszt lie outside of my scope,[18] but a few do not, such as the *Malédiction* (Curse) and

---

[18] So, unfortunately, does the *Scherzo diabolico* of Alkan (pub. 1857).

the *Totentanz* (Dance of Death), both for piano and orchestra – and both with solo parts that are more conventionally 'devilish' also, especially the *Totentanz*.

Ghosts and spirits, on the borderlines of religion, are well-represented in the period – the eerie *tremolandi*, which gave the nickname '*Geister*' ('Ghost') to Beethoven's Piano Trio Op.70/1 (for an example see Chapter Twenty-Four (iii)), the use of the same technique with widely spaced instruments (flute, cello and piano) in var. VI of the set that makes up Hummel's Trio in A major Op. 78 (*c*.1818) (Ex. 11.35a),

Ex. 11.35a: Hummel, Trio in A major Op.78/var. VI, bb. 1–6.

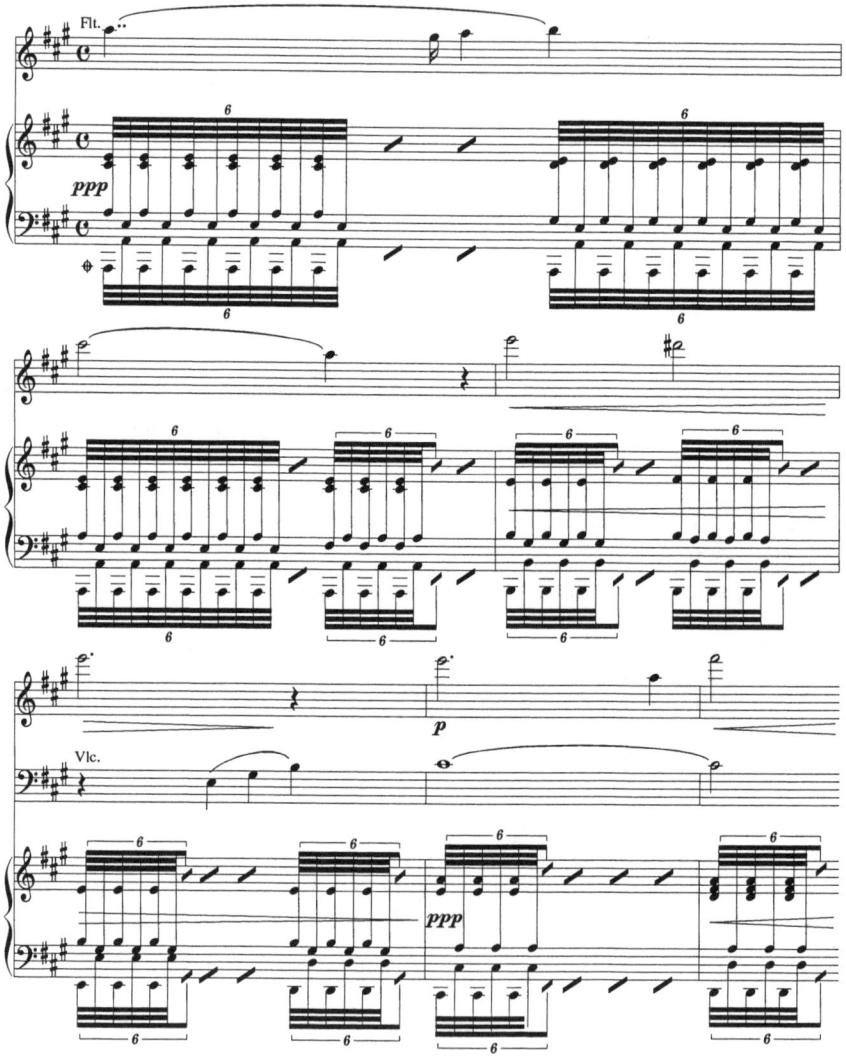

reversing the texture with the piano on top (Ex. 11.35b),

Ex. 11.35b: Op. 78/var. VI, bb. 9–16.

and the last of Czerny's 6 *Brilliant Rondos* Op. 657, The Sailor's Grave, also revelling in *tremolo* with the melody in the bass (Ex. 11.36).

Ex. 11.36: from Czerny, *6 Brilliant Rondos* Op. 657/6.

Clara Wieck's Op. 5, the *Quatre pièces caractéristiques*, (composed between 1835 and 1836, before she became Frau Schumann) contain two pieces in this vein: the first is an 'Impromptu: Le Sabbat', headed Allegro furioso (Ex. 11.37), which revels in ambiguities in melody, rhythm and harmony,

Ex. 11.37: Clara Wieck, *Quatre pièces caractéristiques* Op. 5/1, bb. 1–10.

and the last, 'Le Ballet des Revenants' [Ghost-ballet], the opening of which is given in Chapter Twenty-One below, Ex. 21.26; Ex. 11.38 gives the original and – in terms of pianistic insight as well as dramatic sensibility – highly effective ending, with the ghosts reluctantly melting back into the shadows.

Ex. 11.38: Clara Wieck, *Quatre pièces caractéristiques* Op. 5/4, ending.

Occasionally the pieces feature spirits which are well-known folk-entities, such as the Lorelei, but these cases are better discussed under the heading of Personification (see Chapter Nine above).

CHAPTER TWELVE

Received Forms 1: The Minuet (and Scherzo)

Two genres which, because of the simplicity of their outline, their popularity and their longevity, carried over from a previous era into that under discussion, were the minuet and the rondo, the second of which is the subject of the next chapter. One comes across the enigmatic *Siciliana* or *Siciliano* occasionally, but this had long lost sight of its obscure dance-origins, and become a 'style' in the sense of the 'hunting style'. In compound time, most commonly in 6/8, its leisurely tempo and a characteristic lilting rhythm ♩. ♪♪ ♩ ♪ gave it the character of a slow pastoral jig. It was immortalised by Mozart in his use of it in minor keys, as in the distraught Adagio of the Piano Sonata in F major, K. 280 (189e),[1] the beautiful slow movement of the A major Piano Concerto K. 488 and, above all, the magnificent Rondo in A minor K. 511.[2]

(i) The minuet as component

Although the minuet (*menuet*[Fr.], *Menuett, Menuetto* [Ger.] or *minuetto* [It.]) was not a core member of the Baroque suite of dances – Allemande, Courante, Sarabande and Gigue (in their various national nomenclatures) – its ubiquity almost made it a contender: it also led a separate existence outside the suite. In moderate or slow triple time and of French aristocratic origin, the suite survived as a dance and as an instrumental piece through and beyond the Classical period, the simplicity of the overall shape,

$$M^a :\|M^b :\| T^a(\text{or } M2^a) :\| T^b(\text{or } M2^b) :\| M^a \mid M^b \|$$
(where M = minuet and T = trio)

– with the a-sections ending in the dominant (in major-key works) or relative major (in minor-key ones) – making it a useful foil to the new more intellectually orientated sonata-allegro movements. Consequently it became almost a founder-

---

[1] See Chapter Fourteen (iv) including examples.
[2] See Chapter Thirteen (v) for a discussion of this piece.

member of the symphony, string quartet, sonata, even, to an extent, the concerto,[3] and it continued to make its presence felt in the later scherzo.

As an important component of the piano sonata – especially the two-movement form – from the beginning, the minuet was accepted by composers from early on in the letter if not always in the spirit. Thus some leeway was allowed them for a measure of experimentation in other ways, and this threatened to become a feature of the Classical minuet: Mozart's and Haydn's contrapuntal targeting of this movement in their symphonies and (especially) their chamber works are among the joys of the type. Haydn's Op. 76/2 in D minor with its tonic-key minuet in stark unaccompanied two-part canon at the octave earned it the nickname *Hexenmenuett* [Witches' Minuet] and there are a number of examples in Mozart including his String Quintet in D major K. 593/iii and the C minor Wind Serenade K. 388 (384a)/iii – which he arranged for string quintet (K. 406 (516b) – with each section of the minuet in two-part canon, and each section of the trio in two-part canon *al rovescio* (backwards).

Such techniques are not confined to these genres, however. Haydn's two-movement Piano Sonata in E flat major (H:XVI:25) of 1773 has, as its finale, a minuet in two-part canon at the octave, unaccompanied (except for a few instances of third-doubling) and with *Imitazione* written under the lower part. In H:XVI:26/ii in A major, he gives us a *Menuetto al Rovescio*, in which the second parts (the 'b' sections) of both minuet and trio are the same as the 'a' sections but played backwards: Ex. 12.1 gives the last four bars of the M^a section, reversed to become the first four of the M^b section.

Ex. 12.1: J. Haydn. Piano Sonata in A major H:XVI:26/ii, end of M^a into M^b.

Because of the minuet's tendency to repeat or imitate material, whether on the level of sections, phrases, figures or even single notes, and because of its origin in the physical dance, there are times when one senses that this kind of latent physicality translates itself, through the composer's notation and the player's performance, into musical gesture and articulation. This is, of course, not confined to the minuet or even to dances in general: it has been suggested that eighteenth-century dance has strongly influenced the Classical style itself as well as its immediate precursors[4]. It is, however, particularly true of the minuet because of the tightness of its form and the fact that it is associated with grace and stylisation, albeit somewhat archaic in this period. In the paired minuets of Haydn's Sonata No. 43 in A flat major (H:XVI:43), the crispness of the first two bars would certainly lose little on the harpsichord (Ex. 12.2a), but the carefully articulated (for the eighteenth century)

---

[3] See 'The Sonata' (Chapter Thirteen) and 'The Concerto' (Chapters Sixteen–Eighteen).
[4] Reichart/DANCE, p. 56.

following bars and most of the rest – particularly the graceful rise and middle-voice slurring in bb. 9 and 10 – would lose much (Ex. 12.2b).

Ex. 12.2a: J. Haydn, Piano Sonata in A flat major H:XVI:43/iii, bb. 0–4.

Ex. 12.2b: H:XVI:43/iii, bb. 8–12.

The different articulations in the minuet finale of No. 59 (H:XVI:49) in E flat major between the wedges of the repeated right-hand notes on different beats contrast, both with the slurred bass duplets, and with the smoother triplets following (Ex. 12.3a).

Ex. 12.3a: J. Haydn, Piano Sonatat in E flat major H:XVI:49/iii. bb. 0–4.

A similar contrast occurs later, this example also showing the register-contrast and a traversing of the period piano's entire compass (Ex. 12.3b).

Ex. 12.3b: H:XVI:49/iii, bb. 24–32.

It is difficult not to detect a similarly choreographic gesture in Mozart's repeated notes in the Andante cantabile middle movement from the Piano Sonata in C major K. 330 (300h, 1783). Although not so called, this is a minuet in F major with a trio in the parallel minor, and the three repeated notes are presented in a variety of pianistic guises calling for a good number of different articulations, making them meaningless on any instrument but the piano, ideally the period piano; Ex. 12.4a gives a selection of these.

Ex. 12.4a; W.M. Mozart, Piano Sonata in C major K. 330 (300h)/ii, opening, bb. 4–5, 12–15, 20–1, 62–3 and 34–5.

When one includes the non-monotonic version of this rhythm, the range of articulations increases (Ex. 12.4b and c).

Ex. 12.4b: K. 330 (300h)/ii, bb. 8–12.

Ex. 12.4c: K. 330 (300h)/ii, bb. 2–3, 3-4, 18-9, 39–40 and 24–6.

Although he did write some, the minuet for piano didn't seem to attract Beethoven very much. All three of his first group of published sonatas Op. 2 have a movement in 3/4 with the minuet-and-trio outline, but only the first is called '*Menuetto*' and its unusual phrase-structure of 4 + 4 + 4 + 2, followed by 2 + 2 + 4 + 2 + 4 bars (with several overlaps) would certainly have made for some interesting socio-choreographic misalignments at court.

The other two works have the corresponding movements labelled 'Scherzo' (of which more shortly). The next sonata, Op. 7 in E flat major has a similar movement and, lacking a title, its *Allegro* direction tilts it towards the Scherzo type; the second part has a hint of the canonic imitation noted in connection with minuets, as does the third (penultimate) movement of Op. 10/3, which is labelled '*Menuetto*' (Ex. 12.5).

Ex. 12.5: Beethoven, Piano Sonata in D major Op. 10/3/iii, bb. 16–25.

With the predominant reversion to the three-movement sonata and the preference for the scherzo henceforth, minuets become much less common. Op. 22 (B flat major), another four-movement work, has one with no indication of tempo, but its graceful opening is dispelled by the second part (Ex. 12.6a and b).

Ex. 12.6a: Beethoven, Piano Sonata in B flat major Op. 22/iii, bb. 0–3.

Ex. 12.6b: Op. 22/iii, bb. 8–12.

Op. 54 in F major has 'In tempo d'un Menuetto' as a tempo-direction over its first movement, no doubt suggested by the lilting rhythm and its repetitions, and Beethoven might easily have used the designation for the first of Op. 90's two movements. Here, a minuet, associated with higher registers, is overlaid on a more unruly scherzo, mostly confined to lower registers, and the duality is hinted at in the opening (Ex. 12.7).

Ex. 12.7: Beethoven, Piano Sonata in E minor, Op. 90/i, bb. 0–14.

However, Beethoven makes ample amends for his neglect of the minuet by couching the theme of one of his greatest sets of variations, those forming the finale of the E major Sonata, Op. 109, in the form of one of the older, slower, more stately Baroque types, that without anacrusis and with a tendency to stress the second beat of the bar (as in Ex. 12.8), either by decoration, harmonic stress, or using one of the three most common rhythmic gambits:

Although this could also be taken as a sarabande, the more 'Classical' minuet seems somehow more appropriate.

Ex. 12.8: Beethoven, Piano Sonata in E major Op. 109/iii, opening.

In spite of there being about as many minuets in Schubert's sonatas as scherzos, they are themselves often closet scherzos with a tendency to boisterousness, especially once honour has been satisfied in a more-or-less normative first section. It may be to do with his well-known reverence for Beethoven, or with the fact that, in the early sonatas at any rate, they are often the finales. The *Menuetto* in A minor from the unfinished hybrid sonata in C major, (D 279, 1815), is an example; Ex. 12.9a shows the opening of the first section and Ex. 12.9b the intensified opening part of the second.

Ex. 12.9a: Schubert, Piano Sonata in C major D 279/iii, bb. 0–4.

Ex. 12.9b: D 279/iii, bb. 16–20.

But on occasion, even in these early sonatas, the movement seems to break its bounds without quite losing the feel of the basic dance. In the *Menuetto* of the E flat major, (D 568, 1817) the rhythm of the little dotted figure in b. 2 is used for the almost parodistic echo in b. 9 leading on to the unexpected turn to the relative minor (Ex. 12.10).

Ex. 12.10a/b: Schubert, Piano Sonata in E flat major D 568/iii, bb. 0–4 and 9–10.

It is itself parodied in the manner of a Swiss mountain song, becomes an inner voice in a three-part texture formed through hand-crossing, and finally generates the melodic material for the entire trio (Ex. 12.10c and d). This sonata was one of only three published during Schubert's lifetime (excluding the sonata-like '*Wanderer*' fantasy).

Ex. 12.10c/d: D 568/iii, bb. 12–15 and 16–18.

This invasion of the minuet by other, often dance, styles is a tendency that will be dealt with in more detail in Chapter Thirty (The Dance), but a few instances are worth mentioning here. In Crotch's Third Piano Sonata in E flat major (1793), the second movement, *Menuetto*, is marked Vivace, resulting in a rather spare country dance far removed from the minuet, an extreme version of Schubert's Swiss-ism just mentioned (Ex. 12.11a).

Ex. 12.11a: Crotch, Piano Sonata No. 3 in E flat major/ii, opening.

Here, it is the trio (Ex. 12.11b) that is closer to the style of the title (though not much so).[5]

Ex. 12.11b: Crotch, Piano Sonata No. 3 in E flat major/ii, trio opening.

J.L. Dussek's Piano Sonata in E flat major, 'The Farewell' (pub. 1800) is rather adventurous in its use of keys: the introduction is in the tonic minor and the ensuing Allegro has a section in E major, the slow movement is in the flattened submediant, B major and the Tempo di Minuetto is in its relative minor, G sharp minor. The tempo direction of this angry minuet is 'piu tosto Allegro' and the hint of desperation (Ex. 12.12a) is intensified in the chromatic second half, although the trio in the parallel major (enharmonic), gives some relief, in spite of being based on the syncopation (bb. 3–4) (Ex. 12.12b).

Ex. 12.12a: J.L. Dussek, Piano Sonata in E flat major/iii, bb. 0–24.

---

[5] I shall return to this work in Chapter Twenty-One.

Ex. 12.12a continued

Ex. 12.12b: J.L. Dussek, Piano Sonata in E flat major/iii, trio opening.

(ii) Free-standing minuets

Free-standing minuets were composed individually and in sets, although as time went on the latter became less common. In spite of his frequent inclusion of the minuet in his piano sonatas, Haydn wrote no others for piano, unless one includes an unauthenticated work in the unusual key of F sharp major. Mozart, on the other hand, wrote a number, including several in his earliest extant compositions – in fact the majority of the piano pieces that comprise the first five Köchel numbers are minuets – K. 1d, 1e (the original 'K. 1'), K. 1f, 2, 4 and 5: perhaps this is not surprising in view of the use of minuet-form for teaching composition.[6] Apart from two works and a piano arrangement of a set of eight orchestral minuets (K. 315a (315g)), he doesn't return to the free-standing minuet until his last years, with the highly-chromatic K.

---

[6] See Chapter Twenty-Nine below.

355 (576b) in D major. Although Mozart's dynamics are relatively bare and, with the exception of the opening *dolce*, baldly unqualified, the piece implies the fullest use of the piano's capabilities of grading and shading with, effectively, a *crescendo-diminuendo* wave implied in each two-bar subphrase (Ex. 12.13a),

Ex. 12.13a: W.A. Mozart, Minuet in D major K. 355 (576b), bb. 1–11.

while the B section calls for even more complicated differentiation of parts as, to use an aquatic analogy, cross-currents are at work (Ex. 12.13b). The need for meticulous voicing in the changing chromatic chords makes this a much more taxing piece to perform than it appears at first sight; it is also a tribute to the capabilities of the early piano.

Ex. 12.13b: K. 355 (576b), bb. 17–22.

Apart from sets for public occasions and balls, or domestic gatherings that sought to imitate them, the minuet fell out of fashion in the nineteenth century except for its appearance in *divertimenti* or diversionary pieces,[7] as a character-variation in a set,[8] or occasionally in contexts in which a conscious archaism was intended.

Their spirit is frequently found, however, permeating other musical areas, usually slow movements, such as the Andante second movement of Schubert's A major

---

[7] Such as No. 3 of Ries' *Twelve Trifles*.
[8] This will be briefly dealt with in Chapter Fifteen: Variations.

Sonata, D 664, in spite of its unorthodox 7-bar periods (Ex. 12.14): the fact that repeated chords and indeed this particular rhythm occurs in the sonata and elsewhere does not detract from this.

Ex. 12.14: Schubert, Piano Sonata in A major D 664/ii, bb. 1-7.

Similarly, the corresponding movement (Allegretto non troppo) in J.B. Cramer's Sonata Op. 25/3, has the grace and phrase-structure of a minuet (Ex. 12.15a), and presents the material in the parallel minor, trio-like, as a centrepiece to the movement (Ex. 12.15b).

Ex. 12.15a: J.B. Cramer, Piano Sonata in E flat major Op. 25/3/ii, bb. 0–8.

Ex. 12.15b: Op. 25/3/ii, 'trio'.

Ex. 12.15b continued

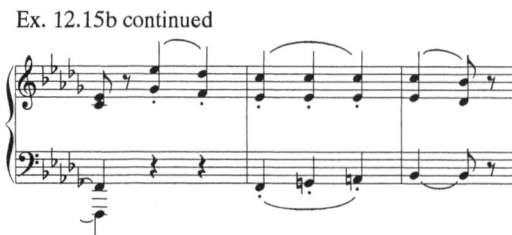

The first sonata of this Op. 25 set has a short middle movement in E flat minor with the direction 'Grave e Sostenuto' and the inexplicable title of '*Choral*', but seems, for much of its length, to be an example of the serious French minuet[9] (Ex. 12.16), and the 'motto'-type at that, with the rhythm $|^3_4 \, \rfloor \; \rfloor \, \rfloor \, \rfloor \, \rfloor|$.

Ex. 12.16: J.B. Cramer, Piano Sonata in E flat major Op. 25/1/ii, opening.

This type was particularly popular in London, and would have been more so after the French Revolution, when fleeing French aristocrats found a safe haven in Britain. Pinto's A flat major Sonata Op. 3 No. 1 also has a slow movement which is very minuet-like, with hints of dance-movement in the *forzato* third beats (Ex. 12.17); although this is headed Adagio, it is qualified rhythmically by 'con giusto'.

Ex. 12.17: Pinto, Piano Sonata in A flat major Op. 3/1/ii, bb. 1–9.

Sarah Bennett Reichart mentions minuets becoming 'unlabelled slow movements' in

---

[9] Another instance, from Schubert, is given as Ex. 12.14 above.

the Classical period, quoting Mozart and Beethoven[10]. She also reminds us that the latter often dropped the direction *quasi-* or *alla-menuetto* between sketch and final version.

Vestiges of the minuet can also be found in themes or songs imported from elsewhere for rondo or variation treatment, many of them from an earlier period in time. The title and words of the theme on which Thomas Haigh based his *Fantasia*,[11] 'Cease, rude Boreas', does not prepare us for its minuet-like demeanour, until we realize that it is in fact an older ballad-opera tune from 1730 with the more fitting title 'How happy are young lovers' (Ex. 12.18).

Ex. 12.18: Haigh, *Fantasia*, 'Cease, rude Boreas', theme.

Similarly, the comic song 'Will Putty', which Samuel Wesley uses for a rondo (*c*.1809), does not seem very apt for a theme which, marked Andante grazioso, is imbued with the grace of the serious French minuet, down to the rhyming 'feminine' cadences. The game is given away finally in b. 7 with the semiquavers, sung to nonsense syllables, and its mocking left hand (Ex. 12.19).

Ex. 12.19: S. Wesley, Rondo in A major, theme ('Will Putty')

(iii) The scherzo

Even though, in its general cut and title, the type does have Baroque precedents, for the purposes of this chapter, the scherzo ('joke') can be taken as a fast, jocular form of the minuet, with the same tripartite form and triple metre. The credit for establishing it in our period belongs to Beethoven: Haydn's famous use of the title for the minuets in his set of six string quartets Op. 33 is misleading, as they are not distinguishable in type and shape from his others. Although, as mentioned above, Beethoven's First Piano Sonata Op. 2/1 contains a movement called a minuet, it gets rather out of hand in its second section and his next sonata, and subsequent ones, have a scherzo. He returns to the minuet in his sonatas on only three subsequent occasions.

---

[10] In Reichart/DANCE, p. 165.
[11] This is actually a set of variations (See Chapter Fifteen (vi)).

If the general intent of the scherzo is a joke, or jokes, then it, or they, are at the expense of the listener, and are perpetrated on all levels. The first of Hummel's *Bagatelles* Op. 107 (pub. c.1825), a Scherzo in F major shows some of the subterfuges. The opening (Ex. 12.20a) at first sounds more like melodic than accompanying material, at least when the chords appear, and when the melody does arrive, the ambiguity is perpetuated by an imitative texture that becomes overt imitation after the second double barline (bb. 6ff.).

Ex. 12.20a: Hummel, *Bagatelle* in F major Op. 107/1, opening.

This is further underlined by tossing the now fragmented material between the hands and introducing inversion, leading to undermining of rhythm, which will be exploited in the 'trio' (in the subdominant, B flat major, Ex. 12.20b). There is much rhythmic interplay also, the differences between these rhythms being exploited

♪♪♪, ♪♪ and ♪♪♪

as well as the displacement of the anacrucial function (see Ex. 12.20a, x and x1). Rapid change of registers, harmonies, dynamics and melodic direction are also disconcerting, and the zany ending pulls many of these together in such a way that the listener isn't really quite sure whether the performer has 'fluffed' or not (Ex. 12.20c).

Ex. 12.20b: Op. 107/1, bb, 24–30.

Ex. 12.20c: Op. 107/1, ending.

Schubert does similar things in the scherzo of one of his A minor sonatas written about the same time (D 845, Ex. 12.21) but overlays a phrasal imbalance, especially the 5-bar units,

Ex. 12.21: Schubert, Piano Sonata in A minor D 845/iii, bb. 0–5.

and Tomásek also plays with phrases and melody/accompaniment confusions in the scherzo from an A major sonata (Ex. 12.22a) with slightly unnerving pattering in the bass register at the end of the section (Ex. 12.22b).

Ex. 12.22a/b: Tomásek, Piano Sonata in A major/ii, opening and end of first section.

R. Schumann gives a lively example in the scherzo section of the *Scherzo ed Intermezzo* in his first Piano Sonata F sharp minor, Op. 11 (1832–5, Ex. 12.23a)

Ex. 12.23a: R. Schumann, Piano Sonata in F sharp minor Op. 11/iii, bb. 0–5.

and even the *Intermezzo* ('trio') section in D major is not free of jokes as its direction – Lento *alla burla, ma pomposo* – suggests (Ex. 12.23b),

Ex. 12.23b: Op. 11/iii, *Intermezzo*.

while the whole thing threatens to fall apart in a strange and wild free passage which is better illustrated than described (Ex. 12.23c).

Ex. 12.23c: Op. 11/iii, end of *Intermezzo*.

The gossamer orchestral scherzo-writing of Mendelssohn, and its transference to the piano, is too well known to require any comment; a vestige of it can, perhaps, be seen in his sister's works, specifically in the scherzo (in the remote B minor) of Fanny Hensel-Mendelssohn's Piano Sonata in G minor (1843), a subtle study in modal unease (Ex. 12.24a) allowing no pause for phrasal breathing,

Ex. 12.24a: Fanny Mendelssohn, Piano Sonata in G minor/ii, bb. 0–10.

while the trio section underlines this with eerie use of *tremolandi*, *una corda* pedal and the upper register (Ex. 12.24b).

Ex. 12.24b: Piano Sonata in G minor/ii, 'trio'

Eerie also, but at the opposite end of the keyboard, is Thalberg's free-standing *Scherzo* in C sharp minor Op. 38, although here we are talking hobgoblins rather than demons (Ex. 12.25).

Ex. 12.25: Thalberg, *Scherzo* in C sharp minor Op. 38, bb. 10–13.

We come to the pinnacle with Chopin's four essays in this style, extended works that nevertheless keep many of the traits of the genre. The second of these, in D flat major (Op. 31, Presto, 1837) begins ominously in B flat minor (Ex. 12.26a), showing the stark contrasts – dynamic, register, density and texture, rhythm and articulation – that have already been noted,

Ex. 12.26a: Chopin, *Scherzo* No. 2 in D flat major Op. 31, bb. 1–27.

Ex. 12.26a continued

and when the music reaches the relative stability of the home key, it is still frenetic, hurtling down the keyboard and doubling back on itself (Ex. 12.26b).

Ex. 12.26b: Op. 31, bb. 42–56.

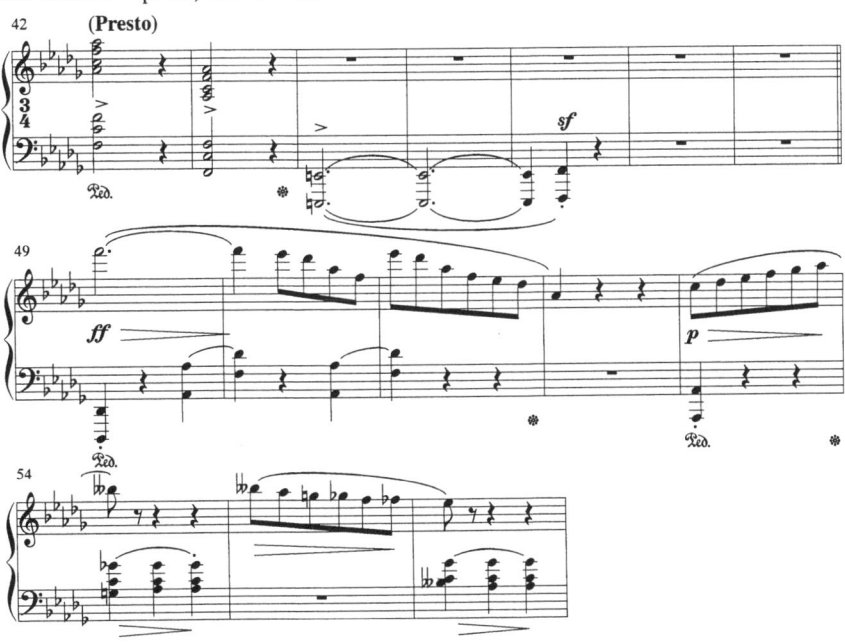

This quality remains even in the more tranquil trio section in A major, the melody wafting away like a wisp of smoke (Ex.12.26c).

Ex. 12.26c: Op. 31, bb. 265–84.

Three of Chopin's *Scherzi* are of a darker type that has come to be known as the 'demonic scherzo', which came into its own in this period and, indeed, outlasted the period also: Alkan wrote a free-standing *Scherzo focoso* (fiery) and one of his *Douze études* (in all the minor keys) is a scherzo *diabolico*. The type became almost a feature in chamber music including piano: the second movement (scherzo) of C.M. von Weber's Flute Trio in G minor (J 259 of 1819) is an example, exploiting the contrasting sonorities of the instruments and of the piano itself, as well as highlighting these with large gaps (Ex. 12.27).

Ex. 12.27: C.M. von Weber, Flute Trio in G minor J 259/ii, bb. 1–12.

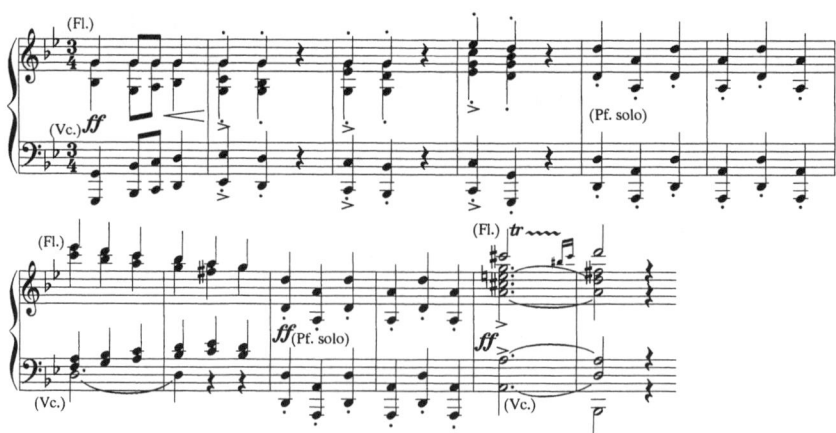

INFLUENCES 237

Another instance, from Hummel's E flat minor Piano Quintet Op. 87 is of particular interest for a number of reasons,[12] not least its scoring (violin, viola, cello, double bass with piano, favouring the middle and, especially, the lower registers). The theme that opens the quintet (Ex. 12.28a, x, y and z) gives rise to the motifs on which the scherzo is based (Ex. 12.28b, x1, y1 and z1).

Ex. 12.28a/b: Hummel, Piano Quintet in E flat minor Op. 87/i, opening and /ii opening.

Here again we have the contrasts in register, texture, dynamics and so on, compounded by the extra colouristic possibilities afforded by the instrumentation, bearing in mind that period, or period-copy, string instruments are also more colourful and incisive than their modern counterparts. The flattened sixth in the relative major context (Ex. 12.28c) also adds to the modal undermining.

Ex. 12.28c: Op. 87/ii, bb. 22–6.

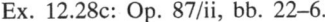

The trio section, in the parallel major (Ex. 12.28d) contrasts also with running quavers and a major version of the x1/y1 amalgamation seen in Ex. 12.28b.

Ex. 12.28d: Op. 87/ii, trio, opening.

---

[12] These will be detailed in Chapter Twenty-Five (ii).

What is surprising here, however, is what appears to be a series of reminiscences of this piece in the Chopin piece mentioned above, the second *Scherzo* in D flat major, which opens in the relative, B flat minor. First there is the proximity of key, an unusual minor version of a strong flat key (E flat minor – although written with a key-signature of three flats) and the closeness of Chopin's opening epigram, in stark octaves and lower-middle and bass registers (Ex. 12.26a), to Hummel's is difficult to accept as coincidental, as is the dominant/flat sixth relationship (marked y2 in Chopin). And like Hummel, (the end of Ex. 12.28b) the younger composer also has a protracted version (Ex. 12.26a, bb. 20–22), although with Chopin, Hummel's quizzical statement becomes a provocative question – and, a little later, possibly an even more provocative answer (Ex. 12.26b bb. 44–6).

Both composers quickly pass through the relative major, although where Hummel ends the first part of the scherzo, Chopin commences his 'trio' (Ex. 12.26c). There is a corresponding case when Hummel's coda (Ex. 12.28c) is compared with Chopin's similar material and, again, for the latter it becomes a point of departure; he also isolates a motivic scrap in his 'trio' (Ex. 12.26c, bb. 267–9 and especially bb. 277–81). Both also use a kind of tautological doubling-back, Chopin's (Ex. 12.26b, bb. 53–6) more so than Hummel's (Ex. 12.28d), and both extend and twist their opening motifs later in the movement, Hummel in the piano's reply in Ex. 12.29a

Ex. 12.29a: Hummel, Piano Quintet in E flat minor Op. 87/ii, bb. 52–4.

and Chopin in Ex. 12.29b, although the greater length and comparative freedom of Chopin's free-standing work gives him leisure to develop it more (bb. 492ff).

Ex. 12.29b: Chopin, *Scherzo* No. 2 in D flat major Op. 31 bb. 145–9.

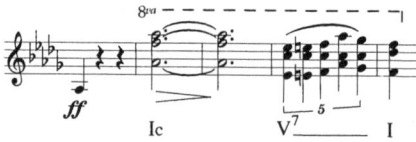

In doing so, he created a new genre; perhaps the Hummel work was one of a 'range of early influences that left their trace even as they were transcended'.[13]

The adjective *scherzando* was occasionally elevated to a title, and the diminutives *scherzino* and *scherzetto* were also used to denote lighter and/or shorter forms.

---

[13] Samson/BALLADES, p. 1.

(iv) Trios

The trio of the minuet-trio-minuet triptych traditionally contrasted in texture with its companion, in melodic material and frequently in mode, or, later on, key. In orchestral and many chamber works, it was scored for three instruments – often soloists – or in three parts, hence its name. On the early piano the possibility of reproducing, or at least approximating, this 'scoring' was possible, as we have seen, and at times this was carried further in that the technical features predominant in the minuet would also be contrasted or varied in the trio. This is already evident from some of the examples given above and a few others will suffice: the Trio of Potter's Piano Sonata in E minor Op. 4, headed *Tempo di Menuetto*, (Ex. 12.30a) contrasts with its minuet (Ex. 12.30b) in mode, character, pace and pianistic technique,

Ex. 12.30a/b: Potter, Piano Sonata in E minor Op. 4/iii, trio, bb. 0–3 and minuet, bb. 0–4.

as does Schubert's, in his last sonata (in B flat major, D 960) although not as obviously (Ex. 12.31a and b).

Ex. 12.31a/b: Schubert, Piano Sonata in B flat major D 960/iii, trio, opening and scherzo, bb. 1–4.

Both of Chopin's mature solo-sonatas have scherzi of the demonic kind and both their keys are, untraditionally, different from those of their host sonatas, that of the B flat minor Op. 35 being in E flat minor and that of the B minor Op. 58 a third away in E flat major. The first (E flat minor) has its unnamed trio in its relative major, G flat, Più lento, in which the obsessive ♩♪♪♪ ♩ rhythm is transmuted to a more leisurely ♩ ♩ ♩♪ ♩ ♩♪ and the dissonances and chromaticism is tamed to gentler diatonic added sixths, with a swaying waltz-melody. Also contrasting is the fact that, with a few small exceptions, all the gradations of volume in the trio are *diminuendi*, whereas the bulk of those in the scherzo are *crescendi*, often cumulative.

The B minor Sonata's scherzo, in E flat major, casts its trio (again unnamed) in B major and again there is something of a Florestan/Eusebius contrast, but with family likenesses also. The writhing scherzo melody-line is underpinned by a cadential inner-voice scrap (Ex. 12.32a) and their textural relationship is inverted in the trio, where it is turned into a more gently twisting inner melody with the 'scrap' elongated into a more leisurely counter-line above (Ex. 12.32b).

Ex. 12.32a/b: Chopin, Sonata in B minor Op. 58/ii, bb. 0–3 and 'trio', opening.

The greatest scherzo in these works, and one of the greatest in piano literature is, of course, the finale of the B flat minor Sonata, where, unrelieved by a trio, a Promethean closet-demon strains at its chains, breaking them only at the end.

CHAPTER THIRTEEN

Received Forms 2: The Rondo

(i) General

The other single piece which, analogous to the minuet, enjoyed a dual existence both within larger schemes (sonata, chamber music, symphony and concerto) and as an independent movement, was the rondo. This was already popular in both guises in the eighteenth century, but the free-standing rondo became the basis of a veritable industry during the later part of that century and the first third of the next. Its basic principle – an ancient one not only in music but in poetry also – was the return of a well-defined theme alternating with sections of episodic material.

At first only the names of the better-known composers enabled some of these pieces to stand out from the mass but as the market, and the production to satisfy it, increased, more distinctive titles became necessary; these were most often provided by publishers, but composers also soon realised their selling power.

The first step in drawing attention to such works was by adding qualifiers to the titles, causing a small rash of *Rondo célèbre*-s and *favori/e*-s, which, together with the composer's name, was usually sufficient to make them hot property. There were also many 'Brilliant' (or *brillant*) rondos, the word usually intended in the technical sense, which were for public performance, whether this was to be intimate and familial, or larger *salon*/concert, and the appendage '*de salon*' had the same meaning, but was less showy.

Programmatic titles were a great resource also. These could play on the sentiments of the domestic buyers, such as Cramer's *All' amica lontana* ('To the Distant Lady-friend'), his *Rondeau expressif Comme il vous plairà* ('As you may like it'), or Czerny's *Le Plaisir* and Hummel's *Rondo mignon*, and '*La Galante*', or incorporate some 'gimmick' such as Field's '*Le midi*' whose coda reproduces a clock chiming twelve, although the title did not appear in the first edition.

Composers could also draw on the fame and popularity of established tunes by using them as the basis of their works, and filling in the episodes with linking material, at best derived in some way from the tunes, or even incorporating further tunes. These tunes were often folk-songs or operatic airs, but could also be based on national dances, or accepted national or regional traits,[1] such as the rondo-finales of

---

[1] This is discussed in Chapter Twenty-One.

Herz's Seventh Piano concerto (*'Rondo espagnol'*) or Hummel's Op. 113 in A flat major (*Rondo alla spagnola*), and his *Rondoletto Russe* (also called *cosaque*), and Ries' *Rondo à la Tedesca*. Sets of rondos were often given catchy titles also; Czerny's *'Talisman Musicale'*, and his *'Passatempi Musicali'* ['Musical Pastimes'] are instances.

The last-mentioned composer, as is evident from opus numbers that reach to 861,[2] was an indefatigable producer of music of all kinds, especially rondos. On the title-page of his *La Jeunesse Musicale: a selection of Popular National and other Airs arranged as Rondos for Pianoforte* (pub. 1841), the publishers, D'Almaine & Co. of London, give a selection of some of his other works in this and related genres, which show the range, not only of the material that he set, but also of the many kinds of character he tried to promulgate. They are all given the French title *Rondeau,* and all are qualified by such types as *élégant, sentimental, brillant, grazioso, pastorale, militaire, écossaise, allemand,* and even *maritime* and *chinoise*. In point of fact, however, they turn out to be simply rondos using operatic arias or national songs.

It tells us much about the domestic market and performers of this music, that the titles upon which Czerny based some of these rondos seemed insufficient in themselves, without extra character being overlaid. One could be forgiven for being unprepared, in the case of *Le Cheval de Bronze*, for a *Rondeau Chinoise*, but *The Blue Bell of Scotland* does rather suggest a provenance not unconnected with matters *Ecossaises,* and *The Rataplan*, as mentioned before,[3] was sufficiently well known not to need the subtitle *Militaire*.

This usage is connected to the equally prevalent *Rondo/eau caractéristique*, a handy blanket-term, as was *Rondo/eau de salon*. The diminutives *Rondino* and *Rondoletto* were also common, implying that they were in a lighter musical vein or that they were easier technically, although it was sometimes difficult to tell the difference: it was more likely to have been a marketing ploy, attempting to attract the ladies by the titles sounding prettier.

Many of these rondos were published in sets of varying numbers, and a single title-page would serve for all the individual pieces when sold separately, or when several were grouped together in books, with the number(s) written in by hand. The typical overall scheme was inherited from Mozart and Haydn and I want to briefly examine a rondo by each.

(ii) A Classical rondo: J. Haydn

Haydn's Rondo finale to his C major Sonata No. 58 (H:XVI:48) of 1789 – one of only two of his later sonatas in two movements – is a characteristically racy *presto* with a theme in two repeated sections, ending on dominant and tonic respectively, whose subtle phrase-structure is belied by its affable exterior (Ex. 13.1a). The first section, T^a, is in two six-bar phrases and the second, T^b, 4 + 4, but when it seems to

---

[2] According to Pazdírek-eds/*UNIVERSAL*.
[3] See Chapter Eleven (i) and Ex. 11.3.

be about to repeat T^a – common practice in such two-part themes (compare minuets) – only four bars appear, to be answered by a six-bar phrase of three two-bar subphrases, the concluding one of which is the opening two bars of T^a. The whole frames the primary triads, I, V and IV and its brightly diatonic feel has the occasional chromatic hint. It is homophonic, with a tiny hint of counterpoint in the answering imitative figures in bb. 12–16 and, perhaps, bb. 24–6. Much attention is given to articulation here, with copious and precise markings (all of which are authentic) and which confirm that the piano is the intended instrument, despite the suitability of the music for the harpsichord on the face of it. The *tessitura* is largely confined to the middle register.

Ex. 13.1a: J. Haydn, Piano Sonata in C major H:XVI:48/iii, bb. 0–33.

The beginning of Episode one, opening with T^a brings a shift into the lower register, which is immediately contrasted by upper and upper-middle, extending the theme and using figuration based upon it (see the end of Ex. 13.1a). The music begins to move towards the dominant with a folk-like passage over a pedal (Ex. 13.1b) and the T^b version (Ex. 13.1a, bb. 20–6) of the theme arrives cadencing firmly in G. A feature of this episode is the constant appearance of the two-quaver anacrusis, occurring also as a downbeat and combining both forms; a modulation back to the tonic brings back the complete theme without repeats.

Ex. 13.1b: H:XVI:48/iii, bb. 45–52.

Episode two begins by plunging us straight into C minor and the bottom register of the piano with yet different combinations of the ♫ | ♩ rhythm with its rhythmic variant ♫ | ♬ complete with the piquancy of the harmonic minor scale's augmented second (Ex. 13.1c).

Ex. 13.1c: H:XVI:48/iii, bb. 122–8.

After a short section in E flat major, the music stops on the dominant of C and the key-signature loses its three flats for the return of the T without repeats, dovetailed with a variant of Ep. 1, now in the tonic, and a short coda gives the the first subphrase of T in each of the three registers (Ex. 13.1d).

Ex. 13.1d: H:XVI:48/iii, ending.

The material here is all firmly based on the theme, with the episodes providing contrast in terms of key, mode, texture, dynamics and register as well as the particular combination of motivic material used. One could say that the instrumental characteristics themselves have a 'say' in the makeup. Haydn's overall shape in the piece is:

Shape: T – Ep. 1(=T) – T^1 – Ep. 2 – T – Coda
Keys: I   V   I   i   I

which can be reduced to A   B   A   C   A.

(iii) A Classical rondo: Mozart

Although using a different approach musically and structurally,[4] Mozart's rondo-finale to his Piano Sonata in D major K. 311 (284c) of 1777, involves the instrument even more. Like Haydn, Mozart chooses the middle register for the bulk of his theme, again in two sections, this time, of two four-bar phrases each ending, like Haydn, on dominant and tonic, but without including the subdominant and not repeated. The motivic elements are clearly discernible here (Ex. 13.2a): the triadic opening (marked x), the decorations of bb. 1 and 3, etc., (*acciaccatura* and unaccented lower auxiliary, marked y) and the semiquaver scale spanning a sixth (z).

Ex. 13.2a: W.A. Mozart, Piano Sonata in D major K. 311 (284c)/iii, bb. 0–16.

---

[4] The fact that this is a sonata-rondo does not affect my discussion.

Ex. 13.2a continued

The texture is single-line melody and accompaniment, except for the chord ending the first half and the third doubling at bb. 2, 4, 10 and 12. The first episode, beginning with octaves in the lower half of the piano, *forte*, is decorated with a variant of the three-quaver figure from b. 1.

Again, as with Haydn's rondo, this is contrasted with the high, soft harmonised passages and ensuing falling scales. The melody of this first episode arrives in b. 41, a falling scalic third doubled at the sixth with the upper line decorated by another variant of *y*, an unaccented (now upper) auxiliary followed by a variant of *x* with an imitation in the left hand, while the scalic fall (*z*) is present in bb. 47–8 and inverted in the bass at b. 44 (Ex. 13.2b).

Ex. 13.2b: K. 311 (284c)/iii, bb. 41–8.

INFLUENCES

The passage from b. 56–8 has almost the status of a second melody in this (dominant) episode and shows its links with the theme in the compound third, falling scale and arpeggio; a coda, confirming the dominant, contradicts it at the last moment and the theme reappears in the tonic.

Bar 119 brings in Episode two, like Haydn, in minor mode, but unlike his parallel minor, this is relative, and once more the motifs are varied further, the *acciaccatura* now becoming a trill and the auxiliary being upper as well as accented (Ex. 13.2c). The thirds, combined with the scale's semiquaver rhythm can be discerned in the left hand, together with its overall descent of a sixth (B down to D), while the triadic fall of the anacrusis has become a falling fifth. Again, texture is part of the process when the repeat of this melody occurs, the hands being reversed with the left hand taking the melody (bb. 127ff.).

Ex. 13.2c: K. 311 (284c)/iii, bb. 119–27.

On its way back to the tonic for the resumption of the theme, the music is sidetracked by a short cadenza, with a concentration of thirds, turns and scales. The return of T is given registral variation (an octave lower) and we have Ep.1 again, but in the tonic. There is a further reprise of T's first half before a short coda. Mozart's rondo-scheme is:

Scheme: T – Ep. 1 – T – Ep. 2 – T – Ep. 1 – T – Coda
Keys: I V I vi I I I I

which can be reduced to   A B   A C   A   B   A
and further reduced to an
overarching triptych: X – Y – X

(iv) Later rondos

These two forms were the basic ones during our period. Most commonly, one of the episodes (usually the second) was in the opposite mode, and, since most rondos were in the major, this continued for some time to be the minor, whether relative or parallel. The other episode tended to be in the dominant or the subdominant.

It is little wonder these pieces were so popular. The form was an extremely satisfying one, with the regular return of the deliberately catchy rondo theme separated by in some way, contrasting (but often related) material in the episodes, some of which could also enshrine an element of not over-taxing technical display. It is easy to see the appeal of the rondo as a teaching piece and, in the case of this type – and of shorter rondos generally – a simpler T – Ep – T shape was used. This is the case, for example, in the 18 rondos making up Czerny's *La Jeunesse Musicale* mentioned above, in which the episodes are usually non-melodic, and this, very often, simply means runs. In his very descriptive *Storm Rondo*, an *Impromptu*, Op. 715, the thunder and lightning of the storm is the theme (in F minor) and the Episode, the calm (*dolce*), in A flat major, which, after another eruption, returns in F minor and the storm ends the piece in that key.

In the case of a rondo based on a well-known air, it became common to add an introduction and this often had some reference to the ensuing melody: some examples can be found in Chapters Twenty-Two and Twenty-Three on improvisation.

The sectional Rondo, occasionally found in Haydn, was also used in longer works in which the episodes were self-contained sections, often in binary form. The ten rondos comprising Czerny's *Talisman Musicale* are of this kind with, or approximating to, the following shape, that of No. 4 in G major. Only the main tonal areas are given; the number of bars in each section is given in parentheses:

A1(8):||A2(8):||B(8):||C(24)||A1:||A2:||D1(16):||D2(12)|Cadenza|A1:||A2:||Coda
Keys: G   C   g   G

The opening melody is typical in its childlike jauntiness and folksy hints (Ex. 13.3).

Ex. 13.3: Czerny, *Talisman Musicale*/4, opening.

Occasionally the reference is operatic, as in the Bellini-ising themes of the fifth and seventh of the *Eight Rondos* Op. 419 (*c*.1837, Exx. 13.4 and 13.5).

Ex. 13.4: Czerny, *Eight Rondos* Op. 419/5, opening.

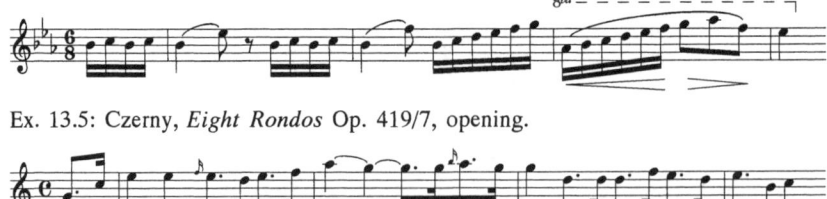

Ex. 13.5: Czerny, *Eight Rondos* Op. 419/7, opening.

INFLUENCES 249

The sheer enormity of Czerny's output in all genres, especially rondos and variations, has already been mentioned, and could not but lead to mediocrity on some, if not several, levels. But this music is not intended to be trailblazing or soul-searching – indeed, to be either of these would be a positive disadvantage and detract from their dual purpose of entertainment and instruction. It was possible to tap into a market such as this one and produce music of reasonable quality, (though not much of it), and composers such as Ries, Moscheles, Hummel, Cramer and Field, among others, managed to make a good living without 'selling out' to any great extent.

No. 4 of Hummel's *Six Bagatelles* Op. 107[5] (pub. *c*.1825 in Leipzig, Ex. 13.6a), the *Rondo mignon* in B flat major, is a lesson in how to make a little go a long way musically and ends up being not entirely without merit.

Ex. 13.6a: Hummel, *Six Bagat*elles Op. 107/4, bb. 0–24.

---

[5] This set also includes the Rondolette russe and the Scherzo discussed elsewhere.

The arpeggio which serves as the opening of the binary theme T^a is left unharmonised, leaving some initial doubt in the listener's ear as to whether it is introductory or thematic, and the next few bars inject a little tension with the pedal-note bass and the neat harmonic turn, using chord vi, passing through v to IV^7 becoming the augmented sixth of vi and resolving onto V/vi instead of the usual V. T^b begins by playing around with the new rhythm that has slipped in unnoticed at the cadence, and a repeat of T^a's opening ends with an inversion of that opening and the introduction of a syncopation. The impression is less of coyness than of cheek.

All of these motifs are used in the rest of the movement and enlivened by catchy devices, such as mock counterpoint – touches characteristic of his teacher Haydn – (Ex. 13.6b),

Ex. 13.6b: Op. 107/4, bb. 36–48.

a keen ear for the possibilities of the instrument itself in making something more of quite mundane gestures as in bb. 8–16 in Ex. 13.6a above, and the manipulation of the episodic material – a skeletal version of the opening four bars – in passages such as in Exx. 13.6c and 13.6d, and later, when a *minore* statement becomes the basis of a mini-development.

Ex. 13.6c: Op. 107/4, bb. 56–60.

Ex. 13.6d: Op. 107/4, bb. 76–80.

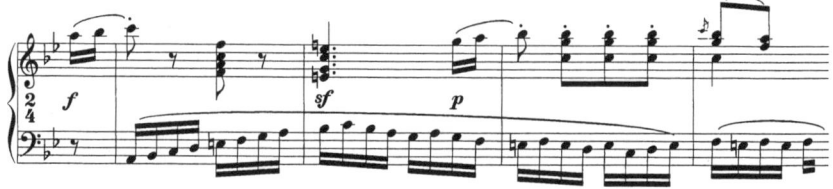

Similarly the *Rondeau brillant* in B minor Op. 109 published simultaneously in Paris, Vienna and London in 1826,[6] opening with Ex. 13.7a and its 'second half' Ex. 13.7b,

Ex. 13.7a/b: Hummel, *Rondeau brillant* in B minor Op. 109, bb. 1–4 and 9–14.

uses his innate feeling for keyboard sonority and articulation to liven up the combinations of ideas (Exx. 13.7c, 13.7d and 13.7e).

Ex. 13.7c: Op. 109, bb. 22–32.

---

[6] This was an arrangement between publishing-houses to prevent piracy – still rife in this period – of works by popular composers. Hummel was a pioneer in the fight to secure copyright for the creator, canvassing, among others, no less than the death-bedridden Beethoven. See Sachs/PIRATES and Sachs/AUTHENTIC.

Ex. 13.7d: Op. 109, bb. 77–83.

Ex. 13.7e: Op. 109, bb. 106–8.

The first episode is in the relative major (D) with a contrasting character, though still related thematically, and the second goes one better, in being set in the key of the ♭VI (G) and changing from 6/8 to common time. In the same composer's Op. 19, the 3/4 theme returns at the end in a 4/4 guise, which may be accounted for by the title of *Rondo quasi una fantasia*.

As the period wore on, the keys used became more adventurous, as one would expect. Czerny's *Rondo Elegante: The Page Inconstant* Op. 414 in A major has the 'Mozartian' shape but with a different key-scheme:

```
            Intro – T – Ep. 1 – T – Ep. 2 – T – Ep. 1 – T – Coda
Key:          I     I     V      I   mod  ♭VI   I     I     I
```

showing the *Terzverwandtschaft* (third-relation) so beloved of the Romantics, and J.L. Dussek, in the finale of his *Grand Military Concerto* Op. 40 (a *Rondo Allegro Militaire* in B flat major), casts the episodes in G minor and the parallel, B flat minor, respectively. J.B. Cramer's *Rondo Brilliant* Op. 72 (pub. 1826) in E major has sections in C major – the long introduction also has an E – C – E scheme – and in D major, and the rondo of his *Two Characteristic Movements* Op. 89 (pub. 1837) entitled *All' amica lontana* has episodes in F major as well as F minor.

Characteristic also is S. Wesley's *The Christmas Carol varied as a Rondo* in E minor (*c.*1810). The 'Old carol' is *God Rest Ye, Merry Gentlemen* in a slightly altered version from the one familiar to us today. It appears in E minor with hymn-like harmonies and the rest of the piece is more in the nature of a variative fantasia than a rondo proper, although the outline can, apart from the obvious *maggiore* episode, be just about discerned. This is partly due to the constant reference to the carol's lines in one of the two or three parts and also the almost perpetual accompanying quaver-movement in one of the other parts. The tune appears in various forms, textures and keys – E minor, A minor, G major, and E major in the central episode – and harmonies; Ex.13.8a–e gives some of these appearances.

Ex. 13.8a–e: S. Wesley, *The Christmas Carol varied as a Rondo.*

The result tends to monotony at the regular tread of the music, and to irritation at the constant hints of imitation, so much so that one almost misses the two-part canon with augmentation (and a hint of *al rovescio* in the inner part, Ex. 13.8f, marked x) eventually becoming a three-part canon.

Ex. 13.8f: S. Wesley, *The Christmas Carol varied as a Rondo*.

With C.M. von Weber's *Rondo brillante (La gaité)* Op. 62 (J 252[7]), written in 1819, we are firmly in the public domain – the concert-hall, or at least the large *salon*. A virtuoso piece, its theme shows a very Hummelian aptitude for dressing up material that is occasionally fairly mundane by judicious decoration or use of the piano, the former in particular being applicable here (Ex. 13.9a).

Ex. 13.9a: C.M. von Weber, *Rondo brillante* Op. 62, bb. 0–8.

The first episode threatens C minor, but this turns out to be an approach to the dominant, B flat major, for the theme, which is also, in fact, a second subject – since

---

[7] The J refers to the numbering in Jähns/*VERZEICHNISS*.

we are dealing with a sonata-rondo – (Ex. 13.9b), derived from the demisemiquaver duplets of b. 1 and the quaver figure of b. 6.

Ex. 13.9b: Op. 62, bb. 48–56.

It is an excellent example of the piano's capacity for distinguishing fine *nuances* and throwing principal thematic material into relief, especially, as here, in close texture; its repeat in octaves in the treble forms a telling contrast.

The second episode coincides with the sonata form's development section, couched mostly in F minor and concentrating on the demisemiquaver duplet and chromatic runs, and includes a colouristic reference to the main theme in the bass register underneath the *Alberti* accompaniment (Ex.13.9c). The reprise presents the thematic material in the tonic and a short coda rounds the piece off in an appropriately bright manner.

Ex. 13.9c: Op. 62, bb. 119–21.

It is interesting to compare this with Moscheles's work of the same name: *La Gaité, A Brilliant Rondo, preceded by An Expressive Slow Movement* Op. 85 in A major, published in London in 1830. The opening of the introduction (Ex. 13.10a) shows some thematic affinity with the rondo's theme – the rising thirds in each of their first bars and the falling scale, marked x and y, respectively – *Allegro giocoso* in 6/8 (Ex. 13.10b, x1 and y1). The first episode in the dominant has a melody which, again, has a family likeness to bb. 3–4 of the opening (Ex. 13.10c, y) and the second episode in the remoter key of B flat major, with another permutation of the thematic material (Ex. 13.10d over a quaver broken-triad bass).

Ex. 13.10a: Moscheles, *La Gaité*, Op. 85, Introduction.

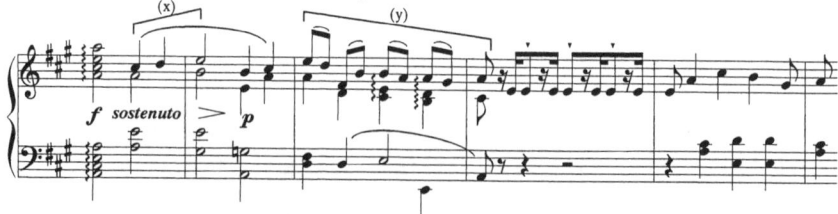

Ex. 13.10b: Op. 85, Rondo theme.

Ex. 13.10c: Op. 85, first episode.

Ex. 13.10d: Op. 85, second episode.

(v) A note on Mozart's K. 511

To regress in time to Mozart is not necessarily to do so in style, especially if the *Rondo* in A minor K. 511 (1787) is in question, a work often singled out as his greatest piece for piano. The use of this key is rare in Mozart; apart from three short vocal items, the only other use is for the great Sonata K. 310 (300d).[8] It also has that combination of musical ingredients which promise, in Mozart, a piece of great emotional depth, insight, and restrained passion:– the *siciliana* rhythm and a minor key. As occasionally happens in this context, the opening presentation of the thematic material is rather deadpan, if not coy, but only on the surface; a gesture of closure in the 5 – 1 fall, a dragging back up by chromatic step, anchored to a tonic

---

[8] This work is discussed in the next chapter, Chapter Fourteen (iii).

pedal and a scalic fall, before reiteration and a more convoluted rise, the cadence delayed until the last moment (Ex.13.11a).

Ex. 13.11a: W.A. Mozart, *Rondo* in A minor K. 511, bb. 0–23.

The 'second half' of this theme is in the relative major and exhibits that difficulty of establishment that can be seen in several of Mozart's minor-key works, especially when he doesn't allow himself the luxury of modulation – the struggle-and-failure in the G minor String Quintet K. 516/i, the roundabout approach in its sister K. 406

(516b)/i (C minor), the Beethovenian 'don't argue' of the early G minor Symphony K. 183 (173d)/i, and so on. Unlike any of these, the relative major here is slipped in unnoticed, and a bid for attention (bb. 10–11) fizzles away into nothing (b. 11). The process of establishment now begins in earnest – not without a hint of backsliding in b. 16, and the exultant trill brings the closure although, within a few effortless bars, we are back in A minor again for a decorated repeat of the opening.

The shape of this rondo is a modification of the 'Mozartian' type outlined earlier in this chapter although the proportions are different:

Sections: A–B–A – C – A – D – A–B–A – Coda
Keys:[9]   a C a   F   a   A   a C a   a

The A section (Ex. 13.11a, bb. 0–8) is so often detached from the A–B–A unit that it is justifiable to see it as a separate component, especially given its treatment, which borders on the developmental. The overall key scheme is an example of *Terzverwandtschaft* more common later in the period and the section in A major leans toward its subdominant, D and even contains a reference to F sharp minor (bb. 112–18).

Improvisatory decoration is the basis of the melodic processing and *quasi-*development in this piece. The poignant opening turn is omnipresent, introducing each section in its original form – the B section (Ex. 13.11a, b. 9), the C section (Ex. 13.11b), the D section (Ex. 13.11c),

Ex. 13.11b: K. 511, bb. 30–33, (C section).

Ex. 13.11c: K. 511, bb. 88–95, (D section).

---

[9] The majors are upper-case, the minors, lower.

and many other places, of which Ex. 13.11d, 13.11e and 13.11g give some examples. Ex. 13.11e and 13.11f also show its integration into the fabric of the music and its development by inversion and rhythmic manipulation, such as the operatic 'sob' of Ex. 13.11f.

Ex. 13.11d: K. 511, bb.–3 and 105.

Ex. 13.11e: K. 511, bb. 26–30.

Ex. 13.11f: K. 511, bb. 85–8.

Ex. 13.11g: K. 511, bb. 97–101.

It creates a subtle dissonance at all appearances, making even the most straightforward parts of this complicated piece appear to be hiding something. It is even incorporated in the harmonic wavering of the C section (Ex. 13.11h).

Chromaticism is the harmonic air that this piece breathes. From the very turn itself and the chromatic auxiliary, as well as the second bar's tortuous crawling through the passage just mentioned, to Ex. 13.11i and to Ex. 13.11j, where, for one moment, we almost glimpse the atonal world of late Liszt in the contorted right-hand line. It also shows the intensification of chromatic decoration that Hummel and Field would extend, breaking down the distinction between the structural and the decorative, (so characteristic of the Romantics) and passing it on to Chopin, Robert Schumann and Liszt.

Ex. 13.11h: K. 511, bb. 68–78.

Ex. 13.11i: K. 511, bb. 116–24.

Ex. 13.11i continued

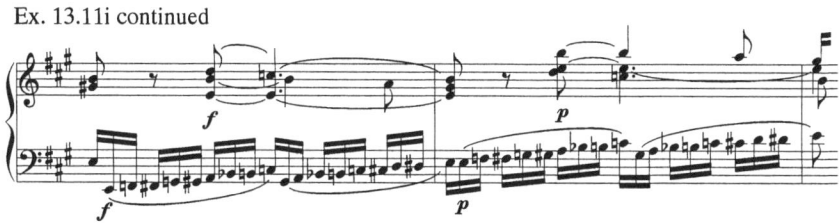

Ex. 13.11j: K. 511, bb. 125–36.

Mozart's pianistic idiom here is also thoroughly early nineteenth century as is his use of the instrument, beginning with an A section firmly and almost exactly entrenched in the middle register, and later coming within a hair's breadth of the topmost and lowest notes of the instrument, e^4 and $F\sharp^1$ respectively.

We are in the world of Romantic piano music here, also in its bittersweet sentiment and knowing irony, nowhere better seen than in the piece's deceptive finish, a perfect expression in music, of the equally deceptive last words of *Wuthering Heights*, when Lockwood, surveying the three graves in the moonlight wonders 'how any one could imagine unquiet slumbers for the sleepers in that quiet earth'.

That was written at the height of Romanticism, 60 years later.

CHAPTER FOURTEEN

Received Forms 3: The Solo Sonata

(i) General

Our current perception of the sonata during the period of this book is of a purely instrumental piece for one or two instruments in several varied movements, or more-or-less discrete sections, at least one of which is in sonata-form or a recognisable variant. We could narrow the description further by saying that the keyboard was almost always a component, in spite of the exceptions involving harp (J. L. Dussek and Bochsa) and other instruments such as the guitar and mandolin (Mauro Giuliani, Paganini, Hummel). The overwhelming presence of the keyboard, however, is largely confirmed by the facts, with the proviso that the trio-sonata from the Baroque was carried over in the form of a 'keyboard sonata with the accompaniment of violin and cello'; however, the fact that '*ad lib*[*itum*]' was usually added gave the game away, in that many of these were not trios in the sense in which we – or, indeed, the last quarter of the period – would apply the term.[1]

Sonatas were published in sets, most usually of three or six and very often contained a mixture of solo- and duo-sonatas, and trios. Thus, at the beginning of our period, Mozart, on a visit to London in 1764–5, brought out his 'Op. III', a set of six 'sonatas' for keyboard and violin or flute with optional cello (K. 10–15), and Clementi's Op. 2 (written by 1770) comprised three solo sonatas and three in the stock mix-'n'-match format for the eighteenth-century of harpsichord/pianoforte and flute/violin. This was also used for the second of Hummel's three sonatas of his Op. 2a, appearing in London in 1792, while the other two were a piano trio and his first solo sonata in C major. Often, solo piano sonatas were given accompaniments by publishers, or by others at the publisher's commission: the first edition of Mozart's Piano Sonata in B flat major, K. 570 was issued with a violin part and Burney paid the same doubtful compliment to some of Haydn's piano sonatas.

Many published sets show arranging by key, *viz.* Mozart's early violin sonata K. 26–31 in E flat, G, C, D, F and B flat majors, and his first six piano sonatas (K. 279–84/ K. 189d–h and 205b), which are in the same keys, but in the order C, F, B flat, E flat, G and D majors. The final order was a matter for the publisher, who

---

[1] These will be addressed under the heading of 'Accompaniment' in Chapters Twenty-Five and Twenty-Six.

would arrange in order of saleability, with the most 'difficult' – whether technically, emotionally or intellectually – coming late in the sets. As our period progressed, piano sonatas, for reasons that will be examined, decreased in number but grew in size, becoming more of an 'event' in a composer's output.

The narrowing down of the meaning of 'sonata' goes hand in hand with the greater importance and popularity of instrumental music, the change in style from Baroque to Classical,[2] the shift from the harpsichord and clavichord to the piano and, of course, the increasing domestic market with its demands for more solo/duo music centred on the piano. At the same time, lighter and, usually shorter, works would be called *sonatina* – a trend towards the use of the diminutive noted in various other forms also – and, later in the period, Grand Sonata (more usually *Grande sonate*, or *Große Sonate*) would be used, ideally, for large works in which a major musical statement was made, and/or for a virtuoso work, often intended for public performance.

Nevertheless, at the beginning of this period (*c.*1760), the status of the keyboard sonata was not high, even within the realm of instrumental music, sharing this lowliness with its kindred genres the trio and, especially, the duo-sonata. This was partly due to the concentration on the string quartet by the greatest masters of the time, Haydn and Mozart, and partly to the status of keyboard instruments themselves. But it was also due to the domestic, occasionally solitary – even introverted – circumstances of performance and the fact that it was destined for amateurs or *dilettantes* and with the implication (in the common title of *Essercisi*, etc.) that its main purpose was as a kind of practice-piece. C.P.E. Bach's blanket designation of his six sets of sonatas written between 1779 and 1787 as *'Für Kenner und Liebhaber'* [*'For connoisseurs and dilettantes'*], shows the distinction.

Unlike the other instrumental genre, which was still recognisable after its passage from Baroque to Classical styles, the keyboard concerto, the sonata, (as we shall see) was subjected to greater modification, which was to raise it in the general esteem. It was inevitably touched by the increasing status of instrumental music in general, as well as the growing popularity of the piano itself, due to its championing in public by, in particular, J.C. Bach and Mozart. And, in spite of their aforementioned preoccupation with other genres, the latter especially, they and Joseph Haydn (in his later period) set the piano sonata well along the road to equal weighting with the string quartet through their different contributions to the genre.

An overview of Mozart's piano sonatas shows a synthesis of the Northern and Southern styles.[3] Unlike the sonatas of his principal influence – here as in the concerto – J.C. Bach, all of his 18 piano sonatas are in three movements[4] and, with two exceptions, of the fast-slow-fast type. The exceptions, which are also the only two not to have sonata-form first movements, are the sonatas K. 282 (198g), his only one in E flat major, which has the first of the two Menuettos in B flat major and the second (really a long trio) in the tonic, and an Allegro finale. The other exception is K. 331 (300i), his only sonata in A major, opening with the well-

---

[2] This is outlined in Chapter One (iv).

[3] For more on this topic, see Chapter One (iv) and Chapter Ten (i).

[4] Menuetto I and II of K. 282 (198g) count as one movement in the manner of a minuet and trio.

known set of variations in *siciliana* rhythm, again a Menuetto middle movement, and the famous [Rondo]*Alla Turca* finale in, unusually, the parallel minor.

A further influence of J.C. Bach on Mozart is his transmission of the 'Southern European' style, especially in the internal melodic character of the movements, particularly in the first two sonatas. An example of this can be seen in a general way long after Mozart had found his own voice: Ex. 14.1a gives the opening of the Piano Sonata in B flat major K. 333 (315c) of 1783, and Ex. 14.2 (see below) that of Bach's Op. 17/4/i in G major (pub. *c.*1774). Interesting in both is the way in which the strong beat of the second bar is displaced by a variant of that of the first bar, exchanging, in both cases, a short accented passing-note for a longer *appoggiatura* with, in Bach's case, the introduction of a new (dotted) rhythm which is to become prominent later by development or extension.

Ex. 14.1a: W.A. Mozart, Piano Sonata in B flat major K. 333 (315c)/i, bb. 0–6.

This is very much a Mozartian practice and there is an instance here, where the syncopated rhythm of b. 5, | ♪ ♩ ♪ ♪ ♩ ♪ | introduced innocently as a cadential decoration, becomes an important feature of the second subject (Ex. 14.1b)

Ex. 14.1b: K. 333 (315c)/i, bb. 23–6.

and is also used in the development (Ex. 14.1c).

Ex. 14.1c: K. 333 (315c)/i, bb. 73–5.

Also notable are the extension of the opening anacrusis in the second half of Bach b. 3 (Ex. 14.2), and Mozart b. 4 (Ex. 14.1a), and the impulse to fill in a rest and (often) a change of register after an inconclusive cadence by passagework (seen in Mozart bb. 6 and particularly 8, and Bach b. 6 (Ex. 14.2)). Mozart also moves closer to the rhythm of Bach's opening bars at the beginning of his development section. Other common shared features are the presentation of like or similar material in different octaves, the avoidance of too many strong closures and the use of the 'false-relation' modulation.

Ex. 14.2: J.C. Bach, Keyboard Sonata in G major Op. 17/4/i, bb. 0–7.

If there is much more melodic variety in Mozart's movements, and a greater degree of contrast between themes and groups, it is not entirely a matter of a creative gap between the two, rather the cleaving to a more superficial kind of unity on the older man's part – perhaps a distant echo of the Baroque theory of A*ffekten* which proposed that one mood or emotion should dominate an entire movement. Development in Mozart is also more rigorous, especially considering the domestic, non-public realm of the piano sonata of his time.

A further reason for modification of the sonata during this period was that, in contradistinction to the concerto, which had, from the beginning, worn the trappings of its more-or-less public status, this period saw the piano sonata, like chamber music, make the vital transition from the private to the public domain.[5] In fact, in terms of composers' attitudes to it and the kind of music that was poured into it, it would not be a gross exaggeration to say that the sonata, rather than the more obvious concerto, became the solo-instrumental equivalent of the symphony. This is already apparent in Beethoven's first three published sonatas, the Op. 2 set (composed by 1795), not only in the quality of their music and their general cut, but also in their occasional hints at orchestral sonority[6] and their four-movement mould, although he would revert, for the most part, to the 'traditional' three movements for the bulk of his later sonatas.

Before the appearance of Op. 2, however, and in spite of the plethora of examples of works and definitions of 'sonata' by various authorities,[7] the view of what a piano sonata was had begun to crystallise by the time our period began. It can be seen doing so in the works of another important composer of piano sonatas crossing over from Classic to Romantic, the versatile and cosmopolitan Italian, Muzio Clementi, who wrote an important body of works, many of which have two movements. This is

---

[5] See Chapters Twenty-Four and Twenty-Five.

[6] See Chapter Six (ii), Ex. 6.2 for an instance of this.

[7] See entry for 'Sonate' in Rousseau/*DICTIONNAIRE*, in Sulzer/*ALLGEMEINE* and in Koch/*LEXIKON* (1802), as well as 'Vor der Sonate' in Koch/*VERSUCH*.

typical of the Southern fork of the North-/South-European divide discussed in Chapter Ten. On the other hand, all the sonatas of W.F., and of Johann Christoph Friedrich Bach, and the greater part of the output of C.P.E. Bach, Georg Benda (a Bohemian who spent most of his life within the Germanic axis) and Christian Gottlob Neefe (best remembered for having taught the young Beethoven) have the 'traditional' three-movement fast-slow-fast outline of the northern, Germanic, type.

So, a summary here would be on the lines of the description given at the beginning of this section, that a sonata was to be a work of between two and four – and mostly three – separate movements with some degree of variety in tempo and time signature, and with at least the first movement in Classical sonata-form.[8] The other movements could be minuets or scherzos, variations, or rondos, or indeed sonata-rondos.

It became usual for aspiring composers to issue, at their own expense, a set of sonatas dedicated to their teacher as their Opus 1 thereby combining the advantages of appearing in print with throwing themselves at this early stage in their career on the mercy of the relatively uncritical domestic market, thereby at least covering the printing costs, and, at the same time, announcing their didactic pedigree in a famous teacher's (or teachers') name(s). A critic in the influential Leipzig periodical, the *Allegemeine musikalische Zeitung* in 1798–9 wrote:

> Good piano sonatas are written less often now than formerly, when the tendency of every musician who wanted public recognition as an active composer was to begin his career with piano pieces, especially solo sonatas – solo sonatas that may not have shown our present superior taste but still had to excel in craftsmanship if the composer hoped to come off with some distinction for his work. Although piano sonatas were less generally cultivated then, they had relatively more good in them than now, when everyone who knows that 3/5/8/ is a triad writes any old way, as the spirit moves him. This composition mania is now gone so far that in nearly every town of any size music publishers are or will be established that, in order to supply nothing but novelties, accept and publish everything they can engrave. There are always [those] little men who will buy anything without looking so long as it is new. Such works cost nothing more than about a dozen free samples as an honorarium, [plus] paper and ink, whereby the publisher is satisfied. The author sees his name printed, nice and big, in an elegantly flourished title, whereby he has achieved his main purpose.[9]

This did not encourage the highest quality: Sor, writing in his *Mémoires* about Paris in 1813 or 1814, relates that a 'celebrated guitarist' told him that a publisher had said:

> It is one thing to appreciate compositions as a connoisseur, and another as a music seller, [and] it is necessary to write silly trifles for the public. "I like your work, but it would not return me the expense of printing." What is to be done? An author must live.[10]

In spite of their growing popularity, sonatas remained for some time firmly in the private domain. They were rarely played in public concerts until the 1830s in Vienna.

---

[8] See below (ii) for a description and history of this.
[9] Review of Joseph Wölfl's piano sonatas Op. 6, vol. I, pp. 236–7, quoted in Newman/SCE, p. 47.
[10] Bone/GUITAR, p. 338.

Mentions of Clementi sonatas (understandably, given their virtuosity and 'public' feel) crop up on a few occasions in London and around the turn of the century chamber music (including accompanied sonatas) were played there also, but this was the piano in a subordinate role rather than as a solo instrument. Burney makes the point that concerts in London were orchestral, vocal, or both.

(ii) First movements

In terms of figuration, presentation of material, harmony and above all form, the transition from Baroque to Classical can perhaps best be seen in the opening movements of piano sonatas. In terms of form, this movement came to embody one of the most important elements of the new Classical style, the encapsulation of a newly articulated tonal/thematic architectonic structuring, sonata-form.

The various paradoxes involved in this term are legendary. Several scholars contend that it doesn't exist, that it is not a form but a principle. I have some sympathy with this view, especially considering that there are 'slow-movement', and 'concerto'[11] versions, not to mention the form's occurrence in works which are not normally designated as 'sonatas' – the symphony, string quartet and overture. Its intertwining with the rondo, giving us the preferred Classical finale's 'sonata-rondo', and its combination with fugal expositions in the finales of Mozart's 'Jupiter' Symphony and D major String Quintet K. 593 are magnificent examples of its versatility. Furthermore, the discussions or explanations of a recognisable 'textbook' sonata-form that can be applied with reasonable impunity to the huge body of literature from the period were not articulated until around 1840, by which time the form was already floundering and copiously shipping late Romantic water. But, any examination of a representative body of first movements shows an undeniable consensus, and clearly composers – whose training was, in any case, largely by example, copying and studying the best models, or by direct contact with other composer/teachers – were aware of a blueprint that they obviously found not only acceptable, but extremely serviceable, and possibly even inspirational.

The form itself can be seen as an amalgamation of two earlier ones, both of prime importance in the Baroque period and, significantly, particularly characteristic of the dance-movements of the suite, which enriched the solo keyboard literature more than any other genre. Binary form was, as the name implies, in two parts, each of which was usually repeated. The same, or recognisably similar, melodic material was used for each section, the first of which modulated to, and cadenced in, the dominant (V in major keys) or the relative major (in minor keys). The second section often began in this same key and modulated back to the tonic (I), using the A material or a close relative.

```
Melodic ‖: A        :‖: B              :‖
Key        I_____V   ?V_____I__
```

---

[11] Further discussion on this combination is reserved for Chapter Sixteen.

Between the V and the I of the second section, there were often brief excursions to related keys and, if these were notable, the term 'rounded binary' was often used.

It is apparent that the tonal (or key-) structure takes precedence over thematic considerations, and it could be said that the opposite is true in the case of sonata form's other progenitor, ternary form. In this tripartite manifestation, schematised as ABA (or ABA^1), the presence of different melodic (often contrasting) material separates presentations of A, both of which will appear in the tonic, the B section need not be in the dominant and is frequently in another key, the relative for instance.

```
Melodic   A              B            A/A¹
Key       I_____?_____I____
```

(A^1 denotes a variant of, or material closely related to, that of the A section.)

In practice, the distinction between the forms became muddied by a growing tendency, in the eighteenth century, to inject an element of recapitulation of the A section in binary form.

These representations are, of course, simplifications, as is a statement that sonata form can be seen as an amalgamation of the tonal (or key) structure of binary with the recapitulatory shape of ternary. This can be simply shown as follows – below the main section headings of sonata form are given a summary of melodic material and the broad harmonic scheme:

Exposition   Development Recapitulation (or Reprise)

1st sub - *trans* - 2nd sub - codetta :‖:from subs   1st sub - *trans* - 2nd sub - codetta:‖

I_____ *mod*   V/rel_____   (various)   I   ?   I_____

The underlying structure of sonata form is based on the conflict between an established key (the tonic) its replacement (through modulation and key establishment) of another key (the dominant or relative major for the most part), the weakening of this new key in the development and its replacement by the original tonic. Each of the two key-areas is assigned melodic, very often contrasting, material but so-called 'monothematic' structures, in which the same thematic/melodic material is used for both key areas, are not uncommon, a frequent practitioner here being Joseph Haydn. This very basic envelope can be modified: introductions and codas can be added before and after the scheme, and subjects (and transitions, or 'bridge' passages) can be groups, containing several themes. The Development serves to weaken the newly established key – melodically, by breaking up the thematic material into smaller pieces, or motifs and recombining them in various ways, thus undermining the association of theme with key, and harmonically, by various devices such as harmonic and contrapuntal sequences, use of ambiguous harmony, and so on. It can be deduced that psychologically and aesthetically, the return of the tonic key is *the* important moment in sonata form. Furthermore, since the main function of the transition section is to modulate to the new key, its function is obviated in the Reprise; in practice, however, the balance of the work demands its retention to some extent, and it usually remains in a modified form.

Apart from some examples of the misnamed 'monothematic' type, in which the second subject is the same as, or very close to, the first, but in the 'proper' key, sonata form often implied some kind of distinction between the first and second subjects (or subject areas) other than a tonal one, and this set it to some extent at odds with the Baroque theory of *Affekten* in which the dominating character of a movement was preserved largely intact throughout. Given also that the Development section would usually be based – and in many cases exclusively – on material from the first subject, it was important for this subject to be clearly articulated. Simply accompanied arpeggiaic openings were common, and they seem to serve the function of giving information about key, mode and rhythm rather than being designed for development. Thus, in the Developments of Mozart's K. 332 (300k) in F major and K. 545 in C major (both with simple arpeggiaic themes supported by a basic *Alberti* figuration), he neglects to refer to the opening theme in any immediately recognisable version of its original form, including its *Alberti* texture, although the codetta in the exposition of K. 545 is a diminution of the opening theme (Ex. 14.3a/b); the scale figure (bb. 31ff), although occurring in the second half of the theme, is so common in C major works as to be discountable, developmentally speaking, in this context.

Ex. 14.3a/b: W.A. Mozart, Piano Sonata in C major K. 545/i, bb. 1–2 and 26–7.

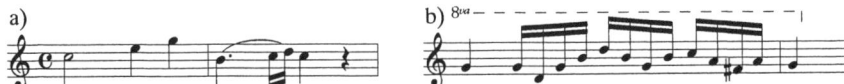

Another common opening texture involving arpeggios is the presentation in unharmonised octaves; again, the presentation of tonal and rhythmic information seems paramount, but Mozart invariably alters the repetitions texturally and it is this version that is used in the development sections. In the case of K. 570 (in B flat major), Mozart uses the opening of his first subject for the second, except that it is now in the piano's lower register and the original second half becomes the basis of a countermelody in the upper register[12] (Ex. 14.4a/b).

Ex. 14.4a/b: W.A. Mozart, Piano Sonata in B flat major K. 570/i, bb. 1–6 and 41–5.

In K. 576 (in D major) the opening theme is treated in a similar way, this time in a counterstatement, but again, in the lower register and again, contrapuntally, and against another version of itself in mock-canon writing (Ex. 14.5a/b).

---

[12] Registers and their implication on the early piano have been discussed in Chapter Three (iii).

Ex. 14.5a/b: W.A. Mozart, Piano Sonata in D major K. 576/i, bb. 0–2 and 8–11.

This treatment is extended and becomes the basis of the first developmental process (Exx. 14.5c and 14.5d).

Ex. 14.5c: K. 576/i, bb. 27–30.

Ex. 14.5d: K. 576/i, bb. 62–7.

Presentation of material, in line with the sonata's growing importance, also became more dramatic, as opposed to becoming simply louder, and here, too, the Classical masters had shown the way. Mozart's A minor Sonata of 1778, K. 310 (300d), gives its desperate first subject with an accompaniment more characteristic of an early nineteenth-century concerto (Ex. 14.6)

Ex. 14.6: W.A. Mozart, Piano Sonata in A minor K. 310 (300d)/i, bb. 1–4.

and Haydn's late E flat major sonata (H:XVI:52, 1794) with drama allied to reflection within a few bars (Ex. 14.7).

Ex. 14.7: J. Haydn, Piano Sonata in E flat major H:XVI:52/i, bb. 1–4.

Hummel's Second Piano Sonata in E flat major (Op. 13, pub. 1805, but composed earlier) is also Janus-faced, with an opening flourish followed by a contrapuntal presentation of an *Alleluia* very similar to that used by Haydn in Symphony No. 30 in C major ('Alleluja'). The presentation is typically 'learned' with a third-species counterpoint using the diminished retrograde of the opening phrase (Ex. 14.8a).

Ex. 14.8a: Hummel, Piano Sonata in E flat major Op. 13/i, bb. 1–8.

This undergoes minimal changes in its later repetitions, in the transition and Development, and opens the reprise without its initial flourish. In the coda, it appears with its *Alleluja* title and has a closing extension (Ex. 14.8b). This sonata is dedicated to his teacher, Haydn, and no doubt homage, and the compliment of a kind of imitation, is intended.

Ex. 14.8b: Op. 13/i, Coda.

Ex. 14.8b continued

Perhaps Schubert also had something of the same intention in his early sonata in C major, D. 279 when he gives us a version of his opening treated in the same way as Hummel (Ex. 14.9a/b).

Ex. 14.9a/b: Schubert, Piano Sonata in C major D. 279/i, bb. 1–4 and 13–15.

At the time of the sonata's composition, Hummel was resident in Vienna and well known as a composer and teacher. In 1814, he emerged as a pianist also. Schubert's regard for Hummel can be gauged from the fact that he dedicated his last three great sonatas to him, a dedication that the publisher later changed after Schubert's untimely death, because Hummel had left Vienna.

In John Field's Op. 1/2 piano sonata in A major, the braggadocio of the opening (Ex. 14.10a) ia soon quelled,

Ex. 14.10a: Field, Piano Sonata in A major Op. 1/2/i, bb. 1–2.

and after another five bars the dotted figure occurs as in Ex. 14.10b.

Ex. 14.10b: Op. 1/2/i, bb. 7–12.

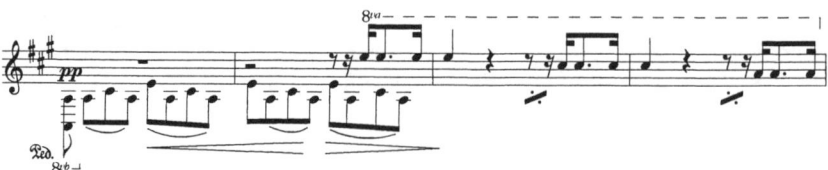

Ex. 14.10b continued

In his first sonata in E flat major we can see the process in reverse (Ex. 14.11a). Here, the gentle opening is only gently interrupted by the chromatic bass echo in b. 5 and the halt in b. 6 does not prepare us for the onslaught to come in the Development (Ex. 14.11b).

Ex. 14.11a: Field, Piano Sonata in E flat major Op. 1/1/i, bb. 0–8.

Ex. 14.11b: Op. 1/1/i, development.

Beethoven's '*Waldstein*' Sonata (Op. 53 in C major) also indulges in deception, in that the opening suggests neither the theme nor the key (Ex. 14.12), and the fact that it is accompanimental and textural does not help.

Ex. 14.12: Beethoven, Piano Sonata in C major Op. 53/i, bb. 1–7.

Subtly deceptive in the long-term is Schubert's last sonata in B flat major, D. 960, where the atmospheric trill on the flat sixth degree (G♭ in Ex. 14.13a) subliminally prepares us for its enharmonic adoption as the key of the second subject, F sharp minor (Ex. 14.13b).

Ex. 14.13a: Schubert, Piano Sonata in B flat major D. 960/i, bb. 0–10.

Ex. 14.13b: D. 960/i, bb. 48–50.

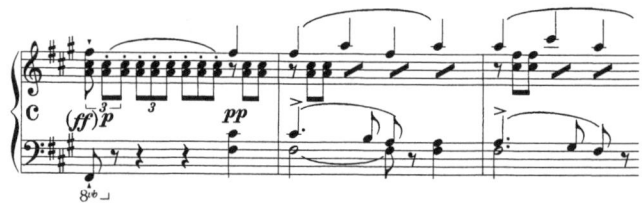

The Op. 10/2 Sonata in F major of Beethoven shows the witty side of deception in its opening in the purported move to IV, which, because of the dominant seventh/augmented sixth pun in bb. 14–15 (Ex. 14.14, marked *) – which the reader can see because of his 'spelling' – does not materialise, bringing us rather to the dominant of chord iii (A minor). This in turn is ignored in a direct shift to the dominant (C major) which is then established in mock laboriousness. This wit appears in all the movements in various ways, especially in the 'mock-fugue' of the finale, referred to in Chapter Three, Ex. 3.10.

Ex. 14.14: Beethoven, Piano Sonata in F major Op. 10/2/i, bb. 0–26.

Ex. 14.14 continued

As one might expect, Beethoven's sonatas show tremendous variety in their methods of presenting subject matter, from the 'Mannheim Rocket' of the first, Op. 2/1, to the rather 'stagey' Maestoso of the last, Op. 111 (1822, Ex. 14.15), similar to the opening of Chopin's B flat minor Op. 35 (1837–9, Ex. 14.16).

Ex. 14.15: Beethoven, Piano Sonata in C minor Op. 111/i, bb. 0–2.

Ex. 14.16: Chopin, Piano Sonata in B flat major Op. 35/i, bb. 1–5.

The three sonatas of Beethoven's Op. 2 are, like some of Hummel's early works, dedicated to Haydn – who was also Beethoven's teacher for a short and turbulent time, during which his arrogance caused the usually benign Haydn to describe him as the

'Grand Mogul'. Here, as is the case in some other of his works, such as with the string quartet Op. 18/1/i and the piano sonata Op. 2/3/i, it is the least obviously significant element of the opening bars which he isolates for the kind of colouristic development which we will find to be a characteristic of improvisatory practice in the period.[13] This little scrap, the flare of the 'rocket', (see Chapter Three, Ex. 3.1) is given against various harmonies, consonant and dissonant, in various voices, and is augmented (bb. 7–8 and 15–19) and finally, shorn of its demisemiquaver run, becomes part of the free inversion which forms the second subject (bb. 20ff.).

(iii) Development Sections

Dealing with Field, earlier, I mentioned the fact that the opening of his first sonata gave no obvious hint of the passion of its Development, but this was by no means new. The piano sonatas of Haydn and Mozart, perhaps more than any other genre in which they worked, are deceptive in their presentation of a socially amenable face but hiding darker intentions. In Mozart, the *Alberti* bass patterns, rarely absent from at least one of the principal subject areas, is very frequently used to build rhythmic dissonant tension at important cadence points, usually associated with the cadential trill; this is also a feature of the piano concertos. But it can also lose its quality of bland accompanimental innocence and be transformed into something more sinister. Ex. 14.17a, from the Development of his first published piano sonata (K. 279 (189d) of early 1775), shows its use in simple but effective imitation, based on a sequence.

Ex. 14.17a: W.A. Mozart, Piano Sonata in C major K. 279 (189d)/i, bb. 44–7.

This movement also shows the surprising strength, and occasional ferocity, of some of Mozart's Development sections: the plunge, *forte*, into the dominant minor after the double-barline (b. 39) is a case in point (Ex. 14.17b),

Ex. 14.17b: K. 279 (189d)/i, bb. 36–40.

---

[13] See Chapter Twenty-Two.

Ex. 14.17b continued

and in the first movement of the next sonata, K. 280 (189e) in F major, written at the same time, he also produces the unexpected dynamic of *forte*, allied to register-exploitation (Ex. 14.18).

Ex. 14.18: W.A. Mozart, Piano Sonata in F major K. 280 (189e)/i, bb. 63–9.

Probably the most striking example of this is in the great A minor sonata K. 310 (300d) where he shows his typical lack of fear of dissonance, and loud, insistent dissonance at that. The subject (Ex. 14.6 above) hammers out, in the right hand, the main rhythm, from which the dotted figure is abstracted and subjected to obsessive repetition in a highly dissonant context (Ex. 14.19a),

Ex. 14.19a: W.A. Mozart, Piano Sonata in A minor K. 310 (300d)/i, bb. 58–62.

and even the fairly inoffensive little cadential *gruppetto* (Ex. 14.19b)

Ex. 14.19b: K. 310 (300d)/i, bb. 70–1.

is given a menacing spin by being used with minor and diminished harmonies in the bass register (Ex. 14.19c).

Ex. 14.19c: K. 310 (300d)/i, bb. 74–9.

This can be viewed in another way, however, as what one might call the 'development' of actual keyboard technique within a movement. It may take the form of extension or intensification, and can be seen particularly clearly in this sonata. Here, the passage in Ex. 14.19a is an intensification of elements from the Codetta (Ex. 14.19d), the two melodic lines in the right hand against a semiquaver pattern and the reiteration of the dotted rhythm in the last bar of the example. At its most basic, this kind of 'development' manifests itself in the addition of decorations to a melodic line: this is dealt with later under the headings of Variations (Chapter Fifteen) and Improvisation 1 (Chapter Twenty-Two). It also has a place in areas such as *reprises* or returns and, of course, in Development sections.

Ex. 14.19d: K. 310 (300d)/i, bb. 41–5.

Ex. 14.19d continued

But the 'development' goes beyond this kind of decorative overlaying and it is not confined to first movements, nor even sonata-form movements. An instance can also be seen in Mozart's K. 280 (189e)/ii (a slow movement, but in full, if miniature sonata form), where the trill-auxiliary figure followed by the rising fourth of the opening (see Ex. 14.21a, section (iv) below) becomes smoothed into a double turn and imitatively – as well as chromatically – intensified by its use in different voices and registers (see Ex. 14.21b, section (iv) below).

One would expect to find this technique, to whatever extent, in those works which were avowedly virtuosic and 'physical', such as the C major sonatas that composers of this time seem to revel in producing early on in their careers:– Beethoven (Op. 2/3, 1796), Hummel (also Op. 2/3, pub. 1792), Weber (J 138, 1812) and so on. The first-mentioned of these is a case in point. The first of its four movements associates each of the main sonata-form areas in the exposition with a particular aspect of piano technique, all of which are developed in the Development section. The first subject is based on the turn (Ex. 14.20a) presented in thirds, against changing harmony and in the bass, and each of these is intensified later in the movement:

Ex. 14.20a: Beethoven, Piano Sonata in C major Op. 2/3/i, bb. 1–13.

from the Development comes the *fausse reprise* in D major, rendering the thirds more difficult (Ex. 14.20b),

Ex. 14.20b: Op.2/3/i, bb. 109–10.

an increased tightness in harmonised and bass presentations (Ex. 14.20c, bb. 129–34) and when presented melodically (bb. 135–8), as well as the further virtuosity shown in the cadenza of the coda, b. 232.

Ex. 14.20c: Op. 2/3/i, bb. 129–38.

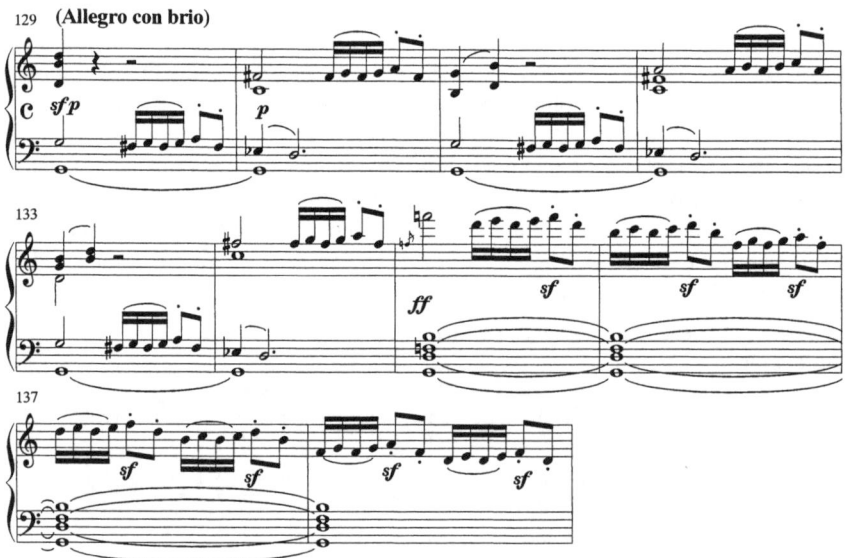

Similarly, the sonata's transition-passage is characterised by arpeggios and broken octaves (Ex. 14.20d)

Ex. 14.20d: Op. 2/3/i, b. 13.

and this, too, is extended in the cascading figure (Ex. 14.20e),

Ex. 14.20e: Op. 2/3/i, bb. 97–8.

while the syncopated figure that ends the first subject (see last two bb. of Ex. 14.20a) also becomes intensified in the Development (Ex. 14.20f) interspersed with the turn figure, and is further played within the reprise. In similar fashion, the lyrical arpeggiaic second melody of the second subject group is extended in the long coda.

Ex. 14.20f: Op. 2/3/i, bb. 123–8.

The other movements of the sonata also engage in this kind of development, the syncopated cadential gesture in the Adagio (Ex. 14.20g) is intensified harmonically, and registrally later (see Chapter Three, Ex. 3.9) and the closeness of touch, hand-shape, instrument and music in the scherzo will be apparent to anyone who has performed it.

Ex. 14.20g: Op. 2/3/ii, bb. 6–7.

The finale (Allegro assai), a sonata-rondo, is also imbued with this physicality. In this movement, the principal areas share most of their musical material, triad, scale, decoration and a falling third (marked x in Ex. 14.20h) and again, are characterised by their individual appropriation of points of piano technique. The 'A1' subject (using the Rondo aspect of the movement) in non-root-position (mostly 6/3) chords with its auxiliary, its rising scale traversing registers and its reliance on wrist staccato; the companion melody showing another aspect of the auxiliary and the scale – now legato (bb. 8–10) –

Ex. 14.20h: Op. 2/3/iv, bb. 0–12.

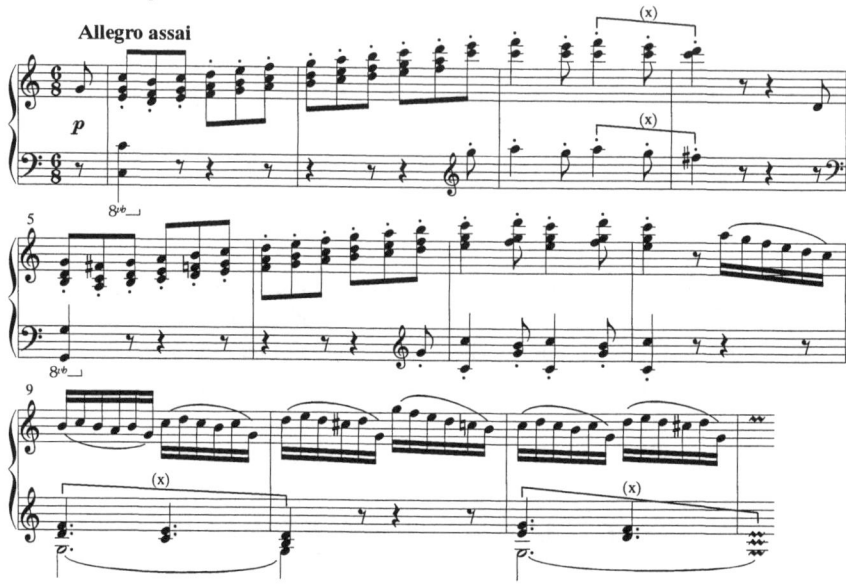

and the second subject (Ex. 14.20i), where the triad is expressed as a diminished and a major arpeggio in different rhythms (also in the accompaniment)

Ex. 14.20i: Op. 2/3/iv, bb. 30–2.

and, within a few bars, converted into the 6/4 (second inversion) form (Ex. 14.20j).

Ex. 14.20j: Op. 2/3/iv, bb. 45–50.

These, in their turn, are developed, extended and intensified in a number of ways, which include the conversion of the triads from the 6/3 form of A1 into octaves for each hand, the staggered configuration in Ex. 14.20k, the central C-section melody (Ex. 14.20l) and the syncopations of Ex. 14.20m.

Ex. 14.20k: Op. 2/3/iv, bb. 87–8.

Ex. 14.20l: Op. 2/3/iv, bb. 103–6.

Ex. 14.20m: Op. 2/3/iv, bb. 119–21.

The opening theme of the 'Appassionata' Sonata (Op. 57 in F minor, 1804–5), an arpeggio, is also subjected to 'development' of the kind in question, as well as the usual ways, being expressed in octaves, *pp*, at the opening, then soon after in *ff* chords staggered rhythmically between the hands, over a single repeated note (bb.134ff) under and over *tremolandi* (bb. 79–93), supported by a different kind of *tremolando* in its guise as the second subject (bb. 35ff.) and under an inverted *Alberti* bass in a pre-echo of the keyboard textures of the late sonatas' variations (bb. 203ff).

The intimate connection between music and instrument in Beethoven's late sonatas has already been discussed in sections (iii) and (iv) of Chapter Six. To that can be added the connection between both of them and Beethoven the player[14] and, by implication, later players, whose contact with this music constantly brings it to the fore. But these works are only a special case of the general symbiosis involving the piano itself and the particular kind of public virtuoso-composer, to whom it gave birth and sustained and who was unique to this period.

(iv) 'Slow' movements

The situation for the rest of the sonata was less prescriptive: if there were two movements, the second was medium- or fast-paced and commonly a minuet, occasionally a rondo or set of variations. This two-movement type, often with

---

[14] Unfortunately, as noted in Chapter Six (iii), 'performer' is inappropriate because of his deafness.

suggestions from the dance – mostly the minuet – was particularly prevalent in the Italian keyboard sonata, in composers such as Domenico Paradies [Paradisi], Domenico Alberti, Baldassare Galuppi and Giovanni Rutini, and many of Domenico Scarlatti's sonatas are so paired. These sonatas, called *Essercizi* and numbered individually, were found grouped according to key in twos and (less commonly) threes, in the two main sources. Although Scarlatti's intentions are not known, there is something of a consensus that he did approve, or would have done.[15] The majority of J.C. Bach's, like his concertos, and many of Joseph Haydn's sonatas are also in two movements – even as late as the last group of three (written in England, during his second trip, for Miss Therése Jansen), of which the second (H:XVI:51 in D major, 1794 or 1795) has an Andante followed by a Presto Finale. Miss Jansen was a pianist whom Haydn met in London, and the dedicatee of his last piano trios.[16] Beethoven adopted similar outlines for his two Op. 49 sonatas: Andante followed by Rondo (Allegro) and Allegro ma non troppo followed by Tempo di Menuetto. These, however, are much earlier than their opus number would suggest. Three other works of his are also in two movements: Op. 54 in F major opens with In tempo d'un Menuetto – but a very undanceable one – and concludes with an Allegretto perpetuum mobile which has a bad-tempered Più Allegro coda.

Beethoven's rather quirky Op. 78, an Adagio movement followed by an Allegro vivace was one of the Master's favourites and if there were such a thing as a 'transitional work' Op. 90 would be a strong candidate. While outside the last 'Great Five' sonatas, it shares, albeit less intensely, their preoccupation with counterpoint, and is the first of his sonatas to use German directions for the movements and without Italian corollaries. The keys of its two movements – E minor followed by E major – mirror that of the last sonata, Op. 111 with C minor and C major and the duality of the movements, though, again, less marked in the Op. 90, can also be seen in Op. 111. This duality is almost Schumannesque, not in terms of style – although Felix Mendelssohn admired the Finale's 'Song Without Words' feel – but rather in the Florestan/Eusebius separation,[17] which Schumann occasionally used to justify the juxtaposition of contrasting pieces. Here the opposition is more one of doing and feeling, objective and subjective, intensification and rarefaction.

When a sonata did have a middle movement, the favoured key in the earlier part of our period is, like the concerto, the subdominant in the case of major-key works, which form the vast majority. This gives way to a desire for modal contrast – already evident in the trios of minuets or scherzos as in all three of Beethoven's Op. 2 – with the relative minor becoming more prominent and, eventually, other, more chromatic, third-relationships, such as the flattened sixth. The pioneering Mozart had already explored this kind of relationship in the A minor sonata, K. 310 (300d, 1778), with its middle movement in F major, as had Clementi in his Op. 7/3 in G minor, slow movement in E flat major (1782), and Beethoven would follow suit in his Op. 10/1 (C minor and A flat major, of ?1795–7), and Dussek's Op. 44 Sonata in E flat major

---

[15] See Boyd/SCARLATTI.
[16] See Landon/CHRONICLE III.
[17] See Chapter Nine (iii) for more on this.

(1800) with its slow movement in B major. Other more remote uses also crept in, such as the major-parallel of the relative minor, the third and the flattened third.

Mozart's middle movements, possibly even more than those of his piano concertos, show the variety possible in this period: most are Andantes (including an *amoroso*, a *Rondeau en Polonaise*, and the occasional *cantabile*) but some are Adagio, beginning with the extra-ordinarily deeply-felt slow movement (in the parallel minor key of F minor) of K. 280 (189e) in F major (Ex. 14.21a, 1775).

Ex. 14.21a: W.A. Mozart, Piano Sonata in F major K. 280 (189e)/ii, bb. 1–10.

This is a case-study in barely controlled grief, the more surprising for coming between two fairly sunny fast movements, and one of a series of minor-key movements in *siciliana* rhythm, including the slow movement of the A major piano concerto K. 488 (in the extremely unusual key of F sharp minor), the finale of the D minor string quartet K. 421 and the great Rondo in A minor, K. 511 for piano solo.[18]

It is a measure of the seriousness of intent on the part of the 19-year-old composer that this F minor Adagio of K. 280 (189e) is couched in a miniature sonata form but, additionally, not of the 'slow-movement' type (lacking a Development section). The opening is full of tragic detail – the minimal accompaniment of a chord to what is essentially a repeated C in the opening bar and its vocal, and unexpected, *portato* up to the tonic which, is presented as a long dissonance exacerbated by the rhythmic echo of the middle voice, the reiterated dissonances of the next bars and the delaying of the perfect cadence until the last possible minute in b. 8. As with similar works from the *Sturm und Drang* period (such as the early G minor Symphony), there is no transition to the relative major for the second subject, simply an abrupt move (see bb. 8–9 in Ex. 14.21a), and the accompaniment is a modified *Alberti* bass (beginning

---

[18] See Chapter Thirteen (v) for a brief treatment of this work.

on a 6/4 inversion) that refuses to allow a perfect cadence until the very end, b. 20. The key of A flat major is only half-confirmed by the disjointed four-bar coda.

The apparent tranquility of this second subject is belied by the augmented sixth and diminished chords and the Development section proper sets the sensibilities of the two subjects against each other, with *p – f* contrasts, and a *fausse reprise* in the dominant minor (Ex. 14.21b). The real *reprise* truncates the first subject by two bars, and the second subject, now in the tonic minor, is, in effect, subjected to further development, with the lyricism turned into tragedy (bb. 43–57), reaching quite unexpected heights of anguish, with, perhaps, some anger, neither of which is quite dispelled by the rhyming coda in the tonic.

Ex. 14.21b: K. 280 (189e)/ii, bb. 25–37.

There is nothing like this in the music of J.C. Bach; the nearest approach is the *Empfindsamkeit*[19] of his brother Emanuel, but it is only an approach. With Mozart we are almost in the world of Romanticism, and the real echoes are in some of the slow movements of Beethoven, although he rarely touches the pathological depth of which Mozart seems capable, This is at its most extreme in the non-public works, such as the slow movement of the D major String Quintet K. 593 and the whole of the G minor String Quintet K. 516, but also appears unexpectedly in the Andante of the G major Piano Concerto K. 453. It was a trait of which the early Romantics were

---

[19] This, and related terms, is discussed in Chapter One (iv).

well aware, and one of the reasons why Mozart, in particular, was accepted as 'one of them' rather than a 'pure' Classic.

The enormous emotional range of Mozart's slow movements is noteworthy, and is matched by his utilisation of the piano in its portrayal of these. The Andante amoroso in E flat major, the middle movement of the next sonata, K. 281 (189f) in B flat major, is not far from the rapt world of some of Schumann's child-oriented pieces at its opening, and moves from quavers through semiquavers to semiquaver triplets with no sense of hurry or jarring (Ex. 14.22).

Ex. 14.22: W.A. Mozart, Piano Sonata in B flat major K. 281 (189f)/ii, bb. 1–15.

Just as many of his piano-concerto slow movements are compared to operatic arias, Mozart goes one better in the sonatas, creating, in effect the aria for piano solo. There was something of this already to be found in the very first sonata in C major (K. 279 (189d), 1775) with its Andante in the subdominant, showing him at his coyest (Ex. 14.23a) with a typically operatic interrupted cadence at bb. 3–4 and the feeling, almost constant with Mozart, that the music is inherently vocal, even though it wouldn't actually work very well in vocal terms.

Ex.14.23a: W.A. Mozart, Piano Sonata in C major K. 279 (189d)/ii, bb. 0–6.

Ex. 14.23a continued

Nevertheless, it takes very little time for even this, surely one of his most ingratiating melodies, to show an aggressive streak (Ex. 14.23b), displacing key, chords, and pulse.

Ex. 14.23b: K. 279 (189d)/ii, bb. 17–28.

The finest example of this kind of emotional landsliding in the piano sonatas is to be found in the central movement of the dramatic A minor sonata (K. 310 (300d). This was written during Mozart's visit to Paris with his mother in 1778 dating from the summer, when she died of fever (Ex. 14.24a). The opening is again ingratiating, full of vocal and theatrical gestures and coloratura decoration.

Ex. 14.24a: W.A. Mozart, Piano Sonata in A minor K. 310 (300d)/ii, bb. 0–14.

Ex. 14.24a continued

The movement shows an early example of *Terzverwandtschaft*, being in F major and is not simply an aria, but in fact an entire miniature operatic *scena*, using the full resources of the 'Viennese' piano of the period. This movement is also a fully-fledged sonata form with a second subject that grows out of the instrument in its rather tricky articulation (Ex. 14.24b).

Ex. 14.24b: K. 310 (300d)/ii, bb. 15–18.

Although the Development section begins an octave and a half lower in sombre mood with full repeated bass chords (Ex. 14.24c), one is still not prepared for the ominous turn of the music when it returns to the lower regions, and its further dissonant intensification spanning, at times, all three registers (bb. 43ff.). Such passion threatens the bounds of Classical decorum and is only barely restrained; and such Romantic upwellings – especially in a mere piano sonata – were amongst the manifestations of Mozart's that caused difficulty in selling his music and attracting subscribers. This music was definitely *non grata* in the Viennese drawing-room of the period.

Ex. 14.24c: K. 310 (300d)/ii, bb. 31–53.

Ex. 14.24c continued

Beethoven, a child of the French Revolution with powerful, rich, and musically cultured patrons providing him with a stipend that enabled him to devote himself to composition, had no such problems, although they would come later in life. He could not but be influenced by his great predecessor in the realm of the piano sonata, and, although his musical mind had less of an operatic, perhaps even simply vocal, bent, the *prima donna* sometimes lurks behind the curtains. The 'noble simplicity' – to use Winckelmann's characterisation of Classical Greek sculpture – of the opening of his first (published) sonata's slow movement,[20] Op. 2/1 with its meticulously marked articulation (Ex. 14.25a), soon becomes more overtly vocal (Ex. 14.25b),

Ex. 14.25a: Beethoven, Piano Sonata in F minor Op. 2/1/ii, bb. 0–4.

Ex. 14.25b: Op. 2/1/ii, bb. 8–12.

and he can no more resist the greasepaint than Mozart can (Ex. 14.25c),

---

[20] This is a reworking of the slow movement of an early piano quartet.

Ex. 14.25c: Op. 2/1/ii, bb. 23–5.

especially on the return of the theme (Ex. 14.25d).

Ex. 14.25d: Op. 2/1/ii, bb. 33–8.

Married to a singer, Elisabeth Röckel, whose brother was an opera-manager, Hummel was no stranger to the operatic voice and this shows in many of his slow movements also. The slow movement of his E flat major Sonata Op. 13 (Adagio con gran espressione) is also in the nature of a scene, with the singer being alternated with distinctly orchestral touches (Ex. 14.26a, b and c),

Ex. 14.26a: Hummel, Piano Sonata in E flat major Op. 13/ii, bb. 16–17.

Ex. 14.26b: Op. 13/ii, bb. 23–4.

Ex. 14.26c: Op.13/ii, bb. 28–30.

and even a duet of some dramatic power (Ex. 14.26d).

Ex. 14.26d: Op. 13/ii, bb. 40–3.

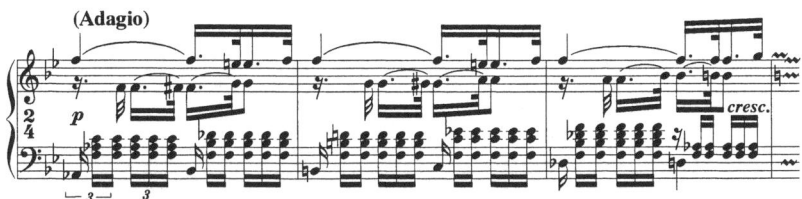

The slow movement of his great F sharp minor Sonata Op. 81 is more of the 'piano-aria', as opposed to the vocal-aria, type which, carrying over the *ff* close of the first movement, begins with an introduction (Ex. 14.27a), a peremptory reference (in the minor) to Bach's D major fugue subject from Book. I of the '48' (Ex.14.27b).

Ex. 14.27a: Hummel, Piano Sonata in F sharp minor Op. 81/ii, opening.

Ex. 14.27b: J.S. Bach, *Das Wohltemperirte Clavier* Bk. I/Fuga V in D major, bb. 1–2.

After this, a rather lugubrious nocturne in B minor gives little hint of the extraordinary wealth of piano textures and registral exploration that is to ensue; this movement really 'takes off' and is one of the best examples of the *cantabile-decorative* style in a sonata of the period. Ex. 14.27c gives a section from the middle of the movement.

Ex. 14.27c: Hummel, Piano Sonata in F sharp minor Op. 81/ii, bb. 15–23.

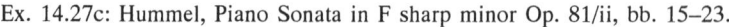

INFLUENCES

Mendelssohn makes no secret of his use of vocal ideas in his piano music, although the sonatas show little of it generally in their slow movements. The exception here is the Op. 6 in E major (1826[21]), whose second movement, in F sharp minor, is headed Tempo di Menuetto with a comparatively long second section in the minuet and a contrasting trio. On its return, however, the minuet is extended, developed and interrupted by a *Recitativo* (so called, Ex. 14.28), marked Adagio e senza tempo

Ex. 14.28: Mendelssohn, Piano Sonata in E major Op. 6/ii, Recitativo.

with a similar opening to that of the (extended) reprise of the first subject of Beethoven's Op. 31/2 in D minor (Ex. 14.29).

Ex. 14.29: Beethoven, Piano Sonata in D minor Op. 31/2/i, bb. 143–8.

---

[21] The opus-numbering of his three sonatas is misleading as to their dates: the Op. 6 was written 14 months before the Op. 106, but four-and-a-half years *after* the Op. 105.

In spite of the free-ness of the music, Mendelssohn actually presents this *recitative* as a four-voice fugal exposition of some ingenuity, follows it with short passages, one chorale-ish in F sharp major (3/4) and another with cascading arpeggios in E major (6/8) before bringing back the *Recitativo* in quasi-canonic imitation. The two passages return in B flat major and (eventually) the home key of E major respectively, and the finale begins without a break.

(v) Overall

Since the sonata's final movement in the period is, for the most part, a rondo or a sonata-rondo and often characterised – folk, pastoral, military, and so on – variations, or, earlier in the period, minuets, these are dealt with in other chapters and do not need to be given special treatment here.

Viewing the genre as a whole in this period, a number of trends can be discerned, of which the first is purely quantitative: the decline in the number of sonatas being produced overall, and per individual composer. This is by no means compensated for by the fact that the size of the individual works themselves was increased or, as some would have had it, inflated. Sonatas were longer, bigger, louder, more difficult and more disparate, but there were far fewer of them.

One reason is due to the development of the 'canon' mentality, the view of music as a set of Great Men – and it was an exclusively male set – who wrote nothing but Great Music that would be an improvement to humanity and would last as long as humankind had wit and taste, an attribute which was paramount in this period, as it had been in the eighteenth century, and is rather too complicated a concept to address in a general book such as this. Music was, like most of the other arts, an encapsulation of basic truths expressed in an individually personal manner and with an impact of great emotional power. Even in its domestic expression, this music was seen as partaking in its small way of the unapproachable greatness of its creator, foothills from which to gaze in awe at the Parnassian clouds. The greatness of the canonic icons was, therefore, not approachable, let alone attainable. But this, of course, did not stop lesser beings from venturing up the wild rocky paths; it just made them watch their steps more carefully and there was a kind of greatness in even trying. In this thrusting, entrepreneurial age, no one liked to fail and especially not to be seen to fail, but a magnificent failure might just be better than not trying at all.

Another reason was the notion of genre applied (though not in name) to music during this time, in the wider meaning of its use in painting, to describe different kinds of subject-matter – still lifes, peasant scenes, landscape, history – and the different techniques and 'messages' they embodied. In this view, the sonata had become, thanks above all to Beethoven – *the* canonic icon *par excellence* – the pianistic analogue of the symphony, and therefore an expression of the highest thoughts and sentiments. Even angels feared to tread on this holy ground.

As a corollary, such audacity was mercilessly criticised by the critics and commentators who became so much more prominent in our period, and this furthered the aura of the sonata as it did the symphony: Brahms' reticence in this latter area is a salutary reminder, as is his wholesale destruction of pieces he considered not to have made the grade. Thus, as noted earlier, composing a sonata became much more of an event than churning out groups of three or six at a time, and it is not surprising that the output of sonatas declined markedly in the last third of this period.[22]

There was also, of course, the more mercenary side in that the production of a few sets of variations on a folk song, swift and painless, was far more lucrative and more appropriate for the new domestic market, than any sonata, and the growing size of this public/private divide can be charted in the designation of pieces as 'de salon' or 'de concert', highlighting comparative interpretative as well as technical difficulty.

However, an additional problem resided within the sonata itself, becoming more noticeable as the period went on, that of an increasing looseness. There were forces that, as it were, sought to fragment the sonata, either by so characterising the movements as to make them like individual members of a set of character-pieces, or by the imposition of other, more-or-less extraneous, features, such as a 'public' type of virtuosity, or a high degree of pianistic colour, or by the inclusion of certain kinds of musical procedure that render the movements more separate – the predomination in movements of counterpoint, fugue, the cantabile-decorative style, and so on. An example is Cogan's Sonata in C major Op. 2/6 with its opening movement a *Capricio [sic] e Ad Libitum*: Adagio, a central fugue in the parallel minor and a concluding *Giga*.

An antidote to this fissile tendency was to link movements, either by implication, such as use of keys, or physically, so that one or more of them were joined – a tendency also seen in the concerto of the period – or to engineer some kind of unifying principle. The use of keys becomes a regular feature for creating somewhat tenuous links and several examples occur in Beethoven's late sonatas, as in the case of the first, Op. 101 in A major, where the first movement's ending is inconclusive, partly due to the elongation of the dominant chord followed immediately by the same note A, now as the mediant of the flattened sixth, F major for the *alla Marcia* second movement. This ends on its tonic F, again on a weaker beat, which in turn becomes the flattened sixth of the ensuing A minor Adagio (Ex. 14.30), a meditation that ends by drawing out its dominant with a reference to the opening of the first movement and finally cadences into A major for the fugue theme.

Ex. 14.30: Beethoven, Piano Sonata in A major Op. 101.

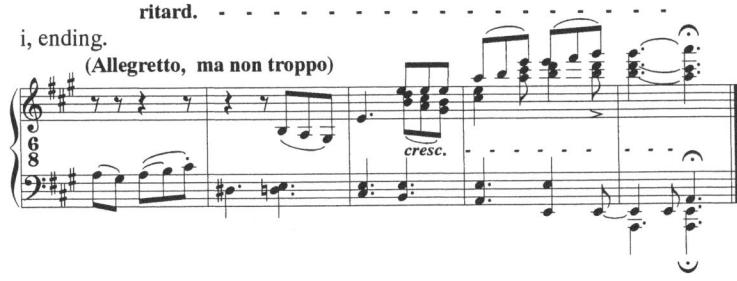

---

[22] See Newman/SSB, 93ff.

Ex. 14.30 continued

Joining of movements in the sense of running one into another or ending, for example on the dominant of the ensuing movement's key, is not particularly common in sonatas of the period and, if present, tends to occur between a slow movement and a faster one, as in the concerto.

The idea of a unifying principle is quite common, ranging from the simple and obvious to the structural and subliminal, requiring an analytical approach or approaches outside of the brief of this book. Amongst the less taxing methods of overall linkage is the use of a 'motto' idea, such as Anton Reicha's, as early as 1804, when, in his Sonata in E flat major Op. 43, he uses repetition, with a *piano* dynamic, as the basis of the opening thematic material of each of the three movements (Ex. 14.31).

Ex. 14.31: Reicha, Piano Sonata in E flat major Op. 43.

John Donaldson has the same idea in his only sonata in G minor, (?1822–3) where his first two movements – both in 3/4 – begin with repeated tonic chords (third on top) followed by a longer note and repeated Gs announce the second (major) episode in the concluding rondo (Ex. 14.32).

Ex. 14.32: Donaldson, Piano Sonata in G minor.

Friedrich Kalkbrenner's *Sonata for the Left Hand (obligato)* – whose title simply means that there is more emphasis than usual on the left-hand, and not that it is a sonata for the left hand alone – Op. 42 (in F minor, pub. 1818, Ex. 14.33), has each of the three movements sharing an opening rising triad followed by a stepwise fall,

Ex. 14.33: Kalkbrenner, Piano Sonata in F minor Op. 42.

and Corri's Sonata *L'Augurio Felice* (pub. 1808) gives the same prominence to a more obviously spelt-out 6/4 of its tonic, B flat major, which has echoes in the openings of the following two movements (Ex. 14.34), and even in the episodes of the finale (Ex. 14.34 iiia–c).

Ex. 14.34: Corri, *L'Augurio Felice*.

The end-point of all these unifying attempts is one of Liszt's greatest pianistic and compositional achievements, the Sonata in B minor, in which the four movements that had begun to become standard are compressed into a single long movement of between 25 and 35 minutes' playing time, and, in addition, the whole is overlaid with a one-movement sonata-form plan:[23]

i Allegro	ii Andante	iii Fugato	iv Allegro prestissimo
Intro & Expo	Development	Reprise	Coda

Essential for this to work is Liszt's creative technique of thematic transformation, especially that involving the two main themes/motives (Ex. 14.35) presented at the beginning.

Ex. 14.35: Liszt, Piano Sonata in B minor.

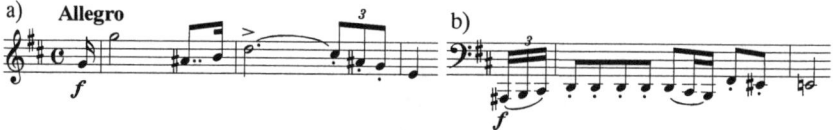

It is not surprising that such an original, profound and dramatic piece was subjected to so much searching for hidden meaning.

---

[23] This is taken from Walker/LISZT II, p. 151.

CHAPTER FIFTEEN

Received Forms 4: Variations

(i) General

An indispensable part of the amateur pianist's staple diet, the popularity of variations gave rise to a rabid demand that composers were only too eager to satisfy. Even the greatest succumbed to this rapidly burgeoning market with its rich pickings, and the lesser made much of their living from it, such as Abbé [Josef] Gelinek and Czerny, the latter with 500 to his credit.[1] The genre was extremely useful and economical: useful because it allowed the aspiring pianist the opportunity to play music by a composer in vogue on a tune in vogue without being a concert pianist; economical because the composer could turn out sets quickly and easily and because he or she could trade on the popularity of the pre-existent theme. Given consumer demand, the conservatism of most of these works is to be expected, a compound of the familiar and the fashionably 'new'.

It is important to remember, then, that sets of variations in this period were very much *Gebrauchsmusik* and not intended primarily as artistic statements of any great moment; one would seek such statements elsewhere, in the sonata for instance. There are, however, exceptions within the variation genre, where the basic compositional technique was the starting-point and not the end of the exercise and overriding musical and structural values obtained. Beethoven's *Diabelli*, and Haydn's F minor sets, Schumann's *Symphonische Etüden*, Mendelssohn's *Variations sérieuses* fulfil their function as variations admirably while transcending the necessarily additive form of the genre with structural unity and in some cases adding further interest by presenting and solving other problems – parody, counterpoint, keyboard technique.

The general binary shape of the tunes used for the sets and the attached variations' adherence to it remained from earlier periods as did the principal Baroque method of varying, best described by the term *Figuralvariation* ['figural variation']. This involved a more-or-less regular increase in melodic/rhythmic activity, the breaking down of the basic beat into progressively smaller units. In more mercenary hands and combined (as it so often was) with *moto perpetuo*, it could result in variations of stultifying predictability and was lampooned among other common procedural *clichés* in Castil-Blaze's *Dictionnaire de Musique Moderne* of 1825:

---

[1] In Nelson/VARIATION, pp. 18–19.

> Ce sont d'abord des simples croches, des triolets, puis des arpèges, des syncopes, des octaves, sans oublier l'adagio dans le mode relatif et le tempo di polacca. Avec les doigts et un peu de goût, un instrumentiste remplira tous les cadres en suivant les modèles donnés.[2]
>
> [First there are simple crotchets, triplets, then arpeggios, syncopations, [and] octaves, without forgetting the adagio in the relative major or minor and the 'tempo di polacca'. With fingers and a little taste, an instrumentalist will fill all the boxes in the manner of the given examples.]

In many sets however, this caricatured succession was alleviated by more fashionable elements, particularly later eighteenth-century *sensibilité* and the individualising of certain variations by characterisation of various kinds. At the same time, the technique of *motivische Arbeit* (an influence from improvisation) militated against a too-obvious shadowing of the melodic, harmonic and phrasal aspects of the theme and pointed the way for a freer treatment with the free (or fantasy) variations, seen in Schumann and later in Liszt, Franck and others.

The variation-theme was primary in every sense of the word; it was what attracted the buyer or listener, and the existence of anything up to half a dozen other sets on the same tune was no deterrent to composer or consumer. Two sources predominated here, the folk/popular[3] tune and the opera aria. The former had traditionally been a source of variations and the more recent burgeoning of its popularity proved a major boost for the industry, providing a large fund of material as well as a set of important model-types for original themes whether avowedly 'in the style of' a particular folk-genre or not. Also, because of the increasingly vernacular nature of eighteenth-century opera, that other great source of variation-themes, the opera aria, had for some time itself been cast in a kind of generalised folk/popular mould; thus, it would be fair to describe many of these themes as 'folk-like' also.

Such a choice of subject-matter was not, of course, without its problems. All folk tunes are intended to be subjected to variative procedures within their own traditions but these were of a kind that demanded a performer versed in the procedures that applied to that particular melody-type. Such procedures would have been both beyond and beneath the buyers of variation-sets in our period and would generally have been at odds with the harmonic, textural and, to some extent, melodic idioms of the time, as we shall see. Its provenance notwithstanding, the subject-matter for variations was not only worked on, but usually also exposed, as a set of data: a folk-like melody, more-or-less sanitised to fit in with the simple Western art-harmony accompanying it which, if it added little to it, at least did not usually detract significantly from it. Since so many of these themes were presented in such a way as to highlight their melodic properties (which is, after all, why they were familiar in the first place), it is not surprising that their subsequent treatment occupies itself almost exclusively with surface aspects. At its worst, the result was the kind of musical tapioca so characteristic of many of the less scrupulously produced sets.

Castile-Blaze's description is not too far wide of the mark and, in a typical set of the period, one would expect to find most of his categories with a few extras:

---

[2] Castil-Blaze/*DICTIONNAIRE*, entry for '*Variation*'.
[3] See Chapters Nineteen, Twenty and Twenty-One.

Figuralvariationen, variations displaying the piano's technical and colouristic properties, some kind of contrapuntal working, some appearance of the opposite mode, change of character and a return to the theme at or towards the end.

(ii) Figural variations

At its most common, this involves an arithmetical division of the theme's basic note-values without increase in the rate of harmonic rhythm, so that for instance, each crotchet becomes progressively two quavers, a quaver triplet, four semiquavers, a semiquaver sextuplet, and perhaps eight demisemiquavers. It was by far the most popular opening procedure, extending over the first three or four variations, occasionally more. Ex. 15.1a–d shows the incipits of the theme 'Fal lal la', (subtitled variously as 'The much admired [or Favorite] (Welch) Air (sung by Mrs Bland) in the *Cherokee*') and of the first three variations on it, written by 'Master [John] Field', probably the young Irishman's first publication.

Ex. 15.1a–d: Field, [Variations on] *Fal lal la*, openings of theme and (b–c) var. 1–3.

The set on the 'March of the Priests' from Mozart's *Magic Flute* by Neefe (1793) also illustrate this technique, but later variations make up for this by changing time-signature (₵ to C and 6/8) as well as key, and, in addition, the beauty and lack of four-square-ness of the theme saves the day.

The progression of variations may not be as literally consecutive as in these examples, but might be interrupted by other types providing localised contrast or, at least, respite, rendering the increase in note-values other than a purely surface feature and making the effect ultimately more telling. Such an insertion or insertions may even give the illusion of reversal of the onward rhythmically reductive motion.

This is part of the effect of the third variation in the group XV–XVIII of Beethoven's C minor set (WoO 80, 1806) where the progression is from triplet quavers (XV) through the same against quadruplet semiquavers (XVI), which in turn remain (XVII) under a two-part contrapuntal right hand (reversed in the last few bars) followed by demisemiquaver sextuplets (XVIII). Similarly, the *sempre legato* fifth variation in the second movement of J.B. Cramer's Piano Sonata Op. 20 is part of a group preceded by a *minore* No. 3 ('***pp*** *e con Espress^e*') and a triplet quaver 'Magiore' [*sic*] as No. 4, followed by a demisemiquaver No. 6.

Indeed, Beethoven is the prime example here, quite capable of making such *Figuralvariation* the whole rhythmic basis of a piece, often his greatest. The *Arietta* of his last sonata survives this treatment because it is only an adjunct to other variative techniques. As early as the first variation this process can be seen. When compared with the theme (see Ex. 15.2a) the variation's melody alone (in Ex. 15.2b) seems a straightforward decoration, the first beat of b. 1 of the variation being a kind of *appoggiatura* on the theme's G (articulated on the second beat) with the intervening semiquaver E being an alternative harmony-note of the theme's original chord of C major. Because, however, the A and E generate their own harmony in the variation (V^7 of ii) the G is presented not as the harmony note, but as an *appoggiatura* on the F (as third of ii); but, by keeping the G in the bass, the second-beat chord keeps some of the character of the theme's V^7 (of C) on its corresponding beat.

Ex. 15.2a: Beethoven, Piano Sonata in C minor Op. 111/ii, bb. 0–5.

Ex. 15.2b: Op. 111/iii/var. [1], bb. 0–2.

The extra subtlety of the two-beat groups on the immediate harmonic level (marked with square brackets) gently nudges the music ahead, creating a counterpoint between the harmonic rhythm in the left hand and that implied by the right hand (with its thematic reminiscences), the more so, since the operative notes are on off-beats within their triplets.

There are less spectacular examples of this kind of double-procedure, but they can also impress in their manipulation of their material to avoid the boredom that poses such a constant danger in this technique. Hummel's variations on a theme from

Gluck's *Armide* (Ex. 15.3) are based on increasing values from the quaver pulse of the theme

Ex. 15.3: Hummel, *Variations sur un thème d'Armide de Gluck* Op. 57/Thema, bb. 0–4.

through the following in consecutive variations:

Further manipulation may include reversing some of the components in the progression and, given adjustments on other levels, can impart some rather more subtle effects than might be expected at face value. One such technique involves the function of the increased note values and whether they cause an increase in momentum or not. If they are of the more-or-less simple arpeggiaic kind, spreading out the chord of the prevailing harmony even with the addition of the odd dissonance, the result will be simply more surface activity and this can be used to actually lower the tension. Similarly, the change from duplets to triplets of the same value can have the same effect since dissonance and consonance in duplets are of the same value, whereas triplets may only have one dissonant note in three, and that very often an unaccented one.

Decoration of a rudimentary kind is prominent; apart from the obvious alternative harmony-notes, auxiliaries and passing-notes of various kinds abound. The first of Beethoven's *Six Variations in D major* Op. 76 (1809, Ex. 15.4a/b) is representative of the tendency in hundreds of sets using this type to open.

Ex. 15.4a/b: Beethoven, *Six Variations in D major* Op. 76, Tema and (b) var. 1 opening.

(iii) Technique

The ease with which *Figuralvariationen* can be made a vehicle for technical display was useful in killing two birds with one stone, but it is this combination that has drawn more bitter scorn than any other from so many commentators both during the period and since. The very increase in note values was sufficient to give the impression of virtuosity and once the player had supplemented the pianistic basics with a few extra figures, he or she could cut a flashy swathe through the drawing rooms of the social circle. There was also the possibility, of course, of omitting the more difficult numbers without great musical damage to the whole.

Some sets of variations, however, were composed with technical considerations so firmly in mind that they become, in effect, a series of *études* connected by a common theme and aim. The prodigious violin technique of Paganini is responsible for a number of these and, coupled with the catchy tune of his *Caprice* No. 24, for solo violin, has been the launch pad for two sets by Brahms (Op. 35 Nos. 1 and 2) and one by Robert Schumann (the *Symphonische Etüden* Op. 13, each one also a variation on the theme), not to mention Liszt and a number of later composers. There is also the increasing number of sets with Grand (*Grandes* or *Grosses*) and/or '*brillantes*' in their titles, having keyboard pyrotechnics as their main aim. Many of these are genuine 'concert-variations' for performance at public recitals, and some have orchestral accompaniment, such as Moscheles' *Alexander* Variations[4] and Hummel's on *Das Fest des Handwerker* Op. 115 (1830).

A disadvantage of the more virtuoso variations is that they can result in long stretches of right-hand orientation with dull left-hand writing. Alleviation of a sort was gained by transferring motion to the latter temporarily – often as one of a right-hand/left-hand pair during a figural group – or by alternating between the hands. This in turn adds the element of registral contrast and brings another kind of virtuosity into play. Deriving ultimately from the *style brisé* technique of Baroque lute music (in which melody and accompaniment are combined in one line of music distributed over the different strings), it is perhaps better known in its adaptation for harpsichord, many of the Allemandes in J.S. Bach's keyboard suites being good examples.

At its simplest, the later use of the technique produces the kind of chordal counterpoint familiar in the second of Beethoven's variations in the finale of the E major Sonata, Op. 109 (Ex. 15.5)

Ex. 15.5: Beethoven, Piano Sonata in E major Op. 109/iii/var. II, bb. 1–4.

---

[4] See Chapter Eleven (i) and Ex. 11.7.

INFLUENCES

and used also by Felix Mendelssohn in his *Fantasia* (actually a set of variations) on *The Last Rose* Op. 15 (1827, Ex. 15.6),

Ex. 15.6: Felix Mendelssohn, *Fantasia on The Last Rose*, Op. 15 [var. 1], bb. 1–3.

although Hummel's use of it in his set on *The Ploughboy*, probably written as a young teenager, shows that it can be quite basic (Op. 1/1, Ex. 15.7).

Ex. 15.7: Hummel, Variations on *The Ploughboy* Op. 1/1/var. 4, bb. 0–2.

Another such development is rapid alternation of chords for which there is a precedent in J.S. Bach's *Goldberg Variations* No. 29, although later examples show wider use of the keyboard, as in the second (Ex. 15.8) and fifth of Ries's *Twelve Trifles* Op 58, in both of Moscheles's *Deux Caprices* Op. 105, and in the Mendelssohn work mentioned above. Some of these are laid out to extract maximum effectiveness from the registral differences.

Ex. 15.8: Ries, from *Twelve Trifles* Op. 58/2.

More general registral exploitation is also common, shown either by direct contrast – leap, theme in different register (Ex. 15.9: Mozart, K. 398 (416e) (1781) on Giovanni Paisiello's 'Salve tu, Domine'), or in an extreme register (the sets in Beethoven's late sonatas) – or the kind of 'over-and-under' writing of Ex. 15.10 (J.B. Cramer's Piano Sonata Op. 20/ii/var. 2).

Ex. 15.9: W.A. Mozart, Variations on 'Salve tu, Domine' K. 398 (416e), var. V, bb. 1–21.

Ex. 15.10: J.B. Cramer, Piano Sonata Op. 20/ii/var. 2, bb. 0–4.

Many of C.P.E. Bach's 'variations' of his recurring themes in the set of sonatas H. 136–40 (W. 50/1–4, 6) *'mit veränderten Reprisen'* ('with varied reprises' – also called *Reprisen-Sonaten* – pub. 1760) involve register changes. Registral exploitation can also be more gradual, by various progressions, passagework, and the presence of more static elements against more mobile ones, as in Ex. 15.11, from Schumann's *Symphonischen Etüden* Op. 13 (1834–7).

Ex. 15.11: R. Schumann, *Symphonischen Etüden* Op. 13/III, bb. 1–4.

(iv) Colour

A more constructive kind of colouring is also to be found, usually in the better sets. This involves harmony, one obvious example of which is the use of the opposite mode, to be discussed later. But there is also the clothing of the theme (or a close derivative) in different, and frequently chromatic, harmonies appearing in most cases during a coda section, or associated with the return of the theme at a later stage in the piece. Again, this seems to be an improvisatory feature akin to what I describe as 'seeing the material in a new light' in Chapter Twenty-Two (iii). This might almost be viewed as a change of character, although I do not treat it as such here.

There is, however, a whole class of variations – though not a large one – which depend on colour as their variative technique. One would expect sets relying on this alone, or primarily, to be short, and this is so; additionally, they occur as movements of larger works rather than being free-standing. An early and beautiful example is the set of variations on his own hymn *Gott erhalte Franz den Kaiser,* which forms the slow movement Haydn's string quartet in C major, Op. 76/3. Here, the melody itself remains unchanged; it is the different textures woven around it that provide the character. This, of course, results in harmonic change, but it remains primarily colouristic, on a par with the contrapuntal and textural components in the variations; Ex. 15.12 gives the incipits of all four variations with the theme marked 'x'. This tune was adopted, as Haydn wished, as the Austrian National Anthem, and the quartet is nicknamed 'The Emperor' [*Kaiserquartett*] for this reason. So popular were the variations that he arranged them for piano.

Ex. 15.12: J. Haydn, String Quartet in C major Op. 76/3/ii, Var. 1–4 openings.

The composer does something very similar in the second movement of the 'Drumroll' Symphony (No. 103 in E flat major). This is one of his 'double-variation' movements, in which two alternating themes are varied. The first, in C minor, is presented almost unclothed and given, in its subsequent variations, minimal but telling colour changes with the addition of, respectively, scraps from the oboe, oboe doubled by flute with bassoons, and it finally appears in full military regalia with horns, trumpets and drums. The colouristic resources of the contemporary orchestra are naturally called into play here, and, even in the string quartet, Haydn played on the subtler, but available differences between violin, viola and cello. With the advent of the piano and its increase in range, colour and power, the colouristic possibilities also became usable in variations as they had been in other genres.

An instance from our period is the set of variations in Schubert's 'Trout' Quintet (piano, violin, viola, cello and double bass) D 667 (1819) in which he uses the melody of his own song *Die Forelle* [The Trout], which is presented at the outset on strings alone (Ex. 15.13a gives the beginning, and the theme is marked x in the variations), appearing on the piano in octaves with a few decorations and the rippling support of the ensemble for the first variation (Ex. 15.13b).

Ex. 15.13a: Schubert, Piano Quintet in A major D 667 ('*Trout*')/iv, theme, bb. 0–8.

Ex. 15.13b: D 667/var. I, bb. 0–4.

The rippling remains in the violin for var. II while the viola takes the theme unchanged and the piano has some echoing phrases (Ex. 15.13c). For var. III, the theme moves down to the cello and double bass (in octaves) while the piano plays decorative whirls and eddies (Ex. 15.13d) and var. IV thunders in in the parallel minor with the tune reduced almost to a harmonic skeleton (Ex. 15.13e). This finishes in D minor and var.V has the tune, minimally varied, on the cello in B flat major (Ex. 15.13f), the second half of which winds its way back to the tonic of D major and the theme returns on violin with the piano playing a close imitation of its accompaniment in Schubert's original song (Ex. 15.13g). The second half of var. V has some developmental characteristics and the piano engages in the kind of chordal *style brisé* mentioned earlier, giving the effect of glinting water (Ex. 15.13h).

Ex. 15.13c: D 667/var. II, bb. 0–3.

Ex. 15.13d: D 667/var. III, bb. 0–2.

Ex. 15.13e: D 667/var. IV, bb. 0–5.

Ex. 15.13f: D 667/var. V, bb. 0–4.

Ex. 15.13g: D. 667/ return of the theme.

Ex. 15.13h: D 667/var. V, bb. 13–16.

If this kind of colouristic variation-type is rare in pieces for solo piano, it is because it would demand a player of virtuoso capabilities to get the most out of the instrument. Thalberg gives an example, in a set of variations on *The Last Rose [of Summer]* (one of the great favourites of the age), which is – exceptionally given that there are only three variations – free-standing. This is his *Air irlandais varié* Op. 73 and, although a little later than our period, it is also an interesting example of the use of the keyboard and of his 'three-handed' technique referred to in Chapter Three (v) and its examples. In the case of the variations, the theme remains virtually unchanged in the 'middle hand' as the Rose is subjected to a series of climatic onslaughts – blowing in the wind, sprinkled with rain, but refusing to be bowed and, whether 'last' or not, surviving triumphantly, perhaps in illustration of its first line: 'Tis the last rose of summer left blooming alone.'

(v) Counterpoint

Ranging from the mildest rhythmic imitation in a couple of parts to the rigours of canon and fugue, some sort of contrapuntal writing usually crept into these works, and was often made a feature of one or a small group of variations. This can be taken as another example of character, the musically antique, or even quaint, simply because it recalls the general flavour of a previous age or reminds one of forms associated with it. The evocation of the French *Ouverture* in No. VIII of Schumann's *Symphonische Etüden* Op. 13 (Ex. 15.14) is an instance, although the contrapuntal level is not high, nor was it intended to be.

Ex. 15.14: R. Schumann, *Symphonische Etüden* Op. 13/Etüde VIII, bb. 1–3.

In many cases mere hints are given: in the first variation in Hummel's *Bagatelles* Op. 107/5 (pub. *c*.1825) the contemplatively chorale-ish theme, which is itself presented with hints of imitation (see Ex. 15.15a), is given the kind of colouristic treatment mentioned earlier, with *quasi*-contrapuntal parts that soon lose their melodic outline (Ex. 15.15b), while the third variation provides a kind of mock species-counterpoint that later runs into three parts (Ex. 15.15c and 15.15d).

Ex. 15.15a: Hummel, *Bagatelles* Op. 107/5, Thème, bb. 0–4.

Ex. 15.15b: Op. 107/5/var. 1, bb. 0–4.

Ex. 15.15c: Op. 107/5/var. 3, bb. 0–1.

Ex. 15 15d: Op. 107/5/var. 3, bb. 4–6.

Beethoven also evokes an earlier form in his 'Eroica' variations, Op. 35 (E flat major, 1802). This begins with an *Introduzione* which is itself a theme-and-three-variations unit in which the bass-line of the theme is used (Ex. 15.16a); because of this, it can be seen as a miniature *passacaglia*.

Ex. 15.16a: Beethoven, 'Eroica' variations Op. 35/ *Introduzione*, bb. 1–9.

In the ensuing variations, he is even more explicit in terms of the 'species' effect mentioned, and draws attention to it by labelling the variations 'a due', 'a tre' and 'a quattro' respectively, with the last two exploiting the piano's registers and not without humour (Ex. 15.16b, c and d).

Ex. 15.16b: Op. 35, *a due*, bb. 0–8.

Ex. 15.16c: Op. 35, *a tre*, bb. 0–8.

Ex. 15.16c continued

Ex. 15.16d: Op. 35, *a quattro*, bb. 0–4.

Rhythm is of the essence here, often pressed into service to give a contrapuntal 'cut' to the music, making use of figures such as ♫ | ♫ and | ♪ ♫ | ♪.

The second of Hummel's later variations on 'The Plough Boy' (Op. 120/1, pub. 1831) is based on the first of these and is one of many that is reminiscent of the type of part-writing found in glees and part-songs, and common in improvisation, a kind of spurious counterpoint based on chord-notes and decorative additions, or on tags that combine a bit of each. Again it has a comic, almost vaudeville, feel to it (Ex. 15.17).

Ex. 15.17: Hummel, Variations on 'The Plough Boy' Op. 120/1/var. 2, bb. 0–14.

318   THE MECHANICAL MUSE

Beethoven has recourse to several types of contrapuntal textures in the *Diabelli* Variations, another, more serious Op. 120 (1819–23). There is a kind of physical/textural counterpoint built into the theme (Ex. 15.18a), in the imitation of the right-hand's fall of a fourth, staggered in the left hand (marked 'x'), in – after the homophony of the opening – the opposition of the hands in b. 8ff, and especially its registral emphasis in bb. 12–16, further highlighted at the end of the theme's second half; this also alludes to the matter of textural 'counterpoint' by having the melody, such as it is, in the left hand for its first half.

Ex. 15.18a: Beethoven, *Diabelli* Variations, Op. 120/Theme, bb. 0–20.

Beethoven refers to the opening textural counterpoint in several of the variations Nos. IV, V, VI, IX, XI (Ex. 15.18b gives the incipits), XII, XIV, XIX, and even XX.

Ex. 15.18b: Op. 120/var. IV, V, VI, IX and XI, openings.

Ex. 15.18b continued.

None of these turn out to be genuine counterpoint, but there is a Fughetta in var. XXIV (Ex. 15.18c) and canonic passages in var. XXX (Ex. 15.18d) as well, of course, as the final fugue (Ex. 15.18e).

Ex. 15.18c: Op. 120/var. XXIV, opening.

Ex. 15.18d: Op. 120/var. XXX, opening.

Ex. 15.18e: Op. 120/Fuga.

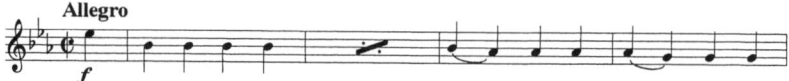

Kollmann, in his set of *Variations on an air of Handel* (Ex. 15.19, known later as 'The Harmonious Blacksmith') has, in his final variation, invertible counterpoint at the 10th, 12th and 14th.

Ex. 15.19: Kollman, *Variations on an air of Handel*, final variation.

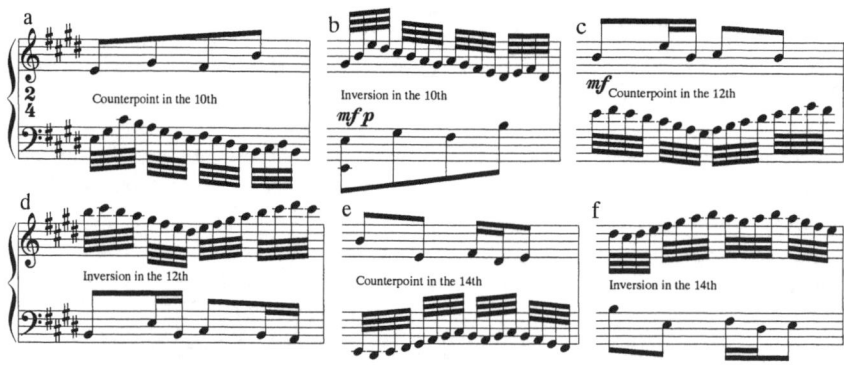

There are also the variation sets that involve canonic writing, which, without aspiring to Bach's mastery in his *Goldberg* or *Von Himmel hoch* cycles, nevertheless make a point of showing the theme in its own right as a canon. Beethoven's '*Canone all'ottava,*' var. VII in the *Eroica* set, is a slightly eccentric instance in its first half and, although it does not belong to our period except in spirit, I cannot resist mention of the particularly beautiful example of No. XIV in Brahms's Op. 9 set on Schumann's theme with its canon at the minor second, although this is only the tip of a contrapuntal iceberg in which subtleties on all levels abound.

My several references to Schumann's *Symphonische Etüden* indicate the general contrapuntal tenor of the whole set. Variation I is of the mock-fugato type, while II and XII feature counterpoints against the theme (or parts of it) relatively unchanged; III and X are vaguely contrapuntal in a *perpetuum mobile* way and IV, V and XI sport canonic writing of varying looseness. Number VI is a kind of staggered *style brisé* and VIII has characteristics of the Baroque French *Ouverture,* as already noted. In general it can be said that the inclusion of counterpoint of whatever rigourousness relieves the monotony of many a poor variation set and adds to many a good one. In the case of the fugues that occasionally crown some of these sets, however, it is the fact of including a fugue rather than its idiom that involves the backward-glancing, as in the Fughetta of the *Diabelli* set, and the fugues of this and the *Eroica* sets.

Another device, which falls very broadly under the contrapuntal heading (although it embodies aspects of several variation types) is one that involves rhythmic syncopation. The usage may be simple, with, for example, the melody 'shadowing' itself in two parts at the octave, third or sixth, as with No. 6 from the set (on *Je suis lindor*) that forms the last movement of Clementi's Sonata in B flat major Op. 12/1 (pub. 1784, revised 1801/2, Ex. 15.20).

Ex. 15.20: Clementi, Piano Sonata in B flat major Op. 12/1/iii/var. 6, opening.

This more 'literal' type fell out of favour, to be replaced by more imaginative versions, such as var. I from Robert Schumann's Op. 1, *Thème sur le nom Abegg varié pour le pianoforte* [Theme on the name 'Abegg' varied for piano, 1829–30], which combines a kind of sublimated *style brisé* with the 'staggered' effect in question (Ex. 15.21).

Ex. 15.21: R. Schumann, *'Abegg' Variations*, Op. 1/var. 1, opening.

Very soon after our period, this technique would reach the complication and effectiveness of Brahms's second variation in his set based – not uncoincidentally perhaps – *On a Theme of Robert Schumann*, and dedicated to Robert's widow, Clara, (Op. 9, 1854), which subtly displaces harmony and harmonic rhythm (Ex. 15.22).

Ex. 15.22: Brahms, *Variations On a Theme of Robert Schumann*, Op. 9/var. 2, opening.

Ex. 15.22 continued

(vi) Opposite mode

It was unusual for a set of variations to be without at least one in the opposite mode to the theme, with a preference for the parallel, occasionally the relative, and more rarely, other keys. As with other topics, this was often accompanied by a change of tempo and became more of a character piece as the period wore on. Stages on the way include J.B. Cramer's close adherence to the theme (Ex. 15.23a) in his Op. 20/ii (while realising the more chromatic implications of the minor chords, Ex. 15.23b),

Ex. 15.23a: J.B. Cramer, Piano Sonata in D major Op. 20/ii, bb. 0–4.

Ex. 15.23b: Op. 20/ii/var. 3, bb. 0–4.

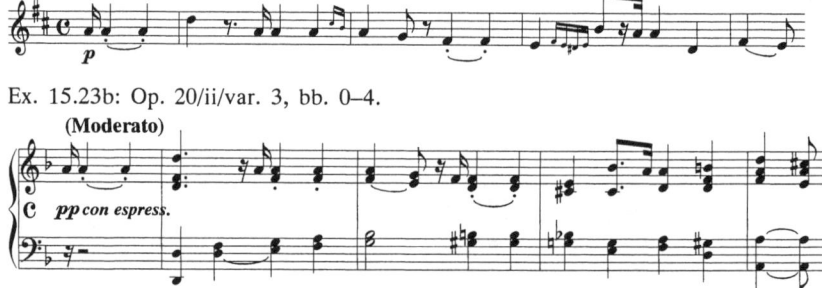

Hummel's Op. 57, where the lure of the major proves too much after eight bars of the *minore,* and his Op. 75 (*Adagio, Variations and Rondo* on 'The Pretty Polly'), where var. 7 (*Sotto voce e sostenuto*), conglomerates simple imitation with textural and registral interplay and chromaticism (Ex. 15.24).

Ex. 15.24: Hummel, *The Pretty Polly*, Op 75/var. 7, opening.

Ex. 15.24 continued

Haigh's 'Scherzo (MINORE)' (fifth) variation in his set on 'Cease, Rude Boreas' in G major is an exception to the rule of greater intensification in minor-key opposite-mode variations (Ex. 15.25, in E minor: the theme is given in Chapter Twelve as Ex. 12.18)

Ex. 15.25: Haigh, Variations on 'Cease, Rude Boreas'/var. 5, opening.

as is the parallel-mode variation found in Mendelssohn's *Variations sérieuses* Op. 54 in D minor (1841). In this case the modal change is into the major, yet is a harmonic development of its theme in the manner of the 'different lights' view noted above. The overall effect is a rather sanctimonious one, and it ends with a 'Mendelssohnian' Victorianism (see Ex. 15.26); the variation succeeds in context, however.

Ex. 15.26: Felix Mendelssohn, *Variations sérieuses* Op. 54/var. 14.

The opposite-mode variation enjoys a higher profile in longer sets and more than one instance may be included, as is the case in C.G. Neefe's nine variations on the Priests' March from *Die Zauberflöte*, with var. 4 (Adagio and *sotto voce*) in the parallel minor, and var. 7 (Andante *e mezza voce*) in the relative minor. In an *Arioso* for violin and keyboard (clavichord or, more likely, piano) in A major, C.P.E. Bach has the third of his five variations in the parallel minor, cadencing in its relative major (C) at the end of the first half and coming back to A minor for the end of the second half. Then, however, he deftly sidesteps into F major for var. 4 and eventually turns the F major local tonic chord into an augmented sixth in preparation for the return to A major in var. 5. In the *Diabelli* set, Beethoven has No. IX, and later a group of three, Nos. XXIX–XXXI, in the parallel (C) minor, the latter lugubriously leading to the fugue in E flat before the final C major variation.

(vii) Alteration of tempo

For the most part, this implies a reduction in speed and, in the majority of sets, simply means the slow variation. Free in tempo and treatment, it is usually the most lyrical and improvisatory part of the piece and favours the *cantabile*-decorative style. It is a character variation in several senses, casting the theme as an operatic aria, portraying the onstage *prima donna* and imitating the particular type of vocal decoration common in such performances whether of the (in the period) 'old-fashioned' *seria*, or the more recent *bel canto* type. Neefe's variation-set on Mozart's 'March of the Priests' (*Die Zauberflöte*), noted in (ii) and (vi) above, has a very *seria*-like var. 4 (Adagio and *minore*), which in its restraint, tempered only by the occasionally missed heartbeat, could have easily issued from the mouth of some grieving queen of antiquity in a Gluckian reform opera (Ex. 15.27).

Ex. 15.27: Neefe, Variations on the 'March of the Priests'/var. 4, bb. 1–4.

As one might expect, Mozart revels in the *cantabile*-decorative variation. In all but one of his sixteen complete sets (including those in the piano sonatas K. 284 (205b) and K. 331 (300i)) only one lacks it, the *Sechs Variationen in F* on an aria from Paisiello's opera *I filosofi immaginarii*, 'Salve tu, Domine', and that contains a *minore* number (without tempo direction) which sports a quite vocal Adagio cadenza (Ex. 15.28), and although it is difficult to conceive of anyone singing the fifth variation (in 6/8) of K. 331/i even at the Adagio specified, it is still very akin to contemporary operatic vocal embellishment (Ex. 15.29).

Ex. 15.28: W.A. Mozart, Variations on 'Salve tu, Domine' K. 398 (416e), b. 27.

Ex. 15.29: W.A. Mozart, Piano Sonata in A major K. 331 (300i)/i/var. V, bb. 1–5.

Yet it is interesting to note that some composers of whom one might have expected more of this kind of writing seem to have indulged in it least. Weber, for example, avoids the *cantabile*-decorative style in his two best-known sets, those on *Vien' quà Dorina bella* Op. 7 (J 53, 1807) – itself an operatic aria – and on *Schöne Minka* ('Air russe') Op. 40 (J 179, 1815); and Clementi, with all his love of Italianate melody and embellishment and his pioneering of the British piano with its *legato* possibilities, reserves this style almost exclusively for slow movements and sections in other kinds of works. Yet, Beethoven, with only one opera to his credit – and that hardly notable for vocal extravagance – uses the style in his Op. 34 (var. 1 and Coda), Op. 35 (a very florid *maggiore* var. XV) and the minor var. XXXI of the *Diabelli* set, somewhat 'over the top'; his intent may have been partly parodistic. Field also seemed to confine this style to non-variation works, although his first variation in the set on *Logie of Buchan* (1799) shows it (Ex. 15.30).

Ex. 15.30: Field, Variations [Rondo] on *Logie of Buchan*/var. 5, bb. 0–8.

326   THE MECHANICAL MUSE

(viii) Closing sections

Apart from the fugues mentioned, this was the least predictable section of all and might simply be a closing variation, perhaps extended (with or without coda features), a return to the theme or a close relative treated similarly, an added coda, a complete section or even a short movement involving, perhaps, a change of character. Some sets draw attention to this in their titles and the formula of *Variations* with *Finale*, *Fugue* or *Rondo* is well known, with additional brilliance (*brillants*, *brillantes*, etc.) in the more public-oriented works. In the *Diabelli* Variations, Beethoven changes the waltz-theme into a Tempo di Minuetto sporting a coda bristling with the sort of demisemiquavers that characterise similar sections in his late variations, and the same kind of increase in frenetic intensity occurs in both his 'Eroica' and *God save the King* sets.

Hummel was fond of ending with a rondo; his set of variations on the Russian tune *Schöne Minka* for flute, cello and piano has a full and brilliant rondo in 6/8 – the theme is 2/4 – and the rondo concluding the '*Pretty Polly*' set is a double-speed, slightly mocking version of the theme.

(ix) Other features

A more drastic form of the technique of 'presenting the theme in a new light' is changing its overall character in some way. There are several instances to be found in the other set of variations written on the C major waltz by Diabelli, by various composers (and, of course, by Beethoven: see Ex. 15.18a for the theme's first half, and section (x) below for further information.) Johann Drechsler presents it as '*Quasi ouverture*', Jacob Freystädtler as a *capriccio* (unheaded) (Ex. 15.31)

Ex. 15.31: Freystädtler, other *Variations on a Waltz by Diabelli* (var. 9), bb. 0–5.

and 'S.R.D.' as a rather fine, though idiosyncratic, four-voice *fuga* including a quirky *stretto* (Ex. 15.32). The initials stood for *Serenissimus Rudolphus Dux*, the official title of The Archduke Rudolph of Austria, a friend and important patron of

Beethoven, for whom the piano sonata in E flat major, Op. 81a (*'Das Lebewohl'* – 'The Farewell') was written and to whom the Fifth Piano Concerto (the *'Emperor'*) was also dedicated.

Ex. 15.32: [Archduke Rudolph], other *Variations on a Waltz by Diabelli* (var. 40), bb. 77–85.

In the composer Tomásek's hands, the theme becomes a *Polonaise*, and Simon Sechter (not surprisingly, considering his reputation as an academician) works it as an '*Imitatio quasi Canon*'(Ex. 15.33).

Ex. 15.33: Sechter, other *Variations on a Waltz by Diabelli* (var. 39), bb. 0–5.

Indeed, Beethoven's own Variation XXXIII, the last one in his set, is a Tempo di Minuetto marked *p grazioso e dolce*. Normally one would expect this kind of alteration to take place, if at all, later in a set, when other less radical procedures had been visited upon it. Beethoven, however, had already departed significantly from the character of Diabelli's fast waltz in his very first variation, where he converts the time-signature to C and writes a 'dotted-rhythm' *Alla Marcia maestoso*.

There is also the possibility of a variation being written in the style of another composer and, as an extreme case, a variation taking on the clearly recognizable contours of another tune. Some of Schumann's Op. 1 *Abegg* variations are distinctly Hummelian, and some of Beethoven's on Diabelli's Waltz suggest some of his contemporaries, while one of the best examples of all of a variation developing into a different (extant) tune occurs in the same set. Variation XXII is headed 'Allegro molto alla "Notte e giorno faticar" di Mozart', and Leporello's aria of that name – the opening number in the opera *Don Giovanni* – is tripped out in octaves, while its status as a variation within the set is preserved, having several clear connections with Diabelli's theme (Ex. 15.34; Ex. 15.18a, above, gives the theme).

Ex. 15.34: Beethoven, *'Diabelli'* Variations, Op. 120/var. XXII, bb. 1–8.

In a similar fashion, in J.L. Dussek's *Rosline Castle with Variations in which is Introduced the Lass of Peaties Mill*, the interloping *Lass* appears as the *maggiore* (third) variation, having superficial connections with the main theme (Ex. 15.35a and 15.35b).

Ex. 15.35a/b: J.L. Dussek, *Rosline Castle with Variations...*/Theme (*Rosline Castle*) bb. 0–8.

In fact, Dussek's first variation (of the 'staggered' type) begins to suggest the contours of the new tune (Ex. 15.35c).

Ex. 15.35c: *Rosline Castle with Variations...*/var. 1, bb. 0–4.

It was also possible for features to come to light in variation sets – which might or might not be discernible in the theme even with hindsight – and develop a personality of their own, so to speak, through several variations. A number of these show themselves in Mozart's variation-finale to the C minor Piano Concerto K. 491 (1786). The theme, on violins (Ex. 15.36a), has a hint of the later syncopation in its phrasing in bb. 3 and 5,

Ex. 15.36a: W.A. Mozart, Piano Concerto in C minor K. 491/iii, bb. 0–8.

and it appears overtly in var. 4, continuing through var. 5 and also appearing in var. 6 (see Ex. 15.36c below). There is even a hint of it in an alternative version of Mozart's piano accompaniment in var. 2, in which the pattern beginning in the bar corresponding to b. 5 of the theme is repeated in each bar.

Also prominent in this context is the dotted-note figure, which, although beginning as a militaristic touch (var. 3, Ex. 15.36b),

Ex. 15.36b: K. 491/iii/var. 3, bb. 0–2.

recurs in mufti in the next one, var. 4, and, equally, the three-quaver anacrusis of var. 5 – whose four-part contrapuntal writing is imbued with it – reappearing in several forms in vars. 6 and 7 (the woodwind interjections), as well as being 'born-again' in var. 8 in 6/8, which persists to the end of the movement (Ex. 15.36c).

Ex. 15.36c: K. 491/iii/var. 4, 5 and 6, openings.

It is also worth mentioning that these features are even more prevalent than my remarks would suggest, since many of Mozart's variations are 'double-variations', that is, where instead of the literal repeat suggested by the theme's repeat-marks, we have a further variation; thus, these features occur almost twice as often. Other examples of this kind of 'set-within-a-set' can be caused by groups of variations with the same technical approach, gradual increase or decrease of pace, or harmonic tendency (for example, increasing chromaticism), or, as we have seen, similar key or mode other than the tonic.

(x) Conclusion

The variation-set is a particularly good example of a 'received form' in that it is probably the oldest musical procedure of all and is recognisable as a form from the Middle Ages – indeed, if birdsong is accepted, the technique may be pre-human. It has evolved constantly, while remaining a recognisable procedure through all musical styles, even transcending those of Western art-music, as the technique remains basic to ethnic music and Jazz, and each period and type of music has enriched its fund of processes, as those periods themselves have been reciprocally enriched. The period of this book has given the variation the particular kinds of character and techniques peculiar – though, of course not exclusive – to Romanticism and, above all, an ideal instrument in the 'new' piano. Also, since many of them are based on popular and well-known tunes, these sets have been ideal for all sorts of purposes, from teaching, in all its forms, to simple enjoyment; they, together with the rondo, have also provided the 'Romantic' composer, newly emancipated from patronage, with an irreplaceable source of income and the comparative security to concentrate on perhaps more satisfying and, perhaps, less immediately saleable, music.

However, as mentioned at the beginning of this chapter, in spite of the basic simplicity of the techniques involved, and the lack of necessity for any underlying form, the greatest composers could express the highest concepts in the form. This resulted in a 'canon' of keyboard-sets stretching from – thinking solely of those in 'living memory' of our period – J.S. Bach's *Goldberg Variations* (pub. c.1741), Mozart's on Gluck's *Unser dummer Pöbel meint* (1764), Haydn's in F minor (H:XVII:6, 1793), Beethoven's *Diabelli* (1819–23) and Brahms' Op. 9 On a Theme of Schumann (1854).

Of particular interest is the *Diabelli* set. The composer-publisher Anton Diabelli, resident in Vienna, had the idea, a potentially lucrative one, of capitalising on the current wave of Austrian nationalist feeling and published a set of variations on a waltz of his composition, each one by a composer native to, resident in, or in some cases then temporarily visiting, Vienna. The result was the grandiloquently entitled *Vaterländischer Künstlerverein./Veränderungen / für das / Piano-Forte / über ein vorgelegtes / Thema / componirt von den vorzüglichsten / Tonsetzern und Virtuosen Wien's / und der k.k. oesterreichischen Staaten.* [Variations for the piano on a given theme, composed by the most distinguished composers and virtuosos of Vienna and the Imperial Austrian States].

The Waltz itself – see Ex. 15.18a above for the first half – was a little *Biedermeyer* trifle that Beethoven, on being presented with it, described as a *Schusterfleck* [a 'cobbler's patch'] and ignored. The possibilities inherent in the very simplicity of the tune, however, began to attract him and, instead of writing the required variation, he produced a set of 33, including (as already noted) an extended fugue. The set was published alongside the other set of 50, which included variations by Hummel, Czerny, Moscheles, Schubert, Mozart's son (also called Wolfgang Amadeus) and the 11-year-old Liszt.

As a final example, the set of *Variations sérieuses*, Op. 54 which Felix Mendelssohn wrote in 1841 as his contribution to help defray the costs of the

INFLUENCES

proposed monument to Beethoven in Bonn, is a fine instance of a set which, at the same time as ticking all the right boxes for its period, is also a masterpiece of the genre. The title is partly a riposte to the prevailing view of variations as being light entertainment and partly a reference to its key of D minor (associated with serious passion), partly to the amount of care that Mendelssohn lavished on the piece and its revisions, and partly to the theme itself (Ex. 15.37a).

Ex. 15.37a: Felix Mendelssohn, *Variations sérieuses* Op. 54/Theme.

The 17 numbers include several of the *style brisé* sort (var. 12 (Ex. 15.37b), var. 16, and the extended coda, var. 17 (Ex. 15.37c), the last half of which is really a further variation),

Ex. 15.37b/c: Op. 54/var. 12, bb. 0–1 and (b) var. 17, bb. 0–1.

and of the 'staggered' kind, var. 5 (Ex. 15.37d), and var. 11,

Ex. 15.37d: Op. 54/var. 5, bb. 0–4.

the very dissonant var. 15 (Ex. 15.37e) and the second half of var. 17, in which Mendelssohn reinterprets var. 5, this time *presto* and *ff*.

Ex. 15.37e: Op. 54/var. 15, bb. 0–3.

There are several contrapuntal variations, requiring a good deal of pianistic control – var. 1 (Ex. 15.37f), the *quasi*-canonic var. 4 (Ex. 15.37g), the *fugato* var. 10 (Ex. 15.37h)

Ex. 15.37f: Op. 54/var. 1, bb. 0–2.

Ex. 15.37g: Op. 54/var. 4, bb. 0–2.

Ex. 15.37h: Op. 54/var. 10, bb. 0–5.

and var. 13, the latter a particularly deft piece of registral awareness and tactile sensitivity (Ex. 15.37i).

Ex. 15.37i: Op. 54/var.13, bb. 0–2.

The opposite-mode variation, var. 14, has already been mentioned (see above, section (vi) and Ex. 15.25).[5]

---

[5] Chapter Twenty examines Clementi's sets of variations on the Irish tune *The Black Joke*.

CHAPTER SIXTEEN

Received Forms 5a: The Concerto 1, Background and Presentation of Material

(i) General

The most prevalent view of our period *vis-à-vis* the piano concerto is of a very small number of works, containing a very high proportion of masterpieces, a somewhat similar situation to the symphony, but a much smaller repertory. Several reasons are proffered: the lack of interest of composers in more-or-less 'vulgar' 'Romantic' display, the intimate and first-hand knowledge of the instrument necessary to write at this level, the expense of hiring an international soloist as well as an orchestra, the fact that the prime orchestral public vehicle for compositional greatness and self-expression, the symphony, was sufficient, and so on.

Few of these can be sustained in practice. Display doesn't, and didn't, have to be 'vulgar', as a glance at any of the better-known pieces will confirm, and in fact, most composers did have, or had had, first-hand experience as virtuoso pianists, and in public at that. The expense of hiring an international soloist needn't have been necessary: in fact, when they were finally persuaded to allow concertos into their concerts, the Philharmonic Society in London initially expected soloists to give their services free, for the *kudos* alone. Also, the growing number of (usually home-grown) executants, as opposed to composer-executants, shows that the market was expanding and fees falling, though this becomes more of a factor towards the end of the period. In any case, the presence of a Moscheles, a Field, a Hummel or a Liszt would amply offset their fees, which were not really so high, and certainly not so in comparison with the contemporary singers, who were notoriously rapacious. Concert appearances were important in boosting sales of sheet-music and attracting commissions and pupils, but the real money was made in publishing and teaching. As for the orchestra, it was already 'on stage', so to speak and the only possible extra payment would be for rehearsals, which, however, could cause production hiccups (see below). It is true that the symphony was the prime public instrumental vehicle for a composer, but a diet of symphonic fare would have very soon produced cultural indigestion in an audience that wanted the sauce of entertainment to palatalise its enlightenment.

The reality in the period is, in fact, the opposite. The conditions were at their best for the concerto. Available was an instrument that was capable of conveying all the *nuances* for which a composer could wish with power and brilliance – the piano – and an even newer instrument (the symphony orchestra) which had become relatively standardised, so that a work written for St Petersburg or Lisbon would be just as playable, other things being equal, in Dublin or Oslo. The form of the concerto itself had been crystallised by, particularly, Mozart and the *venue* for such works, although not yet standardised, was available in the opera house, theatre, ballroom, or the newer breed of concert halls that were springing up all around Europe. The new audience of *bourgeoisie* were determined to be part of the scene and to show off their culture and their clothes. The phrase 'elegant and fashionable society' is hardly ever absent from a concert-criticism of the time in London, for example, and some reviewers complained about the fact that the ladies' wide hats and dresses resulted in two of them taking up enough space for three. Such an audience was wealthy enough to make concert-giving worthwhile, although the financial returns were indirect, as I have said, in the form of sales of music and lessons for the rich.

And what better to entice them than the spectacle of a living legend playing his own works before their very eyes, and of whose divine aura they could partake by trying to emulate in their music-rooms? Again we have to remind ourselves of the ephemerality of performance in an age without recording, or full scores for the most part. For many, such concerts would be a once-in-a-lifetime experience, on which they could dine out or at least tell their grand-children. So why were there so few concertos?

There were, in fact, hundreds of them, probably at least as many as there were symphonies. We do not hear them much nowadays, mainly because they are generally not recorded, as it is far more lucrative for the large recording monopolies to issue yet another set of sure-fire money-spinning Beethoven Symphonies or whatever, than to widen their catalogues: the Canon rules. It is left to a few braver smaller producers to break out of the stultifying mould and take the odd chance, and this has, in recent years, begun to transform our view of the musical past, especially in the period under discussion.

It is important to remember that the whole *raison d'être* of the concerto was to excite and entertain through the performer's virtuosity and the attractiveness of the composer's music, not to uplift or overtax emotionally or intellectually. Trails were not to be blazed here, nor souls bared; these were for the symphony and the sonata to do, and this discouraged the more original composers, while it may have been an advantage for those less so. Many such works are, of course, lacking in the genius of the Masters but if one wants only the greatness of a Beethoven or a Chopin, one should not expect to find it by listening to a Hummel or a Field, whose music provides other, by no means unrelated, pleasures. A love of *sushi* or *canard à l'orange* does not preclude an appreciation for fish and chips or colcannon. Many of the concertos of this period are delightful and fresh, and convey the flavour of this exciting period more than most other genres.

(ii) The orchestra

One must not forget also that the adjustment and, perhaps refinement, of that other, still relatively new, instrument of the time, the concert orchestra, was still ongoing. The typical nineteenth-century equation of bulk with importance was enough to ensure an increase in the size and diversity of audiences and venues, with cities outdoing each other in the scale, amenities and comforts of their theatres and opera houses – not to mention the newer breed of actual concert-halls – so that a larger and more penetrating sound was called for. This, together with a general raising of pitch at the end of the eighteenth century, affected each of the orchestras' instrumental families to a greater or lesser degree.

Of the strings, the violin and viola particularly were physically strengthened in the period around 1800, with the mortising of the neck into the body at an angle to allow for a generally increased string tension and the gradual substitution of stronger and heavier wound strings for the prevailing gut. Both factors also called for internal strengthening of the bass-bar, lengthening of the fingerboard, greatly reinforced bridge, and the use of a chin-rest – the composer-violinist Louis Spohr's invention of about 1820 – took some of the weight off the player's left hand.

The addition of more keys to the woodwind and the influence of the nascent science of acoustics increased reliability, flexibility and range, multi-jointing improved the number and accuracy of finger-holes, and the application of the Boehm system of keys and fingering facilitated versatility and pitching, although tone was felt to have suffered. Similarly, with the invention of the butterfly valve in about 1815, and its use in the brass from the 1830s, the more cumbersome system of crooks fell out of use, and most of the insecurity of pitching associated with lipping and stopping the bell was eliminated, the lower ranges of the instruments were opened up and they could participate to a much greater extent in the increasing chromaticism of the period.

These modifications – especially the last mentioned – took time, not only to develop and apply, but, even more so to be accepted by players and listeners, not to mention composers. Brahms, for example, retained his preference for the natural horn throughout his life, and expressly called for its use as late as 1865, in his Horn Trio Op. 40. The fact is that most orchestras up until 1850 had not changed significantly from the careful numerical and tonal balance of the late Classical orchestra, which still preserved the individual instrumental shades.

The very presence of the orchestra resulted in a number of problems for the concerto-composer, and these were sometimes severe. Skill at writing for the piano did not guarantee an equal aptitude for orchestration, which could result in uninteresting fodder for the orchestral players. But, as against that, orchestras also have to accompany for some of the time, and, in fact, orchestral support in the majority of these works is far from poor throughout, and occasionally as interesting as some of the best symphonic writing and, indeed, surpassing it in the case of Mozart's own concertos and symphonies. The addition of the solo piano guaranteed a combination that was dramatic, colourful and visually interesting, and, of course, the excitement of the virtuoso, seen in multi-faceted splendour as performer, composer and rarely-visiting celebrity, crowned an occasion which, as I have said, was very often the musical experience of a lifetime for the great majority of the audience.

Another problem, however, involved relative standards in different orchestras. My characterisation of the orchestra as a ubiquitous creature tells only part of the story, and a composer had to be extremely careful with his or her writing for it. There were glorious exceptions, of course, such as the Société des Concerts du Conservatoire in Paris, which 'gained repute for polished renditions that eventually established new European performance standards.'[1] This was largely due to the conductor, François-Antoine Habeneck, whose passion for the music of Beethoven ensured the latter's ascendance in France.

However, certainly for the first half of our period, even in the three largest of the European metropolitan centres (London, Paris – Habeneck notwithstanding – and Vienna) standards could not always be relied upon, either in terms of a representative complement of instruments, or in terms of quality, reliability or technical and musical ability. The critic and musical traveller Edward Holmes, after an extensive tour of European musical centres, wrote of conditions in London in 1828: 'The musicians in London, particularly the wind-instrument players, often exasperate a composer by omitting the solos which are set down for them, and, from the lenience of the leader towards these mistakes, the poor author frequently receives the most unjust misrepresentation.'[2] In fact, Habeneck himself was not above rewriting parts of the Beethoven symphonies which didn't appeal to him, a practice which did not endear him to Berlioz especially.[3]

Similarly, Moscheles was accompanied in a concert at Elberfeld by 'a set of fiddlers calling themselves an orchestra' and he had to play his E major Concerto 'with every possible precaution, that the band may not lag behind'.[4] Although Moscheles is in jocular mood in this letter, he is obviously no stranger to this situation, as the next quotation will show.

A third problem was the fact that the kind of rehearsal-schedule that we take for granted today was almost unheard-of for most of the period – in fact a rehearsal at all was by no means guaranteed. Dragonetti, the principal double-bass player in London demanded the same fee, *pro rata*, for a rehearsal as for a concert. Moscheles, this time in England, describes a rehearsal and the subsequent concert in Liverpool in 1825:

> On the 8th of November, at noon, we had the rehearsal in the Concert Room; but what a rehearsal! Wretched is too tame an expression for it. Mori, the London artist, did all that possibly could be done, but what was to be made out of a band consisting of a double quartet and four halting wind-instruments [?] The director of the theatre played the entrepreneur of the concert, Mr. Wilson, the trick of keeping away the orchestral performers, so that I was obliged to play the first movement of the E flat concerto and the Alexander Variations with a bare quartet accompaniment.[5]

---

[1] Cooper/PARIS, 21.
[2] Holmes/RAMBLE, p. 38.
[3] Cooper/PARIS, 33.
[4] Moscheles/LIFE-I, pp. 139–40.
[5] *Op. cit.*, p. 112.

Lessees of concert-halls, theatres, and so on, had near-absolute control over players and often used this power in reprisal for a visitor who could not, or would not, pay them the exorbitant fees they demanded for participating singers, without whose presence many concerts would be doomed. This may have been another reason why piano concertos of the period, if they were published with accompaniment other than a second piano, tended to be issued in the piano-with-string-quartet format.

(iii) The overall shape

If we cleave to the canonic view of music history, the solo concerto's lineage is crystal-clear. From J.S. Bach and Vivaldi through Mozart and, to a lesser extent, J. Haydn, pausing in aweful ecstasy at the feet of Beethoven – Schubert is not a halt on this particular journey – through Mendelssohn and Schumann, to Brahms, and even on to Bartók, Rakhmaninov and Tchaikovsky, the concerto appears a homogeneous form. The picture, however, hides a number of deviations to which I shall allude in passing.

The concerto's division into three movements seems to remain unchanged as does its tempo scheme – broadly, fast-slow-fast – and the manner in which this was generally characterised: an opening to some degree compelling and a light finale, separated by a lyrical movement. This general shape was preserved, no doubt, because it allowed for a wide variety in mood, sound and execution, with the first movement containing whatever 'intellectual' features there were, when audience suspense and attention were at their highest, progressing through the more emotional centrepiece and finishing with a musical *sorbet* whose main function was to clear the palate and leave a pleasant taste.

As in the case of several other genres, the general development of the concerto immediately after Bach can be seen in works of his sons, Wilhelm Friedemann, Johann Christoph Friedrich, Carl Philipp Emanuel and Johann Christian. The last two, Emanuel and Christian, are particularly important and, as we have seen before,[6] represented the main northern and southern European stylistic trends after the Baroque.

With the exception of some early works, all of J.C. Bach's solo concertos were for keyboard – harpsichord in the first of his three sets of six, Op. 1 (published in London in 1763), and with the option of piano in his Opp. 7 and 13 (London, 1770 and 1777 respectively). These sets were an important influence on the young Mozart, who met Bach during his London visit of 1764–65. Indeed, Mozart's first attempts at piano concertos in 1767 consisted of adding orchestral accompaniments to sonata movements for solo keyboard by Paris-based composers such as Johann Gottfried Eckard, Leontzi Honauer, Hermann Friedrich Raupach, Johann Schobert and C.P.E Bach (K. 37, and K. 39–41) and, in late 1770, by J.C. Bach (Op. 5 (K. 107/1–3)). It is clear, however, that when Mozart came to write his own original piano concertos, he was selective in his adoption of the J.C. Bach model. In each of Bach's three sets of six concertos, four are two-movement works with an opening binary movement,

---
[6] See Chapter One (iv).

Allegro for the most part, followed by another fairly fast movement, or a minuet. The remaining two concertos in each set sport an Andante between faster outer movements, giving us the familiar three-movement form.

The two-movement makeup was not confined to Christian Bach: it is also strongly represented in the works of Johann Samuel Schroeter: he, like Bach, also settled in London and also influenced the young Mozart, who wrote cadenzas for three of Schroeter's Op. 3 concertos. This two-movement shape occasionally surfaces in our period, for example in J.L. Dussek's Opp. 18, 30 and 40, and Field's third.[7] It was, however, the more balanced triptych of movements that Mozart used for all his original concertos; only on three occasions in his piano concertos did he use the minuet-finale, and they were all in early works (K. 242, K. 246, and K. 413 (387a)).

(iv) First movement expositions

Even the internal forms of the concerto's individual movements remained close to those of their progenitors. The Baroque Venetian *ritornello*, which J.S. Bach adopted from Vivaldi and transformed with his impeccable sense of structure, became the basic form of the concerto's fast movements. This outline has a simplicity and versatility that made it applicable to all kinds of music, vocal as well as instrumental:

Table 4: Outline of the Baroque Venetian *ritornello*

Section	Key(s)	Content
Tutti 1	tonic	the work's thematic material
Solo 1[8]	tonic, modulating to dominant or relative major	accompanying material from ritornello
Tutti 2	dominant or relative major	may be truncated
Solo 2	dominat, modulating	alternating with tutti
Tutti 3	other related keys	may be truncated
Solo 3	other related keys	modulating to ton
Tutti 4	tonic	thematic material

Each of the two sons of J.S. Bach who concern us here took this *ritornello* as their starting point, but modified and enriched it with their own individual contributions. In Christian Bach's case, in keeping with the general 'southern' leanings of his style, this was to be seen primarily in the less angular, less obviously motivic cut of his themes, and in particular, his casting of the second (dominant or relative major) theme as fluently lyrical melody, moving a step nearer to the thematic distinction

---

[7] Although these may not be entirely *bona fide* imitations of the earlier model – see below.

[8] The solos can, of course, be literally so in the sense of being unaccompanied, but accompanied solo passages are also included here.

(amounting, in many cases, to contrast) characteristic of the key areas in Classical sonata-form.[9]

Similarly, the vast bulk of Emanuel's fast concerto movements are in *ritornello* form, but he placed more emphasis on key-distinction, in particular, a 'fixing' of the dominant or relative major key during the first solo by assigning it a theme of its own. Like his father, Emanuel ensures that *ritornello* material is never far away both in his use of interjected truncated versions, and in the use of *ritornello* motifs in the accompanying orchestral figuration.

It is interesting to note that, as we have seen, Mozart's first essays in the realm of the piano concerto were arrangements of solo keyboard sonatas whose first movements were in binary-sonata form and that, apart from orchestral accompaniments, his main contribution was the construction of the interjecting orchestral *ritornelli* from the given material. He began, therefore, from the structural premise of sonata-form – however primitive its manifestation in his models – and overlaid it with *ritornello* form. Part of his own contribution to the Classical style was a refinement of sonata-form structure, while clothing the motivic carcass of his themes in drapery of a distinctly Italianate mellifluence. At a slightly later date, the more symphonic approach of a Beethoven – especially his C minor Concerto – in the northern Emanuel Bach/Joseph Haydn lineage, would gradually stiffen up the tonal profile as the nineteenth century wore on.

The result of this formal amalgam is that a 'double-exposition' sonata-form envelope fits by far the greater number of concerto first movements up to 1850. 'Sonata-form' in practice allows for such a variety of applications of its underlying principle and so many qualifications and *caveats* are attached – notoriously so in our period – that only the broadest interpretation is necessary and pieces that significantly depart from it can safely be treated as exceptions. Indeed, many works that appear at first sight to be exceptional in this way, such as Beethoven's Fourth Piano Concerto, turn out to be formally – though not necessarily structurally – un-problematic.

An opening orchestral *tutti* presents the themes – or most of them – in two separate groups with a transitional modulating section in between, and a solo entry follows incorporating the same material, a 're-exposition' with solo participation, or dominance, in which the second thematic area appears in the dominant (in major-key works) or relative major (in minor-key ones). In the next section, material is developed and this is followed by a *reprise* closely derived from the first exposition, with thematic material in the tonic key, and involving both *tutti* and soloist.

(v) The concerto's opening

Even in the detail within the movements, the early nineteenth-century piano concerto continued to show its conservatism, its dependance on the Mozartian layout, and its allegiance to audience expectations and the conventions of contemporary public performance. Delaying the solo entry by an opening *tutti* was as important, and for

---

[9] See the scheme in Chapter Fourteen (ii).

the same reason, as the *prima donna*'s non-appearance on stage during the opening few numbers of an opera – to increase audience expectation and allow for the Star's more effective entrance. And, given an excitable body of people, many of whom were more interested in being seen to social advantage rather than as spectators on the musical sideline, the more obvious function of commanding attention should not be overlooked, especially in an age which saw the conductor – if there were one at all – as a curiosity, and, rather like the customary orchestra leader, as *primus inter pares* with no specifically interpretative status and certainly in no position to demand quiet from his social betters.

However, to sustain the listeners throughout a quarter of a movement before the solo fireworks appeared required strategies of a more musical kind also. Since the movement's principal thematic material was presented at the opening of the *tutti*, and since melodic beauty was prized above all other musical attributes by audiences, it was essential that nothing be lost in the chatter. Unlike that other great public work, the symphony, there was no tradition of slow introduction, which would in any case have run the risk of being inappropriate, since, as I have said, the concerto *tutti* itself was largely introductory *vis-à-vis* the soloist.

There are, however, a small number of minor exceptions to this; J.L. Dussek's third concerto in C major, Op. 29 has some 23 soft bars of Larghetto in 3/8, which prefaces the usual kind of opening fortissimo in common time, *tutti*, and Ferdinand Ries begins his Concerto Pastoral (Op. 120 in D major) with a short introduction, effectively on a dominant pedal, which suggests the rumbling of thunder on an otherwise calm day. The case of Josef Antonín Stepán ("Steffan", 1726–97) deserves particular mention, however. This Bohemian composer settled in Vienna in 1741, and 8 of his 38 solo keyboard concertos begin with an Adagio introduction shared between *tutti* and solo. Of particular interest is the B flat major concerto, whose slow introduction is a brooding improvisatory affair in the surprising key of D minor modulating to its relative at the end, forming a V^7 chord in B flat major.

If the introduction could not have its own introduction, an opening call-to-attention was possible, however, something corresponding to the arresting chords of the earlier *premier coup d'archet*, or the more operatic fanfare, or a combination of both, sporting perhaps a characterful rhythmic figure also. Already familiar from Mozart's concertos – K. 271 (E flat major), K. 413 (387a) in F major (Ex. 16.1),

Ex. 16.1: W.A. Mozart, Piano Concerto in F major K. 413 (387a)/i, bb. 1–5.

K. 482 (E flat major) and K. 503 (C major) – it remains in J.B. Cramer's Opp. 10 and 51 (both in E flat major), Weber's second in E flat major, Moscheles's in B flat major (Op. 90) and E flat major (Op. 56) Clementi's in C major (Ex. 16.2)[10],

Ex. 16.2: Clementi, Piano Concerto in C major, *tutti* opening.

J.L. Dussek's in C major (Op. 30) – which it resembles very closely – Field's Sixth in the same key, and others. The general similarity here and the predominance of the keys of C and E flat major is perhaps not accidental and, of course, goes outside of the concerto; the opening of Hummel's E flat major piano sonata is very close to the Moscheles E flat major concerto mentioned. All of these works show the *tutti*'s more functional role in giving the key, mode, basic metre and at least some thematic material within a short space of time.

If the composer decided against this kind of treatment, he or she could always reinforce the material by repetition, first presenting it softly and/or in unison, perhaps, then harmonised and more fully scored (Hummel's A flat major Op. 113, Conradin Kreutzer's Op. 36 in E flat major – a work that, incidentally, shares its first bar with Field's First Concerto also in E flat major – Henri Herz's Fourth in E major Op. 131). An interesting variant of this can be seen in Hummel's last Concerto in F major (Op. posth. No. 1), where the opening melody is constructed in such a way that it has both introductory and thematic features (Ex. 16.3).

Ex. 16.3: Hummel, Piano Concerto in F major Op. posth. No. 1/i, bb. 0–19.

---

[10] The significance of the labels and brackets (r1, m3 etc.) will be made clear in this chapters's section (v), Thematic material (below).

Ex. 16.3 continued

Here, it is associated with a second theme in the first subject area in which those more melodic aspects have been rearranged to give its lyrical manifestation, a practice that seems to have been something of a speciality of Hummel's in his more 'public' work. Since the *tutti* invariably included an *ff* presentation of thematic material – usually the opening – there is something of the tragic/comic masks of the Classical Greek theatre about such themes. The declamatory *fortissimo* so regularly appears in the bass under *tremolando* strings as to render it almost a cliché in these works; for example, see the *tuttis* in Moscheles (Op. 93), Herz (Opp. 131 and 34), Field (Nos. 1 and 3), Hummel (Opp. 85, 89, and posth. 1.) and Chopin (No. 1). In his Third Concerto in G minor, Moscheles gives us a soft harmonised version of his very effective first theme before its subsequent *tutti* treatment, and his Fifth Concerto in C major (Op. 87, Ex. 16.4) opens with an unusual Ic – $V^{13}a$ – Ia cadence in the woodwind, immediately repeated via – $V^{13}a$ – Ia.

Ex. 16.4: Moscheles, Piano Concerto in C major Op. 87/i, bb. 1–4.

Another way of commanding attention and reinforcing the main theme was to present it contrapuntally or *quasi*-canonically. Too much or too strict an application of this kind of treatment would have been inappropriate: just enough of what contemporary critics called 'science', or a few 'learn-ed' touches, such as points of imitation, was sufficient and could be very effective as both J.B. Cramer and Czerny – in his A minor concerto Op. 214 (Ex. 16.5) – found.

Ex. 16.5: Czerny, Piano Concerto in A minor Op. 214/i, bb. 1–18.

Effective too is Moscheles's Fourth Concerto in E major (Op. 64), in which the opening music turns out to be a countermelody to its continuation (Ex. 16.6)

Ex. 16.6: Moscheles, Piano Concerto in E major Op. 64/i, opening.

and Herz's Third Concerto in D minor opens with what feels like an impending fugue (Ex. 16.7), although it is none the less effective for remaining more generally contrapuntal.

Ex. 16.7: Herz, Piano Concerto in D minor, opening.

Ex. 16.7 continued

These, and some other of the better-known composers with international reputations and followings, could afford to pander less to audience taste and even help to expand it. An opening didn't have to be loud and full to be dramatic; it could solicit attention by subtlety and understatedness. Unusual instruments, registers and colouring had been used in the opera house even in the purely instrumental overtures and it would have been surprising if a composer of this period had not availed him (or her) self of the possibilities in the analogous situation of the concerto's opening *ritornello*. Thus, in the Cramer and Czerny works mentioned above, the canonic writing demands some contrast of registers, and they both take pains to maximise this within the dynamic and textural parameters chosen. As evinced in J.B. Cramer's Op. 26 concerto in D major, J.L. Dussek's Op. 22 in B flat major, Herz's in A major Op. 34 and E major Op. 131, Hummel's Op. posth. 1 (see Ex. 16.3 above) and Czerny's Grand Concerto in F major Op. 28 (Ex. 16.8), unison or octave openings were favoured. The similarity of the openings of the last two, in the same key of F major, is interesting, especially as Czerny dedicated his concerto to Hummel.

Ex. 16.8: Czerny, Grand Concerto in F major Op. 28/i, bb. 0–6.

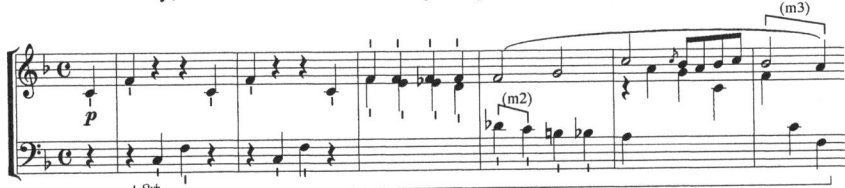

Such colouring becomes more telling in association with the minor mode, and the early Romantics continued the Classical fondness for reserving the darker and more personal utterances for it: the fact that the proportion of major- to minor-key works was to be reversed during our period says much about the early nineteenth-century interest in this. Both Mozart's concertos in D (K. 466) and C minors (K. 491) stand out in the effectiveness of their openings, particularly the earlier, with its weighting towards the lower registers and the uneasiness of its crawling, syncopated material, which maintains an almost constant state of dissonance. I use the term 'material' rather than 'theme', as this must be the only concerto before the twentieth century to be based almost on colour alone. Partaking of the passion of the Queen of the Night (in *The Magic Flute*) and something of the horror of the Commendatore's resurrected effigy (in *Don Giovanni*) – with both of which it shares its key – it was well known and frequently played throughout most of our period and it would have been surprising if it had not been echoed on occasion, even if only by those composers who idolised Mozart, and especially those who, like Hummel and Thomas Attwood, had had the enviable fortune to have been taught first-hand. Attwood died leaving no concertos, but Hummel's best works in this genre – both of them in minor keys – show a similar aptitude for creating atmosphere and suspense through deftness and understatement.

The B minor (Op. 89, 1819) is the only piano concerto in this key to survive from our period. Like its counterpart in A minor of some three years earlier (Op. 85, c.1816), it is symphonic in its large scale and its orchestration as well as its formal cut, and the very effective opening sets the tone and well conveys the general tenor of the piece (Ex. 16.9). A low B on timpani outlines the first and last beats of the 3/4 metre, the last trilled and the first supported by a low *pizzicato* B on double-basses and cellos. After two bars, oboes and clarinets play what turns out to be a basic version of the main subject, elongated and, because of the two introductory bars, slightly uneven in phrasing.

Ex. 16.9: Hummel, Piano Concerto in B minor Op. 89/i, bb. 1–42.

Ex. 16.9 continued

Hummel approaches the dominant on which this phrase ends in a more dramatic way than usual, since the harmony at b. 7 seems to give the impression, by the lightening of the major version of the sub-dominant chord, to be moving to brighter things. However, by immediately afterwards (b. 8) naturalising the G♯ in the bass and having a mirror of this in the treble (E to upper E♭), this is converted into an augmented sixth chord whose resolution is delayed by Ic for a full bar. To push the music onward even more, double-basses and cellos are joined by violas and violins in a *pizzicato* figure that brings their hitherto underlying role into the foreground and this figure remains, in inversion, as a *quasi*-contrapuntal addition to the following answering phrase.

This phrase is based not on the dominant chord but on its more suggestive diminished form, $V^{\flat 9}$. When this resolves onto V in b. 14, the use of an analogous *pizzicato* figure in the bass withholds the root position tonic until the beginning of the next phrase, which states the first subject proper, thus sustaining a momentum that, because of the comparative uniformity of hue, register and harmony, might have threatened to flag. The result is an extremely effective passage with a low but insidious undertow of tension and even a hint of tragedy.

Hummel shifts, without really modulating, to the relative D major for his second subject, but does not linger very long, preferring the minor tonic with some stirring contrapuntal writing, and a passage (bb. 117–31) of which Mendelssohn was probably not unaware when writing his 'Midsummer Night's Dream' overture. A Neapolitan sidestep brings him back to B major and the music calms for the solo entry.

(vi) Thematic material

An interesting feature of many piano concerto opening-movement subjects in this period – the first in particular – is that they seem to exhibit a family likeness. On the rare occasions when the dotted rhythmic motif (marked 'r1' in the examples) is missing, it invariably appears in one of the subsequent melodies, and 'r2', the syncopated cell implying a suspension, is also common. A definite leaning towards the second inversion can be noticed, occurring as a chord, but also, more significantly, in its melodic outline, and this is to be seen in a number of these subjects (marked 'h1' in Exx. 16.2, 16.3, 16.4, 16.5, 16.7, 16.9, 16.11 and 16.13, and in Chapter Seventeen, Exx. 17.5, 17.6 and others). Connecting the minor tonic third with the (major) dominant third (leading-note) (flattened 3 – raised 7), either by leap or otherwise, to outline a diminished fourth, is a slightly unusual manifestation of a more general love for diminished intervals, and this is marked 'm1' in Exx. 16.5, 16.7 and 16.9, as well as in Chapter Seventeen, Exx. 17.6 and 17.7.

Another feature, a common one in the period, is a decoration, or eclipsis, of the dominant note by the lowered sixth, giving rise to a chromatic chord more often than not (marked 'm2' in Exx. 16.3, 16.5, 16.7, 16.8 and 16.9 etc.). Finally, a rhythmic augmentation of 'r1' but manifesting itself melodically, the long *appoggiatura* or accented passing note is useful (as we have seen already) for finishing a phrase or sub-phrase without excessive closure (marked 'm3' in Exx. 16.3, 16.5, 16.7 etc.). These features can be clearly seen in both of Chopin's concertos, in Mendelssohn's and in those of both Robert and Clara Schumann.

The continuation of the opening *ritornello* poses a slight problem that besets major-key works since a double exposition is, effectively, involved. The imposition of sonata-form's harmonic structure on other forms is as much a feature of this (Romantic) period as it was of the previous (Classical) one and to repeat the main structural event – the setting-up of a 'rival' key – after having contradicted it by a return to the tonic, in close proximity and with different, or at least varied, music would result in harmonic confusion. Unless one is contemplating a first movement of Mahlerian – or even Brahmsian – proportions, the obvious answer is not to modulate at this stage, and therein lies a recipe for dullness that not all concertos managed to avoid. Even more reason, then, for diversions involving dramatic harmony and instrumentation.

Hence also, after the first-subject statement, the frequency of transition passages, which are a cue for chromatic writing of a digressive and colouristic, rather than of a strictly functional, kind. Hummel in F major and A flat major (touching on C flat major, Ex. 16.10), and Herz in D major Op. 207 show this tendency, but it also occurs in works in which the first subject itself is of this type, as in Field's Second and, to an extent, Third concertos.

Ex. 16.10: Hummel, Piano Concerto in A flat major, Op. 113/i, bb. 36–49.

Ex. 16.10 continued

Second themes are universally tuneful, diatonic, and unproblematic, being straightforward in outline, rhythm and phrasing, a respite from drama and a point of relaxation in the middle of the *tutti*; C.M. von Weber's from his Op. 11 in C major is surprisingly Italianate; J.B. Cramer's from his Op. 16 in D minor (Ex. 16.11) also evokes sunnier climes, although in some major-key works they may be a little less bland and uneventful than my description might suggest.

Ex. 16.11: J.B. Cramer, Piano Concerto in D minor Op. 16/i, second subject.

Character was evidently important in the presentation of themes and was preserved even in a work like Cramer's Seventh Concerto in E major, Op. 56, which seems to reverse the theme-types, the first being lyrical and the second more vigorous, the latter containing the dotted rhythmic motif (r1) and trills suggestive of the various first subjects discussed.

Again, in these second subjects, the suspicion of cloning nags the listener even more than in first subjects, and many of them do sound as if they have escaped from the opera house. Certainly their jaunty approachability makes for the kind of variety and entertainment value guaranteed to please an audience and keep them interested, for example, J.L. Dussek's B flat major concerto, Op. 22 (Ex. 16.12, pub. 1793), and Hummel, Op. 89 (Ex. 16.13).

Ex. 16.12: J.L. Dussek: Piano Concerto in B flat major Op. 22/i, second subject.

Ex. 16.13: Hummel. Piano Concerto in B minor Op. 89/i, second subject.

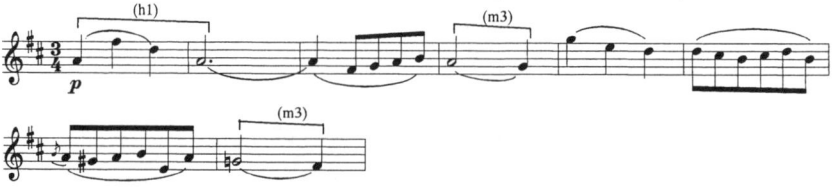

In the *tutti* exposition second subjects tend to appear in the tonic in major-key works and in the relative major in minor-key ones. Exceptions are to be found and include Field's first three concertos (E flat, A flat, E flat majors) and Moscheles's Fourth in E major (all in the dominant), C.M. von Weber's Op. 11 in C major (appearing first in C minor), Chopin's Op. 11 in E minor (appearing in tonic major) and Herz's Fourth in E major, spending most of its time in the relative minor. Exceptional in a different way is J.L. Dussek's Ninth Concerto in G minor Op. 49, in which the first movement's second subject's first half is the corresponding part of the first subject transposed to B flat major – but with the sixth still flattened – and the remainder is related to the rest of the first subject, melodically and rhythmically (Ex. 16.14a/b).

Ex. 16.14a/b: J.L. Dussek, Piano Concerto in G minor Op. 49/i, first and second subjects.

Paisiello's Fourth Concerto in G minor (1770s) presents the second subject in E flat major and remains there until the end of the exposition. In Moscheles's Concerto in E major Op. 64, the main theme (Ex. 16.6 above) returns in the *tutti* as the accompaniment to another theme.

A return to the first subject, or something recognisably similar, allows the orchestra to gather itself up in a last show of strength before the entry of the soloist, although in the event, direct confrontation is usually avoided.

CHAPTER SEVENTEEN

Received Forms 5b: The Concerto 2, The Solo

(i) The solo entry

Although the tradition of the long opening *tutti* unbreached by the soloist remained the norm in the concerto of this time, there were exceptions. Mozart never repeated his experiment of K. 271, where the opening E♭ unison fanfare is answered by the solo piano in a harmonised closing half-phrase (Ex. 17.1): after an immediate restatement, the *ritornello* continues to the soloist's 'real' entry. This gambit is only the most obvious of several daring elements in this, his first masterpiece among the concertos.

Ex. 17.1: W.A. Mozart, Piano Concerto in E flat major K. 271/I, opening.

Similarly, even Beethoven pulled back from the technique used at the beginning of his Fourth Concerto in G major (see next paragraph) to something a little less *outré* in the fifth: loud single orchestral chords on degrees Ia, IVa and V⁷a, each one followed by a short piano *cadenza*, and then the continuation of the *tutti* as one might expect it.

The daring of the G major concerto's opening (1806) was as much in its expectation of immediate audience attention as it was in musical and physical terms. For the early nineteenth-century piano to precede the orchestra was certain to be anticlimactic but, in this case, by careful matching of timbres, the use of complementary material in the band and the solo, the whole process became a pointer to the first structural downbeat on the tonic in b. 14. This trick of withholding the emphatic tonic – a full root-position tonic chord spread over more than one octave including the bass and occurring on the first beat of a bar and phrase and frequently, though not necessarily, at a fairly loud dynamic – or its establishment, was not new. Once true tonal tension became a feature of musical structure during the Classical period, exemplified pre-eminently in sonata-form, the strength of that tension, and usually the length and power of the movement, was to a great extent a function of the degree of security of tonic-establishment. The relationship between the two could give scope for some sophisticated tonal games and musical wit of which the best, though not the only, example within striking distance of the period, is Joseph Haydn.

Although Beethoven's usage was rarely witty, delaying the emphatic tonic was a regular feature in his openings and he develops it through his first two periods, using various ploys and harmonic sleight-of-hand. What is particularly interesting about the G major Concerto's solo piano opening (Ex. 17.2) is that, on the face of it, Beethoven does all the right things to produce an emphatic tonic, and yet, the result is anacrustic and unstable.

Ex. 17.2: Beethoven, Piano Concerto in G major Op. 58/i, opening.

True, the first chord does fulfil most of the conditions as outlined above, but they are subtly undermined. The dynamic is *piano,* and having the third on top compromises its strength, as does the layout, with the doubling of the major third, the chord's close position (and in the bass register too), causing almost a confusion of overtones, far more telling on the period instrument. Metre is indeterminate because of the pause and tie, and the subsequent repetition, without the bottom octave, points away from the chord and further destabilises it by placing it in the guise of an anacrusis.

When this chord I reveals itself on a downbeat (at (1) in Ex. 17.2), it is cast as an *appoggiatura* to V, appears on an offbeat at (2), this time in first inversion and eclipsed by a root-position V. The counter-progression in the bass (marked x) detracts from the top line and makes the supertonic into an immediate goal, to which our chord is annexed as a full crotchet *appoggiatura* (3). When it next appears, it is once again on the first beat of the bar (4), but, by previous implication, and the phrasing (marked in square brackets above the score (a), with subphrases (b)), it still lacks emphasis, with the further indignity of having its third degree eclipsed by the fourth, injecting some of the character of the previous V^7 chord, to which it finally succumbs (without the seventh) in an imperfect cadence. This weighting in favour of the dominant, the half-close itself and the incompleteness of the phrasing creates a structural upbeat that itself needs resolution, but with progressions which should be, to as great an extent as possible, outside of those already used.

The implication here is modulation, but Beethoven chooses not to further weaken the G major tonality it by modulating away *from* it, since, due to the processes described above, it at this stage lacks the tonicity to sustain an outward modulation. Instead he modulates *to* G major from elsewhere and it is here that his insistence on the melodic third, B, becomes vindicated. In the answering phrase-group – on strings alone so as not to detract too much from the purely harmonic game – the B is briefly tonicised as chord III and with a very similar rhythmic profile to the solo's music, the chords move through the progression:

```
Keys:
  I                                                           IV – Ib │ V⁷c – I
  IV                                              Vb           I
  V                                 Vb – I – IVb              ♭VII
  II                      V – Ib    Ib – IV– ♭VIIb
  III    I │ I – V – Ib │ Ib – IV – ♭VIIb
Bars:  6   7              8          9            10           11
```

with the passing secondary dominants syncopated at the expense of their respective tonics and the swing to the subdominant towards the perfect cadence. The orchestral *tutti* ensues.

The sheer magic of this opening was, of course, unrepeatable; Beethoven set himself a unique proposition and it demanded, and received, a unique solution. The whole process presupposed, as I have suggested, an immediately attentive and musically aware audience – which might well have been the case with the surprise of the soloist's beginning the work – or, alternatively, disregard for them altogether.

Few other professional travelling composers could trade on these presuppositions. If Beethoven felt he was writing for posterity, they also, like Shakespeare's Cleopatra, had 'immortal longings' in them, though these had to be tempered by more immediate and more mundane considerations. The soloist's initial entry was still the first among equals *vis-à-vis* the concerto's orchestral opening, and this connection between the two 'entries', not to mention the more obvious one in that they share the same thematic material, meant that links between them were both expected and desirable; the piano appropriated some of the orchestral opening's glory while stamping it with its own instrumental personality.

Thus, in Clementi's C major Concerto and in J.L. Dussek's in F major, the solo entries are simply piano versions of their openings – in fact, Clementi's also exists, in the composer's own transcription, as a piano sonata which Plantinga[1] calls 'rather crude but saleable' (see Chapter Sixteen, Ex. 16.2 for the *tutti* opening). Similarly, the solo entry in Chopin's F minor Concerto is very close to its *tutti*, while many others begin with a lightly decorated statement of the theme in the manner of Mozart's last two concertos. Others that sport an arpeggiaic opening and/or main theme, fill this out with block chords and amalgamate it with a pianistic flourish to give a common type of assertive entry, for example J.B. Cramer's Op. 16 in D minor, J.L. Dussek's in B flat major, Herz's Op. 34 in A major, Chopin's in E minor, Hummel's in E major, Ries' Op. 42 in E flat major, Kalkbrenner's Op. 85 in E minor, and it can be seen in reverse in Beethoven's Third. Even the autumnal melancholy of Ignaz Moscheles's G minor Concerto's *tutti* receives its first blast of winter wind in the piano's entry, impatiently closing the expected perfect cadence (Ex. 17.3).

---

[1] Plantinga/CLEMENTI, p. 163.

Ex. 17.3: Moscheles, Piano Concerto in G minor, piano entry.

This kind of swagger is appropriate enough, but it can pall somewhat with overuse, and, again, other means were sought; if the very unicity and success of Beethoven's solo entry in the G major Concerto put imitation out of the question – in the standard concerto at least – it did not preclude the same sort of ingenuity as some of the orchestral openings we have seen.

Tuttis ended with a coda which, as stated earlier, was generally summary and loud, but in the majority of cases this in turn was followed by something of a more anticipatory – if not more conciliatory – nature, a symbolic withdrawing from the stage ending with a tonic full close, although Herz's Third Concerto, Op. 87 in D minor, ends with a reiterated plagal cadence. Occasionally the expected tonic entry was delayed: Hummel brings the piano in with the unusual direction *Energico e patetico* on the flattened sixth in his F major Concerto Op. posth. 1 – echoing a similar tactic in his previous transition section – before resolving to V (Ex. 17.4), and Moscheles, in his Op. 64, introduces his soloist on the (unflattened) vi, moving to Ib and V.

Ex. 17.4: Hummel, Piano Concerto in F major Op. posth. 1/i, piano entry.

Further delay of the entry could involve the soft prolongation of a final 6/4 –5/3 cadence with the piano entry resolving it. This prolongation could be diatonic (Hummel, Op. 110) or, more tellingly, chromatic (Hummel Op. 113). A classic instance is Chopin's E minor Concerto, which, by dint of interrupted cadences and sensuous elongation of lyrical phrases, creates a gossamer that the piano must crash through. This probably influenced Henselt in his C minor Concerto, which it resembles: indeed, another of his concertos, that in F minor Op. 16, also has affinities with Chopin's in the same key.

Composers who had chosen a striking opening – whether aggressively so or not – at the beginning of the movement, put themselves on their mettle if the solo entry was not going to suffer from anticlimax. Moscheles's *Concerto pathétique* in C minor (no. 7, Op. 93) opens its common-time first movement with a steady crotchet pulse on timpani and double-basses over which a mournful clarinet intones its theme (Ex. 17.5)

Ex. 17.5: Moscheles, *Concerto pathétique* in C minor Op. 93/i, opening *tutti*.

and ends only 55 bars later on an augmented sixth chord, which the piano takes up and rapidly resolves through V to I, the F♯ remaining as an *appoggiatura* in the subsequent arpeggio.

As far as shortening the *tutti* goes, Moscheles had already overstepped this mark in the previous Concerto in B flat major, (No. 6, Op. 90), where the soloist appears in b. 21; this, however, is a shorter than usual work and has more in common with the smaller pieces for soloist and orchestra, such as the concert rondo (to be addressed later) than the full-scale concerto, and its subtitle, *Concert fantastique*, gives him further leeway.

The question of atmosphere is obviously of the essence here, and Moscheles is not the only one to bold-print the emotional or programmatic content of a concerto by appending a title; others were acutely aware of it also. In the B minor Concerto, Hummel manages to reuse the opening in the piano entry without anticlimax. After the music lands in B major, as described above, a serene passage over a tonic pedal is ruffled only by a minor sixth given in the melody and then as part of the harmony. The piano enters playing a simple B major arpeggio on the left hand alone, under which comes the *pizzicati* basses and timpani rhythm as at the opening. Then the music changes to B minor and the piano establishes this with minimal melody (Ex. 17.6). The effect of the opening rhythms is to darken the piano's major mode and virtually drag it down to the minor.

Ex. 17.6: Hummel, Piano Concerto in B minor Op. 89/i, end of first *tutti* and solo entry.

Ex. 17.6 continued

Beethoven's risk in the G major Concerto was even greater, as we have seen, and the price of his solo opening would have bankrupted many another composer. Once it has resolved this opening, however, the entire *tutti* points towards the solo entry. The second subject is itself a modulating cycle-of-fifths sequence, so that at the end of the *tutti* there is more need than usual to underscore the tonic key and he does this by avoiding closure on a number of occasions: at b. 49 by continuing the V^7 chord and 'resolving' onto Ic (as demanded by the melody); at b. 55 Ib is touched on in passing; at bb. 59–60 and 63–4 the issue is dodged again by Ib (and a *p* dynamic in the first case); a momentary diversion at b. 66 proves to be an augmented sixth, and when resolution finally comes in the next bar, it requires underlining, which the tonic pedal literally provides over the next six bars; the solo finally tiptoes in, implying a vii chord over this pedal, and the resolution proper for the section occurs in b. 79, coinciding with the piano's first hint of virtuosity.

In the majority of cases in the early nineteenth-century concerto, the solo entry not only mirrored, but intensified, the dual nature of the first subject's tragic/comic masks effect, and many of the louder entries are in the nature of a *précis* of the *tutti*'s opening, whereas the more lyrical statements are expanded – a situation that seems to obtain even when the soloist reverses the *tutti*'s order of presentation (Field in A flat major, Herz in D minor, Hummel in F major, Ries in D major).

This freedom in treatment and presentation suggests an improvisatory approach at some stage between composition and printing and it extends from simple decoration of given themes (C. Kreutzer, Op. 65) to the freest preludial writing. At perhaps its clearest, it can be seen in Herz's Seventh Concerto (Op. 207 in D major) which is marked – and written – *senza tempo*, and in Czerny's Op. 28 in F major, where the entry, after 11 bars of octaves, has a written-out *cadenza*, so marked.

This last-mentioned work of Czerny's also illustrates another manifestation of improvisatory influence and one on which I remarked earlier: that of bringing the soloist in before his or her time, so to speak, or, to use a different analogy, allowing it to assert itself to the extent of interrupting the *tutti* and leading into its own entry proper. Having given us 11 bars of octaves, a *cadenza* lasting 16 followed by a further 12 bars of fairly free piano-writing, a three-bar *tutti* flourish re-establishes the tonic F, and the piano sails in with a 'proper' entry of the more expected type (Ex. 17.7).

Ex. 17.7: Czerny, Piano Concerto in F major Op. 28/i, 'proper' solo entry.

Chopin seems to anticipate his entry in the F minor Concerto where the ii^{7}b chord (of the prospective ii^{7}b – V$^{(7)}$ – i cadence) is prolonged in the orchestra becoming accompanimental to the soloist's descending flourish, and resolving – a little unconvincingly, I feel – two bars later to give a decorated version of the theme. Improvisatory also is Herz's picking up of a clarinet interjection during the second subject and thundering it out *fortissimo* as his solo entry in the C minor Concerto (Exx. 17.8a and 17.8b).

Ex. 17.8a/b: Herz, Piano Concerto in C minor/i, second subject and (b) solo entry.

The entry in Hummel's A minor Concerto strikes me as a clear case of an improvisatory gesture originating, no doubt, in a particular performance. Like Chopin's E minor after it – and the influence of the former on the latter has been noted by several commentators – the orchestra's *tutti*, after a series of interrupted cadences, settles down to a sinuous lyricism ending on a 6/4 tonic chord. Instead of waiting for a resolution, however, the piano enters *in media res*, with the 6/4 in the left hand and a decorated rising 6/4 arpeggio in the right, finally cadencing after a downward diminished-chord arpeggio for the 'proper entry' (Ex. 17.9, marked *).

Ex. 17.9: Hummel, Piano Concerto in A minor Op. 85/i, solo entry.

A similar effect can be found in J.B. Cramer's Fourth Concerto Op. 38, where the solo has something of a fairground hall-of-mirrors relationship with its main theme – a kind of distorted *déjà vu*, and in Hummel's entry in his F major Op. posth. 1, where the mood-swings and patchwork of thematic reference have all the signs of improvisation (see Ex. 17.4 above, and Chapter Sixteen, Ex. 16.3 for the opening). *À propos* of this and other works, I do not think that the presence of orchestral comments is any reason to doubt the improvisatory origins, since most of them are merely supportive – for example Hummel *op. cit.*, Chopin Op. 11, bb. 140–41 etc. – and could have been added at any time subsequently. Certainly, the sense of a return to 'normality' particularly in harmony and phrasing when the piano finally settles down is generally palpable.

As is sometimes the case with Mozart, the soloist occasionally has a melody (or melodies) within one or other of the subject-groups that does not appear in the orchestra, but for this to be expressed in a distinct theme is rare in our period; more often than not, the derivation from previous *tutti* (or solo) material is clear enough for it to be taken as a derivative, or developmental. In Hummel's E major Concerto, the piano replaces the tutti's original second subject with its own derivative, and this remains throughout the movement. Usually, passagework takes the place of such Mozartian melodic precipitations, even though it may be melodically oriented, as it is for the most part in Hummel, in Chopin, who rated him highly throughout his life,[2] and in much of J.B. Cramer's work. Virtuoso passagework also fills in the orchestra's transitions and coda in the solo exposition and in general this corresponds closely to the *tutti* one, except for the second-subject key; trills, usually double or triple, are obligatory for ending the soloist's exposition.

(ii) The remainder of the movement

The remainder of the movement follows a more-or-less regular sonata-form outline, a Development and a *reprise* with the expected key-orientation. The double-exposition usually ends with a loud orchestral statement of the first subject on a decisive perfect cadence in the dominant or relative major, as in the standard sonata-form. The separation between this and the ensuing Development section is normally clear and may involve rests as well as the general 'full-stop' feeling. When a link is used, it is to lead the music away from its expected path. In Chopin's E minor first movement, the solo exposition ends with a statement of the theme but in the tonic (minor), which modulates quickly to C major, in which key the piano re-enters with the second of the main subjects; in his other concerto (F minor), the exposition ends in the dominant minor, but on an interrupted cadence, thus bringing the music to the 'correct' key of the relative major. Field's link in the third concerto leads him from the dominant (B flat) to F sharp (enharmonic G flat) in three and a half deft bars (Ex. 17.10), and similarly, but not quite as deftly, Hummel's in the A flat major concerto's first movement leads him from dominant to flattened sixth, C major.

Ex. 17.10: Field, Piano Concerto No. 3 in E flat major/i, link to development section.

'Development' may be something of a misnomer in these first movements and, again, the public venue and purpose of the concerto must be appreciated. We have already seen that, because of the double-exposition and of the *ritornello* element in the first part of the movement, there may be insufficient musical time and space to convincingly set up a new key in the manner of the more traditional Classical sonata-form; consequently, a tight tonal argument is neither necessary nor appropriate. This, of course, does not mean that we don't find something approaching it in the works of the greater figures – and indeed, in other works by those selfsame composers who demur when it comes to concertos and some smaller forms.

---

[2] For example in a letter (1845) to Countess Potocka he writes, 'all the great composers, Mozart Haydn, Hummel . . .'

The soloist invariably begins the development with material very similar to its entry, although the more swaggering gestures may have been excised. Melodically speaking, the stock developmental procedure involves a particular application of *motivische Arbeit*, the tossing around of motifs by sections of the orchestra – providing frequent opportunities for the winds to shine – against figuration in the piano, though the technique's application here is nothing like as rigorous or as wayward as it is in improvisation. Tonally, the section takes the form of colouristic explorations of harmony, drawing on the expected repertoire of sequence (melodic and/or harmonic) and so one would expect a fondness for the more highly coloured tonal relationships of the third and its permutations – *Terzverwandtschaft* – especially those that can be made to yield chromatic relationships also, the prime one being the augmented sixth (on the flattened sixth).

The more remote keys, which could involve enharmonic changes, were something of a fashion: in his A flat major first movement in No. 2, Field spends enough time in B and F sharp majors to warrant key-signature changes, although his F sharp major opening in the development of the Third Concerto in E flat major proves to be a brief diversion. Chopin's E minor begins the section in C major and stays there a while; Hummel's A flat and F major concerto developments are, for at least half their extent, in F and F sharp minors respectively, and his E major concerto drops its four sharps for the entire development section, while the first movement of Herz's Op. 34 concerto in A minor passes the development section entirely in D minor. Second-subject material tends to keep its 'relief' character, giving a few moments' repose amid the hurly-burly, and this also applies to any exclusive solo material from the piano's own exposition. The introduction of material that stands out as being or feeling 'new' (whether derived from previous music or not) is very rare and tends to occur later in the period, when the concerto was beginning to loosen up formally. Henselt does introduce such material in the development of the first movement of his Op. 16 Concerto in F minor – a five-part chorale, in effect, played by a '*Quatuor con sordini*' (see Chapter Eleven, Ex. 11.35). This could have been very effective had it not suggested so strongly the cloying piety of the Victorian age; it seems to be the devotional face of the *faux-naïf* second subject (Ex. 17.11), which is almost as unconvincing.

Ex. 17.11: Henselt, Piano Concerto in F minor Op. 16/i, second subject.

Like the opening, the *reprise* usually begins with the *tutti* (often having concluded the development also) giving the first subject or repeating the opening. The section, in effect, combines the two expositions, and one result of this is that the piano in many cases breaks in with its original entry material to take up the second half of the first subject, or even to be its sole bearer, when the repeated *tutti* opening is of the more introductory kind. J.B. Cramer, however, in his Fourth (C major) and Fifth (C minor) concertos, dispenses with the first subject altogether in the reprise, although the piano enters here as it did initially. As a general rule, however, there are few new departures in these *reprises*, the overall feeling being one of consolidation rather than innovation.

There is, however, an interesting and somewhat surprising, omission in most of the concertos of this period, that of the solo *cadenza*. J.L. Dussek's Op. 17 in F major has a *Fermata* on an orchestral 6/4 but this work dates from around the middle years of the 1780s, while Field, uniquely in his Fifth, has a written-in *cadenza in tempo*. Again, there is a mitigating factor here in that the work is particularly programmatic (entitled *L'incendie par l'orage*), and the only *bona-fide* example of a *cadenza*-point in these works that I have managed to find is in Conradin Kreutzer's in E flat major, which asks for a *'Cadenza ad libitum'* seven bars from the end of the movement. It seems contradictory that, in an age in which, as we shall see (Chapters Twenty-Two and Twenty-Three), improvisation was highly prized and expected by all occupants of the musical spectrum, the conventional opportunity for its display – enshrined in every piano concerto of Mozart and Beethoven,[3] no less – should have been shunned.

The principal reason, I think, lies again in the format of concerts in the period, particularly the fact that they included the virtuoso's *'extempore* performance' by which such occasions were crowned, and any formal improvisation apart from this (such as the concerto *cadenza* proper) could well detract from it.

---

[3] Even though the Fifth Concerto ('Emperor') contains the rubric 'Non si fa una cadenza, ma s'attacca subito il seguente', that 'seguente' is 20 bars of typical cadenza stuff. There is also the fact that Beethoven provided mini-cadenzas as the piano interjections at the opening of the movement and extended them in the reprise.

CHAPTER EIGHTEEN

Received Forms 5c: The Concerto 3, Other Movements

(i) The middle movement: keys

The opportunities for contrast that were implicit in the concerto's middle movement was something of which most composers of our period were only too happy to take advantage, and key- and/or mode-changes for this movement are practically universal. Among the extremely rare exceptions are Paisiello's Concerto no. 3 in A major and Cogan's Op. 5 in C major, both of whose middle movements are in the same key as their first. Generally speaking, in the case of major-key concertos the predilection for middle movements in the dominant or subdominant before 1760 was intensified in the following fifty years, with a preference for the latter. This weighting may have been due to Mozart's usage in the majority of his piano concertos, but it changed dramatically during the years from 1810 to 1850, when keys removed by a third – a rarity before 1770 – became a regular feature. Some of these involve modal change, which had always been an option, of course, and that minority of eighteenth-century works of any genre in minor keys almost always featured an escape to the (relative) major in middle movements, and very often the parallel major in finales as well. Exceptions include J.C. Bach's early set of six concertos, the third of which, in D minor, has a middle movement in B flat major (headed Adagio affettuoso con sordini), and whose sixth, in F minor, has one in C minor (Andante), and Paisiello's *Sturm-und-Drang*-influenced G minor Concerto, whose slow movement (Largo) is in C minor with a central section in E flat major.[1]

There are also occasions where an inner movement in a major-key work is in the relative minor, as opposed to the more normative key of the fourth or fifth remove but, given the closeness of the relationship, they are surprisingly uncommon. Examples include Luigi Boccherini's only keyboard concerto[2] (E flat major, with an Adagio slow movement in C minor) and Schobert's in G major (1765) whose deeply felt middle movement, an Andante in E minor, is over half as long again as its first

---

[1] It has proved extremely difficult to date Paisiello's concertos: Michael Robinson's Thematic Catalogue of the composer's works assigns this one to 'before December, 1788'.

[2] No. 487 in Gerard's Catalogue, this has neither been dated, nor fully authenticated.

movement. Some of Mozart's output cleaves to this arrangement, including K. 271, and the heart-rending *siciliana* (in the rare key of F sharp minor) of the A major Concerto K. 488, and so does Beethoven's fourth in G major. This relative minor usage continues in the second half of our period, but is eclipsed by other kinds of third-relationships, which soon become the norm for inner movements. Some examples (all major keys, with the middle-movement key in parentheses) are: Field/6 in C (E), Döhler/1 A (F), Moscheles/4 E (C), J.L. Dussek Op. 27 F (A flat), Beethoven's First and Fifth, C (A flat) and E flat (B), and both of Carl Maria von Weber's C (A flat) and E flat (B).

More typical is *Terzverwandschaft* involving change of mode but not in the relative: this was anticipated even before our period in works such as the concerto attributed to W.F. Bach in G minor (E flat major) (*c*.1751?), C.P.E. Bach's C minor Concerto W 31, (1753–5) with its Adagio in A flat major, and his double Concerto for harpsichord and piano in E flat major (W 47, 1788) having the remoter C major, but also principally by Mozart's sole example, his K. 466 in D minor (B flat major) (1785), Beethoven's Third in C minor (E major) (*c*.1800), and J.L. Dussek's Op. 49 in G minor (E flat major, 1801). It becomes widespread after 1810 with Hummel in A minor (F major), and thereafter something of a *cliché*, with Moscheles's Op. 93 (*Pathétique*) in C minor (A flat major), Op. 64 in E major (C major) and Op. 87 in C major (E minor then C major), Mendelssohn's G minor (E major) and D minor (B flat major) and both his concertos for two pianos A flat major (F major) and E major (C major); Herz's No. 2 Op. 74 in C minor (E major) and his No. 4 Op. 131 in E major (C major) reverses the process.

Similarly, time-signatures usually shift from duple/quadruple to triple (or *vice versa*) between these movements, with a good representation of 6/8 often associated with a pastoral feeling (either so-designated or not) or, more particularly, in *siciliana* rhythm, such as Mozart's already mentioned F sharp minor in K. 488/ii, followed by Field/4/ii in G minor and Czerny/Op. 28/ii in lighter vein, in C major.

(ii) Middle movement: types

In terms of style, middle movements remained true to the tradition of the vocal aria, the piano centre-stage with its orchestral foil, declaiming its *bel canto* with typically operatic decorativeness and, usually, lack of dramatic gesture, in a simple ABA shape. Tempo directions bear this out, an overwhelming preference for the 'gentler' *tempi* – Andante, with Larghetto following on close behind. It is interesting that, although the theorist Heinrich Christoph Koch (in 1802) sees little or no distinction between them, Andante was predominantly associated with triple time-signatures, and Larghetto with quadruple. The use of Largo or Adagio is rare in the period 1770–1810, Beethoven being exceptional, with the slow movements of his first and third concertos using the former, and those of his second and fifth the latter.

During the thirty or so years before our period, there is frequent use of Adagio in concerto slow movements, but this has more to do with the eighteenth-century perception of Adagio as being faster than Largo and slower than Andante (see

Rousseau/ DICTIONNAIRE (1768)), although this was not universal; it was a common marking in C.P.E. Bach's slow movements. By the beginning of the nineteenth century, it was accepted as the slowest tempo, and its use becomes widespread, not least in the movements under discussion.

Occasionally, the predominantly lyrical nature is advertised by a suggestive direction such as *Romance* or *Romanza,* as in Cramer/4, Weber/1, Chopin/1, Hummel/Op. 113, Kreutzer/Op. 65 and Clara Schumann/Op .7, as well as in Mozart's K. 466 – his only use of this term in the piano concertos. Introductions are rare, and, in line with Mozartian precedent, by far the greater number have either the piano or the orchestra beginning the movement alone with the main melodic material, and the other immediately restating this in more-or-less similar form.

The general simplicity of the melodies, the transparency of the ABA formal envelope and the consequent exaltation of content over form and melody over structure in these movements, meant that pianistic indulgence of a lyrical and personal kind was to the fore. And, given the fact that the most common and most prized public performances of these pieces were by their composers, it is not surprising to find that most of Field's slow movements are nocturne-like and that Felix Mendelssohn's have a close affinity to his *Songs Without Words.*

The melodies that form the basis of these movements are of wide variety including the ubiquitous folk/popular and operatic types, and the second movement of Czerny's Concerto in A minor (Ex. 18.1a) is typical, if a trifle 'deadpan'.

Ex. 18.1a: Czerny, Piano Concerto in A minor Op. 214/ii, bb. 1–8.

The tendency to decorate rather than develop was to be expected, given the status of the concerto and its public face, as well as the audience profile and expectations; the result is a body of movements that usher in a new kind of pianism in which the functional and the decorative, the food and the garnishing, become almost indistinguishable. It should come as no surprise that improvisation is very close to the surface in the conception and the performance of these movements.[3] Thus the Czerny melody of Ex. 18.1a becomes Ex. 18.1b.

---

[3] I will expand on this in Chapter Twenty-Two.

Ex. 18.1b: Czerny, Op. 214/ii, decoration of theme.

The slow movement of Hummel's B minor Concerto Op. 89 (1819) transports the listener into the magic realm of German mythology (Ex. 18.2) with its evocation of the nocturnal forest and the *Waldhorn*. Four French horns, intoning a kind of folk-chorale, alternate with the solo piano's delicately decorated commentary.

Ex. 18.2: Hummel, Piano Concerto in B minor Op. 89/ii, bb. 1–2.

This highly evocative movement forms an excellent foil to the more passionate flanking movements, each of which, in its different way, is not without a hint of tragedy.

(iii) The finale

Finales were intended to be the dessert course of the concerto, usually light and fast, rejoicing in uncomplicated surface virtuosity. The general idea was to delight rather than to involve, the *zabaglione* rather than the cheeseboard. Use of the home key in either mode was invariable with, in the case of minor-key works, an occasional reversion to the parallel major at or near the end.

It is interesting, nevertheless, that many minor-key works persisted in the minor mode for their finales, and that this usage had a long lineage, including J.S. Bach's minor-key concertos (violin in A, 2 violins in D, both Triples (A and D) and the F and D minor solo-keyboard works), Paisiello's previously mentioned sole minor-key concerto (No. 4 in G minor), the concerto in the same key attributed to W.F. Bach (*c.*1751?) and C.P.E. Bach's in C minor (W 31, 1753–5). Within the period both of Mozart's minor-key works (K. 466 in D, and K. 491 in C minors), and Beethoven's in C minor, follow suit, as do Dussek (G minor), both of Hummel's minor-key concertos, Czerny (A minor), and Mendelssohn's (G minor and, except for the last section, D minor).

It is in the forms of the finales that we most clearly notice the 'southern' drift. Whereas Emanuel Bach's concerto-finales were, like his first movements, in full *ritornello*-form (but with lighter melodic material), eight of the eighteen by Christian are Minuets or minuet-like, and a couple of the last six (Op. 13), are *Rondeaux*. Since the latter composer was the greater influence on Mozart, it is no surprise to find that, of his 23 authentic piano concertos, two have variation-sets as finales, and eleven of the remainder are Rondos, which includes Mozart's replacement of the original finale of K. 175 in D major with the Rondo, K. 382. Two of these rondos are additionally marked Tempo di Minuetto (or *Menuetto*) and two others contain an interpolated minuet, while the finale of K. 413 (387a) in F major is a plain Tempo di Menuetto. In Beethoven's case, all but one of his piano-concerto finales are Rondos.

This remains the case with the subsequent Romantics, the overwhelming majority of whose finales are in rondo-form, usually so-designated, and with or without any added characterisation (*à l'Hongroise, alla Zingarese*, etc.) There is the occasional sonata–rondo, but the development sections usually lack the rigour of first-movement sonata-form. Although there are some examples of variation finales, they become rarer after Mozart's two of K. 453 and K. 491, and were more common in single-movement works (see below).

As in the case of the middle movements, soloist or orchestra tended to present the principal thematic material alone, although the piano occasionally did so with a clearly subordinate orchestral accompaniment. The generally clear sense of distinction between episodes and surrounding material that we saw in the Rondo (see Chapter Thirteen) is exaggerated in the concerto by the solo/*tutti* alternation, and although occasional attempts were made to cover up the joins, the sectional diversity was seen as a desirable feature and often exploited. Like the solo rondo, one would expect episodes in a variety of keys, almost always including the opposite mode and usually the relative, together with the dominant and the subdominant, and with frequent temporary visits to intermediate keys during the modulatory sections.

In other chapters – Chapters Thirteen (The Rondo), and Nineteen to Twenty-One (The Vernacular), to which the reader is referred – I have already dealt, or will shortly deal, with the kinds of themes to be found in concerto finales. Works in which the finale proves to be of particular interest include Moscheles's Second Concerto in E flat major (Op. 56) where the soft timpani solo opening gives the movement its *polacca* rhythm, Czerny's A minor, whose second episode (in F major) was based on a close relative of Mozart's 'Jupiter' finale (Ex. 18.3), Berger's Concerto in C major, Op. 34 (1808) with its quotation of the rondo-theme of Beethoven's D minor Sonata Op. 31/2 (Ex. 18.4), and the bittersweet *échappée*-figure that opens the finale of Hummel's A minor Concerto (Ex. 18.5).

Ex. 18.3: Czerny, Piano Concerto in A minor/iii.

[Mozart, K. 551 'Jupiter'/iv, opening]

Ex. 18.4: Berger, Piano Concerto in C major Op. 34/iii, opening.

[Beethoven, Op. 31/2/iii]

Ex. 18.5: Hummel, Piano Concerto in A minor Op. 85/iii, opening.

(iv) Overall features

A significant number of piano concertos show linkage of various kinds between two or more of the movements and this, in view of Mozart's exclusive preference for three discrete movements, would seem to be a later, more 'Romantic' trait. There was, however, something of a precedent and it can be seen in a distinction between the Baroque solo-type of concerto – meaning works other than the *Concerto Grosso* that follow the solo concerto's three-movement outline and movement-types, even if they are written for more than one solo instrument – and the *Concerto Grosso*. The latter was much more likely to have linked movements – usually a slow one that often truncated and ended on a dominant or dominant seventh – followed immediately by a faster one, the opening of which usually created a perfect cadence. Such an example of an unresolved implied perfect cadence can be found in J.S. Bach's First Brandenburg Concerto in F major between the second and third movements.

The C minor harpsichord concerto of C.P.E. Bach (W. 31, 1753–5) has its slow movement in A flat major, which, at the end, becomes the augmented sixth chord in C major, resolving onto the dominant for the *attacca* finale in 3/4, and in the fourth of J.S. Schroeter's six cembalo concertos Op. 3 (*c*.1775), the Grazioso middle movement in the dominant key of A major is converted in the last bar (marked Adagio) to an A^7 chord, the soloist adding a few unaccompanied notes to resolve onto D major for the finale (Ex. 18.6).

Ex. 18.6: Schroeter, Cembalo Concerto Op. 3/4/ii–iii.

In Beethoven's five piano concertos, two show a kind of linkage, again between the last two movements. The G major's middle movement is as original and striking as its preceding one, an E minor dialogue – some said an argument – between orchestral strings playing aggressively in dotted octaves and gentle harmonised piano 'points-of-order'. In spite of its being constantly trawled out, it is hard to resist referring to Liszt's description of this movement as 'Orpheus taming the beasts'. The pacified strings end, still with a touch of bad grace, in an E minor which Beethoven has subtly undermined by turning the fairly normal subdominant diversion into something a little less stabilising with the $\sharp vi^7$ chord (suggesting $V^{\flat 9}$ of A minor, b. 68) and delaying the melodic confirmation of the E minor tonic in the last bar (Ex. 18.7). The theme of the third-movement rondo begins in the subdominant (C major) of its key (G major).

Ex. 18.7: Beethoven, Piano Concerto in G major Op. 58/ii–iii.

Ex. 18.7 continued

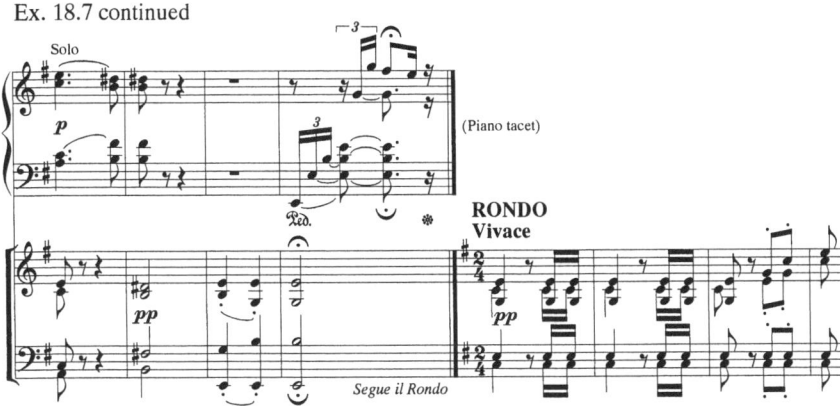

In his last concerto, the 'Emperor' in E flat major, the Adagio un poco mosso is in E major and appears to want to end on the dominant chord, B major. However, by the simple expedient of dropping the unharmonised B to B♭ and following it with a slowed-down solo-piano statement of the ensuing finale's theme, the music moves effortlessly into that movement and its key, E flat major, which is then established.

Field's Fourth Concerto in E flat major has a Sicilienne of 59 bars followed by '*attaca* [sic] *subito il Rondeau*' and Czerny's in A minor, similarly, has a slow movement consisting of 45 bars in E major (see Ex. 18.1a and 18.1b), of which the last is free and ends on the dominant of A (minor). The slow movement of J.L. Dussek's Concerto in F major Op. 27[4] is an ornate Adagio in A flat major which, after a ten-bar *tutti*, modulates to C major as the dominant of the work's tonic, F major, for the concluding rondo.

Hummel's central movement in the A flat major, Op. 113, a typically decorative *Romanze* (Larghetto con moto) in the flattened-sixth key E major has its B and G♯ converted enharmonically near the end to C♭ and A♭ respectively to lead on to the B♭^{7}, the dominant of the dominant of A flat minor that has begun to be established, and a *cadenza* leads to the concluding movement, the rondo, *alla Spagniola* in A flat major. The A minor Concerto Op. 85 also has the last two movements linked by a *cadenza*: the theme of the finale is given in Ex. 18.5 above.

The best-known example of the joining-up of two or more movements in a concerto from this period is probably Mendelssohn's Violin Concerto in E minor (Op. 64, 1844) in which the first and second are linked by a short transition, and the second and third have a modulatory paragraph as a harmonic buffer between them. He had already moved in this direction, however, in the two piano concertos in G minor (Op. 25, 1831), and D minor (Op. 40, 1837).

---

[4] Sometimes called his second, though another also shares this number.

(v) The concert rondo

It soon became apparent that joining a slow middle movement to a faster one formed a unit that could hold its own as a separate concert-piece. And, given the tendency to truncate the slower one, its introductory nature became more obvious when it split off from the concerto proper. Thus, the 'Introduction and ...' format established itself as a satisfying entity that had the virtue of reducing the more emotive characteristics to an anticipatory lead-in, to be crowned by variations, or a rondo (characterised or not), or, very occasionally, both variations and rondo, although this longer type was much more common in solo or chamber works.

However, there was another line of heritage in the concert rondo for piano (or violin) and orchestra, the best-known of which were by Mozart, and, in his case, the form is as old as his first original[5] piano concerto, K. 175 in D major (Dec 1773).

Why he decided, after nine years (1782), to replace the finale of this work with a different rondo is not entirely clear. It may have been because the original movement – a contrapuntal creature with a canonic opening and in full sonata-form to boot, in fact a typically Mozartian sonata-rondo finale – threatened to shift the centre of gravity too much towards the end of the work and was perhaps insufficiently light for the audience. A similar consideration for his audience's point of view may have also been influential in his possible substitution of the original finale of the First Violin Concerto in B flat major, K. 207 with the rondo K. 269 (K. 261a). In any case, his decision with respect to K. 175 produced the free-standing rondo in D major, K. 382 – a theme and variations in spite of its name – that remained one of his best-loved works during his lifetime. This, together with his other rondo for piano and orchestra, K. 386 in A major (thought to have been the original finale for the concerto K. 414 (K. 388a, K. 385p) in the same key) and the free-standing concerted movements for violin and for flute – probably similarly orphaned – gave rise to an important sub-genre of the Romantic period, the one-movement work for piano and orchestra, the concert rondo. However, as we have seen in K. 382, this sub-genre also comprised sets of variations, fantasies, the breakaway unit of the 'introduction-and-Allegro' type just mentioned, and the later *Konzertstück* (see (vi) below).

In the case of the first of these, the rondo, we have already dealt with the topic earlier in Chapter Thirteen (Received Forms 2: The Rondo), and since several examples of variations and fantasies for piano and orchestra have featured in their respective chapters, some general comments only are required at this juncture.

Excluding six fantasies for orchestra by Sigismond Neukomm, three of which were published in Leipzig in 1809, 1810 and 1821 respectively, Berlioz's *Symphonie fantastique* (and possibly Schumann's Fourth Symphony, his original title for which was *Symphonische Phantasie*), fantasies – and variations – for orchestra alone were virtually unknown in this period. It is therefore difficult to imagine the piano-with-orchestra fantasy as anything other than piano solos with orchestral support, and, indeed, perusal of the works bears this out. An instance occurs in the Variations on *Rule, Britannia* by Ries (Ex. 18.8a–g):

---

[5] That is, apart from his arrangements of others' sonatas as concertos.

Ex. 18.8a–g: Ries, Variations on *Rule, Britannia*.

In such works the orchestra usually provides an introduction, even if only a few chords, to frame the soloist's *bravura* flourishes, and functions as a *ritornello*, occasionally, in variation-movements, with a refrain. In the work by Ries the refrain, itself a variant of the opening of the theme (Ex. 18.8a), recurs as a codetta or linking material between the variations and undergoes some development itself later in the piece (Exx. 18.8b–g), including a rabble-rousing reference to Handel's 'Hallelujah' Chorus from the *Messiah* (Ex. 18.8e) and a pianistic attempt at humanisation (Ex. 18.8g).

An interesting illustration of the combining of the two strands leading to the introduction and rondo type – the concert-rondo and the detached slow movement-and-finale aggregate – can be found, appropriately enough, in a work of Mozart's pupil, Hummel. The autograph[6] of the *Gesellschafts-Rondo* (or *Rondeau de société*), Op. 117 is dated September 1829 and the piece was published simultaneously in Vienna, Paris and London in the following year. However, only the slow introduction, 'Introduzone. Adagio con grand espressione' in B minor was written at the time: the 'Rondo. molto vivace' is a rescored and minimally altered version of the finale of an unpublished quartet for harpsichord or piano with the accompaniment of violin, viola and cello in the same key, D major.[7] Sachs[8] gives the 1790s as the date and assigns the quartet the number S 3. Why on earth Hummel should have resurrected part of a piece from his youth – he could have been as young as 12 – can only be due to pressure of work in Weimar where, like J.S. Bach before him and Liszt after him, he was *Kapellmeister*. His *tranche* of annual leave, mostly for concert touring and built into his contract, had to be cancelled in 1829 because of the death of the Grand Duke, and, the following year, he had double leave, with several tours (Paris and London) to compose for.

Yet there is no sense of incongruity in the piece, which has a meditative, almost at times melancholy, Chopinesque introduction, followed by a Mozartian rondo – in fact, the piece perfectly sums up Hummel's historical position and tells us much about the stylistic amalgam that is early Romaticism. An angular, unharmonised – except for its perfect cadence – epigram opens the work in the orchestra, with several of the motifs already mentioned in connection with concertos' first subjects (Ex. 18.9a),[9] and the meandering piano solo following elaborates on these.

Ex. 18.9a: Hummel, Gesellschafts-Rondo Op. 117, 'Introduzione' opening.

This state of affairs is, of course, a godsend for the early nineteenth-century virtuoso–composer. Divested of the constraints of first-movement form and solo/*tutti* etiquette, he or she can indulge in real freedom, and improvisatory impulses, highlighting the lyrical. This is no exception, and Hummel revels in it.

---

[6] British Library Add. 32227, ff. 22–54'.
[7] British Library Add. 32231, ff. 1–12', and Add.32229, ff. 119–39'.
[8] Sachs/CHECKLIST.
[9] See Chapter Sixteen (v) above.

The rondo itself is a delight from beginning to end, an almost perfect example of that unity of effortless art – executive as well as creative – and audience-expectation that is so characteristic of the symphonic finales of Haydn, also Hummel's teacher and his champion. The main theme (see Ex. 18.9b) captures the *frisson* of an expectant early nineteenth-century audience in a manner not dissimilar to that of Mozart at the opening of the *Figaro* overture, and there is something for everyone, *Kenner* and *Liebhaber*, critic and one-nighter, in the music that follows.

Ex. 18.9b: Op. 117/ 'Rondo', opening.

The episodes are couched in B minor and A major and the spontaneously idiomatic piano-writing spiced with contrapuntal ginger, and perfect interaction with the orchestra remind one of ideally partnered dancers. Perhaps the fifty-year-old Hummel was remembering the heady days of the Congress of Vienna for whose balls he used to provide the music as a youth; the crystal and gold of the *Redoutensaal* chandeliers still glisten in this engaging and irresistible music.

(vi) Other works for piano and orchestra

But there were also cases of attempts to unify concertos in more obvious ways. Mozart's F major Concerto, K. 413 (387a) (see Ex. 18.10) is unusual in having virtually the same theme appearing in each of its movements,

Ex. 18.10: W.A. Mozart, Piano Concerto in F major K. 413 (387a).

Berlioz' later use of an *idée fixe*, a theme recurring in various transparent guises, in his five-movement *Symphonie fantastique* of 1830 was originally justified on the grounds of the work's semi-autobiographical programme, as evinced in its full title: *Episode de la Vie d'un Artiste. Symphonie fantastique et monodrame lyrique,* and the technique had a lasting effect on subsequent composers, as soon as the work began to be disseminated.[10] An early example of a concerto with a programme is Steibelt's sixth: *Voyage sur le Mont Bernard* (1816 or earlier), probably drawing on a Cherubini opera with the same literary itinerary – his *Eliza* of 1794 – with its alternative title *Le voyage aux glaciers du Mont St-Bernard.* Field's Fifth Concerto in C major, entitled *L'incendie par l'orage,* is also programmatic, with its storm appearing in the first movement's development section; the other movements are unorthodox also.

A particular manifestation of the free-standing piece for piano and orchestra was the *Konzertstück*. Because of its duration and makeup this partakes of the characters of the fantasy and the linked-movement concerto and is usually programmatic. The best-known example is the first, Weber's *Konzertstück* in F minor, and his previous concertos, including the two for piano, give little indication of the freedom of form of this concert piece. Weber played it to his wife and his pupil Julius Benedict on the day of the *première* of his opera *Der Freischütz*, jocularly giving them a programme for the piece involving the absence and return of a knight from the Crusades. The first two sections are, in effect, an introduction and Allegro: Larghetto affettuoso (improvisatory) and Allegro passionato, respectively, followed by a triumphant march on the Crusader's return, and a brilliant Presto giojoso to finish, full of Hummelian octaves and pearly runs. Perhaps it was in reciprocal homage that the older composer, having already released, for piano and orchestra, a set of variations and a concert-rondo with introduction, chose not only to cast one of his own non-concerto works in a similar programmatic form, the Fantasy Op. 116, but also to entitle it '*Oberons Zauberhorn*' ['Oberon's Magic Horn'] in reference to Weber's opera *Oberon*.

Of the concerted pieces by Liszt that come within the period of this book, the *Grande fantaisie symphonique* (S 120) on themes from Berlioz' *Lélio* remains unpublished, and the others, the two piano concertos, the Fantasy on Beethoven's *Ruins of Athens, Malédiction* and *Totentanz* are either too difficult to date within this book's time-span or have been heavily revised subsequent to it. Suffice it to say that Liszt, to a great extent, did for the concerto what he had for the sonata, in compacting the form into a sectional movement of great virtuosity, in essence, fusing the *Konzertstück* with the concerto.

---

[10] Berlioz asked that a copy of the programme be distributed to the audience, or at least that the titles of the movements were mentioned, whenever the piece was performed; he did add, however, that he hoped the symphony would interest on purely musical grounds.

CHAPTER NINETEEN

Vernacular 1: General

(i) Background

The 'fertilisation from below' that characterises the impact of all things folk on the arts in our period is a recurrent phenomenon in cultural history and often affects style as well as content. In one sense, the interest in vernacular matters is an aspect of the more general preoccupation with the past at which I have looked at in Chapter Ten, and is very much a result of the same needs: a political and social insecurity, engendered by institutional and military upheaval, craves respite and stability. In a climate that, especially in France, saw the aristocracy and their values as artificial, exclusive and ultimately irrelevant, informality and spontaneity were valued for being 'natural'. The very difference, immediately perceptible, between bourgeois and aristocratic social spaces bears this out, the latter's *salons* with formal, carefully placed seating geared towards polite, detached conversation, and the former's drawing-rooms with comfortable furniture, heavy drapery and the ubiquitous piano symbolising familial togetherness. This element is satirised by E.T.A. Hoffmann in *Kreisleriana*, when the poet 'Baron Wallborn', writing to Kapellmeister Kreisler, idealises sentimental, *Biedermeyer* cosiness:

> And finally, Kreisler, what you say about the pleasure that father and mother in their modest household derive from the jangling piano and faltering singing of their small children – I tell you, Johannes, I really believe that amid all the discordant earthly sounds an echo of angelic harmony is to be heard. [1]

Spontaneity and 'naturalness' is shown in the increasing interest shown by the public at large in improvisation, and not only in music, as we shall see (Chapters Twenty-Two and Twenty-Three). Theories of education stressed natural development and play, as opposed to a 'Gradgrind' system in which children were treated as miniature adults. Portrait painters began to concentrate on the natural in their subjects and informality in their settings. As we have already seen in Chapter Nine (i), eighteenth-century portrait painting was raised from its low image, chiefly by Reynolds, who, while posing his aristocratic sitters as Greek sculptures, treated less exalted ones, such as his friend Dr Johnson, in a more realistic way. Indeed genre painting, which specialised in the 'lower' types of subject matter, had already set its sights well down

---

[1] Quoted in Charlton-ed/HOFFMANN, p. 128.

the social scale, even if the message were more moral than nostalgic. This kind of art also became more elevated in the period, mainly because of the morality enshrined in its message: Edward Penny, one of the founder members of the Royal Academy and its first Professor of Painting, for example, made a good living from it and so did the Irishman, William Mulready. The Scots painter, David (later Sir) Wilkie made a great impact with his first Royal Academy exhibit, an unpretentious and charming genre painting called *Village Politicians* (1806). His delightful *The Penny Wedding* (1818) painted for the Prince Regent is equally vernacular and unaffected. The impulse enshrined in genre painting was also to give rise to, on the one hand, 'Chocolate-box art' – since many of the paintings were reproduced as advertisements on the covers of tins containing as diverse items as lip-salve, Gentleman's Relish and chocolate paste – and on the other, the high art of Courbet and Millet.

The growing status of the vernacular in matters of language was also a powerful boost to the folk movement, and it is not surprising that it should arise in association with a language which had no real indigenous literature, which had a low social status, and could not really be located as specific to any particular country, German. Germany, at this time traditionally likened to a patchwork quilt of principalities (some tiny), had no real nationality. Goethe and Schiller could ask, in 1796: 'Deutschland? Aber wo liegt es? Ich weiss das Land nicht zu finden'. ['Germany? But where does it lie? I know the unfound land.']²

French military power in eighteenth-century Europe went hand-in-hand with French (aristocratic) taste and manners and French language. In literature, France had already had her classical age with, principally, Corneille and Racine, based, as such invariably were, on that of Classical antiquity, and when Frederick the Great wished to guide his German subjects' taste in literature, it was through German translations of the literature of France and of Classical antiquity that he proposed to do it. His own city, Berlin, was called '*Klein-Paris*', so great was the dominance of French culture, and French was the language of the court. Napoleon's occupation of Prussia in 1806 was particularly humbling for all Germanic states and led to a reappraisal of German-ness, resulting in Fichte's *Reden an die deutsche Nation* ['Addresses to the German Nation'] given in Berlin in 1807–8 and published in 1808.

Before this, however, the German philosopher and critic Johann Gottfried Herder(1744–1803), a vital early influence on Goethe, believed that the soul of a people resided in their language, and that language evolved from music. As a result of these and other preoccupations, he was an ardent collector of folk-songs, publishing two volumes (1778–9) and, in fact it was he who first coined the term *Volkslied*. He was an important influence on the composers of the Berlin *Lied* School in their quest for a simple, domestic song-style (see Chapter Twenty-Six) and it carried through to C.M. von Weber and Schubert. Goethe himself, under the influence of Herder, cultivated a style of folk poetry in his earlier works, such as *Der Fischer* (1778) and *Erlkönig* (1782), set to music famously by Schubert, and adopted and perfected the four-stress rhyming couplets of popular German balladry, the *Knittelvers*.

---

² *Xenion* 95 in Schiller/*WERKE*.

In Britain, the trend towards the vernacular in poetry can be gauged by the number of ploughman-poets who were fashionable – Robert Burns, John Clare, James Hogg – although they frequently wrote in exalted style as well as vernacular, not to mention dialect, but also in the general attitude of some of the greatest, as with the *Lyrical Ballads* (1798) of William Wordsworth and Samuel Taylor Coleridge. The second edition of 1800 carried a second volume and the famous Preface by Wordsworth, which is an important aesthetic document and something of a clarion-call for the vernacularisation of English poetry, especially in its expanded form in the 1805 edition. Wordsworth writes that the work was 'published as an experiment' in which he proceeds 'by fitting to metrical arrangement a selection of the real language of men in a state of vivid sensation', and, for fear of criticism, goes on to explain his procedure:

> The principal object, then, which I proposed to myself in these poems was to choose incidents and situations from common life, and to relate or describe them throughout, as far as was possible, in a selection of language really used by men; and at the same time to throw over them a certain colouring of imagination, whereby ordinary things should be presented to the mind in an unusual way; and further, and above all, to make these incidents and situations interesting by tracing in them, truly though not ostentatiously, the primary laws of our nature: chiefly as regards the manner in which we associate ideas in a state of excitement. Low and rustic life was generally chosen, because in that condition the essential passions of the heart find a better soil in which they can attain their maturity, are less under restraint, and speak a plainer and more emphatic language; because in that condition of life our elementary feelings co-exist in a state of greater simplicity, and consequently may be more accurately contemplated and more forcibly communicated ... [3]

Another trait of the period is involved here also, that of character. A people would be characterised in their folk-products of which the folk-song, being a living, and long-lived, entity, a testament to history and, in its forming in the individual contributions of generations of singers, a testament to the evolutionary nature of history (which was always upwards) and to the invincibility of the *Volk*, was the prime expression. At the same time, in its association with the land since time immemorial, it partook of the character, immutability and therefore stability, inherent in the natural and the rural.

Although the great Classical civilisations of the Graeco-Roman world also represented stability, these – with the exception of France in the aftermath of the Revolution – were beginning to lose their sway as the ideal models, having had their day in this respect in the eighteenth century, although they continued to have a presence, of course. Similarly, the more general pastoral Arcadian ideal became more particularised, focusing on the more recent past of the living countryside of the various European nations. This was most marked in those areas in which there had been most change, and this had been most radical, among Western countries, in Britain.

As elsewhere, possession of land was the ultimate measure of wealth and the single most defining factor in social ascendancy and empowerment, and was

---
[3] Wordsworth & Coleridge/LYRICAL, pp. 1–2.

frequently depicted in portraits (see Pl. 33, 39 and 41). By the late eighteenth century, most of the agricultural land was in the hands of a comparatively small group of wealthy landowners worked by tenant-farmers who in turn employed landless labourers, many of whom were themselves disenfranchised farmers. The ethos was not simply one of satisfying local needs, but on making profits through more distant, usually urban, markets; and all progress, whether in improved breeding or crop-growing techniques, had profit as its sole aim. In addition, there were more mouths to be fed, with the general rise in population.

But there was still much 'wasted' land. The common land on which village economy largely depended, providing pasturing, turf for fires, and fishing for all, as well as temporary or semi-permanent squattings for the most impoverished, and for itinerant labourers, began to be appropriated by landowners between 1760 and 1830, whose actions were protected by law through the series of 'Enclosure Acts'. Although, in the very short term, this provided labour for those who lost the right to live on the commons, or were no longer able to subsist, in the longer term it created a pool of unused labour and migrant poor. The inhumane New Poor Law of 1834 meant that, apart from labouring, relief was only available in the prison-like workhouse, where separation of men from their families was immediate and permanent. In a classic capitalistic conjunction of landowners' greed, state abetment, legal support and religious acquiescence, the miserable operation was a huge success: the landless, jobless labouring poor were driven into the factory areas to oil the wheels of industry, and into the cities, causing unprecedented expansion, and yet more drastic overcrowding.

Conditions in both of these – factories and cities, which were not one and the same until a little later in the nineteenth century – were so different to what had been left behind, so stressful and so thankless that even the most negative aspects of rural life seemed preferable and, with miserable hindsight, idyllic. The difference in community and also, with more nuclear family units and the fact that the old or infirm, if they left the country at all, had little place if they were not of the affluent classes, also added to a sense of alienation and nostalgia which infected all but the very highest levels of society. In addition to all the other disadvantages, wages were very low – often deliberately kept so, as managers believed that if workers had sufficient to eat they would not turn up for work – and the general subsistence level was on or just below the breadline in most cases, especially in the cotton mills, where the workers were mostly women and children. Any drop in profits was reflected in lower wages and this was not adjusted for fluctuations in the cost of living. In the words of the seamstress in a contemporary poem:

> Oh! God! that bread should be so dear,
> And flesh and blood so cheap![4]

But, in this influx, the country people brought their crafts, their lore and their songs with them: the Scottish laundry-woman with memories of heathered hills and warm hearths, the Kentish drayman telling stories of harvest-home and strong cider, the

---

[4] Thomas Hood, 'The Song of the Shirt', ll. 39–40 in *Poems from Punch* (London, 1908).

Irish labourer singing sad songs of lush green valleys and dark-haired girls. The result was a surge of interest in such music, satisfied by the collection of fresh material and its laundering for consumption in middle-class parlours.

This process had, of course, already begun in the previous century. Bishop Percy's *Reliques of Ancient Poetry*, selections from a handwritten manuscript containing poetry of a wide range of previous periods, aroused great interest in early English poetry and James Macpherson's *Fragments of Ancient Poetry, Collected in the Highlands of Scotland, and Translated from the Galic or Erse Language* (1760) – its very title a compendium of suggestive and seductive 'buzz-words' for eighteenth-century sensibilities – and *Fingal, an Ancient Epic Poem ...composed by Ossian ...Translated from the Galic language, 1762* – both created a sensation, their popularity barely dimmed by the revelation that they were mostly Macpherson's own. The works were praised by Klopstock, Schiller and Goethe, who quotes long passages from *Fingal* in his *Werther*, and this was also one of Napoleon's best-loved books. Herder's *Volkslieder* (1778–9) have already been mentioned and were followed by Burns' *Poems, chiefly in the Scottish Dialect* (1786) – this time certainly not forgeries – and Bunting's *A General Collection of Ancient Irish Music*, (the music notated at a convention of traditional harpers in Belfast in 1792).

Probably the most important of all, in New as well as Old World terms, was Thomas Moore's *Irish Melodies,* appearing between 1808 and 1834, which drew on Bunting for some of its material. The *Melodies* will be discussed below in section (iii). Later collections of folk-based material include *Des Knaben Wunderhorn* [The Boy's Magic Horn], of Arnim and Brentano (1805–8), which remained a rich source for composers for some time, and the Grimm brothers' *Kinder- und Haus-märchen* [Children's and Household Tales] (1812–15).

It could not be long before the traits of folk literature would be transported into art literature either by the retelling of the tales, transposing them into more contemporary settings, adapting the plots or borrowing them, writing in their style, or simply using geographical settings associated with songs and tales. Sir Walter Scott proved himself very adept in several of these ways and the 'Waverley' novels in particular, with their knightly chivalry, sense of adventure and wild landscapes – what the eighteenth-century reader would have seen as 'sublime' – would find many imitators in European literature.

Imitations of folk literary style were very prevalent. The general sense of vernacular simplicity or directness, such as Goethe's earlier poetry at the beginning of our period, and (from the sublime to the not-quite-ridiculous) Wilhelm Müller's later poetry, together with, for example, Wordsworth and Coleridge, and, in effect, many of the published collections of folk material themselves, once they had been sanitised for polite society. In contrast, the use of folk style, involving dialect very often, would impart varying degrees of 'authenticity' to many productions: again, as I have mentioned, the Wordsworth and Coleridge of some of the *Lyrical Ballads*, and the poetry of Robert Burns, James Hogg and John Clare, among the several 'ploughman-poets' discovered, temporarily lionised and then usually dropped, by the higher classes.

(ii) Thomson's 'National Airs'

When the Scottish-born London publisher William Napier was made bankrupt in 1791, he had already published the first volume of *A Selection of the Most Favourite Scots Songs*. His financial rehabilitation was due to the generosity of Haydn, newly arrived in London, who agreed to write the accompaniments for a second volume, entitled *A Selection of Original Scots Songs in Three Parts. The Harmony by Haydn*, brought out in 1792; it attracted almost 400 subscribers. With regard to the airs, Napier, in the preface, claims to have 'carefully studied the simplicity of their character by rejecting the affected Graces and Variations which bad taste or caprice had introduced' and notes that, 'The difficulty of harmonising those wild but expressive melodies, so as to preserve their Effect, has been acknowledged by the most skilful musicians.'

And, in drawing attention to the provision of new words to the songs, his sentiments were to be echoed by many a folk-editor in the ensuing century and a half: 'The original Words, to many of the Songs, being unfit for a work of this nature, others have occasionally been substituted ...' A third volume, Haydn collaborating again, followed three years later. Although the enterprise was on the whole a lucrative one, this last volume did not sell as well as the second.

Napier's fellow-countryman, the Edinburgh publisher George Thomson, an amateur musician, also became interested in folk music, again not in the sense of collecting it but rather in the drawing-room garb in which he heard it performed at the city's concerts. He also had arrangements made for the various chamber groupings that could be expected to be available in British bourgeois homes – voice(s), with piano trio and the addition or substitution of flute. Thomson decided to go 'straight to the top' and approached the most eminent musicians in Europe for his arrangements. He began with Ignaz Pleyel and issued the first part of the *Select Collection of Scottish Airs* in 1793 in Edinburgh.

Thomson's editions were different to Napier's. The latter's were for violin (a written-out part) and simply *basso continuo* (to be realised by the keyboard-player) and he wished the songs to be concluded by playing the tune again (the music for this not provided by Napier – or Haydn). Thomson's, on the other hand, were fully written-out parts. He outlines his requirements in a letter to Hummel in 1826, asking for 'Ritornelles or Symphs [sic], & Accompaniments for the pianoforte, & for the violin, Flute and Violoncello – The Piano Forte to be of itself complete, because it is very often the only Accomp^t. we can have ...'[5] His substitute words were also rather better than most elicited in such enterprises, in spite of including the work of a shepherd (James Hogg) and a ploughman (Robert Burns).

The settings are, however, quite another matter. Of the composers who were involved in the project – Beethoven (126 settings), Weber (for a short time in 1825), Kozeluch, Haydn (187) and Hummel – only the last two had any experience of folk music. Haydn, growing up in a small village, had such music all around him and

---

[5] 3 April 1826, in the British Library, Add. 35,268. fols. 161'–64. Thomson's different spelling for pianoforte are interesting.

when he drew on it, as he occasionally did, for his thematic material – for example, the finale of his 'London' Symphony (Ex. 19.1)

Ex. 19.1: Haydn, Symphony in D major No. 104/iv, bb. 1–6.

and the trio in the minuet of the Op. 76/4 String Quartet ('Sunrise') (Ex. 19.2)

Ex. 19.2: Haydn, String Quartet in B flat major Op. 76/4/iii, bb. 1–9.

– he showed an uncanny aptitude for integrating it into his own high-Classical style. Hummel habitually noted down songs from the areas in which he travelled and some autograph sheets in the *Gesellschaft der Musikfreunde* in Vienna have some of these set for what the catalogue calls '*ein unbekanntes Instrument*' ('an unknown instrument') although the layout – intended for two hands on two staves with treble and bass clefs within a range of $A^1 - f^2$ – and the fingering suggest the harp. Among these is a 'Schottisches Lied', which is in fact the Irish song *Éibhlín a Rúin*, anglicised to 'Eileen Aroon'. This appears in Moore's *Irish Melodies* as *Erin! the tear and the smile in thine eyes* and also known as *Robin Adair*; Moore's work will be discussed in more detail in the ensuing section.

Nevertheless, the settings of all these composers show remarkably little understanding of what made these songs tick. It may be simply a matter of attitude to a relatively easy and lucrative job-of-work: Kozeluch described most of the tunes as 'barbarous music' and the first series he did as 'diabolic', and Beethoven referred to everything as 'Scottish', whether it was Scottish, Irish, Welsh or even English.

It may also be because they were already bowdlerised and were sent to them without words: quite a few of the settings turn out to be unintentionally humorous. Many of them were also difficult, too difficult, in fact, for Thomson to risk publication without first simplifying them. This didn't endear him to the composers and it especially irritated Beethoven. Another problem was that, frequently, the 'additional parts' (for the strings) were not bought, leaving them duo arrangements for piano and voice. Thomson admits this in a later letter to Hummel, saying that although he found the composer's violin, flute and cello parts 'truly delightful' – 'Sorry I am to say that there are not in this large city [Edinburgh] above 3 or 4 families, who ever think of, know, or care for any thing but the Piano Forte part of my Songs!'[6] Thus, the venture was only a moderate success for Thomson and he had

---

[6] Letter of 29 October 1831, in LBl, Add. 32,188, fols. 1–2'. I must confess I find Thomson's assertion difficult to believe.

to subsidise it to some extent from his own private means. For the composers, however, it was lucrative, as can be deduced from the list above and the number of items they were willing to contribute as well, in most cases, as the number of years over which they were associated with the project. It certainly earned Thomson his place in history.

Occasionally, the voice of the composer does break through, however attenuated. In his setting of [*'Tis*] *The Last Rose* [*of Summer*] (see Ex. 19.6a below for the tune) as a set of variations for flute (or violin) and piano, Beethoven provides a rather bland harmonisation for the tune – his version has slight differences, not significant in this context – on the flute, and gives the first of the three variations to the piano solo, an imitative *perpetuum mobile* in triplet quavers (Ex. 19.3a).

Ex. 19.3a: arr. Beethoven, Op. 105/5/ var. 1.

Both the imitation and the constant motion carry over into the next variation, with the triplets now semiquaver quadruplets and the flute with the melody unadorned and doubled by the piano's left hand, against a right-hand descant, (Ex. 19.3b).

Ex. 19.3b: Op. 105/5/ var. 2.

The last variation has a 'boiled-down' version on flute with the piano largely accompanying in arpeggios, now sextuplets. The short coda (see Ex. 19.3c) has the music moving through falling thirds to C flat (flat sixth), where we get a soft snatch of the tune, and a harmonic switch brings us back in muted triumph to the tonic E flat major.

The sequence of works in one crucial period of Beethoven's life is an interesting illustration of this most intractable of composer's willingness to contribute to Thomson's venture:

Op.105   Six National Airs with Variations (c.1818)
Op.106   Piano Sonata No. 29 in B flat major ('Hammerklavier') (1817–18)
Op.107   Ten National Airs with Variations (c.1818)

Ex. 19.3c: Op. 105/5, coda.

(iii) 'Moore's Melodies'

Although Moore is known to us today only through this publication, he was a formidable Classical scholar, publishing his own translation of Anacreon's Odes while still an undergraduate at Trinity College, Dublin, which earned him the nickname 'Anacreontic Moore' – and a well-loved, though little-known, poet, admired by, among others, Byron and Berlioz. His popularity and high status as a *littérateur* can be seen in his many publications on the Continent, and a German edition of his complete works (in English) mentions 'new, complete, and critical editions of "Milton's Works" and "Ossian's Poems"',[7] which were soon to appear. The *Irish Melodies* had enormous influence in Europe and the United States and became the staple diet for the middle- and lower-middle-class drawing-room.

Moore's fitting of his own words to extant tunes was, given the resulting success both in its own terms and in those of the fame/fortune nexus, quite an achievement. Metrical and phraseological difficulties – in spite of the ironing-out of many of these – required a versatile poet. The preoccupations of the texts are those to be expected in the period: love in all its acceptable aspects, melancholy and nationalism, and the nostalgia that tinged just about everything. The language is flowery, skilfully constructed and based on the kind of archaising, sometimes medievalising, versification that was already prevalent in English, and touches of his Classical training can occasionally be detected in the odd extended simile.

---

[7] The 'Advertisement' to Moore/WORKS.

There were problems, however. The poems are frequently at variance with the original, or previously associated text (if known) and one is often aware that the original tune was intended to be faster than Moore's directions and mood prescribe. It still remains a remarkable achievement and its longevity deserved. The melodies were rarely off the parlour-piano music-stand throughout the Georgian and Victorian eras and, indeed, for much of the Edwardian, in Britain, and were a seminal influence on popular music in the United States.[8] It is fair to say that wherever English was spoken, Moore was sung.

The literary aspect of folk-collecting and disseminating had its effect in the musical field also, in terms of providing, whether in themselves or in those works to which they gave rise, operatic *libretti*, calling for incidental music to plays with folk themes or influences, in inspiring instrumental pieces based on the stories, and, of course, in settings of poems. There are analogies here between the treatment of the songs' texts and their music but they must not be pushed too far. The most basic of the diverse ways in which the music itself was also pressed into service was, of course, simply to add an accompaniment to the tunes, whether they were subsequently sung, or played as instrumental pieces. This was the case with the *Irish Melodies*, (or '*Moore's Melodies*' as they were universally known) with 'symphonies and accompaniments' by Sir John Stevenson, a minor Irish composer. The 'symphonies' refer to the purely instrumental component in the piano part, including introductions and interludes, of which more shortly.

Something of the original flavour of the various styles of the Irish originals has to be preserved in some form in the published songs for them to be in any way distinctive or folk-like, or even 'Irish', and the difficulties for the provider of words rests on these flashes of distinctiveness, even in the watered-down versions which remain. There are many tunes in which there are few or no rests for the singer, possibly because they were originally dances (as some clearly were, even if sung) or to allow for the comic effect of the patter-song, of which there is a strong tradition particularly in the Goidelic, northern, branch of the Celtic countries both in the native language and in English.

Moore gets around the problem by slowing them down in his settings – the vast majority of the collection is slow and many of the fast numbers are martial rather than happy – and by using the cadential pause, which is certainly authentic, but not in so many songs as his usage would suggest. In addition, it would be unfair to expect to find the folk performer's subtlety of rhythmic inflection, enlivening a song that, on paper, can look monotonous, in the after-dinner rendition of the bourgeois young lady, however accomplished. Irregular phrasing (by the standards of the drawing-room ballad at any rate) is occasionally a problem, but Moore's versatility places a broad prosodic palette at his disposal, as in 'How dear to me the hour'; Pl. 46 is a facsimile of the first page of the song (issued on its own) by W. Power in Dublin, c.1820. Here long vowels are targeted on the irregular cadence at b. 12 and the pause is called into play to allow singer, accompanist and audience to find their places, so to speak. The poet chooses a pentameter for this song, as opposed to the

---

[8] See Hamm/POPULAR.

usual tetrameter (and occasional trimeter) and the accompaniment wisely opts for the simple underlining of the rhythm here. Pentameter is also used to match the five-bar phrasing in 'The dream of those days' (marked in Ex. 19.4).

Ex. 19.4: arr, Moore, 'The Dream of those days', bb. 7–32.

Elsewhere, Moore matches his rhythm to the irregularity of the tune, giving extra point to a particular line, especially when he makes it a recurring one. In 'Go where glory waits thee', the 3+3+4+3 bar phrasing is underlined by his trochaic trimeter and supported by the predominant aab rhyme-scheme to give extra effect and poignancy to the refrain 'Oh! then remember me', especially as 'me' is rhymed only with 'thee' which rarely appears; and 'be', which appears only once; together they are the only 'male' rhyme in the poem:

> Go where glory waits thee,
> But while Fame elates thee,
> Oh! still remember me.
> When the praise thou meetest
> To thine ear is sweetest,
> Oh! then remember me.
> Other arms may press thee,
> Dearer friends caress thee
> All the joys that bless thee
> Sweeter far may be;
> But when friends are nearest,
> And when joys are dearest,
> Oh! then remember me.

In its appeal to loyalty, its constancy and resignation, and its theme of love in separation, it is a perfect encapsulation of bourgeois sentimentality and could not fail.

Although one is usually very conscious of a folk-song belonging to a particular nation or region, it is often quite difficult to rationalise a stylistic basis for this. The elaborately decorated anacruses of classic Irish songs is clear enough, especially in the Munster tradition – Ex. 19.5 gives an instance from a live folk performance where a plain doh –soh –doh (1 –5 –1, here G –D –G) is extruded into an expressive melisma

Ex. 19.5:

– and the so-called 'Scotch snap' is well-known as is the already mentioned off-tonic ending, modally-altered degree, and so on. There is also the penchant for octave leaps and the very common (and un-Classical) use of conjunct motion followed by a leap (very often a sixth) in the same direction, a good example of which is 'The Last Rose', though it also occurs in 'My Love is like a Red Red Rose' and was not lost on Elgar – especially in the Serenade for Strings, where it is the basis of each of the three movements, and is used to particularly beautiful effect in the slow middle one.

As mentioned, a feature of a number of these and other folk- (or folk-based) tunes is the pause tending to occur before the final cadence of each verse. Moore usually arranges to have it coincide with significant words in the text and it seems to have been derived from the folk-singer's more spontaneous expressive or dramatic usage with, perhaps, a nod in the direction of the *caesura* so familiar to Moore, a device of Classical prosody by which the metrical foot (usually the third or fourth) is divided between two words; the term is used more loosely in modern prosody to mean a pause (mostly governed by the word-sense) near the middle of the line. As used in this musico-poetic context, it highlights in the majority of cases the true highest note – as opposed to decorative note – in the song, which is also very often of melodic significance otherwise, for example being the upper tonic or other primary degree. Moor's E minor setting, 'War Song (Remember the glories of Brien the Brave)' has two, on the flattened seventh (though harmonically presented as the dominant of the relative major) and the upper tonic and they variously coincide with the words 'grave', 'sword', 'shrine', 'blood' and '[to-]night'.

When the upper tonic is in question (or even when this is not the case), the harmonic *cliché* calls for the subdominant, or, less commonly, the submediant chord. The most famous example is "Tis the last rose of summer', the tune (originally 'The groves of Blarney') of which I give in its entirety, since I will refer to it again (Ex. 19.6a). The result is a theatrical, perhaps one should say operatic, gesture and in this particular song, though hardly overladen, there are more added ornaments than usual for Moore, suggesting, perhaps, a genuine, but perhaps dimly remembered folk-performance. The melismatic decoration so common in Celtic folk music, and particularly characteristic of the Irish *corpus*, is hinted at here at bb. 16 and 34 (marked * in Ex. 19.6a), though, as written, it is un-stylistic in its combination of turn and (redundant) slide, although this may be an attempt to reproduce a *portamento*, a basic and prevalent technique in folk-performance.

Ex. 19.6a: arr. Moore, 'Tis the last rose of summer'.

Again, this would be un-stylistic here. In practice, the group is rendered as in Ex. 19.6b, and it is the version which most performers – including many folk musicians – play or sing it.

Ex. 19.6b:

Similarly, 'Though the last glimpse of Erin', using the tune of the better-known 'Coolin' ('*An Cúilfhionn*', or 'White-Haired Boy') is also given extra decorations over and above those already in the tune, placing it closer to its original than most of the *Irish Airs* (Ex. 19.7a).

Ex. 19.7a: arr, Moore, 'Though the last glimpse of Erin' ['The Coolin'].

Here, the trill, which, in its familiar art-music guise, is very rarely a part of Irish traditional vocal performance, is nevertheless fairly comfortable here, and several folk-players have reproduced it in this song. Ex. 19.7b gives an example (transcribed from a live performance on the flute).

Ex. 19.7b:

It is ironic that Moore, in a preface to the third number of his *Melodies*, actually rejects the instigators and performers of these airs, complaining about '... the chief corruptions ... arise from the un-skilful performance of our own [meaning Irish] itinerant musicians from whom, too frequently, the airs are noted down, encumbered by their tasteless decorations, and responsible for all their ignorant anomalies ...', although 'the pure gold of the melody shines through the ungraceful foliage which surrounds it ...'[9]

In similar spirit, despite the patriotic sentiments in these songs, occasionally quite strong and pointed, he carefully distances himself from any association with rebellion or 'trouble-mongering', or indeed, the classes with which these were associated, stressing that the publication 'looks much higher for its audience and its readers – it is found upon the piano-fortes of the rich and the educated – of those who can afford to have their national zeal a little stimulated, without exciting much dread of the excesses into which it may hurry them ...' He was, in spite of this, a friend of Robert Emmet and several other Irish revolutionaries.

The difficulties for the provider of accompaniments to these melodies are more and greater, than in many other 'folk' collections, stemming not only from the 'irregularities' already mentioned, but also from attempting to harmonise in a contemporary style, tunes, many of which were not intended to be accompanied, and/or were couched in the modal system. To the latter type belong songs that do not end upon the tonic chord, perhaps a vestige of the medieval plagal modes whose octave ambitus stretched from a fourth below to a fifth above the *finalis* (or tonic equivalent). In 'Take back the virgin page' – 'Written on returning a blank book', Moore tells us in a footnote – the tune (Ex. 19.8) has all the signs of C major but the final cadences are on D – clearly a poser for tonal, early-nineteenth-century domestically oriented harmony. Stevenson's – the arranger's – problem is here compounded by the fact that there is a danger of repeating the same chord on adjacent strong beats. He opts for an inflection of the repeated A minor harmony of b. 14 in the next bar, by flattening the A, giving a false feeling of minor subdominant that has to be quickly changed in time for the perfect cadence onto the dominant.

Ex. 19.8: arr. Moore, 'Take back the virgin page', bb. 7–16.

---

[9] *Letter to the Marchioness Dowager of Donegal prefixed to the Third Number* in the Leipzig edition (1826).

Ex. 19.8 continued

The similar problem in 'We may roam through this world' is alleviated by its being a merry patter-song and by his treating it simply as the dominant in the imperfect cadence, rather than modulating to it temporarily. 'Lesbia hath a beaming eye' (based on the tune *My Nora Creina* [*Nóra Críonna*][10]), another patter-jig, has a similar situation, aggravated by the addition of a flattened seventh, E♭ (if we think of it in F major), which has to be harmonised. Stevenson's solution (Ex. 19.9) gives an exposed fifth, which could have been avoided by a passing-note (D) instead of the second bass E♭ (marked *); the other alternative would be a bar of dominant minor followed by its parallel major, whose awkwardness would also be lessened by a passing-note.

Ex. 19.9: arr. Moore, 'Lesbia hath a beaming eye', bb. 9–16.

Much better handled is the flattened seventh in 'I wish I was by that dim lake' where Stevenson gives a normative tonal version (Ex. 19.10a) of the later modal cadence, where he neatly sidesteps the implied continuation of the cycle-of-fifths progression that has been made a feature of the harmonic underlay of the accompaniment (Ex. 19.10b). These accompaniments are almost invariably supportive; we look in vain for any of the subtlety of voice/piano interplay which characterises the settings of such composers as Schubert and Schumann. But we should not expect such things in a popular, middle-class, sentimental body of works designed for entertainment and sufficiently simple to be playable and singable by amateurs.

---

[10] This is one of the few cases in which, because of the popularity of the original, Moore has left the tune's real name alongside the title of his poem.

Ex. 19.10a/b: arr. Moore, 'I wish I was by that dim lake', bb. 3–4 and 11–12.

What is interesting is the difference when the 'symphonies' – as the piano introductions were called – are taken into consideration. These are often quite distinct in several – and sometimes in all – ways from the songs with which they are associated, and for the most part, thematic and other such connections are very tenuous. In the very first song, 'Fly not yet' based on the delightful 'Planxty Kelly',[11] with the interesting phrase-pattern of 4 +6 +4 +4 +2 +6 +2 +6 bars for each of its two stanzas, the only connection appears to be the rising octaves, which appear in the song. Similarly, in the song based on 'The Coolin' ('Though the last glimpse', see Ex. 19.7a above), there is little to suggest this tune in the introduction except the E♭– G fall (marked x1 and x2 in Ex. 19.11a), which occurs in the melody (see Ex. 19.7a, b. 2).

Ex. 19.11a: arr. Moore (and Stevenson), 'Though the last glimpse', opening, bb. 0–5.

Apart from that, the cut is mid-Classical or even *galant*. The beginning of the postlude (Ex. 19.11b) is even farther removed, with a jarring change of rhythm and the introduction of an unhelpful flattened sixth. The rhythm of bb. 1 and 3 in this example probably does have its basis in the tune (bb. 5–6 and 6–7 of Ex. 19.7a above) but this has the feel of an unconscious reminiscence rather than a reference. If there is a saving grace, it is the decorated version of the tune later in Ex. 19.11b (marked *). Yet, with its strange mishmash of improvisatory continuation, hints of the folk tune and operatic touches (the interrupted cadence at bb. 7–8 and the flourish in the penultimate bar), it almost convinces, like an inappropriately over-ornate picture-frame.

---

[11] The origin of the word 'Planxty' is unclear, but thought to have affinity with the seventeenth- and eighteenth-century French *plainte* or even the medieval Latin *planctus*, from which it derives. Both mean 'lament' but most of the extant planxtys are fast.

Ex. 19.11b: 'Though the last glimpse', piano postlude.

An impression of the attempt to appropriate style through reference is strengthened by, for example, the out-of-the-blue, half-remembered quotation from the 'Coolin' in the postlude of 'The harp that once' (marked 'x' in Ex. 19.12). This song is one of a number of examples where the 'symphonies' are in some ways inappropriate for their tunes, as is the introduction to 'And doth not a meeting like this': the coda, using the same material, is only half of its length.

Ex. 19.12: arr. Moore, 'The harp that once', postlude.

One of the most interesting occurs in 'How dear to me the hour', mentioned above because of its unusual rhythm and the pentameter metre. This is mirrored in the irregularity of the introduction (see Pl. 46) including its opening with a different time-signature (common time) in triplet figures. Orchestral effects are suggested in 'St Senanus and the lady', complete with bell and horn-figure.

The overall intention in Stevenson's 'symphonies' seems to be two-fold, both socio-musical. The impression is of an operatic *scena*, with the piano setting the scene to introduce the *prima donna* – or her male equivalent – in arresting music that also elicits the audience's attention, in the rare cases when it would need to do so. It also ensures a more-or-less equal participation for the pianist as well as singer, with persuasive and, at the same time, relatively easy, material; when the singer sings, however, there is no contest.

There are a couple of duet songs and, as is the case in 'St Senanus', dialogue songs with the possibility of the same, as well as the effect suggested in 'Echo' to be sung 'By another voice'. This practice reminds one of the occasional performance of Schubert's *Erlkönig*, for example, as a duet between narrator and child. Moore also includes a Scena, 'Before the battle', for four voices in which all but the bass has solo material; the melodic style and the manner of Moore's layout has affinities with English glees. Moore, in addition to his many other talents, was also a performer, reciting his verses and singing the *Melodies* to his own guitar accompaniment, winning the approval of, amongst others, Moscheles, who did, however, comment that 'le genre est petit'. He nevertheless dedicated his *Hibernian Impromptu* which introduced two 'favourite airs' to 'Thomas Moore Esq'.

CHAPTER TWENTY

Vernacular 2: Inclusion

(i) General

I have examined Moore's work in more detail here than is usual because, more than any other source, perhaps, his publications represent the 'classic' versions of many of the 'folk' tunes used by nineteenth-century composers and illustrate the various problems in providing them with convincing settings and accompaniments. They are also of more general importance because, through them, one gets a particularly good picture of the tastes – especially, but not exclusively, literary and musical – and the preoccupations of the society that so avidly devoured them privately and publicly in the drawing room, the ballroom and the concert-hall.

So prevalent was the folk 'industry', not least in music, that no composer could avoid it, or did so at his or her peril. Although very much a bourgeois preserve, the higher reaches of society were not immune either: the German composer–violin-virtuoso Spohr describes an evening he spent with the Duke of Sussex on a visit to London in about 1820:

> During a conversation we had upon the subject of English national songs, the Duke sent for his guitar and sang to me some English and Irish national songs, which afterwards suggested to me the idea of working up some of the most popular of these as a pot-pourri for my instrument, and of introducing the same at my concert.[1]

This evening must have been a welcome change for Spohr, as, on his own evidence,[2] the treatment of musicians by the aristocracy of all kinds in London was notoriously atrocious. The work referred to was the *Pot-pourri on Irish Themes* for violin and orchestra Op. 59, published in Leipzig in 1823 – 'the second of my works written in London', as a footnote to the above quotation informs us.

Such opportunism was usual, but Moscheles, living in London from 1826–46, turned it into a fine art. On a visit to Sir Walter Scott in 1828, the latter gave him some Scottish airs, on which the composer–pianist immediately improvised, to the delight of the assembled guests.[3] The following year, 'Sir Walter Scott's favourite strains of the Scottish Bards by "J. Moscheles"' [*sic*] duly appeared and was reviewed

---

[1] Spohr/AUTOBIOGRAPHY, pp. 90–91.
[2] See quotation in op. *cit.*, p. 52.
[3] Moscheles/LIFE, I, pp. 203–4.

in the London periodical *The Harmonicon*. The reviewer (probably William Ayrton, the editor) presumed it to be 'M. Moscheles' recollections of his extemporaneous effusion when on a visit to Sir Walter Scott, who on that occasion produced two or three of his favourite Caledonian airs, and asked the pianist to play them ...'[4] Moscheles' business sense had already been stimulated in advance of his Scottish visit, however, and is playfully ribbed in the same periodical by the author of a regular column 'Diary of a Dilettante': though given in good part, it is by no means caricature, and, as a matter of fact, all the songs mentioned are genuine.

> Moscheles gave a concert at the Assembly Rooms this evening, but the company scarcely filled one-fourth of the seats. He played many things, and amongst these, "Anticipations of Scotland," a new composition, in which he, perhaps, introduced the old song, "I dreamt a golden dream". He will, doubtless, publish this, and most probably write another under the title of Le Retour de l'Écosse [sic], wherein he may give us the beautiful Scotish [sic] air, "There's nae luck", followed by another almost as good, "Todlen Hame" ("Toddling home").[5]

Similarly, in 1826, a trip to Ireland had produced the *Recollections of Ireland* (*Souvenirs d'Irlande*) Op. 69 which, when he played it at a musical *soirée* in Paris in 1830, was thus commented upon: 'The "Recollections of Ireland" are among the most perfect productions of their kind. They are truly *Souvenirs*, displaying everywhere local character; and, if the expression may be used, indigenous melody ...'[6] It is a fact, however, that in the world of '*Adieu*-s/Farewells', '*Retour*-s/Returns' and 'Recollections', Moscheles was simply the first among equals.

Another insight, albeit a humorous one, occurs in a little-known and rather forgettable novel of the period, dedicated, incidentally, to Moore, at whose suggestion it was written. This is *The Aylmers* (pub. 1827), by Thomas Haynes Bayly, a minor poet of the sentimental type, in which the principal character – clearly a self-portrait on Bayley's part – describes a music-party at the home of a Lady Sampson; the tongue-in-cheek commentary should not detract from the fact that it is based on much first-hand experience:

> The overture being at length over, the vocal music commenced; a professional young lady of second-rate fame began with a bravura, which had all the merit of a solo on the flute, as it consisted of a continual running up and down the notes without one articulate word. Lady Sampson was languid during this exhibition, and at its conclusion exclaimed, 'Science has its charms, but I sigh for nature and a ballad. Come, my sweet friend, favour us with your wood-notes wild'. Her particular friend, a Miss Barrage, who, declaring she was incapable of complying with her request, drew off her gloves and commenced a prelude. Lady Sampson looked round on her guests, shaking her head at all whisperers, and then glided among the benches saying, 'Now you *will* have a treat. She is interesting, soul-stirring – alas! too much for me'.
> She sank into a chair, rested her cheek upon her hand, and gazed upon the performer with a full conviction that her own figure would be compared, by those around her, to a marble statue, personifying silent sensibility.

---

[4] *The Harmonicon*, June 1829, p. 136.
[5] *The Harmonicon*, February 1828, p. 135.
[6] *Op. cit.*, February 1830, p. 115.

Her pale protégée now commenced her ballad, describing the rise, decline, and fall of a lily. How, in the first verse, in 'sweetest sunshine', it sipp'd 'dewdrops' of comfort; but in the second verse came the 'noughts' and the 'blights', and the 'wind' so 'unkind', and all was concluded with a quavering assurance that the lily was found 'dead' in its 'bed'.
Lady Sampson started from her statuary attitude, wiped away a tear, and waved her hand in token of her approbation.[7]

(ii) The single movement

More interesting, in most cases, than the simple setting of folk tunes is their use as a basis for, or as inclusions in, other compositions. The scope and enormous extent of such usage can be seen in any of the catalogues of the publishers of the period, as well as lists advertising the available repertory on the flyleaves of published pieces. Typical is the publisher Corri's 'NATIONAL MELODIES / Consisting of the most Admired / Airs / OF / England, Ireland, Scotland & Wales, / Arranged as Rondos, or with Variations / for the / Piano Forte / and an Introductory Movement to each / Composed by / The most eminent Authors'. This includes 'You Gentlemen of England' (English) as a rondo by J.B. Cramer; 'Ar hyd y Nos' or 'The Live Long Night' (Welsh), as variations by Latour; 'The Corn Riggs' (Scottish) as a rondo by Dance; and 'The Bunch of Green Rushes' (Irish) as a rondo by Cramer. Collections of this kind sold well and, for supplying a piece or two, each contributor did well. Also, each piece was dedicated to someone (often a Miss) and this also bumped up sales as well as immortalising a friend or acknowledging a favour. Czerny, as indefatigable a composer of rondos as we have seen him to be of variations,[8] goes one better, dedicating a rondo on 'Rule Britannia' to 'the British Navy' and trumping even this in the dedication of an equally patriotic rondo – on *God Save the Queen* – to 'the British Nation'.

Folk tunes (in the sense in which we have been using the term) were occasionally inserted as numbers in more miscellaneous collections (for example, the third of Hummel's *3 Capriccios für Klavier*, Op. 105 which is a 'Rondo Styrien') and also used for particular movements in larger works. The most basic form of this usage is simply a setting of the tune for the instrument or instruments in question with few or no extra appurtenances, and this was to be found most frequently in sonatas and concertos. Thus, a setting of an Irish song *Captain O'Kane* forms the central (Andante) movement of Pinto's rather hybrid Sonatina Op. 4/3 – flanked by a Marcia and a Waltz – in which the return of the first half of the tune is subject to a small amount of variation, and Field used the 'Scottish tune' *Within a Mile of Edinboro' Town* as the slow movement to his first Concerto in E flat major (before 1799), giving the work a wonderful sense of central repose and adding the sort of relaxed piano figuration that came so easily to him: Ex. 20.1 is from a solo piano version published in London in 1835, but is not substantially different from the concerto.

---

[7] T H Bayly, *The Aylmers*. Batsford, London 1827, pp. 46–7.
[8] Cf. the 500 sets mentioned in Chapter Fifteen (i).

Ex. 20.1: Field, after Piano Concerto No. 1 in E flat major/ii, bb. 21/2.

(iii) Rondo

Not quite such a soft option, but still relatively easy and non-time-consuming, was the use of a folk tune or two as the basis of a rondo, whether free-standing or as part of a cyclic work. This did not call for anything elaborate: because the tune was well-known and well-loved, once it had been harmonised it could recur unchanged (or perhaps transposed) in the repeat of the A section, with free material – or even other folk tunes – in the other episodes. Apart from the simple fact that a folk tune is used, there is nothing else specifically 'vernacular' about such settings and the procedures involved have been dealt with in Chapter Thirteen, to which the reader is referred.

(iv) Variations

Although requiring more in terms of actual compositional graft, the use of a folk tune as the basis of a set of variations was, in essence, no different from using any other tune – except, of course, the 'quirks' that some of these particular tunes tended to have. As we have seen in Chapter Fifteen (Variations), the tune became, in effect, a motivic, rhythmic and harmonic template and (as in the case of the folk-based rondo just dealt with) the reader is referred back to that chapter.

In view of the prevalence – and lucrativeness – of such settings, however, it may be interesting to compare a composer's response in two different settings of the same tune in different contexts. Clementi's two variation-settings of the Irish tune *The Black Joke*, are separated by about a decade, the earlier a free-standing one dating from 1771 with 21 variations, and the other the finale of the third of his 'Œuvre 1' piano sonatas (?1781) with eight. The difference in numbers is to be expected, and although, in essence, all eight variations in the sonata-set are taken from the free-standing set, the former are less taxing in every way. The connection between the two sets is shown in Table 5 below.

Table 5: Two versions of Clementi's variations on *The Black Joke*.

Sonata		Free Set	Changes made in the later Sonata version
1	=	8	
2	=	4	Dotted notes in l.h. become undotted with a rest
3	=	5	1st half, minor changes; 2nd half, adds more interest
4	=	11	Minor alterations (mostly filling-out of texture)
5	=	9	
6	=	10	
7	=	16	Opening bar changed
8	=	6	Bass thinned and a few other changes

Although the tune, a violinistic jig in 6/8 called *Air Anglais*, is sixteen bars long, it divides, less obviously, into two sections of six plus ten bars each (Ex. 20.2a),

Ex. 20.2a: Irish folk song, *The Black Joke* (Clementi's setting).

giving the following outline:

    Phrase 1 ||: [bb. 1–2; 3–4; 5–6] :|
    Phrases 2 and 3 |: [bb. 7–8; 9–10] [11–12; 13–14; 15–16] :||

The theme is the same in both sets and so is its very simple accompaniment: a dotted crotchet on every main beat, unobtrusively emphasising its character with 'open string' drones. Preserving the six quavers per bar, Clementi builds up the pace over the first six variations in the later set, adding decorations (snaps and trills) with much interplay between hands and registers. Some of these – vars. 1 (Ex. 20.2b) and 3 (Ex. 20.2c), and perhaps part of 6 – have the feel of authentic folk decoration about them, with 6 also suggestive of a common fiddle variation-technique using 'open strings' and a hunting flavour to 5. Variation 7 is harmonically, texturally and rhythmically more static, concentrating on crotchet-quaver figuration, whereas 8 fills in the remaining quaver on occasion. In the earlier set, variations 9 and 10 form a pair, the left-hand of the former becoming the right-hand of the latter with added octaves. Variation 11, Andante, (Ex. 20.2d) offers some respite while preserving a kind of 'folkiness' in its several pairs of consecutive fifths.

Ex. 20.2b/c/d: Clementi, *op. cit.*, openings of var. 1, 3 and 11.

The next two variations are Allegro, exploiting registers, and lead to a group in the parallel minor area, comprising vars. 14 (Andante con moto), 15 (Pia[no] con espressione) in B flat major, a repeat of 14, then 16 and 17 and a repeat of 16, in close four-part texture. This group hangs together very much as a unit sharing a freedom built into each one and a tendency towards slower harmonic rhythm as well as the enormous contrasts in articulation, texture and melodic contour between the 'halves' of each individual number. Variations 18 and 20 (in a faster tempo) have Tyrolean or Swiss flavours (Exx. 20.2e and 20.2f respectively) flanking No.19, which is reminiscent of the Dublin street-song '[Sweet] Molly Malone' (or 'Alive! Alive-o!').

Ex. 20.2e/f: Clementi, *op. cit.*, openings of var. 18 and 20.

The last variation, No. 21, begins as a chromatic parody on this, but progresses to dissonance in what may well be an attempt at musical black humour, an oblique and subtle reference to the original title, which is not mentioned in the sonata version. Leon Plantinga comes to a similar conclusion, although he describes it as 'perhaps an exercise in calculated vulgarity'.[9] Pl. 47 gives this variation in a facsimile of Welcker's first edition.

(v) Fantasia etc.

Fantasies and related types, with a folk tune as their basis, were very popular. The freedom of treatment in these forms precludes any discussion here, since improvisation will be discussed in Chapters Twenty-Two and Twenty-Three. Similarly, in those fantasy-types which are nothing, or little, more than sets of variations, the remarks from section (iv) above apply, especially as variation-technique, however loose, has a strong presence in improvisatory pieces anyway. In addition, any folky quirks in the tunes would hardly be noticed, given the shock-value to which composers often resort when in improvisational overdrive.

---

[9] In Plantinga/CLEMENTI, pp. 40–41.

CHAPTER TWENTY-ONE

Vernacular 3: Regional Styles

(i) Terminology

This chapter attempts to examine some of the more discrete folk-styles as they were perceived during the period, those associated with national and regional areas. One of the problems with the use of the description 'national' here, however, is that it was applied both very generally and very particularly. The term was most often used to draw attention to the fact that a folk song was included in a particular piece.

At its widest, it was more-or-less vaguely geographical and could simply mean characteristic, in some way, of a country, an area, and even a (sub-)continent or a city. Thus the 'air dans le style Indien de l'Opéra Obéron' (by Weber), used by Hummel in his Op. 116 fantasy for piano and orchestra (*Oberons Zauberhorn*), betrays no hint of either the great art or folk traditions of that subcontinent, the perceived 'Indian-ness' of the *air* from the Weber's opera being more the result of its displaced rhythms and the vaguely modal suggestions in the harmony (Ex. 21.1).

Ex. 21.1: C.M. von Weber, *Oberon*/Finale, 'Indian Air.'

In similar fashion the 'Air Américain Lilly [Minnie] Dale', which Thalberg varies in his Op. 74 (Ex. 21.2), is very much of the vaguely Celticised type that became the mainstay of American parlour music in the nineteenth century,

Ex. 21.2: *Lilly* [or *Minnie*] *Dale*.

while the 'Air Anglais' with variations Op. 72 turns out to be a composed air, Bishop's 'Home Sweet Home', whose popularity did, admittedly, confer folk status on it.

Used in its most general, and commonest, sense, 'national' referred to a nation, country or area that had a geographical, linguistic and/or political identity, and the problems in our period can immediately be seen. 'Nations' were mostly embryonic at this time, and many had yet to emerge. While Greece (1830) and Belgium (1831) succeeded in their emergence, Ireland (1798) and Poland (attempts in 1831 and 1846), did not. In spite of their respective distinct cultures and languages – although these were quite closely related to each other – Ireland and Scotland were denied political nationhood during this period, because, ironically, of the sociolinguistic richness of a parallel, shared culture with England – and that in the English language. On the other hand, Germany, in a similar position (though for largely different reasons), did attain the status of a nation during the period.[1]

In Britain, under the general heading of 'National Airs' were lumped together Irish, Scottish, Welsh, Cornish, and Manx, as well as English tunes, and we have already seen that some of these were interchanged, through ignorance of the provenance of the tunes, in error, or through lack of concern. And what of Switzerland, geographically distinct, but sharing the languages of three other countries apart from regional dialects such as Romansh? Yet, with its yodelling and its *Kühreihen* or *Ranz des vaches* (herdsman's song), Switzerland produced one of the most distinct musical sounds among nineteenth-century folk models. 'National' could also be applied to areas and provinces, such as Wales (British for a long period, as we have seen), Tyrol and Styria (both Austrian), and Savoy/Savoie (French).

Tyrol and Savoy had both been 'in the news' in the early years of the nineteenth century: the former had been taken from Austria and given to Bavaria, and had its resulting revolution crushed in 1809; the latter was annexed by France during the revolutionary period. All these Alpine areas shared their folk-musical traits with Switzerland and were characterised by arpeggiaic tunes with a characteristic tendency to turn back on themselves, and with leaps in imitation of the yodellers' register-changes and falsetto. Ex. 21.3 shows an *Air Tyrolien, Der Alpensanger,* the theme of a set of variations by Czerny, where the first variation is an exploitation of the registral features in the tune.

Ex. 21.3: Czerny, *Air Tyrolien*, theme.

A *Tyrolienne* by Saverio Mercadante is the basis for Franz [François] Hünten's set of variations, showing a whit more restraint (Ex. 21.4a) – though it becomes a little more flowery later (Ex. 21.4b) – and the second of Hummel's *III Grandes Valses en forme de Rondeaux*, Op. 103 (*c*.1823), although called simply 'Waltz', is very much of this ilk (Ex. 21.5), particularly when the drone of the four introductory bars are added. Here, he subtly suggests a yodelling effect by prolonging the notes of the 'middle voice'.

---
[1] There is some discussion of this matter in Chapter Nineteen: Vernacular 1.

Ex. 21.4a/b: Hunten, *Variations on a Tyrolienne by Mercadante*/theme and second part.

Ex. 21.5: Hummel, *III Grandes Valses* Op. 103/2, bb. 1–8.

The same kind of technique can be seen in his Op. 105 (*c*.1823), *3 Amusements en forme de Caprices*, No. 3 being a 'Rondo Styrien' (Ex. 21.6). In fact the other two caprices are also in national styles, No. 1 a 'Rondo Suisse' and No. 2 being a 'Rondo autrichien'.

Ex. 21.6: Hummel, *3 Amusements en forme de Caprices* Op. 105/3, bb. 4–8.

The first of Cipriani Potter's *Trois Amusements pour le piano* ('Rondeau à la Suisse'), is one of his last pieces (pub. 1848) and, although much more energetic, has the same traits (Ex. 21.7).

Ex. 21.7: Potter, *Trois Amusements pour le piano*/1, bb. 1–7.

Swiss airs were particularly popular in Britain and a number of all-singing all-dancing 'Swiss families' descended on London during the early nineteenth century, doing the rounds of benefits and private concerts. The 'Styrians of the Alps' and the Rainers (also known as 'The Tyrolese Family' and 'The Tyrolese Minstrels') were the most famous of these, and Moscheles appropriates some of their evident popularity in using the name of the latter prominently in the subtitle of his *The Tyrolese Family / a Divertimento for the piano-forte. / in which are introduced the favourite /*

NATIONAL SWISS AIRS, / sung by / The Tyrolese Family, Rainer, / before the King, at Windsor; / at the nobilities' parties; and at their own concerts in London, Dublin, / Edinburgh. and the principal towns in the United Kingdom.

For once the back-scratching is justifiable, however, as the Rainers saved his annual benefit concert in 1827, when some of the hired singers, indispensable to ensure the success of any London concert, were unable to appear. The Rainers briefly left a private concert and sang in two of the gaps in the benefit. *The Musical Magazine* said of the 'Styrians of the Alps' that 'their simple touching melodies have only to be heard (by those who have any soul) to be appreciated', but a footnote notes that 'their sweet melodies had, unadorned, no charms for English ears.'[2] The reference here is to the prevalent *penchant* of English concert-goers for the more modern and Italianate habit of *impromptu* and sometimes quite florid decoration of melodies – often, the implication is, in inappropriate styles.

As well as the usual praise of native land, nature and love, many of the Rainers' songs were *paeans* to marriage. Even a song entitled 'The Merry Mountain Lad' – the first of the 'introduced' tunes in Moscheles' *Divertimento* mentioned above – which one might have expected to extol wanderlust, begins with quite the opposite sentiment:

> I envy a married man
> Who has a little wife at home,
> Had I one from Switzerland
> I never more would wish to roam.

As is well-known from other similar settings – and by no means confined to Alpine ones – such wives were usually little, unfailingly faithful and unequivocally 'At Home'. Occasionally the effect of the setting borders on the bizarre, as in the fourth of the set, 'A Faithful Wife' (Moscheles gives the German translation, 'Die Treue', also), where the effect of the yodelling is underlined by the piano's held sustaining pedal, *pp* dynamic and change to higher registers (Ex. 21.8).

Ex. 21.8: Moscheles, *The Tyrolese Family*/4 'A Faithful Wife', opening.

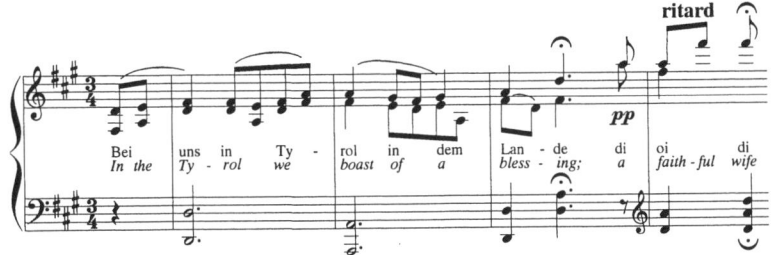

The prevalence of folk tunes is such that several of the styles associated with them are evoked in music, especially piano music, without recourse to actual folk material; it is difficult to ascertain whether this is conscious or not on the composers' parts. I suspect that in most cases it is conscious, as in the rondo finale of Gelinek's B flat

---

[2] *Musical Magazine*, May 1835, p. 80.

major Sonata (Ex. 21.9), and it also indicates the ease with which such 'Alpine' styles can be imitated.

Ex. 21.9: Gelinek, Piano Sonata in B flat major/iii, theme.

In Burton's Piano Sonata in D major (Op. 1, 1766–7) both of the outer movements are folksy, both in 6/8 and with pedal-points, and Crotch's Third Piano Sonata in E flat major (1793) has, as the third of its four movements, a bucolic Presto in 3/4 using, much of the time, the same music as the second movement, a minuet and trio, (see Chapter Twelve (i), Ex. 12.11).

There is a touch of heterophony here whereby in the octave doubling, the upper part only is decorated in a number of ways (Ex. 21.10a–c). This is unusual in art-music before the twentieth century, and belongs, in western Europe at least, to the realm of the 'real' folk music of, especially, instrumental groups, although the technique could, and still can, be found in the psalm-singing of Gaelic Scots.

Ex. 21.10a–c: Crotch, Piano Sonata in E flat major/iii, opening and subsequent variation.

Similarly, the rondo finale of J.B. Cramer's *Concerto da Camera*, for piano with two violins, flute, viola and cello (pub. 1813) has an Irish feel to it (Ex. 21.11)

Ex. 21.11: J.B. Cramer, *Concerto da Camera*/iii, theme.

and the corresponding movement in his Third Piano Concerto is reminiscent of a country-dance (Ex. 21.12a). The same material also crops up in the episodes, in the orchestral *tutti* (Ex. 21.12b) and in the *minore*, with self-parody worthy of Gilbert and Sullivan (Ex. 21.12c); there is also a later variant in 3/8 (Ex. 21.12d).

Ex. 21.12a–d: J.B. Cramer, Piano Concerto No. 3 in D major/iii, opening and episodes.

On occasion, there is the feeling of pick-and-mix about some melodic material that exhibits a number of folk-traits, however vaguely. There are several examples from Ries, such as the Rondo, Op. 106/2 (Ex. 21.13) the quirkiness of whose theme is a ragbag of folksy elements that is ultimately unsatisfactory.

Ex. 21.13: Ries, Rondo Op. 106/2, bb. 1–10.

Yet Ries had plenty of experience of folk-based writing, as the list of his compositions on the Frontispiece of a French edition, (Richault) of his sonata for piano duet (Op. 47, pub. 1817) shows; they include variations on '*airs nationaux suedois*', *airs russes*, *air allemand* and *irlandais*, '*thème hongrois*', polonaise, 'pollacca', and *écossaise*.

(ii) Southern Europe: The tarantella

Mention of these last three is a reminder that, for many regions or nations of Europe, the perception of their folk styles was largely, if not entirely, conditioned by characteristic dances, and this was especially true of the southern regions – particularly Spain and Italy and their provinces, though not by any means confined to them, as we have seen.

The principal dances associated with Italy during our period were the *saltarello* and the *tarantella*, and they are so similar as to be, at times, almost indistinguishable. Both were folk dances and, in their manifestations in the bulk of the literature dealt with within the scope of this book, both are fast, in compound duple time, and with regular phrasing. In art-music, the *tarantella*, its name taken from the city of Taranto, is immortalised in the finales of Mendelssohn's *Italian Symphony*[3] and the G minor Piano Concerto of Saint-Saëns, but it also makes several appearances in piano music of this period. Its features include repeated notes and repeated leaps, scalic motion, and the mordent decoration as well as the predominance of ♩♩♩ and ♩ ♩ rhythms in 6/8 time and the alternation of major with minor.

The *tarantella* of Moscheles's *Romance & Tarantelle brillante* Op. 101, which was written for his daughter Emilie, shows most of these features. After the moody Romance in F major, with *stringendo*, *appassionato* and *agitato* directions amongst others, the dance begins (Ex. 21.14a), returning later with varying harmonies (Ex. 21.14b).

Ex. 21.14a/b: Moscheles, *Romance & Tarantelle brillante* Op. 101, (a) *Tarantelle* with (b) later varied harmonies.

There are also some interesting textural usages in the piece – the theme returns in the bass, as it does in his friend, Mendelssohn's, *Italian Symphony* movement mentioned above, and the leaps in the dance are matched by registral leaps (Ex. 21.14c). Ultimately, however, the piece suffers from a little too much harmonic padding.

---

[3] Although he heads the movement 'Saltarello' and the musico-critical jury is still out on the question of which of the two themes is which.

Ex. 21.14c: Op. 101, from the *Tarantelle*.

Pixis's *Caprice brillante sur une Tarantelle favorite Napolitaine* Op. 108 is like Moscheles's and Mendelssohn's in that it is in A minor, and also in being headed Allegro vivace – as, in fact, were most concert *tarantellas* – but it has a much wider harmonic range, beginning with the theme in A minor (Ex. 21.15a) and passing through C and G minors and A major, (with one of the extended cadences also typical of the dance, Ex. 21.15b), and ending with the theme in the original A minor.

Ex. 21.15a/b: Pixis, *Caprice brillante* ... Op. 108/ Introduction and (b) *Tarantelle*.

The last of Heller's *Promenades d'un Solitaire* Op. 78 [*Spaziergänge eines Einsamen* in the original (pub. 1851)], an Assai vivace in G minor, is quite tarantella-like despite its 2/4 key-signature: Ex. 21.16a gives the opening, and Ex. 21.16b a later development.

Ex. 21.16a: Heller, *Promenades d'un Solit*aire Op 78/6, opening.

Ex. 21.16b: Op. 78/6, middle of movement.

G.A. Macfarren's second piano sonata (entitled *Ma Cousine*) (pub. 1845), with a pastorale-like opening, a Canzonet in the style of a Song Without Words, and a Mendelssohnian scherzo and trio, has a finale, 'Prestissimo assai. *alla Tarantella*', in A major. This movement, after playing around the dominant degree for a while (Ex. 21.17a), including an effect like cranking up an early motor-car (in common with which it, too, takes some time to get going: Ex. 21.17b), becomes a little more interesting and manages to sound at times quite 'British' in spite of its title.

Ex. 21.17a/b: Macfarren, *Ma Cousine*/iii, opening and lead-in to *Tarantella*.

It is less successful in avoiding monotony, primarily because of the repetition mentioned, but also because the mordent figure is as omnipresent in its rondo (*tarantella*) theme as the repeated-note one is in its first episode. A further episode, marked *cantando* in F major with the dance triplet-motion murmuring in the bass under a slower-moving right-hand melody, is a welcome repose.

An example of a *tarantella* exists in Beethoven's sketches and Chopin has left a single little gem, the *Tarantelle* Op. 43 of 1841. By this time, he was a past master at encapsulating the soul and gestures, as well as the social feel, of dance-forms in his dance-music – beautifully crafted salon pieces that are, nevertheless, quite susceptible to public performances, as we know.[4] The piece, with its succession of 16- or 32-bar blocks characteristically alternating soft and loud, has the feel of a whirling *perpetuum mobile* although strictly speaking it is not, and even in the soft sections the harmonically and rhythmically restless bass-line gives the feeling of a coiled spring (Ex. 21.18a and b).

Ex. 21.18a/b: Chopin, *Tarantelle* in A flat major Op. 43, bb. 51–5 and 84–5.

In addition, the feeling of closure at the end of the first section, however weak and last-minute, is dispelled by loud startling E♭ octaves and the sharply contrasting sonorities of their reiteration (Ex. 21.18c and bb. 28ff).

Ex. 21.18c: Op. 43, bb. 17–21.

(iii) Southern Europe: Spanish dances

Several Spanish dances were in vogue, and were occasionally danced (as we shall see below), but utilised more as signifiers of the national/regional style, such as the *bolero, fandango* and *seguidilla*. All in triple metre and all to some extent accompanied by the dancers' singing or vocalising, the *bolero*, in moderate tempo, was the most common and it is still danced today in some of the Spanish provinces. Unlike the genuine folk provenance of the other two, the *bolero* was supposed to have been invented by a Spanish dancer around 1780. One of the problems here is

---

[4] See Chapter Thirty.

that several rhythms are associated with the dance, at first ³⁄₄ ♩ ♩ ♩ |♩. ♪♫| or ³⁄₄ 𝄾 ♪♫♫♫ |♩. ♪♫|, but at the beginning of the nineteenth century it became almost the same as the polonaise rhythm:– ³⁄₄ |♫♫ ♫♫ ♩|, the semiquaver duplet occasionally replaced by a triplet; one has therefore to look for other traits to distinguish the two dances. The finale of Ries' Fourth Piano Concerto in C minor has a theme whose rhythm is a variant of that of the first given above (Ex. 21.19) but the piano entry incorporates 'Scotch' snaps,

Ex. 21.19: Ries, Piano Concerto No. 4 in C minor/iii, theme.

and although Thalberg's *Bolero* Op. 71/3 has the sprightliness associated with the dance, as well as a decoration common in Spanish music, (marked (x) in Ex. 21.20), it is difficult to find anything else particularly Iberian.

Ex. 21.20: Thalberg, *Bolero* Op. 71/3, theme.

The same applies, to a lesser extent, in the case of Chopin's *Bolero* in C/A major Op. 19 (*c*.1833). The musical interest is greater here, however, and there are also some matters of general interest. The *bolero* was usually danced by a couple, who performed both together and, in the quicker more virtuoso episodes, solo. It is possible to see a vestige of this in the layout of Chopin's piece, the solos being the faster sections of bb. 76–87 and 168–78. The first of these is framed by pauses that, together with *ritenutos*, also occur at other important junctures (for example at b. 33 introducing the Più lento) and they can be seen as representations of the *bien parado* (the momentary holding of a stationary pose), which coincided with the ends of sections of the dance. In the same way, the introductory promenade (the *paseo*) is suggested in the opening repeated octaves (*risoluto* with pauses), in the *tremolando* of the guitar by the ensuing triplets, and in the now rather clichéd Spanish ♭II – I chord-pairing of b. 4 (Ex. 21.21a) and articulated with the characteristic triplet decoration in b. 118 (Ex. 21.21b) and elsewhere.

Ex. 21.21a/b: Chopin, *Bolero* in C major Op. 19, bb. 1–6 and 118–19.

The *seguidilla* makes an appearance in Czerny's *Reminiscences of Russia, Spain, Norway (3 Brilliant Rondinos on National Airs)* Op. 520 as the '*Seguilla Espagnole*' of No. 2 (Ex. 21.22),

Ex. 21.22: Czerny, *Reminiscences ... Op. 520/2, Seguilla.*

and a *fandango* is part of a piece – which also includes a *guaracha*, an Afro–Cuban dance related to the *habanera*, and a 'Danza de Village' – dedicated to the Spanish Ambassador to England in R.W. Evans' *Serenada Espanõla* [sic] for piano with 1 or 2 flutes *ad lib*. The *fandango* sports a passage for the 'harmonica' (Ex. 21.23).

Ex. 21.23: R.W. Evans, *Serenada Espanõla*/2, passage for 'harmonica.'

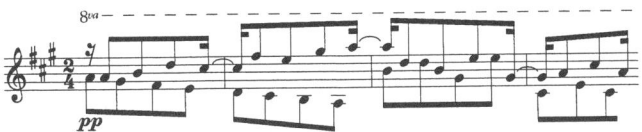

This instrument, properly called 'armonica', was a type of musical glasses associated with Benjamin Franklin because of his mechanically improved version of the instrument, in which moistened glasses were stroked or otherwise excited to produce an ethereal sound that captivated, among others, Goethe, Franz Anton Mesmer (the inventor of Mesmerism, who used its unearthly sounds to hypnotise his subjects) and Mozart (who wrote one of his last works for it, the lovely Quintet for armonica, flute, oboe, viola and cello, K. 617). In the early nineteenth century, there was also a keyboard version of the armonica, and a domestic piano patented by John Day in 1816 incorporated a frame of musical glasses that could be played at the same time as the piano, or separately. Rosamond Harding says that the idea could also be applied to a square or grand piano.[5] No doubt it was such a hybrid instrument that Evans had in mind.

A variation headed '*fandango*' occurs in the last of Pinto's *Three Favorite Airs with Variations* for piano, his Op. 2. There are various character variations among the three sets, including a *marche*, a *pastorale*, the '*relieg*' (with '*e u x*' added in ink) that I have mentioned before (Chapter Eleven (vii)), and national dances – *siciliano*, waltz (in 6/8), *polacca*, and *polonaise*. The *fandango* begins, incongruously, like a hornpipe, and although there is a retreat from this, the English dance is never too far away (Ex. 21.24).

Ex. 21.24: Pinto, *Three Favorite Airs with Variations*, Op. 2/3, bb. 1–6.

Robert Schumann incorporated his Fandango in F sharp minor (1832) into the opening movement of his first piano sonata in the same key (pub. 1836, Ex. 21.25), prefacing it with a slow introduction.

Ex. 21.25: R. Schumann, Piano Sonata in F sharp minor Op. 11/i, bb. 52–7.

At the same time, Clara Schumann also incorporated the same material in the last of her *Quatres pièces caractéristiques* Op. 5 (1835 or 1836), the 'Scène fantastique: le ballet des revenants', where she uses the fifths – suitably diminished in view of her

---

[5] Harding/PIANOFORTE, pp. 265–6.

title – and a close relative of the melody (Ex. 21.26; see also Chapter Eleven, Ex. 11.38 (Più moderato)).

Ex. 21.26: C. Schumann, *Quatres pièces caractéristiques* Op. 5/4, the left hand melody.

An extract from the *Morning Post*, quoted on the cover of a d'Almaine edition of three of Daniel-François-Esprit Auber's ballads, gives an interesting sidelight on the popularity of exotic dances, or dances in an exotic context, in this case a Spanish *cachucha* from an opera. It also shows, in a more general economical sense, the bandwagon of the nascent popular music industry in action.

> Fashion, capricious in music as in matters of graver import, has been more than usually judicious this season in the selection of a favourite melody. We allude, of course, to LA GITANA, or the New Cachucha – an Air nightly heard in our Concert, Ball, and Drawing Rooms, to the sweet strains of which the sylph-like Taglioni[6] figures in the Spanish Bohemian[7] Dance in the Ballet of La Gitana.[8] This charming melody appears to have inspired both native and foreign Composers: Herz has already adapted it in his own inimitable style; Burrowes has transformed it into an elegant Rondo; Czerny has graced it with tasteful variations; and Thalberg will doubtless make it into the *motivo* of a grand Fantasia: with its dulcet notes Weippert summons the lovers of Terpsichore; and Royalty owns[9] the spell, and commands its constant repetition. It required but the genius of a Moore to adapt fitting words, to render the Air equally popular with our fair vocalists; and those who had the good fortune to hear the wild gipsy lay, 'Come wander with me,' sung by Madam Dorus Gras, will not be likely to forget the effect it produced.[10]

As this quotation accurately predicts, Thalberg duly did use La Gitana as the '*motivo*' of his '*Fantasia* [or *Divertissement*] *on Benedict's* The Gypsy'[11] which appeared as his Op. 34 in 1839.

(iv) Eastern Europe: *polonaise*, polka

The Eastern European presence in the literature of national dances is a strong one, partly because of political events, partly because a number of great and prominent composers hailed from the area, and partly because the musical material was taken up by some of the greatest composers. The changing political map of Europe, from the

---

[6] The reference is to the Italian dancer, Marie Taglioni.
[7] The word 'Bohemian' is used here in its contemporary sense of 'Gypsy'.
[8] This was Benedict's opera *The Gypsy's Warning*, (perf. 1838).
[9] The word is here used in the sense of 'admits to'.
[10] *Morning Post*, 3 February 1838.
[11] See fn. 8 above.

tweaking of boundaries to the wholesale appropriation of regions and countries by others – such as the partition of Poland (1795) and the Polish uprising of 1830 – caused a similar feeling of displacement and nostalgia to that which we have seen in the west.[12]

The Italian name *polacca* was usually used for a faster form of the same Polish dance as *polonaise*, the French name that was applied long before our period. This was a stately processional dance in triple time without upbeat and with the characteristic rhythm of | ♩ ♫ ♫ ♫ | and a cadential rhythm of | ♫ ♫ ♩ ♩ |. Of similar overall shape to the minuet (A – B (often called 'trio') – A), it was very popular in Germany as an instrumental piece, examples being written by J.S. Bach, Telemann, W.F. Bach, Schobert, Mozart and Beethoven (his Op. 89 in C major). But the *polonaise* as a character-piece began to be cultivated in Poland itself from the beginning of the nineteenth century also, those by Prince Oginski for piano or piano duet becoming well-known, and examples were also written by Zywny and Elsner, who both taught Chopin, and by Kurpinski.

These last two approach the *polonaise* differently from each other although there is some overlap. The 14 by Kurpinski are mostly gentle works, Moderato being the predominating direction, and a number of the trio sections are marked '*dolce*'; the Allegro pomposo of the seventh and the Allegro deciso of the ninth are exceptional. With Chopin, however, the predominant direction is *maestoso*, and, although he doesn't use the word, they are mostly *pomposo* also – even swaggering, as in the case of the A major, Op. 40/1 (Ex. 21.27a).

Ex. 21.27a: Chopin, *Polonaise* No. 3 in A major Op. 40/1, opening.

They are comparatively sparing in their use of the characteristic rhythms, although the second of the thumbprints given above is quite prevalent (Ex. 21.27b) and it is occasionally modified by dotting one or more notes; the first is fairly scarce.

Ex. 21.27b: Op. 40/1, bb. 55–6.

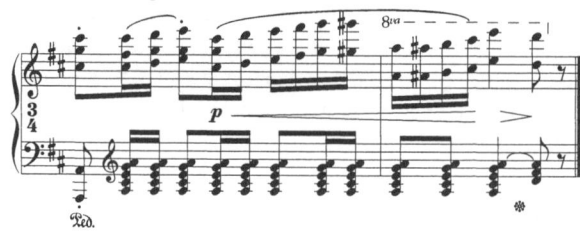

---

[12] See Chapter Nineteen, Vernacular 1: General.

These rhythms are used – again sparingly in both cases – as an introduction, for example in Kurpinski's *Polonaise IX* in D major and, in a modified form, in the previous one in C major (though it opens in C minor, Ex. 21.28),

Ex. 21.28: Kurpinski, *Polonaise VIII* in C major, bb. 1–3.

and at the beginning of Chopin's posthumous No. 11 in G sharp minor (Ex. 21.29).

Ex. 21.29: Chopin, *Polonaise* in G sharp minor, bb. 1–3.

Kurpinski also reserves it for some of his trios, again as introductions (No. II, No. VII and No. XIII), but also later, to generate tension as in the second half of the Trio of No. II in D minor (see Ex. 21.31b below). Chopin tends to feature it as punctuation, as in Op. 40/1 (see Ex. 21.27b) – in this case also to elucidate the harmonic context and exploit register-contrast – and when right-hand activity is diminished, as in Opp. 26/1 in C sharp minor (Ex. 21.30), 26/2 in E flat minor and Op. 40/1 in A major.

Ex. 21.30: Chopin, *Polonaise* No. 1 in C sharp minor Op. 26/1, bb. 3–5.

Kurpinski's *polonaises* lack the range of Chopin's in every way; in terms of pianism this is a result of the different audiences each had in mind. The impression in the older man's work is that the restraint of the *salon* is in question, even though many were written for dancing[13] and, although this does not preclude emotional range, it certainly restricts the more showy elements. This range can be seen in the *Polonaise* II (D minor/F major, 1812) where the D minor introduction begins with a

---

[13] Some were originally written for piano, some as transcriptions, the original orchestral versions being lost: see Przybylski-ed./KURPINSKI-m.

call to attention (ex. 21.31a), only to be answered plaintively before we arrive at the main body of the piece in bb. 6–7 (see also Ex. 21.31b).

Ex. 21.31a: Kurpinski, *Polonaise* II, bb.1–9.

Ex. 21.31b: from the main body of the work.

In Chopin's hands this becomes more like the approach of a ghostly army (see Ex. 21.32, from Op. 26/2) or even a hollow *étude* (Ex. 21.33). In general, Chopin's *polonaises* are concert pieces, but of unusually wide emotional range for this period.

Ex. 21.32: Chopin, *Polonaise* No. 2 in E flat minor Op. 26/2, opening.

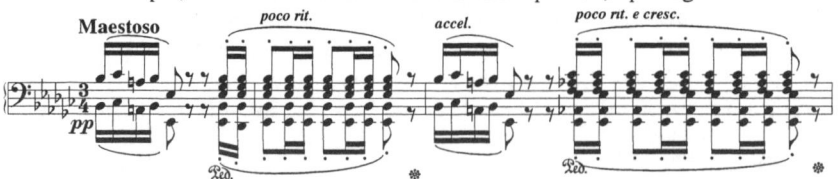

Ex. 21.33: Chopin, *Polonaise* No. 5 in F sharp minor Op. 44, bb. 1–10.

Both composers write idiomatically for the piano with full awareness of its sonorities, as in Kurpinski's *Polonaise* in E flat major (Ex. 21.34), where the bass register is highlighted for the melody, contrasting in register and dynamics with the outburst in bb. 24–5.

Ex. 21.34: Kurpinski, *Polonaise* in E flat major, bb. 20–25.

Chopin's C minor *Polonaise* uses this gambit also, but extends it to form the first half of the *Polonaise* (Ex. 21.35a); here, the contrasting outburst is also represented, at the beginning of the second half (Ex. 21.35b).

Ex. 21.35a/b: Chopin, *Polonaise* No. 4 in C minor, Op. 40/2, bb. 1–11 and 35–6.

Ex. 21.25a/b continued

Mozart's son, Wolfgang Amadeus Mozart (*Fils*), wrote 4 *Polonaises mélancoliques* in C major, and in A, F and G minors as his Op. 22, and Corri's Piano Sonata in B flat major ('*L'Augurio Felice*' of 1808) has a rather British-sounding 'Polonoise' (Allegretto) as its finale (Ex. 21.36a), also using the cadential rhythm (Ex. 21.36b).

Ex. 21.36a/b: Corri, *L'Augurio Felice*/iii, bb. 1–5 and later cadential passage.

There is a trio in C minor '*piu* [sic] *lento e piangendo*' and an extended coda, *Martiale*, in which the '*polonaise* rhythm' is featured (Ex. 21.36c).

Ex. 21.36c: : Corri, *L'Augurio Felice*/iii, coda.

Weber has two works under this heading, the *Grande Polonaise* J 59 in E flat major (1808) and the *Polacca brillante* in E major J 268 which is subtitled 'L'hilarité', both virtuoso works with episodes containing developmental features.

Hummel's *La bella Capricciosa* Op. 55 was written in Vienna between 1811 and 1815, as a *polonaise*, a *polacca* or a *capriccio* but always with the direction Alla Polacca on the tune. It appeared in a serial publication, *Répertoire de musique pour les dames, Ouvrage périodique et progressif composé par J. N. Hummel* [[A] *music-book for ladies, a serial progressive publication by J.N. Hummel*] and reissued at a later date by Artaria and it says much for the technique and musicality of the collective '*dames*' of Vienna that Hummel could address such a long and rather complicated piece to them. The theme, in keeping with my observations above about the characteristic rhythmic features in the case of Kurpinski and Chopin, also sports the cadential cell (Ex. 21.37a) but not the accompanimental rhythm, preferring the plain quaver-outline (Ex. 21.37b).

Ex. 21.37a/b, Hummel, *La bella Capricciosa* Op. 55/Alla Polacca, bb. 9–10 and (b) opening.

There are other features, of course: the *polacca*'s lightness and syncopation, such as the passage in Ex. 21.37c, and there is a 'trio', though not so called.

Ex. 21.37c: Op. 55/Alla Polacca, bb. 11–14.

This appears first (*Con anime e duolo*) in the remote key of B minor, then the tonic minor and finally in a major-minor version very skilfully used as an agent of modulation back to the home key, not for the return of the *polacca*, but of a condensed version of the introduction before the final, developed statement of the same. Like so much of the music of the *Kleinmeisters* of our period, this fine piece little deserves its neglect.

In spite of its nominal similarity, the polka, appearing in the last third of our period, was Bohemian, and, like the waltz, was a lively dance for couples, though, unlike the waltz, in 2/4. It became as popular as the waltz, and the dance-marathons of the Strausses, Jullien and Musard, contained alternating sets of the two dances. It was also popular as a domestic dance, with the quadrille and the more local dances – strathspeys and reels in Britain, for example – but it also appears as an instrumental *salon* piece, mostly for solo piano. A crossover between the two worlds is seen in Moscheles's *Les Polka* [sic] *des Salons* / *precédés d'une Introduction* / *arrés* [sic, meaning *'arrangés']* *pour pianoforte* with the footnote *'The subjects of the favorite Polkas are introduced by permission of Mr. Jullien.'* Its melodic vapidity (Ex. 21.38) is typical of the polkas for dancing.

Ex. 21.38: Moscheles, *Les Polka des Salons*, first theme.

The *Polka originale, grand mouvement de danse* Op. 4 by Best is quite another matter (Ex. 21.39a), a fully-fledged concert-piece from 1847 with a good sense of drive in spite of the occasional Victorianism (for example the *grazioso* section, Ex. 21.39b).

Ex. 21.39a: Best, *Polka originale, grand mouvement de danse* Op. 4, opening.

Ex. 21.39b: Op. 4, *Grazioso* section, bb. 1–6.

As we have seen in Chapter Fifteen, many of these dance-types turn up as character-variations in sets, especially the *polonaise*, and one is reminded of Elsner's statement in a letter to his Viennese publisher Breitkopf & Härtel in 1811, to the effect that almost anything could be converted into a *polonaise*. As instances, there are Marschner's arrangement for piano (Op. 48) of an *'Air favori'* from his own opera *Der Vampyr* with an introduction and *variations brillantes* of which one is a Tempo di Polacca including a *minore* section, and No. 2 of Pinto's *Three Favorite Airs with Variations* Op. 2 (1801, referred to above) has a *polacca* as variation 9 (Ex. 21.40a),

Ex. 21.40a: Pinto, *Three Favorite Airs with Variations* Op. 2/2/var. 9, bb. 1–4.

and No. 3 has an Allegro and rather un-Polish *polonaise* as variation 7 (Ex. 21.40b).

Ex. 21.40b: Op. 2/3/var. 7, bb. 1–6.

The first of Kollmann's Variations on an *Air of Handel* (the so-called 'Harmonious Blacksmith' mentioned previously, 1808) is a rather incongruous *Polacca* Allegretto, and the second of Ries' variations on Arne's *Rule Britannia* is an even more incongruous *polacca* (Ex. 21.41). The dance also features as the third of his *15 Easy Pieces* Op. 124, and in the rondo of his Piano Trio in G minor.

Ex. 21.41: Ries, *Variations on Rule Britannia*, var. 2.

More interesting still is the Tempo di Polacca finale of Moscheles's E flat major Piano Concerto Op. 56 (Ex. 21.42), with its homage to the openings of both Beethoven's Violin Concerto and Hummel's B minor Piano Concerto: a solo timpani statement of the rhythm and an off-tonic piano entry,

Ex. 21.42: Moscheles, Piano Concerto in E flat major Op. 56/iii, bb. opening.

and when Tomásek sent in his contribution to the *other 'Diabelli'* Variations, it was a *polonaise*, Tempo giusto (Ex. 21.43).

Ex. 21.43: Tomásek, from *Variations on a Waltz by Diabelli* (var. 43).

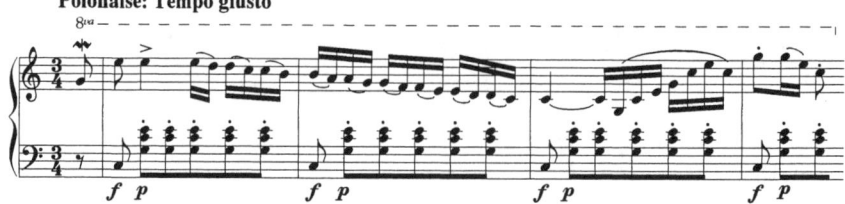

(v) Eastern Europe: the mazurka

However, the early nineteenth century's prime expression of the folk-inspired national dances of Eastern Europe in general and Poland in particular is, of course, the mazurka, a form which, like several others, Chopin made his own.

If the stateliness of the *polonaise* as a dance is compromised by its usage in art-music, the same is true of the mazurka, the problem being compounded by the fact that the term is a loose one. It is also a composite one, covering three regional dances from the Polish provinces: from Chopin's own area, Mazowsze (Mazovia), came the lively *oberek* (or *obertas*), a vigorous round dance with leaping and heel-clicking for the men, the slightly slower *mazur* (or *mazurek*, known generally as the mazurka, occasionally *mazourka*), a dance for couples and, from the nearby area of Kujavy, the *kujawiak*, another couple-dance, slower than the mazurka.[14] Chopin's output in this genre comprises all three types under the title of 'mazurka', and several can occur within a single piece, as in Op. 7/1, where the characters of the opening and the central *sotto voce* sections are quite different. This is also true of some of the dances themselves. The *kujawiak*, for example, can also have alternating slower and faster sections.

In spite of their differing tempi and traits, all three types share features that show their descent from the ancient *polska*, the most immediately striking of which is rhythm. The basic triple metre of the prevalent art-instrumental form in 3/4 is subjected to various combinations of rhythmic decoration, the crotchet becoming quavers, dotted quaver-semiquaver (also with a rest substituting for the dot) or triplets.

These were often used as variants of each other, in subsequent repetition and this is encapsulated in the melodies from Chopin's Op. 6/2 (Ex. 21.44a/b). The beginning of this last example instances another type of rhythmic variation also very prevalent, the use of syncopation, the stress falling on the second or third of the three beats and often representing the stamping of the dancers' feet, especially in the *oberek*.

---

[14] These tempo-characterisations are rather generalised: there was a degree of overlap. The reader is referred to the entry for 'Mazurka' in the New Grove for more detailed information.

Ex. 21.44a/b: Chopin, *Mazurka* in C sharp minor Op. 6/2, bb. 8–12 and 16–20.

A version of this, taken from folk usage in the original dances themselves, is the use of hemiola, as in Chopin's Op. 59/3 (Ex. 21.45).

Ex. 21.45: Chopin, *Mazurka* in F sharp minor Op. 59/3, bb. 138–48.

An earlier mazurka, Op. 17/1, uses hemiola in the middle section (Ex. 21.46), where the 2/4 underlay remains at variance with the ensuing melody, causing subtle interactions and disjunctures – note the 'false return' to 3/4 at the end – on all musical levels.

Ex. 21.46: Chopin, *Mazurka* in B flat major Op. 17/1, bb. 41–53.

Given the variety possible in rhythm alone and given the wealth of invention in Chopin's mazurkas, melodic typicalities resist detection. There are some recurring features, however, such as the upward sweep characteristic of, but not confined to, the faster *oberek* types, for example, Op. 59/3 (Ex. 21.47), Op. 56/1, 41/3, Op. 6/3 (Ex. 21.46 above) and at its most obvious in Op. 7/1 (Ex. 21.48).

Ex. 21.47: Chopin, *Mazurka* in F sharp minor Op. 59/3, opening.

Ex. 21.48: Chopin, *Mazurka* in B flat major Op. 7/1, opening.

Some of these show a feature in common with Celtic folk music as discussed previously, the use of scalic and disjunct motion in the same direction. A piquant melodic presence, also derived from folk music, is the use of the F, *Fa*, or Lydian mode, a Polish favourite with its raised fourth (Exx. 21.49 and 21.50)

Ex. 21.49: Chopin, *Mazurka* in C major Op. 56/2, bb. 5–6.

Ex. 21.50: Chopin, *Mazurka* in B flat major Op. 17/1, opening.

and strikingly combined with another favourite, the use of the submediant (lowered or natural, as in the haunting middle section (in G flat major) of Op. 7/1 in B flat major (Ex. 21.51)), or the subdominant (Op. 17/1, see Ex. 21.46 above and Op. 68/1).

Ex. 21.51: Chopin, *Mazurka* in B flat major Op. 7/1, bb. 44–7.

The use of the Lydian fourth in a minor-key context results in another characteristic example of Eastern European folk-reference, the augmented second, evident in Ex. 21.51, extended in Op. 59/3 (see Ex. 21.47 above) and poignantly articulated in b. 6 of Op. 63/3 (Ex. 21.52);

Ex. 21.52: Chopin, *Mazurka* in C sharp minor Op. 63/3, bb. 0–8.

the same can also occur, of course, between the lowered submediant and the (raised) leading-note, characteristic also of several modal usages in Eastern European folk music. Also modal is the use of the minor seventh, which occasionally occurs.

The folk basis of much of this music should prepare us for some incursions from performance practice, and this can be seen most clearly in the use of decorations, not always used in the expected sense. Chopin uses the symbol for the mordent (∿) on a number of occasions for emphasis and it would appear that the decorative notes are to be played before the beat, since the written-out version of the off-the-beat variety is very common[15] (see Exx. 21.47 above, 21.56c and 21.60 below). He will also use it to perpetuate or emphasise a dissonance – in Op. 7/1 (Ex. 21.53), to underline the dissonance of the passing note D –

Ex. 21.53, Chopin, *Mazurka* in B flat major Op. 7/1 bb. 11–12.

as he does the trill, which is used in this style without its concluding turn, simply for emphasis and interest, shriven of any cadential responsibility, as in Op. 6/2 (Ex. 21.54) and Op. 7/1 (see b. 3, Ex. 21.48 above).

Ex. 21.54: Chopin, *Mazurka* in C sharp minor Op. 6/2 bb. 14–15.

---

[15] There is some confusion between the triplet used as a rhythmic decoration and its incorporation of the upper or lower auxiliary. The performer, as so often, is the most convincing arbiter here.

When Chopin intends its usage to be of the quasi-cadential kind, he tends to show it clearly as in bb. 10 and 11 of Op. 6/4, and there is an extraordinary halfway-house at the end of the 'Mazurka for Emile Gaillard', where the ten-bar trill is partly functional (to prolong the upper tonic pedal) and partly, at the very last minute, cadential.

The *acciaccatura* is very common and, like many other decorations, imparting rhythmic emphasis and bite when used in the accepted manner, of which one example – a chordal one – will suffice (Op. 68/3, Ex. 21.55).

Ex. 21.55: Chopin, *Mazurka* in F major Op. 68/3 b. 18.

But the ubiquity of this decoration in almost all folk musics, and the various forms it can take, are also represented here in some measure, and there is an inevitable overlap between melodic and harmonic function here. In Op. 6/2 it both emphasises the second beat while at the same time attenuating the starkness of the falling fifth and also being reminiscent of the figure of two bars earlier of which this bar is a variant (see Ex. 21.44a above). It suggests a subliminal upper pedal of almost Schenkerian implication in bb. 117–21 of Op. 17/4 (Ex. 21.56a) and an example of its frequent use to resolve a dissonance can be found in the same extraordinary piece (Ex. 21.56b).

Ex. 21.56a/b: *Mazurka* in A minor Op. 17/4 bb. 116–24 and 40–41.

It is a gorgeous sublimation of the *kujawiak*, a compendium of ornamental practice in this style, and an insight into the patriotic and musical soul of Chopin: Ex. 21.56c gives the opening.

Ex. 21.56c: Op. 17/4 bb. 1–20.

As has been mentioned, decorations, of course, can also involve harmonic alteration, or at least inflection. They can prepare us for an unexpected harmonic twist as in Op. 50/1 (Ex. 21.57),

Ex. 21.57: Chopin, *Mazurka* in G major Op. 50/1, bb. 11–13.

and in Op. 7/1 (Ex. 21.58) a different chord (the subdominant) is momentarily suggested by the *acciaccatura*; in the following bar, the (tonic) chord is completed by the small notes.

Ex. 21.58: Chopin, *Mazurka* in B flat major Op. 7/1, bb. 8–10.

I have already strayed into harmony, and it is in the mazurkas that some of Chopin's most daring chromaticism can be found. On the more general level, features include the alternation of parallel major and minor modes, occasionally distinguishing sections, as in Op. 59/1 and Op.17/4, but frequently used as harmonic or modal variation. The same effect is felt in the use of dominant minor harmony also: Op. 7/2 bb. 5–8[16] and Op. 30/2 bb. 1–8. There is also a predilection for chords of the dominant major or minor ninth, those expressed as VII^7 or – in both the major and minor context – VII$^{\flat 7}$. One of many examples is Op. 17/3 in A flat major (Ex. 21.59), where both versions appear.

Ex. 21.59: Chopin, *Mazurka* in A flat major Op. 17/3, opening.

That most of these works were for private consumption and not public performance accounts for the daring that pervades them, but so does Chopin's appropriation of elements of a folk style and his moulding of them into new combinations within his own personal style. They are also utterly pianistic, and this is as much part of their essence as any of the features mentioned.

(vi) Effects of texture

I have dealt with the use of actual folk tunes or versions of them, or the extraction of some more-or-less characteristic traits and the conglomeration of these into a kind of stylistic *cassoulet*. I have also dealt with the use of characteristic national and regional dances and dance-rhythms as folk-signifiers. But there were also other ways of suggesting the vernacular, for example the imitation of folk textures or attributes suggestive – obvious or not – of folk instruments.

The use of pedal-notes would immediately suggest the bagpipe in any of its many forms with its characteristic drone, simple or compound, or the open string(s) of the folk fiddle, while grace-notes – especially those un-adjacent to the principal note – would also suggest these same instruments, particularly with the tendency of the bagpipe open chanter to revert to the basic pitch giving the characteristic 'warblers'. Not only were both bagpipes and fiddles common in Poland in the early nineteenth century, but several versions of them were common – at least five kinds of bagpipe (including the *dudy, koziol, gajdy* and *koza*) and several smaller string instruments (the *mazanki, suka, basy* and *zlóbcoki*) – and we have already seen examples of their imitation in the Chopin mazurkas. Indeed, Chopin occasionally goes beyond merely suggestive use and, in the case of the *Sotto voce* introduction to Op. 6/2, with its triple drone, off-beat rhythm, folk-like decoration and use of an inner voice couched at

---

[16] Even though this may switch to the major at the last moment.

the top of the piano's bass register, gives us a momentary glimpse of a village folk band (Ex. 21.60).

Ex. 21.60: Chopin, *Mazurka* in C sharp minor Op. 6/2, opening.

More specific than either of these instruments in terms of geographical or national area was the *cimbalom*, a Hungarian dulcimer played with wooden or covered beaters. Characteristic of the instrument are the grace-note skip and the 'roll' or '*tremolo*' used to sustain the notes. An example of the former can be found in Schubert's *Hungarian Melody*, D 817 (1824, Ex. 21.61)

Ex. 21.61: Schubert, *Hungarian Melody* D 817, bb. 1–19.

Ex. 21.61 continued

and it, as well as the *tremolo,* is to be found in much of Liszt's music, especially the *Hungarian Rhapsodies* (issued as *Magyar rhapsodiák* or *Rhapsodies hongroises,* and composed between 1839 and 1847); a good instance being found at the beginning of No. 11: Ex. 21.62 gives the opening of the final version, (pub. 1853).

Ex. 21.62: Liszt, *Hungarian Rhapsody* No. 11, opening.

The use of folk music, stories, crafts and general traits never really went beyond surface signification, a kind of exotic titillation, aural or otherwise, the appropriation of which matched the more obvious one of labour from the areas, hemispheres and classes whose sole *raison d'être* was to produce it. Nascent capitalism was already underpinned by its primary tenet that wherever the vast profits from such appropriations went, it would never be to the producers or promulgators, whose individual expendability was a cast-iron guarantee of their continued collective acquiescence.

CHAPTER TWENTY-TWO

Improvisation 1: General

(i) General

Of all the influences which I posit as being operative on keyboard music in its movement from the Classical to the Romantic periods, improvisation is the least considered and perhaps the least approachable, for the obvious and understandable reason that it is, by its nature, incapable of true fixation either in notation or in any other more-or-less permanent form. And unfortunately, in the present time, what we cannot repeatedly access, we at best mistrust, at worst dismiss.

Yet, improvisation was an accepted and necessary part of any composer/performer's attainments in the public domain during the first forty years of the nineteenth century, even though it subsequently fell out of favour during that same century and, although it has since been banished from art-music – with far-reaching results – its importance and prevalence can hardly be underestimated. In spite of this, it is interesting that the several famous women performers of the period seemed not to have indulged in it. This may have been because it was considered unseemly for a lady; more likely, however, it was because artistic creativity, in the sense of exhibiting, publishing, performing or selling the fruits of one's art, became an exclusively male preserve and women were expected to show their creative talents strictly in the biological sense.

Improvisation is constantly referred to, and clearly, from the advertisements or 'notices' alone, was considered the highlight of most concerts which involved the piano. Thus, during the London leg of his concert-tour in 1830, *The Times* of June 29 of that year advertised a benefit concert for the violinist de Bériot mentioning what was obviously the main attraction first:

> Mr. Hummel (his last appearance in this country) will give an EXTEMPORANEOUS PERFORMANCE at Mr. de BERIOT'S MORNING CONCERT on Monday, the 5th of July ...

and Joel Sachs notes that in the Paris tour of 1825, Hummel's[1] very popular concerts fell into a regular format. This was, typically, three instrumental or orchestral pieces

---

[1] Hummel will feature much in this chapter because, being generally accepted as the greatest improviser for much of the period – alongside Beethoven, before the latter's retreat from public performance – his improvisations are comparatively well-documented.

of which two were by himself and in which he partook as a performer, interspersed with two or more smaller vocal items, and rounding the whole off with his improvisation. Table 6 gives an example from April 29, starting 8:00 pm:

Table 6: A typical Hummel concert of 1824[2]

1. Septet Op. 74 by Hummel (with the composer at the piano, and listing the other player's names).
2. Air (unidentified) sung by Mlle. Cinti.
3. Sonata for piano and violin by Hummel, played by himself and Lafont.
4. Variations for oboe (Hummel, Op. 102).
5. 'Airs suisses, variés et executés par Lafont'.
6. Vocal quartet by Rossini.
7. Improvisation by Hummel.

As with so many other matters in this period, which we view from our later and loaded perspective, contemporary practice in this difficult area requires considerable adjustment in our expectations and our understanding, especially as we have no comprehensive guide to the 'practice' in this case. As we shall see, any notion of 'reflex action' or unthinking flailing in *impromptu* playing would have been out of the question. Some kind of working definition or general description is necessary.

Definitions, however, are dangerous, and often misleading in their narrowness of scope, but they do concentrate and eliminate, if they are not taken too literally. By this token, improvisation might be 'defined' as the near-simultaneous creation and realisation of an art-product, and it is by no means confined to music, or even to the piano, in the period, although it is on this instrument that it finds its most characteristic, most common, and, perhaps highest, expression.

All of the great preoccupations of the period, and those that we associate most closely with the Romantic *ethos,* were brought together in improvisation. Generally, the artists' own elevation of the instinctual over the contrived, of art over craft, of creativity over composition, and the overriding need to impress with the emotional force of his or her own personality – a personality that had to be recognisably stamped on a series of artworks of universal appeal. These were exhibited in an age where the *bourgeoisie* could identify with individuality (artistic and emotional), with self-improvement (in terms of virtuosity on the one hand and earning power on the other) and with self-sufficiency without need of pedigree, especially aristocratic pedigree.[3]

---

[2] Sachs/HUMMEL, p. 22.

[3] It is interesting, therefore, how many composers sought to indulge in what Solomon, in Solomon/BEETHOVEN calls the 'nobility pretense', referring to Beethoven's own practice. Having so recently broken away – though many, in fact did not – from the artistic serfdom inherent in much *ancien régime* patronage, being revealers of a new artistic religion was clearly insufficient.

(ii) Improvisation outside of music

There are many examples of the preoccupation with improvisatory practice or general features throughout our period and creativity is, of course, paramount. Works in which the initial inspiration or intuitive creativity was in some way apparent, were especially prized, and led, in many instances, to their creators' playing-down of conscious crafting, in favour of unfettered utterance. This is clear in Lamartine's *Avertissement* [preface] to his *Harmonies poétiques et religieuses:*[4]

> Here are four books of poetry written as they were felt, without connection, without sequence, without apparent transitions: nature has these, but does not show them; real poetry, without pretence, which shows less the poet, than the man himself [*poésies ... qui sentent moins le poète que l'homme même*] the intimate and involuntary revelation of his everyday impressions, pages from his inner life ...
>
> [Voici quatre livres de poésies écrites comme elles ont été senties, sans liaison, sans suite, sans transition apparente: la nature en a, mais n'en montre pas; poésies réelles et non feintes, qui sentent moins le poète que l'homme même, révélation intime et involontaire de ses impressions de chaque jour, pages de sa vie intérieure ...][5]

Wordsworth asserts that 'all good poetry is the spontaneous overflow of powerful feelings'[6] and Shelley makes the distinction between conscious and unconscious quite clear when he writes that '... when composition begins, inspiration is already on the decline, and the most glorious poetry that has ever been communicated to the world is probably a feeble shadow of the original conception of the Poet'.[7] Keats puts it most succinctly in one of his 'Axioms in Poetry': 'That if Poetry comes not as naturally as the Leaves to a tree it had better not come at all.'[8]

Although truly improvisational painting had to wait until the twentieth century for its full flowering, painters also took steps to narrow the gap between inspiration and finished picture. One way of doing this is evinced in the growing habit of painting scenes directly, out-of-doors, rather than working them up in the studio afterwards, and, also, remaining topographically faithful to the original scene. Similarly, the Turner paintings discovered in the National Gallery in London in 1939, were at first thought to be unfinished sketches, but turned out to be the result of painstaking effort, yet preserving the freedom and spontaneity of the sketch. This path would find a culminatory point later in the century in Impressionism of which, indeed, Turner might be seen as the first practitioner.

Improvisation in the non-musical performing arts was also known in the period. Moscheles describes an occasion upon which he 'listened with delight' to the famous *Improvisatore*, Pistrucci, 'as he enlarged, in well-sounding harmonious verses, on a

---

[4] This is briefly looked at in Chapter Eleven (vii) in terms of Liszt's response to it in his set of piano pieces of the same name.

[5] Lamartine/*HARMONIES*, p. 1.

[6] Wordsworth/LYRICAL, Preface, p. 3.

[7] Shelley/DEFENCE, p. 13

[8] In a letter to John Taylor, dated 27 February 1818.

chance theme suggested by the public.'[9] and he makes another revealing, very 'Romantic' remark: 'It gives me food for thought in my own improvisations ... I must constantly make comparisons between the sister arts: they are all closely allied.'[10] In fact, a description of one of Pistrucci's public 'concerts' was given in a London periodical in 1823 and the commentator mentions his improvising poetry in different styles, 'without the slightest hesitation or the least apparent effort'. On the subject of *Orestes,* 'he declaimed, in a succession of smooth stanzas, for upwards of ten minutes' and came more up to date with the *Battle of Waterloo* and *Count Ugolino,* which he 'delivered in a chant, accompanied by a few simple chords on the pianoforte'. This latter was probably in the vein of the Gothic Novels, Ugolino being a Medieval intriguer who was eventually locked in a tower with members of his family, and forced into cannibalism through starvation. Pistrucci also included, for good measure, a pastoral scene with several characters and complete with songs and choruses!

(iii) Characteristics of musical improvisation

Virtuosity

These characteristics are easy to deduce from descriptions and composers' writings in our period and are to be guessed anyway. Virtuosity was clearly expected, almost always referred to, and often in hyperbolic terms. Speaking of Beethoven's improvisations, Czerny talks of 'unheard-of bravura and facility',[11] 'brilliant and astonishing in the extreme', 'novel, brilliant feats of difficulty',[12] and so on, and says that, when improvising, '[in] the speeds of the scales, double trills, leaps, etc, nobody matched his skill, not even Hummel.' ['In der Geschwindigkeit der Scalen Doppeltriller, Sprünge, etc. kam ihm keiner gleich auch Hummel nicht.'][13] Czerny was in a strong position to comment thus, as he had been a pupil of Beethoven's, enjoying the Master's respect, and a good friend of Hummel's. He also makes the interesting observation that Beethoven's virtuosity in *impromptu* performances was almost always of a higher order than in his written-out pieces.

Emotional content

This supranatural aura also bathed another aspect of *extempore* performances in the period, their high emotional content. Moscheles, another great improviser of the age, tells us that, when improvising at the Danish court during his tour of 1829, 'I ... let myself go like a racehorse – fire, passion, even coquettishness – I tried everything to act on the royal nerves'[14] and von Seyfried, describing the range in Beethoven's

---

[9] Moscheles/LIFE, I, p. 79.
[10] *Loc. cit.*
[11] Sonneck-ed./BEETHOVEN, p. 29.
[12] *Op. cit.*, p. 31.
[13] Czerny/RECOLLECTIONS, p. 22.
[14] Moscheles/LIFE I, p. 232.

impromptu playing in 1799 writes that it 'tore along like a wildly foaming cataract ... and anon he sank down, exhausted, exhaling gentle plaints, dissolving in melancholy'.[15] Czerny remembers him in a *salon* setting making 'such an impression on every listener that frequently there was not a single dry eye, while many broke out into loud sobs ...'[16]

Command of styles

A command of musical styles was required in the period and is also commented on when referring to improvisations. By this I mean not so much that an improviser was required to show familiarity with other periods – although, as we have seen in Chapter Ten (The Past), for example, that could be the subject of some admiration, especially in England, where Handel was the musical patron saint – rather, that he would be *au fait* with the various manners, so to speak, of the period and of those non-current styles that were transmuted for contemporary consumption. Thus, listeners to an improvisation would expect the range of musical topics – many of which have been or will be dealt with in this book as influences – including the *cantabile*-decorative style (florid right-hand filigree-work over a more-or-less regular accompanying left hand) the strict style, also called 'fugue' or 'learned' style (counterpoint, including its more rigorous usage in canon and fugue), the free preludial style, variation-technique[17] and, occasionally, those more general types such as the military or pastoral style.

Implicit here is the practitioner's complete command of all the resources of the period style itself and his – since, as already mentioned, it was unheard-of for women to improvise, in public at any rate – thorough grounding in all aspects of it. In the Piano Schools of the period, there was nearly always a section on improvisation and it usually came at, or towards, the end. There were also some instruction books dedicated solely to improvisation, such as Grétry's *Méthode simple pour apprendre à préluder en peu temps* [Simple method of learning to prelude in a short space of time], pub.1803, and the continuation of the title makes it clear what is expected: *avec toutes les ressources de l'harmonie* [with all the resources of harmony].

One of the great glories of these performances was what can best be described as a stretching of musical conventions, in a way that would not really be acceptable to the same degree (if at all) in 'proper' compositions; this is most easily, but by no means exclusively, seen in the realm of harmony. The musical traveller Holmes quotes a 'good judge' who heard Mozart improvise: '[He] was inspired in modulation, all the profound and mysterious affinities of chords were touched upon as his hand wandered over the keys, there was magic in his fingers .. .'[18] and he makes the more general and useful observation in referring to the 'dillettanti of Germany': 'I have had much

---

[15] Sonneck-ed./BEETHOVEN, p. 36. Commenting on this section, Sonneck writes that, although von Seyfried could be unreliable, 'his personal reminiscences of Beethoven ... are accepted as authentic ..' (ibid. p. 35).

[16] Czerny, in *op. cit.*, p. 31.

[17] This was so common that some sets of variations were actually called 'fantasias', for example Mendelssohn's set on 'The Last Rose'.

[18] Holmes/RAMBLE, p. 149.

pleasure in hearing the improvisation of some of this class, who understood the art of modulation surprisingly well for amateurs ...'[19] and he also talks of 'stringing chords well together'. That Hummel 'modulated through a variety of keys ... and revelled in the mazes of melody and harmony'[20] and that Moscheles blended 'the most striking modulations ... with the most brilliant traits'[21] only serves to underline the kind of diversity and contrast that is also to be found in the other arts. Novalis describes 'truly Romantic prose' in similar terms: 'varied in the highest [degree], wonderful – peculiar turns; rapid leaps – dramatic through and through.' ['Eigentliche romantische Prosa, höchst abwechselnd, wunderbar – sonderliche Wendungen; rasche Sprünge – durchaus dramatisch'][22] And for F. Schlegel, Romantic poetry is something similar:

> It seeks to – and also should – blend together and mingle poetry and prose, genius and criticism, art-poetry and natural poetry [*Naturpoesie*], to give life and sociability to poetry and to make life and society poetic, to poetise wit, fill up and satiate the forms of art with sound cultural matter and awaken them to life with the vibration of humour.[23]

Receptivity

This is too large and complex a feature of improvisation to be allowed much space here, but a few points need to be made. The external (so to speak) awareness of the improviser to a number of factors, musical and otherwise, was an important aspect, and, in a climate in which, in some quarters, suspicions were gnawing about the authenticity of *impromptu* performances, could dispel many doubts about material being prepared beforehand. Even 'hot blood' to quote Cecil Day-Lewis 'stays into familiar gestures'. This is to be seen in a review of a London concert by Henri Herz, in which a critic in the *Harmonicon* grandly intones:

> His extemporaneous performance need hardly be noticed. It was as good, and made up of pretty much the same materials, as such things generally are. And we will take this opportunity of observing, that such exhibitions are, in our opinion, as derogatory to a great musician, as improvisation would be to a great poet.[24]

And three years earlier, the same periodical gave the impression of an improviser having a stock of passages and modulations which he could access and use to patch together a performance. There is bound to be an element of this, of course, and, as any improviser knows, it is difficult to resist re-using a particularly striking or successful gambit, but, for the better practitioners, these come across as no more stilted or obtrusive than the Classical cadential trill.

A prominent facet of receptivity is awareness of the 'audience', especially if it were large and in public, and this is helpful not simply in gauging one's effect, but in determining the direction of the rest, or at least the next part, of the '*extempore*

---

[19] *Op. cit.*, p. 236–7.
[20] *Athenaeum*, 15 May 1830, p. 301.
[21] *Harmonicon*, January 1833, p. 9.
[22] *Fragmente aus den letzten Jahren 1799–1800*, Novalis/*GESAMMELTE*, no. 2714, vol. iv, p. 229.
[23] *Athenäum Fragment*, no. 116, in Schlegel/*KRITISCHE*, vol. II, p. 182. (The translation has been slightly adapted).
[24] *Harmonicon*, July 1833, p. 157.

effusion', as it was sometimes called. This had a particular relevance since improvisation implies a fusion of the functions of composer and performer and, since the results are immediate and cannot be gainsaid, whereas the deliberating composer can revise, alter and calculate his or her musical effects in the long term. Hummel tells of his practice, in his youth when he first began to improvise, of testing the waters with a varied group of listeners:

> I ventured to extemporise before a few persons only, some connoisseurs, others unacquainted with the science, and while so doing, observed quietly how they received it, and what effect my Fantasia produced on both portions of my little, assembled, and mixed public.[25]

If, however, the improviser detects boredom or even stronger feelings in his audience – and the latter was less restrained in many ways than its twenty-first-century counterpart[26] – remedial action was necessary, and this is one of the reasons for the enormous variety, on all musical levels, reported by commentators.

A particularly pointed case of the necessity for such remedial action, also involving this consciousness of the audience, was the simple mistake, the wrong note, notes, chord and so on, which, in the absence of a predetermined procedure – that is, the rest of a pre-composed piece – could spell disaster. We must also not forget that the only possible performance was a live performance: retakes and the subsequent substitutions were not options.

There was mitigation, however. Audiences were particularly aware of the vagaries of performance in this period: many were themselves performers, even if this were only before an adoring family and/or lover, or, more seriously, in the competitive marriage-mart that prevailed in many drawing-rooms. Also the 'wrong note' could reassure, in terms of greater authenticity and, if handled well, bring audience and performer closer together, as well as give the latter impetus for further flights of musical fancy. Commenting on the fact that her teacher, Liszt, sometimes hit wrong notes, his young American pupil Amy Fay – clearly half in love with the great man – tells us that

> it does not trouble him in the least. On the contrary, he rather enjoys it. ... An accident of this kind happened to him in one of the Saturday matinees, when the room was full of distinguished people. ... He was rolling up the piano in a very grand manner indeed, when he struck a semi-tone short of the high note on which he had intended to end. ... [He] instantly went meandering down the piano in harmony with the false note ... and then rolled deliberately up in a second grand sweep this time striking *true*. I never saw a more delicious piece of cleverness. It was so quick-witted and so characteristic of Liszt.[27]

Also noteworthy was the practice, first credited to Hummel, of requesting themes for improvisation from audiences 'on the spot'. This could be tricky, however, as the choice of one involved rejection of another and what might have been interpreted – especially among the well-known, rich and, even more so, titled – as a public slight, could easily rebound on the improviser.

---

[25] Hummel/PIANOFORTE, Pt. III, 2nd Section, Chapter VII, p. 74.
[26] See Chapter Sixteen.
[27] Fay/MUSIC-STUDY, pp. 242–3.

There are also a number of documented cases of improvisers incorporating other chance elements into their performances. Moscheles tells of an occasion on which he incorporated a storm into one of his, improvising 'in conjunction with the elements; for with every flash of lightning I brought my playing to a pause, which allowed the thunder to make itself heard independently'[28] and Gottschalk describes Hummel's similar expertise at a concert in Paris:

> So exceptional was Hummel as an extemporizor [sic] that during a concert in the Erard Hall, Paris, when bells from a nearby church began ringing, he was able to switch immediately from his *Polonaise* "La bella capricciosa", opus 55, into a harmonization of the peal, which he then combined with motifs from the Larghetto Introduzione, capping the whole with a fugue improvised on the main theme of the polacca.[29]

Motivische Arbeit

This last description highlights another vital trait of improvisation, the isolating and manipulation of motivic material. This is analogous to *thematisches Arbeit*, (thematic development) and, indeed, they would blend into each other, if they were ever really as separable as I am suggesting. The difference is in the kind of working, much of it inappropriate in the more ordered compositional world of, for example, a sonata-form movement, and in this context, it is perhaps worth mentioning that music-theory books, until well into the twentieth century, used to refer to the development section in sonata-form as 'the free fantasy'.

This facility for varying, combining and generally discovering latent possibilities was also not confined to music. 'Poetry', according to Shelley, 'awakens and enlarges the mind itself by rendering it the receptacle of a thousand un-apprehended combinations of thought. Poetry lifts the veil from the hidden beauty of the world, and makes familiar objects be as if they were not familiar ...'[30] Novalis is moved to exclaim: 'What an inexhaustible quantity of materials for *new* individual combinations lies around!' ['Welche unerschöpfliche Menge von Materialen zu *neuen* individuellen Kombinationen liegt nicht umher!'][31] and Wordsworth talks of 'Fancy' – that is the imagination – detecting 'lurking affinities' between 'thoughts and images'.[32]

The ability to 'see things in a new light' in improvisation was part of this combinatorial facility. This typically took the form of a slowed-down presentation of the theme with different, usually chromatic, harmonies towards the end of an improvisation and a few examples should suffice. Ex. 22.1a gives the lightly scored opening from the second movement of Hummel's posthumously-published F major Piano Concerto, Op. posth. 1 and Ex. 22.1b shows its darker face, and the only time it reappears at the same register.

---

[28] Moscheles/LIFE. I, p. 20.
[29] Quoted in Barnum/HUMMEL, p. 42
[30] Shelley/DEFENCE, p. 13.
[31] *Fragmente des Jahres 1798* in Novalis/*GESAMMELTE,* Vol. III, p. 35.
[32] Wordsworth/LYRICAL, p. 7.

Ex. 22.1a: Hummel, Piano Concerto in F major Op. posth. 1/ii, opening.

Ex. 22.1b: Op. posth. 1/ii, bb. 63–7.

At the end of his Fantasia Op. 77, after a series of largely colouristic variations (see Chapter Fifteen above) on a melodic scrap, Beethoven also darkens his material, but in addition deepens it, before heartlessly dismissing it (Ex. 22.2).

Ex. 22.2: Beethoven, Fantasia Op. 77, ending.

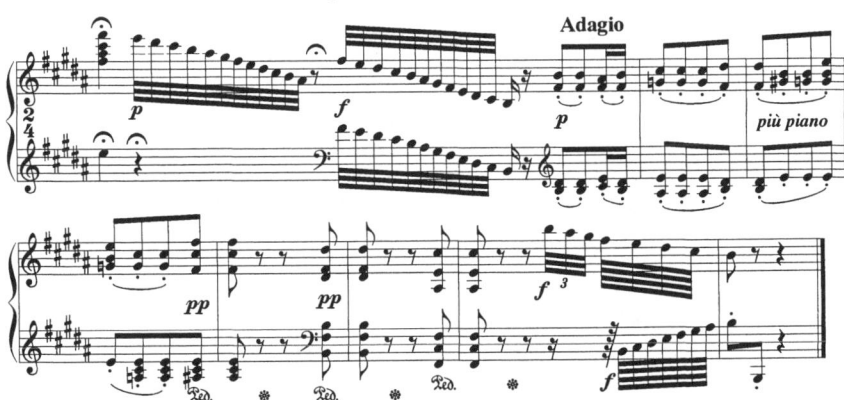

It would be only a short step from this kind of cross-referencing and connecting to the application of the same processes to themes extraneous to the *impromptu* performance itself, in the sense that these belonged to other pre-composed works. Moscheles refers to this kind of creative intrusion: 'I had intended to-day ... to introduce no extraneous subject into my Improvisation, when coming to a pause, the melody, "Das klinget so herrlich" (Zauberflöte) involuntarily forced itself upon me. Two rounds of applause rewarded my treatment of this subject.'[33] The technique was

---

[33] Moscheles/LIFE-I, p. 32.

more consciously used when, for example a performer was improvising in someone else's benefit concert and could compliment them by including some of their music.

(iv) Improvisation and the written score

In outlining the traits of improvisation, it has been necessary to quote descriptions of *extempore performances* for the obvious reason that none of these exist for our examination; the influence of improvisation can, however, be gauged in other ways.[34]

The addition of decorations is often a result of improvisatory tinkering with an extant work, or in subsequent editions and was a feature of performance practice in our period, occasionally remarked upon to its detriment. This can be carried to some length, as with Liszt's 'constantly elaborating variations on standard repertory works, even during performance, a practice which appalled [the violinist-composer] Joachim, among others and which got Liszt a bad name ...'[35] . Such procedures, of course, were the basis of the cantabile-decorative style, so characteristic of, for example, the Nocturnes of Field and Chopin[36] and of numerous slow movements.

The existence of alternative versions of works can also point to *extempore* elaboration, especially if a decorative passage is involved. An instance from the beginning of the period is Variation XI in the finale of Mozart's D major Sonata K. 284 (205b) (early 1775). The opening is given in Ex. 22.3, where the discrepancies, albeit minor ones, between the right-hand part in the autograph (the main staves) and the first edition (the small stave) can be seen.

Ex. 22.3: W.A. Mozart, Piano Sonata in D major K. 284 (205b)/iii var. XI, with alternative.

---

[34] I intend to examine this in greater detail in a forthcoming book.
[35] Walker/LISZT-I, p. 63, fn. 33.
[36] See above Chapter Eleven (vi).

The great increase in, and refinement of, expression-marks and tempo-qualifiers throughout the period is another indicator (see Chapter Eight).

Certain areas in composed music were also either reserved for improvisation, or subjected to it more than others. In the latter category, slow introductions and slow movements – especially those that became themselves introductory to finales – are particularly fertile ground for *extempore* evidence. The most obvious place in this respect, however, is the cadenza, usually in the concerto, where the performer is expected to improvise freely, elaborating on and combining the themes of the work, and there are many examples of written-out cadenzas – both by the composer him- or herself, or sympathetic performers – to show how this works.[37]

The general inroads of improvisatory traits and methods into composed works and compositional style was noted in the period, often disparagingly. The reactionary Gerber deplores this fact in 1817 – incidentally giving a good picture of improvisatory practice at the time:

> At present, ... one can no longer perceive either any definite musical forms or any limits to the influence of the fantasia. Everything goes in all directions but to no fixed destination; the madder, the better! the wilder and stranger, all the more novel and effective; this is an endless straining after distant keys and modulations, enharmonic deviations, ear-splitting dissonances and chromatic progressions, an incessant process and without respite for the listener. In such a way we hear and play nothing but fantasias. Our sonatas are fantasias, our overtures are fantasias and even our symphonies, at least those of Beethoven and his like, are fantasias.[38]

---

[37] The anomaly whereby the early nineteenth-century virtuoso-concerto for piano eschewed this convention has been discussed in Chapter Seventeen (ii).

[38] In a letter to C.H. Rinck, quoted in Schleuning/FANTASIA, p. 15.

CHAPTER TWENTY-THREE

Improvisation 2: Types

As well as its general influence on performance and on compositional style in the period, attempts were also made to 'fix' the phenomenon of improvisation itself in some way. There is evidence that some pianos of the time were fitted with 'recording' devices in the form of a strip of moving paper that could be perforated, giving a rough rendition of the performance. But improvisation gave rise to another type that purported to reproduce a real performance, the fantasy. Before dealing with this however, I will briefly look at a number of sub-genres in which particular aspects of improvisation were encapsulated, so to speak.

(i) Prelude

The nineteenth-century piano prelude is a prime example of a form that fulfilled the prevalent need for short, more-or-less self-contained pieces while gaining some distinction from its title's suggestion of the *impromptu* vein. As in the case of the Character Piece already discussed, there is, in the vast majority of preludes, nothing new or unusual about the general language or structure of these pieces to justify their being viewed as a new departure or genre; when they became legitimised in Chopin's Op. 28 set, providing subsequent generations with the 'typical' prelude, or, more properly *prélude*, these in fact far-from-typical works become indistinguishable from the bulk of character pieces. Indeed, character was so easily perceived in, or imposed upon, members of the Op. 28 set, that titles became attached to them, several of which have persisted until now: the title of No. 15 in D flat major, 'Raindrop', for example, is still current, even though it is only one of two possible contenders for this title. In cases such as these the improvisatory element in the prelude has been neutralised, all contingency banished and the divorce from its principal original function of testing the instrument complete.

The vestiges remain, however, in, for example, the subdued but still restless harmonic searching of No. 4 in E minor (Ex. 23.1),

Ex. 23.1: Chopin, Prelude in E minor Op. 28/4 bb. 0–12.

the exploration of the dotted rhythm and its exhibition in different guises – harmonic, melodic, textural, dynamic – for example, in No. 7 in A major (Ex. 23.2),

Ex. 23.2: Chopin, Prelude in A major Op. 28/7 bb. 0–8.

No. 9 in E major (Ex. 23.3), and No. 20 in E flat major,

Ex. 23.3: Chopin, Prelude in E major Op 28/9 bb. 1–5.

and in the exploration of shapes in No. 18 (F minor, Ex. 23.4), No. 19 (E flat major, Ex. 23.5) and No. 22 (G minor).

Ex. 23.4: Chopin, Prelude in F minor Op. 28/18 bb. 1–9.

Ex. 23.5: Chopin, Prelude in E flat major Op. 28/19 bb. 0–9.

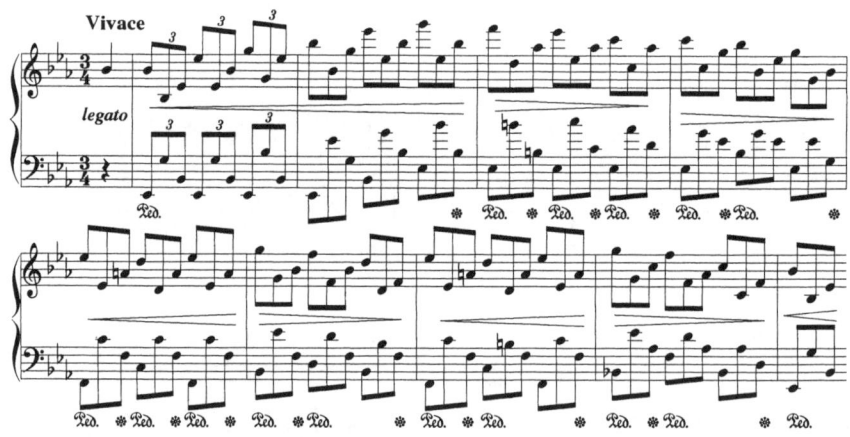

The function of testing the instrument and 'limbering up' before or during a performance may seem mundane now, especially when conditions are such that more-or-less prolonged acquaintance with a particular concert-instrument is the norm where piano recitals are concerned. During this period, however, as we have seen, piano characteristics varied considerably,[1] not only from country to country but from maker to maker[2] and were a matter of professional pride, each having his or her own individual 'sound'. In addition, the instrument was a very sensitive one anyway, and its sound and properties altered according to age and treatment – humidity, how much it was shifted and played, and so on – and touch was of paramount importance, as the instruction books of the period amply demonstrate.[3] Nor should the purely physical aspect, the 'flexing of muscles' be dismissed entirely; it contributes directly to the

---

[1] This has been dealt with in Section I, Instruments.

[2] Mozart's famous letter to his father about the characteristics of the Stein piano and his preferences for it (quoted in Chapter Two (ii)) is the most famous example among many.

[3] See Chapter Two.

typical cut of the written-out prelude – few or no barlines, extensive runs and arpeggios, rapid changes in dynamics – showing its descendence from the unmeasured prelude of the early Baroque suite whose style and function were similar. In this period, the free-standing prelude of this sort is rare, most being introductions to, or sections within, larger works.

Nevertheless, like Chopin, though for a different reason, composers did publish sets of unconnected detachable preludes which could preface other pieces. Moscheles's *50 Preludes in the major and minor keys Intended as short Introductions to any Movement and as preparatory Exercises to the Author's Studies*, (Op. 73, 1827) are of this kind and he dedicated them to the then recently founded Royal Academy of Music in London. All are short and free with no time-signatures, and several glory in having the 'Author's fingering'. Hummel wrote such a set, also intended to be introductory, 'in all the major and minor keys' (Op. 67, pub. *c*.1814–5), of which the first two are typical in their wide-ranging compass and dynamics, (Exx. 23.6a and 23.6b respectively), while cleaving to a small number of figures,

Ex. 23.6a: Hummel, *Vorspiele*, Op. 67/1

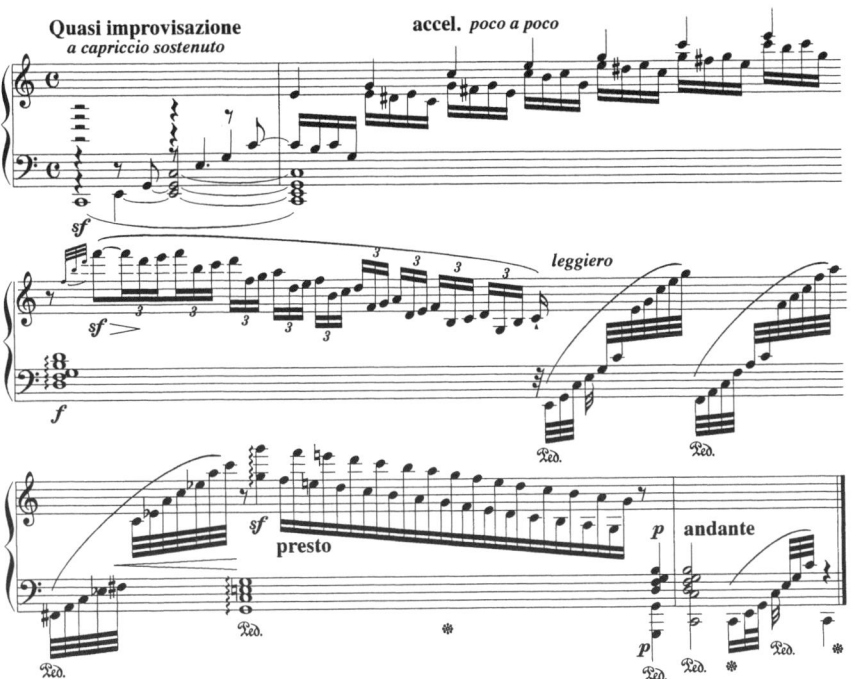

Ex. 23.6b: Op. 67/2.

and this is also a feature of J.B. Cramer's *Pensière musicale: 24 Preludes Melodiques* Op. 91 (late 1830s), from which Ex. 23.7 (No. 13 in B minor) is taken.[4]

Ex. 23.7: J.B. Cramer, *Pensière musicale* Op. 91/13 bb. 0–5.

It is also seen, though less characteristically, in Crotch's Prelude & Air (Ex. 23.8, pub. 1807).

Ex. 23.8: Crotch, Prelude & Air, bb. 1–23.

---

[4] This opening is very reminiscent of that of Hummel's F minor Piano Sonata Op. 20 (pub. 1807).

Ex. 23.8 continued

It is clear from Czerny's *Systematic Introduction to Improvisation on the Pianoforte* that this manual focus was expected, and it is to be seen in most of his examples, two of which are reproduced as Exx. 23.9a and 23.9b. We will see that this was not confined to the prelude, however.

Ex. 23.9a/b: Czerny, *Systematic Introduction* ..., Ex. 10 and (b) Ex. 16.

More important musically was the emotional and psychological 'leading-in' to a piece or movement, a fact that had become acknowledged in the increasing occurrence and weightiness of the slow introduction, hitherto largely confined to the symphonic realm. In his *Systematic Introduction* just mentioned, Czerny describes it as 'akin to a crown of distinction' for a performer to improvise such a lead-in to a piece.[5]

While introductions of this kind were to be commonly found in fantasies and variation-sets, they were extended during this time to piano pieces and even chamber music. When attached to the piano sonata or similar chamber forms with piano, they tended to take on a character similar to that of the symphonic slow introduction immortalised by Haydn in, for example, the London and Paris Symphonies. This is seen typically in Beethoven's piano sonatas and, as with Haydn's symphonic use of the device – uniquely and explicitly so in Symphony No. 103, the 'Drum Roll', probably the apex of this type – Beethoven's is frequently rendered integral to its movement by being reintroduced either wholly or in a truncated form and/or by being linked thematically to its movement.

Although not strictly speaking preludes, these introductions have many of their features and fulfil most of their functions, as that of the *Pathétique* Op. 13 shows.[6] The touch and sonority of the piano are gauged by the weighty full chords that are held, set against the faster lighter ones and by contrasting dynamics (***ff*** –***p***). These demisemiquaver chords, and the runs also, test the response and the decay time and explore the instrument's separate registers[7] in legato-melodic, as well as in percussive, vein. Various other effects appear also: ***sf***, ***fp***, the stress-mark (>), a *crescendo* on repeated notes and a *decrescendo* on a long run, showing also the full range of the registers and their changing sonorities.

Another function of the prelude was as an agent for modulation, largely emptied of rhythmic or thematic content so that a tonal transition could be made between the sections of a larger piece, often carried out by means of a dramatic compromising of the established key. It is in this sense that the verb 'to prelude' (*préluder, preludieren*) was used, as in Czerny's *L'Art de préluder* Op. 300, which was mainly a series of examples to teach the pupil various modulating techniques on the keyboard, varying from the diatonically sequential to the more arrestingly chromatic. The very fact that such books were published shows that the practice was sufficiently prevalent to benefit from a textbook, although it is surprising how few appeared. Perhaps the general feeling was something on the lines of 'You've either got it, or you haven't'.

As far as the written and published literature is concerned, preluding between movements was less common, except, again, in freer works. There is, however, an increase in the incidence of slow or freer introductions to the inner movements of stricter works.[8]

An aspect of this improvisatory encroachment upon the composed is a loosening-up of the slow movement so that it becomes shorter and freer and leads without a break into the ensuing movement, usually a finale. Influence of a particularly preludial kind can be seen at its clearest when such a slow movement finishes by modulating to or towards the key of the following movement. Occasionally there are

---

[5] Czerny/IMPROVISATION, p. 6.
[6] See the discussion in Chapter Six (ii) and the music in Ex. 6.3.
[7] The reader is again referred to Section I for details of this.
[8] See Chapter Eighteen, for example.

thematic or motivic connections between the two, but as there is an increasing frequency of such connections between all movements in this period, this is part of a more general tendency.

One significant outcome of this process of connecting a slower section with an ensuing faster movement is its development into a detachable 'unit', giving rise to works of the very popular 'Adagio and Rondo' or 'Adagio and Variations' type in which the audience (however domestic it may be) is teased into guessing the theme of the main movement – usually, as we have seen, of the popular or folk type – by anticipatory references or a hint of *motivische Arbeit*.[9]

On occasion, these preludial introductions take off into substantial improvisations in which, unlike the avowed Fantasy, the creator feels less obliged to temper his or her effusion with more respectable compositional structuring thus giving us one of the closest approaches to a public improvisation of the time. The Adagio of the *Adagio, Variationen und Rondo über ein beliebtes englisches Lied (The Pretty Polly)*, [*Adagio, Variations and Rondo on a popular English song*], Hummel's Op. 75 (pub. 1817) has been, rightly, noticed as 'outstanding ... as an example of his art in improvisation'.[10]

The Adagio itself has an introduction of 24 bars, Allegro con fuoco – Moderato, which effectively combines the functions of prelude and theme-advertisement. As presented, with the minimum of harmonic support and decorative addition, the theme is very simple (Ex. 23.10).

Ex. 23.10: Hummel, *The Pretty Polly* Op. 75, Thema.

---

[9] See below.
[10] Davis/HUMMEL, p. 171.

Yet in spite of this, there are a number of motifs upon which Hummel the improviser seizes and which he explores in the introduction.

Melodic motifs are few, the most obvious being the *appoggiatura* figure featured in almost every bar involving the fall of a second (marked m1), but also, without change of chord, for its purely rhythmic impact also. The second melodic motif is the falling scale of the theme's second half (m2), and there are also what might be called harmonic motifs, harmonisation in thirds (h1) and, by inversion, sixths (h2). Most important, as so often in improvisation, and especially given the low melodic profile here, are the rhythmic motifs r1, combining the anacrusis-strong beat unit with (mostly) pitch-class identity, the ubiquitous r2 and the very common dotted-note rhythm so common in this period, r3:

Pl. 48 gives the opening of the piece, showing various manipulations and combinations of the motifs identified, and Pl. 49 the Adagio proper, which compounds this aspect.

The increase in the numbers of slow introductions and slow inner movements of the linking type in solo-piano or chamber-piano music seems to coincide with the emergence of an essentially private domestic music conceived primarily with the members of the ensembles themselves in mind – 'chamber' in the eighteenth-century sense – from the drawing-room through the semi-private salon to the public concert venue, a transition looked at in more detail in Chapter Twenty-Five.

(ii) Caprice and *pot-pourri*

If the prelude tended to represent what I have called the manual aspect of improvisation, the Caprice or *Capriccio,* as the name would suggest, did the same for its whimsicality. This was a short piece of free or loose form, generally light and fast and characterised by swift changes in mood with few discernible connections between its sections. By its nature it tended to be short, although there are exceptions.

The *Pot-pourri* was, like the *Capriccio,* more of a procedure or technique than a fully-fledged piece, even though Czerny places it third amongst his six categories of 'Fantasy-Like Improvisation' in his *Systematic Introduction to Improvisation.*[11] In this type, like the Baroque *Quodlibet* – a term occasionally used in our period also – popular well-known tunes were combined. Czerny gives some interesting examples, combining what he calls a 'familiar march' (Ex. 23.11a) with various other tunes, including itself (in canon),

Ex. 23.11a: Czerny, *Systematic Introduction ...,* Ex. 45.

---

[11] The others are (in order): Improvising on a single theme, ditto on several themes, variations, strict and fugal styles, and the *capriccio*.

Mozart's *Bacchuslied* and his 'Ein Mädchen oder Weibchen', the popular *Marlborough* [sometimes '*Marlborouck*'] *s'en va* and 'Rule Britannia' (Ex. 23.11b in the top voice).

Ex. 23.11b: *Systematic Introduction ...*, Ex. 45C

(iii) Fantasy

The fantasy (*fantaisie* [Fr.], *Phantasie* or *Fantasie* [Ger.], *fantasia* [It.] and hybrids) is the quintessential nineteenth-century expression of the *extempore* enshrined in the repeatable. The aim is to convey the impression of a free improvisation but in a manner that will allow for repeated hearings and playings, as with other 'normal' music. Thus the piece is founded on some formal plan, however simple, whether this is preconceived (as happens to some extent in all true improvisations of this period), or, as is more likely, imposed during or after the live performance. In either case, the amount of necessary adjustment is so minimally or cleverly applied that the overall *impromptu* impression is not significantly compromised.

However, the impression of a free improvisation in this period as a hotch-potch of unconnected and off-the-cuff snippets must be resisted. Critics and commentators, as well as the practitioners themselves are at pains to stress the importance of connections between sections of the improvisation, and if, unfortunately, one cannot examine an actual contemporary improvisation to determine whether it is truly structured (in the accepted sense) or not, there is evidence that such a performance had (and was, to some extent expected to have) a format in the sense that similar kinds of procedures tended to be present, whatever their sequence.

Improvisations in public usually began with a preludial introduction leading sooner or later to a theme of some sort. This could be freshly created out of the materials of the prelude (a truly artistic *creatio ex nihilo*), or a melody from one of the composer/ performer's extant works. Occasionally, as a compliment, or a mark of respect or gratitude, perhaps, it could be from a work already given in a concert, especially if it were a benefit concert, or one given to honour a particular composer. Such was the case with Moscheles in the recently buried Weber's benefit concert in London in 1826 when he 'took his subject for improvisation from the Cantata "Festival of Peace", interwoven with "motives" from the "Freyschütz."'[12]

Most common was a popular tune or melody of the 'folk' type discussed in my Chapters on the Vernacular. This last-mentioned, however, could be abused and lay the practitioner open to the charge of playing music that was in whole or in part pre-

---

[12] Moscheles/LIFE I, p. 127.

composed (as we have seen in Chapter Twenty-Two (iii)). To safeguard their reputations, the better improvisers, as I have said, adopted Hummel's practice of inviting melodic suggestions or submissions from the audience, either just before the concert or 'on the spot'.

After the melody's presentation, it would be varied, either freely (including *motivische Arbeit,* the kind of motivic working-out described earlier) or in a set of variations of the more recognisable kind. At some stage the cantabile-decorative, and other, styles would be expected, and some kind of contrapuntal play always impressed, taken as evidence of the composer's 'learned-ness'. The physical aspect of performance was paramount, not only in the more obvious sense of its virtuosity and dexterity, but also in beauty of tone and delicacy of touch.

The overall shape of Beethoven's Op. 77 *Phantasie* (1809) is a good pointer to the general layout. A preludial opening (Ex. 23.12a), confusing in its tonality, gives a hint of a theme,

Ex. 23.12a: Beethoven, *Phantasie* Op. 77, bb. 1–10.

before a vaguely pastoral section in B flat major (Ex. 23.12b)

Ex. 23.12b: Op. 77, bb. 14–38.

and then more preluding with a typically abrupt harmonic shift supported by dynamic contrast. Later, there is a more measured, but still slightly *outré*, modulatory section leading to a theme and variations, most of which are of the colouristic kind described in Chapter Fifteen, where the actual melody (Ex. 23.12c) or harmony hardly changes:

Ex. 23.12c: Op. 77, bb. 157–61.

snippets of some of these are given in Exx. 23.12d–i, and the theme appears in 'different lights' as described in Chapter Twenty-Two (iii), where Ex. 22.2 gives Beethoven's usage towards the end of this *Phantasie*.

Ex. 23.12d: Op. 77, bb. 165–8.

Ex. 23.12e: Op. 77, bb. 181–2.

Ex. 23.12f: Op. 77, bb. 189–91.

Ex. 23.12g: Op. 77, bb. 197–8.

Ex. 23.12h: Op. 77, bb. 205–6.

Ex. 23.12i: Op. 77, bb. 213–14.

A number of other features common in *impromptu* performances and, as a consequence, in the fantasies which purport to be transcriptions of them, also occur here. There is often a musical gesture embodying a physical gesture, or presented through one, which recurs during the work, occasionally giving the feeling of punctuation and acting as a kind of sectional separator. In this case, it is the downward scalic run at the opening (see Ex. 23.12a) which, because of its original ambitus of a diminished fifth, tends to be associated with harmonic instability, although this isn't, in point of fact, always the case. It occurs six times in the introduction (with an additional example of a rising form doubled at the octave) as well as a further five times in the piece, including having the last word (see Chapter Twenty-Two, Ex. 22.2). It furthermore appears as a component in one of the variations (see Ex. 23.12i). In this latter case, it is associated with more abrupt register-contrast as opposed to the generally gradual one built into its longer scale-form.

In the case of Chopin's F minor *Fantaisie* Op. 49, this 'punctuation' takes the form of three bare falling octaves, which he uses as a separator for many of the sections of the piece. Three of the four occurrences are *ff* – Ex. 23.13 gives the first – and the third is *pp*, ushering the magical B major section.

Ex. 23.13: Chopin, *Fantaisie* Op. 49, bb. 52–3.

In Hummel's Op. 18 *Fantaisie*, one can see this physical gesture at work in all aspects of the music and its presence is also to be felt in the general angularity of many of the melodic figures. Another feature that this piece shares with many similar, is the fact that it begins and ends in different keys and (usually) modes, in this case – also common – a third apart though otherwise unrelated: E flat major – G major. This happens also in, for example, Beethoven's Op. 77 (G minor – B major) and Chopin's Op. 49 (more relatedly: F minor – A flat major), both discussed above.

PART THREE

Integration

CHAPTER TWENTY-FOUR

Accompaniment 1a: Chamber Music 1, Classical

(i) Introduction

Given the versatility, popularity and ubiquity of the piano, an increase in its repertory in areas other than that of solo music was to be expected. It was used additionally as an accompanying instrument, as an aid to composition – improvising and teasing out ideas, trying out textures and harmonies, and so on – as a didactic instrument in the sense of teaching the basics of music, or the basics of its own technique to a would-be performer, and as a study instrument, facilitating knowledge of musical repertory in other genres through arrangements.

Although at first glance the idea of the piano *accompanying* one or more other instruments might appear straightforward, the reality is quite otherwise. In music, the meaning of the word can signify functions that are almost in opposition, in the sense that both parity with other instruments, and subordination to them, can be implied. It is also clear that both meanings may hold good for different parts – if not adjacent phrases – of the same piece.

The history of the piano as an accompanying instrument in either sense is bound up with the function of its relative, the harpsichord, in its *continuo* role, not only in the Baroque period, but for much of the Classical also. *Continuo*-playing, or thorough-bass, was a technique by which a harmony-instrument – typically (according to period) keyboard, harp, lute, or guitar – and a bass melody-instrument: cello, bass, bass viol, etc.) combined to reinforce the bass line of a Renaissance or Baroque chamber or orchestral piece, while filling out the harmonies that, in a linear-oriented style, might result in occasional thinness. The harmonic content was expressed in figures (hence the alternative name 'figured bass') and the technique of realisation could become an art in the hands of a master, such as J.S. Bach, who would, at least, embellish the top melody (whether or not it doubled the principal melody-instrument's own) and, at best, add independent parts.

The *continuo*-player also acted as leader (or co-leader with the first violin) and conductor of the ensemble, before the latter function detached itself from other aspects of music-making, becoming a new profession towards the end of our period and during the second half of the nineteenth century. *Continuo*-playing was also a convenient way for composers to be actively involved in the performance of their music in genres in which they might not otherwise have been able to partake.

It was in this capacity that Haydn 'presided at the piano' during performances of his 'London' symphonies in the Salomon concerts of the 1790s in London. There is a little doubt as to the instrument used; the advertisements for, and some accounts of, the concerts mention the harpsichord. On the other hand, Burney, a great champion of the piano (see Section I) specifically cites the 'piano-forte' in his memoirs and H.C. Robbins Landon leans toward the latter instrument.[1] A couple of decades earlier Mozart, as one of the first great piano composer-performers, was to fill the same role in performances of his piano concertos. There are *continuo* figurings for the piano in the *tutti* passages of all the published concertos before 1800 as well as evidence from Mozart's manuscripts and a *continuo* realisation by the composer himself for his second original piano concerto, that in B flat major, K. 238.

One possibility for this apparently anachronistic practice is that, since the publication of a full orchestral (or even chamber) score was, to say the least, a rarity in the first half of our period, the most common form was for solo piano with figuring and a reduction of the *tutti* sections, and this practice continued until comparatively late into the nineteenth century; Pl. 50 shows the first movement's concluding *tutti* of Hummel's Concerto in E major (pub. 1826 and written a year earlier). The general consensus is that a *continuo* support, although not strictly necessary, is appropriate, in terms of performance practice, for eighteenth-century concertos and perhaps for those of the first decade of the nineteenth. The technique continued to be taught: not only was it important for the correct performance of musical styles in which its use was appropriate, but it was also considered an essential component of any musician's training, especially in the case of a composer or a keyboard player, an opinion that survives in many quarters today.

The accompanied keyboard sonata, however, in which the keyboard part was a complete, self-sufficient written-out part accompanied by one or two optional ('*ad lib*[*itum*]') instruments was parallel with, not a replacement for, the *continuo*-accompanied types, and dates from the high Baroque itself, probably the 1730s with the *Pièces de clavecin en sonates avec accompagnement de violon* of Mondonville. These were the model for later composers and developed into the accompanied duet-sonatas and piano trios with which we are familiar.[2] One problem, however, was that the accompanying instruments' parts were often merely to render the top and bass lines more 'melodic' by connecting the notes and – particularly apposite in the case of a harpsichord – adding phrasing and expression. This accounts for the fact that these parts were frequently not even written out, the player merely reading from the piano-part. This is illustrated in Johann Zoffany's painting of *George, 3rd Earl Cowper with the Family of Charles Gore* (c.1775), where the male cellist reads over the shoulder of the female harpsichordist. Solo-keyboard versions of parts of Mozart's

---

[1] Landon/CHRONICLE III, Chapter 1.

[2] Milchmeyer/*PIANOFORTE* gives an additional and more social reason for the desirability of accompanying parts: that the players can feel more relaxed, as the listeners' attention is divided between several players rather than being continuously focused on one (p. 69).

first violin sonatas (K. 6–8) survive, in his father's autograph, in the so-called 'Nannerl Notenbuch'. Conversely, some of Haydn's piano sonatas were published with an *ad lib* violin part by Charles Burney. The pendulum would, however, come to rest and something approaching true equality would obtain in the later works of this type in Mozart and Haydn, to be built on by Schubert, Beethoven (especially) and others.

The result was an enormous increase in this kind of piece which, again, was greatly encouraged by the domestic market and, indeed, the simplicity of much of the writing is one outcome of this market. Once these parts became *obbligato*, the genuine duo-sonata and piano trio came into being.

(ii) Duo sonatas

Many of the features of the Classical style were particularly apt for chamber music in the earlier part of our period: the homophonic texture that distinguished between melody and accompaniment (although contrapuntal writing remained, of course, a useful resource for variety); the favoured type of accompaniment, the *Alberti* bass, which was an unobtrusive yet mobile support and gave the complete harmony with due emphasis on the bass note; and the Classical technique of *redichte*, where the differing *timbres* of piano and melody instrument gave point to the 'echo', as in Mozart's Violin Sonata in G major, K. 301 (293a, Ex. 24.1).

Ex. 24.1: W.A. Mozart, Violin Sonata in G major K. 301 (293a)/i, bb. 28–33.

The sound-character of the early piano was much more suited to blending in with other instruments than its modern equivalent, but it could easily speak with its own distinct voice and provide contrast also, as in the first movement of the Violin Sonata in E minor K. 304 (300c, see Ex. 24.2 below).

It is indeed these matters of texture and timbre, the instrumental setting of the music, so to speak, which show the progression in chamber music as distinct from the general stylistic one, throughout our period; and texture and timbre are, of course, two of the most important defining features of Romanticism in music. They are apparent as early as Mozart's first set of mature violin sonatas (from which Exx. 24.1

and 24.2 are taken) where they are already becoming an important element in the presentation of material.

Ex. 24.2: W.A. Mozart, Violin Sonata in E minor K. 304 (300c)/i, bb. 99–103.

The most basic way in which to exploit this is to delay the entry of one of the participants (usually the melody instrument) before giving it the thematic material, or, instead of delaying, to confine it to fairly unobtrusive accompanying. This tends to be a straightforward exchange of material in outer, faster movements, but usually calls forth some variative ingenuity in the hands of better composers, especially in slower movements in which the emphasis is on the more lyrical, rather than the more overtly intellectual, aspect. Ex. 24.3a/b gives the opening of the finale of the Violin Sonata in E flat major K. 302 (293b) (a two-movement sonata), in which the violin re-presents the theme *forte*, as opposed to the piano's (solo) *piano*, but also has a fuller and more chromatic accompaniment. Mozart's use of *Alberti* bass in parts other than the usual bass-part is characteristic.

Ex. 24.3a/b: W.A. Mozart, Violin Sonata in E flat major K. 302 (293b)/ii, bb. 1–4 and (b) 9–12.

INTEGRATION

As so often in the Classical period, these advances can be seen at their most exposed in minor-key works, as in the E minor Violin Sonata K. 304 (300c) which was completed in Paris in the summer of 1778. Mozart's mother had died of fever on 3 July that year: it is tempting to interpret the passion of the work – especially the first movement – as controlled grief. However, this movement was completed in Mannheim before he went to France. The opening is a *locus classicus* of romantic suspense in which the triads of chords i, V and ii (Ex. 24.4a) are given in octaves, *piano*, the piano beginning low in its bass register. The root-position of chord i is slid through, and the 6/4, the least stable inversion, is emphasised in plain minims while the repetition of this spare three-minim rhythm is compromised only by the crotchet passing-note (bb. 3–4 and 5–6).

Ex. 24.4a: W.A. Mozart, Violin Sonata in E minor K. 304 (300c)/i, bb. 0–24.

A dramatic, obsessive figure follows, again in bare octaves, and the violin takes up the opening melody again, this time showing a more lyrical face with the piano appropriating the passing-note idea, thus dissipating the epigrammatic force of the rhythm in the opening presentation. The small cadential rounding-off (bb. 20–8) shows a standard, if not *cliché* use of the violin to hold a pedal-note, although here it comes in the middle of a sombre piano sandwich and breaks off for a moment of tragedy, with the Neapolitan chord in bb. 23 and 27.

The Development begins with a further presentation, this time with a repeated pedal-note in the piano and a pathetic snatch of canonic overlay (Ex. 24.4b), and the reprise provides yet another guise with the piano accompanying the violin in unsettling repeated chords of German augmented sixth and secondary and primary dominant sevenths respectively.

Ex. 24.4b: K. 304 (300c)/i, bb. 84–96.

Finally, an extended coda gives, for the first time, what might be regarded as one of the more 'normal' types of texture in what might well be an ironic gesture dispelled with a harsh laugh more characteristic of Beethoven.

If this movement was written in Mannheim (of which more shortly) the following melancholic Tempo di Menuetto breathes French air with a whiff of the *clavecinistes*, possibly, in the passing dominant minor and the augmented sixth (Ex. 24.4c).

Ex. 24.4c: K. 304 (300c)/ii, bb. 0–8.

There is a miniature *cadenza* for the piano before the return of the A section,[3] and the E major trio, certainly in its opening phrases, would not be much out of place in a Schubert or early – or even middle-period – Beethoven sonata. Like Haydn's early string quartets, these early violin sonatas have the feeling of divertimentos with four or five movements – especially in that they have two minuets – whereas, like many older solo piano sonatas (including Haydn's), all but one in each of the sets K. 26–31 and K. 301–306 have two movements, not always containing a minuet.

---

[3] That is, the return of the opening material (A) at the end of the minuet's B section as in the scheme A:‖ B:‖ .

Considering that he follows the standardised number of movements in his string quartets (four) and even in his piano sonatas (three), this is more of a reflection of the musico-social status of the duo-sonata than a lack of interest on Mozart's part. His last four violin sonatas, however, have the standard three-movement form of the solo and duo sonata of the Classical period, even if a sop to the *salon* is present in the fact that two have variation-sets for finales. A more serious mood is set immediately by providing an introduction (Largo) to the first movement of the B flat major Sonata K. 454 – rare in Mozart's chamber music. This work gives us an interesting sidelight on Mozart's compositional technique. It was played at a concert in Vienna in the presence of the Emperor Joseph II who, noticing a blank keyboard part, asked to see it. It seems that Mozart played the part from memory, not having had time to write it out. The autograph, with cramped writing using inks of different colours, lends some veracity to the story. A similar story is attached to the G major Sonata K. 379 (373a), which he composed between 11 and 12 o'clock on the night before the performance. Again, this might suggest Mozart's lesser regard for the genre.

It is interesting that, although the piano parts in these works are never unpianistic, there is an orchestral feel to much of the music in the first set of six mature works (K. 301 (293a)–306 (300l). When one considers that they were mostly written during Mozart's visit to Mannheim with his mother, 1777–8, this is not surprising, given the city's strong orchestral tradition under the direction of the Stamitz family and others (many of whom also composed) and the coherence, discipline – Burney's famous remark of 1772, that it was 'an army of generals', is pertinent here – and, not least, characteristic orchestral devices for which it became famous. It may be fanciful to try to detect a sluggish Mannheim 'Rocket' in the Adagio introduction to K. 303 (293c), but it does seem appropriate in the opening of K. 304 (300c), and the 'Steamroller' (*Trommelbaß* [repeated-note] 'drum-bass') is also in evidence in the 'scoring', using the piano's registers as well as those of the violin (see Ex. 24.4a/b above). With reference to register and scoring, Plantinga draws attention to Clementi's 'marvellously lugubrious effect'[4] in his Violin Sonata in B flat major Op. 5/1 (pub. 1780–1, Ex. 24.5).

Ex. 24.5: Clementi, Violin Sonata, from Plantinga/CLEMENTI.

---

[4] Plantinga/CLEMENTI, p. 78.

Beethoven, of course, gained immeasurably from the pioneering of Haydn, one of his teachers, and of Mozart, in which the fully-developed Classical style and already idiomatic writing for the new piano in a relatively new instrumental setting were fused in ready-made models upon which he was not slow to build. The ten violin sonatas do not form as impressive a body of works as the piano sonatas or string quartets, but they contain a fair share of masterpieces, and were successfully published soon after composition. Reflecting his own development as a keyboard-player and composer, and being written for the most part with professional players rather than amateurs in mind, their difficulties were often the subject of criticism in contemporary reviews.

Beethoven himself was aware of this and seems to have wished to draw attention to his care in dealing equally and virtuosically with both instruments, in his title for the 'Kreutzer' sonata of 1803 (Op. 47 in A major): *Sonata per il Piano-forte ed un Violino obligato* [sic], *scritta in uno stilo molto concertante, quasi come d'un Concerto* [Sonata for the piano and violin *obbligato*, written in a very concerted style, rather like a concerto]. On the autograph, this same title had the additional word *brillante* ('... *in uno stilo brillante molto concertante* ...') ['... in a brilliant very concerted style ...'], which was struck out before the work was submitted for publication.

When we come to the cello sonatas, however, Beethoven was on his own, since Mozart and Haydn wrote none, and an example is lacking even in the output of the eighteenth century's greatest champion of the cello as composer and performer, Boccherini, in almost all of whose works, including 11 concertos, the instrument appears. All of Beethoven's five cello sonatas have, from the outset, a partnership based on unforced equality, coupled with a fine ear for avoiding what could threaten to become a lugubriously bass-oriented sonority. The first two (F major and G minor), composed in 1796 and published as Op. 5, were written for performance at the Prussian court by Beethoven himself and the well-known French cellist Jean-Pierre Duport. The latter was attached to the court and taught cello to the King, Wilhelm Friedrich II, for whom Mozart wrote his three 'Prussian' string quartets, K. 575, 589 and 590 of 1789–90, with their prominent and adventurous cello writing. In terms of rewards for their compositional endeavours, Beethoven, who received a gold snuff-box from the king, fared better than Mozart, who, being in dire straits financially, could well have done with something similar.

Surprisingly, for an instrument with such lyrical potential, none of Beethoven's sonatas has a slow movement apart from the last, Op. 102/2. There is some compensation, however: both of the Op. 5 sonatas are in two movements, opening with an expressive Adagio sostenuto leading into a faster movement, and both the Op. 69 in A major and the first of the Op. 102 pair (in C major) have Adagio interludes acting as introductions to their Allegro vivace finales. In other, more radical ways, the cello's parity with the piano is stressed: the opening of Op. 69, presenting the main subject of the movement is entrusted to solo cello for almost six bars and the Allegro fugato finale of the last sonata, Op. 102/2 in D major (complete with a rather comic tonal answer, Ex. 25.6a/b) gives free reign to all kinds of interplay between the instruments, with the contrapuntal texture being quite consciously enhanced throughout by the different registral sonorities of both instruments (Ex. 24.6c and 24.6d).

Ex. 24.6a/b: Beethoven, Cello Sonata No. 5 in D major Op. 102/2/iii, bb. 4–7 and (b) 10-13.

Ex. 24.6c: Op. 102/2/iii, bb. 127–42.

Ex. 24.6d: Op. 102/2/iii, bb. 201–16.

Schubert, like Beethoven, was a fine, though non-virtuoso, pianist but, unlike him, also played the violin to a high standard and regularly took part in chamber ensembles, although this was usually on the viola, Mozart's favourite instrument after the piano. In spite of this, Schubert left little in terms of duo sonatas and they do not in general measure up to the quality contained within his other genres. None of the five were published during his lifetime and there were considerable problems in nomenclature and forms of publication. Thus, the set of three, D 384–5 and D 408 (Op. 137/1–3, 1816) for violin and piano, were called sonatas by Schubert, but published as sonatinas (a reflection of their style and content, not their length, which is not inconsiderable) and his only other was published as a duo, a title justified by the greater independence of the instruments.

The remaining duo sonata was for piano and arpeggione. This instrument was invented by a J.G. Staufer in 1824 in Vienna, a kind of fretted bass *viola da gamba* with six strings tuned like a guitar, hence its other name 'guitar cello'. Schubert's Sonata in A minor, D 821 was written for the instrument's champion, Vincenz Schuster, who also wrote a *Method* for it (pub. 1825); the sonata is nowadays usually played on the cello. The two remaining works for violin and piano, the *Rondeau brillant* in B minor, D 895 (1826) and the *Fantasia* in C major D 934 (1827), were written for the virtuoso violinist Josef Slavík, whose Czech ancestry may have suggested the inclusion of a movement in Hungarian style in each of them. The *Rondeau* was well received, but, according to a review of the first performance of the *Fantasia*, 'the hall gradually emptied' through boredom at the pyrotechnics: in fact the critic himself admits that he left before the end![5]

---

[5] *Der Sammler*, 7 Feb 1828.

(iii) The trio

The trio including keyboard had its roots in the accompanied sonata (as mentioned above) with, at first, simply the addition of a bass instrument, the cello, to strengthen the piano's bass line. Even after this register had been made more interesting, the cello continued to fulfil this function, but the possibility for emancipation was there. In Haydn's chamber music, this took place in the Op. 20 string quartets of 1772 (pub. 1774), but it had to wait until considerably later to be matched in the piano trios. Mozart, however, shows it in his first mature trio, K. 496 in G major (1786), where, after an exposition in which the cello has no real individual voice, the development has all three instruments sharing and discussing the material Ex. 24.7.[6]

Ex. 24.7: W.A. Mozart, Piano Trio in G major K. 496/i, opening of Development section.

By the time of his London visits, and especially during them, Haydn's piano trios were breathing the same musical air as his late symphonies and the quartets, which

---

[6] Mozart uses red and black ink in his MS to distinguish violin and cello.

were being played in public in London in the last decade of the eighteenth century: in fact, the slow movement of the grandest of the trios, No. 40 in F sharp minor, is a transcription of that of the Symphony No. 102. The heavier British piano, with which Haydn could become familiar during his London visits also had a part to play.[7]

With Beethoven and Schubert, the four-movement scheme of the string quartet and symphony was adopted for most of their piano trios, suggesting its increased status in their eyes and also, perhaps, the larger canvas and bolder colours involved in the increasing tendency to treat them in the public, rather than the truly 'chamber', manner. This is clear in the former's choice of this medium to launch his career in print, the three trios of his Op. 1 (1794–5, pub. 1795), and can be seen musically in the finale of the third in C minor which seems un-confinable to any but the most aristocratically proportioned chambers (Ex. 24.8).

Ex. 24.8: Beethoven, Piano Trio in C minor Op. 1/3/iv, bb. 96–9.

It took thirteen years for Beethoven to return to the trio, in the pair of Op. 70 (1808, pub. 1809), and his greater maturity in invention and working-out goes frequently in tandem with striking and daring sonorities. Part of the impact of the latter is to do with the juxtaposition of contrasting passages or sections. The Allegretto of Op. 70/2 shows this clearly with the carefully integrated scoring of interlocked instruments in which piano and cello effortlessly change parts and octaves without disturbing the hypnotic flow of the music (Op. 70/2/ii, bb. 0–8) but later (bb. 16–20) underpinned by thick bass piano chords, *sforzando,* or reinforced with thicker sonorities (bb. 78–81).

Also interesting is the violin's appropriation of accompanimental figuration more usually associated with the piano (Op. 70/2/ ii, bb. 38–42) and a kind of sandwiching effect that is frequently found in these works. Op. 70/2/iv, bb. 19–23 has the piano confining both the other instruments, and the same technique becomes a dramatic gesture in the *fortissimo* opening of the Op. 70/1 trio in D major (see Ex. 24.9a). It is the sound-world of the middle movement of this trio – the only one to be cast in three movements – that gave it its nickname of '*Geister*' (Ghost). Here the drama of oppositions is played out on all levels, but especially in sheer sound, as in Ex. 24.9b

---

[7] If the unintended pun may be forgiven.

and, later (bb. 35–40) where harmonic, rhythmic and melodic motion are reduced to a minimum and the piano's deep *tremolando* is an extremely effective use of the early (especially 'Viennese') instrument's bass register. In spite of their capability, only at the end does he allow the strings to play *tremolandi*, their spaced-out octave Ds giving a marvellously hollow effect against the piano's chromatic descent through its two upper registers.

Ex. 24.9a: Beethoven, Piano Trio in D major Op. 70/1/i, bb. 1–6.

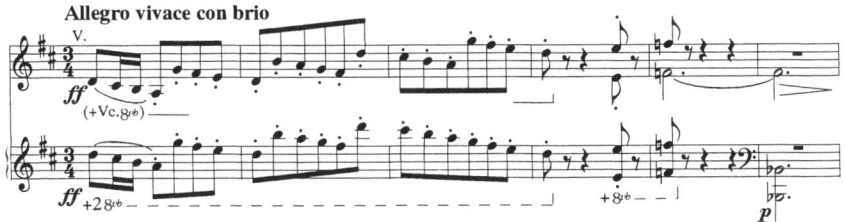

Ex. 24.9b: Op.70/1/ii, bb. 18–26.

Ex. 24.9b continued

Schubert, again surprisingly, has left little in this medium, although in fact the first work to which he gave the title 'sonata' was a single movement in B flat major for piano trio written at the age of fifteen (1812). His next productions in the medium date from the last two years of his life, a Nocturne ('Notturno') in E flat major – 'a singularly empty Adagio, with a few contrasts and modulations' according to Alfred Einstein[8] – and the great trios in B flat major D 898 (Ex. 24.10) and E flat major D 929 (Ex. 24.11). In these, apart from their many other merits, Schubert shows as fine an ear for the sonorities of the medium as Beethoven, in some ways even anticipating the sonority of Brahms' chamber works with piano.

Ex. 24.10: Schubert, Piano Trio in B flat major D 898/iii, bb. 250–60.

---

[8] Einstein/SCHUBERT, p. 316.

Ex. 24.10 continued

Ex. 24.11: Schubert, Piano Trio in E flat major D 929/i, bb. 161–4.

CHAPTER TWENTY-FIVE

Accompaniment 1b: Chamber Music 2, Romantic

(i) Duos and trios

I have already strayed into Romantic territory in the last chapter in dealing with Schubert, and, indeed, perhaps, with Beethoven also. This may be because, of all the extant musical genres in the period, the smaller chamber ensembles are the least susceptible to providing evidence of an interface between the periods; the shading between the periods, always, of course, tenuous, is here imperceptible.

The rise of public concerts, especially the larger, more popular kind with the emphasis on orchestral music, created a demand for showy, brilliant and entertaining music, creating a contrast between the private and public manners and a polarity in compositional application, which I have called, elsewhere, a kind of creative schizophrenia.[1] While the greatest composers could not afford to – nor would (most of the time at least) – sell themselves short in terms of quality, they were quite willing to adapt to a manner of writing that could be described as populist. Haydn had brought this to a fine art in the symphonies he wrote for Paris and London and even in his very un-public string quartets, and he remains probably the greatest exponent of Schiller's ideal of the popular allied to the great. Chopin could manage to keep the letter as well as the spirit of, in particular, the waltz and the mazurka, while at the same time enriching their repertory with great music. But even the greatest, as we have seen,[2] would turn out some pot-boilers for the proverbial quick buck.

It was inevitable that a certain amount of seepage between the 'high' and 'low' styles would occur. As, perhaps, an extreme instance, it shows itself, most unexpectedly, in the late string quartets of Beethoven in, for example, the inclusion of an *Alla danza tedesca* as the fourth movement of the B flat major String Quartet, Op. 130.

The string quartet, however, had already been canonised in the works of Haydn, Mozart and of Beethoven himself, and little vestige of its original domesticity remained; it was now as fit for the highest musical utterance in the private or semi-

---

[1] See Carew/CONSUMPTION, p. 240.
[2] See Chapter Nineteen. Vernacular 1: General.

private field as the symphony was in the public, or as the mass was in the realm of sacred music, and was addressed to the connoisseur, whether participating player or knowledgeable listener. The case of chamber music with piano, whether duo or trio, was very different. As was noted in the last chapter, the low status of piano-chamber music was partly because of its being written with amateurs in mind and partly from the non-*obbligato* nature of the other instrument(s) and their susceptibility to easy substitution, often, as I have said above, having neither independent music, nor even printed parts, of their own, that is, they read from the piano-part: in all senses, *ad libitum*.[3]

There seems to be another kind of polarisation in the duo-sonata – of which the majority were for violin – that between technically very easy pieces and virtuoso ones. Perhaps in parallel to the case of the piano sonata, the duo sonata became less in evidence than the shorter, lighter piece or group of pieces, and variation-sets had pride of place. In the latter category are pieces such as Schubert's Introduction and Variations on his song 'Trock'ne Blumen' D 802 (1824) for flute and piano, and in the former, R. Schumann's *3 Romanzen* Op. 94 (for oboe and piano with violin or clarinet *ad lib.*, 1849) and the *5 Stücke im Volkston* Op. 102 (for cello and piano with violin *ad lib.*, of the same year). Schumann also created an odd hybrid in his addition of piano accompaniments to not only Paganini's hugely virtuosic *Caprices* Op. 1, but also to J.S. Bach's sets of sonatas and partitas for solo violin and sonatas for solo cello.

In the case of the piano trio, in spite of its popularity as a discrete medium, the Romantic love of colour encouraged variations on the basic line-up, with the possibility of substitution of, for example, flute and occasionally clarinet, for the violin, clarinet for viola and, less often, bassoon for cello. The composers' true preferences begin more and more to be betrayed by the thematic material allotted to the usurper: the optional violin in Beethoven's Op. 11 Trio in B flat major (1797) lacks the clarinet's streetwise jauntiness in the finale's appropriation of the terzetto from the popular composer Joseph Weigl's opera *L'Amour marinaro* (perf. 1797), 'Pria ch'io l'impegno' (Ex. 25.1) and its ensuing variations.

Ex. 25.1: Beethoven, Trio in B flat major Op. 11/iii, theme.

What did begin to happen was that such 'alternate' possibilities generated their own 'authentic' ensembles, particularly in the case of the flute, with sonatas and trios for piano, flute and cello. This repertory was enriched by the Danish-naturalised

---

[3] In mentioning this previously, I drew attention to its depiction in a Zoffany painting: see Chapter Twenty-Four (i).

German composer-pianist Friedrich Kuhlau, particularly the three fine sonatas of Op. 83 – in spite of the fact that he was primarily a virtuoso pianist and, apparently, could not play the flute! There is also a rather nice subversion of the by no means obsolete situation in duo sonatas of the time in his stipulation that the piano, rather than the melody-instrument, should be *ad lib* in several works (for example, the *Three Grand Solos*, Op. 57 of 1823 and the *Six Divertimentos* Op. 68 of 1825). Ex. 25.2a gives the opening of his *Grande sonate concertante* in A minor Op. 85 where a chorale-ish piano introduction prepares the way for the flute's off-tonic entry, which soon takes the music out of the depths emotionally into something more robust.

Ex. 25.2a: Kuhlau, *Grande sonate concertante* in A minor Op. 85/i, opening.

The breezy scherzo of the same work shows his happy knack of giving similar music to piano and flute, but tailored to each in such a way that their idiomatic capabilities are brought to the fore: Ex. 25.2b gives the opening (piano solo in octaves) and Ex. 25.2c the flute's 'reply' bringing the music to the dominant minor. His 'trios', incidentally, are for three flutes rather than the accepted ensemble, the exception being the Grand Trio in G major for two flutes and piano (1831).

Ex. 25.2b/c: Op. 85/iii, opening, and (c) opening of second half of scherzo.

In spite of his love for the clarinet, Carl Maria von Weber's only trio was a flute trio, in G minor J 259, written in 1819 during the composition of the opera *Der Freischütz*. (Ex. 12.27 in Chapter Twelve (iii) gives music from the scherzo.) The piece oozes character – in the sense of this period's 'character piece' – from the moody opening, with the melody instruments in temporary canon (Ex. 25.3a),

Ex. 25.3a: C.M. von Weber, Flute Trio in G minor J 259/i, bb. 1–8.

continued in the Baroque-ish presentation of the first subject in b. 28 (Ex. 25.3b), and using it as a coda.

Ex. 25.3b: J 259/i, bb. 28–9.

This first movement is very successful on all levels, combining clear formal shape with Romantic infill. The 'demonic' scherzo has just been mentioned above and the ensuing 'slow' movement is characterful in several ways, although it seems not to be able to make up its mind which character it should adopt. It carries the heading *Schäfers Klage* (Shepherd's Lament), an Andante espressivo in B flat major and in pastoral 6/8 with a *siciliana* rhythm. However, with its pizzicato cello and light detached piano chords providing a guitar-like accompaniment, it sounds more like the operatic *cavatina* than a lament (Ex. 25.3c).

Ex. 25.3c: J 259/iii, bb. 0–4.

The finale begins hesitantly in G minor (Ex. 25.3d) and is a rather unstable movement which doesn't quite manage to unite its minor darkness with its major freneticism.

Ex. 25.3d: J 259/iv, bb. 0–7.

This piece exudes the aura of the opera house, from the scene-setting that appears in all the movements, to the treatment of the instruments, which are presented throughout as operatic/dramatic characters sporting their technical, registral and timbral distinctions but yet engaging in fruitful interplay for much of the time. This is another instance – by no means confined to Weber, and even more evident in the larger chamber groupings – of the bridging of the public/private stylistic divide as chamber music began to don a more fashionable, self-consciously public garb.

Not unconnected with this was the increasing prosperity of the *bourgeoisie* and the development of its drawing-rooms in terms of size and opulence, resulting in larger gatherings. The Mendelssohn *salon* in Berlin was famous for the quality and quantity of the music featured and, under the capable management of Fanny – embodying the nearest an early nineteenth-century woman of talent could approach to a career – the Sunday morning meetings (*Sonntagsmusiken*) often featured a choir and a full orchestra for concerto-performances. A *salon* such as this was clearly nearer to concert-hall than drawing-room and fulfilled an important function in fostering and displaying new talent as well as trying out new pieces, and the Mendelssohns' *clientèle* ranged from Paganini, Weber and Liszt, to Ingres, E.T.A. Hoffmann, Goethe and Hegel.

Indeed, Felix Mendelssohn's youthful set of three piano quartets, all in the minor keys of C (Op. 1, 1822 at the age of nine), F (Op. 2) and B (Op. 3), have a public cut about them, with perhaps even an eye to the gallery – the moody opening of the third (Ex. 25.4) does not suggest cosy domestication – and this applies to subsequent chamber music also, including his sister Fanny [Mendelssohn-] Hensel's later Piano Trio Op. 11 in D minor (1847).

Ex. 25.4: Felix Mendelssohn, Piano Quartet in B minor Op. 3/i, opening.

However, there is no denying the fact that there is a clearly discernible 'slump' in the production of chamber works with piano after *c.*1825, a phenomenon already noted in the case of the piano sonata.[4] Mendelssohn alludes to this in a kind of *apologia* for his turning to chamber music in the late 1830s:

> [A] very important branch of pianoforte music which I am particularly fond of – trios, quartets, and other things with accompaniment – is quite forgotten now, and I feel greatly the want of something new in that line. I should like to do a little towards this. It was with this idea that I lately wrote the sonata for violin, and the one for cello, and I am thinking next of writing a couple of trios.[5]

The first-mentioned work here is the posthumously published Violin Sonata in F major (1838) with no opus number, and the cello sonata – the first of two – of the same year was in the unusual key of B flat major. It is reminiscent of Beethoven in various departments, and not only of his cello sonatas; the approach is largely linear, allowing the cello to shine through. The later cello sonata, Op. 58 in D major, is remarkable for its Adagio slow movement, a combination of piano chorale and cello recitative.

The promised trios duly followed, the D minor Op. 49 a year later (1839), to one of Robert Schumann's critical fanfares (see below). The work opens like another cello sonata, sixteen bars of lyrical but uneasy music in the bass and tenor registers with a prominent D – C♯ – D motif, followed by the violin's entry on, unusually, an augmented chord. The inner movements feature two of Mendelssohn's favourite genres. An Andante con moto tranquillo opens with the solo piano presenting a melody in the typical three-part configuration of the *Songs without Words,* straddling two registers of the period piano. This is repeated when all three instruments join together, although the cello divides itself between outlining the harmonic bass-line and parallel harmonisation of the violin. Similarly, when this theme returns at the end, it is accompanied by new countermelodies. The third movement is also typical, the kind of fairy-like *scherzo* so beloved of Mendelssohn's fans in the period – especially those in Britain – in which the *staccati* and the repeated notes and chords keep the pianist, so to speak, on his or her toes. Technique, also of a virtuoso kind, is very much part and parcel of the finale, based on the kind of foursquare rhythm characteristic of Schumann in similar terrain ♩ ♫ | ♩ ♬ .

The other trio, that in C minor Op. 60 (1845), is as 'instrumental' as the D minor was 'vocal'. There is something very Baroque, specifically Bachian (J.S.), in the opening, with its upward straining against a tonic pedal and regular rhythm in the manner of a Bach concerto *ritornello*. This reverence for the past, particularly Bach and Beethoven was very much part of the age, as we have seen, but was a particular feature of Mendelssohn's music, the legacy of his teacher Carl Friedrich Zelter, a man very much of the Old School and a correspondent of Goethe, whom, indeed, Mendelssohn met and with whom he stayed on several occasions. The reverence is also, of course, the result of the Canon of Great Composers which took surprisingly little time to catch on and which, by this time, was a fact of life as if it were, like the Commandments, set in stone.[6] Schumann – no mean god-maker – alludes to this and

---

[4] See Chapter Fourteen.
[5] Hiller/MENDELSSOHN, pp. 131–2, quoted in Newman/SSB, 302.
[6] See Chapter Ten.

places Mendelssohn fairly and squarely within it, referring, actually, to his D minor Trio:

> It only remains to say something about *Mendelssohn's* Trio, – but only a little, since it is surely already in everyone's hands. It is the trio masterpiece of our time, as in their day were those of Beethoven ... and Schubert ... which in years to come will bring joy to grandchildren and great-grandchildren. ... Mendelssohn ... has raised himself so high that we may well say that he is the Mozart of the nineteenth century, the most brilliant of musicians ... He will also not be the last artist. After Mozart came one Beethoven; the new Mozart will also be followed by a new Beethoven; indeed, he may already be born.[7]

Indeed, he already had been born: Brahms – as Schumann himself was quick to recognise in the famous 'Neue Bahnen' ('New Paths') review of some early works a few years later (1853) – was to be the next name in the Canon. The review quoted is, perhaps, the basis for the received wisdom that the chamber works of Mendelssohn are the only such works of quality between Beethoven and Brahms and the view is helped by the 'slump' in the production of chamber works mentioned above.

It may also be explained by the increasingly ambivalent nature of the genre, the encroachment of the public on the private due to the nature of the Romantic style itself. Colourful, and tending towards the overblown, it favoured the virtuosic, the public heroic gesture as well as the cosily sentimental, and the piano was its ideal instrument with its colour and versatility. Furthermore, arrangements for differing chamber-media of the larger-scale musical classics, brought the orchestral world into the parlour and encouraged imitation of its public style. As early as 1826, a critic in the *Harmonicon* asserted that 'Our age has been called proverbially the "arranging age"'.[8] Add to these features the fact that chamber music became more common in concert programmes as the period wore on, and it becomes clear that a *rapprochement* between the public and private, or chamber and concert, styles was inevitable.

(ii) Larger ensembles

The very fact of increased numbers in ensembles – also a feature of the period in more general terms – helped the process also. Once the addition of a melody-instrument and a bass instrument to the piano had been effected and the problems of ensemble addressed, the way was open for larger groupings, and also for mixed ones. Again it was Mozart who blazed the trail in straining a Classical mould with explosive contents and, again, in a minor-key work – this time something of a favourite, G minor – in his only other completed minor-key chamber work with piano apart from the equally pioneering E minor Violin Sonata (discussed in Chapter Twenty-Four) and a set of variations for violin and piano.

This time, it was a commission by the publisher Hoffmeister for a set of three piano quartets that fired his imagination, not least, perhaps, because there were few precedents for the combination – violin, viola, and cello with piano – to be

---

[7] NZfM, 39 (1853), p. 185.
[8] *Harmonicon*, August 1826, p. 170.

considered. When it became apparent to the publisher that the low uptake among the Viennese *dilettanti*, due to the difficulties on all musical levels of the first, (G minor, K. 478, 1785), would not cover his costs, he cancelled the contract, generously allowing Mozart to keep the advance payment if he agreed not to submit whatever else he'd written. He was, however, so sufficiently advanced on the second, the less problematic K. 493 in E flat major, that he completed it the following year, and it was brought out by another publisher, Artaria in 1787.

In point of fact, the G minor quartet is one of the few works that really do justify the label, albeit a pretty meaningless one, of being 'ahead of its time'. It shares an emotional kinship with the similar, much later, works of the early composer-*virtuosi*. It may simply be that this group had either had contact with Mozart (as had Hummel) or devoutly wished they'd had (as did Spohr) and/or were – understandably – generally influenced by him, as the first great composer who was also a virtuoso pianist (as in the cases of Cramer, Field and Moscheles).

Whatever the reason(s), so 'Romantic' is this work that it is difficult to resist the programmatic. The listener is immediately arrested by the striking epigrammatic opening and its texture, (Ex. 25.5) as well as the piano's self-confidence in its 'answers' and the presentation of the material in so many instrumental, colouristic and emotional guises –

Ex. 25.5: W.A. Mozart, Piano Quartet in G minor K. 478/i, bb/ 1–42.

Ex. 25.5 continued

Ex. 25.5 continued

Ex. 25.5 concluded

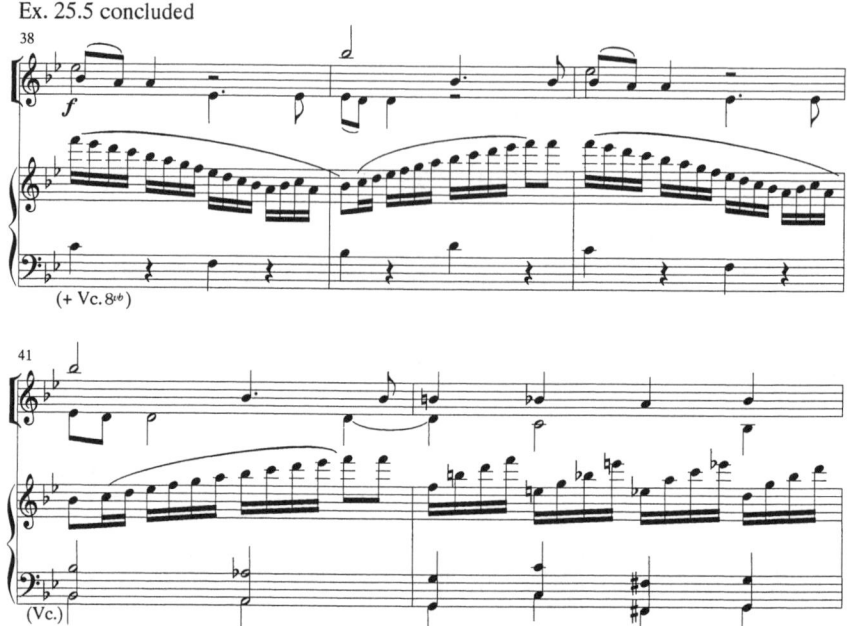

pathetic, on solo strings, in the tonic major with a diminished $V^{\flat 9}b$ inflection (bb. 17–8, marked '1'), firm but not entirely inflexible on piano solo (C minor with the same diminished seventh, bb. 19–20, marked '2'), pleading, on strings solo, with the diminished having now become a German augmented sixth on F, the dominant of the relative major (bb. 21–2, marked '3') and finally in an agreed compromise between the groups with the minor second of the epigram transmuted to a more lyrical and conciliatory minor third (bb. 23–4, marked '4').

The other general fact to note about this work is how much more appropriate it sounds to public rather than private performance. This is not only because of the dramatic quality of the music and its emotional range and intensity, as mentioned, but also because of the *concertante* element, the frequent opposition, or at least contrast, in the piano/strings polarisation, and, especially, the virtuoso nature of the keyboard writing, all of which suggests more a miniature concerto than the stuff of an intimate drawing-room *soirée*. There is also a direct point of contact between private and public here, in that, in the absence of published full scores, piano concertos were often issued in arrangements for piano trio or piano and string quartet – Mozart arranged his own concerti K. 413–15 for the latter combination. Indeed, as we have seen above, the most important change in chamber music during our period was its general outgrowing – though not always in maturity or quality, it has to be said – of the parlour and its appropriation of the concert-hall manner and the wider public ear.

Mozart's work became a launch-pad for subsequent compositions of this type. Each of Beethoven's three piano quartets WoO 36, written in the same year as Mozart's G minor, is modelled on one of the older composer's violin sonatas from the set published in 1781, but he may have been acquainted with the larger work. The increasing importance of the piano's presence in chamber music may be seen in his arranging, or approving the arranging of, several of his own works to include piano, such as the two Serenades in D major – Op. 8 for string trio (1796–7) as the Notturno in D major for piano and viola (1803), and Op. 25 for flute, violin and viola (1801) as the Serenade for piano with flute or violin, Op. 41 (also 1803).

Since Beethoven's early piano quartets were not published until 1828, after his death, it is unlikely that the instrumentation had any influence on contemporary or later composers. Independently of this and due, partly to the increase in the piano's range and volume, and partly to the more public orientation of the music, some of the larger chamber groupings with piano began to include the double bass in addition to the cello and this, with the reduction of the highest string-family representatives to one violin, caused a general darkening of sonority. It also resulted in the greater emphasis on the cello as a solo, rather than as a purely bass, component, and in a casting into relief of the piano's treble register. The two prime examples from the earlier part of the period are the practically unknown piano quintet in the very rare key of E flat minor Op. 87 (1802, pub. *c.*1822) by Hummel and Schubert's extremely well-known 'Trout' Quintet in A major D 667 (1819, pub. ten years later, after his death), so-called because of his using the melody of his song *Die Forelle* [*The Trout*] as the theme for the finale's set of variations. (See Chapter Fifteen (iv) above for examples from this movement).

An interesting halfway house, in terms of its scoring, between the Mozart of the string quintets (with extra viola) and Hummel (with double bass) might be glimpsed in Mendelssohn's Sextet in D major for piano with violin, 2 violas, cello and double bass which, in spite of its late opus number (110) was a product of his fifteenth year, 1824, between his second and third piano quartets.

Having been a pupil of Mozart, Hummel almost certainly knew his G minor quartet and there is an affinity between it and the younger composer's E flat minor Piano Quintet which can be detected both in the presentation of the opening material and in that material itself (compare Ex. 13.28 above and Ex. 25.6a). It is interesting that he uses a key-signature of three flats (E flat major) although the vast bulk of the work (including the whole of the finale) is cast in E flat *minor*.

Ex. 25.6a: Hummel, Piano Quintet in E flat minor Op. 87/i, bb. 1–8.

The economy of Hummel's thematic material is remarkable, that of the whole work arising from the opening bars. Remarkable also is his siting of the first movement's second-subject not in the key of the relative major (G flat, or enharmonically F sharp) but in the remotest key of A major, a tritone from the tonic. This is approached from the E flat minor at the end of the first subject by dropping to D flat, adding a seventh and following with an interrupted cadence, bringing the music to D major – strictly E double flat, the flattened sixth of the relative major G flat – to whose dominant it duly resolves. However, the promised tonic of F sharp major or minor is never reached, since Hummel deftly sidesteps into the relative major of the implied F sharp minor – A major – and straight into the second subject, again closely derived from the opening of the movement (Ex. 25.6b).

Ex. 25.6b: Op. 87/i, bb. 58–63.

Schubert's 'Trout' Quintet was begun during one of his happiest holidays in the, as he described it, 'unimaginably lovely' Austrian countryside at Steyr. In spite of the proximity of their dates and identity of scoring and, occasionally, spirit, it seems that the impetus for this work came not from Hummel's quintet itself, but rather from an arrangement for the same instruments of his Septet in D minor Op. 74, which Hummel had published simultaneously with the original septet version of the work in 1816.

The substitution of woodwinds for strings gave rise to another form that became a standard, the quintet for piano and wind, often including the horn, following Mozart's pioneering example in K. 452 (for piano, oboe, clarinet, horn, and bassoon, 1784), which appears to be the first chamber work to use this combination. Problems of integration abound here, not only in terms of the piano with the individual wind instrument, but in their internal groupings also, and not least in their use as a chordal choir. A judicious use of the instruments' combinatorial possibilities, without too long an exposure to any one, ensures the kind of balance and satisfaction on all levels of which this composer's music is so exemplary.

The 'original' version of the Hummel septet mentioned – the D minor Op. 74 – is scored for piano, flute, oboe, horn, viola, cello and double bass, and points to another example of the chamber group gazing at the wider world outside through the drawing-room casement, the combination of solo woodwind and brass instruments with the less common members of the strings and the piano. Given the greater timbral distinction of these instruments, the problems of ensemble posed are considerable and the tendency to feature them soloistically has to be resisted to some extent. In point of fact, Hummel's handling in this area is, in general, deft: Ex. 25.7 gives the approach to the transition passage (bb. 34ff.) in the first movement, and the quirky *fugato* in the Finale is a little touch of black humour in its setting.

These septets, involving solo representatives from winds and strings with the piano, seem to have generated a small specialised niche of their own involving a succession of composers extending well beyond our period, such as those of Georges Onslow in B flat major Op. 79 (?1840s), Spohr in A minor Op. 140 (1853), Camille Saint-Saëns in E flat major (including, like Hummel's C major septet Op.114, a trumpet, 1881) and Igor Stravinsky (1952–3), together with Leos Janacek's *Concertino* (1925) and Arnold Schoenberg's *Suite* Op. 29 (1925–6): a legacy of no mean importance indeed.

Ex. 25.7: Hummel, Septet in D minor Op. 74/i, bb. 37–50.

Ex. 25.7 continued

CHAPTER TWENTY-SIX

Accompaniment 2a: Song 1

(i) Background

If the piano in Classical chamber music began with the upper hand in terms of its status (in the sense that the added instruments were seen to be accompanying *it*), the situation in vocal music was quite other. The basis of the *Lied* in our period was laid by Christian Gottfried Krause, a lawyer and composer in Berlin, which became the centre for the First and Second Berlin *Lied* Schools. He and a local poet, Ramler, published a collection of anonymous song-settings in 1753 entitled *Oden mit Melodien*. The composers are now known to have included Franz Benda and C.P.E. Bach. This collection was an illustration of Krause's ideas on songwriting (published the year before), showing a new approach to the *Lied*. The emphasis was to be on text and on a melody that should faithfully and, perhaps simplistically, reflect it in an easy setting that would not require a professional singer. Part of a general reaction to Baroque complication and Rococo fussiness – which, with other concerns, also prompted C.W. von Gluck's operatic reforms – the *lied* was to be folk-like, non-chromatic, un-taxing rhythmically and, like the poetry, strophic (that is retaining the same music for each stanza with miniscule changes to accommodate those of the text) with a keyboard accompaniment so supportive and unobtrusive as to be almost unnecessary.

With the ripening of the Classical style and the further development of the piano itself, subsequent composers began to see the style as too simple, including those of the Second Berlin *Lied* School, J.A.P. Schulz, J.F. Reichardt and C.F. Zelter, but also others, such as C.G. Neefe and those of the Swabian School, J.R. Zumsteeg and C.D. Schubart. In terms of the later flowering of the *Lied*, it is significant that the German-speaking lands' greatest poet, Goethe, was so interested in folk poetry that his imitations produced ideal texts to which subsequent composers would constantly return. It is also significant that one of the members of the second Berlin *Lied* school, Zelter, was both the Mendelssohns' mentor and that a composer much influenced by the School, Neefe was Beethoven's teacher at a crucially formative period (ten or eleven years of age).

One of the most telling developments in the Second School was the extra prominence given to the accompaniment, not only its texture, but in the addition of interludes. The great Classical masters, however, had little interest in the *Lied*, although both wrote some. The surprise here is Mozart, whose lyrical gifts generally and, in particular in his secular, staged and religious works, should have made him a sure-fire bet for this kind of composition. He has provided, however, two masterpieces of *Lied* composition, the first of which, *Das Veilchen* K. 476 (1785), was inspired by his discovery of Goethe's poetry, the other by evening – that most Romantic of times– in *Abendempfindung an Laura* K. 523 (1787), which, in that it is through-composed, and in its sustained melancholy, looks away from the eighteenth-century aria to the nineteenth-century *Lied*.

Haydn composed his *XII Lieder für das Clavier* (two books of twelve each) in 1781 but it was Beethoven, who can be said to have created the *Lied* in a sense recognisable in the terms in which we accept the appellation today, who produced in his *An die ferne Geliebte* [To the Distant Beloved] Op. 98 of 1816, the first song cycle. It is arguably both more and less than a song-cycle in that it is a continuous composition, the songs being joined together by piano interludes that are an agent of modulation between keys and aid in changing the mood.

The first song, 'Auf dem Hügel' ('On the Hill', with the direction *Ziemlisch langsam und mit Ausdruck*, [Fairly slow and with expression] and a time-signature of 3/4) has a little interjection between verses, marked both *Ausdrucksvoll* and with its Italian equivalent, *espressivo* (Ex. 26.1a).

Ex. 26.1a: Beethoven, 'Auf dem Hügel', bb. 9–11.

This reappears later in slightly different guises (Ex. 26.1b, c and d),

Ex. 26.1b: 'Auf dem Hügel', bb. 19–21.

Ex. 26.1c: 'Auf dem Hügel', bb. 29–31.

Ex. 26.1d: 'Auf dem Hügel', bb. 39–41.

before it forms the coda, after the music has begun to speed up (*'Nach und nach geschwinder'*, adding *'stringendo'*, in the Italian). This coda (Ex. 26.1e) leads to the second song, 'Wo die Berge so blau' ['Where the Mountains so Blue'], a pastoral in 6/8 with piano echoes. The succession of keys in the songs also shows tonal unity, being E flat, G, A flat (sharing with the parallel minor with which it ends), A flat again, C, and E flat, and the Romantic *penchant* for *Terzverwandtschaft* (third-relationship) is clear.

Ex. 26.1e: 'Auf dem Hügel', coda.

The song-cycle itself was analogous to the set of solo piano pieces grouped together by type and/or interaction. Those song-cycles that were based on poem-cycles were, of course, linked by the poet's ideas and basic 'plot'. Given the great surge of interest in German literature, and the virtual creation of its modern repertory by the Weimar Classics, Goethe and Schiller, who enriched all aspects of this repertory, the scene was set for crossover types such as the poem-cycle, its subject-matter derived from the *Bildungsroman* and its form from the epistolatory novel. Both of these were popular eighteenth-century genres. The purpose of the *Bildungsroman* was to chart and explore the spiritual, or character, development of the main protagonist, often presented as a journey, which could be real as well as being symbolic. This concentration – sometimes to the point of obsession – on one main character and his (and it was predominantly a 'he') inner life would appeal to the increasing self-consciousness and self-confidence of the middle classes. The type had received a great boost in respectability in Goethe's *Wilhelm Meisters Lehrjahre* [Wilhelm Meister's Apprenticeship] in 1795.

It was also Goethe who made a great impact on the epistolary novel, with his *Die Leiden des jungen Werther* [The Sorrows of Young Werther] (1774), which took Europe by storm. This was a type of novel expressed in a series of letters, therefore written in the first person, and of great importance was the effect of place on character and character-development. Thus we see, because of his rejection in love, Werther's emotional disintegration into suicide. The epistolatory form died out soon after the turn of the century, although Tieck's *William Lovell* (1790s) was a late example of the form, as was Jane Austen's youthful novel *Lady Susan* (1793–4); the early form (1797 or before) of her *Sense and Sensibility* was also cast in this mould.

Schubert was a devotee of the Second Berlin School and his first compositional masterpiece was a song, *Gretchen am Spinnrade* (D 118), prompted by his discovery of Goethe's *Faust* and which antedated Beethoven's cycle by two years. Melody, poetry and piano share an equal partnership in which the whole is greater than the sum of the parts. In a letter to Zelter, Goethe had already laid his cards on the table, so to speak, with regard to lyrical poetry, and viewed it in the light of music, as, in a sense almost incomplete without a musical setting.

Schubert's gift for melody guaranteed attractiveness and popularity, but it was his response to the poem, as language, as idea and as an artistic entity inspiring a parallel on the musical level that informs all his great songs. My concern here, however, is with the function and use of the piano in this genre, and Schubert's *œuvre* shows this from the most basic to the most sophisticated.

(ii) Accompaniment

That function, in its most minimal sense of accompaniment, was to support the voice harmonically and rhythmically, but Schubert and the other *Lied*-composers never left it at that for very long. It was also proactive in providing information that might not be available, or at least not immediately discernible, in the melody, such as tonality and mode, harmony, time-signature and rhythm, thereby imparting a great deal of freedom to the vocal line. More subtly, it could partake of, or enhance, ideas and feelings embodied in the text, underline verbal declamation and even impart irony in the opposition of spirit to letter. These functions, combining to give shape and form to the whole song, could also be operative in the larger scale of the song-cycle and act as strands in a structural web of powerful cohesion.

The most basic type of accompaniment, a simple chordal one following the rhythm, is rare, because of the ubiquitousness of the *Alberti* and its almost inseparable association from a great deal of piano music. The effect, however, can be dramatically ominous when used sparingly and judiciously, as in 'Trockne Blumen' ['Withered Flowers'] from Schubert's song-cycle *Die Schöne Müllerin,* where the rejected young miller-lad intends to take the withered flowers given him by his erstwhile love to his grave with him (Ex. 26.2). The vocal line here is almost equally spare, the two half-phrases having the same rhythm, and the harmony, remaining on the E minor tonic until the move to the relative major, the brightness of which is, in a typically Schubertian touch, compromised by the tenor passing-note (B♭), giving a momentary G minor.

Ex. 26.2: Schubert, 'Trockne Blumen', bb. 1–6.

The impression of a death-knell is difficult to resist in the poetic context, as it is in the ensuing song, 'Der Müller und der Bach', ['The Miller and the Stream'] a sublimated dialogue in which the young miller seems to hear the brook commenting on his grief. Here it is intensified by the syncopated rhythm (3/8: ♪ ♩), the same kind of imagery being used, except that the withered flowers are specifically lilies, the flowers of death and purity. The important words in these two lines *Liebe* (love) and *Lilien* (lilies) are each subtly pointed, in the first case by being the highest note the miller-lad sings (F♯) and the hint of diminished chord resolving to the dissonant dominant over tonic pedal, and in the case of 'lilies' by another chromatic chord, this time the Neapolitan, giving us also the first move from the pedal-note (Ex. 26.3).

Ex. 26.3: Schubert, 'Der Müller und der Bach', bb. 1–10.

In fact, basic though it may be, Schubert gives this repeated-note chord accompaniment the status, almost, of a textural/rhythmic motif in the companion song-cycle *Winterreise* [*Winter Journey*], especially when expressed in the cycle's most common time-signature, 2/4. The piece opens with this figure, what German-speaking scholars have called the *gehendes Bewegung* (the impulse to go) ('Gute Nacht', ['Good Night'] Ex. 26.4), in which the young man, having lost a home, a good job with prospects and a lover, leaves the mill by night. Here, the slow rate of harmonic change, the nullification (the end of bb. 2 and 3) and postponement (through the ivb chord in b. 5) of V–i closure underlies the situation where the flesh indeed is willing to go, but the spirit weak.

Ex. 26.4: Schubert, 'Gute Nacht', bb. 1–7.

The familiarity of this song could blind one to the highly unusual contour of the melody, which, in spite of the natural gravitational fall, has the feeling of being drawn down, with its momentary resistance on the F (marked * in Ex. 26.4) overcome, wonderfully illustrating the opening line *Fremd bin ich eingezogen* [A stranger, I was drawn [here]] the more telling when the other meaning for *eingezogen* in the period – 'conscripted' – is taken into account, a meaning all too familiar within the wider context of its period. The repeated-chord device is similarly used as a symbol of motion in 'Der Wegweiser' ['The Sign-post'] (Ex. 26.5a).

Ex. 26.5a: Schubert, 'Der Wegweiser', bb. 0–4.

The pianist can, of course, invest this kind of figure with all kinds of nuances, and passages such as Ex. 26.5b and 26.5c from this song would be unthinkable on any other instrument(s) given their varying degrees of articulation, use of different registers, sustained notes and the illusion of *crescendo* that the skilled performer can impart to the held notes through the repeated G.

Ex. 26.5b: 'Der Wegweiser', bb. 55–64.

Ex. 26.5b continued

Ex. 26.5c: 'Der Wegweiser', bb. 67–74.

Similarly, in 'Rast' ['Rest'], the compulsion to continue walking to keep warm persists even while resting, the wounded feet being a constant reminder, and this is again depicted by a subtle combination of regular rhythm, displaced between the hands with regular harmonic changes, but anchored to a tonic pedal (Ex. 26.6).

Ex. 26.6: Schubert, 'Rast', bb. 1–8.

A different combination of rhythmic regularity and full chords is shown in 'Das Wirtshaus' ['The Inn'], an ironic song in which the young man, now well on the way to mental disintegration, seeks refuge in a graveyard which he describes as an 'inn'. The rhythmic regularity is here on three levels, in the voice with quavers and semiquavers, the piano right hand, with rich chords shadowing the vocal line on the crotchet and quaver level, and the left hand in the lower register with dotted-crotchet and quaver rhythm, all giving the tolling-bell impression. This time, however, the avoidance of the usual major dominant, its use in the minor, and the preponderance of chords ii and IV give a very churchy feel. The overall impression hints at self-pity also.

Another use of this basic technique with tiny but immensely telling inflections occurs in 'Morgengruß' ['Morning Greeting'] from *Die Schöne Müllerin,* where held full-bar chords on the piano are underpinned by a scalic progression in the bass leading from tonic to dominant (Ex. 26.20a below). However this is compromised in a number of ways. Harmonically, the F (b. 4) becomes not the root of the major IV chord, but the third of ii (minor) with a change or register (the added lower octave). The words over this are (in their different verses) *Köpfchen* [little head] – a reference to the girl's starting in surprise, *Fenster* [window] (which was to become one of a number of important symbols in *Winterreise*), *Blümelein,* [little flower], (flowers being, as we have seen to an extent, of symbolic importance also), and *frei* [free]. The next few words are, however, also 'loaded' and the expected dominant harmony is also compromised by its upper auxiliary (A♭ in the bass) giving a diminished chord and by its lower auxiliary (F♯ in the tenor), giving a hint of secondary dominant ninth. The scalic rise is echoed in inversion in the chromatic fall of the next four bars under a broken-chord bass, and the verses finish with a canon between voice and piano.

Broken chords are, of course, a standard resource, yet it is surprising how comparatively little Schubert uses them in the usual way, that is *Alberti* or linear. The former is pressed into service in the opening song, 'Das Wandern', ['To Wander'] of *Die Schöne Müllerin,* where, in a version of the *gehendes Bewegung,* it expresses the simple joy – complete with the 'skip' in the offbeat right-hand chords – and, at this stage, inexperience, of the miller-lad (Ex. 26.7).

Ex. 26.7: Schubert, 'Das Wandern', opening.

Alberti figuration is also used throughout to depict running water, distinguishing, for example the Brook's voice from that of the Miller in 'Der Müller und der Bach' (referred to above), and appearing as soon as the brook is mentioned in 'Der Neugierige' ['The Questioner']: see bb. 23ff (Ex. 26.8), and 41ff. Indeed, Schubert seems to associate triadic writing in general with water, even in his melodic parts.

Ex. 26.8: Schubert, 'Der Neugierige', bb. 23–4.

Naivety is also the aim of the broken-chord right hand in 'Frühlingstraum' ['Dream of Spring'] from *Winterreise*. Schubert tends to reserve major tonality – especially in a minor-key context – for dreams and memories involving the miller-lad's happy past in spring and summer with the miller-maid, as opposed to the lonely and ever-present misery of rejection in the wintry 'now' of his waking world.

Of the six stanzas in this song, 1 and 3 represent the dream, 2 and 4 the reality and 3 and 6 an attempt to reconcile the two. In the settings of verses 1 and 3, there is again more than a hint of irony, the over-precious, consciously *volkstümlich* melody with its lilting rhythm and winsome auxiliaries and the regular triplet rhythm of the accompaniment concentrating on the *cliché*-d cadential progression I – vi – ii – V – I (Ex. 26.9a).

Ex. 26.9a: Schubert, 'Frühlingstraum', opening.

The aim is a false sense of security, to be dispelled by the 'reality' of the second and fourth stanzas, where the birdsong has changed to cocks' crowing and ravens' screeching, with concomitant changes in the accompaniment of texture, mode, rhythm, and chromatic dissonances, making liberal use of the piano's dynamic and registral colouristic possibilities (see Ex. 26.9b). The 'compromise' verses 3 and 6, involve a number of symbolic and real interfaces between the two worlds: the window, on which the condensed frost looks like flowers symbolising the coming-together of past warmth and happiness and present cold and misery (with, in the lines 'the dreamer who saw flowers in winter', a reference to Goethe's *Werther*, to whom the hero of *Winterreise* is comparable) and, in the last verse, another symbol, the eye, as an interface between inner and outer, dream and reality, past and present.

Ex. 26.9b: 'Frühlingstraum', bb. 14–18.

The musical setting of verses 3 and 6 is itself a kind of interface between the contrasting styles of the other two pairs (Ex. 26.9c). The time-signature changes to 2/4, which simply replaces the 6/8 quaver-triplets with paired quavers, while the implied |♩♩♩ ♩♩♩| rhythm is a toned-down version of the *siciliano* rhythm without either the bounce of verses 1 and 3 or the harsher regularity of 2 and 5. There are other compromises also: half of the stanza is in the tonic major and the other half in the parallel minor; in addition, the triadic bass of verses 1 and 4 and the punctuating chords of verses 2 and 5 are combined (and mollified) in verses 3 and 6, while the right-hand pedal is an attenuation of the savage bass *tremolando* (and the 'cock-crow') of verses 2 and 4.

Ex. 26.9c: 'Frühlingstraum', bb. 25–9.

A most interesting feature, to my mind, is the use of a harmonic interface, the octave un-harmonised A's beginning the slower verses 3 and 6, after the A minor broken triad ending verses 2 and 4 (see Ex. 26.9c, b. 2), which then become major; conversely, the same figure ends verse 3 in a minor context, and leading on to the major of verse 4. In all these cases, change of modality is confirmed by an upward tonic arpeggio (Ex. 26.9d). Because of this change to the parallel minor, the piece ends in that mode.

Ex. 26.9d: 'Frühlingstraum', bb. 42–5.

The association of regular broken-chord accompaniment also characterises other songs where the emphasis is on happiness in a rural setting, such as 'Des Müllers Blumen' [SM9:[1] 'The Miller's Flowers'] where it runs in parallel compound thirds and sixths with the vocal line for much of the time, and its use to depict or suggest streams and rivers has already been mentioned. Other, more complicated accompaniments may use this, or the plain chords dealt with earlier, as but one strand in an accompanimental layout.

Interesting in this context is Schubert's penchant for three-part textures – including the vocal part – of which one of those in the piano may be a more obviously 'accompanimental', and the other contributing more subtly. A case in point is SM18 'Trockne Blumen', already noticed as an example of minimal chord-support, with the chords appearing on beats 1 and 3 of the 2/4 rhythm (see Ex. 26.2 above). Later, this takes on the rhythm of the opening vocal phrase (Ex. 26.10a)

Ex. 26.10a: Schubert, 'Trockne Blumen', bb. 11–15.

and this is further compounded by the addition of the third strand, a strange, even wandering figure – the text mentions the vision of the miller's young daughter wandering through the churchyard when her young lover is dead (see Ex. 26.10b). Other examples of this kind of writing will be dealt with under subsequent headings.

On the level of mere accompaniment, the variety that Schubert manages to wring from a small number of basic patterns is huge, but it is not simply a question of variation to avoid monotony: it is also an acute ear for the piano and all its

---

[1] From here on I will use the shortened version of the reference to the song-cycles: SM9 is the ninth song in *Die schöne Müllerin*, and, for example, W14 is the fourteenth in *Winterreise* ('Der greise Kopf').

possibilities, as well as its partnership with the voice as melodic line, as a rich repository of vocal effects, as a vehicle for language as sound, and, within the confines of the poem or cycle as well as in the wider sphere, as a transmitter of information, emotional and factual.

Ex. 26.10b: 'Trockne Blumen', bb. 30–33.

(iii) Introductions and their effects

Occasionally, however, monotony of a deliberate kind can be used creatively, and the ever-resourceful Schubert will tease out other possibilities, by which he will use regularity of figuration to cause a lulling of the senses. An example of this is the surreal 'Die Krähe' [*W*15: 'The Crow'], drawing also on the layering of texture mentioned above. Here, the piano lays out its accompanimental strategy in the five-bar introduction, a *perpetuum mobile* in each of the hands, one with the song's melody representing, in its even quavers, the constant walking of the man, the other with triplet semiquaver arpeggios in a kind of wing-flap, especially in its later form when shared between the hands (bb. 5ff).

This introduction also gives a registral *précis* of the piece, descending from the upper to the lower registers with a slightly unsettling Neapolitan inflection in bb. 3 and 4. Schubert shows the parallel – implicit in Müller's verses – between the two creatures, by the octave or unison doubling of the voice and piano, the melody now being below the accompaniment, which has moved to the upper register and the relative thinness is compensated for by occasional chords (b. 7). Doubling the voice at pitch or octave almost invariably produces an eerie effect, intonation as well as timbre aiding and abetting here, and is a device that Schubert uses several times in *Winterreise* for the same or similar effect, for example 'Die Wetterfahne' ['The Weathercock'], 'Der stürmische Morgen' ['The Stormy Morning'] and 'Irrlicht' ['Will o' the Wisp']. Nor is the effect confined to art music; a similar eeriness results in the Beatles' 'Eleanor Rigby': at the point where the lonely priest Father Mackenzie has just finished burying the eponymous spinster, the cello forsakes its bass line to join Paul McCartney's vocals when the priest wipes the dirt from his hands walking away from the grave. It is the more subtle for its brevity and for not being repeated. In 'Die Krähe', the similar feeling of menace in the situation is underlined in the piano's high right-hand 'wing-flap', and that menace turns to uneasiness, if not slight horror, in the middle section

> Krähe, wunderliches Thier,
> willst mich nicht verlassen?
> Meinst wohl bald als Beute hier
> Meinen Leib zu fassen?

['Crow, strange bird, will you not leave me? Do you mean to take me as your prey soon?']

Here, the melodies separate while remaining, however, in parallel (sixths and thirds) and the harmony oscillates between major and augmented chords, giving the feeling of uneasy hovering (Ex. 26.11).

Ex. 26.11: Schubert, 'Die Krähe', bb. 15–19.

This is preserved even in the modulation, where the ambiguous dominant diminished chord (V^9) is chosen in preference to the dominant or dominant seventh. The same chord (this time in the subdominant) is used to effect the interrupted cadence on the song's last word *Grabe* ('grave', b. 33) and when closure occurs, an octave below, the piano is at its lowest, finally in the bass register proper and its postlude sinks lower still, the last chord, without fifth and with very low third, being within a few notes of the bottom of the compass.

As this song shows, the introductory function, apart from giving listener and occasionally singer, necessary data concerning key, mode, tempo and rhythm, not to mention the opening line of the melody – as in 'Der greise Kopf' [*W*14: 'The Grey head'] – or a version of it – as in 'Irrlicht' [*W*9: 'Will o' The Wisp'] – also involves a degree of scene- and mood-setting. An obvious example from *Winterreise* is 'Die Post' [*W*13: 'The Post'] giving the rattling of the wheels and the sound of the post-horn and, in 'Der Neugierige' [*SM*6: 'The Questioner'], asking the question more clearly than the voice or the rest of the song (Ex. 26.12).

Ex. 26.12: Schubert, 'Der Neugierige', bb. 1–6.

Often it does much more than this. In the miniature tone-poem that is 'Der Lindenbaum' [*W5*: 'The Lime-tree'], the introduction seems at first sight too substantial for the folk-like melody (Ex. 26.13a), but is justified by the need to dispel the strength and passion of the preceding song, 'Erstarrung', of which more shortly.

Ex. 26.13a: Schubert, 'Der Lindenbaum', bb. 1–13.

The melody of 'Der Lindenbaum' itself, with its bland accompaniment, ill prepares us for the middle of the song, but there are hints in the introduction. Here, depiction of the tree is almost literal, the crown of leaves rustling in the winds supported by the strong stem and the swaying of the stronger branches and, in the horn calls (bb. 7–8), an evocation of the forest, that all-important German Romantic symbol and its musical signifier, the *Waldhorn*. Far less easy to explain pictorially (apart from its general feeling of 'rightness') is the auxiliary figure in bb. 2 and 4–5 (left hand). Its import is more musical, referring to the basic melodic/rhythmic motif of the song-cycle, making its first telling (though surreptitious) appearance in *Die Schöne Müllerin*'s 'Morgengruß' (mentioned above) and in the introduction to 'Gute

Nacht' [W1: 'Good Night'] (see bb. 3 (last half-beat)–4) and it is reinforced later in the song in a form which is all-pervading in *Winterreise* (see b. 9, voice and bb. 24–7, piano). Again, pianistic colouring is important here in 'Der Lindenbaum', b. 4's echoing and extending of b. 2 in the bass, this being a presage of the tree's depiction in other seasons later in the song.

The change to the minor mode again shows the present and night time, and under the word *Augen* (eyes, b. 35) the motif is outlined in octaves in the bass and the accompaniment is triplet quavers. The seductive Lorelei-like invitation of the tree – 'come here to me, journeyman [*Geselle*], here you'll find your peace' – prompts a change to major, a thickening of accompaniment and a gracing of the auxiliary motif, showing it in its true – although major – form (Ex. 26.13b).

Ex. 26.13b: 'Der Lindenbaum', b. 40.

This figure also underpins the *kalten Winde* [cold wind] episode (marked in Ex. 26.13c) in which the C natural is the basis of an augmented sixth, which, a few bars later, transforms itself enharmonically into the dominant of ♭II (F♮) (Ex. 26.13d) before subsiding on the dominant pedal.

Ex. 26.13c: 'Der Lindenbaum', bb. 45–46.

Ex. 26.13d: 'Der Lindenbaum', bb. 52–53.

With the preceding number, 'Erstarrung' [W4: 'Numbness'], we enter the realm of obsession and desperation, shown not least by the repetition of lines and words – not common in Müller's verses or in Schubert's settings generally in these cycles. Here, as in the case of 'Die Krähe', the piano introduction presents us with triplets in one hand and a rhythmically regular melody in the other (Ex. 26.14a). Here the *Ur-Motiv* appears on two levels, as a melodic inflection and as a rhythmic spur, a triplet on the last beat of most bars, driving the music forward to the next beat. Schubert's choice of register here is again important, not simply as a timbral device (though this is compelling) but also as a pointer to the different psychological levels inherent in the poetic subsoil.

Ex. 26.14a: Schubert, 'Erstarrung', opening.

The song deals with the young Miller's passage across a snow-covered meadow where he and his ex-love were happy in the good times. The poem contrasts the grass beneath, which represents these, with the cold reality of the snow; again there is an interface between the two worlds in the skin of icy snow, depicted in the triplets, which have the minimum of melodic movement for the most part. The other two levels, represented by the piano's melodic part and, of course, the vocal line itself, are not so simplistically assignable and seem to vacillate between past and present, in a telling comment on the miller-lad's own distraction. This is also made evident in the claustrophobic darting of piano's left-hand octave displacements, which several times are close to the lowest note of the contemporary piano's range on the words *Tritte Spur* [footprints], (Ex. 26.14b).

Ex. 26.14b: 'Erstarrung', bb. 9–11.

On the lines

> Ich will den Boden küssen,
> Durchdringen Eis und Schnee
> Mit meinen heißen Thränen,
> Bis ich die Erde seh'.

> ['I will kiss the ground, [and] with my scalding tears penetrate the ice and snow until I see the earth.']

the piano's triplets are two octaves below in the bass and its melody, which is now in octaves linking two registers (principally middle and upper) has become an arpeggio momentarily thrusting and cutting through the voice to illustrate the tears melting the snow.

Another powerful example, in the *Lied,* of the malleability of the meaning, in practice, of the term 'accompaniment' – if not its outright inappropriateness – is found in 'Auf dem Fluße' [*W7*: 'On the River']. This is a song in which the introduction is of the minimal kind, reminiscent of 'till ready' vamping, giving no indication that this is to preface one of Schubert's very greatest songs. As soon as the voice enters, the bass line shadows it, picking out the main notes until the astonishing key-shift from the dominant root-position chord (of the tonic E minor) to viic, the second inversion of the leading-note D sharp minor, perfectly expressing the '*still*' of 'how still you have become', referring to the stream's ice-cover (Ex. 26.15a). Indeed, it is on the word *Rinde* [crust] that the *Ur-motiv* reappears (b. 15), presaged by its hint in the piano's 'pull-yourself-together' modulation of two bars previously.

Ex. 26.15a: Schubert, 'Auf dem Fluße', bb. 5–15.

As in the last song discussed, the increased agitation and use of the language of direct action –

> In deine Decke grab' ich
> Mit einem spitzen Stein
> Den Namen meiner Liebsten
> Und Stund' und Tag hinein:

['On your surface with a pointed stone I'll scratch my love's name with hour and day beside it']

– calls forth an intensification in the accompaniment, here the adoption of the repeated-chord idea in Ex. 26.15b, each instance embodying a harmonic shift,

Ex. 26.15b: 'Auf dem Fluße', bb. 23–5.

and when specific occasions are mentioned – for example, the first kiss – the semiquavers become triplets.

It is these, alternating between hands and registers, which subside to be followed by one of the great moments in all tonal music. Müller's last verse does not depart from the prosody of the rest of the poem, but Schubert departs from his hitherto strophic setting, and the voice brokenheartedly stammers out the words 'Mein Herz – in diesem Bache – erkennst du nun dein Bild?' ['My heart, in this stream, do you not now see your own image?'] while the bass line has the 'image' of the original vocal melody, now a counter-melody to the voice accompanied by the repeated chords in a further diminution of note-value and the *Ur-Motiv* (*x* in the example) has been further extended into an upsurging stab of pain (Ex. 26.15c).

Ex. 26.15c: 'Auf dem Fluße', bb. 41–9.

In 'Rückblick' [*W8*: 'Backward Glance'], what appears to be a matter of movement to give the bass interest and suggest (in tandem with the right-hand offbeat semiquavers) the feeling of scurrying (Ex. 26.16a), is, on the entry of the voice, transmuted into an uneasy counterpoint, at times *quasi*-canonic, adding greatly to the feeling of being driven along (the words show the young man's reluctance even to stop for breath) (Ex. 26.16b). But when he thinks of his last visit to the town and how very different it was, the mode changes to parallel major and the bass-line goes in parallel motion in (mostly) thirds and sixths (Ex. 26.16c).

Ex. 26.16a: Schubert, 'Rückblick', bb. 1–2.

Ex. 26.16b: 'Rückblick', bb. 10–13.

Ex. 26.16c: 'Rückblick', bb. 28–30.

The 'falling teardrop' motive that opens the introduction to 'Gefror'ne Thränen' [W3: 'Frozen tears'] is given in imitation, thrown into relief by being in the middle and bass registers successively (see Ex. 26.17a), and it turns out to be a counterpoint to the vocal part in the first pair of lines, and to anticipate the second two. This figure is confined to the bass after the move to the relative major (bb.17ff.) and its ending pulls the music down to the very low bass for the next verse, the rhythm (no longer syncopated) underlying the voice in parallel octaves. It remains in this register until the postlude, reaching its most intense when the miller-lad talks of his tears melting all the ice of winter (Ex. 26.17b).

Ex. 26.17a: Schubert, 'Gefror'ne Thränen', bb. 0–7.

Ex. 26.17b: 'Gefror'ne Thränen', bb. 33–40.

It is the use of registers and the period piano's fine response to subtle articulation which gives this its effect. In similar fashion, the build-up on overtones and colours implicit in a passage such as Ex. 26.18 from 'Einsamkeit' [*W*12: 'Loneliness'], and its contrast with what follows, is part and parcel of the effect, which is inimitable on the modern instrument,

Ex. 26.18: Schubert, 'Einsamkeit', bb. 26–34.

Ex. 26.18 continued

as is the darkening of the sound in its drop from upper to lower-middle registers in 'Der greise Kopf' and the pointillistic accompaniment to 'Letzte Hoffnung' [W16: 'Last Hope'], shown in Ex. 26.19.

Ex. 26.19: Schubert, 'Letzte Hoffnung', bb. 0–4.

(iv) Interludes and postludes

We have already seen examples of the interlude (for example in 'Frühlingstraum'). These can partake of some of the functions of introductions in that they may be required to introduce new sections of a song, and they are very frequently repeats of them, or close relatives, especially in strophic settings; this can also apply to postludes. As one might expect, departures from this generalisation tend to be found in the better songs, and some have been discussed already. In some cases the 'interlude' is no more than a couple of bars, but I intend to deal with them as interludes because of the fact that they occur between stanzas (whether or not the mood is different) and because of their effect.

Sometimes they need to be no more than an echo of the voice-part, as in 'Morgengruß' [SM8: 'Morning Greeting'], where, halfway through each stanza, the piano repeats the voice's question, complete with dominant inflection (as mentioned earlier) (see Ex. 26.20a). When, however, it comes between stanzas (and, incidentally, forms the postlude in this strictly strophic song), it again echoes the voice's last *gruppetto*, but an octave lower with the left hand near the bottom of the contemporary instrument.

Interesting also is the preceding line, the last few words of which were repeated in the *gruppetto*. In each of the six verses, this last line deals with some aspect of uneasiness, either obviously in the words – 'Then I must go away again', 'Love's sorrow and care' – or with a reference that will become more ambiguous later in the cycle, and the piano's right hand melody plays in canon with the voice in, perhaps, a hint of irony or warning (Ex. 26.20b).

Ex. 26.20a: Schubert, 'Morgengruß', bb. 4–11.

Ex. 26.20b: 'Morgengruß', bb. 15–23.

In 'Irrlicht' [W9: 'Will-o'-the Wisp'] also, mockery seems to be in question, in the traveller's deception by the Will-o'-the-Wisp and in 'Die Nebensonnen' [W23: 'The False Suns'] where his failing mind deceives him (Ex. 26.21, bb. 8–9, 14–5, and 23–5).

Ex. 26.21: Schubert, 'Die Nebensonnen', bb. 9–16.

Repetition, of course, need not be exact, and echoes can be distorted: Schubert at times extends the self-reference. Thus, in 'Tränenregen' [*SM*10: 'Rain of Tears'], the opening of the introduction (Ex. 26.22a)

Ex. 26.22a: Schubert, 'Tränenregen', bb. 0–4.

is referred to during the first interlude (Ex. 26.22b), in its basic quaver-triplets, in the tied-over quavers and in the tenor reference to the opening melody (marked x), while overlaid with the semi-quaver movement that the mention of *Bach* [stream] immediately calls forth.

Ex. 26.22b: 'Tränenregen', bb. 12–14.

In 'Die Wetterfahne' [*W*2: 'The Weathercock'], the interludes and the postlude recall, but also reinterpret, the blustery opening, as well as – ironically – becoming the unifying point of reference in a song in which the perpetual veering of the weathercock is compared to inconstancy in love. Blustery, too, is the opening of 'Muth' [W22: 'Courage'] and here the interludes egg on the miller-lad with their bravado repetition of the voice's phrases with extra force (bb. 10–11, 29–30 and 41–2) or more overtly mocking in their paraphrase, as in Ex. 26.23a and 26.23b).

Ex. 26.23a: Schubert, 'Muth', bb. 1–11.

Ex. 26.23b: 'Muth', bb. 21–4.

Schubert very often invests a repetition with deeper, or – in the context of a song-cycle – more far-reaching, meaning. A more tragic kind of jibe is to be found in *Winterreise*'s opening song, 'Gute Nacht', where, remembering the happier past with a shift to the major, the young man sings the line 'Das Mädchen sprach von Liebe, die Mutter gar von Eh' [The [miller-] maid spoke of love, the mother even of marriage], in which the word *Liebe* is given a form of the *Ur-Motiv*, only to have it thrown back at him by the piano's pointed dragging back to reality and repeating it against the subsequent line 'nun ist die Welt so trübe' [now the world is so bleak] (Ex. 26.24).

Ex. 26.24: Schubert, 'Gute Nacht', bb. 19–29.

This kind of interplay and self-reference underpins and informs the last song in *Winterreise*, 'Der Leiermann' ['The Hurdy-gurdy player'], reaching the surreal apotheosis of both cycles. Everything in this song is calculated to preserve the feeling of uneasiness which pervades it. The hurdy-gurdy was an ancient stringed instrument in which a wooden resined wheel, turned by a crank, 'bowed' the strings, one or more of which were stopped to give the pitches by tangents worked by a miniature keyboard, the remaining strings being drones. Its long association with beggars and wandering minstrels is apt here, since the wandering miller-lad seems to have come to the end of his journey with another wanderer. Schubert clearly knew the instrument, since he suggests its basic form of three strings, the two drones tuned – as was common – to a fifth, and the melody-string, although he does not always project this in the literal sense, but as three levels: drone-accompaniment, hurdy-gurdy melody and the miller-lad's voice. For most of the time, the two melodies alternate, suggesting not dialogue, but identity and, apart from the 'coda', each entry begins at the same pitch on the tonic (A), and the vocal part stays within the ambitus of a sixth and then an octave, while the piano's melody progresses from a diminished fifth through a sixth to an octave.[2]

The hypnotic effect is maintained by the unchanging tonic-and-dominant drone repeated on the first beat of every bar, by its subversion of any harmonic movement, and by the use of only tonic and dominant chords. The *appoggiatura* inflecting the drone-string in bb. 1 and 2 merely articulates the rhythm and then is discarded. Hypnotic also is the rhythmic minimalisation. The outline of b. 3 remains constant in the piano (Ex. 26.25a), with the exception of bb. 27–8 where it borrows the figure

---

[2] I am treating the piano's melody in separate bars, as the phrasing suggests this.

from the voice, and the note-group in b. 4 never alters (except that it is either harmonically tonic or dominant).

Ex. 26.25a: Schubert, 'Der Leiermann', bb. 1–10.

This again is very suggestive of the instrument in its ability to give articulation by momentarily stopping the wheel. It also highlights the difficulty, given the hurdy-gurdy's short keys, of smoothly moving the hand from one note to a chord, which requires either several sets of keys, or a key or keys to activate the separate, pre-tuned drones (the dominant chord and the third of b. 8 right hand, et al.).[3] The 'tenor-line' rhythm (bb. 7 and 18, for example) is insignificant, being more a matter of texture, although it can be seen as a kind of sublimation of b. 4. The voice-part, similarly, is strictly syllabic throughout and again is basic in its reliance on two rhythms, the unbroken six-quaver kind and the four-quaver-and-crotchet; the introduction of the dotted notes only ruffles the surface.

However, the asymmetry of the phrasing overlays this regularity, producing a slight disjunctive quality, and thereby adding to the unease. The two bars of drone are classic, of course, followed by the two bars of melody, but with the cadence repeated, in effect isolating b. 5 (and the others in which this happens). Thereafter the two-bar alternation between piano and voice is maintained for the body of the song, with the exception of bb. 27–30, where, on the one and only occasion in the song, the piano appropriates a short passage from the voice with an added parallel part (Ex. 26.25b).

Ex. 26.25b: 'Der Leiermann', bb. 25–30.

The effect is wonderfully pathetic, and comes, interestingly, after the words '*immer leer*' [ever empty, referring to the player's money-tray] and '*nimmer still*' [never silent, referring to the almost automatic action of the crank], respectively. Although

---

[3] I mention this merely to show that the possibility was there on some instruments.

INTEGRATION

Müller's prosody in his last verse does not depart from that of the rest of the poem, Schubert chooses to set it differently[4] as a coda, departing from the prevailing texture also in that the piano right hand and the voice appear together, on the lines

> Wunderlicher Alter
> Soll ich mit die geh?
> Willst du meinen Liedern
> Deine Leier drehn?

['Strange old man, shall I go with you? Will you accompany my songs?' (literally: 'Will you rotate [the crank]?')]

with the vocal part ending interrogatively on the high dominant.

In its scaling-down of the *materia musica* to its sparsest, this little masterpiece loses much on the modern piano, requiring a real master to articulate it. On the early nineteenth-century instrument, especially the 'Viennese' one that Schubert would have used, with careful digital control, articulation and phrasing, together with precise application of both common pedals, it is astounding in its capability of, if not quite reproducing a hurdy-gurdy sound, at least in giving the otherworldliness that imbues Müller's text and Schubert's setting.

(v) A note on word-painting

A well-known feature of Schubert's songs is his word-painting, ranging from the subtlest to the deliberately obvious. Many instances have been referred to in earlier contexts in this chapter. Here, I am more interested in the latter kind of onomatopoeic writing and the extent to which it relies on the features of the piano of the period. The cock-crow in 'Frühlingstraum' (W11) is not a bad suggestion of the real thing (see Ex. 26.9b above) as well as acting, in its $V^{\flat 9}c$, as a momentary confirmation of the key in this modulatory sequence. The reminiscence of silent-film accompaniments is an unfortunate hindsight here, but there is, as I have mentioned before, an ironic streak in this song.

The weathercock in 'Die Wetterfahne' (W2) veers not only melodically, but also between registers, and the whiplash of the spread chords (Ex. 26.26)

Ex. 26.26: Schubert, 'Die Wetterfahne', bb. 14–22.

---

[4] See also the 'sobbing' *'Mein herz'* of 'Auf dem Fluße' above.

Ex. 26.26 continued

and the following mockery[5] reaching, at the end, almost to the top of the piano's range, well expresses the self-critical remorse of the words, while the low trills and minor-third *tremolandi* are particularly telling.

The 'turning' figure in 'Der Wegweiser' (W20, Ex. 26.27) suggests the turning of the traveller but also seems almost like a picture of the signpost with its several different fingers, and the 'hidden pathway', which avoids human contact and is the province of wild animals – and, not least, 'from which no-one returns' –

Ex. 26.27: Schubert, 'Der Wegweiser', b. 9.

relies, for its sinister connotations, upon the integrity of the registers on the piano and the clear articulation in the bass which etches out the commentary (see also Ex. 26.5b and c above).

In summary, to hear Schubert's songs, in particular *Winterreise*, accompanied by a piano of the period is an utter revelation.

---

[5] The same kind of figure is used in 'Irrlicht', also in connection with deception (bb. 21–2).

CHAPTER TWENTY-SEVEN

Accompaniment 2b: Song 2

In the realm of the *Lied*, Schubert was certainly a tough act to follow. Chopin's *17 Songs* Op. 74, was a compilation from his nineteen songs, ranging from 1827 to 1847, by Julius Fontana, his faithful copyist and factotum and published posthumously in 1857. These are outside of the matter of this chapter – in spite of the recollection, in 'Wojak' ['The Warrior'] of the horse's pounding hooves in Schubert's *Erlkönig* (D. 328) – as 'with few exceptions they remain in intention and realisation within the sphere of the ephemeral, 'homely' ballad, usually strophic and often based on a national dance.'[1] The collection is a hybrid affair based on popular Polish *salon* song-types, including vaudeville and drinking-songs. Some of the later examples – 'Moja Pieszczotka' ['My Darling'], 'Melodia' ['Melody']) – however, reach beyond the confines of the *salon*.

Carl Loewe also concentrated more on the ballad, but his conviction that the music should serve the text did not preclude enterprising usage of the piano, especially in the occasionally long interludes and when dealing with the supernatural, where he exploits the upper register to good effect (*Die Heinzelmännchen*, [The Brownie]). Some of his settings bear comparison with Schubert's *Erlkönig* and *Edward* in particular, the latter subtitled *Eine altschottische Ballade* (D. 923). Mendelssohn's piano-accompaniments in his songs became so independently developed that they were the spur for the *Lieder ohne Worte*, as already mentioned.

In the light of his strong literary background – his father was a publisher with an excellent library – and passion for literature (especially German of his period), one would expect the *Lied* to figure largely in the output of Schumann. But it comes as something of a surprise to find him expressing the view, as late as 1839, in a letter to his friend Hirschbach, that he considered songwriting to be of secondary importance as an art-form. His concentration on piano composition and piano technique – which he shared with his wife-to-be Clara Wieck, daughter of one of the foremost piano teachers of the time, Friedrich – left little time in any case, although the mastery he achieved in these was to stand him in good stead when he did turn his hand to songwriting.

On his marriage, after myriad difficulties and lawsuits, to Clara in 1840, the flood of songs was remarkable. He produced 140 during what has consequently been called

---

[1] Samson/CHOPIN, p. 101.

this *Liederjahr* ('Year of songs'), an average of one every two-and-a-half days, although many were written in a single day. The texts he chose betray the fact that they were a kind of extended wedding-present of love songs for Clara. As far as texts were concerned, Heinrich Heine was to be for Schumann what Goethe was for Schubert, although, in fact, Schubert himself was a strong influence on Schumann also.

So was Beethoven in general and, in particular, significantly enough, his song-cycle *An die ferne Geliebte* [To the Distant Beloved[2]], which Schumann was in the habit of quoting often – for example in the impassioned *Fantaisie* Op. 17, referring to the distance, real and symbolic, placed between him and Clara by her father. Bearing in mind his contribution to the character-piece and his publication of these in organised sets, it comes as no surprise to find that his approach to *Lieder* was cyclical for the most part, even if he took it upon himself to provide the necessary coherence when using diverse poets and drawing from diverse poem collections such as in *Myrthen*, Op. 25, for example, setting Friedrich Rückert, Goethe, Burns, Heine, Byron and Moore.

That coherence was psychological and emotional and the music expressed it, either in the obvious sense of key relationships between the songs, or by other means, the responsibility often being devolved upon the piano part. His more general tendency, however, was to concentrate on a particular poet for a particular song-group, as on Heine for the *Liederkreis* [Song-cycle] Op. 24 and *Dichterliebe* [Poet's Love] Op. 48, Joseph Eichendorff for the other *Liederkreis* Op. 39 and Adelbert von Chamisso for the *Frauenliebe und -leben* [Woman's Love and Life] Op. 42.

As in Schubert's work in this genre, the variety of accompanimental figures is apparent and the sense of partnership between voice and piano characteristic. In Op. 24/2 'Es treibt mich hin' ['I'm driven to (and fro)'] the piano's introductory bars give the feeling of impatience, the bass-register chords contrasting with the middle, and this impatience changing to urgency, as they are allied to the vocal melody, urging it on (Ex. 27.1).

Ex. 27.1: R. Schumann, *Liederkreis* (Heine) Op. 24/2, 'Es treibt mich hin', bb 4–8.

The next lines show a feature not common in Schubert, especially, and in other composers of *Lieder*, the form of accompaniment that doubles the voice part (octave

---

[2] Briefly mentioned in Chapter Twenty-Six, with Ex. 26.1.

or unison) as the top line in a progression of chords. The chordal context and their close position *vis-à-vis* the melody generally, together with the faster tempo all militate against the eeriness of effect that I mentioned in connection with Schubert in the last chapter.

This kind of writing is very common in Schumann – even to the point (here) of doubling the melismatic vocal decoration (b. 17) and it additionally shows the pianist–composer (in a sense in which Schubert, for example, was not) revelling in the sheer sound of the piano's contribution as pure sonority. This is not, of course, the whole story, but time and time again one gets the feeling of the specifically tactile element in the piano writing. This is most apparent in the slower songs, such as 'Wehmuth', Op. 39/9 ['Melancholy'] with its lingering suspensions (Ex. 27.2).

Ex. 27.2: R. Schumann, *Liederkreis* (Eichendorff) Op. 39/9, 'Wehmuth', bb 1–6.

A fond lingering on dissonances is also apparent in Op. 24/3, 'Ich wandelte unter den Bäumen' ['I wandered under the trees'], initially in the introduction (Ex. 27.3a) but also implied in the slow pulse, and the plain chords, and shows an absolute confidence in the piano's ability to respond to every nuance of voicing and subtlety of dynamics of which the player is capable. We must recall here that the period piano takes palpably more time to reach full volume after striking than the modern one, so some kind of savouring becomes necessary, as with a good wine. The combination of voicing, dynamics, touch and sonority in the introduction to this song show a composer alive to every nuance of the instrument and requiring a player of the utmost sensitivity.

Ex. 27.3a: R. Schumann, *Liederkreis* (Heine) Op. 24/3, 'Ich wandelte', bb 1–6.

Ex. 27.3a continued

The eloquence of the solitary F double-sharp octaves in b. 2 and of the inner voice, and the traversing of the registers is a clear exploitation of timbre when the birds of the forest answer the young man's question, signified by a pause on the $V^{\flat 9}$ chord of the tonic, B major. The bass moves up over two octaves (including the pedal-held F♯) to a close-position chord of G major in slower tempo and *pp* (Ex. 27.3b).

Ex. 27.3b: Op. 24/3, bb. 22–6.

This belief in the piano's powers of eloquence underlies the minimal introduction afforded to what is possibly the greatest of his song-cycles, *Frauenliebe und -leben*, the two hushed chords of a plagal cadence (Ex. 27.4a) that lead into the first song, 'Seit ich ihn gesehen' ['Ever since I saw him'].

Ex. 27.4a: R. Schumann, *Frauenliebe und-leben*, Op. 42/1, 'Seit ich', bb. 1–4.

The young woman has just seen the man of her dreams and is, to put it bluntly, somewhat "gob-smacked" by the experience. Again, the chords shadow the voice with one or two small anticipations, up to the repetition of the falling phrase on the words '*sein Bild mir vor*' [his image before me], which the piano allows to remain in relief as it begins its meandering but sure descent into the extreme bass (Ex. 27.4b). This is in spite of the fact that the sense of the words is of her love's image being ever brighter in the deepest darkness; Schumann clearly favours the dark.

Ex. 27.4b: Op. 42/1, bb. 9–18.

The second of the eight songs, 'Er, der Herrlichste von Allen' ['He, the noblest of all men'] shows a very common accompanimental texture in Schumann, repeated chords in the right hand with octaves in the left (Ex. 27.5).

Ex. 27.5: R. Schumann, *Frauenliebe und-leben*, Op. 42/2, 'Er, der Herrlichste', bb. 5–10.

As we have seen, Schubert's tendency was to create a relationship between voice and left hand, whereas Schumann's is a more structural approach, the bass giving harmonic direction. Partnership, even if strained, is not, however, excluded: the piano seems to mock on the lines *'Holde Lippen, klares Auge'* [fair lips, clear eyes] and even more so at the end of the verses during which, in her sense of personal unworthiness, she thinks to bless his choice of woman and will happily suffer the resultant broken heart. Here, the opening phrase is subjected to register-shifts that are almost manic as the music gallops through a cycle of fifths (dominants, one to a bar, of A, D, G, C, F, B flat and E flat) for a repeat of the first verse.

The cycle, as set by Schumann, is eight poems out of the poet Chamisso's nineteen. Whatever governed his choice, one is grateful for his selectivity: it would be difficult to take much more fluffy self-abasement and twittering adulation from our heroine. Nevertheless, though such sentiments stick in the craw somewhat, it is impossible not to be moved to concern for the young widow in the last song. Schumann sets this as a recitative, in stark and telling contrast to the previous fluttering,[3] with largely conjunct motion and more measured rhythmic tread in D minor, ending on its dominant. Then, in a moment of utter perfection, the piano modulates heart-rendingly to the calm of B flat major and the music of the opening song – or, rather to the piano's part in it – in a postlude more eloquent than any of Chamisso's previous eight poems.

Thus, again, it is the piano that sums up and draws all together.

---

[3] Although it is fair to say that maternal responsibility has brought some toning-down of excitement in the previous song.

CHAPTER TWENTY-EIGHT

Accompaniment 3: Piano Duet and Duo

The ever-increasing dynamic, colouristic and pitch range of the piano together with its usefulness in teaching and as a reproducer of music for other media – especially the orchestra – coupled with the increasing army of domestic players, meant that more was asked of it and that, in houses 'of the better sort' one instrument was not enough. Music was required – and supplied – for more than one performer on one piano and for more than one piano, in each case most usually two: the duet and the duo[1].

(i) The piano duet

Some early seventeenth-century English precedents for virginals exist, by Nicholas Carleton, Thomas Tomkins and John Bull – the last for three hands – but the great rise in popularity coincides with that of the piano. Again it seems that Mozart was the pioneer, as his ensemble works with piano predate his solo sonatas. He wrote the duet-sonata in C major, K. 19d, at the age of nine (1765) during the family's London visit, and the portrait by Johann Nepomuk della Croce shows him and his sister Nannerl playing a keyboard duet with hand-crossing (see Pl. 37); this may well refer to K. 19d, which calls for this technique (see Ex. 28.1 below). Leopold Mozart claimed that this work was the first of its kind, which seems extremely unlikely.

This sonata did not appear in print until 1788, however, and the distinction of producing the first published examples in this genre belongs to Charles Burney whose *Four Sonatas or Duets for two performers on one Piano Forte or Harpsichord* appeared in 1777, followed by a second similar set the following year and, incidentally, a *Sonate à trois mains* about 1780. These pieces were for playing with his (later famous) daughter Fanny, and he commissioned a six-octave piano (C^1–c^4) from Merlin in 1777 especially for duet-playing. As a composer, Burney is generally little more than competent, but his exposure to a wealth of music during his two grand tours of 1770 and 1772 has clearly borne fruit in these sonatas, in which

---

[1] Not included in this chapter are didactic music and arrangements.

French and Italian lyricism is pleasantly blended. There is also evidence of attempts to treat the players as different characters and an ear for the piano's sonority in terms of register, with the greater sustenance of bass and tenor being not simply nodded at, but incorporated in the dialogue as a more individual contribution; Ex. 28.2a and 28.2b provide illustrations.

Ex. 28.1: W.A. Mozart, Duet-Sonata in C major K. 19d/i, bb. 17–21.

Ex. 28.2a: Burney, from *Four Duets*/2/i.

Ex. 28.2b: from *Four Duets*/3/ii.

J.C. Bach, then living in London, followed Burney a year later by including duets in his *Four Sonatas and Two Duetts*, Op. 15 of 1778, followed by a similar set in 1780 as his Op. 18. Mozart, for whom he was a chief influence, had two more duet-sonatas published in Vienna in 1783 as Op. 3 (K. 381 (123a) and K. 358 (186c)):

they were written 1772–4. Two more followed, K. 497 in F major and K. 521 in C major, both published in 1787, the former (1786) sporting one of his very few slow introductions in a chamber work, in keeping with its symphonic cut (Ex. 28.3). He also wrote a set of variations on a probably original theme (K. 501 in G, major 1786).

Ex. 28.3: W.A. Mozart, Duet-Sonata in F major K. 521/i, bb. 1–10.

Muzio Clementi – the butt of Mozart's scorn and disparagement in his letters because of their piano-playing competition before the Emperor Joseph II – released duets early on in his published career, including three, together with three flute/violin sonatas, as his Op. 3 written and published in London in 1779, where, after Burney's sets, such pieces were very fashionable. Ex. 28.4 shows Clementi injecting some light contrapuntal interest into a coda section in the rondo from Op. 3/1.

Ex. 28.4: Clementi, Duet-Sonata Op. 3/1/iii, ending, bb. 59–67.

Ex. 28.4 continued

One of Clementi's three public performances that year was of a duet played with the composer William Dance in April 1779 in London.[2] The duets are an impressive debut, though in competence, rather than in the headier technical vein that caused such a splash with the solo sonatas in Op. 2 (Nos. 2, 4 and 6) published earlier the same year. The first of his Op. 6 is another duet with the glitter of the concert-hall about it; Leon Plantinga suggests that this may have been the work that Clementi played in the already mentioned performance with Dance (April 1779)[3].

Haydn barely dipped his toe in this particular pond; there is a solitary set of variations, the didactic piece *Il Maestro e lo Scolare* ('*Divertimento*') for harpsichord (four hands)[4]. There is also a Partita in F major for harpsichord, four hands, which is attributed to him, but this has not been authenticated and is unlikely to be so. Beethoven added little more to the repertory, with two early sets of variations – WoO 67 on a theme by one of his staunchest patrons, and dedicatee of some of his greatest works, Count Waldstein, and WoO 74, on his own song 'Ich denke dein' – three Marches Op. 45 and a single Sonata in D major, his Op. 6 of 1796–7. His reticence in this genre may not be unconnected with a lack of opportunity for practical performance; playing duets with Beethoven would not have attracted the faint-hearted, something akin, perhaps, to sharing a bivouac with a Rottweiler.

Given the physical closeness of the performers in this medium, its domestic setting, and its association with didacticism (see the next chapter), it is understandable that the focus was on non-virtuosic, non-showy but 'fun' music[5], and lighter music cast in shorter pieces tended to prevail. Variations were common, particularly those on operatic airs or folk tunes, such as Jean Baptiste Chollet's Four Variations with an extended finale on music from Bellini's *Il pirata*. The tune is one of those requiring vocal inflections to make anything of it (Ex. 28.5a), and the rather pallid var. 1 (Ex. 28.5b) and var. 3 (Ex. 28.5c) would, with some adjustments for range, be more effective in the voice than on the piano, and possibly more convincing. This is one of Chollet's few compositions, since, as one of the most important tenors of the first half of the nineteenth century, his *métier* was operatic performance and this piece

---

[2] *Public Advertiser*, 22 April, 1779, quoted in Plantinga/CLEMENTI, p. 53.
[3] Plantinga/CLEMENTI, p.109, fn. 40.
[4] This will be discussed briefly in Chapter Twenty-Nine.
[5] There is, however, a strong didactic bent, as we shall see in the next chapter.

is yet another reminder of how easily the vocal idiom of this period translates into the pianistic in spite of the few awkwardnesses, attributable more to the composer than to the singer.

Ex. 28.5a–c: Chollet, Four Variations on Bellini's *Il pirata*/ Theme, Var. 1 and Var. 3.

But, as well as all the froth of the dances and variations, there were substantial works also. Chopin's early *Introduction, Thème et Variations sur un air national de Moore* (1826) is more solid than its title would suggest, and sonatas of quality were written by Pleyel, Moscheles (Op. 47 in E flat major), J.L. Dussek, Kuhlau and Felix Mendelssohn. Hummel wrote an effective *Sonate ou divertissement* in E flat major (Op. 51, pub. c.1811–15) comprising of a Marcia with a rather neat Mendelssohnian link to an Andante quasi Allegretto in G major, whose opening 'theme' (Ex. 28.6a)

Ex. 28.6a: Hummel, Duet-Sonata in E flat major Op. 51/ii, bb. 0–2.

becomes an accompanimental figure to what gracefully follows (Ex. 28.6b).

Ex. 28.6b: Op. 51/ii. bb. 8–12.

This movement, effectively a short intermezzo, is in turn joined to a concluding rondo via a short free passage shared between the four hands (Ex. 28.6c).

Ex. 28.6c: Op. 51/ii, end, leading to iii.

There is also Hummel's fine duet-sonata in A flat major Op. 92 (1820), a battle-scarred Grave introduction in F minor contrasting bombast with frailty (Ex. 28.7a)

Ex. 28.7a: Hummel, Duet-Sonata in A flat major Op. 92/i, bb. 0–6.

and providing a very sure-footed link to its first movement proper, an aptly-headed Allegro commodo (see Ex. 28.7b). The central Andantino sostenuto in E major, in echo of the Grave, alternates firmness and leniency and the rondo with a slightly pastoral theme draws the opposing elements together. Hummel also wrote a Nocturne in F major Op. 99 with the *ad libitum* addition of two horns, reminding one of

Robert Schumann's original version of the *Andante and Variations* in B flat major for two pianos Op. 46 (1843) which was originally accompanied by a horn and two cellos.

Ex. 28.7b: Op. 92/i, bb. 14–20.

In general, the output of composers in the piano duet and the duo is considerably smaller than their other music for, or including, the piano. The exception here is Schubert, with the added benefit that it is also amongst the best in the genre. Like his *Lied* output, his lack of great public profile and his position as the kingpin in a small, but very active, rewarding and highly appreciative musical circle of friends, focused his attention and efforts on the more domestic genres. A great range of contemporary piano music types is represented – dances (polonaises, *Deutscher*, *Ländler*), marches, fantasies, *divertimenti*, rondos, variations, duos, overtures (not arrangements), sonatas ('*grande*' or not) – and the works span his entire short life, including his first extant composition (a Fantasia in G major, D 1 (1810, at the age of 13)) to within five months of his death (the Rondo in A major, D 951).

This very popular medium also includes pieces for three hands. As well as Burney's *Sonate à trois mains*, already mentioned, there are the three sonatas by Johann Wilhelm Hässler (1747–1822) and three by Friedrich Hugo Dalberg (1760 –1812); the latter also produced one for five hands[6].

---

[6] Information from Newman/SCE, pp. 579–80, p. 662, and p. 576 respectively.

(ii) Two pianos

This medium tends to elicit more public-oriented works, often virtuoso, and a smaller literature would be expected. Three of J.S. Bach's sons (C.P.E., J.C. and W.F.), J.L. Dussek and Clementi all wrote examples and W.A. Mozart provided the Sonata in D major, K. 448 (375a, 1781) as well as the four-voice Fugue in C minor, K. 426 (1783) with its severe and deliberate subject (Ex. 28.8), fugues being, of course, ideal for the two-piano, four-hand format. It must be said, however, that the two-piano repertory was eclipsed during most of our period by the single-piano four-hand works.

Ex. 28.8: W.A. Mozart, Fugue in C minor K. 426, bb. 1–13.

We shall see, however, in the next chapter that the literature of this medium was much swelled by arrangements.

CHAPTER TWENTY-NINE

Didacticism and Dissemination

This chapter will deal with some of the *genres* that have been strongly associated with didacticism in music but with the emphasis on the social sense of teacher-pupil relationship, rather than, for example, the kind of self-sufficient personal training implicit in the exercise or *étude* – including those of the latter whose purpose was more than the basically digital.[1] Thus, solo teaching-pieces, duets and duos, and arrangements are included here because, although the last two categories do have a life outside the schoolroom, so to speak, they were particularly targeted for teaching purposes.

(i) Background

The vicissitudes of musical education in the eighteenth century are too wide and specialised for discussion here. In an age when craftsmanship, rather than 'Art' was the ideal, for the professional musician destined to be a *Kapellmeister* or its municipal counterpart, training was provided by the guilds and, of course, by father – or other relative – to son transmission. Non-professional musical education had fallen into disarray, poorly, if at all, represented in schools because of lack of interest on the part of the organisers – whether Calvinist, Jesuit or, to a lesser extent, Pietist – and despised by the utilitarian secularisation that characterised much Enlightenment thinking. Locke, in England, considered music education to be simply time-wasting; Jean-Jacques Rousseau, however, himself an accomplished musician, argued the psychological and social benefits of exposing children to musical stimuli in *Emile, ou l'Education* (1762) as part of his general shakeup of attitudes to children and their learning potential, wellbeing and general creative development.

Indeed, the Enlightenment's own general credo of accessibility and dissemination of information is shown primarily in the publication, in the last half of the eighteenth century, of the *Encyclopédie*, the full title of which gives a better indication of its intended scope: *Encyclopédie, ou Dictionnaire raisonné des sciences, des arts et des métiers, par une société de gens des lettres*. [Encyclopaedia, or analytical dictionary of the sciences, the arts and the professions, by a society of

---

[1] Dealt with in Chapter Two (vi).

writers]. The work was intended to be a compendium of all knowledge published, in 35 volumes between 1751 and 1780, or more particularly in specialised books on individual subjects, or on specific aspects of the same. With the increase in literacy and the technical advances in printing, cheaper and better-illustrated material was produced, written in the vernacular, sounding less like a dissertation (and so more readable), and by no means confined to the cerebrally educational, including subjects such as dancing, diction, manners and deportment, aimed at the aspiring new class of *bourgeoisie*.[2]

Music, as well as being represented in the *Encyclopédie*, had also its more specialised publications, such as Fux' *Gradus ad Parnassum* and the tutors of J.J. Quantz (on playing the flute), Leopold Mozart (the violin) and C.P.E. Bach (the keyboard, dealt with in Chapter Two (iv)).

(ii) Printing and publishing

But even the significant increase in such publications could hardly have prepared people for the explosion to which the combination of drawing room, affordable piano, affectations of sensibility, the view of music as an attractor of suitors and, perhaps above all, the progress in printing and publishing would give rise early in the following century. Many composers had, of course, supplemented their incomes before this time, and indeed for some, Mozart among them, it was a little more than just supplementation. But in the new century, domestic consumption of music on a hitherto unimagined scale provided a market that enabled composers to rely less and less on the aristocratic patronage – and interference – of their predecessors, though, in fact, not many saw the shift entirely as one of liberation. This new market transformed the music-printing industry resulting in an enormous proliferation of music, and composers were not backward in their response to its demands.

Music-printing, at the beginning of the nineteenth century, used two methods, type and engraving, both of which were undergoing developments and improvements. The former worked on the same principles as letterpress, each note and rest having its own type, but it was becoming increasingly cumbersome, due to the growing number of different kinds of notes and symbols during the late eighteenth and nineteenth centuries, and, in an age where the specialised music-printing house was a rarity, it meant having a musically literate compositor on the staff, something of a luxury for general firms. Also, the process often required several impressions, one for the staves, one for the notes, a further one for texts, and so on. For small amounts of musical script, for instance as examples in books or articles, this was very useful, but in the huge quantities that would soon be the norm, it was unsatisfactory, compromising print-quality and speed of production. It was equally unviable for chamber music and, especially, the large orchestral scores that would later form part – though, because of costs, necessarily a small part – of the music-publisher's output.

---

[2] See Chapter Seven (i) and Pl. 30 and 31.

The second method, engraving, had already reached a high state of development and excellence in art-printing and mapmaking during the eighteenth century and, in its later part, served music-printing equally well, resulting in beautifully produced scores: one has only to remember the firms of Artaria and Torricella in Vienna, and their associations with the Classical and early Romantic composers. The plates, one for each page, were made of pewter or copper with the staves and symbols engraved on them and the notes punched onto them. Corrections could be made fairly easily, the plates were durable enough to support a long print-run, and they could be stored for later editions. Additionally, illustrations could be engraved for title pages and frontispieces.

However, given this Age of Progress, it was a newly invented method, lithography, that became standard. The result of the Bavarian actor and playwright Alois Senefelder's need to publish his own plays as cheaply as possible, it was a revolutionary method, with material written onto stone (hence the process' name) and treated with acid, throwing the written material very slightly into relief and allowing for contact-printing of a large number of copies very cheaply and quickly. It was Senefelder himself who saw the particular advantages in his system for music-printing, and within a decade of his first attempts at music in 1796, it had become widespread in Europe. His first print-run, 120 copies of 12 songs by his friend Franz Gleissner, took less than a fortnight – and that included in the work's composition! Subsequent improvements allowed for manuscript, using the prescribed ink and paper, to be transferred directly onto the metal plates that replaced the cumbersome stone, thus allowing the composer to participate directly in the process at a late stage compared with other printing methods, not to mention the attractive possibility of musical self-publication.

Among the first to avail themselves of this possibility were C.M. von Weber, in the case of his piano variations Op. 2, and Wagner, who wrote out all 450 pages of his opera *Tannhäuser* in full score in 1845, for their immediate transfer to the plates. In spite of the fact that these were now made of metal rather than the original stone, the method continued to be called lithography, and was adopted by all the major music-printers, although music engraving still continued on a large scale, since this technique produced clearer work. Nevertheless, in a period in which thrift and economy were middle-class bywords, the fact that lithography was a quarter of the cost of engraving spoke loudly in its favour and the fact that it was ideal for illustrations – multicoloured ones as well as monochrome – was certainly no disadvantage. The results were soon to grace the publications of sentimental and patriotic ballads, making them even more acceptable in the drawing-room. This boom in music-printing caused a mushrooming of new publishing firms, many of which are still in business, such as Chappell, Boosey, Cramer, Novello and Eulenberg. Parallel developments in transport technology provided for quicker and safer ways of carrying goods and people, including the new railway and steamship, and assisted greatly in the dissemination of printed music.

Hand-in-hand with these developments, as a result of them but also, in turn, abetting them, was the expansion of the press – newspapers, periodicals, yearbooks, and occasional publications – and especially the more dedicated musical press. This allowed for advertising of concerts, of instruments for sale, of various musical services and of recent or reissued publications thus boosting sales and keeping composers' names and works in the forefront of readers' minds. These were often reinforced by biographical notices and items of news, including the trivia, on the one hand, and the lurid *'exposés'* on the other, which we associate almost without thinking with the mass media of our own time. In this connection, Liszt wrote that people 'want to know the colour of your bedroom slippers, the cut of your dressing gown' and that the press 'eager to profit from this pitiable curiosity ... heap[s] ... anecdote upon anecdote, falsehood upon falsehood.'[3] (He himself, it has to be said, benefited considerably from such published details, however.) The press also allowed for critical perusal of concerts and publications fulfilling an important function in terms of quality-control and rendering a career-boost to many an up-and-coming composer, although partisanship and camp-following – to the point of blatant puffing – was easy enough to find. The public 'war' in the newspapers between Herz and Thalberg in New York during the 1840s is a prime example of such and showed the power of the nascent popular press in keeping the public interested in the careers of the two protagonists.[4]

Yet another beneficiary of the printing and publishing revolution was the subject of this chapter, the didactic sphere, as evinced in the proliferation of 'schools' or 'methods' of piano-playing in the early nineteenth century. As worthy descendants from their eighteenth-century counterparts, these were not solely technical manuals but were 'compleat' in the sense that they began from first musical principles and proceeded to a quite advanced educational stage as far as non-institutionalised and non-personalised professional training was concerned. They included practice material of all kinds, from five-finger exercises to fully fledged multi-section or multi-movement pieces, often of sufficient quality to warrant their being placed, and published, alongside their composers' own non-didactic works, and even resulting, on occasion, in prime examples of their type and genre: Chopin's *Trois nouvelles études*, (1839) written for the treatise upon which Moscheles and Fétis collaborated, the *Méthode des méthodes* (1840), are a case in point.

(iii) The solo didactic piece

But, in an age where music, particularly piano music, was being made accessible as never before, the production of separate pieces and sets of pieces for children and beginners burgeoned. One would expect much of this material to be concerned with the basics of digital and manual development, but not in as bald a fashion as in the schools or the clearly titled 'Exercises'. What is interesting is how quickly a literature based on accessible and popular pieces – just the sort that children of middle-class homes would be used to hearing – grew up. What is, perhaps, surprising is that, in echo of their involvement with the folk-industry as perpetrated by Thomson *et al*, the

---

[3] Liszt/JOURNEY, p. 14.
[4] See Loesser/MEN, pp. 48–51.

greatest and most famous musicians in Europe were happy to write pieces of this sort.

Many are straightforward in their titling, such as Henri Bertini's *25 Etudes Faciles et Progressives* Op. 100, Herz' *Collection d'Exercices, Passages, Préludes, Sonates, Rondos, Variations, et autres Morceaux d'une difficulté progressif* [... 'and other pieces of progressive difficulty'], and Lecarpentier's *Méthode de Piano pour les Enfans* [sic], and among its 'Récréations' are a 'Walse [sic] allemand', 'Galop favori, motif du quadrille de Venise', a 'Ronde montagnarde', and several pieces by 'Mlle Loïsa Puget' including 'Mon rocher de Saint Malo'. Carl Czerny is extremely prominent in this, as in other areas (variations, rondos) with titles such as *Etudes pour la jeunesse*: 26 very easy preludes for the pianoforte Op. 694 (pub. 1842), *24 Irish Airs as Studies*, Op. 684, *Amusemens de la jeunesse*: 6 overtures on National airs for pianoforte, Op. 710 (pub. 1842) his *24 Petites Pièces en Rondeaux et Variations ... à l'usage de la Jeunesse* Op. 455, which includes Moore's 'The Minstrel Boy'. A list of his various publications with the title 'School' alone, which deal with playing techniques, will illustrate how few pedagogical stones he left unturned:

The School of Velocity, Op. 299
The Preliminary School of Velocity, Op. 636
The School of Legato and Staccato, Op. 335
The School of Embellishments, Turns and Shakes, Op. 335
The School of Virtuosity, Op. 365
Die Schule des Fugenspiels [*The School of Fugue-playing*], Op. 400
The School of Expression, Op. 613
Kinderklavierschule [*The Child's Piano School*], Op. 825
Das moderne Klavierspiel [*The School of modern Piano Forte Playing*], Op. 837
Complete Theoretical and Practical Pianoforte School, Op. 500

Several composers are explicit about their aims and methods. The fourth edition – showing the popularity of such productions – of J.B. Cramer's *Instructions for the Piano Forte (with additions & improvements)* has an 'Introduction to the Public', where he states that:

> Every day's experience proves that introducing popular Airs as Lessons for the practice of Learners, greatly promotes their application and improvement; as they have the satisfaction to observe that this species of Lesson affords more entertainment to their hearers, than long uninteresting compositions: on which account I have introduced many popular subjects, for part of the Lessons, and arranged them in a familiar style (- January 1st, 1825).

Some, however, are almost misleading: Ladurner wrote a *Fantasie in C (absichtlich / für fortsch-reitende Schüler im Clavierspielen / zur angenehm und nützlich unterhaltenden Anwendung / einiger technischer Uebungs-Formen / mit beigefügten Fingersatze / und für ein CLAVIER von 5 Octaven)* [*Fantasy in C (specifically for improving students of piano-playing to maintain some system of technical exercises through agreeable and useful application for a five-octave piano)*], which turns out to be mostly passagework of the following type, with right- and left-hand echoing each other much of the time.

The necessity to shine in the parlour is demonstrated in a note to an advertisement inside the front cover of Czerny's *New School of Velocity* Op. 834 by the publisher Robert Cocks & Co, for *The Vesper Hymn* (transcribed by W. Vincent Wallace):

> The interest thrown into this fine melody, making it heard in all the different parts as it runs through the piece, shows what can be made of a very simple Theme in the hands of a man of taste and genius. It is showy and useful for practice, and, although brilliant, is not difficult for tolerably good performers.

Wallace presents the hymn in various registers in what is, basically, a colouristic setting.

Czerny's own rather charmingly titled *100 Royal Bouquet Valses for the Piano by Lanner and Strauss, arranged for such as cannot reach the Octave. 12 books Each 3/-* is also a reminder of how lucrative this business could be. For comparison with this price of three shillings per book – a comparison which, because of myriad other factors, such as cost-of-living, relative costs of fuel, value of currency, and so on, can only be of the very roughest – a concert ticket in London was around half-a-guinea (10 shillings and sixpence), which was about sixpence less than a (female) mill-operative in a Lancashire factory earned in a week.[5] One did not see many mill-girls at the Philharmonic Society's concerts. However, the middle- and upper-classes, who benefited from this appalling system, were not so strapped for cash and could well afford such luxuries. Sales could also be boosted by targeting particular parts of the market, as in the case of Czerny's Op. 690, *Les Jeunes Militaires*, which comprises of 12 Rondinos '*on the most popular marches*', dedicated to the 'Pupils of Mr. Nunn, Bury St. Edmunds'; as well as being a welcome 'plug' for the dedicatee's musical establishment – this one is unusual in that it is run by a man – it would guarantee Czerny generations of sales there. His dedication of the *Invitation à la Danse: Divertissement Elegant* Op. 482 ('dans le style brillant et moderne') to '… Young ladies at Mrs. and the Mi∫ses Milfords' School, Walthamstow' would have had the same effect, especially when the 'Mi∫ses' broke away from the 'Mrs.' and branched out on their own.

(iv) The piano duet

In spite of the emphasis being on lighter music, as suggested in the last chapter, there is also a substantial literature of didactic pieces here also, and they are particularly useful in involving children and beginners in music-making on the piano in spite of very limited technique. The subtitle of a four-hand harpsichord *Divertimento* by Haydn already mentioned, says it all: his *Sonata a quattro mani* subtitled *Il maestro e lo scolare* of around 1768–70. This is a theme followed by a set

---

[5] See Hobsbawm/REVOLUTION, p. 56.

of variations in increasing note-values and of progressive difficulty, the *Scolare* playing the *Maestro*'s music a bar or two later and a couple of octaves above. The result is that, apart from the cadences at the ends of sections when both play together, each variation is a simple mini-canon. Although a little on the dull side, it probably succeeded in its aim. Ex. 29.1a gives the opening of the *Tema*

Ex. 29.1a: J. Haydn, Divertimento *Il maestro lo scolare* H:XVIIa:1, Tema.

and Ex. 29.1b part of the concluding Tempo di Menuetto, in which, at last, the two play together for the most part.

Ex. 29.1b: H:XVIIa:1, from Tempo di Menuetto.

Czerny's *Fantaisie* duet on motifs from Bellini's *I puritani* also has an easy and dull *Secondo* part, although in No. 2, on different motifs from the same work, the pupil gets the tune at one point. It would be fanciful, though tempting, to make any connection between this and the fact that it appears bound into the tenth of a series of beautifully bound volumes of piano music in the Royal Music Library in the British Library, London, all stamped with 'Princess Victoria' on their cover panels. Further down the social scale is a collection called *The Sisters*, attesting to the prevailing gender of the domestic commoners as do its contents, both in style and in the diminutive titles of *Rondino* and *Rondoletto* as well as the common *Rondo*.

(v) Two pianos

In view of my remarks under this same heading (section (ii)) in the previous chapter, one would expect the didactic to have a very small representation in the two-piano medium also. Czerny's *New School of Velocity* Op. 834 (the original of which was *Die höhere Stufe der Virtuosität* ['A higher degree of virtuosity']) shows, again, his interest in pedagogy and in pedagogical institutions. His *Preface* to this work states:

> To all the Studies, both in the old [that is, his *Étude de la velocité*] and in the present work, I have added an *ad libitum* accompaniment for a second pianoforte, for those who enjoy the great advantage of having two Pianos at their command. As this accompaniment is in part concertante and partly also a filling up of the harmony, the efforts of the teacher (particularly in large music schools) will be attended with much greater and more speedy success by his accompanying, than by any other method of instruction. (Vienna 1854).

Chopin's still popular *Rondo* in C major Op. 73 (1828) was published after his death, as was Hummel's *Introduction and Rondo* in E flat major Op. posth. 5.

(vi) Arrangements

As mentioned in the last chapter, arrangements counted for much of the duet and duo repertories, in fact the Chopin rondo just mentioned was itself an arrangement from a solo piece. The Mozart *Fugue* in C minor, also mentioned in the last chapter, shows some of the vicissitudes of arranging: composed in 1783 for two pianos, it was arranged for strings (quartet or orchestra) in 1788, with an introduction, as K. 546 and this in turn was arranged for two pianos. Beethoven's symphonies were arranged several times by different composers, including Hummel and Moscheles, and Liszt paid the same compliment to his Ninth as well as many of his own orchestral works.

Arranging was also a lucrative way of prolonging the shelf (or drawing-room) life of many a solo piece, whether *favori* or not, and if simplification were involved, a further *tranche* of the market could be accessed. It became common for popular successful composers to have simultaneous arrangements issued with pieces. Thus Hummel's *Air à la Tyrolienne avec Variations* Op. 118 (*c*.1829) for soprano and orchestra, which he wrote for the dedicatee, the singer Madame Malibran to première in London, was simultaneously published for voice and piano, piano duet, piano solo, piano with string quartet, piano and violin and piano and cello – not to mention its simultaneous publication in some of these forms in different cities! Indeed, it was the duet version of this very work which was also included in Princess Victoria's tenth volume mentioned above, with '*Victoria*' in childish copperplate on the title-page.[6] Czerny, also featuring in this volume (as we have seen), arranged his *Grand Coronation March* for Victoria – now Queen – as a duet, which the publishers dedicated to her.

---

[6] British Library R.M.25.i.8.

As well as a composer's self-arrangement, there was much back-scratching also. When Czerny and Georges Bizet got together to issue a simplified edition of Thalberg's *L'art du chant appliqué au piano* – itself consisting of piano arrangements of vocal (mostly operatic) pieces – they appended 12 new numbers, some arranged as duets, and Hünten similarly arranged a *tyrolienne* of Mercadante's, as did Czerny in the case of Alphonse Leduc's *Trois fantaisies gracieuses* Op. 163 *bis*, obviously with beginners in mind.

There is didacticism in the broader sense associated with arrangements for one or more pianos in our period also. Given the, by present standards, comparative infrequency and great expense of orchestral concerts, the obvious lack of any kind of recording, and the fact that orchestral full scores – and even, to an extent, chamber scores – were very rarely published for most of the period, arrangements of standard orchestral works were essential for becoming familiar with the repertory. This applied particularly to music-lovers living away from the larger conurbations. Anyone who had a piano, or, even better, two, could become well-versed in the master-works and other repertories. In fact, this would be the way in which most people of the period came to know, for example, the symphonies and orchestral works of Haydn, Mozart and Beethoven.

An interesting light is thrown on this lack of contemporary knowledge of a repertory, the highlights of which anyone with any love of music would nowadays take for granted, in a publication of a selection of Mozart's symphonies. In an 'Extract from Ewar & Co's General Catalogue of Pianoforte Music, section B, Piano-Forte 4 hands' we find the following:

> Mozart, W. A. Twelve Grand Symphonies, Posthumous Works, now first published: Arranged by C. Czerny - No. 13, in C minor .. 6s.0d. 14, in D .. 4s. 0d. 15, in E .. 5s. 0d. 16, in C .. 4s. 0d. 17, in B .. do. Every Month One Number will be published until complete. Should any doubt exist as to the authenticity of these Symphonies, the Publishers are satisfied that no Musician, Professional or Amateur, will question it, after the perusal of any one of them; but, as a further proof, they submit to the Reader the following attestation: – 'We, the undersigned, who are well acquainted with the Works of the immortal Mozart, throughout his career, as also his style and handwriting, affirm, that the above Symphonies have been laid before us in the Original Score; and, after a careful examination, we declare them to be in the genuine handwriting of Wolfgang Amade Mozart. – Vienna, 9th June 1847.' 'R. G. Kiesewetter Carl Czerny Adalbert Gyrowetz Anton Schmidt Leopold von Sonnleitner Aloys Fuchs'.

Arrangements were of indispensable value also in not only familiarising amateurs with the concerto repertory, but with furnishing professionals with the wherewithal to practice without the expense of an orchestra – especially given the cavalier attitude to rehearsals.[7] These could be performed without orchestra, of course, in the form of, usually, piano-quartet arrangements, and several were arranged and published in that way for chamber use, including Mozart's own arrangements of some of his concertos. But the more common was the solo-piano part with the orchestral interludes in small notes and, where necessary, some provision for the orchestral thematic material to be

---

[7] See Chapter Sixteen (ii).

incorporated into the solo part when both were playing simultaneously in the original.

However, the most useful form of all was the two-piano version, one of which was an orchestral reduction. This sums up the view of the piano in the period in its capacity as an exciting and powerful virtuoso-instrument and at the same time as capable of reproducing to a significant extent, the orchestral colours also.

A rather quaint footnote to the uses of didactic music and its presentation is the case of an amateur composer called 'Flora' whose speciality was to construct her scores in the form of flowering shrubs, in which the ligatures and, occasionally the barlines, were branches or leaves and the flowers notes (see the back cover of this volume). All of these are delicately coloured, clearly aimed at children, and the 'cue' 'for the accommodation of her Pupils' at the bottom of the piece shows how the system works. I have not been able to discover much about 'Flora', but it is clear she was female, a piano teacher and an amateur composer. She may have possibly been Tyrolean or Swiss, judging by her own melodies and her choice of others' to arrange. The use of 'wasps' for sharps is charming, although one wonders why she did not choose bees. I fear the identity of 'Flora' is doomed to remain one of the great musicological mysteries of our period, impervious to scholarship.

CHAPTER THIRTY

The Dance

(i) Suite dances

The Baroque dance-suite, with its movements all in the same key (though not necessarily the same mode) and intended to be played as a whole, is to be seen as an early example of the consistent use of character in (keyboard) music in that, as we have seen[1] with the sets by François Couperin in particular, most of the movements have humanised, and frequently emotionalised, titles. But, of course, the dances themselves also have character in the choreographic sense – tempo, expression, time-signature, quality of anacrusis, type of melody, not to mention rhythm and social requirements. The basic core of the suite were the four principal dances, *allemande*, *courante*, *sarabande* and *gigue* (or their close equivalents in other languages) could be seen as representing the politically important empires of Western Europe, a geographical cross with the United Kingdom and the southern Latin countries forming the upright and France and the Austro-Germanic Empire the crossbar: it may not be too naïve to see the threat of the emerging nationalist movements. These core dances were often joined by a sprinkling of less common ones, such as the *bourrée*, the *gavotte* (a descendant of which is still very much alive and well in Brittany) and other movements (*rondeau*, *prélude*, and so on). Despite some loss of individuality, these characters remained after most of them were no longer used for actual dancing, as was already becoming the case in the Baroque period itself.

Although the production of dance-suites of this kind died out soon after 1750, to be replaced by the instrumental sonata, there are occasional examples of suites or various of their constituent members as well as related dances being written, although in the spirit of antiquarianism rather than revivalism. While one might not be surprised (in view of their titles) to find a *Giga* complete with imitative entry (see Ex. 30.1) or a Saraband (in 3/2) among Kollmann's *Variations on an Air of Handel*[2] (1808), in which each of the nine variations has its own, usually dance-, character (the whole set itself thus making up a Handelian type of suite),

---

[1] See Chapter Nine (iv).
[2] The theme is the Air from Handel's fifth suite in E major, later known as the 'Harmonious Blacksmith', although Kollmann makes some changes, including the substitution of his own trochaic rhythm - ˘ for Handel's iambic ˘ - .

Ex. 30.1: Kollmann, *Variations on an Air of Handel/Giga*, opening.

or a Courante as the fifth item of Cramer's *Divertimento nello stile antico* (1808), one is perhaps less prepared for Mozart's *Eine kleine Gigue* in G major, K. 574 (1789, see Ex. 30.3a), until one remembers his 'crash-course' in Handel around this time. The piece was inspired by the concluding *Gigue* in Handel's eighth suite in F minor (Ex. 30.2)

Ex. 30.2: Handel, Keyboard Suite No. 8 in F minor/*Gigue*, opening.

and written out *impromptu* in Leipzig for the court organist, Engel, which is why it is sometimes called the '*Leipziger Giga*'.

Ex. 30.3a: W.A. Mozart, *Eine kleine Gigue* K. 574, opening.

Mozart also appropriates Handel's inversion of the theme in the second half of the piece (Ex. 30.3b), though not as completely as the older composer.

Ex. 30.3b: K, 574, opening of second half.

Other experiments in this form include Moscheles's somewhat skittish Op. 58 (Ex. 30.4),

Ex. 30.4: Moscheles, Giga Op. 58, opening.

Valentin Alkan's *Bourré d'Auvergne*, Op. 29 (1846) and especially the rather gothic – or perhaps I should say 'Gothick' – gigue of his *Gigue et air de ballet dans le style ancien* Op. 24 of two years earlier.[3] Ex. 30.5a gives the two-part fugal opening and Ex. 30.5b a later *stretto*.

Ex. 30.5a/b: Alkan, *Gigue et air de ballet ... Op 24/Gigue*, opening and (b) *stretto*.

Such pieces, however, were, as I have suggested, usually in the nature of exercises in quaint charm or a 'romantic' harking-back to a vanished and more genteel age. The whole of Philip Cogan's Op. 2/6 Sonata of 1784 is along these lines, opening with an Adagio headed *Capriccio e Ad libitum* in C major followed by a competent, if a trifle straightlaced, *Fugue* in the parallel minor (Ex. 30.6a) finishing off with a Prestissimo *Giga* (Ex. 30.6b).

---

[3] Excluded here are such specialised directions as "In the old style" and its permutations, as these belong in Chapter Ten.

Ex. 30.6a: Cogan, Piano Sonata in C major Op. 2/6/ii, bb. 1–12.

Ex. 30.6b: Op. 2/6/iii, bb. 0–8.

Similarly archaising is the untitled third movement of George Jackson's Sonata in D major, Op. 4 (?1780), which seems to want to be a jig in the style of Arne but lacks the essential seamlessness that characterises good examples of this sublimated dance. In rhythmic and harmonic terms, bb. 7–8 as written are particularly unconvincing, and only a little less so if the second G were to be preceded by a natural accidental (Ex. 30.7).

Ex. 30.7: Jackson, Piano Sonata in D major Op. 4/iii, bb. 0–9.

Ex. 30.7 continued

Beethoven's *Bagatelle* in D major Op. 119/3 is headed 'à l'Allemande', whose 'country-ness' is suggested in the drones (Ex. 30.8) and the simplicity and layout in terms of repetitions – like the minuet-and-trio with a 'trio'-derived coda three times as long as any of the sections – bears comparison with the various sets of dances written for the public ballrooms, of which more later.

Ex. 30.8: Beethoven, *Bagatelle* in D major Op. 119/3, bb. 0–8.

I have already discussed the minuet (and its attributes) as a character piece for solo piano, but, as the only suite-dance to survive, still danced, into the early nineteenth century, it merits a few more words here. It was aristocratic and graceful, danced by a succession of individual couples, allowing them to meet and touch on occasion, and there was a strict observance of social precedence in the order of couples (beginning with the highest). Although the floor-patterns were well-defined and uncomplicated in themselves, they allowed scope for development and variation, and the interpolation of complex steps from other dances. As with so many of the courtly dances, there was a strong element of competition on all levels.

(ii) Country-dance (*contredanse*)

The bourgeois preference for informality, its emphasis on social intimacy and the centrality of the drawing-room as the hub of family life and entertainment was better expressed in its adoption of round-dances – allowing for closer proximity with simpler steps and with no need for the services of a dancing-master – than the more formal up-market display dances, and for these purposes the English country dance was ideal. Beginning with two unisex lines, its emphasis on figures – the patterns made by the participants – rather than complicated steps, allowed for various couplings and closer and more frequent contact and was not associated with any one class, mixtures being common (within reason, of course). The dance, which was eventually confined neither to the country nor to England, became popular throughout Europe in the eighteenth century, and was greatly welcomed in France where more graceful French steps were added and the line-format was changed to a round for eight. This form also enjoyed great popularity everywhere in Europe, and the French and English types were danced side-by-side: the name, *'contredanse'*, was a French phonetic corruption of 'country dance', and it was a welcome antidote to the more theatrical aristocratic court-dances, particularly to their most long-lived representative, the minuet. Such was the popularity of Musard's orchestra and its playing *contredanses* for public balls in 1835, that publishers were mainly interested in these and in *quadrilles*, and wouldn't accept even opera scores for publication unless they included material that could be easily converted to *contredanses*.[4]

The *contredanse* spawned simpler forms, such as the *cotillon* and the *cadrille* or quadrille, a foursome dance, as the name suggests, and various combinations were made into sets, composers often entitling them with the names of the presiding host or, more often, hostess, on the occasion of their first use and their title pages often carry the puff '... as danced at the nobility's balls' or 'in the houses of the aristocracy and nobility'. These sets of dance-music are entirely functional, their whole *raison d'être* is to accompany the thud of pump on parquet; the music is, consequently, of little value outside of this.

(iii) The Waltz

One dance, however, was to embody all the qualities which the *bourgeoisie* held dear and which characterised their social ascendancy. The waltz was informal, with no prescribed steps or patterns, danced by couples in intimate bodily contact whirling in and out of a floorful of others similar. Like so many other appropriations of the new class it came from below socially, belonging to a group of (mostly) triple-time dances known simply as *Deutscher* (German dances) featuring embracing couples and with names derived from words which, like *Walzen* itself, drew attention to the characteristic motion of twirling or twisting – *Dreher, Weller, Spinner* – and the generic term, *Ländler*, was originally a kind of slow waltz, but there was so much cross-fertilisation that it was eventually impossible to distinguish the types from each other, and 'Waltz' became the blanket term.

Because of the numbers of dancers, their peasant garb (including hobnail boots for the men) and the vigour of the movements – the female partner was frequently thrown over the shoulders of the male – the general freeness, and the association with inns and alcohol, these were outdoor dances popular in the Vienna Woods and suburbs in the *Heurigen*, the vineyard inns that retained their rural simplicity, despite their being close to the glitter of an already dance-crazy Vienna. It was not long before these happy abandoned dances infiltrated Viennese society.

The city already had a public venue for dancing, the *Redoutensaal*, consisting of a large and a smaller ballroom capable of accommodating some 3,000 people, and it is a measure of the huge increase in the popularity of public dancing that two more were

---

[4] In a review by the anonymous N. in 'Revue de la semaine', *Gazette musicale de Paris* 2/30, (26 July 1835) p. 252. Quoted in Cooper/PARIS, p. 144, fn. 84, p. 252.

added, in 1807 and 1808. The first of these, the *Sperl*, had a beer-garden and became a great haven for tourists, and an idea of the sumptuousness of the *Apollo-Säle* [*Apollosäle*], 1808, catering for 4,000 (or in some accounts, 6,000), included five great pillared dance-halls with crystal chandeliers and mirrored walls, together with a couple of dozen rococo-styled drawing rooms, three glass-domed gardens with waterfalls and swans and thirteen kitchens.[5] Similar establishments in other cities also included gaming-rooms and concert-halls.

Given the later hierarchisation of music into the almost immiscible categories of 'art' 'folk', 'popular' – or whatever terms different ages use – it can come as a surprise that composers, including the very greatest, were more than happy to supply dances, individually or (more commonly) in sets for public as well as private dancing. And the choice of this gay, elegant and, above all – under the iron hand of Metternich and his secret police – politically stable city to host the Congress of Vienna (1815–16) where the Good and Great of Europe gathered to apportion out their continent, was a great boost.

Between 1787 and his death four years later, Mozart's only duty as imperial *Kammermusicus* was to provide sets of dances – *Contredanses, Deutscher* (or *Teutscher*) and minuets – for the court balls, and he wrote seven sets in his last year alone, not counting individual items. After his death, it fell to Haydn to do the same, and Beethoven's first orchestral work in Vienna were the *Redoutensaal* Dances (1795). The young virtuoso Hummel was commissioned to compose the dances for the *Apollosäle* opening.

In the hands of Josef Lanner, and the Strauss dynasty, the waltz would sweep Europe in an unprecedented craze, and even a cholera epidemic in Vienna that claimed hundreds of lives every day, could not dampen the populace's enthusiasm and persuade them to stay at home. In a famous comic poem, Byron shows his ambivalence towards the waltz, while giving us a good picture of the dance's influence, especially in superseding the older types. It also shows the shock and outrage that the apparent abandonment and the unprecedented body-postures in public places provoked in most parts of Europe, and the view of it as what I have elsewhere described as choreographic rape:[6]

> Endearing Waltz! – to thy more melting tune,
> Bow Irish jig and ancient rigadoon.
> Scotch reels, avaunt! and country-dance, forego
> Your future claims to each fantastic toe!
> Waltz – Waltz alone – both legs and arms demands,
> Liberal of feet and lavish of her hands;
> Hands which may freely range in public sight
> Where ne'er before – but – pray "put out the light."[7]

This heady cocktail of music, movement and eroticism was experienced even earlier (1771) by Goethe's Werther during a ball in a country house:

---

[5] See Fantel/STRAUSS, p. 32.
[6] Carew/CONSUMPTION, p. 255.
[7] 'The Waltz: An Apostrophic Hymn' in Byron/WORKS, p. 143.

And when at last we changed to waltzing ... all the couples revolved around one another like celestial spheres ... Never have I danced so well! I was no longer a mortal being. To hold that loveliest creature in my arms and to whirl with her like the wind so that the surroundings disappeared – truly, Wilhelm, I swore to myself that a girl whom I loved, on whom I might have claims, should never be allowed to waltz with another man save myself, even if it would spell ruin for me.[8]

This dance-craze provided a very lucrative additional domestic market for composers, especially in arrangements of orchestral dances, which, following the models of Lanner and the Strausses, were grouped into little suites, complete with introductions and codas, and these arrangements would soon be supplemented by others specially written for the drawing-room piano.

The changing taste in this area can be seen neatly encapsulated in a tabulation (see Table 7 below) of the output of one of the most popular and admired piano virtuoso-performers in the early nineteenth century with whom I have already associated these dances, J.N. Hummel. Apart from a set of variations for piano and small orchestra and a military march, both from about 1798, the Op. 16 with which the list begins was his first full orchestral publication, written the same year as he was appointed Haydn's successor at Esterháza[9].

Opp. 24, 27 and 28 each have one piece headed [*à la*] *Militaire* (although there are many others that could quite easily be so headed); the last of the *Deutsche* of Op. 31 is called 'Die Cyclopen'; the fifth of the Op. 45 set is 'Alla Spagnuola'; and Op. 91 contains dances entitled 'La Chasse' and 'Alla Turca'. With the exception of the *Hungarian Dances* (Op. 23) all of which are in 2/4 time, the entire remainder are 3/4, except that the rather grand 'Intrada' of Op. 45 (not included in the 12 dances) is a 'Marcia con moto' in alla breve time. It is interesting that the variety of the dances – *Deutscher*, minuets, *ecossaises*, *Ländler* – has been reduced to waltzes and *polonaises* by the end of the list.

As an impression of the music, Ex. 30.9a gives the opening of the first *Hungarian Dance* in A major (Andante), Ex. 30.9b that of the third in F major,

Ex. 30.09a: Hummel, *Hungarian Dance* in A major Op. 23/1, opening.

Ex. 30.9b: *Hungarian Dance* in F major Op. 23/3, opening.

---

[8] *Die Leiden des jungen Werther* (The Sorrows of Young Werther, 1774) tr Elizabeth Mayer and Louise Bogan in The Oxford Library of Short Novels, vol. I (Oxford, 1990), p. 18. The extract is from Werther's letter of 16 June 1771, to the recipient of all the letters, his friend Wilhelm.

[9] He was certainly no novice, however, since the famous Trumpet Concerto was written at the end of 1803, though it had to wait 154 years for publication!

Table 7: Dance output of J.N. Hummel

Opus/ S No.[10]	Title	Date of composition	Remarks
16	6 German Dances & 12 Trios	1804	Pf arr. pub. c.1805
23	7 Hungarian Dances	1805?	Pf arr. pub. c.1806
24	12 Minuets & 7 Trios ('for the small *Redoutensaal* in the 1807 *Carneval*')	1806	Pf arr. pub. c.1807
25	12 German Dances with Battle Coda	1807	Pf arr. pub. c.1807
27	12 Minuets & Trios ('for the opening of the *Apollo Saal* 1808')	1808	Pf arr. pub. c.1808
28	12 German Dances Set 2 ('for the *Apollo Saal*')	1808	Pf arr. pub. c.1808
29	12 German Dances [& Coda] ('for the Great *Redoutensaal*')	1808	Pf arr. pub. c.1808
31	6 Minuets and 6 German Dances for the *Apollo Saal* Set 3	1809	Pf arr. pub. c.1810
S 80	*Contredanse* in B♭	c.1810?	unpub.
S 81	5 *Ecossais*	c.1810?	unpub.
39	10 German Dances for the *Apollo Saal* Set 4	1811	Pf arr. pub. c.1811
40	12 German Dances [& Coda] 'zum Römischen Kaiser'	1811	Pf arr. pub. c.1811
44	12 German Dances & Coda 'zur St. Catherinen Redoute'	1811	Pf arr. pub. c.1812
45	12 German Dances [& Introduction] for the *Apollo Saal* Set 5	1811	Pf arr. pub. c.1812
70	6 Polonaises[11]	?	Pf arr. pub. c.1815
S 104	12 Waltzes & Coda	1817	Pf arr. pub. c.1828
91	6 Waltzes with trios and a large Battle Coda	1820	Pf arr. pub. c.1821

and Ex. 30.10 the melodies of some of the Op. 27 set, which was for the opening of the *Apollosaal* in 1808. These are pleasant enough pieces, Hummel probably having learnt from Mozart (whose pupil he was) in this area, and there is some evidence of thematic cross-reference between member-dances – the rising arpeggios in Nos. 1, 2, 3 and 4, the turn figure in 5, 6, 7 and 8, and the dotted figure in 9 and 12. Bearing in mind the festive nature of most of the dances, and the restrictions on thematic variety and development, likenesses are bound to occur. This, however, is not an isolated

---

[10] The S is the supplementary number given in Sachs/CHECKLIST.
[11] The published piano arrangement describes them as 'Six POLONOISES FAVORITES'.

case. The only other dances for piano that Hummel wrote are presented as rondos, the 3 waltz-rondos of Op. 103 (*Grandes Valses en forme de Rondeaux*, 1823, pub. 1824: see below) and the 'Scotch Contradance-Rondo' Op. posth. 3 (pub. 1839).

Ex. 30.10: Hummel, *12 Minuets & Trios* Op. 27/1–4, openings.

The fact that many dances were for domestic dancing, the simple shape which, in the absence of a prescribed form, usually turned out to be some kind of alternating rondo, the lack of necessity of taking any kind of choreographic prescription (steps, figures, and so on) into account, the tendency to rely on foursquare phrasing and, of course, the more-or-less constant 'um-cha-cha' pulse outlining the harmonic framework, thus freeing up the melodic line – all of these made the waltz and related types ideal for improvising, and it is clear that this was the procedure in much of the extant music. We also have documentary evidence of it. During the Congress of Vienna (1814–5, when all was dancing[12]) the virtuoso violinist-composer Louis Spohr remembers an evening when Hummel improvised waltzes for the dancers.

> I especially remember with great pleasure one evening when he improvised in so splendid a manner as I never since heard him whether in public or in private. The company were about to break up, when some ladies, who thought it too early, entreated *Hummel* to play a few more walzes [sic] for them. Obliging and galant as he was to the ladies, he seated himself at the piano, and played the wished for walzes, to which the young folks in the adjoining room began to dance. I, and some other artists, attracted by his play, grouped ourselves round the instrument with our hats already in our hands, and listened attentively. *Hummel* no sooner observed this, that he converted his play into a free phantasia of improvisation, but which constantly preserved the walz-rhythm, so that the dancers were not disturbed. He then took from me and others who had executed their own compositions during the evening a few easily combined themes and figures, which he interwove into his walzes and varied them in every recurrence with a constantly increasing richness and piquancy of expression. Indeed, at length, he even made them serve as fugue-themes, and let loose all his science in counterpoint without disturbing the walzers in their pleasures. Then he returned to the galant style, and in conclusion passed into a

---

[12] One of the participants, when asked how the Congress was going, replied famously 'Il ne marche pas; il danse' ('It doesn't march; it dances', punning on the several meanings of *marcher*).

bravoura, such as from him even has seldom been heard. In this finale, the themes taken up were still constantly heard, so that the whole rounded off and terminated in real artistic style. The hearers were enraptured, and praised the young ladies' love of dancing, that had conduced to so rich a feast of artistic excellence.[13]

In the sad absence of any record of such improvisations, an idea of this kind of continuity and spinning-out can be gained from the second of the above-mentioned Op. 103 waltz-rondos (published as *III Grandes Valses en forme de Rondeaux*). Ex. 21.5 (in Chapter Twenty-One) shows the opening and Ex. 30.11 gives the material from some of the other sections; there is also much of the simple figural variation of material, which all the virtuoso-composers could do with their eyes closed.

Ex. 30.11: Hummel, *III Grandes Valses ...* Op. 103/2

Another way to guarantee continuity was more literal: many of the German-Swiss and Austro-German folk songs and regional dances had sections in continuous melody, a kind of *perpetuum mobile*, and once the style was grasped, it was easy to perpetuate the shapes. An 'À la Styrienne' by Hummel (the third of his *Amusements en forme de Caprices* Op. 105) shows the technique. The movement of the opening (see Chapter Twenty-One, Ex. 21.6) is rarely departed from and, for variety, is used in several parts, including the accompaniment: Ex. 30.12 gives music from the third section from the London musical publication *The Harmonicon* in 1824. This kind of texture also characterises Hummel's contribution to Diabelli's other set of variations.

Ex. 30.12: Hummel, *Amusements...* Op. 105/3, last section.

---

[13] Spohr/AUTOBIOGRAPHY, pp. 191–2.

Ex. 30.12 continued

An interesting variant of domestic dancing occurs associated with one of this composer's waltzes, the 'New Vienna Waltz, with three trios' which also appeared in *The Harmonicon* in 1824.[14] After the title, the following appears:

> In Germany the third Trio is sung by the Waltzers, and accompanied. It is intended for two Tenors and two Basses, and performed an octave lower than printed. It may be sung by four Sopranos, or even three will be sufficient; but in the latter case, the inner part, which is printed in small notes, must be omitted.[15]

Pl. 51 gives this trio and, clearly, wordbooks would not be necessary. This is surprisingly effective *in situ*.

Schubert, when on form, was very much a party-animal, and on many occasions played and improvised for dancing at the *Schubertiade*, the musico-social gatherings of friends devoted to his music. When two friends of his were married in 1826, Schubert improvised all the dance-music for the celebrations at the piano and, apparently, would let no one else play. This aura of improvisation carries over into his works in this genre; the early ones, and the Collection of 36 *Originaltänze* (or *Erster Walzer*) [Original Dances or First waltzes], D. 365, published by Cappi and Diabelli, are imbued with it. This was Schubert's first purely instrumental publication, composed between 1816 and 1821 and published as Op. 9 in 1821. The composition of some of the dances – the three *Atzenbrugger Tänze*, nos. 29–31 of the collection – took place during a holiday at Atzenbrugg with a party of his young friends, which was like an extended *Schubertiad* with dancing, concerts and charades. There is a watercolour (now in the Schubert Museum, Vienna) by one of the participants, the artist Leopold Kupelwieser of the group playing charades painted during this visit. The fact that the Op. 9 set – like several others – has a key-plan might also suggest an improvisatory provenance, or at least, the hint that they belonged to one 'sitting'. The same holiday provided some of the dances for his next publication of this sort also, his Op. 18 of two years later. This included 17 *Ländler*, and 9 *Ecossaises* as well as 12 waltzes, the *Ländler* being distinguishable by their folk-dependency.

Mention of Diabelli the publisher brings to mind Diabelli the composer (again) and entrepreneur, in the form of another waltz which he himself wrote as a theme for a set of variations, one by each of the composers living in, or visiting, Vienna at the time,[16] the whole set to be published as a kind of national monument to Austrian music. It is not insignificant that he chose what had become the Austrian national

---

[14] I can find no reference to this piece in Zimmerschied/CATALOGUE or in Sachs/CHECKLIST.
[15] *Harmonicon*, Vol. II, Pt. II, (1824), p. 46.
[16] See Chapter Fifteen, Ex. 15.19 for its first half.

dance as the vehicle, fast and racy, complete with syncopations, and a good sense of the keyboard built in. Schubert and Hummel were both contributors, together with the 11-year-old Liszt. Their contributions – and the work itself – have been noted in Chapter Fifteen.

As Schubert developed, so did his dance-music also and, although it never lost the feeling of spontaneity, the greater maturity and inclusion of more taxing matters for the listener rendered them less suitable for lucrative publication, in the eyes of the publishers. This was the fate of the 12 *Ländler* composed in 1823 (D 790), which, like so much of his music was published posthumously, in this case in 1864.

Schumann wrote that Chopin's waltzes were written for princesses to dance, though it is difficult to see why, unless the exuberance breaking through the 3/4 restraint is in some way analogous to the comparative abandon of the waltz in the context of a court ball. Apparently he

> agonised almost as much over the waltzes as over the ballades. They cannot be dismissed as hackwork, even the hackwork of genius. They are beautifully finished miniatures which accept the atmosphere of the salon and the conventions of the society dance and elevate both into a sophisticated art-form.[17]

There is certainly, in the early works, the feel of the 'live' dance, with the orchestral 'take your partners' and laying-down of the beat – see the openings repectively of the *Grande Valse Brillante* Op. 18 (1831, Ex. 30.13), that in A flat major, Op. 34/1 (1838, Ex. 30.14) or that in F major Op. 34/3 (1838, Ex. 30.15).

Ex. 30.13: Chopin, *Grande Valse Brillante* in E flat major Op. 18, bb. 1–20.

[17] Samson/CHOPIN, p. 122.

Ex. 30.14: Chopin, Waltz in A flat major Op. 34/1, bb. 1-28.

Ex. 30.15: Chopin, Waltz in F major Op. 34/3, bb. 1–8.

The exuberant swing of the dance is rarely absent even if muted (Op. 64/3, 1846–7, Ex. 30.16)

Ex. 30.16: Chopin, Waltz in A flat major Op. 64/3, bb. 1–9.

Ex. 30.16 continued

or even transmuted into an ecstatic swaying (Op. 34/1, 1835, (bb. 17ff. in Ex. 30.14 above and Op. 34/2, 1831, Ex. 30.17) or perhaps nostalgia (Op. 69/1, 1835).

Ex. 30.17: Chopin, Waltz in A minor Op. 34/2, bb. 1–11.

He also manages to transfer the choreographic gestures to the piano: there is a real feel of steps in Op. 18, for example, the foot-stamp propelling the bodies (Ex. 30.13, bb. 5ff.) and the turning motion of bb. 9ff and bb.17ff in the same example. Op. 70/1 (1833) has a similar effect (Ex. 30.18).

Ex. 30.18: Chopin, Waltz in G flat major Op. 70/1, bb. 0–8.

But, in spite of this, these pieces, 'too profound'[18] for the *salon*, were also never meant for the ballroom: it remains to the pianist and the piano itself to dance the music out, as indeed it does, in its way, the whole history of this period.

---

[18] Samson/CHOPIN, p. 128.

Select Bibliography

NB: Standard secondary literature has not been included, except where specifically relevant.

Adam/*METHODE*: Louis Adam, *Méthode de Piano* (Paris, 1802)
Adlung/*MUSICA*: Jakob Adlung, *Musica mechanica Organoedi* (Berlin, 1768, ed. J.L. Albrecht; facs. 1961)
Anderson-ed/BEETHOVEN: Emily Anderson ed. & tr., *The Letters of Beethoven* (London, 1961)
Anderson-ed/MOZART: Emily Anderson ed. & tr., *The Letters of Mozart and his Family* (London, 1938; 2nd edn, ed. M. Carolan and A.H. King, 1966)
Athenaeum: *The Athenaeum: Journal of Literature, Science, the Fine Arts, Music and the Drama* (London, 1827–1921)
Bach/ESSAY: Carl Philipp Emanuel Bach, *Essay on the True Art of Playing Keyboard Instruments* (tr. & ed. W.J. Mitchell, London, 1974; or. edn: *Versuch über die wahre Art das Clavier zu spielen*, 2 pts, Berlin, 1753 & 1762)
Barnum/HUMMEL: Marion P. Barnum, *A Comprehensive Project in Piano Literature and an Essay on J.N. Hummel and his Treatise on Piano Playing*. D.M.A. diss. (unpub.) (U. of Iowa, 1971).
Beaud/CAPITALISM: Michael Beaud, *A History of Capitalism, 1500–1980* (tr. T. Dickman and A. Lefebvre, (London, 1984 or. edn: *Histoire du Capitalisme, 1500–1800,* Paris, 1981)
Bent-ed/ANALYSIS: Ian D. Bent, ed., *Music Analysis in the Nineteenth Century*, 2 vols (Cambridge, 1994)
Berlioz/TREATISE: Hugh Macdonald, ed. & tr., *Berlioz's Orchestration Treatise: A Translation and Commentary* (Cambridge, 2002)
Blake/POETRY: William Blake, *The Poetry and Prose of William Blake*, ed. D.V. Erdman, 4th edn (New York, 1970)
Bone/GUITAR: Philip J. Bone, *The Guitar and Mandolin: Biographies of Celebrated Players and Composers* (London, 1954)
Boyd/SCARLATTI: Malcolm Boyd, *Domenico Scarlatti - Master of Music* (London, 1986)
Brancour/*INSTRUMENTS*: René Brancour, *Histoire des instruments de musique* (Paris, 1921)
Branson/FIELD: David Branson, *John Field and Chopin* (London, 1972)

Burney/HISTORY: Charles Burney, *A General History of Music from the Earliest Ages to the Present Period, to which is prefixed, a Dissertation on the Music of the Ancients* ed. F. Mercer (London 1935; facs. 1957; or. edn in 4 vols, London, 1776–89)

Byron/WORKS: George Gordon Byron, *The Works of Lord Byron*, Wordsworth Editions, (Hertfordshire, UK, 1994)

Carew/COMPOSER/PEFORMER: Derek Carew, *An Examination of the Composer/Performer Relationship in the Piano Style of J.N. Hummel* (Ph.D. diss., unpub., U. of Leicester, 1984)

Carew/CONSUMPTION: Derek Carew, 'The Consumption of Music' in Jim Samson, ed., *The Cambridge History of Nineteenth-Century Music* (Cambridge, 2002)

Carew/PARADIGM: Derek Carew, 'Hummel's op. 81: A Paradigm for Brahms's Op. 2?' (*Ad Parnassum*, vol 3, Issue 6, October 2005)

Castil-Blaze/*DICTIONNAIRE*: François-Henri-Joseph Blaze, *Dictionnaire de Musique Moderne* (Paris, 1821)

Charlton-ed/HOFFMANN: David Charlton ed., tr. Martyn Clarke, *E.T.A. Hoffmann's Musical Writings: 'Kreisleriana' – 'The Poet and the Composer' – Music Criticism* (Cambridge, 1989)

Chua/ABSOLUTE: Daniel K.L. Chua, *Absolute Music and the Construction of Meaning* (Cambridge, 1999)

Closson/PIANO: Ernest Closson, *History of the Piano*, tr. D. Ames, ed. & rev. R. Golding (London, 1974; or. ed. 1944, tr. Eng., 1947)

Cole/PIANOFORTE: Michael Cole, *The Pianoforte in the Classical Era* (Oxford, 1998)

Colt/COLLECTION: C.F. Colt with A. Miall, *The Early Piano* (London, 1981)

Cooper/PARIS: Jeffrey Cooper, *The Rise of Instrumental Music and Concert Series in Paris, 1828–1871* (Ann Arbor, 1983)

Cooper/REVISIONS: Barry Cooper, 'Beethoven's revisions to his Fourth Piano Concerto' in Robin Stowell, ed., *Performing Beethoven* (Cambridge, 1994),

Cramer-ed/*MAGAZIN*: Carl Friedrich Cramer ed., *Magazin der Musik* (Hamburg, 1783-6)

Cramer/STUDIO: Johann Baptist Cramer, *Studio per il pianoforte*, 2 sets (London, 1804 & 1810)

Czerny/PIANOFORTE: Carl Czerny, *Complete Theoretical and Practical Pianoforte School*, Op. 500 (Eng. tr., Vienna, 1839); or. *Vollständige theoretisch-praktische Pianoforte-Schule*, Op. 500 (Vienna, 1839)

Czerny/RECOLLECTIONS: Carl Czerny, 'Recollections from My Life' tr. E. Sanders (*The Musical Quarterly* XLII (1956); or. *Erinnerungen aus meinem Leben* (MS in the Gesellschaft der Musikfreunde, Vienna, 1842)

Czerny/IMPROVISATION: Carl Czerny, *A Systematic Introduction to Improvisation on the Pianoforte*, Opus 200 tr. A.L. Mitchell (New York, 1983); or. *Systematische Anleitung zum Fantasieren auf dem Pianoforte* (Cassel, 1836)

Dale/PIANOFORTE: Kathleen Dale, *Nineteenth-Century Piano Music* (London, 1954)

Davis/HUMMEL: Richard Davis, 'The Music of J.N. Hummel, Its Derivations and Development', (*The Music Review,* XXVI (1965)
Diderot & d'Alembert eds., *Encyclopédie, ou Dictionnaire raisonné des sciences, des arts et des métiers, par une société de gens des lettres* (Paris & Neuchâtel, 1751–65; supplements, Amsterdam, 1776–7)
Eigeldinger/CHOPIN: Jean-Jacques Eigeldinger, *Chopin: Pianist and Teacher,* tr. Naomi Shohet with Krysia Osostowicz and Roy Howat, ed. Roy Howat (Cambridge, 1986); or. *Chopin vu par ses élèves* (Neuchâtel, 1970)
Einstein/SCHUBERT: Alfred Einstein, tr. D. Ascoli, *Schubert* (London, 1951)
Fantel/STRAUSS: Hans Fantel, *Johann Strauss: Father and Son, and Their Era* (Newton Abbott, 1971)
Fay/MUSIC-STUDY: Amy Fay, *Music-Study in Germany in the Nineteenth Century* (Dover, 1965; or. Chicago, 1880)
Goethe/SELECTED: J.W. von Goethe, *Selected Verse,* tr. & ed. David Luke (London, 1985, or. pub. 1964)
Grove/MUSIC: *The New Grove Dictionary of Music and Musicians,* ed. S. Sadie, 20 vols (London, 1980)
Grove/INSTRUMENTS: *The New Grove Dictionary of Musical Instruments,* ed. S. Sadie, 3 vols (New York, 1983)
Hamm/POPULAR: Charles Hamm, *Popular Song in America* (New York, 1979)
Harding/PIANO-FORTE: Rosamond E.M. Harding, *The Piano-Forte: Its History Traced to the Great Exhibition of 1851,* 2nd ed. (Cambridge, 1978)
Head/ORIENTALISM: Matthew Head, *Orientalism, Masquerade and Mozart's Turkish music* (London, 2000)
Hellyer-ed./SEPTET-m: Roger Hellyer, ed., J. N. Hummel, *Military Septet Op. 114* (London, 1970)
Hiller/MENDELSSOHN: Ferdinand Hiller, *Mendelssohn: Letters and Recollections* (Cologne, 1874), tr. M.E. von Glehn from or. Ger. (Cologne, 1874)
Hobsbawm/REVOLUTION: E.J. Hobsbawm, *The Age of Revolution* (London, 1988, or. pub. 1962)
Holmes/RAMBLE: [Edward Holmes], *A Ramble Among the Musicians of Germany* (London, 1828)
Hüllmandel/CLAVECIN: Rita Benton, tr., 'Hüllmandel's Article on the Clavecin in the Encyclopédie méthodique' in the *Galpin Society Journal* xv (1962)
Hummel/PIANOFORTE: Johann Nepomuk Hummel, *A Complete Theoretical and Practical Course of Instruction on the Art of Playing the Pianoforte* (London, 1829); or. *Ausführliche theoretisch-practische Anweisung zum Piano-Forte-Spiel* (Vienna, 1828)
Jähns/*VERZEICHNISS*: Friedrich Wilhelm Jähns, *Carl Maria von Weber in seinen Werken: chronologisch-thematisches Verzeichniss seiner sämmtlichen Compositionen* [Thematic Catalogue] (Berlin, 1871)
Johnson/LETTERS: Samuel Johnson, *Letters to Mrs. Piozzi* (London, 1780)
Koch/LEXIKON: Heinrich Christoph Koch, *Musikalisches Lexikon welches die theoretische und praktische Tonkunst, encyclopädisch bearbeitet, alle alten und*

neuen Kunstwörter erklärt, und die alten und neuen Instrumente beschrieben, enthält. (Frankfurt am Main, 1802/1817)

Koch/*VERSUCH*: Heinrich Christoph Koch, *Versuch einer Anleitung zur Composition* (Rudolstadt & Leipzig, 1782–93)

Komlós/FORTEPIANOS: Katalin Komlós, *Fortepianos and Their Music: Germany, Austria, and England, 1760–1800* (Oxford, 1995)

Koszewscy-eds/KURPINSKI-m: [Pieces by] *Karol Kurpinski*, ed. Andrzej & Krystyna Koszewscy (Cracow, 1992)

Lamartine/*HARMONIES*: Alphonse de Lamartine, *Harmonies poétiques et réligeuses* (Paris, 1830)

Landon/CHRONICLE: H.C. Robbins Landon, *Haydn: Chronicle and Works*, 5 vols (London, 1976–80)

Langley-ed./FIELD-m: Robin Langley ed., *John Field: Nocturnes and Related Pieces* (London, 1997)

Latcham/STRINGING: Michael Latcham, *The Stringing, Scaling and Pitch of Hammerflügel built in the Southern German and Viennese Traditions 1780–1820*, 2 vols (Musikverlag Berndt Katzbichler, 2000)

Leppert & McClary/MUSIC: Richard Leppert & Susan McClary, *Music and Society* (Cambridge, 1987 rep. 1996)

Liszt/JOURNEY: Franz Liszt, *An Artist's Journey: Lettres d'un bachelier ès musique*, tr. and annotated Charles Suttoni (Chicago & London, 1989). The letters date from 1835–41.

Liszt/*SCHRIFTEN*, Franz Liszt, *Gesammelte Schriften* ed. L. Ramann (Leipzig 1880–83)

LLoyd-Jones/BLOOD: Hugh Lloyd-Jones, *Blood for the Ghosts: Classical Influences in the Nineteenth and Twentieth Centuries* (London, 1982)

Loesser/MEN: Arthur Loesser, *Men, Women and Pianos* (New York, 1954)

Matthews/BEETHOVEN: Denis Matthews, *Beethoven Piano Sonatas* (London, 1967)

Maunder/KEYBOARD: Richard Maunder, *Keyboard Instruments in Eighteenth-Century Vienna* (Oxford, 1998)

Milchmeyer/*PIANOFORTE*: J.P. Milchmeyer, *Die wahre Art das Pianoforte zu spielen* (Dresden, 1797)

Moore/MELODIES: Thomas Moore, *Moore's Irish melodies with Symphonies and Accompaniments by Sir John Stevenson, Mus. Doc. and Sir Henry Bishop* ('Popular Centenary Edition', Dublin, 1879)

Moore/WORKS: T. Moore, *The Works of Thomas Moore, Esq. accurately printed from the last original editions. with additional notes. complete In one volume* (Leipzig, 1826)

Morrow/CRITICISM: M.S. Morrow, *German Music Criticism in the Late Eighteenth Century: Aesthetic Issues in Instrumental Music* (Cambridge, 1997)

Moscheles/LIFE: Constance Moscheles, *Life of Moscheles by his Wife*, tr. A.D. Coleridge (London, 1873)

Musical Magazine, 1 vol. (London, 1835)

Nelson/VARIATION: Robert U. Nelson, *The Technique of Variation* (Berkeley & Los Angeles, 1949)

NZfM: *Neue Zeitschrift für Musik* (Leipzig, 1834 onwards)

Newman/PERFORMANCE: William S. Newman, *Performance Practices in Beethoven's Piano Sonatas* (New York, 1971)

Newman/PIANOS: William S. Newman, 'Beethoven's Pianos versus his Piano Ideals' *Journal of the American Musicological Society*, xxiii (1970)

Newman/SBE: William S. Newman, *The Sonata in the Baroque Era* (Chapel Hill, 1959, 4/1983)

Newman/SCE: William S. Newman, *The Sonata in the Classic Era* (Chapel Hill, 1963, 3/1983)

Newman/SSB: William S. Newman, *The Sonata Since Beethoven* (Chapel Hill, 1969, 3/1983)

Novalis/*GESAMMELTE*: *Novalis [Friedrich von Hardenberg], Gesammelte Werke*, ed. Carl Seelig (Zurich, 1945)

Parrish/CRITICISMS: Carl Parrish, 'Criticisms of the Piano When It Was New', in *The Musical Quarterly*, vol. XXX (1944)

Pazdírek-eds/*UNIVERSAL*: B & F Pazdírek-eds, *Universal-Handbuch der Musikliteratur* (Vienna, 1904–10)

Piggott/FIELD: Patrick Piggott, *The Life and Music of John Field 1782–1837: Creator of the Nocturne* (London, 1973).

Plantinga/CLEMENTI: Leon B. Plantinga, *Clementi: His Life and Music* (London, 1977)

Pollens/PIANOFORTE: Stewart Pollens, *The Early Pianoforte* (Cambridge, 1995)

Rees/CYCLOPAEDIA: Abraham Rees, *Cyclopedia: or Universal Dictionary of Arts, Sciences, and Literature*, 41 vols with 6 vols of plates (New York, 1810–24)

Reichart/DANCE S.B. Reichart, *The influence of eighteenth-century social dance on the Viennese Classical style*, PhD diss. (City U. of New York, 1984)

Reynolds/DISCOURSES: Sir Joshua Reynolds, *A Discourse delivered to the students of the Royal Academy, on the Distribution of the Prizes, December 10 1788, by the President* (London, 1789)

Ripin/KEYBOARD E.M. Ripin, ed., *Keyboard Instruments: Studies in Keyboard Organology, 1500–1800* (New York, 1971)

Rosenblum/PERFORMANCE: S.P. Rosenblum, *Performance Practices in Classical Piano Music: Their Principles and Applications* (Bloomington & Indianapolis, 1988)

Rousseau/*DICTIONNAIRE*: Jean-Jacques, *Dictionnaire de musique* (Paris, 1768)

Rowland/PEDALLING: David Rowland, *A history of pianoforte pedalling* (Cambridge, 1993)

Rowland/NOCTURNE: David Rowland, 'The nocturne: development of a new style' in Samson-ed./HISTORY

Russell/HARPSICHORD: Raymond Russell, *The Harpsichord and Clavichord: An Introductory Study*, 2nd ed. rev. H Schott (London, 1973)

Sachs/AUTHENTIC: Joel Sachs, 'Authentic English and French Editions of J.N. Hummel' in *Journal of the American Musicological Society*, XXV, (1972), pp. 203–39

Sachs/CHECKLIST: Joel Sachs, 'A Checklist of the Works of Johann Nepomuk Hummel' in *Notes*, XXX (1974)

Sachs/HUMMEL: Joel Sachs, *Kapellmeister Hummel in England and France* (Detroit, 1977)

Sachs/PIRATES: Joel Sachs, 'Hummel and the Pirates: The Struggle for Musical Copyright' in *The Musical Quarterly*, LIX (1973)

Samson/BALLADES, Jim Samson, *Chopin: The Four Ballades* (Cambridge, 1992)

Samson/CHOPIN: Jim Samson, *The Music of Chopin* (Oxford, 1994; 1st ed. 1985)

Samson/HISTORY: Jim Samson, ed., *The Cambridge History of Nineteenth-Century Music* (Cambridge, 2001)

Samson/VIRTUOSITY, Jim Samson, *Virtuosity and the Musical Work: The Transcendental Studies of Liszt* (Cambridge, 2003)

Schiller/*GEDICHTE*: J.C.F. von Schiller, *Schillers Gedichte* (Leipzig, n.d. [c.1830])

Schiller/*WERKE*: J.C.F. von Schiller, *Sämtliche Werke*, ed. Fricke, Göpfert & Stubenrauch, (Munich, 1958ff)

Schindler/BEETHOVEN: tr. I Moscheles, *The Life of Beethoven*, (London and Boston, 1841); or. *Biographie von Ludwig van Beethoven*, (Münster, 1840)

Schlegel/*KRITISCHE*: F.W. von Schlegel, *Kritische Ausgabe*, ed. H. Eichner (Munich & Vienna, 1967)

Schleuning/FANTASIA: Peter Schleunung, *The Fantasia*, vols 11 & 12 of *Anthology of Music* (Cologne, 1962)

Schubart/*IDEEN*: Daniel Schubart, *Ideen zu einer Ästhetik der Tonkunst* (Vienna, 1806)

Schumann/*JUGENDBRIEFE*: Robert Schumann, *Jugendbriefe*, 2nd edn., ed. Clara Schumann (Leipzig, 1886)

Shelley/DEFENCE: Shelley, *A Defence of Poetry*, (1821, pub. London, 1840)

Solomon/BEETHOVEN: Maynard Solomon, *Beethoven* (London, 1980; or. pub. 1978)

Sonneck-ed./BEETHOVEN: Oscar G.T. Sonneck ed., *Beethoven: Impressions of Contemporaries* (New York, 1926)

Spohr/AUTOBIOGRAPHY: Louis Spohr, *Louis Spohr's Autobiography* Eng. tr. (London, 1865)

Staël/*LITTERATURE*: Anne-Louise-Germaine Necker ['Madame'] de Staël, ed. Paul Van Tieghem *De la littérature considerée dans ses rapports avec les institutions sociales* (Geneva & Paris, 1950)

Sulzer/*ALLGEMEINE*: Johann Georg Sulzer, *Allgemeine Theorie der schönen Künste* [etc.], (Leipzig, 1771–4)

Temperley-ed/LONDON-m: Nicholas Temperley ed., *The London Pianoforte School* (New York & London, 1987)

Thayer/BEETHOVEN: Alexander Wheelock Thayer, *The Life of Ludwig van Beethoven*, 3 vols, (New York, 1921)

Todd-ed./SCHUMANN: R. Larry Todd ed., *Schumann and His World* (Princeton, 1994)

Türk/SCHOOL: D.G. Türk, *School of Clavier Playing*, tr. & int. Raymond H. Haggh (Lincoln, 1982); or. *Klavierschule, oder Anweisung zum Klavierspielen für Lehrer und Lernende* (Leipzig, 1789)

Virgil [Publius Vergilius Maro], *Eclogues* ed. Sir Roger Mynors (Oxford, 1969) or. 42–39 B.C.

Walker/LISZT I: Alan Walker, *Franz Liszt, Vol I: The Virtuoso Years 1811–1847* (London, 1983)

Walker/LISZT II: Alan Walker, *Franz Liszt, Vol I: The Weimar Years 1848–1861* (London, 1989)

Wolff/BACH: Christoph Wolff, 'New research on Bach's Musical Offering,' *The Musical Quarterly* 57/3 (July 1971)

Wordsworth/POETICAL: *The Poetical Works of William Wordsworth*, ed. Ernest de Selincourt, rev. Helen Darbishire, 5 vols, (Oxford, 1949–59)

Zimmerschied/*HUMMEL*: Dieter Zimmerschied, *Thematisches Verzeichnis der Werke Johann Nepomuk Hummels* (Hofheim am Taunus, 1971)

Index

Words, names etc.

The use of underlined type in page-numbers denotes that the indexed item is the subject of its own (named) section within the page-numbers given.

If an item is referred to in a footnote 12 on page 492, the index reads '492n12', and if it also appears on the same page, the index would read '492, 492n12'.

Page-numbers in parentheses means that the index item is referred to by implication. For example, mention of a Beethoven work without his name in a footnote would give rise to a parenthesised reference, '(231n4)' under his name, but the work mentioned would simply be indexed in the same way but without parentheses: '231n4'.

A page-number followed by 'q' means that the entry appears in an indented quotation on that page; if there are more than one, they are numbered 1, 2, etc. Thus the word 'ballad', which appears in the second indented quotation on page 394, is indexed as '394q2'. Again, if it also appears outside of the quotation on the same page, it will be additionally indexed as '394'.

A capital 'T' with a number appearing after a page-reference means that the item appears in the (numbered) Table on that page. 'Pl.' or 'Pls.' mean that the index item is the subject of a plate or several plates, with the number(s) of the plate(s) given.

Index entries should be treated as root-words which imply their various grammatical forms, so 'patent' also includes the references for 'patents', 'patented', 'patenting', 'patentee', etc. Conversely, to find references for 'bracing' in the index, look up 'brace'.

Performance directions ('*allegro*', '*con dolore*' etc.) are grouped alphabetically under 'directions' and are not given separate entries.

Musical (scored) examples are not given in the index for reasons of space, but there will be a reference to the page-number(s) on which they occur, either under the entry for the work itself or that for its genre (if individual works are not detailed).

Biographical information is not given for writers who appear in the bibliography.

An asterisked word means that it has its own entry in *The Companion to the Mechanical Muse: the Piano, Pianism and Piano Music, c. 1760–1850.*

Composers' entries

Works entered under composers' names are grouped under medium (Keyboard, Operas, etc.) and then in categories (Sonatas, Variations etc.) according to opus or other number, if known; otherwise they are alphabetical. If there is a small number of entries, works are either not categorised under media or genres, but simply listed alphabetically, or the individual items are not named, but occur on the pages after the composer's name.

Abbreviations

Where given, keys of works in upper-case represent major keys, lower-case minors; the musical symbols ♯ and ♭ are used rather than 'sharp' and 'flat'.

Am.	American	hn	French horn
arr.	arranged, arrangement	Hun.	Hungarian
attr.	attributed	Ir.	Irish
Aus.	Austrian	It.	Italian
bef.	before	Jap.	Japanese
bn	bassoon	kb	keyboard
Boh.	Bohemian	Lat.	Latin
Br.	British	Mor.	Moravian
c. (in dates)	around (time/date)	Neth.	Netherlandish
C (in a date)	century	ob	oboe
c c	clavichord	orch.	orchestra/orchestral
comp.	composer	pf	piano
cl	clarinet	pf2	piano duet
Cz.	Czechoslovakian	2pf	2 pianos
db	double bass	Pol.	Polish
Du.	Dutch	pub.	[first] published
ed.	editor, edited by	Sc.	Scottish
Eng.	English	str	string(s)
Flm.	Flemish	Swi.	Swiss
fig.	figure	UK	United Kingdom
fl	flute	va	viola
fl. (in dates)	flourished	vn	violin
Fr.	French	vc	cello
Ger.	German	Wel.	Welsh
hc	harpsichord		

INDEX

ABA form/shape [see 'form (musical)']
*Abel, Carl [Karl] [Friedrich (Ger. comp., 1723–87) 9
accompany, accompaniment, -al, accompanist xx, 105, 143, 205–9, 210, 262n1, 276, 282, 285, 306, 329, 384, 388, 419, 435, 460–530, 513, 527, 538q
   'ad lib.[itum]' instruments 460, 461, 476, 528, (529), 538q; Lied, -er, song [see 'song']; supplied for solo piano sonatas 262, 461, 475
Adam, Louis (Jean) (Fr. teacher, 1758–1848) 90–91, 91n5–6, 101
*'additional keys' 57, Pl. 6
ad lib.[itum] [see also 'accompany' and 'chamber music'] 173, 262, 361, 460, 461, 476, 528, (529), 538q, 543
Adlung, Jacob (Ger. musical theorist, 1699–1762) 6n13
aesthetic(s), -al xix, 42, 114, 148, 169, 268, 377
*Affections [Affects], Doctrine of (Affektenlehre) 134, 265, 269
Affektenlehre [see 'Affections, Doctrine of']
*Agricola, Johann Friedrich (Ger. comp., 1720–74) 5, 6n13
agriculture, Agricultural Revolution (160), 378
*Alberti, Domenico (It. comp., c.1710–40) 284
*Alberti bass 37, 92, 205, 206, (206–7), 269, 276, 283, 285, 461, 462, 492, 496
*Alkan [Morhange], (Charles-)Valentin (Fr. comp., 1813–88) 110, 213n19, 236, 543
   Solo Pf: *Bourrée d'Auvergne* 543; *Scherzo diabolico* 213n19, 236; *Gigue et air de ballet* .... 543; *Scherzo focoso* 236
   Pedal-Pf: 110
*Alla turca [see also 'Turkish'] 105–6, 264
*allemand(e) [see 'dances (named)']
*Allgemeine musikalische Zeitung [AmZ] (Ger. music periodical, 1798/9–1848) 266
Allgemeine Musik-Zeitung [AMZ] (Ger. music periodical, 1827/8) 59
Alps, Alpine 28, 401, 402, 403, 404
Ancient Style, 'old[en]' style [see 'antico, stile' and 'past']
Anderson, Emily (Ir. editor & translator, 1891–1962) 30n6, 202n13
Anglo-German action 33
animal(s) 28, (38), 137, 137q, Pls. 33–5, 146, Pl. 39, 170, 193, 195, 196, 197, 434, 516, 517, 526
antico, stile; all'antico; style ancien, Ancient Style 176–81, 178–9, 180–81, 182, 183, 543, 543n3, 544–5
*Apollo-Säle [Apollosäle] [see 'dance-hall']
Arcadia, -n, -nism 170, 175, 181, 377
archaic (style), archaism, archaising [see also 'past' and 'stile antico'] 176, 178–9, 193, 218, 383, 541, 544–5
aristocrat(ic), aristocracy 8, 38, (48), 97, 134, 137, 144, 146, (Pl. 39), Pl. 41, 169, (178), 228, 375, 376, 393, 402, 403, 470, 532, 545, 546
*armonica, (h-), (glass) 111, 411, 412
army, armies [see 'military']
*Arnaut de Zwolle, Henri (Neth. writer, late C14th/early C15th–1466) 3
*Arne, Thomas Augustine (Eng. comp., 1710–78) 177, 186, 370–71, 421, 451, 544
*arpeggione ('guitar cello') 468
arrangement (of music) xviii, 380, 459, 480, 538–40, 538, 548
*Artaria & Co. (Viennese publishers, 1765–1868; different from following) 140, 158n19, 419, 481, 533
Artaria, Matthias (Aus. publisher, 1793–1835; different from preceding) 158
*Athenaeum, The (Eng. musical periodical, 1827–1921) 169
*Athenäum, Das (Ger. literary journal, 1798–1800) 169, 436n23
attributes (human) in music 147, 153–7, 165
*Attwood, Thomas (Eng. comp., 1765–1838) 346
Auber, Daniel-François-Esprit (Fr. comp., 1782–1871) 413
audience(s), concert-goers, hearers, listener(s) xix, 12, (38), 187, 230, (302), 335, 336, 338, 340, 341, 345, 349, 351, 353, 364, 370, 373, 384, 392, 403, 415, 435, 436–7, 449, 460n2, 468, 475
Aufklärung [see 'Enlightenment']
Augener (Eng. firm of music publishers, 1853–1910) 180n12, 181
*Ayrton, William (Eng. editor of *The*

Harmonicon, 1777–1858) 394

*Bach, Carl Philipp Emanuel (Ger. comp., 1714–88) 6, 14, 16, 29, 31, <u>35–8</u>, 139, 139n3, 148, 263, 266, 286, 308, 324, 338, 363, 364, 365, 366, 367, 489, 530
   Solo Kb: 15, 31, 36, 39, 148, (148q3), 308
   Chamber: 324, 530
   Kb Concertos: 338, 340, 363, 364, 365, 366, 367
   Vesuch 15, <u>33–8</u>, 139n3
*Bach, Johann [John] Christian ('London Bach', Ger. comp., 1735–82) 8, 9, 14, 18, 29, 29q, (181), 263, 264, 265, 284, 286, 338–9, 339, 362, 366, 524, 530
   Solo Kb: 264, 265, 284, 338
   Chamber: 524, 530
   Concertos: (hc & pf) 284, 338–9, 362, 366
*Bach, Johann Christoph Friedrich ('Bückeburg Bach'; Ger. comp., 1732–95) 266, 338
*Bach, Johann Sebastian (Ger. comp., 1685–1750) 5, 6, 6q, 18, 35, 39, 60, 63, 135, 138–9, 139, 157, 169, 181–2, 182, 293, 306, 307, 320, 330, 338, 339, 365, 367, 372, 414, 459, 475, 479, 530
   Solo vn & vc: 475
   Solo Kb: 18, 39, 60, 63, 138–9, 182, 193, 293, 307, 320, 330
   Concertos: 365, 367
   The Musical Offering 6
*Bach, Wilhelm Friedemann (Ger. comp., 1710–84) 6, (181) 266, 338, 363, 365, 414, 530
   polonaises 414; Kb Concerto in g (attr.) 363, 365
*Backers, Americus (Du. kb-maker, ?–1778) 8, 10, 11, 57, 116
*Bahrent, Johann ['John Brent'] (Ger. pf maker in USA, *fl.* 1775) 10
*Balbastre [Balbâtre], Claude-Bénigne (Fr. organist, 1727–99) 9, 16, 155
ball (dancing), ballroom 226, 335, 373, 393, 413q, 545, 546, 547, 553
*ballade(s) 238n13
ballet 170, 216, 413q, 543
Barnum, Marion P. (Am. musicologist) 438n29
*Baroque (period) xx, 14, 53, 134, 135, 143, 150, 182, 186, 217, 222, 229, 262, 263, 265, 267, 269, 301, 306, 320, 338, 339, 367, 450, 459, 460, 477, 479, 489, 541
barrel organ [*see also* 'hurdy-gurdy'] xviii
Bartók, Béla (Hun. comp., 1881–1945) 338
*Bartolozzi, Therese [Theresa] (*née* Jansen) [*see* 'Jansen']
basso continuo [*see also* 'harpsichord'] 56, 380, 459–60, <u>Pl. 50</u>
bassoon [*see also* 'pedal' *and* 'stop'] 310, 475, 486
battle 133–4, <u>Pl. 31</u>, 185, 186n2, 549T7
*battle-pieces [*see* 'military']
Beatles, The (Br. pop group, 1956–70) 500
Bebung [*see also* 'vibrato'] 35, 36, 107
Bechstein (Ger. firm of pf makers, 1853–now) 120
*Beethoven, Ludwig van (Ger. comp., 1770–1827) xviii, 12, 19, 62, 63, <u>63–77</u>, 92, 107, 119–20, 119n7, 120–121, <u>123–30</u>, 139, 142, 143, 153, 158, 165, 165n25, 166, 166n26, 170, 175, 182, 185, 191, 193, 201, 202, 202n13, 220–3, 229, 251n6, 258, 265, 266, 273, 274–6, 283, 283n14, 284, 286, 291–2, 295, 296, 297–8, 301, 303–4, 304, 306, 307, 316–17, 318–20, 320, (321), 324, 325, 326, 326–7, 327, 327–8, 330, 331, 335, 337, 338, 340, 351–3, 353, 354, 356, 361, (361n3), 363, 365, 366–7, 368–9, 380, 381, 382–3, 408, 414, 421, 431n1, 432n3, 434, 434n11–12, 434–5, 435n15–16, 439, 448, 452–5, 455, 461, 464, 466–8, 470–72, 474, 475, 479, 480q, 480, 484–5, 485, 490–91, 492, 518, 526, 538, 545, 547
   Solo Pf: 54, 142, 158, 165, 193, 414, 439, 452–5, 455, 545; Sonatas 229, 448 ; late (<u>123–30</u>), 265, 283, 297, 307; Op. 2: 64–7, 68, 69, 71–3, 119–20, 220, 229, 265, 275, 276, 279–83, 284, 291–2; Op. 7: 220; Op. 10: 68, 69, 73, 143, 165, 220, 274, 284; Op. 13: 19, 69–71, 92, 120–23, 159, 165; Op. 14/1:139; Op. 22: 165, 221; Op. 26: 165, 185; Op. 27/2: 142; Op. 31/2: 295, 366–7; Op. 49: 284; Op. 53: 67–8, 73–4, 158, 165, 273; Op. 54: 221, 284; Op. 57: 283; Op. 78: 284; Op. 81a: 327; Op. 90: 165, 221–2, 284; Op.

101: 185, 297–8; Op. 106: 68, 69, 74–6, 123–30, 382; Op. 109: 221, 306; Op. 110: 158; Op. 111: 275, 284, 304; Variations 165, 303–4, 325, 326; Op. 35: 165, 305, 316–17, 320, 321, 326; Op. 120: 318–20, 321, 324, 325, 326, 327, 327–8, 330
  Chamber: 185, 382–3, 466, 485, 526; vc & pf 165, 466–8, 479; Pf trios 123, (123q), 470–72, 475, 480q; Pf Quartets 484, 485; Str Quartets 130, 470, 474; Op. 18/1:276; Op. 130: 158, 474; *Grosse Fuge* 158
  Orch.: *Redoutensaal Dances* 547; Overture: *The Ruins of Athens* 374; Pf Concertos 338, 340, 361, 363, 366, 368–9; No. 1: (361), 363; No. 3: 166, 340, 353, (361), 363, 365; No. 4: 76–7, 340, 351–3, 354, 356, (361), 363, 368–9; No. 5: 153, 327, (361), 361n3, 363, 369; Vn Concerto Op. 61: 421; Symphonies 335, 337, 470, 538; 'Battle' Symphony' 191; No. 3: 165; No. 6: 170, 175; No. 9: 38
  Vocal: *Fidelio* (opera) (325); 'Ich denke dein' (song) 526; Song-cycles: *An die ferne Geliebte* 490–91, 492, 518; *Gellert Lieder* 165
bell(s), bell-like 52, 90, 105, 109, 392, 438q, 496
*Bellini, Vincenzo (It. comp., 1801–35) 248, 526, 527, 537
*Benda, Franz [Frantisek] (Boh. comp., 1709–86) 489
*Benda, Georg (Anton) [Jirí Antonín] (Boh. comp., 1722–95) 266
*Benedict, Sir Julius (Ger. [Br. nationalised] comp., 1804–85) 53, 374, 413q, 413, 413n8, (413n11)
*Bennett, Sir William Sterndale (Eng. comp., 1816–75) 155, 197
Bent, Ian D(avid) (Eng. musicologist) 31n9
*Berger, Ludwig (Ger. comp., 1777–1839) 92, 366,
*Bériot, Charles-Auguste de (Bel. violinist, 1802–70) 431
Berlin (Germany) 59q1, 59, 376, 478, 489, 492; *Berlin *Lied* Schools 376, 489, 492
*Berlioz, (Louis-)Hector (Fr. comp., 1803–69) 108, 108n9–10, 190, 337, 370, 373–4, 374n10, 383
  Symphonie fantastique 190, 370, 373–4, 374n10; *Lélio* 374
  (Grand) traité d'instrumentation 108, 108n9–10
*Bertini, Henri(-Jérôme) (Fr. comp., 1798–1876) 42, 49, 100–101, Pl. 11, 213, 535
Best, W(illiam) T(homas) (Eng. organist, 1826–97) 420
*Beyer, Adam (?Ger. [Br. nationalised] kb-maker, 1774–?) 107
*bichord [see 'string']
*binary form [see 'form']
bird(s) 137, Pl. 34, 196, 197, 197q2, 330, 497, 498, 500, 515, 547
*Bishop, Sir Henry R(owley) (Eng. comp., 1786–1855) 400
Bizet, Georges (Alexandre César Léopold) (Fr. comp., 1838–75) 539
*Blanchet (Fr. firm of hc makers, 18th century) 10
Bland, Mrs (It. [Br. naturalised] soprano, 1769–1838) 303
Blewitt, Jonathan (Eng. comp., 1782–1853) 191
*Boccherini, (Ridolfo) Luigi, (It. comp., 1743–1805) 362, 362n, 466
Bochsa, (Robert) Nicholas Charles (Fr. comp., 1789–1856) 197, 262
*Böhner, (Johann) Ludwig [Louis] (Ger. pianist, 1787–1860) 153, (375)
*Boieldieu, (François-)Adrien (Fr. comp., 1775–1834) 91
bolero [see 'dance']
Bone, Philip (Eng. musicologist) 266n10
Boosey (Br. firm of music-publishers, founded c. 1795) [now Boosey & Hawkes] 533
*Bösendorfer (Aus. firm of pf makers, 1828–now) 11
Boyd, C. Malcolm (Eng. musicologist) 284
*brace, bracing Pl. 2, 12, 13, 30q2, 58, 62
*Brahms, Johannes (Ger. comp., 1833–97) 50, 140n5, 169, (178), 296–7, 306, 320, 321–2, 330, 336, 338, 348, 472, 480
Brancour, René (Fr. musicologist) 16n49
Breitkopf & Härtel (Ger. music-publishers, 1719–now) 420
'Brent, John' [see 'Bahrent']
*Broadwood, John (Sc. kb-maker, 1732–1812) Pl. 3, Pls. 12–13, Pl. 23 9, 10, 11, 12, 13, 14, 26 Fig. 7, 29, 56,

57, 58, 61, 62, 69, 103, 114, 116, 116q, 120, 124, 125
*Brodmann, Joseph (Aus. kb instrument maker) 11
*Browne-Camus family (Aus. aristocrats, patrons of Beethoven) 165
Bull, John (Eng. comp., ?1562/3–1628) 523
Buntebart, Gabriel (Ger. [Br. Naturalised] kb-maker *fl.* 1769–95) 8, 10
*Bunting, Edward (Ir. folk-song collector, 1773–1843) 379
*Burney, Charles (Eng. music historian, 1726–1814) 8, 9, 18, 29, 29n2, 29n4, 30, 262, 267, 460, 461, 465, 523–4, 525
*Burns, Robert (Sc. author and comp., 1759–96) 377, 379, 380, (386), 518
Burrowes, John (Freckleton) (Eng. comp., 1787–1852) 413q
*Burton, John (Eng. comp., 1730–82) 18, 194–5, 404

caccia, stile di [*see also* 'hunt'] 195
cachucha [*see* 'dance']
*cadenza [*see also* 'concerto'] 68, 76, 92, 211, (233), 247, 248, 280, 339, 351, 357, 361, 369
*Canon, The, canonic [*see also* 'Great men'] 169, 296, 330, 335, 338, 479, 480
*canon (device), -ic 218, 220, 253, 269, 296, 315, 319, 320, 332, 343, 345, 370, 435, 450, 464, 476, 496, 507, 510
*cantabile 44, 142, 293, 297, 324, 325, (363), 435, 440, 452
  -decorative style 293, 297, 324, 325, (363), 435, 440, 452
*canzonet 408
*Cappi, Pietro (Aus. music publisher, *fl. c.* 1790–1830) 552
*capriccio, caprice 155, 157, 326, 402, 419, 543
*carillon 9, 9n27, 109, 173, 173n10, 174
Carleton, Nicholas (Eng. comp., c. 1570-75–1630) 523
*casework [*see* 'piano, case']
*Castil-Blaze [Blaze, François Henri Joseph] (Fr. writer, 1784–1857) 301–2, 302, 302n2
'Celestial harp' [*see* 'stop']
cello, [violoncello], cellist 34, 108, 188, 191, 214, 237, 262, 310, 312, 346,

372, 380, 381, 382, 404, 412, 459, 460, 466–8, 468, 469, 475, 477, 479q, 485, 486, 480, 485, 500, 529
*cembalo, cimbalo 18, 19, (109)
cembalo stop [*see* 'stop']
chace [*see* 'chase']
chamber-concert xx
chamber music (general) 236, 241, 262, 267, 370, 380, 448, 450, <u>459–88</u>, 489, 525
  '*ad lib.*[*itum*]' instruments 173, 262, 460, 461, (475), 528, (529)
Chappell (Br. firm of music-publishers and pf makers, 1810–now) 533
character (person) 145q, 148q3, 150, 153, 394, 491, 524
character (musical general) 42, 48, 49, 77, <u>133–216</u>, 181q, 195, 242, 297, 302, 303, 309, 315, 322, 324, 326, 341, 349, 380, 394, 414, 541
*character-[characteristic] piece (xx), 77, (<u>133–166</u>), 136, 149, 297, 414, 442, 476, 518
*Charlotte Sophia, Queen of G.B and Ireland (1744–1818) 8, 9
Charlton, David (Eng. musicologist) 375n1
chase, *chasse* [*see also* 'hunt'] 193
*Cherubini, Luigi (Carlo Zanobi Salvadore Maria) (It. comp., 1760–1842) 374
child, -ren, -hood, -like [*see also* 'painting'] xviii, 101, 144, Pl. 36, Pl. 37, 167, 204–5, 248, 287, 335, 375q, 375, 378, 392, 480q, 531, 534, (535), (535q), (536), 536, 538, 540
*Chollet, Jean Baptiste (Marie) (Fr. singer, 1798–1892) 526–7
*Chopin, Fryderyk Franciszek [Frédéric François] (Pol. comp., 1810–49) xviii, 34, 42, 44, 45, 53, <u>80–83</u>, 95–8, 135, 140n5, 151, 151n14–15, 153, 182–3, 209, 234–6, 238, 239–40, 260, 275, 335, 343, 348, 353, 354, 355, 357, 358, 359, (359n2), 360, 364, 372, 408–9, 410–11, 414, 415, 416–17, 417–18, 419, 422, 422–8, 428–9, 440, 442, 442–4, 445, 455, 474, 517, 517n1, 527, 534, 538, 553–6
  Solo Pf: Ballades 553q; *Bolero* 410–11; *Etudes* 21, 42, 53, 80–83 182–3, 534; *Fantaisie* Op. 49: 455; *Mazurkas* 422–8, 428–9, 474; *Nocturnes* 95–7, 135, (209), 440; *Polonaises* 414–18; *Préludes* 80, 442–4; Scherzos 234–6; Pf Sonatas

239–40, 275; *Tarantella* 408–9;
Waltzes 474, 553–6
Chamber: *Introduction, Thème et Variations ... Moore* (pf2) 527; *Rondo* Op. 73 (2pf) 538
Orch.: Pf Concertos 343, 348, 350, 353–60, 364
Vocal: *17 Songs* 517
choreography, choreographic [*see also* 'ballet' and 'dance'] 220, (541–56), 541, 550, 555
Chorton ('choir pitch') [*see* 'pitch']
Chua, Daniel (Am. musicologist) 169, 169n4, 170n7–8,
*cimbalom 5, 429
*Cinti[-Damoreau] [*née* Montalant] Laure (Cinthie), Mlle. (Fr. soprano, 1801–63) 432
class(es) (social) 378, 379, 388, 393, 430, 532, 533, 534, 536
    aristocracy [*see* 'aristocrat']
    bourgeois, *bourgeoisie* (middle-class) 48, 118, 140, 146, 335, 375, 380, 384, 386, 389, 393, 432, 478, 491, 532, 533, 534, 536, 545, 546;
    peasant [*see* 'labour']
*Classic(s), -al (general) xx, 145, 146, 169–75, 291, 324, 343, (375), 376, 377, 383, 390n11
*Classic, -al, -ism (music) 53, 118, 118–23, 138, 142, 143, 177, 218, 222, 229, 263, 265, 266, 267, 287, 290, 340, 345, 348, 351, 359, 381, 431, 436, 459–73, 489, 533
    style 14, 16, 263, 267, 381, 436, 459–73, 489
*clavecin 17, 18, 19
*claveciniste(s) 118, 182, 464
*clavichord(s) 3, 6, 7, 10, 15, 16, 16q, 19, 20 Fig. 1, 28, 33, 35, 35q, 36, 38, 38q, 39q, 87, 88, 89, 103, 108, 109, 110, 112–3, 143, 157, 263, 324
    pedal-clavichord 110
*clavier(e) 30q2, 38q, 87, 112–3T2, 113n(3), 144, Pl. 26
*Clementi, Muzio (It. [Br. nationalised] comp., 1752–1832) 19, 19n60, 31–3, 34, 38, 40, 42, 48, 53, 57, Pl. 28, 63, 63, 91, (103), 116q, 118, 142, 143, 159–62, 168, 265, 267, 284, 321, 325, 333n5, 342, 353, 353n1, 396–99, Pl. 47, 399n9, 465, 465n4, 525–6, 526, 526n2–3, 530

Solo Pf: *Musical Characteristics ...* 53; *Variations on The Black Joke* 333n5, 396–99, 397T5, Pl. 47, 399n9; Sonatas 267, 353; Op. 1: 396–99, 397T5, 399n9; Op. 2: 19, 526; Op. 7: 284; Op. 12: 321; Op. 25:143; Op. 33: 57, Pl. 6; Op. 40: 31; Op. 50 159–62
Chamber: 465, 525–6, 530
Orch.: Pf Concerto 342, 353
Pedagogical: *Gradus ad Parnassum* 40, 42, 142, 143, 159
Closson, Ernest (Bel. musicologist, 1870–1950) 9n29, 17, 17n51, 17n53, 17n54
Coenen, Jan (Du. kb-maker) 111
Cogan [Coogan], Philip (Ir. comp., 1748–1833) 142–3, 143, 297, 362, 543–4
Cole, Michael (Eng. musicologist) 3n4, 5n11, 7, 7n17, 8, 8n20–22, 10n31–2, 61n20, 111, 111n16, 112n20, 116–17, 117, 117n1–2
Collard & Collard (Br. firm of pf makers, 1767–1971) 104, Pl. 26, 115
colour, -istic, (musical) [for piano, *see* 'piano sound'] 198, 237, 255, 309–14, 345, 377q, 470, 481, 503, 536, 536q, 540
*Colt Clavier Collection (UK) 56, 105, 107, 110, 114, 114n22, 115
*combination [keyboard] instruments [*see under* 'piano']
*compass [*see under* 'piano sound']
*compensation (compensated) (frame) [*see* 'piano frame']
composer-performer, -pianist xx, 140, 148, 334, 336, (353), 393, 431, (432), 437, 460
compositor [*see* 'printing']
*concert(s) 241, 380, 403, 413, 413q, 431– 432, 440, 451, 474, 534, 536, 539
    season 413q
concert-goers [*see* 'audience']
concert-halls, -rooms 12, 39q, 254, 335, 336, (337), 338, 393, 413q, 468, 478, 484, 526, 547
Concert Rondo 355, 370–73
concert-season [*see* 'concert']
*Concert Spirituel (concert-series in Paris, 1725–90) 9, 17
*concerto(s) (generally) 115, 218, 218n3, 241, 265, 284, 298, 334–74, 478
*concerto(s) for keyboard xx, 12, 18, 263, 287, 298, 334–74, 395–6, 404–5, 441,

441n37, 484
   arranged/published 338, (395–6), 484, 539; Concert Rondo 355, 370–73; *da camera* 404; first movt 339–61; last movt (finale) 338, 365–7, 404–5; middle movt 298, 338, 362–5, 395–6; *ritornello* [*see separate entry*]; soloist(s) 351–9, 441, 441n37
*concerto(s) (piano(s)) [*see* 'concertos for keyboard']
Concerto Grosso 367
**Concerts of Antient Music* (London concert organisation, 1776–92) 178
*conductor [*see also* 'leader (orchestral)'] 341, 459
*Congress of Vienna [*see* 'Vienna']
*continuo (-playing) [*see* 'basso continuo']
*contrapuntal [*see* 'counterpoint']
Cooper, Barry (Eng. musicologist) 76
Cooper, Jeffrey (Eng. musicologist) 337n1, 337n3, 546n4
copy, -ist (music) 517
copyright 251n6
Cornetton ('cornet pitch') [*see* 'pitch']
*Corri, Domenico (It. [Br. naturalised] comp., 1746–1825) 190, 193, 299, 395, 418
*counterpoint, contrapuntal 14, 49, 138, 184, 243, 250, 268, 269, 297, 301, 315–22, 303, 304, 309, 329, 343–4, (345), 347, 370, 435, 452, 461, 466–7, 507, 525, 550q
   canon [*see separate entry*]; imitation [*see separate entry*]; mock (spurious), *quasi-* 250, 315, 317; *passacaglia* [*see also separate entry*] 316; species 271, 315, 316
*Couperin, François (Fr. comp., 1668–1733) 13 (13n44), 36, 38, 153–5, 155, 157, 541
craft, craftsman, -ship 4, (16q), 114, 115, 116q, 266q1, 378, 408, 432, 433, 531
Cramer, Carl Friedrich (Ger. writer on music, 1752–1807) 16, 16n47, 148, (148q3), 148n12
*Cramer, Henri (?Fr. comp., *fl.* 1840) 190, 198, 212–3
*Cramer, Johann [John] Baptist (Ger [Br. naturalised] comp., 1771–1858) 31, 32, 42, 43, 48, 53–4, 109, 139, 142, 166, 173–4, 176–8, 181, 186, 190, 195–6, 227–8, 241, 249, 252, 304, 307–8, 322, 342, 343, 345, 349, 353, 358, 359, 360, 364, 395, 404–5, 446, 481, 535, 542
   Solo Pf: *The Chase* 195–6; *Divertimento nello stile antico* 542; *Dulce et Utile* 42–3, 53–4; *Harvest Home* 173, 174, 176, 186; *Kutusoff's Victory* 186; *Pensière musicale* 446; *The Two Styles* 176–7; *2 Characteristic Movements* 252, 241; Rondos: *All' amica lontana* 241, 252, 395; Pf Sonatas: Op. 20: 32, 304, 307–8, 322; Op. 25: 109, 227–8
   Orch.: Pf Concertos 360; No. 1: 342; No. 2: 349, 353; No. 3: 345, 404–5; No. 4: 358, 360, 364; No. 5: 360; No. 6: 174, 342; No. 7: 349; *Concerto da Camera* 404
   Pedagogical: *Instructions for the Piano Forte ...* 535, (535q); *New Studio* 142; *Studio per il pianoforte* 42, 139, 142; *Twelve New Studies* Op. 96: 166
Craw, Howard Allen (Am. musicologist) 190n4
*Cristofori, Bartolom[m]eo (It. kb-maker, 1655–1732) 4, 5, 6, 7, 7q, 8, 13, 22 Fig. 3, 25, 33, 56, 57, 88
   Pianos: (1720): 4, 7, (56), 88; (1722): 4, (56), 88; (1726) 5, Pl. 1, 22, (56), 57, 88
critic(s), critical, criticism, critique 140, 140n5, 148, 148n8–10, 149, 296, 335, 337, 373, 406n3, 436q1, 451, 468, 480, 516, 534
*cross-stringing, overstringing 61, 104
*Crotch, William (Eng. comp., 1775–1847) 223–4, 404, 446–7
*Czerny, Carl (Aus. comp., 1791–1857) 40, 50, 55, 101, 101n11, 135, 143, 155, 166, 185–6, 186, 190, 193, 215, 241, 242, 248–9, 249, 252, 301, 330, 343–4, 357, 363, 364–5, 366, 366–7, 369, 395, 401, 411, 413q, 434, 434n13, 435, 435n16, 447, 448, 448n5, 450, (450n11), 450–51, 535, 536, 537, 538, 539, 539q,
   Solo Pf: *Impromptu Sentimental* Op. 580: 212; *Invitation à la Danse* Op. 482: 536; *Souvenir à Schönbrun ...* 166; *La Reine, Nocturne* 143; *Toccata* 55; Rondos: 155, 175, 185–6, 193, 215, 241, 242, 248, 252, 301, 330, 395, 401, 411,

413q
Chamber: *Fantaisie ... 'I puritani'* (pf2) 537; *Grand Coronation March* (pf2) 538
Orch.: Pf Concertos etc. 343–4, 357, 364–5, 366, 366–7, 369; *Grandes Variations Brillantes* Op. 236: 186, 190; *Le Retour de Kalisch* 186
Pedagogical: *Amusemens de la jeunesse ... 535; L'Art de préluder* 448; *L'art du chant ...* 539; *Character Etudes* 135; *Pianoforte School* 101, 101n11, 535; *Etudes pour la jeunesse ...* 535; *Grand Characteristic Studies* 135; *24 Irish Airs as Studies* 535; *Les Jeunes Militaires* 536; *Kinderklavierschule* 535; *Das moderne Klavierspiel* 535; *New School of Velocity* 536, 538; *24 Petites Pièces en Rondeaux et Variations ...* 535; *Preliminary School of Velocity* 535; *100 Royal Bouquet Valses ...* 536; *School of Embellishments ...* 535; *School of Expression* 535; *School of Legato and Staccato* 535; School of Velocity 40, 535; *School of Virtuo*sity 535; *Schule des Fugenspiels* 535; *Systematic Introduction to Improvisation ...* 447–8, 448n5, 450–51, 450n11

*Dalberg, Friedrich Hugo, freiherr von (Ger. comp., 1760–1812) 529
D'Almaine & Co. (Br. firm of music publishers and instrument makers, c. 1834–60; originally Goulding & Co.) 104, 242, 413
*damper(s), damping [*see also* 'pedal, sustaining'] 5, 21, 23, 27 Fig. 8, 31, 86, 120, 142
dance(s), dancing (general) xx, 5, 115, 135, 218, 218n4, 223, 228, 284, 373, 384, (406–28), 413–28, 517, 527, 529, 532, 541–56
 -hall [*see separate entry*]; -marathons (Vienna etc.) 420; national [*see also separate entry*] 406–28, 517; regional 428, 551
 *-suite [for individual dances *see* 'dance(s) (named)'] 541–5
dance(s) (named) 406–9, 413–28, 422–8
 allemande 217, 405, 535, 541, 545; *bolero* 409–11; *bourrée* 541; *cachucha* 413, 413q; *cadrille* [*see* 'quadrille' in this entry]; *contredanse* 545–6, 547, 549T7, 550; *cotillon* 546; country-dance 223–4, 404, 545–6, 547q; *courante* 217, 541, 542; 'Danza de Village' 411; *Deutscher* [*Teutscher*] 529, 546, 547, 548, 549T7; *Dreher* [*see* 'waltz' in this entry]; *écossaise* 405, 548, 549T7; *fandango* 409, 411, 412–13; *galop* 535; *gavotte* 541; *gigue, giga* 217, 541, 542–3, 543, 543–4, 544, 544–5; *guaracha* 411; *habanera* 411; hornpipe 412; jig 217, 397, 544–5; *kujawiak* 422, 426; *Ländler* [*see* 'waltz' in this entry]; *mazur(ek)* 422; *mazurka (mazourka)* 163, 422–8; minuet, menuetto etc. [*see separate entry*]; *oberek, obertas* 422, 424; *polacca* (*tempo* di) 45, 302q, 366, 405, 412, 414, 419, 421, 438q; *polka* 413–22; *polonaise* 285, 327, 405, 410, 412, 413–22, 422, 438q, 529, 548, 549T7; 'Polonoise' 418, 549n11; *polska* 422; *quadrille* (quadrille) 420, 535, 546; quickstep (quick step) 191; reel 420, 547q; -rhythm 428; rigadoon 547q; round- (*ronde*) 535; *saltarello* 155, 406, 406n3; *sarabande* 217, 222, 541; *seguidilla* 409; *seguilla* 411; *siciliana, siciliano, sicilienne* 217, 264, 285, 369, 412, 477, 498; *sicilienne* [*see* 'siciliana' in this entry]; *Spinner* [*see* 'waltz' in this entry]; strathspey 420; suite [*see separate entry*]; *tarantella* 406–9, (406n3); *tedesco, tedesca* 186, 474; *valse* (*Valse*) [*see* 'waltz' in this entry]
 waltz 186, 240, 330, 395, 401–2, 412, 419, 535, 546–56; *Dreher* 546; *Ländler* 529, 546, 548; shock of 547; *Spinner* 546; *Weller* 546
 Weller [*see under* 'Waltz' in this entry]
*Dance, William (Eng. comp., 1755–1840) 395, 526
dance-hall(s) [*see also* 'ball, -room'] 373, 546–7
 Apollo-Säle [*Apollosäle*] (Vienna) 547, 549T7, 549; Redoutensaal (Vienna) 373, 546, 549T7; *Sperl* (Vienna) 547
'Danza de Village' [*see* 'dance']
Davis, Richard (Eng. musicologist) 449n10
*Day, John (Eng. soldier and ? pf maker, *fl.* 1816) 412

dedication(s) 41, (41n27), 153, 159, 165–6, 271, 272, 395, 445
*Del Mela, P. Domenico (It. kb-maker, *fl.* 1739) 5
Deutscher [*see* 'dance, (named)']
*Diabelli, Anton (Aus. comp., 1781–1858) 318, 330, 422, 551, 552
Dibdin, Charles (Eng. comp., 1745–1814) 9
didactic, -ism [*see also* 'pupil', 'student' *and* 'teach (music)'] 49, 134, 136, 165n23, 198, (249), 459, 531–40,
d'Indy [*see* 'Indy, d'']
direction(s) (performance) 140, 144, 147–9, 466
  accelerando 123; *accento* 149; *adagio* 363, 466; *affetto, con* 142, 155; *affettuoso* 142, 149; *agitando* 149; *agitato* 142, 149; *allegramente* 142; *allegresse* 199; *allegrissimo* 142; *andante* 363; *andantino* 177, 528; *anima, anime, con* 159, 164, 419; *animando* 149; *amore, con* 149; *amoroso* 142, 149, 285, 287; *appassionato* 124, 142, 147, 149; *arpa, quasi* 149; *arpeggiato* 149; *auflebend* 158; *Ausdruck (mit), ausdrucksvoll* 490; *brillante* 306, 420, 466; *burla, alla* 232; *calando* 143, 149; *calmato* 149; *cantabile* 142, 186, 202, 285, 293, 324, 325, (363), 435, 440, 452; *cantando* 408; *commodo* 528; *deciso* 414; *deliberando* 159; *delicatamante* 149; *delicatezza, con* 142, 149; *delicatissimamente* 142; *delicato* 142; *dignità, con* 149; *disperazione, con* 149, 159; *dolce* 149, 186, 327, 414; *dolcissimo* 149; *dolente* 158; *dolore, con* 150; *duolo, con* 186, 419; emotionalised 144; energetic 180q1; *energico* 142, 149, 354; *espressione* [*con*] 142, 149, 174, 292, 398; *espressivamente* 149; *espressivo* 142, 177, 202, 490; *fièrement* 143; *flebile* 149; *forzato* 228; *furia, con* 159; *furioso* 215; *gefühlvoll* 148; generic 147; *geschwind(er)* 491; *giocoso* 195; *giusto (con)* 228; *giusto (tempo)* 139, 176, 422; *grandezza, con* 149; *grandioso* 200; *grandissima, -e* 149; *grave* 228, 528; *grazia, con* 149; *grazioso, gratioso* 142, 148q2, 163, 177, 229, 327, 367, 420; *gusto, con* 149; *hongrois(e), all', à l'* 366; *innocente* 142, 165, 173;
  klagend 158; *lamentando* 159; *lamentoso* 166; *languendo* 149; *languente* 159; *larghetto* 190, 202, 363, 438q; *largo* 190, 363; *lebhaft* 185; *legato* 31, 45, 123, 186, 281, 325, 448; *lento* 149, 418; lively 148q2; *maestoso* 142, 149, 190, 275, 327, 414; *mancando* 149; *marcato, -a* 149; *marcia, alla* 149, 185, 186, 327, 548; *marschmässig* 185; *martiale* 190, 418; *meditando* 159; *melanconia, con* 164; *melancolico, mélancolique* 163, 418; *mesto* 143; *mezza voce* 49q; *misurata, -o* 149; *moderato* 414; *moderatissimo* 142; *moderazione, con* 149; *morendo* 143, 149; *naïf, naïveté, avec* 165; *ordinario (tempo)* 139; *parlando* 149; *passione, con* 149; *patetico, pathetico* 143, 147, 159, 163, 213, 354; *perdendo le forze* 158; *perdendosi* 109, 143, 149; *più tosto* 224; *plangendo* 149, 418; *pomposo* 233, 414; ... *possibile* (with other directions) 149; *precipitato* 149; *precisione, con* 149; *prestissimo* 142, 543; *presto* 242; *pulito* 149; *religioso* 211, (213), 213; *risoluto* 123, 124, 411; *ritardando (rit)* 123; *ritenuto (rit)* 411; *rubato* 98, 150; *rührend* 148; *rustico* 173, 186; *schwermütig* 148; *semplicamente* 149; *semplice* 142; *sentimentale* 163, 165; *sentimento (con)* 124; *sforzando* 470; *smania, con* 149; *smorzando, smorz.* 128, 143, 149; *soave* 142; *solemno, solenelle* 190; *somma ..., con* (with other directions) 149; *sostenuto* 89, 95, 149, 159, 186, 228, 528; *sotto voce* 49q, 149, 324, 422, 428; specific (more) 147; *spiritoso* 142, 186; *spirituoso* 174; *staccato* [*see also* separate entry] 281, 479; *strepitoso* 142; *stringendo* 491; *Tedesca, à la* [*see* 'dance']; *teneramente* 149; *tenero* 149; *tormento, con* 149; *tragico, -a* 159; *tranquillo* 142, 149, 174, 479; *vacillando* 149; *veemente* 149; *vif* 165; *vivace* 185; *vivacessimo* 142; *vivacissimo* 142; *vivo (con)* 164; *ziemlisch* 490; *zingarese, alla* 366
dissemination of music 531–40
*Dittersdorf, Carl Ditters von [Ditters, Carl] (Aus. comp., 1739–99) 170
divertimento, divertimenti, divertissement 186, 226, 464, 526, 527, 529

*Doctrine of Affections, (*Affektenlehre*) [*see* 'Affections, Doctrine of']
*Döhler, Theodor (von) (Aus. pianist, 1814–56) 53, 363
domestic [*see also* 'market'] [*for* piano *see under entry*] 6, 12, 13, 28, 56, 57, 103, 104, 110, 134, 147, 158, 226, 241, 265, 266, 296, 297, 376, 420, 449, 450, 523, 526, 532, 537, 548, 550, 552
Donaldson, John (Sc. comp., ?–1865) 298–9
Donizetti, Gaetano (It. comp., 1797–1848) xviii
double bass 188–9, 237, 310, 337, 346, 355, 459, 485, (486)
    inclusion of in chamber music 188–9, 237, 310, (459), 485–6
*double-escapement action [*see under* 'piano, action']
*down-striking [*see* 'piano, action']
*Dragonetti, Domenico (It [Br. naturalised] bass-player, 1763–1846) 337
drawing-room (drawing room), parlour xix, xx, 10, 114, 147, 204, 290, 306, 375, 379. 380, 383, 384, 393, 400, 413q, 437, 450, 478, 480, 484, 486, 532, 538, 545, 547
dream(s), -y, -ing 150, 151, 168, 198–205, 210, 394q1, 497, 498
*Drechsler, Johann (Boh. comp., 1782–1852) 326
drum(s) 105, 106, 107, (108), 184, 191, 192, 310, 346, 355, 366
'drum-bass' (*see* '*Trommelbaß*' *and* 'Mannheim, orchestra')
due corde [*see* 'pedal']
**dulce melos* 3
*dulcimer [*see also* 'Hackbrett' *and* '*Pantalon*'] 3, 3n2, 5, 429
*Dulcken, Louis (Fl. kb-maker, *fl.* 1785–1816) 87
Dunhill, Rosemary (Eng. musicologist) 8n21
*Duport, Jean-Pierre *l'aîné* (Fr. cellist, 1741–1818) 466
*Dussek, Jan Ladislav (Boh. comp., 1760–1812) 33, 56, 118, 142, 166, 172–3, 174, 190, 190n4, 193–4, 210, 224–5, 252, 262, 284, 328, 339, 341, 342, 345, 349, 350, 353, 361, 363, 365, 369, 527, 530
    Solo Pf: *La Chasse* 193–4; *La consolation* 210–11; *Fantaisie* in F 172–3, 190; *Rosline Castle* ... 328; Sonatas: 'The Farewell' 224–5; Op. 25: 193; '*Elégie harmonique ...*' 166; Op. 44: 284–5; in B♭ 174
    Chamber: 530; Sonata (pf2) 527
    Orch: Pf/hc Concerti: Op. 17: 353, 361; Op. 22: 345, 349, 353; Op. 27: 363, 369; Op. 29: 341; Op. 30: 339, 340; Op. 40: 187, 252, 339; Op. 49/50: 350, 363, 365; Op. 70: 142

Eckard [Eckardt, Eckart], Johann Gottfried (Ger. comp., 1735–1809) 18, 338
eclogue (*ecloga, ekloge*) 171, 171n9, 173
**écossaise*(s) [*see* 'dance, named']
Edge, Dexter (Am. musicologist) 9n24
education, educative [*see also* 'didactic', 'pupil' *and* 'student'] 193, 375, 531–40,
Ehrlich (Ger. kb-maker, *fl. c.* 1840) 104
Eigeldinger, Jean-Jacques (Fr. musicologist) 35n13, 97n8, 104n4
Einstein, Alfred (Aus. [Am. naturalised] writer, 1880–1952) 472, 472n8
Elgar, Edward (Eng. comp., 1857–1934) 130, 130n15, 386
*Eliason, Edward (?Br. comp., *fl.* early C19th) 50
*Elsner, Józef Antoni Franciszek (Pol. teacher of Chopin, 1769–1854) 414, 420
emotion(s), -al, -ism 135, 137–43, 143, 144, 147, 148, 149, 151, 157–65, 196, 256, 263, 265, 288, 296, 335, 355, 370, 386, 415, 416, 432, 476, 481, 484, 500, 518, 541
**empfindsamer Stil* [*see* '*Empfindsamkeit*']
**Empfindsamkeit* (*empfindsamer Stil*) [*see also* 'C. P. E. Bach'] 14 , 37, 143
Engel, K. I (Ger. organist, *fl.* 1789) 542
*'English' Piano School [*see* 'London Piano School']
'English (single) action' [*see* 'piano, action']
engrave, engraving (of music) [*see* 'printing']
*Enlightenment (*Aufklärung*), The 133, 134, 145, 146, 167
entrepreneur, -ial, -ship 118, 167, 296, 337q
equal temperament [*see* 'temperament']
*Erard, Pierre (Fr. pf maker, 1796–1855), nephew of S. Erard 12, 13, 27 Fig. 8, 33, 34, 35, 81, 114, 120, (438q)

*Erard, Sébastien (Fr. pf maker, 1752–1831) 10, 12, 33, 107
*escapement [see under 'piano, action']
Escudier, Léon (Fr. firm of music publishers, c. 1842–c. 1876) 97
*Esterházy Family (and members of) (141, 141n10), 185
*étude (general) xix, 39–53, 306, 416, 531, 538, 538q
Etüde (Ger.) (general) [see also 'Studie']
Eulenberg (Ger. firm of music-publishers, 1874–now) 533
Evans, R W (Eng, comp., fl. early C19th) 411, 412
*Ewer & Co. (Br. firm of music-publishers, fl. early C19th) 539
extra keys [see 'keys, additional']

*fandango [see 'dance']
*fantaisie, Fantasie [see 'improvisation']
*fantasy, Fantasy etc. [see also 'improvisation'] 50, 172–3, 185, 223, 252, 370, 399, 448, 449, 450, 451–5, 529
Fantel, Hans (Aus. musicologist) 547n5
fashion, -able, in vogue xix, 8, 10q, 116, 145q, 146, 158, 226, 302, 335, 360, 413q, 478
*Fay, Amy (Am. pupil of Liszt) 437, (437q2), 437n27
female, feminine [see 'woman']
*Ferrini, Giovanni (It. kb-maker, ?–1758) 5
*Fétis, François-Joseph (Bel. musicologist, 1784–1871) 52–3
fiddle, fiddler(s), 134, 337
*Field, John (Ir. comp., 1782–1837) 12, 31, 43, 44, 50, 92–5, 115, 115n25, 118, 175, 187, 205–09, 241, 249, 259, 272–3, 303, 325, 334, 335, 339, 342, 348, 350, 357, 359, 360, 361, 363, 364, 369, 374, 395–6, 440, 481
    Solo Pf; Introduction ... 'Come Again, Come Again' 101–102; Pastorale in A (Nocturne 17A; piano quintet) 93–4; Le midi 241; Sonatas 272–3; Nocturnes 93, Pl. 10, 94–5, 175, 205–09, 364, 440; Variations 92, 303, 325; Exercices 44
    Orch.: Pf Concertos 364; No. 1: 342, 343, 350, 395–6; No. 2: 348, 350, 357, 360; No. 3: 339, 343, 348, 350, 359, 360; No. 4: 363, 369; No. 5: 175, 361, 374; No. 6: 187, 342, 363; No. 7: 93, 115
*Figuralvariationen (figural variations) [see 'variation']
*figured bass [see 'basso continuo']
*finger(s), -ing (digit, -al) 16q1, 16q2, 36–7, 38, 38q, 39, 45, 49q, 61, 180q2–81q1, 181, 183, 302q, 515, 516
'Flora' (music teacher in London) 198, 540, Pl. back cover
Flotow, [Baron] Friedrich Freiherr von (Ger. comp., 1812–83) xviii
flower(s) 134, 146, Pl. 32, 198, 395q, 492, 493, 496, 497, 499, (540), Pl. back cover
    lily, Lilien 395q, 493; little, Blümelein 496; music written in the form of [see also 'Flora'] 540, Pl. back cover; rose(s) 198, Pl. 32, 314
*folk, -sy, -like [see also 'vernacular'] xix, 167, 185, 193, 212, 216, 248, 297, 302, 365, 375–430, 449, 502, 534, 547, 551
Fontana, Julian (Pol. writer, amanuensis to Chopin, 1810–65) 517
Forkel, Johann Nikolaus (Ger. musicologist 1749–1818) 6
form, shape (musical) 135, 267, 301, 363, 372, 450, 477
    ABA (229), 363; additive 301; binary 14, 248, 250, 267, 268, 301, 338; sonata- [see separate entry]; ternary 267, 268
frame [see 'piano']
Franck, César (Auguste-Jean-Guillaume-Hubert) (Bel. [Fr. naturalised] comp., 1822–90) 302
Franklin, Benjamin (Am. Statesman, 1706–90) 411
*Frederick the Great [Frederick II of Prussia] (Ger. emperor, 1712–86) 6, 112, 376
French Overture (ouverture) (style) 138, 176, 315, 320
French Revolution xvii, 134, 147, 167, 228, 377,
fret(s), (-ted) 468
Freystädtler, Jacob (Aus. comp., 1761–1841) 326
*Friederici [Friedrichs], Christian Ernst (Ger. kb-maker, 1709–80) 103
Frühromantik, -er 169
*Fuchs, Aloys (Aus. musicologist, 1799–1853) 539q
fuga, fugato [see 'fugue']
fughetta [see also 'fugue'] 182, 319, 321

*fugue, *fuga*, fugal 53, 73, 123, 124, 157, 182, 183, 267, 274, 296, 297, 319, 320, 321, 324, 326, 332, 344–5, 435, 438q, 450n11, 466–7, 486, 530, 543, 543–4, 550q
fundamental [*see* 'harmonics']
*Fux, Johann Joseph (Aus. music theorist, 1660–1741) 532

galante, style 14, 16, 37, 143, 177, 390
*galant style [*see* '*galant, style*']
*Gallenberg, (Wenzel) Robert, Graf von (Ger. comp., 1783–1839) 153, 166
*Galuppi, Baldassare (It. comp., 1706–85) 284
*Ganer, Christopher (Ger. kb-maker, *fl.* 1774–1809) 114
Gebrauchsmusik 301
*Geib (Ger. [Br. & Am. naturalised] firm of pf makers and music publishers, last half of C18th–first half of C19th) 13
Geigenwerk xviii, xviiin2, 3, 3n1, 108
*Gelinek [Gelineck, Jelinek], Joseph ['Abbé'] (Cz. comp., 1758–1825) 301, 403–4
gender [*see also* 'woman' *and* 'man'] 154, 431
genouillère(s) 18, (23), <u>86–7</u>, 105, 107, (108q)
*Gerber, Ernst Ludwig (Ger. music scholar, 1746–1819) 441, (441q), 441n38
gesture 15, 218, 256, 281, 288, 360, 363, 408, 436, 455, 464, 470, 555
*gigue, giga [*see* 'dance']
*Gilbert and Sullivan (Br. light-opera librettist and comp., collaborated 1869–96) 404
Gildon, John (Eng. comp., *fl.* early C19th) 191, <u>192T3</u>, <u>Pl. 43</u>
Giuliani, Mauro (Giuseppe Sergio Pantaleo) (It. comp., 1781–1829) 262
*Giustini, Lodovico (It. comp., 1685–1743) <u>Pl. 4</u>, 7, 18
*glass harmonica [*see* 'armonica']
*glee(s) 317, 392
Gleissner, Franz (Ger. comp. and lithographer, 1759–1818) 533
Glockenspiel [*see also* carillon] 109
*Gluck, Christoph Willibald, Ritter von (Ger. comp., 1714–87) 304–5, 330, 489
Goermans, Jacques (Fr. kb instrument maker, ?–1789) 10
Gothic(k) (gothic) 166, 168, 434, 543

*Gottschalk, Louis Moreau (Am. comp., 1829–69) 153, 163, 438
Goulding & Co. (Br. firm of music publishers, 1786–1834, then becoming Goulding & D'Almaine)
*Gounod, Charles (François) (Fr. comp., 1818–93) 110, 150, 212
gradability, gradation (of tone) [*see also* 'piano'] (16q), 28, 30q1, 49q, 86, 107, 226, 240
*Graf, Conrad, (Ger. [Aus. naturalised] pf maker, 1782–1851) 11
Grand Tour, The 169, (523)
grave, graveyard 153, 168, 215, 261, 386, 492, 496, 499, 500
great(est) composers [*see also* 'Greats'] 39q, 134, 296, 330, 474, 479
'Great Men' 169, 296
Greats, The (great composers) xx, xxi, 474, 479, 534–5, 547
*Grétry, André-Ernest-Modeste (Fr. comp., 1741–1813) 435
guaracha [*see* 'dance']
guitar(s), -ist 262, 266, 392, 393q, 411, 459, 468, 477
*'guitar cello' (arpeggione) 468
*Gyrowetz Adalbert (Boh. comp., 1763–1850) 539q

habanera [*see* 'dance']
*Habeneck, François-Antoine (Fr. conductor, 1781–1849) 337
Hackbrett 5
*Haigh, Thomas (Eng. comp., 1769–1808) 172, 174, 229, 323
*'halo' [*see* 'piano, sound']
Hamm, Charles (Edward) (Am. musicologist) 384n8
*Handel [Händel, Hendel], George Frideric [Georg Friederich (Friedrich)] (Ger. (Br. naturalised] comp., 1685–1759) (xviii), 8, 93, 138, 150, 157, 176, 177, 178, 181, 182, 186, 320, 372, 421, 435, 541–2, 541n2, 542–3
  Solo Kb Suites: 138, 320, 421, 541–2, 541n2
  Zadok the Priest (anthem) 177
  Oratorios: *Deborah* 186, 186n2; *Messiah* xviii, 8, 372; *Saul* 30q1; *Susannah* 150
Hanon, Charles-Louis (Fr. musical pedagogue, 1819–1900) 40
*Harding, Rosamond E(velyn) M(ary) (Eng. musicologist) 3n4, 4n5, 33n10, 58n5,

61n18, 86n1–2, 103, 103n1, 104n2, 104n2–3, 114n23, 115n26, 117n3, 412, 412n5
*harmonica [*see* 'armonica']
harmonics, overtones, partials 52, 60n13, 100, 352
*harmonium 86
harps, -er [*see also* 'imitation', 'pedal' and 'stop'] 3, 87, 104, 262, 379, 381, 459
*harpsichord(s) Pl. 3, 3, 5, 7, 10q, 13q, 16, 17q1, 17q3, 18, 19, 21 Fig. 2, 28–9, 33, 35, 35q, 38, 86, 87, 88, 89, 103, 108, 109, 110, 111, 111q, 112–13, 115, 118, 120, 135, 141, 144, 153, 154, 157, 180, 182, 191, 193, 218, 243, 262, 263, 306, 372, 459, 460, 523, 526, 536
  pedal-harpsichord 110
*Haschka, Georg (Aus. pf maker, 1772–1828) 105, 106, Pl. 17, Pl. 18, 107, Pl. 19, 114, 114n23
*Hässler, Johann Wilhelm (Ger. comp., 1747–1822) 529
*Hawkins, [John] Isaac (Eng. [Am. naturalised] kb-maker, 1772–1854) 103, 108
*Haydn, (Franz) Joseph (Aus. comp., 1732– 1809) xvii, 19, 53, 62, 103, 139–40, 140, 141, 142, 174, 185, 189, 218–19, 225, 229, 242–5, 250, 262, 263, 268, 284, 301, 309–10, 330, 338, 340, 352, 359n2, 373, 380–81, 448, 460, 461, 464, 466, 469–70, 474, (489), 490, 526, (526n4), 536–7, 539, 547, 548
  Solo Kb: 19, 139–40, 140, 141–2; unauthenticated minuet 225; Sonatas 35–9, 139, 140–42, 218–9, 242, 242–5, 262, 263, 271, 284, 461, 464; Variations in f 301, 330
  Chamber: 218, 469; *Il Maestro e lo Scola*re (hcd2) 526, 526n4, 536–7; Partita in F (hcd2) (attr.) 526; Str Quartets xvii, 218, 229, 309–10, 381, 464, 469, 474; Pf Trios 284, 469, 470
  Orch: Symphonies 271, 373, 448, 460, 469, 539; No. 30: 271; *London* Symphonies 310, 381, 448, 464, 470, 474; *Paris* Symphonies 448, 474; Trumpet Concerto 189
  Vocal: *Gott erhalte Franz den Kaiser* 309–10; *XII Lieder ...* 490; *Missa in angustiis* ('*Nelson*') 185; *Missa in tempore belli* ('*Paukenmesse*') 185; *A Selection of Original Scots Songs in Three Parts ...* 380
*Haydn, (Johann) Michael (Aus. comp., 1737–1806) 115
Head, Matthew (Br. musicologist) 105n6
hearer(s) [*see* 'audience']
*Hebenstreit, Pantaleon (Ger. instrument maker, 1667–1750) 5
*Heilman, Matthäus (Ger. kb-maker, 1744–98) 24, Fig. 5
*Heller, Stephen [István] (Hun [Fr. naturalised] comp., 1813–88) 53, 155, 164–5, 165, 173, 174, 190–1, 193, 407–8
  Solo Pf: *Die Jagd (La chasse)* 193; *Les Maturins* 165; *Miscelannés* 155, 173; *Promenades d'un Solitaire* 164–5, 407–8; *Silvana* 174; *3 Character pieces* 190–91
Hellyer, Roger (Br. musicologist) 188n3
hemiola rhythm 178, 179, 423
*Henderson, J (Br. kb instrument maker, *fl.* 1825–35) 56
*Henselt [Hänselt], (Georg Martin) Adolf [Adolph] (von) (Ger. comp., 1814–89) 53, 163, 213, 354–5, 360
*Herder, Johann Gottfried (Ger. philosopher, 1744–1803) 376, 379
*Hérold, (Louis Joseph) Ferdinand (Fr. comp., 1791–1833) 197
*Herschel, Sir William [Friedrich Wilhelm] (Ger. comp., 1738–1822) 18
*Herz, Henri [Heinrich] (Ger. [Fr. naturalised] comp., 1803–88) 33, 34, 195, 242, 342, 348, 350, 353, 354, 357, 360, 363, 413q, 436, (436q2), 534
  Solo Pf: *Collection d'Exercices ...* 535; *Fantaisie chivalresque*195; *Fantaisie ... Otello ...* 33; *Trois airs variés* 195
  Orch.: Pf Concertos 242, 342, 343, 344–5, 348, 350, 353, 354, 357, 360, 363
heterophonic, heterophony [*see* 'texture']
Heurigen 546
Hipkins, Alfred (James) (Eng. writer on music, 1826–1903) 61, (61n19)
*Hoffmann, E. T. A. (Ger. author and comp., 1776–1822) 153, 168, 375, 375n1, 478
Hoffmann, Johann Wilhelm (Ger. kb

INDEX

instrument maker, 1764–1809) 12
Hoffmeister, Franz Anton (Aus. music-
  publisher, 1754–1812) 480–81
*Holmes, Edward (Eng. music critic,
  1797–1859) 337, 337n2, 435–6,
  435n18, (436), 436n19
homophony, homophonic [see 'texture']
Honauer, Leontzi (Aus. [Fr. naturalised]
  comp., c. 1730–c. 1790) 338
horn (French) 119n7, 193, 310, 336, 392,
  486, 502, 528, 529
*hornpipe [see 'dance']
*Hüllmandel [Hullmandel], Nicolas-Joseph
  [Jean Nicolas, James Nicholas] (Fr.
  comp., 1756–1823) 17, 17n55
humidity 12, 28, 444
humour(ous) 148q3, 181, 316, 381, 399,
  436q1, 486
*Hummel, Johann Nepomuk (Ger. comp.,
  1770–1837) (12n40), 30, 31, 31n7,
  45–8, 50, 51, 58–9, 59n6, 87, 101,
  101n12, 118, 155, 164, 170, 178–9,
  179, 182–3, 188–9, 214–5, 230–31,
  237–8, 241, 242, 249, 249–52, 259,
  262, 271–2, 272, 279, 292–4, 304–5,
  306, 307, 315–16, 334, 335, 342–3,
  343, 346–7, 348–9, 353, 354, 355–6,
  357, 358, 359, 359n2, 360, 363, 364,
  365, 365–6, 366, 369, 372–3, 374,
  380, 381, 395, 400, 401–2, 419, 421,
  431–2, 431n1, 432, 432n2, 434, 436,
  437, 438, 438q, 438–9, 445–6, 446n4,
  449–50, 449n10, 452, 455, 460, 481,
  485–6, 486, 527–9, 538, 547, 548–52,
  548n9, 549T7, 553
  Solo Pf: *3 Amusements en forme de
    Caprices* 402; *Bagatellen für
    Klavier* 164, 230–31, 241, 242,
    249–50, 249n5, 315–16; *La Bella
    Capricciosa* 155, 419, 438q; *3
    Capriccios für Klavier* 87, 395,
    402, 551–2; *Fantaisie* in E♭ Op. 18:
    46-8, 455; *Recollections of
    Paganini* 50; Preludes 445–6; *24
    Grandes Etudes* 45-6, 182–3;
    Répértoire de musique ... 419;
    Rondos: *3 amusements en forme des
    Caprices* 87, 395, 402, 551–2; *III
    Grandes Valses* ... 401–2, 550,
    551; Rondos: 241, 251–2, 550; Pf
    Sonatas Op. 2/3: 279; Op. 13:
    271–2, 292–3, 342; Op. 20:
    446n4; Op. 81: 293–4; Op. 106:
    178–9, 179; Variations: *Adagio ...
    on 'The Pretty Polly'* 322–3, 326,
    449–50, Pls. 48–9; *Air à la
    Tyrolienne ...* 538; *on a theme from
    'Armide'* 304–5; *on 'The
    Ploughboy'* Op. 1/1 307; on 'The
    Ploughboy' Op. 120 317
  Guitar & Mandolin 262
  Chamber: *Adagio ... 'Schöne Minka'*
    (fl, vc, pf) 214–15, 326; *Air à la
    Tyrolienne ...* (pf & vn) 538; Air à
    la Tyrolienne ... 538; *Introduction
    and Rondo* Op. posth. 5 (2pf) 538;
    Nocturne Op. 99: 528–9; Pf Quintet
    Op. 87: 237–8, 485–6; Septet Op.
    74: 432, 486–8; Septet Op. 114
    188–9, 486; Duet-Sonata (pf2) Op.
    92: 528–9; *Sonate ou
    divertissement* (pf2) Op. 51: 527–8
  Orch.: Dances: 547, 548, 549–50,
    549T7; Ballet-music 170; Pf
    Concertos etc. 346, 358; Op. 85:
    343, 346, 358, 363, 365–6,
    366–7, 369; Op. 89: 343, 346–7,
    349–50, 355–6, 365, 365–6, 421;
    Op. 110: 353, 354, 358, 460, Pl.
    50; Op. 113: 242, 342, 348–9,
    354, 364, 369; Op. posth. 1: 51,
    342–3, 354, 357, 358, 438–9;
    Variations ...'Castor et Pollux'
    170, (548): *Das Fest des
    Handwerker* 306; *Gesellschafts-
    rondo* 372–3; *Oberons Zauberhorn*
    374, 400; Trumpet Concerto 189,
    548n9; Variations (ob & orch.) 432
  Vocal: *Air à la Tyrolienne* ... New
    Vienna Waltz ... 552, 552q, Pl. 51
  Pedagogical: Pianoforte School
    (1821-5) 12n40, 31n7, 59, 59n7,
    87, 101, 101n12
hunt, -ing, -er *caccia*, chase, *chasse*138,
  193–6, 197, 217, 398
  style, flavour 193–6, 217, 398
*Hünten, Franz [François] (Ger. [Fr.
  naturalised] comp., 1793–1878) 34,
  401–2, 539; *Variations on a
  Tyrolioenne by Mercadante* 401–2, 539
*hurdy-gurdy, 513, 515

illuminations (fireworks) 191–2, 192T3,
  Pl. 43
illustration(s) (artwork) 133–4, Pls.
  30–31, 533
image(s), imagery [see also 'song', 'text']
  438, 493, 506, 521

imitation, imitative [see also pedal' and 'stop'] (117), 178, 218, 230, 243, 253, 271, 276, 279, 315, 322, 382
*impromptu [see also 'improvise'] 186, 212, 542
*improvise, improvisation, inprovisatory xix, xixn3, 6, 120, 151, 248, 258, 276, 278, 302, 309, 317, 324, 341, 357, 358, 360, 361, 364, 372, 374, 375, 390, 393, 399, 431–55, 459, (542), 550–51, 550–51q, 551, 552
    types 442–55; caprice, *capriccio* 155, 157, 326, 450–51, 543; fantasy etc. 399, 413q, 435n17, 441n38, 448, 449, 450, 451–5, 529, 539, 550; *impromptu* 186, 403, 542; *pot-pourri* 393q, 450–51; prelude [see also 'prélude'] 157, 394q2, 442–50; *quodlibet* 450
Industrial Revolution xvii, 147–8, 167
Indy, [Paul Marie Théodore] Vincent d' (Fr. comp., 1851–1931) xviii
inlay [see 'piano, case']
interlude(s) 466, 509–15

*Jackson, George K(nowil) (Eng. [Am. naturalised] comp., 1757–1822) 544–5
Jähns, Friedrich Wilhelm (Ger. musicologist, 1809–88) 254n7
Janáček, Leos (Cz. comp., 1854–1928) 486
*Janissary music [see 'Turkish music']
*Jansen, Thérése [Theresa] (Ger. [Eng. naturalised] pianist, pupil of Clementi) 57, 284
*Joachim, Joseph (Hun. [Aus. nationalised] violinist, 1831–1907) 51, 440
jodel [see 'yodel']
Joseph II, Holy Roman Emperor (Aus. ruler, 1741–90) 53, 465, 525
journal(s) (periodical) [see 'magazine' and 'press']
*Jullien, Louis (George etc. etc.) (Fr. comp., 1812–60) 420
jumps, skips [see 'leaps']

*Kalkbrenner, Frédéric [Friedrich Wilhelm Michael] (Ger. [Fr. naturalised] comp., 1785–1849) 34, 55, 135, 155, 163–4, 299, 353
    Solo Pf: *Essais sur différents caractères* 135, 163–4; *La femme du marin* 155; *Sonata for the Left Hand* 29
    Orch.: Pf Concerto Op. 85: 353

    Pedagogical: *Traité d'harmonie* ... 55
*Kammermusicus 547
Kammerton ('chamber pitch') [see 'pitch']
*Kapellmeister 372, 531
Keeble, John (Eng. comp., c. 1711–1786) 147
*key (on instrument) [see also 'key-dip'] 37, 37n21, 38, 57, Pl. 6, 107, 111, 435, 514
    'additional' 57, Pl. 6
*keyboard (= instrument) 541, 553
*keyboard (= manual; general) 38, 103, 105, (431), 513; shifting of [see 'pedal, una corda']
*key-dip 29, 31, 31q
Kiallmark, George (Eng. comp., fl. early C19th) 186
*Kiesewetter, Raphael Georg (Aus. musicologist, 1773–1850) 539q
*Kirckman [Kirchmann, Kirkman] (firm of Ger. [Br. naturalised] kb-makers, 1770–1898) 8, 25 Fig. 6, 115, Pl. 27, 116q
Klavier [see also 'clavichord', 'harpsichord' and 'piano'] 38
Kleinmeister(s) 419
*knee-lever, knee-pedal [see 'genouillère']
Knittelvers 376
*Koch Heinrich Christoph (Ger. musical theorist, 1749–1816) 265n7, 363
*Kollmann, Augustus (Eng. comp., 1789–1845) 90, 320, 421, 541–2
Komlós, Katalin (Hun. musicologist) 3n4, 31n8, 57n2
*Konzertstück [see also 'concert rondo'] 370, 374
*Kotzwara [Koczwara], Franz [Frantisek, Francis] (Boh. comp., c. 1750–1791) 191
*Kozeluch [Kotzeluch, Kozeluh], Leopold Jan Antonín, Ioannes Antoninus] (Boh. comp., 1747–1818) 380, 381
*Kreutzer [Kreuzer], Conradin [Conrad] (Ger. comp., 1780–1849) 342, 357, 361, 364
*Kuhlau, (Daniel) Friedrich [Frederik] (Rudolph) (Ger. [Dan. naturalised] comp., 1786–1832) 476, 527
    Sonata (pf2) 527; Flute Sonatas 476; *Grande sonate concertante* (fl & pf) Op. 85: 475; Grand Trio in G (2fl & pf) 475; *6 Divertimentos* (2fl) 476; *3 Grand Solos* (2fl) 476
*Kuhnau [Kuhn, Cuno], Johann (Ger.

comp., 1660–1722) 135
*Kühreihen (Swiss mountain song) [see also 'Ranz des vaches'] 91, 401
*kujawiak [see 'dance']
*Kullak, Theodor (Ger. comp., 1818–82) 149
*Kurpinski, Karol Kazimierz (Pol. comp., 1785–1857) 414, 415, 415n13, 415–16, 417, 419

labour(ers), workers [see also 'peasant'] 48, 378, 379, 430
*Ladurner, Josef Alois (Aus. comp., 1769–1851) 535–6
Lafont, Charles Philippe (Fr. violinist, 1781–1839) 432
*Ländler [see 'dance, (named)']
Landon, H. C. Robbins (Am. musicologist) 140n6, 141, (141n8), 141n9, 284n16, 460, 460n1
Langley, Robin (Eng. musicologist) 205n17
*Lanner, Josef (Karl Franz) (Aus. comp., 1801–43) 536, 547, 548
Latcham, Michael (Eng. musicologist) 3n4, 11, 11n35, 57, 57n3–4, 59n8–10, 60n13–15, 62n21
Latour, (comp., *fl.* early C19th) 395
*Latrobe [La Trobe], Christian Ignatius (Eng. comp., 1758–1836) 174–5
leader (orchestral) [see also 'conductor'] 337, 459
leap(s), jump(s), skip, sweep 30q2, 51, 154, 348, 386, 401, 406, 422, 424, 428, 436, 496
Lecarpentier, (Fr. comp., *fl.* early C19th) 535
Lechantre, Mme (Fr. pianist, *fl.*1768) 9
*Leduc, Alphonse (Fr. comp., 1804–68) 539
leg(s) [see 'piano']
'legato' style (in performance) 30, (45), (325)
*Lemière [Le Mière, Lemierre] de Corvey, Jean Frédéric Auguste (Breton comp., 1770–1832) 192–3, Pls. 44–5
Leppert, Richard, (Am. musicologist) 147, 147n3–4
lessons (music-) [see 'teach']
lessons (pieces) 180q1, 535q
letterpress [see 'printing']
*Lichnowsky (Aus aristocratic family, patrons of Beethoven) 165
*lid-swell [see 'swell']

*Lied(er) [see 'song']
Life Class (art education) 145, Pl. 38, 170
lighting xvii, 144, 145, 373, 547
lightning 137, Pl. 35, 248, 438
listener [see 'audience']
*Liszt, Franz [Ferenc] (Hun. comp., 1811–86) 34, 42, 43, 50, 51, 52, 53, 83–5, 135, 136, 136n1, 153, 166, 198, 211–12, 213–14, 259, 260, 300, 306, 334, 368, 372, 374, 430, 437, 437q2, 440, 440n35, 478, 534, 534n3, 538, 553
   Solo Pf: *Album d'un voyageur* 212; *Années de pèlerinage* 212; *[3] Apparitions* 211; *Après une lecture du Dante* 166; *Bénédiction papale (Urbi et orbi)* 211; *Clochette* 52; *Consolations* 211; *Etudes d'éxécution transcendente* 52, 85; *12 grandes études* 85; *3 Konzert-Etüden* 84–5; *Etude en 48/en douze exercices ...* 50; *Grandes Etudes de Paganini* 50, 5,1 52; *24 Grandes études* 50, 52; *Harmonies poétiques et religieuses* (85), 211–12; *Historical Portraits* 153; *Hungarian Rhapsodies* 51, 227, 430; *In festo transfiguronis* 211; *2 Légendes* 166, 211; *Liebesträume* 198; *La Marquise de Blocqueville* 153; Pf Sonata 300; *Sancta Dorothea* 211; *Variation on a Waltz by Diabelli* 330, 553
   Orch.: Pf Concertos etc. 374; *Fantasy on 'Ruins of Athens'* 374; *Grand fantaisie symphonique* 374; *Malédiction* 213, 374; *Totentanz* 214, 374
   Writings; *Journey* 534n3
lithography [see 'printing']
Loesser, Arthur (Br. writer) 534n4
*Loewe, Carl (Ger. comp., 1796–1869) 517
*London Piano School 30, 31, (202n14)
Longman and Broderip (Br. publishers & instrument makers, 1767–1810) 57
Lortzing, [Gustav] Albert (Ger. comp., 1801–51) xviii
loud pedal [see 'pedal (types), damper']
*Louis Ferdinand, Prince of Prussia (Ger. comp., 1772–1806) 166
*lute(s) [see also 'imitation', 'pedal' and 'stop'] 87, 108, 109, 306, 459
Lütge, William (Aus. musicologist) 57n2

McClary, Susan (Am. musicologist) 147n3–4
*Macfarren, Sir George (Alexander) (Eng. comp., 1813–87) 166, 408
*MacFarren, Walter (Cecil) (Eng. comp., 1826–1905) 158–9
*Magazin der Musik (ed. C F. Cramer, pub. 1783–4) 16, 16n47, 148, (148q3), 148n12
magazine(s) [see 'newspaper' and 'press']
Mahler, Gustav (Aus. comp., 1860–1911) 348
male [see 'man']
*Malibran [née Garcia], Maria [Madame] (Spanish soprano, 1808–36) 149–50, 185, 242, 538
man, men 146, 170, 431, 433q, 460
*mandolin 262
*Mannheim (Germany) orchestra 275, 465
march(es), *marche, marcia*, martial 152, 184, 185, 186, 190, 191, 195, 203, 384, 395, 412, 450, 527, 529, 536
*Marius, Jean (Fr. instrument-maker, ?–1720) 4, 7, 13, 109n12
market, market-driven, marketability 115, 118, 147, 242, 249, 263, 266, 297, 301, 334, 378, 532, 538, 548
Marpurg, Friedrich Wilhelm (Ger. music theorist, 1718–95) 37
*Marschner, Heinrich August (Ger. comp., 1795–1861) 420
martial [see 'march']
mass media [see 'media']
mass production 63, 112, 116q, (241)
*Mattheson, Johann (Ger. comp., 1681–1764) 5
Matthews, Denis (Eng. musicologist) 119n7
Maunder, Richard (Eng. musicologist) 9n24, 112, 141, 141n10
*Mayer, Charles (Ger. comp., 1799–1862) 48
*mazurka [see 'dance']
Mazzinghi, Joseph (Eng. comp., 1765–1844) 158
media (mass media) [see also 'news' and 'newspapers'] (129), 534
medieval [see 'Middle Ages']
*Méhul, Etienne-Nicolas (Fr. comp., 1763– 1817) 143
*Mendelssohn[Bartholdy] [Hensel], Fanny [Cäcile] (Ger. comp., 1805–47) xviii, 233–4, 478, 489

Pf Sonata in g 233–4; Pf Trio Op. 11: 478
*Mendelssohn[-Bartholdy], [Jakob Ludwig] Felix (Ger. comp., 1809–47) xviii, 51, 53, 233, 284, 295, 296, 301, 307, 323, 330–33, 347, 348, 363, 364, 366, 369, 406, (406n3), 408, 435n17, 478–80, 479n5, 480q1, 485, 489, 527
  Solo Pf: 233; *Fantasia on The Last Rose* 307, 435n17; *Lieder ohne Worte* 284, 364, 479, 517; Sonatas 295, 295n21, 296; *Variations sérieuses* 301, 323, 330–33
  Chamber: 480; Sonata (pf2) 527; Cello Sonatas 479; Vn Sonata Op. posth 479; Pf Trios 479q, 479, 480q; Pf Quartets 485; Sextet (pf, vn, 2va, vc & db) 485
  Orch: Overture: *A Midsummer Night's Dream* 347; *Italian Symphony* 406, (406n3); Pf Concertos 348, 364, 365, 369; Vn Concerto in e 51, 369
menuet [see 'minuet']
Menuett, -o [see 'minuet']
*Mercadante, (Giuseppe) Saverio (Raffaele) (It. comp., 1795–1870) 401–2, 539
Mercken, Johann Kilian (Fr. naturalised kb instrument maker, *fl.* 1770) 10
*Merlin, John Joseph (Fl. [Br. naturalised] instrument maker, 1735–1803) 13, 29, 86, Pl. 20, 110–11, 523
*Method(s) (*Méthode*) (for teaching), Schools [see also 'education', 'school' and 'teaching'] 35–9, 39, 44, 90–91, 91n6, 182, 435, 534, 535, 536, 538
*metre, metrical (prosodic) (94), 383, 384, 385, 386, 391, 394, 541n2
*Meyerbeer, Giacomo (Ger. comp., 1791– 1864) xviii
Middle Ages, medieval [see also 'mode'] 167, 330, 383, 388, 390n11, 434
middle class(es) [see also 'bourgeois'] 118, 379, 383
Milchmeyer, Johann Peter (Ger. musical theorist, *c.* 1750–1818) 37, 38–9, 38n23, 39n24–26, 118, 118n5, 460n2
*military etc. 7, 165, 173, 184–91, 192, 193, 203, 329, 375, 416, 435, 465
  battle piece 107, 191–3, 549T7
mill(s) [see also 'child', 'factory', 'labour' and 'woman'] xvii, xviii, 378, 494, 536
Minasi, Carlo (It. [Br. naturalised] comp., *fl.* early C19th) 185
*minuet(s), *menuet, Menuett, -o, minuetto*

xx, 148q2, 172–3, <u>217–29</u>, 239, 241, 242, 263, 263n4, 266, 283, 284, 295, 296, 326, 404, 414, 464, 464n3, 537, 545, 546, 549T7

Mitchell, William J. (Am. musicologist) 36

*mode, modal 233, 237, 245, 269, 284, 303, 309, <u>322–4</u>, 386, 388, 424, 428, 498, 501, 541

*moderator [see 'pedal']

moderno, stile, modern style 177, 182. 183

Momigny, Jérôme-Joseph de (Bel. music theorist, 1762–1842) 31

*Mondonville, Jean-Joseph Cassanéa de (Fr. comp., 1711–72) 460

*Moore, Thomas (Ir. comp., 1779–1852) 307, 379, 381, <u>383–92</u>, Pl. 46, 393, 394, 413q, 518, 527, 535

Mori, Nicolas (Eng. comp., 1796/7–1839) 337q

Morrow, Mary Sue (Am. musicologist) 148, 148n8–10

Moscheles, Charlotte [née Embden] (Ger. [Br. naturalised] wife of I. Moscheles, 1805–89) 34, (166)

*Moscheles, Ignaz (Cz. [Ger. nationalised] comp., 1794–1870) 34, 34n11, 35, 41, 48–50, 50, 52–3, 53, 57, 109–110, 118, 135, 143, 149, 149–50, 155, 155–7, 162, 165, 166, 180–2, 182, 187, 199–201, 202, 249, 255–6, 306, 307, 330, 334, 337, 337n4–5, 342, 343, 344, 350, 353–4, 354, 355, 363, 366, 392, 393–4, 393n3, 402–3, 406–7, 421, 433–4, 434n9–10, 434n14, 436, 438, 438n28, 445, 451, 451n12, 481, 527, 538, 543

Solo Pf: *L' Ambition* ... 165; *Characteristic Tribute to Malibran* 149, 149–50; *2 Caprices* 307; *La Fougue* 165; *Gems à la Paganini* ... 50; *Giga* 543; *Hibernian impromptu* 392; *La petite babillarde* 155–7; *Romance & tarantella brillante* 166, 406–7; *Sir Walter Scott's favourite* ... 393–4; *La tenerezza* 155; *The Tyrolese Family* ...402–3; *La Gaité* 255–6; *Rondo Expressif* ... 166; Studies: *24 Characteristic Compositions* 48–9, 135, 143, 180–82; *Characteristische Studien* 49–50, 199–201; *4 Grandes Etudes de Concert* 109–10, 199; *50 Preludes* ... 41, 445; (with Fétis) *Etudes de perfectionnement* 52;

Variation on a Waltz by Diabelli 330

Chamber: *Hommage à Weber* ... (pf2) 149; Sonata (pf2) 527; *Hommage à Haendel* (2pf) 149–50; *La belle Union* (2pf) 57, 166

Orch.: Pf Concertos etc. No. 2: 324, 366, 421–2; No. 3: 162, 343, 353–4; No. 4: 344, 337, 350, 354, 363; No. 5: 363; No. 6: 342, 355; No. 7: 162, 343, 355, 363; *Alexander Variations* 187, 306, 337q

Pedagogical: (with Fétis) *Complete system of Instruction* 52–3

moto perpetuo [*see also* 'perpetuum mobile'] 301

*Mozart, Maria Anna (Walburga Ignatia)'[Nannerl'] (Aus. musician, sister of W. A. Mozart, (1751–1829) 144, <u>Pls. 36–7</u>, 461, 523

*Mozart, (Johann Georg) Leopold (Aus. comp. 1719–87) 30n6, 37, 38, 523, 144, <u>Pls 36–7</u>

*Mozart, Wolfgang Amadeus (Aus. comp., 1756–91) 7, 7n18, 11, 30, 30n6, 31, 35, 53, 56, 62, 105, 115, 118, 118n6, 119, 122, 142, 144, <u>Pls 36–7</u>, 177, 184, 190, 217, 218, 220, 225–6, 229, <u>245–7</u>, 252, <u>256–61</u>, 262, 263, 264, 265, 267, 269–70, 276–9, 284, 285–90, 290, 291, 303, 307–8, 324, 328–9, 330, 335, 336, 338, 339, 340, 341–2, 345–6, 351, 353, 358, 359n2, 361, 362, 363, 364, 365, 366, 367, 370, 372, 373, 412, 414, 435, 440, 444n2, 460, 460–1, 461–5, 466, 468, 469, 469n6, 474, 480q, 480–84, 485, 486, (489), 490, 523, 524–5, 530, 538, 539, 539q, 542–3, 547

Solo Pf: *(29) Contredanses* (orch., arr. pf) 184; *Eine kleine Gigue* 542–3; Rondo K. 511: 217, <u>256–61</u>, 285; *Marche funebre del Sigr Maestro Contrapunto* 155, 184; Minuets 225–6; Pf Sonatas: K. 279–84 (189d–h & 205b) 119, 142, 217, 262, 263, 263n4, 276–7, 279, 287–8, 440; K. 310 (300d) 256, 270, 277–9, 284, 288–91, K. 311 (284c) <u>245–7</u>; K. 330 (300h) 220; K. 331: 105–6, 263–4, 324–5; K. 332 (300k) 269; K. 333 (315c) 142, 264; K. 537: 19; K. 545: 269,

K. 570: 262, 269; K. 576: 269–70; Variations: on 'Salve tu, Domine' 307–8, 324–5; on 'Unser dummer Pöbel meint' 330
Chamber: 465 423; Pf Duet: Sonatas: K. 19d 523–4, ?Pl. 37; K. 381 (123a) 524; K. 358: 524; K. 497: 525; K. 521: 525; Variations: K. 501: 525; Two pf: Sonata K. 448 (375a) 530; Fugue K. 426: 530, 538; Introduction & Fugue K. 546: 538; Vn Sonatas K. 6–8: 460–61; K. 26–31: 262, 464; K. 301–306: 464, 465; K. 301 (293a): 461; K. 302 (293b): 462; K. 303 (293c): 465; K 304 (300c): 461–2, 463–4, 465, 480; K. 379 (373a): 465; K. 454: 465; K. 481: (465); K. 526: (465); K. 547: (465); Pf Trios: K. 10–15: 262; K. 496: 262, 469; Pf Quartets K. 478: 480–484, 485; K. 493: 481; Concertos arranged for pf. quartet 539; Pf & winds quintet K. 452: 486; Str Quartets: 465; K. 421: 31, 285; 'Prussian' 466; Introduction & Fugue K. 546 (arr. of K. 426) 538; Str. Quintets: K. 406 (516b): 218, 257–8; K. 516: 257, 286; K. 593: 218, 267, 286; Pf. concertos K. 413–15 arr. for pf & str. quartet 484; Quintet (fl, ob, va, vc and armonica) K. 617: 412; Wind Serenade K. 388 (384a) 218
Orch.: *Contredanses* 184, 547; Introduction and Fugue K. 546 (str arr. of K. 426) 538; Minuets 547; Pf Concertos etc. 285, 287, 335, 336, 338, 361, 362, 366, 367; K. 37: 338, (361); K. 39–41: 338, (361); K. 107: 338, (361); K. 175 (361), 366, 370; K. 242: 339, (361); K. 246: 339, (361); K. 238: (361), 460; K. 271: 341, 351, (361), 363; K. 413–15: 339, 341–2, (361), 366, 370, 373, 484; K. 453: 286, (361), 366; K. 466: 345, (361), 363, 364 , 365; K. 482: 342, (361); K. 488: 217, 285, (361), 363; K. 491: 184, 328–9, 345, (361), 365, 366; K. 503: 342, (361); K537: (353), (361); K595: 19, (353), (361); Rondo K. 382: 366, 370; Rondo K. 386: 370; Vn Concertos etc. 370; Rondo K. 269 (261a): 370; Symphonies 336, 539, 539q; K183 (173d): 258, 285; K. 444 (425a): 115; K. 551: 267, 366–7

Vocal: Songs: *Abendempfindung an Laura* 490; *Bacchuslied* 451; *Das Veilchen* 490; Operas: *Don Giovanni* 327, 345; *La clemenza di Tito* 190; *Le nozze di Figaro* overture 373; *Die Zauberflöte* 303, 324, 345, 439, 451

Mozart, ['Wolfgang Amadeus *fils*'] Franz Xavier Wolfgang (Aus. comp., 1791–1844, son of W. A. Mozart) 163, 330, 418

*Müller, Matthias (Ger. kb-maker, c. 1770–1844) 103

*Musard, Philippe (Fr. conductor, 1793–1859) 420, 546

*musical glasses [see 'armonica']

*'nag's head swell' [see 'swell']
*nameplate(s) 10
*'Nannerl' [see Mozart, M. A.']
*Napier, William (Sc. music publisher, ?1740/41–1812) 380

nature, (rural etc.), natural 196–8, 147, (336), 375, 377q. 394q2, 433q, 436q1, 499

*Neefe, Christian Gottlob (Ger. comp., 1748–98) 266, 303, 324, 489

Nelson, Robert U(rel) (Am. musicologist) 301n1

Neukomm, Sigismond Ritter von (Aus. comp., 1778–1858) 370

Newman, William S(tein). (Am. musicologist) 16n46, 266n9, 297n22, 529n6

newspaper(s) [see also 'magazine' and 'press'] 533–4

Nicolai, [Carl] Otto [Ehrenfried] (Ger. comp., 1810–49) xviii

noble, -men, nobility, titled [see also 'aristocrat'] 137, (145q), 145, 146, 165, 178, 291, 403, 437, 522, 546

Nocturne 93–7, 95n7, 175, 198, 205–9, 293, 364, 440, (472), 528

nostalgia, nostalgic [see also 'past'] 109, 167, 176, 179, 378, 383, 414, 555

notes inégales 138

Novello (& Co.) (Br. firm of music-publishers, 1829–now) 533

*Oginski, Prince Michal Kazimierz (Pol. comp., 1728–1800) 414

old masters [*see* 'painting']
Onslow, (André) Georges (Louis) (Fr. comp., 1784–1853) 486
orchestra (in concerto) <u>336–8</u>
    rehearsal(s) 336, 337, 337q, 539, (599n7)
*'orchestra in the drawing-room' [*see* 'piano']
*organ xviii, 5, 9, 14, 18, 83, 86, 110, 111, 113, 135, 155, 176–7
organ swell [*see* 'swell']
*ouverture [*see also* 'French Overture'] 138, 315, 320
*overture (general) 267, 345, 394q2, 529
*overstringing [*see* 'cross-stringing']
*overtones [*see* 'harmonics']

*Paganini, Niccolò (It. violinist, 1782–1840) 50–52, 100, 151, 262, 306, 475, 478
    Wks for Guitar 262
    Caprices, Op. 1 (solo vn) 51, 306, 475; Vn Concerto No. 2: 51
painting 144–6, Pls. 36–41, 168, 296, 375–6, 433
    child, -ren 144, Pls 36–7, 375; 'Chocolate-box art' 376; genre 296, 375–6, 376; 'grand manner' 145; history 145, 296; Impressionism and Turner 433; landscape 137, 146, 212, 296; life-class 145, Pl. 38; lower form(s)/ style(s) of 145q; moral(ity) 376; nostalgia 375; old masters 144, 145; out of doors 433; peasant scenes 296 portrait (-ure) 144–6, 145q, Pls. 36–41, (149–53), 153, 169, 375; musical <u>149–53</u>, 153; Renaissance masters 145; sketch, -ing 433; still life 296; techniques 296; watercolour 134, 144, 552
*Paisiello, Giovanni (It. comp., 1740–1816) 307–8, 324, 350, 362, 362n1, 365
*Pantalon 5, 113
*Pape, Jean Henri (Ger. [Fr.naturalised] pf maker, 1789–1875) 34, 104, 115
*Paradies [Paradisi], Domenico (It. comp., 1707–91) 284
Paradis [Paradies], Maria Theresia von (Aus. pianist, 1759–1824) 53
parlour [*see* 'drawing-room']
Parrish, Karl (Am. musicologist) 16n47, 17n50, 17n52
Parry, Sir [Charles] Hubert [Hastings] (Eng. comp., 1848–1918) xviii
partials [*see* 'harmonics']
partita(s) [*see also* 'suite'] 138, 526
passacaglia 316
past, the [*see also* 'nostalgia'] 109, <u>167–83</u>, 375, 435, 497, 498, 504, 512, (543)
    style(s) <u>176–83</u>, 435, 543, 543n3
*pastoral(e), -s (style) 90q, <u>169–75</u>, 186, 193, 212, 217, 408, 412, 434, 435, 452, 528
patron, -age 178, 330, 532
patter-song 384, 389
Pauer, Ernst (Aus. music editor) 181
Paulirinus, Paulus [of Prague] (Cz. writer on music, 1413–after 1471) 110
Pazdírek, Bohumil and Frantisek (Cz. editors, 1839–1919 and 1848–1915) 242n2
peasant(s), -ry [*see also* 'labour'] 146, 296, 546
*pedal(s) (general), -ling xix, 11, 18, 86, 87 96, 105, 114, 115, 116, 120, 143, 180, 211, 403
*pedal(s) (types)
    bassoon, 'di Fagotto' 87, 105, 107; damper <u>88–101</u>, 120; 'di Fagotto' [*see* 'bassoon' in this entry]; divided <u>101–2</u>, Pl. 15, (107); drum 106, 107; *due corde* 88, Pls. 7–8, 128; *forte* <u>88–101</u>; *Jeu Céleste* 88; Jeu de buffe 88; lid-swell, 'nag's head swell' 13, 87, 107; loud [*see* 'sustaining' in this entry]; moderator 88, 101, 101q, 105, 107; *piano, pianissimo* 88; *Pianozug* 88; shift [*see also* 'una corda' *in this entry*] 88, 105, 125; soft [*see also 'una corda' in this entry*] <u>87–8</u>, 91q2, 101, (101q), 102, 515; *sordino* [*see also* 'harp' *in this entry*] 87; sustaining [*see also* 'damper' *and* 'forte' *in this en*try] <u>88–101</u>, 105, 122, 143, 177n11, 211, 403, 515; 'third' 101; *tuute le corde* 125; *una corda* 5, 11, 88, 105, 107, 111, 125, 233; *volti subito* 115
*pedalboard 109, 110
pedal-clavichord [*see* 'clavichord']
pedal-harpsichord [*see* 'harpsichord']
*pedal-piano [*see* 'piano types']
Péronard, Balthazar (Fr. kb instrument maker, *fl.* 1771) 10
*perpetuum mobile [*see also* 'moto perpetuo'] 44, 138, 176, 200, (253), 284, (301), 320, 382, 409, 500, 551

personification, personifying 144–66, 216
*Philharmonic Society (London) 114, 334, 536
*piano (instrument)
  accompanying, accompaniment(s) [see separate entry; also 'chamber' and 'song'] xx, 10q, 56, 59, 103, 115, 136, 267, 459–88, 489–522
  action 29–55, 116q
    down-striking 111, 115; 'English single' action 8, 10, 25, Fig. 6; escapement, double-, repetition 7, 13, 22, 23, 27, Fig. 8, 31q, 33, 43; shifting of (excluding *una corda*) 86
  arrangement(s) [see 'piano music']
  articulation 31, 44, 71, 76, 141, 220, 234, 251, 398, 494, 508, 515
  as aid to composition 459
  ascendancy of 29
  as [*basso*] *continuo* 56, 461
  as cultural icon xviii
  as curiosity 112
  as furniture xviii, 112, 114, 115
  as teaching (didactic) instrument 459, 523, 523n1, 526, 526n5, 531–40
  case, casing 6, 12, 60, 104, 116q
  cheap (comparatively) 8, 18q, 31q, 114
  characteristics of 245
  classisic simplicity of (early) 114
  combination instruments 5, 9, 13, 109, 110–12
  compass [see 'piano sound, range]
  domestic [see separate entry]
  durability of 12, 30q2, 31q, (104)
  facility (in playing) 33
  factory (-ies) [see 'workshop' in this entry]
  fashionable 116
  forms of (generally) 103–5
  frame xviii, 12, 104
    cast-iron xviii, 58, 60, 113, 115
    compensation Pl. 2, 12, 13, 26 Fig. 7, 60
  function(s) of 56, (103–15), 112–15;
  imitating other instruments [see also 'bassoon', 'harp', 'lute'] 108–10
  instructions [labels] for repairs 10, 104, Pl. 15
  legs 6, 113, 114, Pl. 28, 115
  literature [see 'piano music']
  'orchestra in the drawing-room' 107, (480)
  orchestral effects on 104, 107–8, 108q, 233

  portable (relatively) 8, 10q, Pl. 21
  reception of (9n26), 13–18
  'Schools' [see 'Method']
  stands, trestles 103, 113
  teaching [see under 'teaching']
  tuner, tuning 29q, 37, 60
  universal instrument 107
  variable 120
  versatility 103–15, 136, 191, 459
  workshops/factories 11, 12, 115, 120
piano droit [see 'piano types']
piano ensembles and functions 380, 414, 450, 459–88, 479q, 480–88, 523–30;
  duet (pf2) xx, 110, 185, 414, 460, 523–9, 531, 536–7, 538, 539; duo (2pf) xx, 263, 461, 465, 529, 530, 538, 538, 539, 540; duo (pf & other instrument) 461–8, 474–80; larger ensembles 478, 480–88; sonatas (chamber) 524, 529; trios 380, 460, 461, 469–73, 474–80, 479q
piano (names) [see 'piano types']
piano music (generally)
  arrangements xviii, xx, 459, 523n1, 524, (529), 530, 538–40
  bel canto (324)
  colour, use of 309–14, 503
  counterpoint, use of 315–22
  problems of performance on modern instruments 94, 122, 122n9, 129, 135, 515
  sonata(s) 218, 262–300, 448, 475, 479
  tactile element in 519
piano sonata [see 'piano music']
piano sound 5, 42, 116–30, 444, 519
  of early piano, generally 5, 42, 116–30, 444
  blending easily with other instruments 12, 31q, 35q, 461
  'halo' 31, 89, 90, 96
  harmonics [see 'overtones' in this entry]
  'orchestra in the drawing-room' 107, (480)
  orchestral, orchestral effects on 107–8, 104, 108q, 110, 119
  overtones 52, 61, 100, 117, 508
  range, compass [see also 'keys, additional'] 56, 56–8, 60, 64, 68, (69), 181, 219, 261, 310, 445, 485, 523, 526
  register(s), registral 56, 61–2, 63, 64, 69, 71, 72, 73, 74, 75, 76, 77, 78, 80, (81), 83, 86, (89), (93), 95,

(101), 102, 122, 123, 124, 125, 129, (154), 160, 181, 193, 199, 200, 202, 203, 219, 221, 230, 231, 233–4, 234, (235), (236), 237, 238, 243, 244, 245, (246), 247, 255, 261, 264, 269, 269n12, 277, 278, 279, 281, 293, 306, 307, 316, 318, 322, 332, 352, 397, 398, 403, 406, 415, 438–9, 448, 455, 463, 465, 467, 469, 471, 478, 479, 494, 496, 497, 498, 500, 501, 503, 504, 505, 506, 507, 508, 509, (514), 516, 518, 520, 521, 522, 524
piano types, and named
  'Animo-Corde' 108
  boudoir 104; British *versus* 'Viennese' 29–35, 31, 31q, 56, 62
  cabinet 56, 104
  clavecin à maillets 4
  Clavier-Instrument 4
  'Claviol' 108
  Claviorgan, '-um' 9n28, 86, 110, 114, Pl. 20
  'Conductor's' 114
  cottage 56, 105, 114, Pl. 23
  'Ditanaklasis' 103
  droit 104
  duoclave 110
  electronic 117
  'Eolodicon' 108
  'Euphonicon' Pl. front cover, 108
  Flugel/klavier 103
  Giraggenflügel, 'Giraffe' 104, 107
  Hammerflügel 103
  'Lyraflügel' 56, Pl. 17, 87
  'Orphika' 113
  pianino 104
  pedal-piano 110
  'Piano-Viole' 108
  piccolo 104
  'Plectroeuphon' 108
  portable [*see also* 'Conductor's' *in this entry*] 103, 113–4, Pl. 21
  Pyramid 11
  'sloping backwards' 104, 115
  sostenente 107
  square 28, 118
  upright 5, 11, 56, 87, 103, 104, 108, 110, 113, 116
  upright grand Pl. 28, (103)
  upright square 103
  vertical 104
  'Viennese' *versus* British 29–35, 31, 31q, 56, 62

  'Violicembalo' 108
  'wing' 103
piano(forte) organisé 9
Pianoforte Schools [*see* 'Method']
*Pierson [Pearson], Henry Hugo [Hugh] (Br. [Ger. naturalised] comp., 1815–73) 165
Piggott, Patrick (Ir. musicologist) 115n25
*Pinto, George Frederick (Eng. comp., 1785–1806) 179–80, 190, 212–13, 228, 395, 412, 420–21
piracy (musical) 251n6
pitch (instrument or voice) 56, 58–60, 112, 336
  Chorton 58, (59q1); *Cornetton* 59; *Kammerton* 58, (59q1); orchestral 59q1; raising 12, 59, 336; singers a problem 59q1, (59n6); standardisation 58, (59q1); theatre 58q1
*Pixis, Johann Peter (Ger. comp., 1788–1874) 34, 166, 190, 407
Plantinga, Leon (Am. musicologist) 19n60, 53, 53n33–4, 353n1, 399, 399n9, 465, 465n4, 526, 526n1–2
plate(s) (printing) [*see* 'printing']
*Pleyel, Ignace Joseph [Ignaz Josef] (Aus. [Fr. naturalised] comp., 1757–1831) 12, 34, 35, 380, 527
*Pohlmann, Johannes (Ger. kb-maker, *fl.* 1767–93) 9, 18q
**polacca* [*see* 'dance']
polka [*see* 'dance']
Pollens, Stewart (Am. musicologist) 3n4, 4n5–8, 5n9, 6n15, 9n25, 10n30, 13n43, 111, 111n17, 112n18
**polonaise* [*see* 'dance']
'Polonoise' [*see also* 'dance, polonaise'] 418, 549n11
polyphony, polyphonic [*see* 'texture']
portrait(s), -ure [*see* 'painting']
  musical 149–53, 153,
postlude(s) [*see* 'song']
pot-pourri [*see* 'improvisation']
*Potter, (Philip) Cipriani (Hambly) [Hambley] (Eng. comp., 1792–1871) 40, 54, 89–90, 149, 155, 174, 179, 239, 402
Power (James and William) (Ir. firm of music publishers and instrument makers. *fl.* 1802–38) 384
**Prellmechanik, Prellzungenmechanik* [action] 6, 7, 11, 23 Fig. 4, 24 Fig. 5
*prelude (general) 42, 157, 186, 394q2,

442–50
prélude (genre, movement) 110, 120, (442–50), 541
preluding [*see* 'improvisation']
press, the [*see also* 'newspaper'] 533–4
press (printing) [*see* 'printing']
print, -ing 140, 266, 266q1, 357, 460, 532, 532–4
*programme (program) music, programmatic 135, 157, 202, 355, 361, 373–4, 374n10
promenade concerts [*see* 'concert']
Przybylski, T. (Pol. editor of music) 415n13
*psaltery 3
public, (the) (16), 133, 140. 168, 226, 254, 263, 267, 297, 334, 359, 375, 478, 480, 484, 532
publish, er, -ing, publication, 133, 140, 158, 262, 266q1, 334, 419, 466, 480–81, 486, 532–4
*Puget, Loïsa [Louise-Françoise] (Fr. comp., 1810–89) 535
pupil [*see also* 'didactic', 'education', 'teacher' *and* 'student'] 334, 448, 532, 540
pyrotechnic(s) [*see also* 'piano music' *and* 'virtuoso'] 306, 468

*Quantz, Johann Joachim (Ger. theorist, 1697–1773) 37, 38
quill(s) 3, 13, 28, 30q1, 112
*quodlibet [*see* 'improvise']

Raay, Joannes van (Du. kb-maker, *fl.* 1825) 107
Rainer Family, The ('The Styrians of the Alps'; 'The Tyrolese Family/Minstrels') 402–3
Rakhmaninov, Sergey (Vasil'yevich) (Russian comp., 1873–1943) 338
Rameau, Jean-Philippe (Fr. comp., 1683–1764) 155
range [*see under* 'piano sound']
Ranz des vaches (Swiss mountain song) [*see also* 'Kühreihen'] 91, 401
Raupach, Hermann Friedrich (Ger. comp., 1728–78) 338
Redoutensaal [Redouten-Saal] (Vienna) [*see also* 'dance-hall'] 373
regimental music [*see* 'military music']
region, -al [*see also* 'folk'] 386, 400–30, 551
*register(s) (in piano) [*see under* 'piano sound']
rehearsal (s) [*see* 'orchestra']
*Reicha, [Rejcha] Antoine(-Joseph) [Antonín, Anton] (Cz. [Fr. naturalised] comp., 1770–1836) 298
*Reichardt, Johann Friedrich (Ger. comp., 1752–1814) 87, 489
Reichart, Sarah Bennett (Am. musicologist) 218n4, 228, 229n10
religion, religious 90q, 137, 168, 210–16, 378, 412
Renaissance (period) 53, 145, 146, 170, 459
reverie(s), *rêverie* 151, 198, 199, 208, 211
revolution(s), uprising(s) [*see also* 'Agricultural', 'French' *and* 'Industrial'] 134, 147, 147–8, 167, 228, 377, 401
Revolution, French xvii, 134, 147, 167, 228, 377, 401
Revolution, Industrial xvii, 115, 118, 147, 147–8
rhythm (prosodic) [*see* 'metre, prosodic']
Richault, (Fr. firm of music publishers, 1805–98) 405
*Ries, Ferdinand (Ger. comp., 1784–1838) 155, 158, 163, 166, 186, 190, 201–4, 226n7, 242, 249, 307, 341, 353, 357, 370–72, 405, 410, 421
  Solo Pf: *La cappriciosa* 155; *The Dream* 190, 201–4; *15 Easy pieces* 421; *Fantasia à la mode* 190; *Grand Military Divertimento* 186; *Rondo* Op. 106/2: 405; *Rondo à la Tedesca* 242; *Trois airs favoris* 158; *Twelve Trifles* 155, 163, 226n7, 307; *Variety* 186
  Chamber: Sonata for pf duet Op. 47: 405; Pf Trio in g 421
  Orch.: Pf Concertos etc. 341, 353, 357, 410; *Variations on Rule Britannia* 370–72, 421
Rinck, Johann Christian Heinrich (Ger. comp., 1770–1846) 441n38
Ripin, Edwin M (Am. musicologist) 9n24
ritornelles 380
ritornello, ritornello form 14, 339–40, 340, 345, 348, 351, 359, 366, 372
Robert Cocks & Co. (Br. music publishers; 1823–1904) 536
Robinson, Michael (Eng. musicologist) 362n1
Röckel, Elisabeth (Ger. singer, wife of Hummel) 59n6, 292
rocket(s) [*see also* 'Mannheim'] 191–2,

192T3, Pl. 43, 276
*Rococo 489, 547
Rolfe (Br. firm of pf makers, 1785– 1888) 116q
roll [*see* 'tremolo']
*Rölling, C. L. (Aus. pf-maker) 113
romance, *romanza*, Romance, Romanze 90q, 192q, 193, 364, 369
*Romantic, -ism (period or style) xx, 16, 118, 134, 137, 138, 146, 157, 169, 191, 196, 205, 252, 260, 261, 265, 267, 286, 290, 330, 334, 345, 348, 366, 367, 370, 372, 431, 432, 434, 436, 461, 463, 474–88, 475, 477, 480, 481, 490, 491, 502, 533, 543
rondino 536, 537
*rondo(s) (genre) *Rondeau*, *-x* xix, xx, 135, 148q2, 155, 156n18, 157, 158, 185, 186, 195, 210, 211, 217, 229, 241–61, 283, 285, 296, 330, 366, 369, 395, 396, 404, 413q, 421, 525, 528, 529, 535, 537, 541, 550
sonata- [*see* 'sonata-form']
rondoletto 242, 537
rondino 242
rose(s) [*see* 'flower']
Rosenblum, Sandra (Am. musicologist) 61n17, 122, 122n8–9, 143, 143n12–13
*Rosenhain, Jacob [Jakob, Jacques] (Ger. comp., 1813–94) 53
rosewood [*see* 'wood']
*Rossini, Gioachino (Antonio) (It. comp., 1792–1868) 107, 432
Rowland, David (Eng. musicologist) 86n2, 87n4, 205n15
royal, -ty (kings, etc.) (8), 9, 165, 166, 324, 413q, 434, 537, 538, 553
*Royal Academy of Music (London) 41, 445
Royal College of Music (London) 23
Royal Family [*see* 'royal']
Royal Music Library (British Library, London UK) 537
*Rudolph (Johann Joseph Rainer), (S. R. D., (*Serenissimus Rudolphus Dux*), Archduke of Austria (Aus. comp., 1788–1831) 202, 326–7
Russell Collection [of early keyboard instruments] (Edinburgh) [*see also* 'Russell, Raymond'] 11n33
Russell, Raymond (Eng. writer on music, 1922–64) [*see also* 'Russell Collection'] 11n33, 111, 111n15

Russia(n), *russe* 92, 93, 97, 110, 186n2, 405
Rutini, Giovanni Marco [Giovanni Maria, Giovanni Placido] (It. comp., 1723–97) 284

Sachs, Joel (Am. musicologist) 251n6, 372, 372n8, 431–2, 432n2, 549n10
*Saint-Lambert, ?Michel de (Fr. music theorist, *fl. c.* 1700) 38
Saint-Saëns, (Charles) Camille (Fr. comp., 1835–1921) 406, 486
*Salomon, Johann Peter (Ger [Br. naturalised] impresario, 1745–1815) 460
salon xix, xx, 10, 153, 198, 241, 254, 408, 415, 420, 450, 465, 478, 517, 553q, 556
saltarello [*see* 'dance']
Samson, Jim (Br. [Northern Ir.] musicologist) 50, 50n31, 238n13, 517n1, 553n17, 556n18
*Scarlatti, (Giuseppe) Domenico (It. comp., 1685–1757) 7, 37, 135, 180q2, (181), 182, 284, 284n15
scene, *scena* 289, 292, 501
*Schantz [Schanz], Johann (Aus. pf maker, *c.*1762–1828) 11
Schenker, Heinrich (Pol. [Aus naturalised] musical analyst, 1868–1935) 426
scherzetto 238
scherzino 238
scherzo xx, 135, 178–9, 189, 218, 220, 221, 222, 229–38, 239, 240, 241, 266, 408, 476, 477, 479
*Schindler, Anton Felix (Mor. biographer of Beethoven, 1795–1864) 130n13
Schleip, Johann Christian (Ger. pf maker, *fl.* 1825) 87
Schleuning, Peter (Ger. musicologist) 441n38
Schmahl, (Ger. firm of kb instrument makers, *c.* 1675–1774) 114
Schmid, Johann Baptist (Aus. pianist, *fl.* 1763) 9
Schmid[t], Anton (Boh. [Aus. naturalised] musicologist, 1787–1857) 539q
Schnell, Jean-Jacques (?Fr. pf maker, 1740–after1790)
*Schobert, Johann [Jean] (Ger. [Fr. naturalised] comp., 1735–67) 338, 362, 414
Schoenberg [Schönberg], Arnold (Franz Walter) (Aus. comp., 1874–1951) 486

Schoene & Company (?Br. kb-makers, 1784–1820) 9
'school(s)' (musical methods) [see 'Method']
*Schroeter, Johann Samuel (Ger. [Br. naturalised] comp., 1752–88) 339, 367–8
*Schröter, Christoph Gottlieb (Ger. kb-maker, 1699–1782) 4
*Schubart, Christian Friedrich Daniel (Ger. author, 1739–91) 5n12, 16, 16n46, 489
*Schubert, Franz (Peter) (Aus. comp., 1796–1828) 88, 222–3, 226–7, 228n9, 231, 239, 272, 274, 310–14, 330, 376, 389, 429–30, 461, 464, 468, 470, 472–3, 475, 480q, 485, 486, 492, 492–516, 517, 518, 519, 521, 529, 552, 553

    Solo Pf: *Ecossaises* 552; *Hungarian Melody* 429–30; *12 Ländler* D 790: 552, 553; *36 Origiltänze* 552; *Atzenbrugger Tänze* 552; *Variation on a Waltz by Diabelli* 330, 553; *Waltzes* 552; *'Wanderer' Fantasy* 223; Pf Sonatas: last three (239), 272; D 279: 222–3, 272; D 568: 223; D 664: 226–7; D 845: 231; D 960: 239, 274

    Chamber: 529; Fantasia (pf2) D 1: 529; Rondo (pf2) D 951: 529; Variations on 'Trock'ne Blumen' (fl & pf) D 802: 475; Vn Sonatas etc. 468; Arpeggione Sonata 468; Pf Trios etc.: 472–3; 'Trout' Quintet 310–14, 485, 486

    Vocal: Songs 389; accompaniments 88, (389), 492–516, 521; *An mein Klavier* 16n46; *Ave Maria* 212; *Edward* 517; *Erlkönig* 376, 392, 517; *Die Forelle* 16n46, 310, 485; *Gretchen am Spinnrade* 492; *Morgenlied* 88:

    Song-Cycles: 504, 512

    Die schöne Müllerin 492–3, 496, 496–7, 499–500, 499n1, 501, 502, 509–10, 511; 1. Das Wandern 496; 6. Der Neugierige 496–7, 501; 8. Morgengruß 496, 502, 509–10; 9. Des Müllers Blumen 499; 10. Tränenregen 511; 18. Trockne Blumen 92–3, 499–500; 19. Der Müller und der Bach 493, 496

    Winterreise 493–6, 497–9, 499n1, 500–1, 502, 502–9, 509, 510–11, 511–15, 515–16; 1.Gute Nacht 494, 502–3, 512–13 ; 2. Die Wetterfahne 500, 511–12, 515–16; 3. Gefror'ne Thränen 507–8; 4. Erstarrung 502, 503–5; 5. Der Lindenbaum 502–3; 7. Auf dem Fluße 505–6, 515n4; 8. Rückblick 506–7; 9. Irrlicht 500, 501, 510; 10. Rast 495; 11. Frühlingstraum 497–9, 515; 12. Einsamkeit 508–9; 13. Die Post 501; 14. Der greise Kopf 501, 509; 15. Die Krähe 500–1, 504; 16. Letzte Hoffnung 509; 18. Der stürmische Morgen 500; 20. Der Wegweiser 494–5, 516; 21. Das Wirthshaus 496; 22. Muth 512; 23. Die Nebensonnen 510–11; 24. Der Leiermann 513–15

Schubertiad(e) 552

*Schulz [Schultz], Joann Abraham Peter (Ger. comp., 1747–1800) 489

*Schumann [*née* Wieck], Clara (Josephine) (Ger. comp., wife of R. Schumann, 1819–96) 80, 100, 150, 152, 153, 215–16, 321, 348, 364, 412–13, 517–18, 518

*Schumann, Robert (Ger. comp., 1810–56) xviii, 33, 41, 42, 50, 52, 54, 77–80, 97–100, 110, 135, 140n5, 150–3, 152n16, 198, 198n12, 204–5, 207, 232–3, 260, 284, 287, 301, 302, 306, 308–9, 315, 320, 321, 321–2, 330, 338, 348, 370, 389, 412, 475, 479–80, (480q), 480, 517–22, 529, 553

    Solo Pf (in Opus no. order): *'Abegg' variations* 98, 321, 327; *Fandango* 412; *Papillons* 98–100, 198; *Toccata* 54; *Carnaval* 33, 52, 77–80, 97–8, 100, 135, 150–53, (240), (284); *Studien nach ... Paganini* 41, 42, 50; Sonata No. 1: 232–3, 412; *Symphonische Etüden* 301, 306, 308–9, 315, 320; *Kinderszenen* 204–5, 207; *Kreisleriana* 153; *Phantasie* 151; *Blumenstück* 198; Pedal-piano: *Skizzen* 110; *Studien* 110

    Chamber: *Andante and Variations* (2pf + 2vc & hn) 529; *3 Romanzen* (vc & pf, vn/cl *ad lib*.) 475; *5 Stücke im Volkston* (vc & pf, vn *ad lib*.) 475

    Orch.: *Manfred* xviii; Pf Concerto in a (338), 348; Symphony No. 4: 370

INDEX

Vocal: Songs 389, 517–22; Song-cycles 518–20, 520–22; *Genoveva* (opera) xviii; *Jugendbriefe* 152n16
*Schuster, Vincenz (Aus. arpeggione player, *fl.* early C19th) 468
season (= temper wood, etc.) [*see* 'wood']
season (concert-) [*see under* 'concert']
*Sechter, Simon (Boh. [Aus. naturalised] music theorist, 1788–1867) 327
seguidilla [*see* 'dance']
seguilla [*see* 'dance']
Senefelder, Alois (Cz. [Ger. naturalised] actor, inventor of lithography, 1771–1834) 533
sensibilité [*see also* 'sensibility', 'sensitive' *and* 'taste'] 302
sensibility [*see also* 'sensibilité', 'sensitive' *and* 'taste'] 48q, 137, 138, 149, 216, 286, 394q2, 532
sensitive, sensitivity [*see also* 'sensibilité', 'sensibility' *and* 'taste'] xix, 31q, 137, 146, 519
sentimental [*see also* 'sentiment'] 148, 159, 212, 386, 389, 394
seraphin 104
Serenissimus Rudolphus Dux (S. R. D.) [*see* 'Rudolph, Archduke']
serpent(s) (musical instrument(s)) 148
*Seyfried, Ignaz (Xaver), Ritter von (Aus. comp., 1776–1841) 434–5, 435n15
shape (musical) [*see* 'form']
shift (of keyboard) [*see* 'pedal, *una corda*' and 'piano action']
*Shudi [Schudi, Tschudi, Tshudi], Burkat [Burkhardt] (Swi. [Br. naturalised] kb-maker, 1702–73) Pl. 3; 8, 9, 11, 14
siciliana, siciliano, sicilienne [*see* 'dance']
Silbermann, Gottfried (Ger. kb-maker, 1683–1753) 5, 6q, 6, 9, 57, 112
*Silbermann, Johann Heinrich (Ger. kb instrument maker, 1727–99) 9, 87, 103
singer(s), vocalist(s) 112, (149–50), 185, 292, 334, 338, 377, 384, 403, 413q, 489, 501
*Smart, Sir George (Thomas) (Eng. conductor, 1776–1867) 114
Smith, Thomas (Eng. comp., *fl.* early C19th) 193
Socher, Johann (Ger. kb-maker, *fl. c.*1742) 6, 57
society, social xvii, (14), 118, 146, 220, 276, 306, 341, 375–6, 377, 378, 392, 393, 436q1, 460n2, 465, 531, 541, 545, 553q
soft pedal [*see* 'pedal']
Solomon, Maynard (Am. musicologist) 130, 130n14, 165n25
*sonata(s) (as genre) [*see also individual composers*] xx, 157, 217, 218, 218n3, 241, 262–300, (266q1), 301, 335, 461, 529, 541
  accompanied [*see separate entry*]; - allegro 217; arranged by key (when published) 262; duet- 460; duo- 262, 263, 460, 474–80; keyboard sonata (generally) 157, 263, 265, 283–4, 296, 301, 475; keyboard 'with the accompaniment of ...' 262; piano [*see under* 'piano music']; solo- 262–300; trio- 262, 263; unifying principle 298
*sonata-form (general) 193, 202, 262, 266, 267, 267–9, 289, 340, 351, 359, 372, 438
  as an amalgamation of/with earlier forms 340; diagram of 268; combined with fugue 267; concerto version 267, 340, 340–1, 343, 359; Development section 268, 269, 276–83, 286, 359, 359–60, 438, 464; 'doesn't exist' 267; 'monothematic' 268, 269; Recapitulation/Reprise 268, 278, 308; slow-movement version 267, (283–96); sonata-rondo 245n4, 254, 266, 267, 296
song(s), -like, *Lied*, *-er* [*see also* 'Berlin *Lied* Schools'] xx, 229, 489–522;
  accompaniment (keyboard) 489–522; cycle 490, 491, 492, 504, 509–10, 512; drinking- 517; interlude(s) 489, 490, 509–15; introduction(s) 500–9, 518, 519, 520; postlude(s) 501, 507, 509–15; setting 489, 506, 509, 515, 517; singer 489, 501; text 489, 490, 492, 493, 496, 499, 500, 504, 506, 507, 509, 515, 518
*song-cycle [*see under* 'song']
Sonneck, Oscar G(eorge) T(heodore) (Am. musicologist) 434n11–12, 435n15
sonority [*see* 'piano sound']
Sor [Sors], (Joseph) Fernando (Macari) (Sp. [Catalan] comp., 1778–1839) 266
sordino, sordini (mute(s)) 213, 360; (pedal) [*see* 'pedal' *and* 'stop']
sound of piano [*see under* 'piano']
*soundboard 3, 28, 29, 30q2, 56, 62, 106, 108, 115, 117

sound-box 108
*Southwell, William (Ir. kb instrument maker, 1756–1842) 57, 103, 104, 115
*Späth, Franz Jakob (Ger. kb instrument maker, 1714–86) 30q2, 114
Sperl (Vienna) [see also 'dance-hall'] 547
spinet 103, 112–13
*Spohr Louis [Ludewig, Ludwig] (Ger. comp., 1784–1859) 123, 336, 393, 393n1–2, 481, 486, 550, (550–1q), 551n13
spruce [see 'wood']
*S. R. D. (*Serenissimus Rudolphus Dux*) [see 'Rudolph, Archduke']
*Stamitz Family (Boh. comps. in Mannheim) 465
Stanford, Sir Charles Villiers (Ir. comp., 1852–1924) xviii
*Staufer, J. G. (Aus. inventor of arpeggione) 468
Steffan [see 'Stepán']
*Steibelt, Daniel (Ger. comp., 1765–1823) 91, 92, 175, 197–8, 374
*Stein, Johann (Georg) Andreas (Ger. kb-maker, 1728–92) 7, 11, 12, 30q2, 35, 57, 62, 111, 117
*Steinway (Am. pf making firm, 1836–now) xviii, 120
*Stepán [Steffan, Steffani, Stephan, Stephani], Josef Antonín [Joseph Anton; Giuseppe Antoni] (Boh. [Aus. naturalised] comp., 1726–97) 341
*Stevenson, Sir John (Andrew) (Ir. comp., 1761–1833) 384, 389, 392
Steward, Dr. John (Eng. pf maker, *fl.* Wolverhampton *c.* 1742) , 108. Pl. front cover
stile antico [see 'antico'] [see also 'archaic']
stile di caccia [see 'caccia'] [see also 'hunt']
stile galante [see 'galant']
stile moderno [see 'moderno, stile']
Stodart, Robert (Sc. kb instrument maker, 1748–1831) 11, 116, 116q
*Stodart, William (Eng. pf maker, *fl. c.* 1790–1837) Pl. 2, 13, 29, 60n16, 103
*stop(s) [hand-stops] 5, (5n10), 18, 86–7, 105, 107, 109, 111, 116, 191
  bassoon [see also 'fagotto' in this entry] 87, 109; 'Celestial harp' 111; cembalo 109; fagotto [see also 'bassoon' in this entry] 87; harp [see also 'sordino' in this entry] 87, 111; lute 87, 107, 109; sordino [see also 'harp' in this entry] 87; Turkish music 191
*Strauss Family (Aus. comps.) (xviii), 420, 547, 547n5, 548
Stravinsky, Igor (Fyodorovich) (Russ. [Fr. & Am. naturalised] comp., 1882–1971) 486
*Streicher, Johann Andreas (Ger. [Aus. naturalised] pf maker, 1761–1833) 11, 12, 35, 57n2,
*Streicher [*née* Stein], Nanette (Maria Anna) (Ger. [Aus. naturalised] pf maker, 1769–1833) 12, 57n2
string, stringing (on/in instruments)[see also 'string instruments' *and entries for individual string instruments*]xviii, 3, 5, (13q), 29, 56–85, 86, 88, 100, 104, 108, 109, 111, 115, 116, 117, 120, 124, 143, 336, 397–8, 513
strings, string instruments (general) [*see also entries for individual string instruments*] 13q, 107, 237, 336, 353, 368, 481; orchestral section 368
student(s) [see also 'didactic' *and* 'pupil'] 144, 170
Studie (Ger.), *Studio* (It.) (general) [*see* '*étude*' *and* '*Etüde*']
study [see '*étude*' *and* '*Etüde*']
Sturm und Drang ['Storm and Stress'] (artistic movement) 16, 141, 285
style(s), stylistic, stylisation (general musical) xix, 36, 48q, 135q, 143, 181, 183, 218, 372, 403, 435–6, 468, 474, 543, 553q,
  'old[en]' [see also 'past' in this entry and also separate entry] 543n3
  past [see also separate entry] 176–83, 435, 543, 543n3
style brisé (technique) 306, 312, 320, 321, 331
style galant [see 'galant, style']
style, 'old[en]' [see 'style']
'The Styrians of the Alps' (The Rainer Family; 'The Tyrolese Family/ Minstrels') 402–3
*suite 139, 157, 217, 267, 541
Sulzer, Johann Georg (Swi. theorist, 1720–79) 265n7
sustaining pedal [see 'pedal']
swell-box [see 'swell']
*swell, 13, 14, 87, 107
  -box 14; lid- 13, 107; 'nag's head' 13, 87; Venetian 14, 87
*symphony (as genre), symphonic 218,

241, 267, 296, 334, 335, 341, 346, 373, 448, 474, 475, 525
'symphonies' (= accompaniments) 380, 384, 390, 391, 392
symphony-concert xx
syncopate, -d, syncopation [see 'rhythm']

*tangent(s) 3, 6, 7, 35, 513
*tarantella [see 'dance']
*Taskin, Pascal(-Joseph) (Flm. [Fr. naturalised] kb instrument maker, 1723–93) 16–17
taste 29q, 38, 48q, 152, 266q1, 296, 302q, 345, 380, 393, 536q
Tchaikovsky, Pyotr Il'yich (Russian comp., 1840–93) 191, 338
teach, -er, -ing (music) [see also 'didactic', 'education', 'pupil' and 'student'] x, 117, 198, 266, 271, 334, 335, 531, (531–40), 538q, 540, 538q, 540
Telemann, Georg Philipp (Ger. comp., 1681–1767) xviii, 414
Tellefsen, Thomas (Dyke Acland) (Norweigen [Fr. naturalised] pianist, 1823–74) 97
*temperament 37, 59–60, 112, 117
temper(ing) [see 'string']
Temperley, Nicholas (Eng. musicologist) 202, 202n14
tension (string etc.) [see 'string']
*ternary form [see 'form']
*Terzverwandtschaft (211), 252, 258, 284, 289, 360, 455, 491
tetrachord (stringing) [see 'string']
*Teutscher [Deutscher] [see 'dance, Deutscher']
text (script, generally) [see under 'song']
texture, textural, density 14, 16, 53, 71, 143, 183, 207, 223, 234, 237, 239, 240, 243, 246, 253, 255, 309, 318, 345, 398, 404, 428–30, 459, 461, 462, 466, 481, 493, 514
*Thalberg, Sigismond (Fortuné François) (Ger./Aus. comp., 1812–71) 34, 44, 53, 83–4, 234, 314, 400, 410, (413q), 413, 534, 539
  Solo Pf: *Air anglais varié* 400; *Air irlandais varié* 314; *[2] Airs Russes variés* 83–4; *Bolero* 410; *Fantasia on 'The Gypsy'* (413q), 413; *Grande fantaisie ... 'Il Trovatore'* 83; Scherzo in c♯ 234; *Variations on 'Lilly [Minnie] Dale'* 400; *L' art du chant appliqué au piano* 44, 539

Thayer, Alexander Wheelock (Am. writer on music, biographer of Beethoven, 1817–97) 123n11, 166n26
theatre, theatrical [see also 'drama' and 'opera'] 335, 336, 337q, 338, 386
third-relationship [see 'Terzverwandtschaft']
*Thomson, George (Sc. publisher, 1757–1851) 380–83, 534
*thorough-bass [see 'basso continuo']
*'three-handed effect' (Thalberg) 314
thumb (use of) [see also 'finger'] 36, 37, 45
timber [see 'wood']
title(s) (name(s)) 135, 138, 144, 147, 155, 157, 158, 196, 241, 242, 355, 413, 533, 541, 546;
  descriptive 135, (196), 355; distinctive (157), 241; given by comp. 355; given by publishers 241; heading(s) 144; -page(s) 266q1, 533, 546; qualifiers added to 241; selling power of 196, 241
title (Earl etc.) [see 'noble']
title-page 242, 266q1
*toccata, toccatina 53–4
*toccatina [see 'toccata']
Todd, E. Larry (Am. musicologist) 198n12
*Tomásek, Václav Jan Kritel [Tomaschek, Wenzel Johann] (Boh comp., 1774–1850) 171, 231–2, 327, 422
Tomkins, Thomas (Wel. comp., 1572–1656) 523
*Tomkison, Thomas (Eng. kb-maker, *fl.* 1798–1853) 114, Pl. 24, 116q
*tone-poem 502
topic(s) (musical) 170, 184–216, 322
Torricella (Sw. [Aus. naturalised] firm of music-printers, early 1770s–1786) 533
tragic, tragedy, Tragedy 146, 159, 285, 286, 347, 365, 463, 512
training [see 'teaching']
transformation, thematic [see also 'Liszt'] 300
*transposing pianos 59, 111–12
tree(s) [see also 'wood'] 144, Pl. 36, 146, Pl. 41, 433, 519, 540, Pl. back cover
  linden, lime 502–3
*tremolando [see 'tremolo']
*tremolo, tremolando, roll 69, 70, 92, 214, 215, 233–4, 283, 343, 411, 429, 439, 471, 498, 516
triangle (instrument) 105, 106, 107
*trichord [see 'string']
*trio-sonata [see 'sonata']

Trommelbaß (*see also* 'Mannheim, orchestra') 465
*Türk, Daniel Gottlob (Ger. theorist, 1750–1813) 37, 37n18–19
*Turkey, Turkish, Turks, Janissary 105–7, 184, 191
turn, -ed, -ing (woodwork) [*see* 'piano, legs']
types, (human) 153–7
typing (of music) [*see* 'printing']
'The Tyrolese Minstrels/Family' (The Rainer Family; 'The Styrians of the Alps') 402–3

Übung 39
*una corda [*see* 'pedal']
'universal instrument' (piano as) [*see* 'piano (general)']
unmeasured (i.e. no time-signature) 124
Ur-Motiv 504, 505, 506

*valse [*see under* 'dance (named)']
Van der Hoef (Du. kb instrument maker 107
van Raay [*see* 'Raay']
*variation(s)[-set(s)] (general), variant xix, xx, 91, 92, 105, 135, 157, 183, 184, 186, 195, 226, 226n8, 229, 266, 278, 283, 296, 297, 301–3, 366, 370, 372, 380, 382, 395, 396–9, 404, 405, 412, 420, 426, 435, 435n17, 448, 450n11, 453, 462, 465, 475, 480, 525, 526, (526n4), 527, 529, 535, 537, 538, 541–2, 551, 548
   alteration of tempo 324–6; as entertainment 331; as part of larger work 91, 105, 266, 296, 309, 366, 396–9, 475; character- 226, 226n8, 303, 309, 322, 324, 326, 412, 420; closing (section(s)) 326; colour, use of, colouristic 303, 309–14, 453; counterpoint, use of 303, 309, 315–22, 332; double- (on two alternating themes) 310; double (where repeats (following the theme) are also varied) 329; fantasy- [*see also* 'improvisation'] 302, 435n17; features coming to light gradually 328–9; figural, figuration, *Figuralvariation(en)* 301, 303, 303–5, 306, 398, 551; free-standing 92, 157, 309, 366, (382), 396–9; grouping together of 329, 398; in finales 465; opposite mode, use of 303, 322–4; 'set-within-a-set' 329; teaching

material, as 330; technique 306–9; theme(s): 297, 302, 303, 323, 326, 330, 396–9, 405, 526
*Venetian swell [*see* 'swell']
Verdi, Giuseppe (Fortunino Francesco) (It. comp., 1813–1901) xviii
Verel (Fr. kb instrument maker, *fl.* early C19th)) 113, Pl. 21
vernacular [*see also* 'folk'] xix, 167, 302, 375–430, 451, 474n2, 532
vibration(s) [*see also* 'vibrato' and '*Bebung*'] 30q2, 62, 88, 89, 100, 108
*vibrato [*see also* '*Bebung*' and 'vibration'] 16q, 35q, 35, 122n9
Victoria, Princess and (1837–1901) Queen of Great Britain 115, 323, 360, 384, 420
*Vienna (Austria), Congress of 373, 547, 550, 550n12
*viol(s) 459
viola 108, 237, 310, 312, 336, 347, 372, 404, 412, 475, 480, 485, 486
viola da gamba 468
violin(s), violinistic 3, 38, 50, 52, 108, 188, 191, 237, 262, 310, 312, 336, 347, 370, 372, 380, 393, 397, (398), 404, 432, 459, 463, 468, 475, 479q, 479, 480, 484, 485, 525
   fiddle, fiddler(s), 134, 337
violoncello(s) [*see* 'cello']
virginals 523
virtuoso(s), virtuosity [*see also* 'piano music'] xix, 5, 44, 50, 118, 178, 279, 280, 283, 297, 306, 314, 334, 336, 356, 372, 410, 418, 434, 466, 468, 479, 480, 481
Vivaldi, Antonio (Lucio) (It. comp., 1678–1741) 338, 339
Vogler, Georg Joseph [Abbé Vogler] (Ger. comp., 1749–1814) 170
*voice, vocal [*see also* 'song'] 44, 107, 116q, 118, 150, 153, 199, 203, 223, 226, 240, 285, 288, 291, 293, 295, 401–2, 432, 479, 504, 519, 520, 526, 527
Volk 377
*Volkslied 376, (379)
volkstümlich [*see also* 'folk'] 497
*volti subito (device for turning pages) 115
Voss, Charles (Eng. comp., *fl.* early C19th) 198–9

Wachtl (Aus. kb-maker, *fl. c.* 1808) 57
Wagner, Richard (Ger. comp., 1813–83)

xviii, 533
*Waldstein, Ferdinand Ernst Joseph Gabriel, Count von (Boh. [Ger. naturalised] aristocrat, patron of Beethoven 1762–1823) (165)
Walker, Alan (Br. [Canadian naturalised] musicologist) 440n35
Wallace, (William) Vincent (Ir. comp., 1812–65) 536
Walsh, Henry (Ir. pianist, *fl.*1768) 9
*Walter, (Gabriel) Anton (Ger. [Aus. naturalised] pf maker, 1752–1826) 11, 12
*waltz [*see under* 'dance (named)']
*Weber, Carl Maria (Friedrich Ernst) von (Ger. comp., 1786–1826), 107, 143, 182, 236, 254–5, 279, 325, 342, 349, 350, 363, 364, 374, 376, 380, 400, 418, 451, 476–8, 478, 533
    Solo Pf: *Adagio patetico* in c♯ 143; *Grande Polonaise* 418; *Polacca brillante* 418; *La gaité* 254–5; Sonata in C 279; Variations: *on an Original Theme* 533; *on 'Vien'quà Dorina bella'* 325; *on 'Schone Minka'* 325
    Chamber: Trio (fl, vc, pf) 236, 476–8
    Orch.: Pf Concertos etc. 342, 349, 350, 363, 364, 374
    Vocal: *Festival of Peace* (cantata) 451; *Der Freischütz* (opera) 374, 451, 476; *Oberon* (opera) 374, 400
Weigl, Joseph (Aus. comp., 1766–1846) 475
Weippert, John M. (?Br. harpist and publisher, *fl.* 1836–48) 413q
Welcker (Br. firm of music publishers, *c.* 1762–78) 399
Weltman [Veltman], Andries (Du. kb instrument maker, 1730–96) 13
*Wesley, Samuel (Eng. comp., 1766–1837) 229, 252–4
Wesley, Samuel Sebastian (Eng. comp., 1810–76, son of preceding) 188
Wieck, Clara [*see* 'C. Schumann']
*Wieck, (Johann Gottlob) Friederich (Ger. pf teacher,1785–1873; father of Clara Schumann and teacher of R. Schumann) 517
Williams, Peter (Frederic) (Eng. musicologist) 9n28

Willis & Co. (London and Dublin, music dealers, *fl.* early C19th)) 104
wind instruments (excluding brass), section [*see also individual entries*] 59, 59q1, 107, 329, 336, 337, 337q, 360, 486
wit, -ty [*see also* 'humour'] 274, 296, 352, 436q1, (437q2)
Wolff, Christoph (Ger. musiocologist) 6n14
Wolff, Edward (Edouard) (Pol. comp., 1816–80) 53
*Wölfl, [Wölffl, Woelfl] Joseph (Aus. comp., 1773–1812) 266n9
woman, lady etc., xviii, (xix), 10q, 49, 114, (144), 145, 146, Pl. 40, 147, (149q3), 152q, (154), 155–6, 185, 242, (321), 378, (379), 384, 394q, 403, (419), 431, 435, 460, 478, 496, 500, 512, 521, 522, (522n3), 536, 537, 550q, 551q
wood, -en (timber) 62, 88, 429, 513 cherry 114, 114n23; crossbanding 114; fir 62; grain 62; mahogany 114; pine 62; rosewood 114; satinwood 114 ; seasoning 62, 115; spruce 28; stain 114, 114n23; veneer 114; walnut 114
-worker(s) (*legnaioli*) 4
woodwind [*see under* 'wind instruments']
*word-painting 515–16
*Wornum [Wornham], Robert (Eng. kb instrument maker, 1780–1852) 56, 58, 104
Wunderkind 144

*yodel(ling) 401–2, 403

*Zelter, Carl Friedrich (Ger. comp., 1758–1832) 479, 489, 492
Zimmermann, Guillaume (Fr pf maker, *fl.* 1780s) 10
Zimmerschied, Dieter (Ger. musicologist) 552n14
zither 3
*Zumpe, Johannes (Ger. kb–maker, *fl.* 1735–83) 8–10, 18q, 25, 57
*Zumsteeg [Zum Steeg], Johann Rudolf (Ger comp., 1760–1802) 489
*Zywny, Wojciech [Adalbert] [Zivny, Vojtech; Zhyvny, Ziwny, Zwiny] (Boh. [Pol. naturalised] teacher; 1756–1842, teacher of Chopin) 414